AMERICAN
JEWRY
and the
HOLOCAUST

AMERICAN

JEWRY

and the

HOLOCAUST

The American Jewish Joint Distribution Committee, 1939—1945

Yehuda Bauer

The Institute of Contemporary Jewry
The Hebrew University, Jerusalem

Wayne State University Press
Detroit, 1981

Library of Congress Cataloging in Publication Data

Bauer, Yehuda.
  American Jewry and the Holocaust.

  Bibliography: p.
  Includes index.
  1. Holocaust, Jewish (1939–1945)
2. World War, 1939–1945—Jews—Rescue. 3. Jews
in Europe—Charities. 4. American Jewish Joint
Distribution Committee. I. Title.
D810.J4B3158   943.086   80-26035
ISBN 0-8143-1672-7

Grateful acknowledgment is made to the Morris and Emma Schaver
Publication Fund for Jewish Studies for financial assistance in the publi-
cation of this volume.

Contents

5

maps

tables

Abbreviations
of Organizations

AFSC	American Friends Service Committee
AJ	Armée juive
AJB	Association des juifs de Belgique
AJC	American Jewish Committee
BEL-HICEM	Belgique-HICEM
BuF	Bevölkerungswesen und Fürsorge
CAR	Comité d'assistance aux refugiés
CC	Consistoire central
CCOJA	Commission central des organisations juives d'assistance
CDJ	Comité de défense des juifs
CENTOS	Centrala Opieki nad Sierotami
CFA	Committee for the Assistance of European Jewish Refugees in Shanghai
CGD	Comité general de défense
CLN	Comitato di Liberazione Nazionale
CNDJ	Comité national de défense des juifs
CPR	Commission for Polish Relief
CRIF	Conseil représentatif des israélites de France

DELASEM	Delagazione Assistenza Emigranti e Profughi Ebrei
DORSA	Dominican Republic Settlement Association
EFI	Entr'aide français israélite
EIF	Éclaireurs israélites de France
FFI	Forces françaises d'intérieur
FPO	Farainikte Partisaner Organizacje
FSJ	Fédération des sociétés juives
HIAS	Hebrew Sheltering and Immigrant Aid Society
HICEM	HIAS-ICA-EMIGDIRECT
IC	International Committee (Shanghai)
ICA	Jewish Colonisation Association
IGCR	Inter-Governmental Committee on Refugees
IKG	Israelitische Kultusgemeinde
IRC	International Red Cross
JA	Jewish Agency
JDC	American Jewish Joint Distribution Committee
JNF	Jewish National Fund
JSH	Jüdische Soziale Hilfe
JSS	Jüdische Soziale Selbsthilfe
JTA	Jewish Telegraphic Agency
JUS	Jüdische Unterstützungsstelle
KEOKH	Külföldieket Ellenörzö Oorszagos Központi Hatoság
KK	Koordinatzie-Komitet; *also called* Koordinirungs-Komisie fun di Iddishe Hilfs and Sozial-Gesellshaftn
LPZ	Left Poalei Zion
MJS	Mouvement de la jeunesse sioniste
MOI	Main d'oeuvre immigré
NRO	Naczelna Rada Opiekuncza
NRS	National Refugee Service

NSV	Nationalsozialistische Volkswohl-fahrt
OMZSA	Országos Magyar Zsido Sëgito Akcio
ONE	Oeuvre national d'enfance
ORT	Organization for Rehabilitation and Training
OSE	Oeuvre secours aux enfants
PEC	Palestine Economic Corporation
PZ	Poalei Zion
RELICO	Committee for Relief of the War-Stricken Jewish Population
RGO	Rada Glowna Opiekuncza
RSHA	Reichssicherheitshauptamt
RV	Reichsvertretung der deutschen Juden
RVE	Reichsvereinigung der Juden in Deutschland
RWR	Russian War Relief
SA	Sturm Abteilung
SACRA	Shanghai Ashkenazi Collaborating Relief Association
SD	Sicherheitsdienst
SIG	Schweizerischer Israelitischer Ge-meindebund
SJUF	Schweizerischer Jüdischer Unter-stützungsfond für Flüchtlinge
SKSS	Stołeczny Komitet Samopomocy Społecznej
SLS	Slovenska L'udová Strana
SOCOBO	Sociedad Colonizadora de Bolivia
SS	Schutzstaffel
TOPOROL	Towarzystwo Popierania Rolnictwa
TOZ	Towarzystwo Ochrony Zdrowia
UGIF	Union générale des israélites de France
ÚHÚ	Ústredný Hospodárský Úrad

UJA	United Jewish Appeal
UJRE	Union des juifs pour la résistance et l'entr'aide
UNRRA	United National Relief and Rehabilitation Administration
UPA	United Palestine Appeal
USJ	Union des sociétés juives
ÚŽ	Ústredna Židov
VH	Va'ad Hahatzalah
VSIA	Verband Schweizerischer Israelitischer Armenpflegen
WIZO	Women's International Zionist Organization
WJC	World Jewish Congress
YMCA	Young Men's Christian Association
WRB	War Refugee Board
ZA	Zentralausschuss für Hilfe und Aufbau
ŻETOS	Żydowskie Towarzystwo Opieki Społecznej
ŻOB	Żydowska Organizacja Bojowa

Preface

This book has two purposes. One is to describe the endeavors of a great charitable agency, the American Jewish Joint Distribution Committee, to extend help to European Jewry during the Holocaust. The other is to continue the history of this organization begun in *My Brother's Keeper* (Philadelphia, Pa.: The Jewish Publication Society of America, 1974). The present work is meant to stand on its own as a contribution to the history of the Holocaust, but it also follows up the problems and events described in the earlier volume. While a great deal has already been written regarding the policies of the U.S. government towards the Jews during the period 1939–45, the story of Jewish efforts at self-help has not yet been told. Outside aid to European Jews was very largely in the hands of the JDC (or "Joint," as it was also called), the central Jewish body for aid and welfare in the world; the other Jewish communities in the free world had neither the financial means nor the administrative and political experience of the American organization, and it was natural for suffering Jewish groups anywhere to turn to JDC for help.

The present volume, however, is not intended as an organizational history. It deals only cursorily with the American background of JDC and concentrates on its activities abroad. Two main areas are covered: aid emanating from the United States or from JDC's European headquarters during the war; and self-help initiated or executed in the countries under Nazi occupation, including Germany. Such local efforts are described if they were the work of groups or individuals who had represented JDC in their countries prior to the war and continued their activities under Nazi domination, legally or illegally, or if they involved people

13

who pretended that they were in contact with JDC and whose work was recognized by the parent organization after the event. The theme of this book, therefore, is Jewish self-help, whether American-based or initiated locally under JDC's name.

The reader will find that the chapters which follow are organized into broad chronological divisions. After an introduction outlining JDC's prewar history and its attempt to aid European Jews before 1939, the years of American neutrality are dealt with. Until the Japanese attack on Pearl Harbor in December, 1941, JDC maintained contact with Jewish communities in Europe, and the story of its welfare efforts there falls naturally into geographically determined sections. These were years when hunger, epidemic, and humiliation were known, but mass murder was still inconceivable. There follows the period of destruction—1942 to 1944—when JDC's activities involve separate stories: those of the New York center; of the local European communities and committees, now cut off from New York; and of the headquarters at Lisbon, which increasingly pursued independent policies. Saly Mayer, JDC's unofficial representative in Switzerland throughout most of the war, also emerges as a significant force. The final part of the book deals with the later period of the war. While it concentrates on the complicated negotiations with the Nazis for ransom and release with which Saly Mayer was concerned, JDC's attempts to help Jews in Shanghai, North Africa, and the Soviet Union are also described. Finally, the last months of Nazi Germany are considered from JDC's point of view.

The documentary materials which lie behind this history are contained in a variety of sources. I have relied most heavily on JDC's own archives, which contain a very large number of reports, letters, and memoranda; within these archives the Saly Mayer papers were especially important. Other important archival sources included the Public Records Office in London, the Yad Vashem Archives in Jerusalem, the War Refugee Board Papers in the Franklin D. Roosevelt Library at Hyde Park, New York, and the Yiddish Scientific Institution Archives in New York City, as well as some smaller archives, among which the Moreshet Archive at Giv'at Haviva, Israel, was most useful. These sources enabled me to understand and evaluate some of the criticisms leveled at JDC throughout the period, and they also helped to establish the facts of events when the JDC archives were incomplete, inaccurate, or simply did not contain the necessary materials. Contemporary newspapers were another significant source of

14

information. The Selected Bibliography indicates my indebtedness to many previously published works, and I have also tried, to the extent that it was possible, to take account in my notes of research completed by others while this book was being written.

I would like to take this opportunity of expressing my deeply felt thanks to Samuel L. Haber, now the honorary executive vice-chairman of JDC, whose constant and friendly prodding had a large share in producing this volume. Thanks are also due to other good friends, such as Boris Smolar and Herbert Katzki, who read chapters of the manuscript and made important comments. I should, however, emphatically state that no one made any attempt to influence or censor the manuscript, and that all criticism was invited by myself, freely given, and accepted or rejected at my own discretion.

My special gratitude is due to Mrs. Rose Klepfisz, JDC archivist, without whose help in checking notes this book could never have been completed. Between the time of my reading the papers in New York and my completion of the final draft of the manuscript, many files, including the Saly Mayer papers, were reorganized, and all notes regarding them had to be rewritten. Mrs. Klepfisz and her staff spent much time settling this problem in a most helpful and conscientious way.

In a sense, while retaining sole responsibility for everything that this book contains, I consciously tried to make it into as much of a collective venture as I could. Our group of researchers at the Institute of Contemporary Jewry in Jerusalem read and commented on parts of the manuscript. I am especially indebted to my research assistant and good friend, Dr. Aharon Weiss, to Dr. Israel Gutman, Dr. Shmuel Krakowsky, Dr. Livia Rothkirchen, and Dr. Menahem Kaufman for their important comments, and to my colleague and friend, Professor Moshe Davis, for his constant encouragement. My daughter Danit, who had the dubious pleasure of typing part of the original manuscript, bore her fate with fortitude.

Finally, as in all my work, my kibbutz had a large if unconscious share in the effort. The background of a warm and sympathetic commune was a great help in writing this book.

Kibbutz Shoval
March, 1980

Introduction

Nazi Antisemitism and the Holocaust

The event that we have come to call the Holocaust—the planned mass murder of the European Jews—was made possible by the confluence of a number of factors: a brutal dictatorship, the development of modern technology, a bureaucracy that not only executed orders but initiated them, and a war. All these were necessary, but not sufficient, conditions for the Holocaust to happen. The addition of that old, deep-seated malaise of gentile society called antisemitism made these conditions sufficient.*

Nazi antisemitism invented nothing new. Its picture of "the Jew" as the devil had been inherited from traditional Christian Jew-hatred;[1] the description of the Jew as the parasite feeding on the bodies of other nations, incapable of a separate corporate existence—which in a way contradicted the satanic imagery—had been developed in the second half of the nineteenth century; the further development of these themes into an imagined threat of a Jewish world government out to control gentile society can also be traced to premodern Europe, though it received its modern garb in the notorious *Protocols of the Elders of Zion* in 1905.[2] The combination of these major and some minor trends into a hatred of murderous import was the achievement of the Nazi movement in the 1920s.

Connected with its antisemitism was the Nazi rebellion against the civilizing mission of Judaism and Christianity in the

---

*I prefer the spellings *antisemitism* and *antisemitic* to the more customary *anti-Semitism* and *anti-Semitic*. The Jew-hating movement that invented the terms in the 1870s attacked Jews, not some nonexistent "Semitism."

modern world, a rebellion that has since been picked up by others. It denied the sanctity of human life; it opposed humanism, pacifism, socialism, liberalism. In short, it stood against all those trends in modern society that would build a world based on the interaction between a free individual and a peace-loving society around him. It saw these trends as stemming from Judaism, and declared Judaism to be a warping of the true nature of man, which supposedly found its highest expression in a struggle for power, in war. Nazism denied monotheistic religion; by denying the equality of all humans it denied the fatherhood of God. Moses, Jesus, Marx, and Lenin were all Jewish revolutionaries against the true call of nature. Judaism was, in the Nazi perception, a mortal, universal danger to the natural hierarchy of human society built on the superiority of some races over others. It had to be fought and eliminated in order to build a new order based on Germanic hegemony.[3]

The tragic irony of Nazism was that it imputed its own guilt to the Jews. Nazi intentions to dominate the world, subvert existing governments, and enslave their societies were real, but in Nazi ideology these aims were those of the archenemy, the Jewish devil. In reality, the Jewish people were powerless. They were a tiny minority scattered all over the globe, heirs to a culture that was neither better nor worse, but simply different. However, they were heirs also to that ancient hatred against them that was based, ultimately, on the fact of being different, and it was that predisposition of European society to antisemitism that made the Nazi accusations stick.[4]

Antisemitism was not just one of the aspects of Nazi ideology. Rather, it was one of its two central pillars, the other being the demand for world domination by the Germanic peoples. Nazi racialism was, in a very real sense, a by-product of its antisemitism. After all, in Nazi eyes the Aryan race included such peoples as Russians, Poles, or Czechs, who were nevertheless seen as subhumans. Only the Germanic peoples were fully human. Japanese were "honorary Aryans." So were Arabs, whose leader, the mufti of Jerusalem, Hajj Amin el-Husseini, was an ally of the Nazi movement. Blacks were not really humans, but an intermediary stage between the animal world and humanity—but the Nazis never faced the problems of blacks, largely because they did not really meet them. The only non-Aryans in Europe were the Jews. Racist Nazi doctrine was therefore largely a cover for antisemitism. Antisemitism stood at the center, not only of ideology, but of the decisive actions of the Nazi regime.

18

One might perhaps think that the picture drawn here is exaggerated, that antisemitism, while important, took second place to other, more central motivating forces in the Nazi makeup. One wishes this were true; unfortunately, it is not. The apocalyptic vision of the Nazi leaders was of an imminent threat by "International Jewry" to the physical survival of the German people, and Germany had to be prepared for war before that satanic force could strike. Thus, in his instructions to Hermann Göring for the four-year plan in 1936, Hitler says that Germany must be ready for war within four years because "the loss of months may cause damage that will be irreparable in hundreds of years." The victory of International Jewry, "whose most radical expression is Bolshevism . . . will not this time lead to new Versailles treaties but to the final destruction, that is the extermination of the German people."[5] Similar expressions could be quoted from Nazi sources for the years leading up to the war in 1939.[6] The Nazis posited a Jewish world power controlling both the Bolshevik East and the capitalist West. The war was started to break this imaginary stranglehold and assure Germany of the basis from which it could start its drive for hegemony. In a very real sense, therefore, the Nazi attack on the world, costing millions of lives and causing havoc and destruction unequaled before or since, was at least in part an ideologically or pseudoreligiously motivated struggle against the imaginary Jewish adversary. Antisemitism was a central cause of World War II.

This analysis, while hardly open to doubt in light of the documentation now available, is yet very hard to grasp, let alone to accept.[7] If this is so a generation and more after the event, how much more difficult it was to understand the Nazi argumentation in the late thirties, when much of what we know today was unknown to those whose lives were threatened or affected. In this extreme form, Nazi Jew-hatred was utterly outside the experience of a world which still saw itself as civilized, and neither the Jews nor their non-Jewish friends could comprehend it. The Jews were the products of a civilization which stood in stark contradiction to all the premises of Nazism. It was totally incomprehensible to them that people should exist who denied the sanctity of human life, or who excluded some people from humanity altogether. They were therefore outwitted at every point, easily misled, and murdered precisely because they could not accept the reality of a world in which such murder was possible. "The Jew is not a human being; he is a manifestation of the process of decom-

19

position," as a Nazi source put it.[8] Once the Jew was put outside the universe of human obligation, he could be destroyed, or sold, or stored, as occasion demanded. The dehumanization of Jews had started with the dehumanization of the society which gave rise to Nazism, but the intended victims were quite unaware of the wider implications of the development of Nazism taking place before their very eyes.

Yet it must be emphasized that the Nazis did not actually form a plan to annihilate the Jews prior to early 1941.[9] As late as May, 1940, Heinrich Himmler, chief of the SS and future executioner of the Jewish people, could argue against mass murder as a policy towards subject populations.[10] The logical consequences of Nazi ideology may have been forming in Adolf Hitler's mind before 1941, or even before 1939, but all the evidence indicates that no plans for the murder of Jews were discussed or formulated at that time. Rather, from 1933 to 1940, Nazi policy escalated from emigrating Jews (up till 1938) to expelling them (1938–1940); in 1940 two plans for mass deportation (to an area in eastern Poland or to Madagascar) were very seriously considered. It was only with the planned attack on the Soviet Union, accompanied by the United States' obvious lack of interest in the fate of the Jews, that the way was clear to mass destruction. The stages towards the "Final Solution," the name that the Nazis gave to the mass murder of the Jews, were not preplanned, however it might seem after the event. They grew out of the basic Nazi worldview and were influenced by the pragmatic opportunities of "solving" the Jewish problem as these unfolded. The sale or export of Jews to potentially hostile countries prior to 1941 was justified ideologically by saying that, on the one hand, emigrating Jews would cause antisemitism in the receiving countries (thereby increasing sympathy towards antisemitic Germany), and that, on the other, the influx of Jews would introduce a fatal social illness into these societies (causing them to become easy prey to Nazi Germany).[11] This attitude prevailed before the war began and enabled over half of German Jewry to escape—though some were caught again in the course of German conquests in Europe.

After the decision to murder the Jews was taken, probably around the middle of March, 1941, and transmitted orally, the destruction began, first of all in the newly conquered territories in the USSR. It is really immaterial whether a second decision was taken at some point to expand the murder to the rest of Europe, or whether such a second order was not necessary.[12] The Rubicon had been crossed. Mass murder was now sanctioned.

In the face of all this, what could the Jews do? The Jewish people in the world of the thirties were politically powerless. They could beg and plead, and they did. But they were not popular anywhere, and they had no real influence. Essentially they were left to their own devices, but were also divided among themselves. There were strictly traditional religious Jews who only sought to be left alone to worship God in their own way and eke out a living as middlemen and artisans in Eastern Europe; there were socialists and communists dreaming of a new world in which they could forget their Jewishness—that is, their different-ness—and merge with a universal brotherhood oblivious to na-tional origins; there were middle-class and intellectual Jews, pri-marily in the West, who were in the process of a swift assimila-tion and submergence in the host cultures and who wanted to have nothing to do with their background or anybody who might remind them of it. There were Jewish nationalists—Zionists—who believed that the Jews were a nation scattered among all others; this nation had to be collected again and settled in Palestine so as to avoid destruction by the forces of antisemitism without and assimilation within. Finally, there were good-natured philan-thropists, mainly in North America, Britain, and France, who viewed the regeneration of Jewish Palestine as a valuable contri-bution to the solution of the problems of East European Jews, but whose aim was not Zionism. Rather, they hoped for the further scattering of Jews and the furtherance of conditions in which Jews would become equal citizens in democratic societies, just another religious community which ultimately would merge completely with its surroundings. Such views were particularly popular among the Jewish upper-middle classes in the United States. They did not involve abdicating responsibility for Jews outside the United States; on the contrary, aid to their coreligionists was a time-honored concept. When the Nazis came to power, the or-ganization that came to the aid of European Jewry was an Ameri-can agency led by just such benevolent philanthropists.

The First Twenty-five Years of JDC

The American Jewish Joint Distribution Committee (JDC) was founded in November, 1914, as a purely practical step to facilitate the distribution of funds collected by two committees, one Orthodox and one chiefly Reform, which had been organized a few months before to aid Jews in the Middle East and elsewhere. In 1915, a Jewish Labor committee was founded for the same purpose and soon joined it. It was therefore a "joint" committee; hence the awkward name. But in fact, though Orthodox and Labor members served as officers, it was the German Jewish element, predominantly non-Orthodox, Americanized, and liberal-minded, that directed JDC from its inception. These men had become wealthy in America, and their religious and moral tradition obliged them to share some part of their wealth with "our co-religionists," "our less fortunate brethren." They did so willingly but condescendingly. Those they helped were foreigners; if American aid could help them to rebuild their lives so that they could achieve in their own countries what German Jews had achieved in America—equality and a sense of identification with their land of residence—so much the better. There would be fewer poverty-stricken Jews to take care of in New York and other places in the United States.

Between 1914 and 1929—that is, to the beginning of the Great Depression—JDC collected the very considerable sum of $78.7 million from American Jews to help Jews overseas. It never intended to become a permanent organization; its leaders thought that after the damage to Jewish life in Europe by the war was repaired, JDC would go out of business. But in fact, the need for help in Eastern Europe grew, both in Poland, where Jews suffered from intensifying economic discrimination, and in the Soviet Union, where a large-scale effort was made to settle Jews on the land. This latter attempt at social engineering was made through an agreement between JDC, a Jewish capitalist organization, and the Soviet government; predictably, anti-Bolshevik circles in the United States, and especially the Zionist movement, bitterly attacked JDC for squandering Jewish resources in Communist-dominated Russia.

The leadership of JDC remained in the hands of the German Jewish aristocracy until the end of the 1930s, though professional social workers, administrators, and other experts were beginning to come to the fore. There was a close alliance between JDC and the American Jewish Committee (AJC), the political organization of the non-Zionist elite of American Jewry, which was led until his death in 1929 by Louis Marshall, the acknowledged leader of American Jewry as a whole. Felix M. Warburg, one of the original founders, scion of a famous Hamburg banking family, and the son-in-law of the great Jewish banker Jacob M. Schiff, was the undisputed leader of JDC until his death in 1937, and in fact it could be said that between 1929 and 1937 he assumed the mantle that had fallen from Louis Marshall's shoulders. Warburg also exerted the most decisive individual influence in AJC, so that in many ways the two groups were merely different organizational expressions of the same elite. After Warburg's death, Paul Baerwald took his place in JDC. Baerwald was a banker—of German Jewish origin, of course—associated with Lazar Frères; a well-meaning and intelligent if somewhat rigid and unimaginative man, he fell short of supplying the kind of leadership his predecessor had given. Cyrus S. Adler was Warburg's successor at AJC, and while the alliance between the two organizations remained very much intact, the lack of the kind of guidance that both had enjoyed in the twenties and early thirties was clearly felt.

Bernhard Kahn represented JDC in Europe from the 1920s until he retired in 1938. To millions of European Jews, Kahn was "Mr. Joint." An early Zionist, this Swedish-born and German-educated economist and social worker, possessed of a tremendous knowledge of Jewish life and tradition, was an ideal interpreter of the desires of the American philanthropic organization to its European clients. He was pedantic, his figures were always accurate, his inclinations were conservative, and his aim was to help Jews help themselves. At the same time, he identified with those he aided, and he did not hesitate to defend them against the New York office whenever he felt he had to.

At the end of the thirties, Edward M. M. Warburg, Felix's son, emerged as the new predominant force among the laymen, but it was the professional leadership that became more and more significant. Joseph C. Hyman, longtime secretary of JDC, came to occupy the more distinguished but less influential post of vice-chairman. Moses A. Leavitt, a professional social administrator (originally a chemical engineer), returned to JDC from the Palestine Economic Corporation (PEC), a company set up by the Zionists of the Louis Brandeis wing and the AJC-JDC group for economic work in Palestine. Leavitt became secretary of JDC in 1939, and he called upon Joseph J. Schwartz, a young social worker from the Brooklyn Jewish Federation, to be his assistant secretary. When Leavitt briefly returned to the PEC, Schwartz acted as secretary until he left for Europe early in 1940; Leavitt then came back to JDC for good.

Leavitt was helped by a growing staff of experts, both in New York and in Paris, JDC's European headquarters. A forceful man with considerable organizational gifts, he dominated not only the New York staff but the committees of laymen, who were dependent on the information he supplied. They increasingly tended to accept his expert advice. The major committees were the Executive Committee, which met about once a month, and the smaller Administrative Committee, which saw to the day-to-day running of the organization. The Board of Directors, which met once a year, and the annual meeting of the membership involved bodies too large to participate in the actual decision-making process. Other committees were the Budget and Scope Committee, which passed on financial matters, area committees such as those on Latin America and Poland, and functional committees such as the Cultural Committee chaired by Cyrus Adler. Leavitt and his people condensed the information supplied by the European director and his staff, presenting it to the Administrative and Budget and Scope committees, which would then in most cases decide the issues or call upon the Executive Committee to approve the decisions formally. Except for the Budget and Scope Committee, however, the special committees tended to wither away in the tremendous upheavals of World War II. JDC was then trying desperately to meet crises, and there was little time for long-range planning.

The general trend in American Jewry during the decades between the wars was against the unification of organizations. Divided into Reform, Conservative, and Orthodox religious groups, and innumerable political, social, and cultural institutions, American Jewry resisted all attempts to create unity out of its diversity. Yet JDC nevertheless succeeded in building for itself a virtual monopoly in the field of overseas aid. This is not to say that its position went unchallenged. JDC was constantly fighting to preserve it against other organizations which were trying to enter the field. But by and large, despite—or perhaps because of—its oligarchic leadership, JDC remained in effect the sole representative of American Jewry's desire to aid its brethren in Europe and elsewhere.

JDC spent, in the decade 1929–39, a total of $24.4 million. However, this money was collected and spent very unevenly. In 1931–35, only $4.3 million were spent abroad, just at the time that much larger sums were needed. Another $8.5 million were spent in 1936–38, and the same amount in 1939 alone. JDC could

24

only spend as much as American Jewry was prepared to give it. One may ask, of course, whether JDC did all it could to get as much money as possible, but an examination of the organization's fund-raising material in the thirties and forties leads to the conclusion that it did indeed invest a very considerable effort in painting a realistic picture of the plight of Jews abroad, hoping to make American Jews open their hearts and, in consequence, their pockets. Yet it must not be forgotten that the late 1930s were a time of growing antisemitism, that the Depression had hit American Jews as well as other American citizens, and that the traditional Jewish saying, "Your own town's poor have priority," applied to the situation in the United States. Jews gave money—if they were in a position to give anything at all—to local hospitals and old-age homes, to religious institutions and Jewish schools, and overseas aid came second. The figures speak a fairly clear language nevertheless. They show that despite the second wave of economic depression that hit the United States in 1938–39, JDC income was increasing, probably because, in addition to whatever JDC did to increase donations, the news media had supplied a great deal of information about the fate of European Jewry.

After 1933, the year Adolf Hitler came to power in Germany, JDC concentrated on dealing with three main problems: the flight of refugees from Germany, Austria, and Czechoslovakia; the maintenance of the Jewish communities in Central Europe; and the terrible economic and social situation of East European Jews. In 1939, for instance, out of the total expenditure of $8.5 million, $3.25 million went to support refugees in the European countries to which they fled, while an additional $600,000 were spent to settle some of them in Latin America. Of the rest, $2.18 million were spent on Jews in Central Europe, and $1.25 million went to Eastern Europe.

The Flight of Jews from Germany and Austria

From 1935 on, it was clear to the most shortsighted observer that only emigration could offer a real answer to the problems of German Jewry. Nevertheless, contrary to claims made after the event, no one knew or could have known what was in store for European Jews. Prophets of doom there were, no doubt, but they prophesied persecution, war, pogroms, economic ruin, and slave labor, not physical destruction. Most Jewish observers and men of affairs expected to have fifteen to twenty years in which to emi-

25

grate the bulk of Central European Jewry, and they thought they would be able to accomplish the task in that period of time. In fact, they had four years, from 1935 to 1939, or at most eight, if one counts the years from the Nazi rise to power in 1933 until all emigration became impossible in 1941.

Table 1 shows that a surprisingly high percentage of the 500,000 German and 200,000 Austrian Jews did manage to escape, despite the fact that most countries refused to open their gate to Jewish refugees. The figures include both organized emigration—roughly half of those who fled—and emigration effected through private initiative. The accuracy of these figures, however, is problematical. The JDC archives contain contradictory data, which derive partly from lack of uniformity in defining Jewish emigration. It is often unclear whether the figures include people of Jewish descent or Jews by Nazi definition who neither saw themselves as Jews nor registered as such. For example, one estimate puts the total number of Jews and persons of Jewish descent in Germany in 1933 at 625,000, and the equivalent number in Austria in 1938 at 280,000–290,000. The Reichsvereinigung der Juden in Deutschland (RVE) estimated that in 1933 there had been 522,700 "full" Jews in Germany, including nonprofessing ones.[13]

Table 1: Jewish Emigration from Central Europe, 1933–39

From	1933	1934	1935	1936	1937	1938	1939	Total
Germany	37,000	23,000	21,000	25,000	23,000	47,400	68,000	244,400
Austria						62,958	54,451	117,409
Bohemia and Moravia							43,000	43,000

	Grand total	**404,809**

The need was truly overwhelming in all sectors. Of course, JDC expenditures for the upkeep of Jews in Germany and in the countries it annexed in 1938 and 1939, and for refugees from there, were intimately connected. As far as Central Europe itself was concerned, since 1935 it had been standard JDC policy not to send dollars to Germany so as not to be guilty of helping the Hitler regime. The only exception to this rule was a relatively small sum of money given to the Quakers, the American Friends

Service Committee (AFSC), which was used largely for undercover aid to persecuted individuals in Germany. By 1939, the money transfer was effected by giving emigrants who had reached freedom dollars with which to repay money they had handed over in local currency to Jewish communities in their respective countries.

In April, 1933, all countrywide German Jewish social and welfare institutions were united in a single committee, the Zentralausschuss für Hilfe und Aufbau (ZA). Until 1939, the ZA was practically identical with the Reichsvertretung der deutschen Juden (RV), established in September, 1933, as the political representation of German Jewry. However, in 1938, a new policy had been introduced by the Nazi regime—namely, to squeeze the Jews dry and deprive them of their property, and then to drive them out. In August, 1938, Adolf Eichmann, the SS commissar for Jewish emigration, began to execute the plan in newly annexed Austria. Under these circumstances, the RV was no longer satisfactory to either Jews or Nazis, and after a good deal of wavering and negotiating, a new organization was finally approved by the Gestapo in July, 1939: the Reichsvereinigung der Juden in Deutschland (RVE). Like its predecessor, the RVE was ultimately the result of Jewish initiative, and while it was placed under more direct and threatening supervision by the Gestapo, its personnel was taken over from the old RV. At its head stood Rabbi Leo Baeck; finance and emigration questions were handled by Julius Seligsohn, Paul Meyerheim, and Paul Eppstein. These men continued to head the ZA, where Otto Hirsch was also a leader. JDC, whose contacts were largely with Hirsch and Meyerheim, contributed about 30 percent of the ZA budget, so its influence was considerable.

The establishment of the RV in 1933 was, in a sense, a definite break with tradition. There had never before been a united communal organization for all of German Jewry because Jews had organized in communities within the old German states and provinces. Moreover, differences in religious observance had prevented unification, as had the bitter struggle between Zionists and anti-Zionists during the decades preceding the Nazi era. The situation in Austria, however, was quite different. The Israelitische Kultusgemeinde (IKG) of Vienna was not solely a municipal Jewish community, but also represented the relatively few Jews in the Austrian provinces. The much stronger ethnicity of Viennese Jews, who were predominantly of Polish (Galician) ori-

27

gin, perhaps contributed to this difference. When the Nazis came to Austria in 1938, Dr. Josef Löwenherz became chairman of the IKG. Unlike the German organizations, which reflected the strong and ancient tradition of German Jewry, the IKG, representing a relatively new community under tremendous pressure, did not show much inclination to evade or otherwise thwart Nazi designs. Pressure by Gestapo officials, who wanted to demonstrate how to get rid of the Jews quickly and efficiently caused a very swift emigration movement. Unhampered by legalities still ingrained in the German system, Nazis in Austria were free to use open terrorism and imprisonment in concentration camps to prod the Jews to leave. Most young Jews had left Austria by the end of 1939, and only 55,000–60,000 confessing Jews, most of them old people, remained. Table 2 illustrates the number of Jews remaining in other Central European countries at that time.

Table 2: Jews in Central Europe at the End of 1939

	Jews	"Non-Aryans"*	Total	Jews before Hitler
Germany	200,000–225,000	65,000	265,000–290,000	522,000 (1933)
Austria	55,000	70,000	125,000	186,000 (1938)
Bohemia and Moravia	75,000 (including 20,000 refugees)	15,000	90,000	110,000 (early 1939)

*Christians of Jewish descent or persons of partly Jewish parentage. For the sources for this table, see n. 1.

The major problem in emigration was where to turn. All the prospective countries of immigration were extremely dubious about receiving Jewish emigrants from Europe. Most potential Jewish emigrants were middle-class people—merchants, intellectuals, clerks, and a sprinkling of artisans. But the economic crisis still held most of the world in its grip, and receiving countries had large and unsolved problems of unemployment to deal with. Middle-class immigrants were therefore unwanted. Furthermore, antisemitism was rampant, especially in the United States of the thirties, which did not make the absorption of Jews any easier. In Palestine, after a period of relatively free immigration which reached a peak when 62,000 Jews entered the country in 1935, the

28

British government severely limited entry because of growing resistance by the Arabs. Nevertheless, as table 3 shows, relatively
large numbers managed to enter the various countries.[14] The
number entering the United States increased significantly after
President Roosevelt intervened in late 1935 to ease administrative
restrictions in the quota system instituted under President Hoover
in 1930. In Palestine, illegal immigration added some 17,000 persons to the legal migration in 1938–39, and most of these came
from Central Europe. Illegal migration also accounted for a fairly
high proportion of entrants into America. The evidence, therefore, contradicts the view that Jews did little to save themselves.
Large numbers of people managed to escape; in Germany and
Austria, these amounted to 60 percent of Jews who identified
with Judaism and were organized in Jewish communities. Even of
the unorganized group of people of Jewish descent, 40 percent
managed to leave. These figures would seem to prove those historians wrong who claim that the organized Jewish community, by
its passivity, contributed to the destruction of the Jews and that
Jews would have been better off without it.

Table 3: Jewish Emigration by Area, 1933–39 (Estimated)

Safe Areas	Total	Areas Later German-Occupied	Total
United States	85,000	Belgium	15,000
Latin America	85,000	France	30,000
Palestine	80,000	Holland	27,000
Shanghai	18,000	Other	38,000
Australia and Africa	7,000		
Britain	42,000		
Switzerland	12,000		
Grand totals	**329,000**		**110,000**

Because of the preference given to young emigrants by
countries of refuge, and also as a result of demographic processes
that long preceded the Nazi regime, Central European Jewry in
1939 consisted largely of an ageing population in increasing need
of welfare. In Germany at the end of 1939, for example, some
52,000 persons had to be fully supported. Winter help had to be

provided to over 70,000 persons, and there were only 9,555 school-aged children, who attended 127 elementary, 7 secondary, and 5 other (presumably vocational) schools. On the other hand, there were 91 institutions for the aged and 52 percent of the Jews were over fifty years old.[15] There were 6,000 more deaths than births in 1938, and 6,300 more in 1939.

JDC's share in providing help was considerable in 1938–39. Its funds went to the ZA in Germany and the IKG in Austria, and the ingenious transfer arrangement itself meant that emigration was pushed at the same time as local institutions were helped to maintain themselves. Migrants were aided at every stage of their often torturous wanderings; illegal immigrants stranded in South America, or in the Aegean Sea on the way to Palestine, were sent help; and in the summer of 1939, in the famous case of the refugee ship *Saint Louis*, JDC paid tremendous sums to save over 900 Jewish refugees from being returned to Germany.[16] The Jewish Agency, attempting to get as many Jews as possible into Palestine, also received help—though it was often reluctantly given, because JDC argued that the Zionists should pay for this emigration themselves and not preempt money which should go to Jews fleeing elsewhere. Through its support of HICEM, the Jewish emigration society, JDC paid for a significant proportion of Jewish migration, and its funds activated societies aiding refugees in England and South American countries.[17]

Inevitably, welfare and emigration touched upon political issues. Theoretically AJC was JDC's political ally, looking after Jewish rights in foreign countries. Yet in fact, in the world of the late thirties, politics and social work could not be separated. JDC had had a significant share in the unsuccessful attempt to solve the refugee problem through international action: it had been involved both in James G. McDonald's High Commission for Refugees (Jewish and Others) Coming from Germany, set up by the League of Nations in 1933, and in the Evian Conference of July, 1938. It cooperated fully with the Inter-Governmental Committee on Refugees (IGCR) set up in London after Evian, and in 1939 it established the so-called Coordinating Foundation to provide capital outside of Germany with which Jewish refugees from Nazi Europe would be settled. This foundation was part of an abortive plan by the president of the German State Bank, Hjalmar Schacht, and the director of IGCR, George Rublee, to enable Central European Jews to escape with some of their capital and thus be more acceptable to receiving countries.

30

All these schemes came to nothing. Most of the world was essentially uninterested in the fate of the Jews. The Jews who did save themselves did so through Jewish efforts and individual infiltration into various countries. When war broke out, about 110,000 Jewish refugees were spread all over Europe. It was clear that they could not stay there, but it would be extremely difficult to move them to other havens. In fact, Morris D. Waldman, Secretary of AJC, thought that the efforts at an international solution to the refugee problem had been a double-edged sword, and that emigration possibilities had actually lessened. "Many countries are said to have closed their doors in the expectation that through the efforts of the Winterton-Rublee Committee (IGCR), refugees from Germany might bring some money with them, types of immigrants to be preferred to the destitute refugees who had been admitted in the past."[18]

The Pre-Holocaust Tragedy of Polish Jewry

If refugees from Nazi-controlled areas were the main preoccupation of JDC at the outbreak of war, the situation in Eastern Europe was almost as pressing. The case of the Polish Jews has been fully described elsewhere.[19] Open and violent Polish antisemitism did recede somewhat in the spring of 1939 in the face of the increasing German threat to Poland, but the basic condition of 3.3 million Polish Jews was characterized by terrible poverty, including near starvation for about one-third of them, by political helplessness, and by the hostility of the majority of the population. In addition, Polish Jewry was plagued by political dissension: the anti-Zionist socialist Bund party, the non-Zionist Orthodox Agudat Israel, and the different and warring Zionist factions were about equally strong, and these groups were unable to agree about policy. The Polish government, a semifascist regime of army officers, wanted to get rid of the Jews by emigration. This was, of course, out of the question. Countries of immigration certainly would not receive Polish Jews when they refused admission to most German Jews, and Palestine was all but closed by the British. Polish Jewry could not stay where it was; neither could it leave. The government did, however, support the Zionists, because Zionism seemed to promise a chance of getting rid of at least some Jews.

In such a situation, JDC could only offer palliative solutions: banks where artisans and small traders could get loans free of

31

interest; children's homes and food for hungry children, dispensed largely by the Centrala Opieki nad Sierotami (CENTOS), a JDC-sponsored organization; and health institutions organized by TOZ, another JDC creation. Paradoxically, however, JDC, an American group still controlled by non-Zionist liberals, was an agent of national unification in Poland. By late August, 1939, it had managed to establish a committee for social and welfare work, led by the Lodz industrialist Karol Sachs, in which Zionist, Orthodox, and assimilationist elements participated; the Bund also agreed to cooperate with it. On September 2, 1939, a day after the war began, the Warsaw office of JDC cabled New York that the Central Committee had finally been established.

A development could already be discerned in prewar Poland which was to mark one of the major trends in the history of the Holocaust as well as the history of JDC. Contrary to the situation in Germany, where JDC relied on the ZA to receive and spend JDC money, there was a very active and influential JDC office in Warsaw. An effective staff had been built up there since the early 1920s, which in time became almost autonomous. The somewhat supercilious and patronizing attitude of many German Jews (whether in Germany, America, or Palestine) toward their Polish brethren certainly had something to do with it, but be that as it may, JDC officers thought that they had to supervise the spending of JDC funds in Poland very closely.

It is unfortunately impossible to examine in detail why and how the Warsaw JDC office came to be manned and administered the way it did. It is, however, a fact that the team in charge was a most remarkable collection of individuals, including Isaac Giterman, David Guzik, Leib Neustadt, and the famous historian Emmanuel Ringelblum, to mention just the chief names. Most of the staff were left-wing Zionists—which is rather surprising, considering the tendencies of JDC's American leadership—and very active in Polish Jewish life. Giterman was a supporter of the Hitachdut-ZS, the moderate socialist wing of Zionism, whereas Ringelblum and a number of other JDC officials were members of the Left Poalei Zion, a Marxist Zionist faction which, until the war, refused to participate in Zionist congresses because of its opposition to collaboration with bourgeois Zionist representatives. It would be hard to imagine a more unlikely recruiting ground for the conservative-minded philanthropic American Jewish organization. The fact that the JDC office in Warsaw was not just another local representative of a foreign philanthropic

32

agency, but a tremendously active and vital part of the community's social, cultural, and political elite, made all the difference in the frightful situation that lay ahead.

The Central Committee was very largely the achievement of Giterman and the Warsaw staff. Another typical activity was the response of this staff when the Nazis expelled 18,000 Jews of Polish citizenship living in Germany and 5,000 of these unfortunates found themselves in a Polish border village named Zbaszyn in late October, 1938. With the Poles refusing to admit these refugees into Poland, Ringelblum and Giterman themselves went and organized the necessary help, although this was contrary to the standard JDC practice of letting local organizations do the work. Equally significantly, both men later were among the ardent supporters of Jewish resistance to the Germans in the Warsaw ghetto.

JDC was also active in other East European countries, such as Lithuania, Rumania, and eastern Czechoslovakia. In the face of an ever more serious deterioration of the situation of Jews in those countries, palliative solutions similar to those in Poland were offered, but with less money and therefore less effect.

European Jewry on the Eve of War

The outlook in 1939 was bleak. JDC tried to get local communities to raise money from their richer members. While it is true that some communities could have done much more, and some in fact did do quite a lot, in most communities there were simply no reserves available for social and welfare work. There were exceptions. In Switzerland, for instance, the head of the Jewish community, Saly Mayer, heard what was termed a "pep talk" from Morris C. Troper, JDC's European director, who claimed that "it was hardly fair that American money should be used until he was convinced that the maximum amount possible had been raised in his own community." Mayer did in fact obtain increased sums from members of his community (which numbered only 18,000).[20] On the other hand, there were many extremely wealthy Jews in Hungary, but the community leadership there had degenerated to a frightening degree. There were internecine quarrels, a lack of public and community spirit, and mass conversions. Little help was forthcoming for the many Hungarian Jews who needed it, especially those in the territories annexed from Czechoslovakia in early 1939.

It is evident that the many complicated problems could not

possibly be handled from New York, given the relatively slow means of transportation and communication. Ever since the early twenties, JDC had tried to remedy this situation by having a central office responsible for the whole of Europe. Until the rise of the Nazis, this office was located in Berlin, and the New York leadership delegated some authority to it. In 1939, however, the center of JDC activity in Europe was in Paris, where JDC's European Executive Council was located, with Morris C. Troper as chairman or European director. The other members of the council were relatively junior staff, and in the crucial summer of 1939, it was Troper who was JDC in Europe, just as Bernhard Kahn had been until late in 1938. Troper emerges from JDC correspondence as a warm human being with compassion and a sense of humor, but he apparently never became very popular either in Europe or with his own people in America. He had become involved in JDC affairs by being head of the firm that JDC used for all its accounting business—obviously a very important aspect of the work of a public philanthropic organization. But he never quite shook off the image of a "mere" accountant, and while his letters and memoranda reflect quick intelligence, broad vision, and seemingly considerable powers of decision, that is not the impression one gathers from later testimonies of people with whom he worked.

In late August, 1939, JDC and HICEM called an emergency conference in Paris of their main representatives, who discussed arrangements to be made in case war broke out. A rare and interesting motion picture taken on that occasion shows Troper, Joseph C. Hyman, who had come from New York to participate in the proceedings, Saly Mayer from Switzerland, Gertrude van Tijn of Holland, Max Gottschalk of Belgium, Isaac Giterman of Poland, Marie Schmolka of Prague, Otto Hirsch of Berlin, and others. The main decision taken by JDC in the wake of that conference was to transfer large amounts of money to Poland for the second half of 1939 and to keep its cash reserves in European banks as low as possible.[21] In the midst of the conference, Giterman rushed back to Warsaw to be at his post when hostilities began. That was the last time his colleagues saw him. On September 1, German soldiers crossed the Polish border. Night descended over the Jewish people in Europe.

34

1

A Time of Chaos

The American Scene, 1939–1940

At the Paris meeting of JDC's European leaders in August, 1939, European Director Morris C. Troper announced that $400,000 would be made available to the committees represented in order to tide them over the first few difficult months (over one-half of the sum went to the Warsaw JDC). It was hoped that by the end of 1939 the war might be over or the situation stabilized. In New York, the outbreak of war caused a good deal of confusion. On September 5, President Roosevelt declared U.S. neutrality in the European conflict, whereupon James N. Rosenberg, summarizing the position of JDC's Executive Committee, wrote in a letter to the entire organization that "our course must be to lean over backward" to avoid engaging in any relief work that might infringe the country's laws. He foresaw "frightfully difficult problems" in determining whether JDC was doing anything that might aid the belligerents. "We must not and cannot let our desire to help suffering cause us to lose our moorings. Our rule must be 'When in doubt, ask the State Department.' "[1] His words appear to echo the stand taken by AJC, which after all was the political organization of JDC's leadership.

In order to strengthen Paul Baerwald's weak leadership, Edward M. M. Warburg, son of the founder, now became cochairman. JDC, however, feared that it might be perceived as too sectarian by non-Jewish Americans, a fear which led one member of the Executive Committee to express his belief that it might not be desir-

35

able "to particularize as between Polish Jews and Polish non-Jews." Joseph Rosen, the man who had guided JDC's social engineering venture in Russia in the twenties and thirties, and who was better acquainted with European realities than JDC's assimilated leaders, thought that European Jews had to secure adequate representation, or else they might not receive their due share of aid. Morris D. Waldman, secretary of AJC, tried to influence JDC in the direction of his organization's policies. He suggested the establishment of a strong AJC-JDC staff in neutral Holland to watch the situation. This action would be an exact repetition of that taken during World War I. "We should exercise the greatest caution in avoiding giving the impression that we Jews have special interests in the present situation. . . . Jews in Europe are not the only victims of the present turmoil." If Jews were given a fair share of management and field personnel in any nonsectarian aid effort, then they would not have to "segregate [themselves] from other groups."[2]

Some time passed before JDC's leadership realized that American neutrality was increasingly to be "bent backward" to help Britain; when the realization came, what was interpreted as helping Britain became a major JDC objective. In clashes between the interests of the British blockade and the extension of help to European Jews, majority decisions of the Executive Committee tended to support the blockade. This was so despite a series of changes in the membership of the committee in 1939 and 1940.

Under pressure from Jewish organizations—mainly the Council of Federations and Welfare Funds—the AJC had been forced into a Council of Jewish Organizations with the American Jewish Congress, B'nai Brith, and the Labor Committee. The pressure, however, was not strong enough to unite American Jewry in any effective way, and the Council of Jewish Organizations was a failure. Nevertheless, it did reflect a new reality—the rise of East European Jews as the decisive influence in American Jewish life and the corresponding weakening of the old American German Jewish aristocracy. This situation coincided with the emergence of professional leadership in all of the major Jewish groups and the acceptance of that leadership by the lay members. These trends expressed themselves in the demand raised by the American Jewish Congress that the membership of JDC's Executive Committee be broadened to include a representative of the congress.

JDC did not accept the idea of an American Jewish Congress representative. But in November, 1939, it did agree to choose seven names out of a list submitted by that organization, provided the new members would sit as individuals and not as representatives of any group. The American Jewish Congress was connected with the World Jewish Congress (WJC), which Joseph Hyman characterized as "wholly political and international in its objectives and scope." JDC, however, was "an American organization," bound by Roosevelt's declaration of neutrality. Including members of the American Jewish Congress, even as individuals, meant that others representing Orthodox and Labor interests would have to be added to create the desired balance. Among these new members were Morris Rothenberg, a Zionist, Hirsch Manischewitz of the Orthodox group, and Max M. Warburg, Felix Warburg's brother, who had reached the safety of America from Hamburg in 1938.[3]

The effect of these changes was in a sense the opposite of that intended by the American Jewish Congress and other groups. The Executive Committee became an unwieldy body unsuited for rapid decision making, and the steering group had to rely increasingly on the Administrative Committee, which ran day-to-day affairs. Even more than before, decisions were taken informally, by telephone or in consultation at the office, and it was through these arrangements that the professional staff gained more and more influence as time went on.

The Financial Squeeze

A major issue for JDC was its perennial struggle with the United Palestine Appeal (UPA) over scarce charity dollars. The growing strength of the fund-raising bodies united in the Council of Federations and Welfare Funds influenced the reluctant UPA and JDC to coalesce and establish the United Jewish Appeal (UJA). After a first effort on a temporary basis in 1939, another agreement was patched up in early 1940 for the 1940 campaign. This provided that, of the first $11 million collected, the National Refugee Service (NRS), established in 1938 to look after new Jewish immigrants to the United States, would receive $3.5 million, while JDC would get $5.25 million and UPA $2.5 million. JDC was very worried about its financial position, because as 1939 closed it had a deficit of $1.8 million, and the outlook for 1940 was anything but bright. As it turned out, the apprehension was justified. Total JDC income for 1940 slumped sharply and indebtedness increased. JDC leaders calculated that, of the dollars for overseas collected in America, JDC was getting 60 percent and UPA 40 percent. But the number of refugees entering Palestine was small, and in the existing emergency it was more important to save Jews or help them by relief work than to provide for building up the National Home. UPA of course argued that, in the long run as well as the short, the base in Palestine should have priority.

JDC's financial problems multiplied during 1940. With the beginning of the war, emigration work underwent a crisis. Emigration from Europe had been organized by HICEM (formally, HIAS-ICA-EMIGDIRECT), which was essentially a combination of the JDC-supported Hebrew Sheltering and Immigrant Aid Society (HIAS) and the London-based Jewish Colonisation Association (ICA), but the HICEM was registered in France and could not look after refugees from Nazi-controlled territories. Moreover, the brunt of HICEM expenditures in 1940 had to be borne by JDC (amounting to $240,000). Prior to the war, Paris HICEM had obtained so-called individual clearances, payments from American relatives and other sources for the emigration of Central European Jews, which were paid out for tickets and other necessities. In return, the emigrants paid in their marks in Berlin, Vienna, or Prague for use in their local communities. A similar arrangement had functioned through London via the International Trade and Investment Agency, a special financial organ set up by the Warburg family. Now, with HICEM in France out of the picture, JDC accepted an offer by its Dutch affiliate (led by David Cohen and Gertrude van Tijn) and transmitted funds to Amsterdam for these emigration arrangements. Relatives in the United States and elsewhere also sent money, either directly to Amsterdam or to HIAS or NRS in New York, and thus enabled emigration to proceed.

For a number of practical reasons, Troper transferred the whole operation of direct emigration out of Nazi territory to Brussels at the beginning of 1940. A special HICEM affiliate, BELHICEM, was entrusted with this operation under the effective leadership of Alice R. Emanuel; emigration from Allied-controlled territory remained largely under HICEM. When Germany invaded the Low Countries on May 10, 1940, Emanuel fled Brussels, and most of the records of the Service de transmigration, as it was called, were lost. HIAS and NRS advised JDC that they could not really cope with the deposits from relatives, and JDC reluctantly agreed to establish a Transmigration Bureau in its own offices and under its own name. By the end of 1940, this bureau had become a vast operation, and by June, 1941, $3.77 million had been accepted from relatives for 29,000 prospective emigrants. This sum almost doubled by the end of the year, but JDC then refused to accept any more deposits because the practical possibilities of escaping from Europe had decreased. When America entered the war in December, 1941, the Transmigration Bureau went into liquidation and returned unexpended funds to the givers.[4]

Emigration was in fact the main burden on JDC's budget in 1940–41. With the UJA fund-raising campaign going from bad to worse in 1940, allocations began to be cut drastically towards March of that year. Thus the allocation to Belgium, which had been $80,000 in December, 1939, went down to $60,000 in January, 1940, and $40,000 in March. All of Europe received $660,000 in January and February, but only $440,000 in March. Allocations for emigration had been running at $35,000 a month until March, and then were reduced to $20,000 until June, and to $10,000 in the summer. They reached a nadir with an allocation of $5,000 in November, 1940.

The pressure from Europe, the feeling that if JDC went out to raise funds independently more could be obtained, and general bitterness toward the Zionists and their Palestine-oriented campaigns made JDC decide, in late 1940, to dissolve UJA and strike out on its own. Preparations for independent fund-raising were made. But counterpressure from the Council of Federations and Welfare Funds was decisive: no money could be raised without its help, and it was tired of the constant bickering between Zionists and non-Zionists. In the end, both sides were forced into a new UJA agreement, which was signed on March 5, 1941. With fewer immigrants coming in, NRS would receive only $2 million of the first $8.8 million. JDC would get $4.275 million and UPA $2.525 million.[5] Stringent economies and drastic cuts had reduced JDC deficits to less than $1 million by the end of 1940, and the same level of expenditure as that of late 1940 was maintained in 1941. What this meant in terms of human suffering that could have been alleviated with more money is very difficult to estimate.

What caused the reduction in income to all of the overseas funds? There is no doubt that the rise of a virulent American antisemitism in the late thirties made its mark in 1940–41. A Gallup poll in April, 1938, indicated that 58 percent of Americans thought that the persecution of European Jews was partly or entirely their own fault. In July, 1939, 31.9 percent of those asked thought that Jews had too much power in the business world and that steps should be taken to prevent them from accumulating it; 10.1 percent expressed the view that Jews should be deported from America. Even as late as July, 1942, 44 percent of those polled thought that Jews had too much power and influence in America.[6] In the light of these sentiments, many contributors thought that JDC should stress loyalty to America and that spending too much money on overseas causes might be detrimental to the position of American Jews.

JDC, especially in the person of Morris Troper, tried its best to counteract these beliefs. In April, 1940, Troper declared that American Jews should realize what budget cuts meant to those who now looked to them, and to them alone, for help. Some 60 percent of German Jews would lose the visas they had obtained with difficulty if present budgetary levels were maintained, because no funds would be available for tickets. However, the response was not encouraging. A contributor from Denver, Colorado, argued that contributions would dry up unless support for refugees anywhere but in the United States were abandoned. The American Red Cross or the Friends would be better suited to handle the overseas problems. "The new order must be met courageously," his letter said, and JDC must stop asking for money.[7] Even Baerwald asked in June, 1940, whether JDC should not direct its first attention to helping the Allies with their refugee problems (for example, by taking care of British children), rather than continuing to deal with Jewish questions.[8]

Troper, and later Joseph J. Schwartz, fought vigorously against these tendencies, aided by most of the professionals and laymen in the New York organization. In a moving appeal to the Board of Directors on September 9, 1940, Troper declared:

> Where I stand before you this morning, I am not here as Morris Troper alone; I am here as Hirsch of Berlin, Loewenherz of Vienna, as Giterman, Guzik and Neustadt of Poland, as Eppler of Budapest and Friedmann of Prague, as Fueredi of Bratislava and Grodzensky of Lithuania, as Van Tijn of Amsterdam and Ussoskin of Roumania, as Valobra of Italy and d'Esaguy of Lisbon. . . . They have nothing to look forward to except starvation, disease and ultimate extinction. . . . Ours is the sacred task of keeping our brethren alive—if not all, then at least some. . . . The problem is one and indivisible for all the Jews of the world.[9]

JDC propaganda used every report out of Europe, every effective speaker; the evidence for this is overwhelming. It was not the fault of the organization that American Jews failed to respond, or that on occasion even some of its own leaders despaired.

On the other hand, important organizational changes were made that tended in the long run to strengthen JDC's effectiveness in spite of the budget cuts. Joseph Schwartz, who had become secretary of JDC in 1939, was asked in April, 1940, whether he would go to Europe to assist, and ultimately take the place of, Morris Troper. On May 3, Schwartz left for Europe. Moses A. Leavitt was recalled from the PEC and began his second term as secretary. He was to serve the organization in that capacity, and then as executive vice-chairman, until his death in 1965. Young professionals were sent to Europe, Cuba, and other places as occasion demanded: Emanuel Rosen to Italy, Bertrand S. Jacobson to Rumania, Moses W. Beckelman to Lithuania, Herbert Katzki to Paris, and Laura Margolis to Havana, among others. In February, 1941, Paul Baerwald resigned his chairmanship, and Edward M. M. Warburg became de jure what he had been for some time de facto: head of JDC. Essentially, however, the period from spring, 1940, until well beyond the end of the war is that of Joseph Schwartz, a powerful and many-sided figure who vitally influenced not only JDC but American Jewry as a whole.

Schwartz—"Packy" to his closest friends—was a tall, black-haired man with a large mouth and a large nose. In fact, everything about him was large and generous: his hands, his smile, his voice. Born in the Ukraine, he had come from a rabbinical family that settled in the United States when he was a small boy. He grew up in Baltimore, Maryland, studied at what later became Yeshiva University, and was ordained an Orthodox rabbi in 1922. Not satisfied with this achievement, however, he went on to Yale University and became an orientalist with a good knowledge of Arabic and Hebrew. He received his Ph.D. in 1927, and afterwards spent some time in Egypt at Cairo University and in Palestine. The economic crisis in 1929 prevented him from entering academic life as he had planned, though for some time he earned his living teaching German at Long Island University. For a short time he worked as a rabbi but then decided he did not like to; in later life he was no longer observant.

In the thirties, Schwartz accepted a post at the Brooklyn Federation of Jewish Charities, where he spent almost ten years as executive director before becoming secretary of JDC. His rabbinical background and his wide reading in academic disciplines made him both a man of the world and a lover of all things Jewish; more especially, he was deeply committed to the Jewish people as they actually were, with their manifold qualities and problems. He was at once a trained administrator, a social worker used to dealing with people, and a man who had learned how best to spend scarce charity dollars.

Schwartz was not an easy person to get along with. He was never petty or vengeful, but he was apt to get impatient with slowness or inefficiency. He was intensely loyal to his organization—so much so that he tended to forget or gloss over his own fights with JDC and try to defend positions with which he actually disagreed. Above all, this man with his well-developed sense of humor and occasional sharp sarcasm was an ardent defender of Jews everywhere. At first hesitant and sometimes defeated in his battles with the New York office, he soon emerged as the single most influential personality in JDC councils during the war. The period of World War II and its aftermath—the heroic period in the history of JDC and the most tragic period in Jewish history—was indelibly marked with his charismatic personality.

JDC, Refugees, and the French Debacle in 1940

Morris Troper was in Rome on May 9, 1940, and by telephone ordered Alice Emanuel to leave Belgium immediately. On May 10, the Germans invaded the Low Countries and moved into France. On May 14, both Troper and Joseph Schwartz arrived in Paris. Seeing the dangers of the situation, they decided on a quick tour of the continent, going first to Switzerland, where they discussed with Saly Mayer, head of the Swiss Jewish community organization, the possibility of his becoming the local JDC representative. The idea was that if JDC were forced to leave Europe altogether, Mayer would serve as a conduit of funds and information, provided, of course, that Switzerland remained neutral. Mayer accepted—marking another important milestone in the history of JDC.

From Switzerland the two went on to Italy and then Budapest, where they met with Otto Hirsch of RVE, Josef Löwenherz of the Vienna Jewish community, and leaders from Bohemia, Slovakia, Yugoslavia, and Rumania. Emigration procedures were discussed, including illegal immigration to Palestine—of which more must be said later. On June 10, Troper and Schwartz got back to Paris. Most of the JDC personnel had already been evacuated to Angers, where JDC had opened an office in April, 1939, and a staff member was sent to Bordeaux to establish a foothold there. JDC was the last Jewish organization to quit Paris, leaving on

June 11, after it had been advised by the American embassy that there was nothing more the organization could do there. Troper, Schwartz, Herbert Katzki, and four secretaries left in one car and joined the legions of refugees crowding French roads away from the German invaders. There was almost no food or gasoline, and there was a continual danger of German air attacks. European JDC had become a refugee.

With a great deal of resourcefulness and sheer luck, they finally made it to Bordeaux, the temporary seat of the French government, on June 15. They found total anarchy, and it was clear that no work could be done from there. Troper and his staff were evicted from one hotel after another, and he decided to send Schwartz to Lisbon to find out whether an office could be established in that city. Schwartz left on June 18, reaching Portugal a few days later. What happened in Bordeaux is perhaps best described by quoting Troper's report to the Executive Committee on July 8, 1940.

> Bordeaux, a city normally of some 300,000 people now had a population of one million. . . . One spent hours trying to find a place to eat. . . . Money was of little value. . . . We were isolated. . . . The air was filled with all kinds of rumors. . . . It developed that these rumors were true, that the Reynaud government had resigned, that Pétain had become Prime Minister and that an armistice with the Germans and Italians was being sought. . . . The Germans were advancing and were expected to reach Bordeaux any day, any hour. . . . We all decided that the staff had to be gotten out of Bordeaux . . . and that one of us should try to get to Lisbon. . . . There was uneasiness about severing, even for a temporary period, relations with the JDC, especially among those of our staff who were stateless or who had Polish or German passports. . . . It was almost impossible to receive a Portuguese visa unless one had . . . the necessary permission to proceed to some other point beyond Portugal. . . . On Wednesday (June 18) an announcement was made that after 12 o'clock that night no automobile would be allowed to leave Bordeaux. We decided to get busy and to get out before the deadline. . . . We spent the night in the automobile, proceeding in the early morning to Bayonne where we hoped to obtain Portuguese and Spanish visas for Katzki, Miss Manson and Miss Cohen. . . . They waited in line with hundreds of others from 9.30 in the morning until 6 o'clock in the evening at the Portuguese Consulate before they finally received their visas.[10]

Some sources estimate the number of Jewish refugees crowding Bordeaux at the time at about 30,000. Approximately a third of these were looking for a way to enter Portugal; Spain, destroyed by civil war and ruled by a fascist dictator, could not be considered a haven. At this juncture occurred one of the most extraordinary incidents in the history of the Holocaust. The Portuguese consul general at Bordeaux was a man named Aristides de Sousa-Mendes, a devout Catholic of Marrano extraction whose ancestors had been converted by force on the expulsion of the Jews from the Iberian peninsula. Mendes had a very large family—thirteen children at the time—and a brother who was the Portuguese minister to Poland in 1939. From May 10, 1940, the Portuguese government's instructions regarding the granting of transit visas were unequivocal: visas were to be granted to people with money, provided that they had a legal permit to enter a country of final destination. Jews in any case were to be barred.

It is not quite clear who or what made up the consul's mind to risk his career and his future to help the refugees. One story has it that Rabbi Chaim H. Kruger, a Polish refugee from Belgium, was offered the hospitality of Mendes's home, together with his wife and five children. Kruger is said to have persuaded the consul to disregard his government's instructions. Other accounts seem to indicate that the plight of the refugees aroused his deep Christian convictions. Mendes's family, especially his wife and two of his sons, certainly shared his views. What is most probable is that it was a combination of principles firmly held and immediate impressions of refugee problems through individuals such as Kruger that made up his mind.[11]

The result was one of the most fantastically successful rescue operations to occur during the war. Mendes, single-handedly and in contravention of his government's instructions, stamped a very large number of Portuguese visas in passports or temporary travel documents, and he did so without asking for payment. The number of these visas must have been close to 10,000, and that is the approximate number of refugees who actually reached Portugal in the summer of 1940. Not all of them received their visas from Mendes, but a very high proportion must have. It is not clear how long the granting of visas at Bordeaux lasted, but it can not have been more than a couple of weeks. Mendes was of course recalled by his government, which apparently sent two officials from Lisbon to bring him back. On his way to the Spanish frontier he stopped at Bayonne, where the local Portuguese vice-consul, on instructions from Lisbon, was refusing to issue visas. Using his authority as the vice-consul's superior, Mendes spent a day there granting them, and then proceeded to Hendaye, where the Spanish authorities, faced with a very large crowd of refugees in possession of Portuguese visas, had closed the border to await instructions from Madrid and Lisbon. What happened then is not quite clear. Either Mendes advised the refugees to cross the border at other points or he went across at Hendaye, certifying to the Spaniards that the visas in the refugees' passports were genuine. In any case, on his intervention, the refugees went through.[12]

The story of Mendes is perhaps the most amazing instance of an individual's help to Jews (and others) during the Holocaust. There is no doubt that many thousands of persons were saved by the courageous act of a single man acting out of religious and moral conviction. When one considers that throughout the war Switzerland saved some 25,000 Jews, or that not more than a few thousand managed to squeeze through Turkey to Palestine from 1940 to 1944, the 10,000 or so Mendes saved are a symbol of what true humanitarianism can achieve, or could have achieved.

Mendes returned to Lisbon, was hauled before an inquiry committee, and was fired from the Portuguese foreign service for not obeying instructions. Unable to find any other employment, burdened with debts and obliged to support a large family, he worked for a short time for the Jewish refugee committee at Lisbon and then drifted from one occupation to another until he finally died in poverty in 1954, forgotten by everyone. He does not seem to have regretted his great act of rescue. His daughter Joana says that he stated that if thousands of Jews had to suffer because of one Catholic (Hitler was, at least on paper, a Catholic), it was perfectly all right for one Catholic to suffer for thousands of Jews. Some of his children emigrated to the United States, and in the 1960s Yad Vashem, the Martyrs and Heroes' Remembrance Authority in Israel, planted a tree in his memory—a belated recognition of an act worthy of a Catholic saint or a Jewish tzaddik.[13]

JDC in Portugal and Spain, 1939–1941

The record of Franco's Spain regarding Jewish refugees has been the subject of much controversy. What is beyond doubt, however, is that the Spanish government refused throughout the war to allow any official Jewish relief agency to open offices on its territory. Jewish refugees had to obtain transit visas through Portugal in order to obtain transit visas through Spain, which meant that they had to acquire visas to some final destination first. In a minority of cases these were U.S. visas; usually, however, they were visas to Cuba, the Dominican Republic, or some other Central or South American republic. In most instances such visas were either forged or sold to the refugees by representatives of these countries with the understanding that they would not be honored. In a small number of instances they might be genuine and enable the holder to claim entry. In June, 1940, Troper thought that the prices for visas sold in Bordeaux were "very reasonable. . . . So are visas for Haiti, and, yes, for San Domingo, and for any country willing to do business."[14]

The first mass influx to Portugal was therefore quasi-legal. There were different categories of refugees: French, German and Austrian, Czech, Belgian, Dutch, Polish, and stateless. There were those who needed no assistance because they were wealthy or had relatives on the other side of the ocean who would look after them; or they were well-known intellectuals; or they had political connections in Britain or America or with the various governments-in-exile. On the other end of the scale were those who desperately needed assistance, and it was these people who began to turn to JDC and to HIAS, which also had an office, opened by Dr. James Bernstein and Ilya Dijour, in the Portuguese capital.

In line with traditional JDC practice, much of the relief work was done through the local community, which was very small but rather well organized. At the head of the community stood Moses B. Amzalak, a well-known professor, and there was a refugee committee, the Commisão Portuguesa de Assistencia aos Judeos Refugiados, headed by a young doctor, Augusto d'Esaguy. The secretary was a man who was to play a very important role in the rescue operations in the peninsula, Samuel Sequerra. D'Esaguy and Amzalak had a good relationship with the heads of the all-powerful police in Lisbon, and it was obvious that the best way of dealing with the refugees already in the country was to strengthen and subsidize the local committee. This was done, at considerable expense, because JDC believed that the local authorities must be kept happy about the refugees already in the country so that additional people might be allowed to enter. The HIAS office took over the visa and other arrangements.

JDC tried to have HIAS deal with the emigration transport arrangements as well, but in the end this became the main preoccupation of Schwartz and his staff. Originally the American Express Lines shipping company was prepared to transport emigrants to the New World, but as the European situation became more complicated, it preferred American citizens who were returning home. Only two Spanish ships were available, on a very limited basis, sailing usually from Seville to the American continent. The only real possibility for arranging transport was therefore to use the medium-sized Portuguese ships: the *Nyassa*, *Guinee*, *Teneriffe*, *Serpapinto*, *Magallanes*, *Mouzinho*, and *Colonial*. American visas were issued only after proof of a booked passage had been given, and JDC had to buy berths for emigrants from Germany and German-controlled territory without knowing whether the people concerned would manage to arrive on time. Unused berths still had to be paid for, and sometimes, especially in 1941, the shipping company would not agree to book individual berths, but only blocks of places or even the whole ship. The financial risk was great, but it was the only way of saving those that could still be saved.

JDC and HICEM transported large numbers of refugees to the United States, Cuba, the West Indies, and other places. Additional people went who made private arrangements. But the refugees had to be maintained while waiting for ships, and it was JDC's task to do that. A camp was established at Caldas de Rainha, and other refugees were maintained in a few small places along the coast and at Oporto. The numbers were relatively small, because most of those entering during the first mass influx managed to leave very soon; of those who stayed on, many had funds or could obtain them from relatives abroad. At the end of 1940, there were 1,500 refugees (out of a total of 8,000 in Portugal) supported by d'Esaguy's committee with JDC funds—though the New York office admitted that because of budget cuts the assistance had been reduced to below subsistence level.

The question of how many refugees got away through Portugal in the summer of 1940 is of central importance: it was beyond doubt the largest number of Jews to escape the Nazis during the war itself by flight to the West. Yet it was largely chance that made this mass escape possible: people took advantage of the availability of Portuguese transit visas and the generally chaotic conditions. The majority seem to have been German and other Central and East European Jewish refugees, among them such well-known individuals as Marc Chagall and Leon Feuchtwanger. Non-Jews were either political refugees, British soldiers trying to reach home, or French officials and officers. According to JDC accounts, about 90 percent of the refugees were Jews.

In November, 1940, the number of Jewish refugees then in Portugal was estimated by JDC at 10,000. In Feburary, 1941, d'Esaguy estimated that 32,000 refugees had gone through Portugal in the first months after the fall of France. My own estimate is that in 1940 some 25,000 Jewish refugees passed through the two countries, and another 15,000 came in 1941. If this is approximately correct, then about 40,000 Jews must have entered Spain between the fall of France and early 1942.[15]

How many of these 40,000 were Jews who reached Lisbon straight from Germany or Austria, and how many were French or Belgian? For 1941, it appears that most came from the Reich, which can be explained by the fact that the Germans permitted Jewish emigration until the summer of 1941, finally prohibiting it only in November of that year. The decision to murder the Jews en masse was in all probability taken early in 1941, apparently in March.[16] For several months in 1941, therefore, both German policies—emigration and murder—ran concurrently, one being pursued in Central Europe and the other in the newly conquered Russian territories, where more than 1 million Jews were killed by the end of the year.

In principle, Spanish transit visas could be obtained in Marseilles, provided Portuguese visas and French exit permits had been stamped into the passports first. Early in September, 1940, a French-Spanish border station at Cerbére was opened and twenty-five refugees a day could pass through there. But in November, the Spanish consulate at Marseilles received instructions that from then on every application would be decided upon separately in Madrid. This meant that many refugees decided to try to cross the Pyrenees border surreptitiously. At first it was possible simply to walk seven kilometers around the Spanish border posts in the seaside area where the hills were very low. Some refugees who were apprehended by the Spanish police were handed over to the Vichy authorities, but there are no figures on how many of these cases there were.[17]

The goal of these illegal emigrants was Barcelona. Emigrants arriving with legal visas from the Reich were also often stranded in Barcelona while waiting for a ship or for a renewal of their visas if these had expired in the meantime. Most of the refugees, especially those who had crossed the border illegally, were put into the concentration camp of Miranda de Ebro, where food was bad and housing was worse, and where mortality was high. Suffering at Miranda was worst during the period under review—until early in 1942. Some were relatively lucky and were placed in forced residence in Barcelona or village resorts, but all of them needed help, as did others who had managed to get to Madrid and hoped to continue their journey into Portugal or to one of the Spanish ports.

Not only did the Spaniards not allow Jewish organizations into Spain, but non-Jewish aid associations were not admitted either, so that AFSC, JDC's oldest ally, could not help. It was not until July, 1941, that Philip B. Conard of the Friends was allowed to visit Spain. Even then no change was effected. JDC had to try to help through various temporary arrangements. For example, one such consisted of handing out money to refugees in Madrid through Moshe Eisen, a refugee who worked as a doorman in a hotel there. A slightly more permanent solution was to transmit funds to Dorsey Stephens, wife of the American military attaché, who had offered her services under the general auspices of Virginia Chase Weddell, wife of the ambassador. When Mrs. Weddell had to stop her own activities in September, 1941, after some nine months of work, Mrs. Stephens continued alone until the middle of August, 1942. Between $1,000 and $1,500 a month were transferred to these women, who then tried their best to administer aid to refugees in Madrid and some other places.

The major headache was of course Barcelona. The Viennese IKG, headed by Josef Löwenherz, had sent there a man named Fred Max Oberländer, apparently a non-Jew, who had been in the fountain pen business. His firm, Ofir, opened a branch in Barcelona. His origins, the background for his activity, his contacts with German and Jewish groups—all these are somewhat of a mystery. What is clear is that, for lack of a better method, JDC-Lisbon began sending him funds which he then distributed in Barcelona and at Miranda. Whether this was done efficiently or not is a moot point; at any rate, it appears that Oberländer used some of the money to "grease the palms" of Spanish officials, to use Joseph Schwartz's language. This may have been necessary, but it ultimately worked to Oberländer's disadvantage, because in September, 1941, after some nine months sojourn, he had to leave Barcelona.

Fortunately, JDC found a better solution to the problem of Barcelona. Samuel Sequerra, who had a Portuguese passport and was therefore permitted to enter Spain, volunteered to take over work in the city, and he arrived just as Oberländer was leaving. American Treasury licenses for the transfer of money for charitable purposes to Europe had been granted for Spain since June, 1941, so that Sequerra could use official funds. Support for the refugees in Barcelona was minimal, however, amounting to about one peseta a day, which, according to Sequerra, bought about one cup of coffee. Some 600 refugees were receiving financial aid, and about double that number were somehow supporting themselves. The last 122 emigrants from the Reich arrived in Barcelona in August and September, 1941, and after that Sequerra had to look after illegal entrants.[18]

Iberian attitudes toward the Jewish refugees depended largely on the varying fortunes of the warring countries. The Portuguese authorities hardened their stance in the spring of 1941, after the great German victories in the Balkans and North Africa. In May, they threatened to arrest the refugees for their failure to leave Portugal, and JDC departed from its stated policy by intervening directly with the Portuguese minister in Washington, J. A. de Bianchi. This action apparently had the desired effect, because no more was heard about this particular threat. The entry of Russia into the war in June, 1941, in its turn meant that the Portuguese absolutely refused to accept anyone who admitted having been born in Russian-controlled territory.[19]

The difficulties were compounded by American immigration policies. These policies have recently received considerable attention and can be considered well researched. What this research shows is that the Roosevelt administration was under heavy restrictionist pressure just when a liberal immigration policy was the only hope for many threatened individuals in Europe. The quota of 30,244 for Germany, Austria, and Czechoslovakia combined, had it been fully used, might have saved a considerable portion of the Jews in those countries between 1939 and 1941. Such a policy was blocked, however, by the efforts of Breckinridge Long, who in January, 1940, had become assistant secretary for special problems at the State Department, and who had added a paranoiac fear of aliens, radicals, and Jews to his earlier admiration of Italian fascism. His friendship with the president enabled him to influence Roosevelt, for whom the question of visas was clearly a secondary matter. With isolationist sentiment in the United States swiftly changing into a mania for security against imagined threats from "radicals" and foreigners, Roosevelt was in no mood to intervene to save a few refugees. In April, 1940, he was even forced to veto a bill that was to have caused the deportation of certain classes of aliens from America.[20]

Liberals in general and Jewish bodies in particular had no real knowledge of the attitudes prevalent in the State Department. It seemed to them that nothing much had changed since late 1939, when visa policies were relatively very liberal. They were not aware that in June and July, 1940, just a few months after Long entered his new post, Avra Warren, head of the visa section, had journeyed to Europe and advised consular officials in effect to curtail drastically the entry of refugees into the United States. The reason given was that Nazi agents and other security risks might enter in the guise of refugees. In the fiscal year 1940 (July, 1939, to June, 1940), 21,000 persons managed to immigrate to the United States directly from Germany; in fiscal 1941, when the new, unpublicized regulations were in effect, only 4,000 entered. Another 4,150 came between July and December, 1941.

Antisemitic sentiments were spreading in America generally; Warren's assistant, for example, submitted a memorandum claiming that the Jews were in league with Hitler because their hyper-emotional antics only served to impede the Allied war effort. As Saul S. Friedman puts it: "Hostility toward aliens, refugees or Jews, in the form of dismissals and job turndowns became so pronounced in 1940–41 that officials in Washington had second thoughts about the propriety of legal restrictions on their employment."[21] After a short period of relative relaxation early in 1941, a regulation was issued to the consuls in June, 1941, that forbade the granting of visas to persons who had close relatives in German-controlled territory. In July, most American consulates in German-held areas were closed in any case, and it became almost impossible to get a visa.

Much, of course, depended on the attitude of the consuls, because they ultimately made the decisions regarding visas, at least until mid-1941, within the State Department regulations. Consul Young at Lisbon, for instance, was not known for his liberal attitude. Ilya Dijour of HIAS criticized his behavior, and other complaints were channeled through George S. Messersmith of the State Department to the visa section. Even more explicit was some of the Jewish criticism of the consul at Barcelona. In October, 1941, with 184 refugees there, of whom 122 held expired U.S. visas, he refused to give letters confirming that the refugees had handed in new applications; they were thereupon threatened by the authorities with expulsion to France. In November, the situation worsened, and Schwartz cabled to New York: "Avra's boy continued unfriendly although granting few visas where absolutely necessary."[22]

Despite these policies, HIAS and JDC managed to get almost

all of the refugees out of Portugal and Spain, so that at the beginning of 1942, there were only 1,000 left in each of the two countries; those in Spain were largely interned at Miranda.

JDC struggled for the solution of practical problems in practical ways. Yet it seems that its lack of awareness of what was really going on at the policy-making level in Washington stemmed from more than simply lack of information. The people at the New York office were constitutionally incapable of serious questioning, let alone serious criticism, of an administration that stood between the Jewish community and antisemitism or worse. JDC's attitude was brought out clearly in an incident which occured early in 1940, involving a diplomatic pouch containing reports of the Warsaw JDC office for Morris Troper. The material was handed to the American consulate in Brussels, which refused to give it to Troper, although he was in the city and needed the material for discussions with Warsaw JDC officers who had come to Belgium for consultations. JDC-New York contacted Assistant Secretary Long and asked for the contents of the pouch to be delivered to Troper. Long refused, telling JDC that the pouch would be delivered to Washington, where it would be examined and then delivered, should it be found "that such a delivery may properly be made by the Department." Joseph Hyman's letter to Long of March 1, 1940, is typical of the attitude that characterized the New York office. Not only was there no word of protest, but Hyman went so far as to express his "very real appreciation to you for your courtesy in this matter and for the consideration you have given to our suggestion." He continued: "As an American organization it is, of course, our desire to conform in the closest degree with the requirements of the service and the policy of our government, and we trust that the Department has not been embarrassed by this request."[23]

Behind these developments, behind the figures and the facts, lay the stories of the thousands of people who were trying to flee from the Nazi regime. One such story was brought back by Troper from Spain early in 1941. A young Polish Jew in the Polish army fled to Rumania after Poland's defeat in September, 1939, managing to take his wife and two-year-old daughter with him. The wife's sister lived in France, and the soldier volunteered for the Polish forces there, again taking his family with him. During the German offensive in the spring of 1940, the wife lost all contact with her husband at the front, and, though in her fourth month of pregnancy with her second baby, she took her daughter and fled from Paris. As Troper put it, she "let herself be driven by the stream of the frightened masses" and finally arrived in Marseilles. There her daughter fell ill with dysentery, and she had to nurse her back to health. She wrote to a person in the United States who was also known to her husband and received an answer enclosing a letter by him. It appeared that he had been able to escape German imprisonment and had crossed into Spain illegally. He was then at Miranda doing hard labor. She wrote asking him to wait for her. The woman could not get a French exit permit, so she crossed the border illegally, now about eight months pregnant, with her first child in her arms. She obtained permission to visit her husband, only to find that he had been shot dead by Spanish policemen in the camp the very morning she arrived. The young woman had to be taken to a lunatic asylum.[24]

Another case, with a different outcome, concerned not an individual but the whole Jewish community in the Grand Duchy of Luxemburg. There were about 3,500 Jews living there in 1939; some 1,500 fled in the spring of 1940 to Belgium and France. About 800 of those who were left in late 1940 were citizens of Luxemburg whose families had been living there or had come from the neighboring Alsace region a hundred or more years before. Another 200 families, or about 800 persons, were recent refugee immigrants. The remaining 100 families were mainly citizens and immigrants who had come from Eastern Europe or Germany before 1935. The person most active in contacts between the community and the outside world was Albert Nussbaum, secretary to the aid society Ezra, and, after May, 1940, head of the consistory of Luxemburg Jews.

Some JDC help had been given to the families in Luxemburg prior to 1940. With the conquest of the country in that year, Luxemburg was annexed to the Reich, and the Jews became wards of the RVE, the roof organization of German Jewry. In August, 1940, the relatively mild military occupation regime gave way to civilian Nazi administration. Luxemburg Jews began to make frantic attempts to reach safe havens. Twenty-six Luxemburgers with expired U.S. visas arrived at the Franco-Spanish border on August 24, 1940, and thirty-two others followed. On September 12, Rabbi Robert Serebrennik of Luxemburg was told by the Gestapo that all Jews must leave the place by September 26. Nussbaum tried to find an asylum for his community, and first of all for the Luxemburg citizens among them. Augusto

d'Esaguy of the Commisão Portuguesa de Assistencia aos Judeos
Refugiados negotiated with the Portuguese police, and JDC was
induced to offer a guarantee that they would be supported in
Portugal, though Nussbaum was told on September 26 that "no
guarantee either for emigration or maintenance" could be given.
The Luxemburg government-in-exile, itself still in the first stages
of organization, offered help and negotiated with other exile gov-
ernments, such as that of Belgium and General Charles de
Gaulle's movement, which had overseas territories outside of the
German reach.[25]

In the meantime, the Germans had relented somewhat and
allowed for an extension of their ultimatum. On October 8, 150
persons with Cuban visas left for Irun, Spain, on their way to
Lisbon. JDC, meanwhile, also approached the Luxemburg government, and while no hard-and-fast government guarantee
could be offered because of lack of funds, it wanted to help. On
November 11, 203 Luxemburgers arrived at the Spanish border
with doubtful visas, were rejected, and had to go to French internment camps. JDC was investigated by the Portuguese police,
or, in Schwartz's colorful language, "were called by brassbuttons
explain our part. They fully satisfied responsibility elsewhere but
whole matter extremely sensitive." D'Esaguy was told that those
who were refused entry had been sent back on the orders of
Antonio Salazar, the Portuguese dictator, himself: "Portugal
would not become a dumping ground for refugees." The Cuban
visas were invalid, and Moses Leavitt induced Troper to tell
Nussbaum "that we would do everything possible towards arranging orderly emigration, but that they [the Jewish community!] must see that similar expulsions did not occur again." The
failure to comprehend the real situation was still deep enough to
make Troper (or perhaps the New York office through Troper)
express a belief that if only the neutral countries would refuse to
accept refugees dumped by the Germans, Germany might change
her tactics and prefer "ordered emigration."[26]

Nussbaum did not relent. Through Moses Amzalak, he submitted a memorandum explaining the situation directly to Salazar.
JDC, through its affiliate dealing with emigration to the Dominican
Republic, picked 51 of those in French camps for emigration overseas at the end of 1940. Small groups of Luxemburgers were un-
ceremoniously deported by the Germans into the unoccupied zone
of France. Approximately 100 got out to Portugal in May and June,
1941, including Rabbi Serebrennik. Schwartz in Lisbon tried to

obtain Panamanian visas for some of those that remained, and a last group of 133, apparently from French camps, arrived in Spain in October, 1941. Most of those in camps got out of France before 1942.

It is difficult not to engage in some speculation regarding this typical incident. JDC did not have enough funds in 1940–41 to pay the $200,000 for transportation and the $25,000 monthly needed for the 2,000 Luxemburg Jews. Had it had them, would more Jews of that small community been saved? Quite possibly. D'Esaguy called Nussbaum a Quisling because he had negotiated with the Germans regarding a mass exodus from his country, which again suggests that d'Esaguy completely misunderstood the real situation. Lastly, it seems that here is additional proof for the argument that at the end of 1940 the Germans were still thinking in terms of expelling the Jews to the West (possibly to Madagascar) rather than sending them eastward to be murdered. They were, if one wishes to look at the situation with hindsight, trying to force the Jews into an expulsion which would have saved their lives. It is disturbing to think that more money might indeed have saved them.[27]

The suffering of the refugees had a profound emotional effect on those whose task, or calling, it was to deal with it—the JDC workers. This was true not only of the men and women in the field, but also of those holding responsible positions in New York and Lisbon. Perhaps among the first American Jews to grasp the depth of Jewish despair in Europe, the Warburgs and Leavitts and Tropers sometimes, though rarely, allowed themselves to pour out their true feelings in private correspondence. They all would have subscribed, one feels, to Troper's words in a letter to his wife—words of genuine feeling, because they were not intended for public consumption—on November 15, 1940.

> The pity of it all is not the physical aspect to most of them [the refugees]—but honest, decent-looking men come to me in tears and in quivering voices lament the fact that they are losing the respect of their little children! Think of it—they are sorry they ever escaped. A ship goes off, but what we need is a bridge—a bridge that hundreds of thousands could cross—like over a rainbow—from despair to hope or even to despair with dignity.[28]

2

"Despair with Dignity": Jews in Central Europe, 1939–1941

Morris Troper's definition—"despair with dignity"—fitted the mood of German Jewry in the last years of its existence perfectly. It also fitted that of Czech Jewry, and, to a lesser degree, that of Austrian Jewry. These three communities of what was known as Greater Germany, however, had different social physiognomies, and though they suffered identical fates, they and their relationship with JDC must be treated, up to a point, separately.

The people with whom JDC had the closest contact among the German Jewish leadership were Dr. Otto Hirsch, Dr. Julius L. Seligsohn, Dr. Paul Eppstein, and Paul W. Meyerheim. Hirsch was the director of the RVE, the comprehensive organization set up by German Jewry and accepted by the Nazis in July, 1939, in place of the RV, which had been based on more autonomous local units and had in effect been destroyed during the November, 1938, pogrom. The leaders of the RVE were more or less the same as those of the RV. Rabbi Leo Baeck, the venerated head of German Jewry, was still the official president, and the different offices, formerly the different organizations of German Jewry, were maintained. The Hilfsverein der deutschen Juden, set up in 1901 to aid in East European Jewish emigration to America and elsewhere, now became the emigration section of the RVE dealing with emigration to places other than Palestine. The Palästina-Amt—the Palestine Office connected with the Jewish Agency for Palestine (JA)—was responsible for emigration to that country, and remained so even after war had broken out between Germany and Britain, the mandatory power ruling Palestine. It too was part of the RVE.

The RVE reacted to the beginning of the war in September, 1939, by intensifying its search for emigration possibilities. But the spirit had changed. Terror loomed and became increasingly oppressive. In November, 1940, Seligsohn disappeared into a concentration camp and died there in early 1942. Eppstein became the head of the emigration section, and after June, 1941, when Hirsch was sent to a concentration camp, he became the effective leader of the RVE. Direct contact was maintained, as before, between JDC-Lisbon and Paul Meyerheim, the financial secretary of the RVE, in whom Troper and Schwartz had full confidence.

Throughout Germany, Jews were subjected to a night curfew immediately upon the outbreak of war on September 3. On September 9, radios were taken away, and in February, 1940, clothing coupons were taken—Jews could no longer renew their clothing. From July, 1940, special hours were introduced for Jews to buy food—late hours, when there usually was not much left over. As time went on, meat, eggs, milk, and other commodities were forbidden to Jews. But two blows descended which were even harder than those already outlined: early in September, 1939, between 5,000 and 10,000 Polish and stateless Jews were arrested and put into concentration camps (practically none of these survived), and forced labor was gradually instituted.

The labor provision, at least, had some ironic repercussions. It provided Jews with an opportunity to earn wages, though in 1941 they averaged only 20 marks a day, or about 50 to 60 percent of what German workers were getting. Even more important, Jews were placed largely into essential war industries. By October, 1941, 18,700 Jewish workers were employed in Berlin's industries, of whom 10,474 were working in metal trades. This was not only an important quantitative problem for the Nazis, but also a qualitative one: Jews were considered to be very good, if not the best, workers some firms had, and there was therefore later some reluctance to release them when the Nazis wanted to ship them away to their deaths.[1]

Living conditions became increasingly unbearable, and from

57

early 1940, with the deportation of more than 1,000 Jews from Stettin into what was planned to become a Jewish reservation in the Nisko area near Lublin, the specter of deportation began to hang over German Jews. But the Nazis themselves did not decide on their policy of mass murder until late 1940 or early 1941, and the Jews, still believing in a moral world where mass murder was simply impossible, did not realize what was in store for them. In fact, a series of letters written from June to November, 1942, by leading members of the RVE (and especially a letter by Baeck in November) point to a failure to realize what deportation meant, even at that late date.[2]

The situation in the first months of the war in Austria and the Nazi Protectorate of Bohemia and Moravia was essentially the same as that in Germany. In Austria, Jews were treated in the same way as in Germany—they became German *subjects*, not citizens. However, the RVE was not permitted to look after them. In the Czech lands, non-Jews became German-protected citizens, but Jews became subjects ruled by German orders. The Nazis found it convenient to keep the central Jewish bodies in Berlin, Vienna, and Prague separate.

In Austria, all stateless (that is, chiefly Polish) Jews were sent to concentration camps; from September 25, 1939, an 8:00 P.M. curfew was imposed. Deportations to the Nisko reservation started earlier than in Germany. Some 5,000 persons were sent from Vienna and the Czech town of Moravská Ostrava to Poland in October and November, 1939.[3] These deportations in effect ceased at the end of 1939. The social and economic situation did not become any better, however. Evictions from apartments, closing of orphanages, reduction of the hours permitted for shopping, and all the other humiliations and defamatory ordinances were enacted in Vienna and Prague as they were in Berlin. In Vienna, where the community had not been wealthy to start with, these steps produced catastrophe. Community revenues fell from 2 million marks in 1939 to 0.3 million in 1940; this decline was aggravated by the fact that forced labor (with its attendant starvation wages) was not officially introduced until March, 1941. In January, 1940, the "non-Aryans"—converted or nonconfessing Jews, and some half-Jews—were forced to join the Jewish community. In September, 1939, there were 66,260 Jews and 2,944 "non-Aryans" in Vienna, and 90,147 Jews and "non-Aryans" in the Protectorate early in 1940. There were no Jews left in Austria outside of Vienna, and the social situation of the Viennese Jews was even worse than that of German Jews. At the end of 1940, when only 48,465 Jews were still in Vienna, two-thirds of them were women, of whom three-fourths were over forty-five years old. Only 3,000 children under eighteen were left. Because of their ages and sex, it was even more difficult to emigrate Viennese Jews after 1940 than those of Berlin.[4] Table 4 affords a basis for comparing the size of the Jewish populations in Germany, Austria, and the Protectorate in the early years of the war, but the figures are not necessarily very accurate.[5]

Table 4: The Jewish Population in Central Europe, 1939–41

	Germany	Austria	Protectorate
end 1939	225,000	55,000	90,147
end 1940	190,000	48,465 (53,604)*	not available
end 1941	151,370	46,300	83,900

*Based on Rosenkranz; see n. 5 to this chapter.

JDC and Jewish Emigration from Central Europe

One of the escape routes from Greater Germany was by way of Italy. Until that country joined the war in June, 1940, 1,139 refugees from Germany entered Italy with visas to the western hemisphere, but not all of them managed to continue their journey. One of the hazards they encountered was that French authorities considered Jewish refugees from Germany to be German, and therefore hostile aliens. On September 25, 1939, 30 such unfortunates were taken off the S. S. *Virgilio* at Marseilles, and another 58 off another ship at Algiers on October 14. The position of the Jewish emigrant, considered an enemy by the Germans and a hostile alien by the Allies, could not have been more dramatically illustrated.[6]

Other avenues of escape were still open: the road through Asia, via Siberia, led to Shanghai and Japan; the road to the West led through the Low Countries until the spring of 1940. After June, 1940, Lisbon and some of the Spanish ports were in effect the only possible escape points in Europe.

The RVE, faced with this deteriorating situation, at first aimed at two objectives: to move neutral states and the United

States to "influence Germany [so] as to prevent a sudden and brutal attack" on the Jews; and to utilize every possible avenue of escape, at whatever cost.[7] This policy ran into difficulties on both counts. It proved to be practically impossible to persuade either the United States or neutral countries to influence Germany in any way. With hindsight one can argue that the only possible influence on Germany in the Jewish question would have had to have been expressed by readiness to absorb Jewish refugees, but this readiness was precisely what the western world did not show. South American and Central American republics might be willing on occasion to sell visas for a great deal of money; however, neither JDC nor the Jews of Europe could pay the kind of money they demanded. In January, 1941, the Prague community asked JDC to advance money outside the budget for bonds which would guarantee to the Cuban government that the refugees' living expenses would be paid after they arrived in Havana. These Cuban bonds amounted to $2,800 per person per visa. Of course this appeal was hopeless. JDC replied that it could not pay, but it would turn to the individuals' relatives. Nothing is known of the fate of those for whom the applications were made.[8]

JDC budgetary cutbacks were a deathblow to many seekers of visas. After the war, Joseph Schwartz maintained that no visas were lost for lack of funds. His statement is quite true for those who already had visas—they were most probably all taken out. But lack of funds prevented the purchase of rescue visas from Latin American officials, and shipments of people to Shanghai were similarly blocked. Thousands must have had their hopes dashed when JDC was forced to reduce its monthly budgets to Germany from $75,000 in January, 1940, to $40,000 in March, and to $27,000 in July. The cost of passages for visa-holders soared to $180 via Italy and $250 via Japan. One hundred passengers via Japan would exhaust the total monthly budget of the RVE.

At first JDC saw itself hampered by U.S. regulations that did not allow American organizations to pay passages for immigrants, but it soon emerged that as the money really belonged to the Hilfsverein, to whom it had been allocated in return for marks paid in by emigrants in Germany to their respective communities, JDC could use it. Some members of the Administrative Committee asked whether it was right to use "philanthropic funds to pay for transportation of persons with limited means when these facilities [the ships that were becoming very scarce] could be availed of by people having adequate funds."[9] But Warburg and Troper made short shrift of this objection. As time went on, ships and berths were preempted for JDC's refugee clients as much as possible.

The responsibilities assumed by JDC, HICEM in Europe, and HIAS in New York changed in response to changing realities. JDC was reluctant to shoulder the burden of providing for emigration from Europe, but as 1940 wore on, it became clear that it would have to book the ships while HICEM arranged for visas and transportation to the ports and for emigration from all ports of exit other than Lisbon. In 1939, JDC allocated $454,000 to HICEM, 38 percent of the HICEM budget. In 1940 it paid $313,772 (51.6 percent), and in 1941 $578,000 (86 percent). It was the old story of JDC acting as a financing and supervisory agency, while remaining ready to jump in and undertake the work if there were no other choice.[10]

Despite all the hindrances, a small trickle of refugees from Prague and larger numbers from Germany and Austria continued to escape throughout 1940. In January, 1941, Paul Meyerheim and Josef Löwenherz were allowed to leave their countries for discussions with Joseph Schwartz and Herbert Katzki in Lisbon. They intended to discuss emigration possibilities with JDC. The two men were quite different. Löwenherz was the cowed, frightened head of a vanishing community, whose first-hand knowledge of Gestapo methods had brought him to see in emigration the sole hope for Viennese Jewry. Meyerheim was the delegate of a community that knew it was in deep trouble, yet he was determined; he would go back to Berlin to continue to fight for survival of the Jews in Germany.

Löwenherz "reiterated again and again that the solution of the Jewish problem in Vienna can be met only through emigration, prompt and in substantial numbers." JDC did not like sending people to Shanghai, though that city seemed to offer an avenue of escape in light of the restrictive immigration policies of the countries in the western hemisphere; nobody could tell whether the Japanese rule in Shanghai might not force the Jews into a situation in China no better than that in Germany. But Löwenherz wanted Shanghai, as "his only thought" was to move as many people out of Vienna as possible. Meyerheim wanted JDC to explore any possibilities of entry into the West Indies, because U.S. consulates had in effect stopped the issuance of new visas in the summer of 1940. However, there were rumors of a change in the attitude of the United States, and from about January 15, 1941, some U.S. consuls did resume issuing visas, though on a limited basis.[11]

Some of the dangers of the situation were clear to the two emissaries from the dying communities. If the United States entered the war, "the worst might be expected for the Jewish people in [Old Germany] and Vienna." It was possible that those Jews still in Germany would be expelled to Poland or elsewhere—perhaps to Madagascar, in accordance with a German plan, known to the RVE, which had been formulated in July, 1940, and abandoned at just about the time when Meyerheim and Löwenherz went to Lisbon. The mentally ill Jews of Vienna had been taken to Poland in the 1939–40 deportations. "It is plain that the plan is to eliminate these unfortunates," Schwartz reported to New York. Meyerheim wanted visas for Baeck, Hirsch, Eppstein, a few others, and himself. Most of these were obtained, but they were never used.[12]

An incident typical of the abyss that was opening between the Jews under Nazi control and those in the free world occurred during these Lisbon talks. Transports of Jews had been pushed over the borders of Yugoslavia from Austria by the Gestapo—without papers, of course. The Jews of Yugoslavia, especially the community at Zagreb, protested. They had no funds, no emigration possibilities, and no housing for the new arrivals. JDC supported the Zagreb Jews, and Löwenherz was accused in effect of collaborating with the Gestapo in arranging these transports. The accusation was true; there was little else he could have done but obey Gestapo instructions. Yet rather than facing JDC's unrealistic attitude, he chose to prevaricate and protest his innocence. JDC was forced to support the refugees, though it really had no money to do so. It did not believe one moment in Löwenherz's protestations.[13]

It must be admitted that Löwenherz probably had a more realistic appreciation of the dangers the German and Viennese communities were facing than did Meyerheim and others in Berlin. The discussions in Lisbon took place in mid-January, 1941. As late as August of that year, after the decision for mass murder had been made and emigration had become almost impossible, Dr. Cora Berliner, a leader of German Jewry, could still write to Troper that she had qualms about sending people to Spain "when we do not know exactly that they will be able to proceed from there someplace else." But apparently Schwartz and his team in Lisbon could see things more clearly and accurately. An almost comical incident occurred when the New York office questioned subsidies to a Swiss-based organization called the Comité international pour le placement des intellectuels refugiés. This organization was run by Marie Ginzburg, who was also involved in Jewish student affairs. On April 30, 1941, the *New York Post* reported that the committee had provided Polish Jewish intellectuals with forged passports and brought some of them out to France. Paul Baerwald commented on May 1, "I am shocked." In a memo which went to Lisbon he added, "I do not suppose we are getting a detailed accounting of the money we give her . . . we ought to be quite sure that the money was spent for [legitimate] purposes, and not for the purposes, no matter how tragically necessary they were, which are spoken of in this article." Schwartz of course knew very well where the money was going, but there was no point in arguing with New York. By April, 1942, exactly a year later, the situation had changed. After hearing how 312 intellectuals had been helped to escape, Baerwald wrote another memo: "I believe the JDC can be well pleased with having done its part."[14]

The Closing of Exits

In early 1941, the Gestapo noose over Berlin and Viennese Jews was tightening. In March, Hirsch was arrested, Seligsohn was dying in a concentration camp, and a frightened and compliant Eppstein was taking over the RVE. While time was running out in Berlin, the *New York Herald Tribune* reported on March 15 that Rear Admiral Emory S. Laud, head of the U.S. Maritime Commission, had refused permission for the S.S. *Washington,* an American ship with 1,700 passenger berths, to sail on the Lisbon-New York route. On April 24, Portugal announced that it would issue no more transit visas—a reaction to German victories in the spring of 1941. The Japanese route had been closed since the third week in March. But the people in Berlin were still fighting for time and exit routes. On May 25, they asked the Lisbon office to direct American boats to Vigo, Spain, and to intervene in Japan to lift the ban. With the relative easing of U.S. restrictions in January, U.S. visas were available for about half of the monthly U.S. immigration quota. The Portuguese rescinded their ban, and in June batches of refugees with U.S. and Latin American (mainly Cuban) visas began arriving again.[15]

Almost immediately, however, the situation again worsened, although at first, JDC in New York and Lisbon had no more than an inkling of what was developing on the American side. They heard that new regulations were coming into force in June which would deny visas to persons with close relatives still in Germany. On June 7, Troper suggested the closing of the Berlin JDC office. The situation became desperate at the end of June. In July, U.S. consulates in German-held territories were closed down, leaving Latin American visas as the only way of getting out of Germany. There still were 1,000–1,200 persons in Greater Germany who had obtained U.S. visas before the closing of the consulates, and they had to be taken out. On August 5, there were still 1,000 U.S. visa-holders, 1,500 holders of Latin American visas, and a few others left in Germany. JDC finally began to understand what was at stake. Troper had told New York on July 19 that he was willing to pay up to $360 per passage, provided he could take the people out: they could not leave Germany until they had proved that they had reserved a passage to the western hemisphere. As autumn came on, prices of Latin American visas rose, and James G. McDonald, a great friend of the Jews and then chairman of the Presidential Advisory Committee on Political Refugees, met with Roosevelt on September 9 to try to persuade him to instruct the State Department to put a "helpful interpretation" on immigration regulations. It was of no avail. The influence of Long and the restrictionists on Roosevelt at this stage was too great; the president did not care to intervene.[16]

On September 19, 1941, the Nazis forced German Jews to wear the yellow star. Jews were marked now, in preparation for the Final Solution which had been decided upon some six months before. On September 6, the Nazis forbade the emigration of people between the ages of eighteen and forty-five. The RVE still managed to get people into Spain and Portugal. Three families left Germany for Spain on September 11, and three more were allowed to leave on October 14. On October 17, twenty-one German Jews with Dominican visas arrived at the Spanish border. Sixteen were admitted into Barcelona. It appears that this was the last German Jewish group to escape.[17]

In November, the Nazis finally terminated the official emigration of European Jews under their control. Alois Brunner, the Gestapo hangman of Viennese Jewry, told Löwenherz on November 5 that no more Jews would be allowed to leave Vienna. But before the final liquidation of the Jewish communities of Greater Germany could take place, a formality had to be seen to. The Germans were, after all, murdering their own subjects (*Staatsangehörige*), albeit they were persons of a lower grade than Aryan citizens (*Staatsbürger*). The property of Jews deported from the

Reich could not ordinarily be appropriated by the state because there might be heirs, insurance claims, and so forth. To regulate all these matters, an implementation order of the Reich citizenship law (the Nuremberg law of 1935) appeared on November 26, 1941, which said that a Jew whose usual residence was outside of the Reich could not be a subject of the Reich. "Usual residence" (*gewöhnlicher Aufenthalt*) was defined as "sojourn abroad under circumstances that make it clear that he does not stay there only temporarily." If he were transported to his death, then obviously the circumstances indicated that he would not stay only temporarily, but the order also covered all those who had emigrated or fled. Furthermore, subject to certain conditions, such as claims by Aryan creditors or heirs, all property left behind would be appropriated by the state. In this way, the biblical question "Have you murdered, and inherited as well?" received its proper Nazi answer.

Always behind the figures and the facts there were human beings trying desperately to escape. The residents of a boys' home at Floersheim near Frankfurt, for example, were trying in 1941 to get into Ecuador. The problem was to get entry permits for fifty boys and four adults. After long negotiations, the government of Ecuador agreed to accept them and give them visas without deposits (deposits usually meant bribes) on the condition that heads of Jewish families in Ecuador were found to guarantee their education. A committee of the Jewish community at Quito, headed by Oscar Rocca, tried and failed to get fifty Jewish families to accept the responsibility. "We only succeeded to obtain ten certificates signed for the above-referred purpose." The committee then tried to house the children in a school, but found there was no building that would be regarded as suitable by the authorities. It was clear to the JDC emissary in Quito that the children would not necessarily be suited for the agricultural work for which they were intended, but the local Jews said that the children should be brought in first, and then one would see what would happen. They appealed to the president of Ecuador to admit the children even without the guarantees, but he refused. The date was December 6, 1941. It was too late in any case. It must be assumed that none of the group survived.[18]

By the time all exits to freedom had closed, the door to hell had been opened. Five transports left Vienna for Poland between mid-February and mid-March, 1941, carrying a total of 5,004 persons. Deportations from Berlin to Lodz started on October 18 and proceeded thereafter throughout 1942. By the end of 1941, some 25,000 German Jews had been deported. JDC knew about the deportations, but eyewitness reports ceased after the end of October, and no more reached it until much later. On December 7, the United States was forced into the war, and an entirely new situation came into being.

What were the results of the tremendous efforts to get Jews out of Greater Germany? The figures in table 5 seem to speak a fairly clear language.[19] A total of 41,500 left Germany and Austria in 1940 and 1941. Between the outbreak of war and the end of 1939, some 16,000 left Germany and 14,000 left Austria, for a grand total of approximately 71,000 persons who escaped death during the first period of the war. Most if not all of these fled to the safety of Britian or the Americas, to Shanghai or to Palestine. Table 6 shows the numbers and destinations of emigrants from Austria; no satisfactory parallel figures could be obtained for Germany.[20] Only a very small number would have remained in Belgium or Holland at the beginning of the war and been caught by the Germans. These 71,000 were about 20 percent of the German and Austrian Jews still in their countries of birth when the war began. A high proportion of these people were saved through the united effort of their communities, of HICEM, of the Zionist groups, and of JDC. Had there been more funds available, probably more could have been done, even in a hostile and unconcerned world.

Table 5: Jewish Emigration from Germany and Austria, 1939–41

	Sept.–Dec., 1939	*1940*	*1941*
Germany	16,000	16,000	13,000
Austria	14,000(?)	6,500	6,000

Table 6: Jewish Emigration from Austria by Area, 1939–41

	Total Emigrants	*United States*	*Palestine*	*Latin America*	*Shanghai*
end 1939	116,994	24,682	7,837		
end 1940	122,000	28,012	8,900	11,000	
end 1941	128,500	28,615	9,195	11,580	18,124

3

JDC in Poland, 1939–1941

Nowhere do JDC's rescue attempts during the Holocaust stand out as clearly as in the area of the greatest tragedy—Poland. Nowhere in Europe was the local JDC office as independent of the New York center as in Poland. The story of Warsaw's JDC office in the twenty-eight months between the conquest of Poland by the Germans in September, 1939, and the Japanese attack on Pearl Harbor in December, 1941, is the story of Polish Jews trying to help themselves, sometimes with the aid of their American brethren, sometimes against the wishes of the U.S. parent organization, in face of literally impossible odds.

There were some 3.3 million Jews in Poland in 1939, forming about 10 percent of the population. Living in a violently antisemitic environment, in a country torn asunder by an economic crisis which had not abated since the early twenties, the Jews were in a most unenviable position. It was estimated that 30 percent of Polish Jews were living on the verge of starvation even before the war.[1] Yet there was a plethora of cultural, political, and religious institutions through which to carry on a vital social life. JDC occupied a central place in this mass of impoverished people. It had been the main, and at times the only, Jewish organization from abroad which by its action showed that at least some Jews elsewhere cared about them. JDC established a great network of loan banks (*kassas*) and of free loan banks (*Gmilut Hessed Kassas*) which kept about one-third of Polish Jewry afloat economically in the face of an antisemitic boycott of increasing viciousness. JDC supported schools and cultural institutions, and a delicate balance was kept in the support given to the three main political movements of Polish Jewry: the socialist, antinationalist Bund, the ultrareligious camp of Agudat Israel, and the faction-ridden Zionist national movement.

On September 1, 1939, World War II began with the attack of Nazi Germany on a haughty, ill-prepared, and utterly inefficient Polish army. On that day, a municipal social service committee, the Stołeczny Komitet Samopomocy Społecznej (SKSS) was set up by the Polish authorities in Warsaw, ostensibly for all Polish citizens. Coincidentally, and as a result of prewar efforts that had nothing to do with the outbreak of war, JDC managed to establish a central committee of Jewish social organizations, the first such group in Poland since the eighteenth century, on September 2. But even while it was being organized, its chairman, the Lodz industrialist Karol Sachs, was already fleeing for his life to Paris. In Warsaw, Leib Neustadt, Giterman's deputy, took over the chairmanship. Giterman himself left the capital, probably on September 7, in the wake of a Polish broadcast advising civilians to leave the capital for the eastern parts of the country. Giterman apparently thought that his well-known anti-Nazi stand would endanger him after the probable German conquest. On September 19, the central committee took the name Koordinatzie-Komitet (KK; also called the Koordinirungs-Komisie fun di Iddishe Hilf und Sozial-Gesellshaftn).[2] Neustadt was chairman, and the secretary was the famous historian Dr. Emmanuel Ringelblum, a JDC official. The KK succeeded in gaining recognition from the SKSS as representing the Jewish population in Warsaw and received an allocation of bread and funds from them; it also received $215,000 as a last transmission from Paris.[3] Soup kitchens were opened by the KK and temporary shelters (*punktn*) were established for residents who had been bombed out in the frightful havoc wreaked by German aircraft during the brief and violent September campaign, and for refugees who began streaming into the city. The total number of those killed in the bombing was about 25,000, of whom some one-third were Jews, and it was later estimated that 25 percent of Warsaw's Jewish houses were destroyed. Among the dead was Neustadt's wife, and he was wounded. Some 9,000 Jewish people received direct help from the KK.[4]

Before the war, there had been 2,212,000 Jews in what now

became German-controlled Poland. When the September war ended with the capitulation of Warsaw on September 27, 1939, the Germans immediately evicted large numbers of Jews from more than 100 places in territories they annexed to the Reich: western Poland, which they called the Warthegau, and southwestern Poland, renamed Ostoberschlesien. Of an original population in these areas of 692,000 Jews, some 460,000 remained, at least at first. The others were expelled into central Poland, which the Germans named the Generalgouvernement (GG), and in which a civilian administration headed by Hans Frank began to function on October 26, 1939. During the fighting itself and immediately following it, hundreds of thousands of Jews fled eastward from German-occupied Poland to the Russian-controlled areas, but many of them came back in the winter of 1939–40. Nevertheless, 200,000–250,000 Jews from German Poland remained in the East. It has been estimated that 20,000 were killed in the September campaign, and the total number of Jews, not counting the many casualties of the evacuations and the attendant pogroms, who lived in western and central Poland at the end of 1939 can be set at roughly 1.8–1.9 million.[5]

The expulsions took place mainly in northwestern occupied Poland, but spread elsewhere as well, until about a quarter of west Polish Jewry—roughly 610,000 people—had been turned into refugees. The expulsions occurred in two main waves: immediately following the German conquest and between April and September, 1940. Among others, Jews of forty-five larger towns, including Kalisz and Poznan, were expelled, and 100,000 of them fled to Warsaw and the surrounding area. As a result of an order by the Nazi provincial governor on September 19, 1940, 50,000 people, old residents and refugees, were driven from the Warsaw district into the capital, swelling the Jewish refugee population there to 150,000.[6]

The Economic Plight of Polish Jews

The problem of sheer physical survivial became most urgent, especially in Warsaw, which had 360,000 Jews by late 1939. Among the Jewish population were 173,000 individuals seeking to earn a living, and 95,000 of these were wage-earners. The immediate and almost total destruction of Jewish enterprises upon German entry into the city, together with the confiscation of machines, tools, raw materials, and goods in shops that survived, caused severe unemployment in a Jewish community which even before the war had suffered widespread poverty. One survey made in May, 1940, showed that only 40 percent of the 95,000 Jewish workers had found some kind of work under the Nazis.[7] Other Nazi actions compounded the economic problems of the Jews in Warsaw and elsewhere in Poland.

German regulations in October-December, 1939, effected the transfer of Jewish-owned businesses to German commissars (*Treuhänder*); payments or purchases by Jews were limited to 500 zloty (zl.). There were 5 zl. to the dollar before the war, but its value fell sharply after the German victory. By the spring of 1940, JDC managed to get 10 or 11 zl. to the dollar; on the black market, rates were three to five time higher. Any payment above 500 zl. had to be deposited in a blocked account. A Jew could receive from his own bank account only 250 zl. a month, and cash holdings per family were limited to 2,000 zl.

Wherever Jews were unable to circumvent them, Nazi regulations effectively strangled business. No purchases of raw materials were possible, and no transactions of any kind could be effected. According to an order of January 31, 1940, new enterprises in Warsaw could in any case be set up only by Aryans. Jewish lawyers were barred; pensioners lost their pensions; peddlers were limited to Jewish streets. By early 1940, all Jewish house owners were deprived of their property and Jewish employees dismissed from all non-Jewish businesses or Jewish enterprises run by Aryan commissars.[8] In July, 1940, a discussion among officials of the Kraków-based German administration made it clear that Jews had been completely removed from industry, wholesale trade, land ownership, banking, insurance, and other important economic activities. They shortly would be removed from small trade, and ultimately from crafts and peddling as well.[9]

On October 26, 1939, Frank issued an order that made forced labor mandatory for all Jews between the ages of fourteen and sixty.[10] In fact, however, random kidnappings of Jews from the streets for forced and usually degrading labor, which had begun immediately upon the German conquest, continued. It was dangerous for people to leave their homes. Germans, aided by Polish hooligans who specialized in recognizing Jews, would seize men and women to perform hard and unpaid labor for the day. Insults, beatings, and even murder were common. The Warsaw Judenrat (Jewish Council), which was founded on October 4,

Europe in 1938–1939 and Concentration Camps in Germany. Reproduced by permission from Martin Gilbert, *Final Journey* (Tel Aviv: Steimatzky and *Jerusalem Post*, 1979).

71

1939, preferred to supply the Germans with the required number of laborers if only the kidnappings would cease. A Judenrat-organized work battalion, the Batalion Pracy, therefore came into existence. It supplied close to 1,000 laborers daily in November, 1939; the number rose slowly, until in August, 1940, it reached 9,000 daily. Workers were assigned to a variety of places, including the German army, German private firms, and the Warsaw city government. How they were treated depended greatly upon where they were sent. The regular army, for example, was relatively mild, but the SS, the elite troops, were violent and brutal. The trouble was that from the very beginning forced labor increasingly became the responsibility of the SS and its branches: the Sicherheitsdienst (SD), the intelligence organ; the Gestapo, the political police; and the "regular police." SS Chief Heinrich Himmler held onto this lucrative slave labor preserve, despite attempts by Frank's civilian government to penetrate it.

The Warsaw Judenrat paid the laborers paltry sums of money—at first three and then four zl. daily—but quickly ran into difficulties in meeting even these modest commitments. A system was therefore established whereby all Jewish adults were obliged to present themselves for forced labor six or even nine days a month. Individuals with enough money resorted to paying refugees and unemployed persons to work in their stead, and in this way most people got paid. Moreover, later in 1940, a whole system of economic transactions grew up around forced labor because laborers were sometimes able to steal food or obtain it from Poles with whom they had contact at work in exchange for items brought from Jewish homes. In August, 1940, the Warsaw Judenrat was required to send 1,400 laborers to the Lublin district. These first groups were largely made up of volunteers who hoped to find work and pay. The frightful conditions in these labor camps, however, quickly changed the workers' attitude, and the Judenrat was forced to send food, blankets, and other items.[11] The organization of these supplies through its subsidized agencies became one of JDC's main areas of activity. Tables 7, 8, and 9 illustrate the kinds of resources, both monetary and organizational, that JDC had at its disposal in Poland during the early years of the war.[12]

The economic and social condition of Polish Jewry under Nazi rule can best be illustrated by a description of life in Warsaw, both because the information regarding other places is not as detailed and because Warsaw, with about one-fourth of the

Table 7: Official JDC Cash Receipts and Expenditures, Poland, 1939–41

	Sept.–Dec., 1939	1940	Jan.–Sept., 1941	Total
Receipts (millions of zl.)	4.449	7.45	5.8	17.699*
Expenditures (millions of zl.)	3.65	7.5	6.55	23

*Dollar equivalents are difficult to compute; the zloty stood at about 100 to the dollar in 1941.

Table 8: Official JDC Expenditures, Poland, 1940

Use	Cost in zl.	Percent of Total Cost
Food and clothing in GG	5,831,940	56.98
Warthegau (Lodz area)	355,400	3.47
Ostoberschlesien (Zagłębie area)	344,000	3.36
TOZ and other health costs	1,485,516	14.51
CENTOS	1,353,000	13.21
ORT and vocational training	273,777	2.67
Administration	594,345	5.80
Totals	**10,238,062** (approx. $205,000)	**100**

Table 9: Total JDC Income and Expenditures for Poland, 1939–41

	Total Income	Total Expenditures	Polish Appropriations	Percent of Total Budget
1939	$8,138,160	$8,447,784	$1,258,742	14.8
1940	$6,308,342	$6,179,577	$859,942	13.8
1941	$6,078,769	$5,716,908	$972,000	17.0

Jewish population of the GG, contained the largest single group of Jews.

The number of Warsaw Jews who earned their living by paid work was relatively small, especially after the establishment of the ghetto on November 15, 1940. The pittance the Judenrat paid for forced labor was utterly insufficient to keep body and soul together. Jews therefore lived to a large extent either on their cash reserves or by the sale of their possessions. Their goods were coveted by the Poles, and especially by the peasants, who could barter their produce for clothes, tools, luxury articles, or machinery. But most Jews had no reserves of any kind; they sold what they had and then attempted to live on a combination of occasional work, public charity, begging, stealing, or smuggling. The refugees especially were natural candidates for starvation, disease, and death. Food consisted mainly of bread and potatoes. A family which could eat bread every day was considered lucky. This fact does not contradict stories about coffeehouses and nightclubs where good food could be obtained for large sums of money: these places were frequented by the smugglers and other illegal operators who were the new aristocracy of a society distorted by the rule of a vicious enemy. A tiny percentage of the ghetto population after November, 1940, they were usually in some way partners of Germans in murky business ventures. Yet many of them also fulfilled a vital social function, smuggling food into the ghetto against the rules of the Nazi authorities. They contributed a great deal to keeping the ghetto alive; they were daring, in their own way heroic, and unscrupulous.[13]

Prices rose, and in February-March, 1940, even before the ghetto was established, they were between five and ten times higher than the prewar level.[14] By April, the price of bread had again doubled.[15] Official food allocations clearly reflected a German intention to cause starvation among the Jews. In May, the Judenrat reported:

> The reduction of food allocation on May 14 has caused fear among the Jewish population because it creates a most difficult situation. The Jews will get one kilo of bread a week, whereas the rest of the population will get 1,750 grammes weekly. When one considers that even this latter amount is scarcely sufficient for the feeding of an adult person, one must conclude that the reduced portions for Jews are literally starvation rations.[16]

Forced laborers for the Germans received slightly bigger rations, but everyone in the ghetto had to pay for these official allocations.

Another major problem was the lack of coal. The winter of 1939–40 was particularly cold, and temperatures of −25 degrees centigrade were common. Many people, especially children, tried to escape the intense cold by staying in bed for whole days.

These deprivations were added to the terrible congestion. Almost 400,000 people were crammed into the ghetto established in an area of Warsaw previously occupied by 150,000. One result was epidemics, especially of two types of typhoid fever. The fever began early in 1940, and by April of that year 861 persons had been hospitalized. Of these, 104 died—the first of many. As the epidemic grew worse, the Judenrat and its German supervisors began a so-called disinfection campaign. Rapacious Polish doctors and their Jewish henchmen, accompanied by Polish police, would visit a block of houses, throw out all the possessions, take away bedding, and steal large amounts of property. Often the bedding did not return from the disinfection plant; when it did, it was often damaged and torn. Worst of all, the inhabitants of the block were marched to primitive bathhouses, where they were forced to stand naked in the freezing cold until the hot shower was ready for them, and then wait for more hours until their clothes were returned, damp and ruined after disinfection. This process caused the deaths of large numbers of people and untold misery to many more. It was, of course, also accompanied by graft. Certainly it increased rather than decreased the danger of epidemic.[17]

Another important restriction was that the Jews were not free to receive postal matter. From June, 1940, cables could be received only through the Judenrat. In time there was only one post office, located in the ghetto, that served Jews; overcrowding, inefficiency, and loss resulted as a matter of course. This was by no means a secondary matter: until the outbreak of the German-Soviet war in June, 1941, people—mostly young men—who had escaped to the Russian-held areas kept sending food parcels to their relatives and friends in the west. Thus, between December 1, 1940, and March 22, 1941, 197,758 parcels arrived in Warsaw alone, 84.3 percent of them from the USSR.[18] These parcels often proved decisive in keeping people alive. When they were lost, or rather stolen, the results could be fatal. Postal connections with other neutral countries were at first less important, but they also became vital in the period between the Nazi attack on Russia and the American entry into the war. JDC did whatever it could to encourage Americans to send food parcels. However, problems arose connected with the British blockade of Nazi Germany. The

British did not want to allow food parcels from American Jews or anyone else to go into Nazi-held areas because, it was argued, this would release the Germans from their obligation to feed the local population, including Jews. Until well into 1943, the British did not understand that the Nazis had no wish to feed any Jews.

One point must be stressed: had Jews obeyed all the restrictions, they would probably soon have ceased to exist. They were not allowed any normal economic activity, they could not hold money or travel, and, after the establishment of the various ghettos, they were forbidden on pain of death to leave them. They received rations too scanty to keep them alive and yet were forbidden to obtain food in any other way. Of course they circumvented all or most of these restrictions and broke all or most of the rules imposed on them. They suffered terribly, especially during 1941, but all the indications are that by 1942 they had established a modus operandi that would probably have enabled them to survive the war had the Nazis not embarked on mass murder. In Warsaw, 43,239 deaths were officially registered in 1941 (10 percent of the population), although the true number was probably higher, because not all deaths were registered.[19] The figure for January-May, 1942, was 22,760. Undoubtedly more deaths were prevented by the fact that the Jews simply did not obey Nazi orders.[20] By May-June, 1942, the typhoid epidemic had spent itself—the weakest had succumbed.

This picture of mass starvation and epidemics was not true of all of the Jewish communities in the GG. Places like Czestochowa in the southwest and Radom, south of Warsaw, for instance, suffered from grim poverty; there were forced labor, beatings, occasional murders, and humiliation. But there was no mass starvation. The same is true of a number of smaller places, such as Piotrków Trybunalski and Hrubieszów. In most other ghettos, including Lublin, Kraków, and Kielce, mass starvation and epidemics did occur, and the suffering was very bad. Warsaw, however, was undoubtedly the worst place, and it is against this background that one must understand the policies of the Warsaw office of JDC.

The Warsaw JDC Office

The increasing German pressure and the hostility of most of Polish society apart, any independent social organization such as JDC had to contend with the emergence of the Judenräte. These

Jewish Councils were nominated all over Poland as part of a set German policy formulated in an order by Reinhardt Heydrich, head of the Reichssicherheitshauptamt (RSHA), the SS office responsible for all police and repressive activities, including those of the security police and the Gestapo. The order was given on September 21, 1939, while the Polish campaign was still in progress. It now seems that it was not designed to prepare for the mass murder of the Jews; rather, it provided for the elimination of Jews from the social and economic life of Poland through ghettoization and then expulsion.[21] The Nazis thought in terms of a reservation near Lublin, on the new border with the USSR, where they would concentrate most or all of the Jews under their rule. When this plan failed because of the objections of Frank and his administration, the idea was revived of expelling all European Jews to Madagascar. It seems quite clear that the notion took hold especially after the conquest of France in June, 1940, because Madagascar was a French colonial possession. The term "Final Solution" at that point meant banishment to the island, though what the Nazis had in mind was not some idyllic Jewish self-government. Madagascar would become a grim concentration camp in a deadly tropical environment, with a possibility of ransom by American Jewry. This stage in Nazi planning for the Jews lasted at least until October–November, 1940. In October, some 9,000 Jews of the Baden-Pfalz area in western Germany were expelled into southern France in the expectation of a further expulsion from French ports to Madagascar.[22]

The Judenräte and the ghettos were at first intended to be convenient tools for this policy of isolation, decimation by disease, and finally expulsion. The composition of any given Judenrat, however, depended very much on the local German authority. Often the Jews themselves elected or chose the head of their community; often too, Judenräte simply maintained, wholly or in part, prewar leadership. In Warsaw, for instance, the Polish-nominated head of the Jewish community, Mauricy Maisels, had fled from the city when war broke out. On September 15, 1939, the Poles nominated a Jewish citizens' committee consisting of five men, among them Adam Czerniakow and Marek Lichtenbaum. On September 23, while Warsaw was still in Polish hands, Czerniakow was named head of the Jewish community by the Polish mayor. On October 4, the Nazis, now ruling the city, told Czerniakow to choose a twenty-four-man Judenrat, of which he was to be the head. Like Czerniakow himself, who had been the head of the influential Artisans' Society before the war, many of the members of this first Judenrat had belonged to the prewar Kehilla, the Jewish communal council (which in 1939 was a body nominated by the Polish government). These Jewish communal workers were confirmed by the Nazis as Jewish representatives.

A high proportion of the top political leaders of Polish Jewry managed to flee abroad, either during the September war or in the ensuing months. This meant that Polish Jewry was deprived of its acknowledged leadership and that the Judenräte (and particularly the important Warsaw Judenrat) were composed of men who neither commanded general support nor had the necessary political experience. Victor Alter and Henryk Erlich of the Bund fled to the east; Apolinarius Hartglass, Moshe Sneh, and Ignacy Szwarcbart of the General Zionists, Avraham Bialopolski of the Zionist-labor group Poalei Zion (PZ), Zerah Wahrhaftig of the religious-labor-Zionist Hapoel Hamizrahi, Rabbi Itzhok Meir Levin of Agudat Israel, and Szmul Zygielbojm of the Bund also joined the exodus in late 1939 and early 1940, fleeing to America, Britain, and Palestine. (The Jewish section of the Polish Communist party did not then exist, because the whole party had been purged by Stalin in 1938.) Of all these groups, only the Bund managed to establish a leadership to replace the leaders that escaped. Maurycy Orzech and Abrasha Blum took the places of Alter and Zygielbojm. On the other hand, some of the leaders of the small Left Poalei Zion (LPZ), a leftist opposition to the official Zionist movement, did not try to get away. The LPZ was Marxist, Zionist, and Yiddishist (that is, advocated Yiddish as a Jewish national language), characteristics which both isolated it from all the other parties and made escape to Palestine, the Soviet Union, or the West very difficult because it lacked the appropriate political connections. Shachne Sagan, Adolf Berman, and Emmanuel Ringelblum stayed in Warsaw, though other party leaders, such as Itzhak Lev, fled to the east. Paradoxically, however, it was among the small LPZ group that JDC found some of its most devoted workers: there could hardly have been a greater ideological contrast than that between the conservative leadership of the American-Jewish philanthropic organization and the East European Marxist-Zionist splinter party.

The decisive event in the history of the Jews in Poland in those first war years was of course the establishment of the ghettos. The first ghetto was set up at Piotrków Trybunalski in October, 1939, and the second, established at Lodz on February 2,

1940, was hermetically closed on May 30. Other smaller places followed. By October, 1940, 350,000 out of the 1.9 million Polish Jews under German rule were in ghettos. The main period of ghettoization came between then and April, 1941. On November 15, 1940, Warsaw ghetto was set up. Ghetto Kraków followed in March, 1941, and some ghettos in western Poland—Czestochowa, Bedzin—were established even later. Why ghettoization proceeded so slowly has not really been satisfactorily explained, but the fact that it did would seem to contradict the adage of the immediate and efficient responses of German bureaucracy. The term "ghetto" was itself misleading when applied to these places in which entire Jewish populations were entombed; they were in effect concentration camps, rather than anything resembling the original medieval concept of a largely voluntary closing in of an ethnic and religious minority for its own protection. In this disastrous situation, a desperate need arose for what one might call alternative leadership: groups and individuals that would try to strengthen the powers of resistance of the Jewish minority, that would provide material and spiritual help, and that might even search for forms of organized resistance to the Nazi regime in Poland. JDC was perhaps the major example of such a focus of resistance.

JDC in Poland was fortunate to have the services of a group of gifted individuals, of whom the leading four received the collective name of "directors" from the inmates of the Warsaw ghetto: Isaac Giterman, Leib Neustadt, Isaac Borinstein, and David Guzik. Although he did not share the name, it seems permissable to add Emmanuel Ringelblum, who appears to have had considerable influence in JDC councils. These men excelled in clear-sighted assessments of the developing situation; they also enjoyed very close relations, though not always smooth ones, with the so-called Jewish public bodies, the underground parties and groups with their second-line leadership.[23] It was these public bodies that formed the backbone of the self-help organized by JDC, working through social agencies such as CENTOS, the JDC-sponsored society originally set up for the protection of orphans; TOZ, the society for the protection of health; the Organization for Rehabilitation and Training (ORT), the vocational school system; and various school organizations. Many of the surviving Jewish intelligentsia, especially in Warsaw, flocked to JDC in order to help and to work.[24]

The front organization JDC created in Warsaw became

known as ŻETOS, from the Polish name, Żydowskie Towarzystwo Opieki Społecznej (Jewish Society for Social Help). It developed from the Jewish KK during the siege of Warsaw. Until the end of 1941, the protection of the American-based JDC was fairly effective in maintaining ŻETOS as an institution relatively independent of the Judenrat. Officially, ŻETOS was responsible for the organization of public kitchens and the support of children's homes, hospitals, and other forms of aid in Warsaw. In this it competed with, or rather overshadowed, the Judenrat's own welfare department. From the fall of 1939, ŻETOS was directed by a so-called Public Committee, which unofficially represented the underground political parties, from the Bund to the right-wing Zionists. At the head of the committee stood Emmanuel Ringelblum, representing JDC.

Also from the days of the September war dated the spontaneous emergence of the "house committees." Buildings in Warsaw, as elsewhere in Poland, were generally built in squares around a central yard. They were almost fortresslike, promoting feelings of community and of sharing a common fate. Committees were organized in most such houses to help the poor, look after children, seek material aid, and foster cultural life. About the middle of 1940, ŻETOS, in response to Ringelblum's prodding, began to group them under its own leadership. The committees were of different kinds. Some were well organized, socially conscious, and active; others were poor and less well arranged; some were even corrupt. Generally, however, they succeeded. They alleviated suffering, provided children's corners which in many cases became covers for elementary schools (Jewish schools were illegal until September, 1941, when a few were permitted to open), and organized cultural activities that were quite consciously designed to fortify the morale of a starving and sick population. Poorer committees received subsidies from ŻETOS that were financed by a system of taxation devised by Ringelblum and his Public Committee.

The house committees were limited mainly to Warsaw, though there are traces of their existence in Piotrków and a few other places.[25] The Judenrat occasionally tried to acquire control over the house committees or use them for its own purposes. Adam Czerniakow even tried to persuade them to raise funds for the public kitchens, which in Warsaw were sponsored by the Judenrat. The committees refused, reminding Czerniakow of the way in which he had organized forced labor. In some cases the

Warsaw kitchens, mainly those for children and refugees, were run by "patronats," special bodies recruited largely from surrounding house committees which agreed to support the kitchens together with ŻETOS. In many instances kitchens were run by political parties or groups and became assembly points for illegal political activity, while also saving members of the group from starvation. These groups and their kitchens became alternative homes, substitutes for a warmth and security that was swiftly disappearing. Children's kitchens, on the other hand, whether run by patronats, CENTOS, or TOZ, were in the most cases also covers for illegal schooling, in other towns as well as in Warsaw. Tables 10 and 11 provide examples of two representative community budgets.

The centerpiece of Ringelblum's work in the area of cultural activity, however, was the Oneg Shabbat (Friday Evening Pleasure of the Sabbath), of which he was the organizer and chairman. This was a clandestine group of economists, historians,

Table 10: Welfare Activities, Warsaw, May, 1941

Use	Zlotys
Kitchens (local population)	255,150
Refugee punktn (for soup kitchens)	339,830
Food for children	396,900
Subtotal (direct feeding)	991,880
TOZ	50,000
Hospitals (other than TOZ?)	60,000
CENTOS	100,000
Children's homes (internats)	105,600
Social aid (to intellectuals?)	180,000
ŻETOS	165,000*
Old-age homes and orphanages (other than CENTOS?)	83,000
JDC administration	4,520
Subtotal (other expenditures)	748,120
Grand total	**1,740,000** **(about $174,000)**

*ŻETOS was financed by a head tax collected by the Judenrat and by a voluntary collection, which provided 618,714 and 133,936 zl. respectively at the end of 1940 (for an unknown period). The JDC subsidy was in addition.

Table 11: Monthly Budget in Zlotys, Rzeszow (Kraków District)*

Income		Expenditures		Debts
JDC	19,000.00	Kitchens	1,665.72	15,662
Local Judenrat	250.00	Passover	13,919.00	
Payments for meals	84.70	Children	3,000.00	
Other	1,103.30	Medical	1,177.25	
Total	20,438.00	Burials	45.00	
	(approx. $4,000)	Coal	25.00	
		Administration	112.00	
		Other	27.31	
		Total	**19,971.68**	
			(approx. $3,950)	

*Rzeszow (Yiddish: Reishe) had around 14,000 Jewish inhabitants. This budget was submitted on April 30, 1940 (YV, 355-16).

physicians, rabbis, political leaders, and others whose main aim was to collect material dealing with everything they saw happening around them and preserve it for future generations. Among others, Oneg Shabbat commissioned a since famous study of the effects of starvation upon human bodies. Done by a group of doctors, it was included in the materials finally committed to caches by Ringelblum and found amid the two-thirds of the Oneg Shabbat material uncovered so far.[26] Hundreds of essays, articles, and reports relating to what was happening all over Poland were collected by Oneg Shabbat and personally checked by Ringelblum for objectivity and accuracy.

Unfortunately, there is no material documenting the discussion among JDC's leaders in Poland. It is known that the four directors and Ringelblum were in daily contact and carefully planned their activities, but one can only guess the logic that moved them to resist Nazi policies by their active, though unarmed, resistance and that led them into conflict with the policies of the Judenrat and of Czerniakow. The conflict was not overt; JDC supported the legal institutions, such as those run by the Judenrat's welfare department, and generally did not hesitate to support the Judenrat when it felt that the official leadership was doing useful work. The directors do not seem to have opposed Czerniakow personally. But it is evident from Ringelblum's strictures of the Judenrat in his writings, as well as from the fact that JDC knowingly supported institutions and groups that opposed it, that JDC was critical of the official policies. In any case, underground workers had great confidence in JDC, and by and large its public image was very positive.[27] There was some criticism in Warsaw; Chaim A. Kaplan, one of the foremost diarists of the ghetto, wrote a number of passages criticizing bureaucratic ways at the JDC office. More significantly, he thought that JDC's distribution of food from abroad in early 1940, and especially the transport of matzot for Passover, was an ill-organized failure.[28] It was obviously difficult to please everyone, though with all due respect to Kaplan, one should point out that his criticisms are not repeated elsewhere.

Apparently there was a connection between JDC and some of the leftist groups, no doubt as a result of the personal inclinations of the Warsaw JDC leaders. CENTOS in Warsaw came to be run by Adolf Berman of the LPZ after the flight from Warsaw in September, 1939, of his predecessor, Aharon Goldin. Leib Neustadt relinquished his prewar post as vice-president of CENTOS, but through him CENTOS was assured of a central position in JDC's concerns. TOZ was directed by Dr. Israel Milejkowski, who belonged to both LPZ and Oneg Shabbat. Chief of the nursing school, founded by JDC in the early 1920s, was Luba Bilecka, wife of Abrasha Blum, one of the chief leaders of the Bund. The ŻE-TOS Public Committee consisted of six members, with Ringelblum as chairman; of these, Shachne Sagan of LPZ and Maurycy Orzech of the Bund were apparently close to Ringelblum, as was Abraham Gepner, who as a wealthy industrialist had been very active in JDC's prewar work. Gepner was one of the two Judenrat members to support the underground in the ghetto and its preparations for the great uprising.[29]

Warsaw was of course a focal point for JDC's policy of aid to the suffering Jewish masses, whose numbers were continually being added to by refugees. The plight of the refugees, and especially of the children, was probably the most frightful aspect of ghetto life. Housing was very scarce: refugees were crowded into schoolhouses, synagogues, and other public buildings, and special centers were set up for them. In many cases they had nothing but the clothes they stood up in, and these clothes soon began falling apart. There was no way of feeding these multitudes; the efforts that were made soon failed. JDC was the only hope, but the paltry sums at its disposal did not allow effective action. Kaplan's diary records of the winter of 1940–41:

On days of cold so fierce as to be unendurable, entire families bundled up in rags wander about not begging but merely moaning with heartrending voices. A father and mother with their sick little children, crying and wailing, fill the street with the sound of their sobs. No one turns to them, no one offers them a penny, because the number of panhandlers has hardened our hearts.[30]

What was JDC's policy in Warsaw in regard to refugees? How did it allocate its meager resources? What agonies did the men go through who made the decisions? We shall probably never know.

The JSS: JDC's Front Organization

In trying to formulate a policy for all of Poland, JDC had to take into account differences between four areas: Warsaw; the eastern part of Poland annexed by the Russians; the GG; and the western territories annexed by the Reich. In Warsaw, JDC acted through ŻETOS, CENTOS, TOZ, and other groups, and thus could exercise direct control. Table 12 illustrates the scope of CENTOS and TOZ activities during the first two years of the war.[31]

Table 12: Child Care in the GG, 1941–42

	In 31 CENTOS Homes	In 68 CENTOS Day Homes	In TOZ Hospitals
1941	3,000	5,000	23,019
1942	3,700	11,000	(not known)
	Fed in Warsaw Special Kitchens	Fed in Warsaw Children's Homes	Fed in Warsaw Children's Corners
Sept., 1941	29,167	(not known)	(not known)
Oct.–Nov., 1941	29,516	15,425	4,391

In the east, 1.3 million Jews were living under Russian rule in late 1939. Obviously all JDC contact with these areas was cut off immediately after the Soviet-German partition of Poland. Yet, incredibly, a lone JDC representative named Benzion Horowitz, of whom nothing else is known, was sent out from Warsaw to distribute funds in the area in late October and early November, 1939. It is said that he handed out 220,000 (or 350,000) zl. (about $10,000). He left and the refugees were taken care of by Soviet methods until the Nazis came in 1941.[32]

Apart from Warsaw, the area where JDC could be most effective was the GG. As early as September 2, 1939, with the establishment of the central committee of Jewish social organizations that became the KK, Chairman Leib Neustadt tried to shift official responsibility for relief work to other than JDC shoulders. He named Dr. Michael Weichert, a one-time actor and cultural worker who since 1933 had been an official of the Artisans' Society, to be vice-chairman of the KK. Weichert was to play an important and very controversial role in the history of the Holocaust. He survived the war and was tried and acquitted on charges of collaboration with the Germans. His memoirs and papers form an important source for our understanding of Polish Jewry's fate.

There were two American agencies active in Poland immediately after the German conquest: the American Red Cross, represented by William MacDonald, and the Commission for Polish Relief (CPR), represented by John Hartigan and Columba P. Murray. Both were voluntary agencies, but the Germans knew that they were in close touch with the U.S. government. Not surprisingly, JDC turned to them and, according to Weichert, it was their intervention that led to the establishment of the Jüdische Soziale Selbsthilfe (JSS), a Jewish self-help association for the GG.[33] In time, JSS was recognized by the Nazis in its role as the Jewish constituent of the only independent local organization that was allowed to function—an overall welfare association named Naczelna Rada Opiekuncza (NRO), which also had Polish and Ukrainian components.[34] Weichert was nominated by the JDC directors to be the Jewish representative with NRO and, as Kraków rather than Warsaw became the Nazi capital of the GG, he began to spend more and more time at the new seat of power. At first he had contacts with the Gestapo only, but this changed as Frank's civilian administration took over. By January, 1940, JSS was under civilian Nazi control: first under the welfare organization Nationalisozialistiche Volkswohlfahrt (NSV), and then under the Bevölkerungswesen und Fürsorge (BuF), the welfare department of the Frank administration.

Weichert's organizational talents were undoubtedly considerable, and he set about creating a network of local aid committees, trying to keep them as independent of the Polish Judenräte as he could; in this he was no more successful than he was in his attempts to have his organization treat with the Nazis on a more or less normal civilian footing. JDC insisted from the beginning that all JSS goods be stored in JDC warehouses—quite clearly it did not have unlimited trust in Weichert, because the distribution of allocations from NRO, as well as of goods he acquired with JDC money, were dependent on German approval. Weichert's relationship with the Nazis developed slowly, and initially he was not free to move about; moreover, he was not known at first by the Jewish communities, so that in the fall of 1939 and in early 1940 the local committees were either established spontaneously or by Neustadt and David Guzik in JDC's behalf.

Early in February, 1940, partly perhaps because of American influence, but partly also because the Germans wanted some semblance of order introduced into the chaos they had created, a meeting took place in Kraków between Isaac Borinstein of the JDC, Weichert, and a Dr. Fritz Arlt, head of the BuF. A second meeting took place on February 14, 1940, between Arlt, members of the Warsaw Judenrat, JDC, and JSS.[35] The Germans took their time over the official constitution of NRO and its constituent bodies. It was not until March 29, 1940, that the NRO statutes were approved; the JSS statutes followed in May. All JSS contacts abroad were to go via the German Red Cross, and in general JSS was to be bound hand and foot by German regulations. JDC had no choice. It too was obliged to work through JSS and had to distribute the money it received from abroad largely through it. Yet JDC maintained as tight a control over JSS as it could. The JSS presidium, approved by the Germans in September, 1940, was nominated by Giterman, Gepner, and Czerniakow, and included Weichert and the head of the Kraków Judenrat, Dr. Marek Biberstein. Provincial "advisers" were nominated for the four GG districts of Warsaw, Radom, Kraków, and Lublin, and "delegates" for the local committees.[36] The official setting up of the JSS in May, 1940, was immediately followed by the establishment of a JDC office in Kraków under Borinstein, an action taken in response to German attempts to close the Warsaw office late in 1940 and their demand that JDC open one in the capital of the GG. Giterman and his friends, however, successfully resisted Nazi pressure to close down JDC in Warsaw, which remained the center of Jewish life in Poland.[37]

The next step after the official establishment of JSS was

another meeting in Warsaw in early June, which apparently took place thanks to the appearance of the CPR mission. Representatives of the German Red Cross and even of the German Foreign Ministry consented to come, along with BuF and the constituent bodies of NRO. Borinstein and Weichert represented JDC and JSS. At this and a subsequent meeting, the Jews asked for 30 percent of all the food distributed in Warsaw by NRO, and for 25 percent elsewhere, amounts that reflected both population numbers and, to a certain degree, needs. The Poles did not agree, however, and after much haggling 17 percent was agreed upon.[38] (This was to change to 16 percent after the annexation of East Galicia to the GG in August, 1941.) As the situation of the Jews was incomparably worse than that of the Poles, 17 percent of the food distributed as charity represented fairly harsh discrimination. Table 13 indicates the total food shipments to JDC-JSS from June, 1940, to July, 1941.[39]

Table 13: Food Shipments to JDC-JSS, June, 1940–July, 1941

	June, 1940	*Oct., 1940*	*Apr., 1941*	*July, 1941*
Origin	CPR	CPR(?)	American Red Cross-JDC	CPR-JDC
Wagons		29		
Matzot (tons)			35	
Fats (tons)	95			
Wheat (tons)	231	350		
Milk (tins)	440,000			12,000

According to Weichert, the JSS budget was about 1 million zl. monthly (about $100,000 at first; in 1941, closer to $50,000) between spring, 1940, and the end of 1941. Roughly half came from JDC in cash, and the other half was the money value of the 17 percent of NRO food allocations.[40] Both JDC and the Germans supervised the distribution of JSS funds, and such supervision seems to have been Borinstein's main task in Kraków. However, JDC representatives never participated in official monthly meetings between JSS and the BuF or NRO. JSS operated mainly by transferring funds and food to local committees which were divided into three categories: those that could cover up to 50 percent of their budget, those that managed up to 25 percent, and those that could not cover anything at all. It bombarded BuF with memoranda on welfare—defined as the provision of food for the poor in public kitchens, of clothes, of help to "deserving individuals" (mainly intellectuals), of agricultural and other vocational training, and the creation of tailor and shoemaker shops.

The whole JSS network existed, nominally, as an agency separate from the Judenräte. This was officially stated in a BuF circular of January 20, 1942. Weichert obviously placed great importance on this independence, yet it also seems abundantly clear that it was fictitious. Thus, in Radom, Lublin, and elsewhere, the heads of the Judenräte were also the local JSS representatives.[41] In his memoirs Weichert tries to argue two points: that he and his organization were not as dependent on Nazi authorities as were the Judenräte, because he had access to civilian German officials who were easier to deal with; and that his interventions were often successful. Both of these claims are difficult to accept. Weichert was part of an official structure, tied both to the NRO and to BuF. It would seem that he was considerably less independent than some of the more enterprising Judenräte.[42] His most vigorous attempt—to prevent the expulsion of Jews from Kraków in the summer of 1940 and again in 1941—did not make the slightest impression on the Germans. The BuF itself, with which Weichert dealt, was a rather unimportant branch of the German bureaucracy. His organization's occasional successes were limited either to the temporary postponement of anti-Jewish measures or to the alleviation of suffering in cases where no central German institution was involved. A certain freedom of action existed on the local levels within the large German bureaucracy that developed in the GG, and Weichert and his various committees sometimes managed to capitalize on it. But the surviving materials relating to individual communities suggest that it was the Judenräte rather than JSS who actually exploited this freedom. However, JSS did succeed, along with Judenräte in Warsaw, Sosnowice, and elsewhere, in establishing agricultural training centers which in practice became focal points for the illegal work of Zionist-socialist youth movements.

The JSS soon expanded its operations to include attempts to help the many thousands of Jewish workers in Nazi slave labor camps. These camps were created on a provisional basis, largely on the eastern borders of the GG where fortifications against the Russians were dug, but they were also built elsewhere in the GG on various amelioration and construction jobs, such as the damming of rivers or the repairing and building of bridges. Workers had practically no machines, very little food, and the treatment was brutal. Most were housed in windowless, leaky wooden barracks with totally inadequate sanitary arrangements. At first, workers who had managed to survive a certain period of labor were usually allowed to go home. Later camps became more permanent, but the Judenräte were permitted to rotate the workers in them until late 1941. In December, 1940, there were fifty-four such camps, holding 30,000 workers. In 1941, these numbers increased rapidly. The incidence of disease and mortality was high.[43] Weichert's attempts to intervene with BuF and alleviate conditions in the camps seem to have been successful in some cases, but direct intervention by the Judenräte was usually more effective. A case in point was the labor camp at Belzec, near Lublin (not to be confused with the death camp set up there in 1942), with 12,000–14,000 Jewish workers. Weichert asked Nazi authorities if food might be brought in; this request was granted late in 1940 and early in 1941—at additional expense to the Lublin Judenrat, of course.

Early in 1941, JDC sent out a circular advising all aid organizations in the GG that from then on, direct administration would be handled by JSS. However, it was not allowed to operate outside the GG. Early requests to set up a JSS network in the Warthegau and in Ostoberschlesien were disallowed by the Nazis. On the other hand, East Galicia became a JSS responsibility when the Nazis conquered that territory in August, 1941. Weichert went to Lwów in November of that year and named Dr. Leib Landau as the local JDC representative. (In January, 1942, Landau became a member of the JSS presidium.) By early 1942, JSS claimed to have 412 local committees, of which 56 were in East Galicia. There were very few ghettos without social aid committees, so these figures probably represent fairly accurately the number of Jewish communities still in existence at that time.

JSS had inspectors in the persons of officials who lived in the large towns and were responsible for the smooth running of the JSS committees in their areas. But JSS did not have workers who could advise local committees in the difficult situations that they had to face, and the organization had to turn to JDC. Four of the JDC instructors—altogether there were certainly not more than ten—are known to us by name: Mordechai Goldfarb, Israel Falk, Jozef Szalman, and Abe Zychlinski. All of these men devoted their lives to the vain attempt to ease human suffering. None survived the war.

On a GG scale, JSS had its own problems with the JDC affiliates, CENTOS and TOZ. (ŻETOS in Warsaw was completely independent.) It was not until January, 1941, that JSS and the two aid organizations reached an agreement regarding the amount of support each of them would receive, even though JSS covered only part of their budget.[44] CENTOS especially developed a feverish activity, and in the period July–October, 1941, it was at work in 143 places in the GG. It ran 26 homes and 62 "children's corners," with a grand total of 12,299 children. It also ran 122 kitchens where 47,167 children ate, and 15 summer "half-colonies," whatever that term meant in ghetto conditions, for 6,413 children. These activities were of course vital, yet they probably did not reach more than 15 or 20 percent of the children, or about one-third of the needy.[45]

JSS was also helped by the NRO, largely with funds received from abroad and a meager German allocation. According to Weichert, until July, 1942, when both NRO and JSS were dissolved, the NRO gave 4,845,000 zl. (about $250,000) to JSS under the 17 percent agreement of 1940. This figure would work out at 200,000 zl. ($10,000) a month, yet Weichert claims to have had a 1 million zl. monthly budget, of which JDC supplied half. It is not quite clear where the other half, or possibly the fourth quarter, came from.[46] Occasionally funds levied from Jews by the Nazis were handed back to them. One such very rare occasion came when the welfare tax, which Governor Frank imposed on Poles and Jews alike on July 6, 1940, was not totally appropriated by the Nazis. After much supplication, small parts of it were handed back, but only in Lublin, Tarnów, Ostrów Lubelski, Hrubieszów, and a few other towns. JSS attempts to lay hands on other sources, such as blocked Jewish accounts, succeeded only to a very small extent. The Germans suggested that Weichert take over the Jewish post office and establish a casino or a lottery, but he refused.[47]

There is no doubt that Weichert tried hard to get more money and more food, that the funds he received were spent conscientiously, and that they preserved many lives for as long as was possible. Weichert was a very ambitious man, and one may even conclude from his memoirs that he fancied himself a great leader of men. This attitude was reflected in his dealings with JDC, and therefore JDC's relations with him became increasingly guarded. He tried to take over the welfare activities in Warsaw as well as in the rest of the GG by establishing a JSS in

Warsaw as part of the Judenrat, using his good relations with
Czerniakow toward that end. He even tried to name Dr. Isaac
Schipper, a well-known historian, to head the office. But his
actions ran directly counter to JDC's interests, and its directors
very emphatically kept him out. The welfare department of the
Judenrat, and even ŻETOS, occasionally went under the name of
JSS, but this was a matter of camouflage. Hierarchical arrangements seem to have been kept vague on purpose, and in fact it
was JDC through ŻETOS that controlled welfare activities in the
capital. It would seem that keeping Weichert out of Warsaw was
a precondition for the successful development of an anti-Nazi
underground, financed and backed and identified on its "civilian" side by ŻETOS and the house committees. At any rate, no
parallel development of welfare and social aid groups into a
resistance movement can be traced elsewhere in Poland.

JDC and JSS tried to aid the Jewish population by appealing to the German economic interest: why not utilize the Jews to
develop the economy of German-occupied Poland or serve German interests directly? These attempts were not as quixotic as
they may seem. Vacillations in German policy were marked and
sometimes rather significant. After stealing Jewish property on a
vast scale in 1940, the Nazis tried to utilize Jewish labor and
know-how. Heinz Auerswald, the Nazi in charge of the Warsaw
ghetto, ordered the organization of the Warsaw Transferstelle,
an economic office to exploit the ghetto, in May, 1941, and this
office was paralleled in other towns all over the GG. Weichert
submitted a memo to the BuF on January 31, 1940; the aim was
to persuade the Germans to develop the Jewish economy in Poland.[48] In May, 1941, Weichert was called to see a Dr. Emmer-
ich, head of the Reichskuratorium für Wirtschaft (Reich Economic Development Directorate), one of Göring's men. Other
negotiations took place throughout the year, continuing as late
as March, 1942, when Weichert met with a Dr. Burkhardt, of the
Gruppe Handwerk (Artisans' Group). Some results were obtained, and civilian groups such as these served as intermediaries for the German army in placing orders with Jewish producers. Later these orders proved to save lives temporarily—the
producers' murders were postponed.[49]

With the cooler relations now prevailing between Weichert
and JDC, some JDC suggestions were rejected in Kraków. Weichert, for example, rejected a JDC proposal to raise additional
funds by taking loans from wealthy Jews against promises of

repayment after the war. This had become a major source of funds in Warsaw, even though it was illegal as far as the Germans were concerned, and also against the policy of JDC-New York. JSS refused. Weichert obviously lacked the courage of the JDC directors. On the other hand, he tried to float a public loan, with German approval, which was actually obtained in April, 1942. Czerniakow made a similar move. An attempt by Weichert to have his loan floated in Warsaw as well was rejected by the Warsaw Judenrat. In the end, none of these schemes matured.[50]

JDC in Western Poland

JDC tried to find a way to operate in the western annexed territories, but all these attempts ended in failure. There were then two main concentrations of Jews; in Lodz in the Warthegau, where the ghetto was established in May, 1940; and in Ostoberschlesien in an area called Zaglębie, where a group of Jewish communities was established (as in Sosnowice and Bedzin) which became ghettos in 1942.[51] In Lodz, an elderly industrialist named Mordechai Haim Rumkowski was head of the Judenrat. Rumkowski ran the ghetto with an iron hand and was completely subservient to the Nazis. In Zaglębie, the Nazis organized a central Judenrat at Sosnowice for all the communities in the area and Moshe (Muniek) Merin was named head of it. Rumkowski at least though that by turning the Jews into slaves to the Germans he was protecting their lives. Merin had no discernible ideological proclivities. He was simply a pliable Nazi tool.

The Nazis made any contact between the GG and the annexed western areas increasingly difficult, until in 1940 it became virtually impossible. The Lodz ghetto was most thoroughly sealed off. Giterman visited it once in June, 1940, but all contact ceased after that. JDC was faced with the choice between sending aid to Rumkowski and Merin and relying on them to distribute it or not sending anything at all. It chose the former course and thereby inevitably strengthened the two tyrants. The Nazis were interested in helping the two men, and this pressure no doubt also influenced JDC. A kind of tax was exacted on JDC income in favor of Rumkowski, a sum of 50,000 marks (about $20,000) from every transfer of JDC funds to Poland. This was justified to New York by the fact that Lodz ghetto was, after Warsaw, the largest in Poland, with a population in 1940 of about 160,000 (JDC's estimate was 175,000);[52] Giterman thought that it was inconceivable that aid should be denied to such a large concentration of suffering people.

A JDC report on Lodz of October, 1940—clearly based on Giterman's one visit to the city in June—shows that Giterman did not quite understand conditions there. The report says that the situation was aggravated by Rumkowski, who was seventy-two years old and was "despised and hated by every inhabitant of the ghetto . . . working hand in hand with the Nazi officials outside the ghetto he has robbed the Jews of their money and valuables." Furthermore, he met with the Nazis outside the ghetto, and they "of course, are kept in ignorance by Rumkowski of the real conditions that prevail in the ghetto." If this analysis represents Giterman's thinking, he must have thought, very naively, that if the Germans knew what was happening they would put an end to Rumkowski's rule.[53]

The situation with Moshe Merin and his Zagłębie group of ghettos was only slightly different. He too managed to get 50,000 zl. monthly ($5,000 in 1940) from JDC at German command. In October, 1940, he was reported to be a dynamic person, "in constant touch with the German authorities." Reports regarding Merin emanating from Poland became increasingly critical. The New York office clearly did not understand them. In October, 1940, an internal report said that a "Senior Council of Jews in Sosnowitz [Sosnowice] . . . has been formed to supervise welfare work in their behalf."[54] The good people in their comfortable American homes transformed bloodthirsty murderers into nice folk who wanted their Jews to have a council supervising welfare.

We have seen that JDC representatives in Lisbon met with Paul Meyerheim of the Berlin RVE in January, 1941. According to a report sent to New York at the end of his conversations with the Lisbon office, Meyerheim had had a meeting with the Warsaw office people in Berlin. One can imagine that what the Warsaw directors had to say about Merin was bitterly critical. In New York, in an atmosphere removed from Nazi Poland by a whole world, their opinion was rendered in the language of a liberal society. "They seem to have some suspicion that he is too closely associated with the authorities."[55] Yet it seems that Merin did at first get something from the Nazis in return from his services. There was no starvation in the Zagłębie area such as in Lodz, and most of the committees which JDC reported as active in the west were active in Ostoberschlesien.[56]

Money and Food for Polish Jewry

With the outbreak of war, the unity of JDC as an organization was disrupted. Within a few months, three essentially separate entities emerged, all of them operating quite legitimately in JDC's name. One was the mother organization at its headquarters in New York; another was the European director and his staff in Lisbon. The third, in a way the most important, was the JDC in the conquered countries of Europe, and first and foremost in Poland. It was not unnatural that the policies pursued by the three branches of JDC should have been different and sometimes even contradictory. Personal and cultural differences among individuals played a part, but it was mainly differences in the political, economic, and social conditions as they developed in the various countries subjugated by the Nazis that led to local policies that conflicted with those set in America. Particularly in Poland, funds were handled and raised in ways that quite definitely did not reflect the wishes of the New York office.

The funds allocated to Poland during 1939–41 amounted to a sizable portion of the JDC budget. JDC's fund-raising crisis is obvious in the figures set out in table 9, which also reflect Poland's place in the context of JDC's other concerns. But in a way these figures are misleading, because they do not represent actual expenditures in Poland, but rather the allocations decided upon in New York. How did JDC transfer funds into Poland? What additional funds were raised by the directors? The questions are much more easily asked than answered.

First, it is futile to translate expenditures into exact amounts in dollars. JDC got a rate of exchange on its dollars which was double the official one, but which still remained at about 10 to 20 percent of the free market exchange rate. Second, there was no necessary relation between the appropriations in New York and actual expenditures in Poland, because the latter depended both on German agreement to transfers and on the initiative shown by Warsaw in raising local funds. Transfers began in spring, 1940. Until then, JDC reserves accumulated before the war were utilized. Weichert tells the story of the JDC cashier fleeing to the east early in September, 1939, with the keys of the safe in his pocket. David Guzik is said to have broken open the safe and found $40,000 in cash in it.[57]

It is also known that Leib Neustadt took on loans from people who still had some wealth, promising repayment after the

94

war. While JDC-New York did not at first protest much against this method of fund-raising, it soon objected loudly. A stream of instructions, harsher and harsher in tone, went out to Warsaw forbidding the taking up of loans. Neustadt was also specifically warned against entering into any commitments above the authorized budget. Troper seems to have sympathized with the New York directives, and in any case they were presented by Moses Leavitt on February 28, 1940, as though he had initiated them. "In view of the many problems surrounding these transactions, Mr. Troper had decided that no unofficial money should be accepted by the Warsaw office."[58] In a way, these instructions reflected a serious difference of opinion which developed within the JDC leadership in New York. In December, 1939, Troper suggested that, contrary to established JDC policy, dollars should be sent to Poland—that is, into Germany, in order to avoid starvation among Polish Jews. His plan appears to have been supported by Alexander Kahn, the lay leader responsible for the committee on Poland and eastern Europe, by Max M. Warburg, and by Jonah B. Wise, JDC's veteran fund-raiser and treasurer. Harold Linder, James N. Rosenberg, and Solomon Lowenstein represented the opposition, arguing that it would be disloyal to Britain as well as to American policy if money were sent to Germany. JDC obviously could not do anything for Polish Jewry, and it should therefore limit itself to the border countries and abandon Poland altogether.[59]

In late January and early February, 1940, Neustadt and Guzik got German permission to go to Brussels, where they discussed with Troper a scheme, based on the fact that Jewish emigration from Germany, Austria, and Bohemia was still permitted, to transfer funds to Poland. Emigrants paid in money to their community treasuries and received part of it back in dollars once they reached their destination abroad. In this way JDC financed operations in Germany without transferring dollars there. The Berlin, Prague, and Vienna communities now agreed to transfer part of these funds to Warsaw, in accordance with a predetermined budget at an agreed rate of exchange. The Germans did not object, because no German funds were involved. Guzik asked for 3 million zl. monthly, or $300,000 at the JDC exchange rate,[60] but this amount was obviously impossible, and it was not until later in the spring that the transfers began. For all of 1940, according to JDC-Warsaw, 7.5 million zl. ($750,000) were received by transfer, which of course was much less than the bare minimum necessary to do what JDC was in any case doing in Poland.[61] But Rosenberg said in New York, "JDC is, after all, only a disbursing agent to the Jews of America, and it cannot disburse more than it expects to receive."[62]

The situation in Poland was getting worse, and Neustadt and his friends apparently did not follow instructions. Troper was caught between two fires, as he told Leavitt over the telephone from Budapest on June 7, 1940.

> Well, you know Neustadt, I have instructed him several times that all he has a right to spend is the actual zloty payments we clear with him. Nevertheless, he tells me about large deficits and I am very firm with him and shall continue to tell him we will not be responsible in any way except for the actual cash he gets.[63]

JDC figures, in or out of Poland, are contradictory and unreliable in detail, and because cables and reports from Warsaw were subject to German censorship, JDC expenditure accounts have to be treated cautiously. Sums obtained as loans to be repaid after the war obviously would not appear in any official account, but we do know that by February, 1940, loans for $250,000 were contracted, and one report from Poland for 1940 mentioned the sum of 236,442 zl. under "loans," though this might mean official loans from Polish banks.[64] Only Guzik among the directors survived the war, but he died in an air crash soon after and so could not answer questions. Most of the people who received little slips of paper for the money they gave JDC did not survive the Holocaust, nor did they leave any heirs who knew of the transaction. The few that did received their money back in full, but no picture of the real JDC budget can be deduced from that. A JDC suggestion to send sums from relatives in the United States to Poland via the clearance arrangement in Germany was apparently not agreed to by the Germans.[65] Most of the sums actually cleared came from Berlin or Vienna, and only small sums via Prague.[66]

How the directors used the funds at their disposal is no more certain than how the money was raised. Again one must rely on official reports, and the figures they record must be interpreted. For the year 1940, for example, total JDC expenditures in Poland were given both as 7.5 million zl. (table 7) and as 10,238,062 zl. (table 8). It is of course possible that JDC-Warsaw included the money raised by illegal loans in their 1940 report of expenditures. The funds for Rumkowski and Merin were deducted from the transfers in any case, and JDC had little to do with them. The percentages given in table 8, however, do indicate what the priorities were.

Another JDC document from the spring of 1941 reflects a continuing emphasis on emergency feeding and children. The Jewish population of the GG is there estimated at 1,570,000. Of these, 480,000 were estimated to live in Warsaw, which probably was an overestimate. Some 300,000 of these were unemployed persons and refugees in dire need. JDC proposed dividing the funds available for welfare and social work as follows: 60 percent to Warsaw; 6 percent to the Warsaw district; 14 percent to the Lublin district; 11 percent to the Radom district; and 9 percent to the Kraków district. Obviously JDC was aware of the relatively easier situation in the last two areas.[67] Funds sufficient to meet the minimal budgetary requirements, however, were far beyond the wildest hopes of JDC in Poland. When a budget was projected for the first six months of 1942, 33.5 million zl. were needed to feed 300,000 adults and 30,000 children. CENTOS would cost another 11.6 million, TOZ 9.6 million, refugee care 6.2 million, and so on, for an astronomical total of 72.1 million zl. (including 5 million for East Galicia).[68] This sum would have represented more than JDC's budget for all of its work all over the world.

JDC-Warsaw tried to overcome these vast problems in another way. If transfers of cash were limited and the amount of cash that could be borrowed locally were diminishing because of the impoverishment of the few wealthy Jews, could not emergency help be obtained through food shipments? There were two possible ways: from JDC-New York or from other aid organizations, mainly of course American ones, who could send general shipments into Poland. JSS would then get its 17 percent share. JDC therefore obtained help from abroad by asking for shipments of food and medicine. Small amounts were received from an aid organization in Zürich, Hilfsaktion für Notleidende Juden in Polen, behind which stood the American Federation of Polish Jews. Polish Jews were also supported by Dr. Alfred Silberschein, a veteran Zionist leader from Galicia, who ran a relief organization in Geneva called the Committee for Relief of the War-Stricken Jewish Population (RELICO), which was a part of the WJC office. Most Hilfsaktion aid went to Weichert's JSS, but goods were stored in JDC warehouses and distributed with JDC's consent. There seem to have been at least six shipments between July, 1940, and February, 1941, totaling almost twenty-six tons.[69] Polish Jewry could not be helped by such small-scale shipments.

JDC-Warsaw decided, early in 1940, to try to get a considerable shipment of food into Poland as a special Passover gesture. Neustadt and Guzik arranged for this during their discussions in Brussels, and JDC decided to spend part of its appropriation to Poland on it. One gets the impression that the timing for Passover was motivated not only by traditional considerations—matzot for Passover had always been a gesture treasured both by the givers and by the recipients—but also by the hope that it would facilitate German approval. The Germans, whatever their reasons, did not object, customs duties were low, and JDC used its representatives in neutral countries to prepare the shipment. In the end, the shipment did not arrive until the second half of Passover week and consisted of 137 railway wagons of food (603 tons of matzot, 350 tons of grains, 29.4 tons of fats and meat) and 12,000 tins of condensed milk. Most of the wagons came from Rumania, Yugoslavia, and Lithuania. Distribution was planned by JDC and effected through JSS; 47 percent went to Warsaw and its district. It was estimated that 560,000 adults and 75,000 children received the food as a one-time gift. One can imagine what the situation was in Poland, if a shipment of less than 1,000 tons of food for a Jewish population of under 2 million created such an uproar, demanded such an expenditure of effort and organization, and aroused many comments, mostly favorable.[70]

The success of the shipment encouraged JDC-Warsaw to try again, and from about June, 1940, there is plenty of evidence of attempts to organize another one. Two JDC officials, the American Bertrand S. Jacobson in Rumania and Joseph Blum, a local representative in Hungary, were particularly active in trying to get the New York office to agree. An admission by the American Red Cross that shipments to Poland were not distributed impartially strengthened the hands of those advocating the shipment, and Troper seems to have supported it.[71] Food was actually bought in Rumania in September, and permits were obtained in Slovakia and from the Germans in Poland.[72]

However, the group in JDC's New York leadership that wanted to prevent any indirect help to Germany demurred. The rift among leading Jews was symptomatic of the tragic situation in which they found themselves. Some of them felt that they could not oppose Britain's blockade of Germany and thus lay themselves open to the charge of indirectly supporting the Nazis. The food had to be bought in such doubtfully neutral countries as Slovakia, Rumania, and Yugoslavia. Their attitude was strengthened by an almost unbelievable naiveté regarding Nazi methods. They argued that feeding civilian populations in the war area was a responsibility of the German government, and any food shipments would free Germany from its obligation to provide food. Joseph Schwartz in Lisbon might send exasperated cables to New York, but he was told on November 19, 1940, that he should explain to JDC-Warsaw that "everybody feels this problem up to Hirsch's country [Germany]." Schwartz wanted to know whether this decision was final. "Making this Hirsch's problem [has] little practical value." JDC-New York thereupon requested a report by a special subcommittee composed of Paul Baerwald, Harold Linder, and Alfred Jaretzki, Jr.; they reported on December 16 that, as food would have to be paid for in dollars to countries such as Slovakia, they were opposed to the shipments. Schwartz cabled to Jacobson and Blum on December 20 that the decision was final: "Suggest you do nothing." An attempt by Leavitt, Hyman, and Alexander Kahn in April, 1941, to push through a decision to buy food for Poland and Russia was again thwarted by some of the conservative members of the Administrative Committee.[73]

JDC-Warsaw, however, was not dependent on official JDC shipments only. Schwartz especially, but also Troper, Meyerheim in Berlin, and Jacobson and Blum in the Balkans were helpful in finding alternative sources, of which the chief ones were the American Red Cross and the CPR. The latter, under its very energetic chairman Maurice Pate, was especially active in Poland. JDC had allocated $250,000 to it in January, 1940, and smaller amounts were given later; it also supported shipments by the American Red Cross.[74] The CPR spent $996,000 in Poland; 3,500 tons of food, 251 tons of clothes, and 150 tons of medicines reached that country. But from May, 1940, on, limitations were placed on the organization's actions, until in 1941 they had to cease altogether, and all aid to Poland was handed over to NRO. Throughout, JDC-JSS received their 17 percent. The German Red Cross seems to have cooperated, and a number of food shipments got through, though we unfortunately know little of the negotiations that must have taken place to effect them.

In its official report for 1940, JDC estimated the value of the shipments it received at 7,235,000 zl.[75] In other words, the shipments nearly doubled its budget. But in actual fact these food supplies meant more than is suggested by their monetary equivalent. For one thing, Polish Jews could not normally get good food, even if cash were supplied through transfers from Germany. Secondly, the shipments reminded the sufferers that their brethren abroad, and some at least of the civilized non-Jewish community, had not abandoned them. Yet even so, the amounts were insignificant compared with the need. Misery and near starvation had been the lot of large sections of Polish Jewry even before the war, but now soup kitchens were the order of the day. The very considerable importance of the JDC in the life of Polish Jews stemmed in the first place from its involvement in establishing these kitchens.

The fact that one-tenth of Warsaw's Jewish population died in 1941 despite the efforts of JDC reflects the financial weakness of JDC-Warsaw in 1940 and 1941. The refugees were hardest hit, because in most places it proved impossible to overcome the feeling that hungry local Jews should be considered first. This was especially so in Warsaw, where an estimated total of 130,000 refugees congregated at the peak of the hunger crisis in the spring of 1941. By September, a high death rate had reduced the number to 115,000. The situation was simply beyond description. All writers agree that JDC was doing whatever it could through its agencies, but that was not nearly enough. A report preserved in the Ringelblum archive estimates the number of those who needed social help at 250,000 out of a ghetto population in spring, 1941, of 418,000. Table 10 shows that of these, less than one-half received any food at all. The overwhelming majority of those fed were refugees, but the problem was unsolved, to put it mildly, because the food provided in the kitchens furnished only 200–300 calories for each person, or just over 10 percent of what was needed to keep the people alive.[76]

There were about thirty-six official refugee shelters where these masses of refugees were slowly dying of hunger or of the typhoid epidemic. Frantic attempts were made to extend some kind of help, but not only was there no money, there was no food to be bought, because it was more difficult for public bodies to engage in smuggling than it was for individuals. Mostly housed in former schools, synagogues, or cinemas, lacking heat or adequate sanitary arrangements, the refugees succumbed to the weakness caused by hunger. Ringelblum's Oneg Shabbat group sent its reporters to these shelters.

> I see how a Jew lies there with his Talit [prayer shawl] and tefillin [phylacteries], wrapped in his rough, torn rags. He lies on his wooden bunk together with his five little children, and looks out into the world through the snow-covered, frozen, filthy window;

he only sees what his fantasy wishes him to see. Perhaps he sees himself standing again in his township of Zirodow with his ritual butcher's knife in one hand and a chicken in the other—slaughtering, so he can bring home to his family some money, bread, meat and all those good things that he usually brings home. He looks at me disapprovingly, glances angrily, then looks in sorrow and despair at his little swallows that are lying there pressed one into the other, and then turns his head again toward the window. Only the eyes are aglow with an inner fire. Perhaps he is praying to his God who misled him so disgustingly, or perhaps he is blessing the sufferings and trials that his God brought upon him and his community of Jews—who knows?

It was often impossible even to move the dead, and scenes that the world later learned about from places like Bergen-Belsen were first seen in the Warsaw ghetto. "Later," says the reporter,

> I became aware of a girl of maybe 14 years lying on a bunk . . . and next to her lay, half uncovered, with the naked buttocks turned to the outside, the body of a child of about six years. . . . It was only the doctor's hysterical laughter that woke me from my frozen stance. . . . "Kiss my behind," yelled the doctor, pointing to the dead child's buttocks. He said it in the child's name, to the whole world.[77]

These refugees were sometimes victims of Judenrat officials out for money. Those expelled from Pruszkow, for instance, were held up for ransom of 5,000 zl. by being placed into a so-called disinfection plant and told they would not be let out unless they paid the money.[78] The officials demanded more money, and only the intervention of JSS or ŻETOS saved them. Demoralized and hungry, some of them nevertheless tried at first to establish organizations by towns of origin (*Landsmanschaftn*) or engage in cultural activities. Youths especially were active in these fields.[79] But all of these attempts floundered against the inexorable grimness of hunger.

Could JDC and its agencies have done more? In the summer of 1940, just as the need was growing bigger, JDC had to cut its budgets, resulting in temporary closure of the kitchens. Despite unbelievable odds, and apparently with money obtained from illegal loans, work was intensified in 1941. Yet it was but a drop in the bucket. During the worst of the typhoid epidemic, one writer of Ringelblum's Oneg Shabbat, Peretz Opoczynski, accused the Polish Jews of a frightful lack of foresight. Had they given JDC their money when they still had some, they might have helped. But by 1941 the Nazis had taken it. "When the Jews, in the personality of the weak JDC suddenly realized that one actually could give something to Jacob [the Jews] and not everything to Esau [the Nazis], there was nothing to give away anymore."[80]

In the spring of 1941, JDC estimated that some 950,000 of the 1.8 million Jews in German-controlled Poland needed help, but at best only 300,000 would get it: 225,000 adults and 75,000 children through the kitchen program. In addition, 3,000 children in CENTOS homes, 5,000 in day homes, and 1,000 old people would benefit.[81] According to a summary made in 1942, this program was at least partly carried out: an average of 295,000 soup portions were distributed daily to some 260,000 people, apparently including 42,000 children, throughout the GG. Apart from these, 3,700 children in homes and the 1,000 old-age pensioners had also received something. Yet JDC estimated that some 50,000 starving children had not received any care at all.[82] Looking forward to 1942, JDC wanted to feed at least as many as in 1941. There was no need to, as it turned out.

Looking after children followed closely after the general feeding program on JDC's list of priorities. There was no clear dividing line between the two activities in any case, or indeed between the second and a third, arranging for adequate health services. CENTOS established institutions that were designed to save children from the physical, educational, and moral effects of the ghetto. Foremost among these were the so-called children's corners, organized early in 1941 by the house committees and usually manned by members of youth organizations such as the Tsukunft (Future) groups of the Bund and by Zionist youth movements. Some food was distributed, and the children's play was usually combined with one or another form of instruction, depending on the affiliation of the young counselors. "For the children in the house, the corners were an inexhaustible source of joy, lust for life, energy, partly even a school for the development of a communal, social feeling."[83] Not all of these corners survived to the end of the year. Opoczynski, a Zionist, claimed that instruction, education, and play were sometimes conducted in Polish, a language foreign to many of the children. The struggle over ethnic identity was conducted even in the ghetto, and even over the children.

Day homes were organized for refugee children and for children of *obozniks,* men who had been forced into labor camps outside Warsaw. CENTOS even tried to organize summer vacation camps. For a short time the Germans gave permission for Jewish children to go and bathe in the Vistula, though at odd times and strictly separated from Aryans. The Judenräte also aided children, and Czerniakow in Warsaw, especially, tried to establish playgrounds and play gardens.

In smaller towns the problem of feeding children was at least manageable, and there was no mass begging of starving children in the streets, but the situation in Warsaw was a different matter. Opoczynski estimated that in 1941 there were 3,000 child beggars in the ghetto. Approximately 10,000 children in Warsaw were part or full orphans, but there were only 2,000 children in Warsaw's twelve children's homes, one of which was run by the Judenrat and the rest by CENTOS. The 3,000–4,000 daily rations of bread CENTOS distributed to the street beggars left 90 percent of them uncared for.[84]

TOZ tried to compete with CENTOS by setting up its own feeding centers for children, and complained bitterly at the end of 1940 when JDC decided to concentrate its support for such activities with CENTOS. JDC did not succeed in eliminating the competition between the two groups altogether, but generally speaking TOZ concentrated on health services to both adults and children. It ran ambulatories, advice and information centers, hospitals, clinics, and sanatoria, which was quite a feat under the prevailing conditions. A mental hospital at Zofiówka and a tuberculosis hospital at Otwock were kept going until the very end in 1942. In the midst of chaos and misery in Warsaw, a training school for nurses, originally founded by JDC in 1921, was kept in existence by Luba Bilecka. The school was attached to the Jewish hospital at Czyste Street, and then transferred with the hospital into the ghetto. The training of nurses continued unabated, and there was enough practical work for them to do. They were particularly active during the peak of the typhoid epidemic in 1941 and worked all through the great deportation period in the summer of 1942. In the end, most of the trainees were deported and murdered. A few of them managed to hide, among them Luba Bilecka herself.[85]

Constructive Aid and Cultural Activities, 1940–1941

In the midst of catastrophe, JDC attempted to provide what it termed "constructive aid"—establishing artisans and craftsmen in their occupations and providing for vocational training. These activities were in the best JDC tradition of helping others to help themselves, but a great deal of optimism and steadfastness was needed to maintain such a tradition in 1940 and 1941. Working through the JSS and its own inspectors, JDC helped to reestablish some few craftsmen in their occupations, using special ORT allocations from New York. JDC was proud of this aid, "which all this time assists 2,000 persons to begin to earn their own livelihoods through the purchase of small machinery, the establishment of collective workshops, etc."[86] Should one marvel at the naiveté of responsible social workers trying to discern a ray of hope in the setting up of 2,000 artisans when thousands were dying of hunger—or should one admire the tremendous will to live that is obvious in their acts? JDC must have assumed that one had to do all one could to alleviate suffering in the hope that the war would soon end with Germany's defeat—of that there was never a doubt.[87] The Jewish people of Poland would have to pull through until then. It was this positive attitude that led to moral resistance and later to physical resistance as well.

A different role altogether was played by Towarzystwo Popierania Rolnictwa (TOPOROL), a prewar JDC-sponsored organization for the support of agriculture, which was resuscitated in Warsaw with the help of ORT towards the end of 1940. TOPOROL was also active outside Warsaw, supervising a number of agricultural training centers throughout the GG. But its center of activity was the Warsaw ghetto, where it provided three major services: training courses for farmers and gardeners; gardening plots within the ghetto; and employment for large numbers of young people outside the ghetto. For example, in its report for the first half of 1941, TOPOROL claimed that 591 persons attended its study courses, which included botany, zoology, chemistry, agricultural economics, gardening, and other topics. The gardening plot program, carried on with some help from the Judenrat, used every available piece of ground in the narrow ghetto confines for vegetable gardens and flowers for sale to the Aryan quarters. The irony is self-evident: starving Jews produced fragrant flowers in a stinking ghetto for tender Aryan noses. Vegetables for consumption in the ghetto were also grown in appreciable quantities in balcony gardens developed by the organization.

TOPOROL's chief endeavor, however, was the provision of jobs outside the ghetto on farms run by Polish or German owners or supervisors. Jewish farms had of course been confiscated much earlier, but some former Jewish properties were run by commissars who were willing to use Jewish labor. Furthermore, farm laborers were scarce in the GG in the spring of 1941, largely because of the mass conscription of Poles for work in Germany. The Germans were not eager to reintroduce Jews into areas that had already been declared "free of Jews" (*judenrein*), and some high German officials, such as Heinz Auerswald in Warsaw, balked at the idea of letting them out of the ghetto. But there was no hard-and-fast German policy, and economic pressures were allowed to prevail. The German Labor Office in Warsaw gave only 240 permits for Jews to work outside the ghetto in spring, 1941, but TOPOROL, with the connivance of some German officials, managed to smuggle out thousands—how many exactly is unknown. As late as November, 1941, some 1,000 Jews were still working on these farms, although most of the work was of course done in the summer months.[88]

The farm labor program enabled as many young people as possible to escape from ghetto conditions for as long as possible, and TOPOROL noted with satisfaction that they came back to Warsaw healthy and heavier. In addition, the Zionist youth movements used the opportunity to prepare their membership for agricultural work in Palestine, thus raising morale and providing the members with a sense of purpose. Zionist-socialists of the Dror and Hashomer Hatzair movements went to Grochów and other places, Betar members went to the Hrubieszów area, and so on. There is no doubt that these activities were a milestone on the road toward a resistance mentality.

JDC's Policy in Poland

JDC placed great stress on morale-building activities. In this ŻETOS, led by Emmanuel Ringelblum, was of primary importance, but diarists and memoirists also mention lectures and courses held under the auspices of house committees or soup kitchens, quite apart from similar activities conducted by the Judenrat. The kitchens were, as we have seen, often handed over to underground political groups. Youth movements also utilized these convenient gathering points, not only in Warsaw but elsewhere. The beginnings of underground activities were inevitably cultural and discussion meetings. From them developed an underground press. Ringelblum was the JDC worker most intimately concerned with these developments, but we find Giterman involved as well.

Simply put, JDC-Warsaw's main effort was directed to keeping as many Jews as possible alive. It struggled against the German desire to humiliate, dispossess, and starve out the Jews, against the frightful conditions of ghetto life; it struggled with and against the Judenräte, being both an official American-based organization and a local institution headed by leftists who were moving increasingly toward a radical anti-German stand. JDC's strength was its insistence on a close liaison with the accepted—now underground—political leadership. ŻETOS in Warsaw had a public committee of politicians, and CENTOS and TOZ were led by politicians. But the Warsaw directors did not submit to public control anymore than other JDC branches did, nor did they submit easily to control by their own organization. Their independence and determination to do their job made them engage in policies that may not have won the approval of New York, but that helped the Jews of Poland. They must have felt that with contacts to the outside becoming increasingly tenuous, they were the best judges of what should or should not be done—and so indeed they were.

Nevertheless, ultimately the strength of JDC-Warsaw lay precisely in its ties with the United States. These ties guaranteed its legal existence until December, 1941, and the American allocations of money that came via Germany and Austria formed the basis of its operations. Without those funds, no action would have been possible. It was in no small part due to JDC's efforts that, early in 1942, a first kind of balance was found that might have enabled Polish Jews to survive under ghetto conditions. But in the meantime, on June 22, 1941, the Germans had attacked the USSR, and on December 7, 1941, the Japanese attack on Pearl Harbor had brought the United States into war. The first of these events brought with it the beginnings of the mass murder of European Jews; the second made their protection by the United States impossible. Polish Jewry was doomed.

4

A Case of Rescue: Lithuania

There were only a few instances of successful rescue of European Jews in the course of the war. In all of them, resourceful individuals overcame bureaucratic or political obstacles by a combination of willpower, luck, and sheer daring—and were thereby instrumental in saving endangered people. The pattern can be clearly discerned in the case of the Polish Jewish refugees in Lithuania and their rescue to Japan, Shanghai, and Palestine.

After World War I, a serious quarrel over Vilna, the ancient capital of Lithuania, marred the relations between Poland and Lithuania, both of them republics carved out of the chaos of 1917–18. A Polish army gained control of the city, and until 1939, Vilna was Polish. Its population of 290,000 included Poles, Lithuanians, and 60,000 Jews. An additional 25,000 Jews lived in the countryside around the city. On August 23, 1939, the Nazis and the Soviets signed a nonaggression pact which triggered the outbreak of World War II. The Soviets invaded Poland on September 17, and seized Vilna two days later. Originally included in the German sphere of interest, Lithuania was transferred to the Soviet sphere by a secret protocol of September 28, 1939. On October 10, the Lithuanian foreign minister was forced to sign an agreement with the USSR, according to which Vilna would revert to Lithuania, but Soviet army and air force units would occupy bases throughout that country.

These sudden, dramatic changes reunited Lithuanian Jewry, of which Vilna Jews had always considered themselves a part, and which then totaled some 250,000 souls. Most Vilna Jews remained after the Soviets left, except those who had been taken prisoner by the Nazis or the Soviets, had been exiled by the Russians immediately after their occupation of the town, or were among the hundreds of persons who chose to leave with the Russians before the Lithuanians entered the city. The Russians had dismantled Elektrik, a radio factory manned largely by Jewish workers, and these followed the Russians for economic reasons. Others had taken part in pro-Communist activities during the brief Russian occupation and thought it safer to leave. The rest stayed on.

The Lithuanian army officially entered Vilna on October 28, 1939; a pogrom lasting until October 31 immediately broke out, instigated by right-wing Poles, mainly youths, but carried out with the connivance of Lithuanian authorities. They accused the Jews of starting demonstrations against the drastic impoverishment caused by a 250 percent devaluation resulting from the conversion to Lithuanian currency. One Jew was killed and some 200 wounded, and an attempt was made by the Jews to set up a self-defense organization. One source claims that this group prevented more deaths; at any rate, further pogroms expected to take place on November 10–11, traditional dates for anti-Jewish disturbances in Vilna, did not occur, largely because of very determined Jewish protests to the Lithuanian authorities. These protests culminated in a threat by the Jewish representative, Dr. Jacob Wigodsky, to the Lithuanian general Skuvas that the Jews would turn to the Soviets for protection.[1]

As early as September, 1939, it was clear that Lithuania might become a neutral island in the midst of a spreading sea of war. JDC, with a long record of aid to the 155,000 Lithuanian Jews and to the 85,000 Jews in Vilna and its environs, saw that this potential outpost of rescue had to be manned without delay. European Director Morris C. Troper sent one of his best young men to Lithuania, an American Jew named Moses W. Beckelman, who arrived on October 11, 1939. Isaac Giterman, head of the Warsaw JDC office, arrived soon after, a refugee himself.

As a result of a policy promulgated by Reinhardt Heydrich, head of the RSHA, village Jews in areas to be annexed directly to the Reich were to be deported, largely to the newly created GG in central Poland.[2] This policy was implemented in the district of

108

Suwalki, an area wedged between Lithuania and eastern Prussia, where some 15,000 Jews were living. Immediately following the German occupation, all livestock belonging to Jews was requisitioned, all money and valuables registered and put into blocked accounts (or practically, confiscated), and all houses requisitioned and their inhabitants forced to live in barns and stables. "In one case the Germans set fire to the granary of a Jewish wheat dealer and then charged him 90% of the wheat stored in the granary for putting out the fire."[3] Then humiliations and beatings started, culminating in direct expulsion of part of the Jewish population into the GG and of another part into the no-man's-land on the Lithuanian border. The Jews were told that they were to make room for Germans to be repatriated from the Baltic states (a dim echo of Heydrich's instructions); their papers and passports were taken from them, and they were then told to make their way into Lithuania, but warned against returning to German-occupied territory on pain of death.

Those who were forced into the border area endured unbelievable suffering. They were exposed to gunfire from both sides and were not allowed to buy food, but they had no money anyway.

> They had been visited by German guards and searched to the skin again and again to make sure they had not succeeded in hiding some money or valuables. One man with a bandaged leg had had the wound opened because the Germans had ripped off the bandage to see whether he was hiding any money. With the aid of some of the peasants, some of whom I saw standing about crying while we talked to the refugees, they had built crude unroofed thatched huts which offered some protection against wind but none against rain.[4]

The first expulsions took place during the last days of October, just as the Lithuanians entered Vilna.[5] Beckelman turned to the Lithuanian vice-premier, Każys Bizauskas, and pleaded with him to accept the refugees, promising JDC support for them. Bizauskas told him that while Lithuania could absorb 500 or 1,000 such refugees easily, this would simply constitute an invitation to the Germans to send in thousands more, which of course Lithuania could not accept. As a result of Beckelman's interventions and those of other Jewish groups, a Lithuanian investigative commission in which Beckelman and the representative of HIAS, Yehoshua Razovsky, participated, was sent out on November 5, 1939. As a result of its report, the Lithuanians accepted a number of the refugees, estimated at between 1,600 and 2,400. The latter figure seems to be closer to the truth. In any case, most of these refugees were not actually formally admitted, but rather were smuggled across the border at great danger to themselves by local village Jews on the Lithuanian side. One of them especially, whose name is unknown, became famous as a kind of latter-day Samson who himself carried a large number of children and sick persons and led others into the relative safety of Lithuania.

Polish Jewish Refugees in Lithuania

The Suwalki refugees were but a prelude to the bigger problem that had to be faced—the stream of Jewish refugees from Poland who began arriving in Vilna after October 10, when it was announced that the town was about to be transferred to Lithuania. After September 7, 1939, when the dying Polish regime had called upon civilians to leave Warsaw, large numbers of Jews had left the city and turned east, hoping that some kind of Polish resistance would continue there. Refugees from other places joined them, and when the Russians crossed into Poland, the fleeing crowds soon found themselves under Soviet occupation. Many refugees clutched at the hope that a further move into neutral Lithuania might be a stepping-stone to Palestine or elsewhere. Entry into Vilna was completely free until the Lithuanians occupied the city, and almost free until the middle of November.

Many refugees decided to make the move to Vilna, among them three distinct groups who had very good grounds for not staying in Russian-occupied Poland. One of these was the Zionist youth organizations. In their temporary quarters at Kovel, the Dror Zionist-socialists decided to move; the Hashomer Hatzair leadership at Rovno wavered, but in the end followed some of its rank-and-file and made a similar decision. The Betar movement had concentrated at Vilna in the first place, and decided to stay there; other groups, such as Gordonia, Akiva, Bne Akiva, and Hanoar Hatzioni followed suit. Approximately 600 of the activists of all these movements reached the city by the middle of November, and 1,400 more came after that date, crossing into Lithuania illegally before the hermetic closure of the border by the Soviets and an unusually severe winter made further attempts hopeless about the middle of January, 1940. These illegal crossings took place mainly between Lida on the Polish side and Eisiskes in Lithuania, but some youth-group refugees came via Oshmyany and Svencionys (Swienczany) further north. They were well organized; individuals picked from the different movements went to the border area to establish contact with the smugglers of the region. Usually money had to be paid to the professional smugglers for each group. If caught, groups had to expect Soviet labor camps or worse. Some of the individuals then making their way with such difficulty to Vilna were to achieve fame later on. The left-wing youth organizations decided, during the period of what became known as the "Vilna concentration," to send back a number of their leaders into Nazi-occupied Poland in order to organize and lead Jewish youth under the new terrible conditions. Back to Poland went Mordechai Anielewicz, later the commander of the Warsaw ghetto rebellion, his deputy, Yitzhak Zuckermann, and many others. These acts of voluntary return to Nazi-controlled Poland set the youth movements apart from the political parties, whose leaders escaped from the country and had no intention of going back.

Another group who tended to use the same methods of crossing were students of yeshivot and their rabbis. Whole rabbinical schools were transferred to Lithuania in this way, because it was obvious that they could only hope to survive in a place where Soviet authorities or the Nazis would have no control over them. These yeshivot, one of which was the famous yeshiva of Mir, numbered about another 2,000 persons.

The third group was composed of the leaders of Jewish parties in Poland, a fair percentage of whom made their way into Vilna. Among them were journalists, lawyers, politicians, and writers, and they hoped they might escape from Lithuania to safety. There were such men as Dr. Moshe Sneh, leader of the General Zionists in Poland (who was to become head of the Haganah, the Jewish underground military organization, in Palestine a year later); Dr. Zerah Wahrhaftig, leader of Hapoel Hamizrahi, a religious Zionist-socialist movement (who later fled to the United States and ultimately became a minister in the Israeli government); Menachem Begin, leader of Betar (who became head of the Irgun Zvai Leumi, the anti-British Jewish underground in Palestine, and in 1977 the prime minister of Israel); and Abraham Mendelsohn, a well-known leader of the anti-Zionist Bund party.

In other words, in what was known as *Yerushalayim de'Litta* ("Jerusalem in Lithuania") in the city of Vilna, there congregated late in 1939 and early in 1940 a group of about 14,000 Jewish refugees, among whom there could be found a high proportion of

111

the spiritual and political leadership of Polish Jewry. Apart from these, there were also simple Jews who had fled the Germans and the Soviets and were desperately trying to get out—anywhere, at any cost—just like so many other Jewish refugees elsewhere. Some 70 percent of the refugees had come from the German-occupied areas of Poland, the rest coming from the Soviet-controlled eastern part. There were 2,440 rabbinical students with 171 rabbis; 2,065 others were from the *halutzim* (pioneering Zionist youth), of whom about 600 belonged to Hashomer Hatzair, 580 to Hehalutz-Dror, 400 to Hanoar Hatzioni, and the rest to other movements.

Outside Help to the Refugees

For JDC, as well as for other aid organizations, Lithuania in late 1939 was unique in the sense that it was the only opening to suffering Polish Jewry through which help could come.[6] However, as JDC stated very clearly, initiatives by organizations and individuals within the Lithuanian Jewish community were the sine qua non of any additional help from the outside.[7] Locally active were the Palestine Office of JA—in effect, the Zionist organization in Kovno (Kaunas) under Zvi Brick; the towering personality of Rabbi Chayim Ozer Grodzenski and his group of Orthodox Jews in Vilna; the Ezra aid organization in Kovno, which undertook to look after the Suwalki refugees; a local refugee committee in Vilna; and others. Foreign organizations or persons active on the scene were the American Polish Relief Fund, whose representative, H. Foster Anderson, resided in Lithuania; Gilbert Redfern, who for a time represented American agencies connected with the Hoover Committee; and a Mr. Kaiser, who for a very brief period represented the British-based Committee of Polish Jews. Apart from these, there were HIAS and JDC; HIAS was represented by Yehoshua Razovsky, a local Jew, and JDC by Beckelman. Isaac Giterman remained in Vilna until early in 1940, when he left on a fateful journey that was to have taken him via Sweden to Amsterdam. It ended, instead, with a German bullet during the first phase of the Warsaw ghetto rebellion in January, 1943, after a glorious chapter of moral and physical resistance.

The refugees were welcomed by Lithuanian Jews, especially those in Vilna. On December 23, 1939, Dr. Jacob Robinson, a well-known Jewish lawyer and a former member of the Lithuanian administration, united all the Jewish aid organizations, local and foreign, into Ezrat Plitim, a general committee dealing with refugees. This happened none too soon, for on December 9, the Lithuanian government nominated a Mr. Alekna to serve as its commissioner for refugees in the Ministry of the Interior. The aim of the Lithuanians at this stage was to combat Polish influence in Vilna, and the Jews could serve as allies in this if they behaved loyally. The Lithuanians most probably wanted to deprive the Vilna Poles of their citizenship and turn them into refugees. On the other hand, given the desperate state of the Lithuanian treasury, foreign aid activities that would bring in much-needed dollars were very welcome. Trying to establish their hold over the money, the government issued an order on January 20, 1940, that all funds from abroad would have to be paid in to the Lithuanian Red Cross, run by General J. Sutkus. The order prompted the formation of a committee, consisting of Anderson, Redfern, and Beckelman, representing the foreign groups. After protracted negotiations, Beckelman reached an agreement with the Lithuanian Red Cross whereby the latter would add 50 percent in Lithuanian money to any sum in foreign currency that the organizations might transfer. That portion of the funds earmarked for Jews was transferred to the committee organized by Robinson. From September, 1939, until the end of 1940, JDC spent $717,000 in Lithuania, about $60,000 (£15,000) of which represented a contribution by South African Jewry.[8] This figure represents about 11.7 percent of the total JDC expenditure in 1940 of $6,103,000. In addition, $25,000 were spent by the JDC Cultural Committee.

The Vilna Ezrat Plitim opened kitchens—at first ten, and later others—to feed the refugees. Housing was a big problem. The solution was communal homes (internats), where organized groups as well as unorganized refugees were housed. By early June, 1940, 6,980 people were fed daily by the kitchens, 8,000 had been given clothing,[9] and medical aid was organized. In a continuation of a JDC tradition holding that "intellectuals" should be helped to overcome their shame at being reduced to seeking social aid, some persons received preferential treatment. A vexing problem in this connection was the demand of a small group of Bundists, numbering with their families perhaps 400 people, to be treated separately so that they would not have to deal with the general committee, which was run by Zionists, Orthodox Jews, and other "reactionaries."

In the end, even the angelically patient Beckelman complained about the "Bund question which is coming out of my ears now." The Bundists were presenting "fantastic and infantile schemes" of administering JDC relief so as to avoid contact with the committee. The trouble Beckelman complained of reflected the fact that twenty-five years before the Jewish Labor Committee had cofounded JDC, and in 1940, some of its leaders, such as Adolph Held, still occupied respected positions in the JDC lay committees. Bundists had always tended to exaggerate the importance of these facts and even threatened JDC in Europe with turning to their colleagues in the United States for direct support. By 1940, Bundist influence in the American socialist Jewish movement had been watered down, both by the American experience, which found Bundist ideology difficult to apply to the new conditions, and by the existence of a Zionist wing. However, JDC was prepared to compromise in order not to lose the cooperation of the Labor Committee leaders. Beckelman managed to patch up an agreement with the small Bund group in Vilna, aided somewhat by a special allocation of $25,000 from the Jewish Labor Committee in New York to help the Bundists stranded in Vilna. It is interesting to note that the money was actually donated by the Rosenwald family of Sears, Roebuck and Company, not usually known for their enthusiastic support of socialist causes, and channeled via Agrojoint, the JDC organization to aid Soviet Jews, and the AFSC to the committee. One is left to wonder what the comrades in Vilna had to say about the help extended to them by the "bloodthirsty capitalists" of America.[10]

The Lithuanian government wanted the Jewish refugees to leave Vilna and disperse in the "old" Lithuanian provinces. The motives were partly political—to emphasize the Lithuanian character of Vilna—but also pragmatic: Lithuanian authorities were moving into the city and needed space. Houses occupied by the refugees could be used for the police, the army, and officials. Immediately upon the formation of Ezrat Plitim, Robinson and some other members met with Alekna and agreed with him to proceed slowly with such a dispersal, which would ultimately be in the refugees' interest if they could find remunerative work outside Vilna. Nominally, only people who had come to the city before the Lithuanian occupation were eligible for refugee status, but this regulation was circumvented by falsifying documents, with the tacit approval of the authorities. The Lithuanians were concerned about the Poles, whom they wanted to keep out, and not about the Jews. Nevertheless, supervision tightened as time went on. On March 1, 1940, refugees were denied free movement in the country and political activity was also proscribed. On

March 28, all inhabitants of Vilna who had not been citizens in October, 1920, when the town was annexed by Poland, were declared to be refugees. Although this action was intended to depolonize the city, it also hit a number of Jews.

On the whole, however, Jewish relations with the government were not unfriendly. On January 5, 1940, in an article in the government paper *Lietuvos Aidas,* Alekna presented a favorable picture of the Jewish refugees to the Lithuanian public. It seems that Lithuanian society was split between a liberal-conservative, older wing of government supporters and a newer radical-nationalist and pro-German wing, and the Jews could still find some understanding among the former.[11] In any case, apart from the Suwalki refugees, who had been more or less successfully resettled in the interior, Jewish refugees dispersed slowly indeed. As late as early 1941, 8,500 of the 12,000 refugees still supported by the JDC-subsidized refugee committee were in the Vilna area.[12]

While all of this supportive activity solved the immediate physical problems of the refugees, they knew that the authorities would press for their emigration. The refugees themselves never had any intention of staying permanently in Lithuania, and some felt politically endangered. The major problem, then, for many of the people who had fled to Vilna was how to get out as quickly as possible. At first the decisive influence in trying to facilitate emigration was the Palestine Office, directed by Zvi Brick. Aided by an effective committee composed of veteran Polish Zionists such as Moshe Sneh, Zerah Wahrhaftig, and Abraham Bialopolski, Brick made frantic attempts to get those Polish Jews who had Palestine immigration certificates, or who had confirmation that they would get them on arrival in Palestine, out of Lithuania. The Lithuanian government tried to be helpful, because of course it wanted to get rid of as many refugees as possible. The Palestine certificates were valid only till March 31, 1940, and then would have to be renewed, which in Lithuania would be most difficult.

Zvi Brick turned to Sweden. Working through the Swedish Jewish community, he managed to get the agreement of the Swedish Red Cross, in the person of Prince Carl, to allocate enough fuel to a Swedish-Russian airline flying between Riga and Stockholm to charter ten aircraft for Jewish refugees. Although French and British diplomatic representatives in Kovno made all kinds of additional difficulties, the air route actually came into operation. All ten flights left Riga between March 20 and March

24, 1940, paid for by JA. By the end of March, 406 people had managed to emigrate to Palestine.[13]

In April, Brick secured German agreement to allow sealed trains carrying Jews to pass through to Trieste via Germany, but JA did not consent because it thought the venture was too risky. However, parallel negotiations with the Russians through the Lithuanian representative in Moscow for exit via Odessa elicited a positive response early in April.

HIAS had always been a close ally of JDC in matters pertaining to emigration, and this relationship was maintained in Lithuania. Of the total amount of foreign aid to potential emigrants from that country, JDC contributed about 80 percent. However, with the tremendous difficulties facing emigrants, only 137 people had managed to get out by April, 1940, to countries other than Palestine; 41 of these went to the United States.[14] Robinson, Brick, and Razovsky were negotiating different escape routes and grappling with the fact that the USSR would not allow transit through its territory to holders of Polish passports. Through the Kovno Soviet consul, Pozdniakov, a Russian agreement was obtained to allow refugees holding "sauf conduits"—(that is, stateless persons, not Polish citizens) to emigrate via the USSR. This agreement was announced by Lithuania on April 22. However, the annexation of Lithuania by the Soviet Union soon put an end to all these efforts.

The Effects of the Soviet Occupation

Prior to the Soviet occupation, a financial problem arose which was to have significant effects on later developments: the Lithuanians wanted to have all foreign welfare funds deposited with the Lithuanian Red Cross, which then would distribute them as it thought fit. Furthermore, foreign organizations should contribute to the administrative expenses of the Red Cross's refugee section. Beckelman fought a successful diplomatic battle over these points: in addition to an agreement to add 50 percent to the sums provided from abroad in their own currency, the Lithuanians also agreed to joint supervision by the Lithuanian Red Cross and the foreign groups, while the former received a small sum of money for its administrative expenses.

Russian troops entered Lithuania on June 15, 1940. On June 17, a "popular" government under Justas Paleckis, a veteran Communist leader, was set up. On July 17, so-called elections were held for a "popular Sejmas" (parliament), which in turn declared Lithuania to be a soviet socialist republic and asked the Supreme Soviet of the USSR to accept it into the Soviet Union. Not surprisingly, this request was acceded to on August 3.

The Jewish population was caught in a vise which proved to be fatal for its relations with the Lithuanians. On the one hand, all discrimination disappeared, especially in education. Jews also could become officials, policemen, and judges, though not quite without restriction. Five Jews sat among the eighty-four members of the Communist parliament; one of the two deputy chairmen of the Supreme Soviet in Lithuania was a Jew, as were one minister and two deputy ministers (commissars). There had been only seventy-four Jews in all the Lithuanian administration in early 1940; there were a very large number afterwards, including, for instance, 44 percent of the officials of the Commissariat for Industry. No wonder, then, that a fair proportion of Jews, especially of the younger generation, supported the new regime, although it was almost universally hated by the local population. On the other hand, when the nationalization decree was promulgated in September, 1940, a full 83 percent of the enterprises taken over by the Soviets were Jewish. All Jewish traders and many artisans were deprived of their livelihoods; Jewish political, cultural, and educational institutions were closed down, and their workers and adherents placed in danger of arrest. The whole complicated structure of Jewish autonomous endeavor was struck down with one blow. A number of Jews were arrested and exiled. Finally, a week before the German invasion, on June 14, 1941, the Soviets arrested and exiled 30,000 people, among them 5,000 Jews.[15]

It is clear, therefore, that the Jews were torn between loyalty and opposition toward a government that was both protecting their lives against Germany and preventing the angry Lithuanians from venting their antisemitism (now fortified by what was interpreted as a Jewish pro-Soviet stand), and yet was suppressing Jewish national and religious expression and also ruining the majority of the Jews economically. Surprisingly enough, no change took place in regard to the refugees for some time. The refugee committee in Vilna continued to operate, and the status of the refugees remained uncertain. In August, the committee decided to provide the refugees with stateless-person papers in order to obviate the danger inherent in holding Polish passports in a Soviet-occupied area.

In the meantime, however, a very dangerous situation developed. Lithuanian assets in the United States were frozen and no more transfers of dollars to Lithuania were permitted; moreover, the elitist group of Zionists, religious leaders, and Bundists was faced with very grim prospects under the new regime and were desperately seeking a way to escape. In New York, Moses Leavitt tried to persuade the Treasury Department to permit the transfer of funds to Vilna on humanitarian grounds, but to no avail. On the other hand, the Polish Relief Fund, Beckelman's colleagues in Lithuania, simply circumvented Treasury regulations without actually violating the law and transferred its funds to Switzerland, and from there to Lithuania. Leavitt absolutely refused to follow suit, Beckelman's increasingly furious letters notwithstanding. "Although we realize that remittances to Switzerland are perfectly legal and require no permission from the Treasury Department, the JDC is very anxious to stay both within the letter and the spirit of our Government's regulations, as well as policy. Consequently, before availing ourselves of this method, we would appreciate knowing what the attitude of the Department is," Leavitt wrote to Washington.[16] The State Department was opposed, as Beckelman was informed on August 23, 1940.

The result was that the Poles had dollars to spend for their refugees, whereas JDC was in trouble. Polish-Americans were apparently much less worried by the danger of being found out and censured than was the Jewish leadership in New York. Not only Beckelman's personal position as an American in Soviet Lithuania was endangered, but also the very existence of the Vilna committee. Its kitchens had to be closed on October 14 and reopened on a self-supporting basis. Beckelman finally wrote in December, 1940, that he would only stay on if JDC were willing to overcome what he termed "bureaucratic scruples." "Considering JDC's inept handling (which putting it mildly) this situation since July," he said, the assumption of responsibility by the Soviet authorities for the refugees would be a better solution than anything else the Jews could reasonably expect. Fortunately for the refugees, Beckelman did not give up. Against all odds, he managed to convince the new leadership of the Lithuanian Red Cross that dollars would soon be sent. In the meantime, the organization advanced him $33,000, and later on another $42,000, in local currency. With this money the refugees could be supported. Also, with educational institutions open to all after the Soviet occupation, young Jewish refugees could and did use the new opportunities, thus somewhat easing the burden on the refugee committees.[17]

118

Emigration to Japan and Palestine

There was little hope for Jewish refugees in Vilna in the summer of 1940 and even less for native Lithuanian Jews. Thousands wanted to escape, to anywhere at any price, but the world was closed. Then, apparently at one of the yeshivot, somebody decided to ask the Dutch consul at Kovno, Philip Reyda, whether there was any Dutch colony which would accept Jews. Not exactly, the consul replied after consulting the Dutch chargé d'affaires in Riga, P. N. Dekker, but there was no need for visas to Curaçao. Of, course, if you actually got there, the authorities would either accept you or not—presumably not. But the main point was that officially no visas were required.

The route to Curaçao was via Japan; to Japan, via Siberia. For that matter, the route to the United States was also via the USSR and Japan. The Soviets might give a transit permit if one got a Japanese transit visa. Obviously, Jewish refugees were led to look for a cooperative Japanese diplomat. Oddly enough, there was a Japanese consul in Kovno, Sempo Sugihara. He had been sent there late in 1939, at the instigation of the Japanese ambassador to Berlin, Hiroshi Oshima, who wanted to find out whether the Germans were preparing to attack the Soviet Union, and when. A listener posted in a neutral country might be useful, and that was Sugihara's main occupation until the Soviets came in June, 1940. At that point Sugihara was told that Japanese commercial interests in the Lithuanian Soviet Socialist Republic would scarcely warrant a consulate; he was to close down by August 31. On about August 1, Sugihara relates, he was surprised to find his modest building beleaguered by a large crowd of refugees, obviously in desperate straits. Most of them held papers from the Dutch consul advising them that they would not need visas for Curaçao. Some had papers for Palestine, a few even for the United States. About 1,000 yeshivot rabbis and students received their papers for Curaçao from Sweden, where the Dutch consul gave them to a local Orthodox rabbi. The Soviets told him that they would issue transit visas if the refugees first got Japanese visas, but the problem was whether Tokyo would agree. Sugihara wired for instructions, but for ten days there was no answer.[18]

On August 11, Sugihara began to hand out Japanese transit visas—without Tokyo's agreement—with the help of Wolfgang Gudke, a German who served as his secretary. On August 20, Tokyo did intervene, and energetically at that. No transit visas should be issued. The captain of the only ship bringing passengers from Vladivostok to Tsuruga in Japan also cabled not to hand out any more visas. But Sugihara did not listen. The first refugees to go to Japan left, it seems, on August 20. Sugihara stamped visas on all and every paper that was presented to him until August 31, when he had to leave Kovno for Germany. It appears he stamped 3,400 transit visas, and of these, 500 were on some kind of paper purporting to give the holder right of entry into Palestine. Most of the rest, about 1,600, were going to Curaçao.[19] Sugihara then disappeared from view; he spent the war years in Germany and Rumania. In 1947, he came back home and was promptly fired—because of the visas to the Polish Jews, he was told.

Parallel to the attempts to obtain visas to Japan went attempts to leave for Palestine. Those persons who held immigration certificates (allocated by Britain and distributed by JA) that had not been used in 1939 had a legal basis for their efforts, and some others were advised by JA just before the Soviets came that their applications for certificates had been approved by the British. The problem now was how to get these persons out. There was a British consulate in Kovno. Just as in the case of the Japanese consulate, it had been told to close by the end of August and actually was shut down September 4. But unlike Sugihara, the consul there refused to grant visas to Palestine, while the British embassy in Moscow demanded that applicants appear in person before it. A JA request that a special official be sent to Moscow to handle the technical work of issuing the certificates was rejected. At the very last moment, the consul at Kovno relented. He would give visas to holders of certificates or JA notifications, but he did not have enough paper and he did not have enough staff. The Jewish groups were willing to help. Paper was found and 250 visas were stamped into passports and sauf conduits. Another 550 papers advising individuals that visas would be granted on arrival in Palestine were prepared and signed on the very morning that the consulate closed its doors. Inventive minds forged another 400 such papers—these were later discovered by British officials in Istanbul, who were decidedly not amused. Normally, official stampings proudly displayed two very British lions. In Kovno, the lions had been miraculously transformed into cats. After all, who in Kovno had ever seen a lion?

The cats proved to be rather costly. The British declared that because of the falsification, a transit camp would be established at

Mersin, Turkey, for holders of these visas. JDC had to allocate
$17,500 to keep the camp going for a number of months. In the
end, a total of $10,000 was spent by Beckelman for emigration to
Palestine, and JDC New York added another $60,000 for the Istan-
bul end. Nonetheless, this proved to be much less than the sum
spent on migration via Japan.[20]

The next problem was how to get out of Russia. Soon after the
Soviets came, Zerah Wahrhaftig and a few other refugees approached the new authorities, the Russian representative Pozdniakov and President Paleckis, requesting permission for the refugees
to leave the Soviet Union. It seems that a meeting with Globecki,
one of the new vice-premiers, took place. On August 28, Soviet
Ambassador Ivan Maisky in London suddenly answered a request
that had been made of him in February, 1940, by Palestine Chief
Rabbi Isaac Halevi Hertzog to allow the transit of refugees via
Russia. Maisky said that refugees could leave for Palestine if they
had Turkish visas. Simultaneously, a list of 700 refugees who
claimed they had visas to various countries was presented to the
Soviets in Lithuania. On other occasions such lists had proved to
be one-way tickets to Soviet concentration camps, but this particular list apparently contributed to a Russian decision to let the refugees out, and not only to Palestine. From the accounts of survivors
one gets the impression that intervention by Beckelman in Moscow
also had something to do with the Russian step.[21]

The Russian emigration procedures had a special Soviet fla-
vor. First an order came to hand over all foreign currency, after
which the authorities declared that people who had visas should
come to Intourist, the official Soviet tourist agency, and acquire
tickets to Odessa or Vladivostok as foreign tourists with foreign
currency (that they were no longer supposed to have). A minimum of one hundred dollars was needed. Some people managed
to buy dollars, others had dollars hidden away, and still others
were aided by JDC and HIAS—at any rate, the money was paid.
Then the authorities required Soviet exit permits, which were
given only after an applicant had filled out a questionnaire, the
main item of which was a long "curriculum," or autobiography.
Youngsters from Warsaw, rabbis from Lublin, and merchants
from Lodz had to prove by their life histories that they intended
no harm to the USSR. Some people were arrested as a result of
these procedures, but most who had Japanese or Palestinian visas
received their exit permits. These were handed out from early
September until November 15, 1940.

121

During that autumn, Beckelman, aiding the would-be emigrants with every means at his disposal, again had to engage in a struggle with Leavitt in New York. The New York office actually tried to stop Jewish migration from Lithuania. In November, 1940, Leavitt asked Beckelman to advise (whom?) against sending Curaçao visa-holders to Japan. Beckelman's answer on November 22 was bitter and clear: he was aware that the visas were invalid, but "nevertheless despite financial burden possibly imposed [on] JDC [as] a result of Japanese stranding we must do nothing which might prevent exit these visaholders firstly because temporary maintenance Japan or Shanghai permits contacting consulates there mobilizing resources relations abroad which impossible here, secondly, reasons which impracticable inadvisable I detail." Leavitt was helpless in the face of Beckelman's actions. He therefore tried to stop the migration by asking HICEM not to send refugees from Lithuania to Japan. HICEM protested on February 1, 1941, that JDC had instructed its European headquarters in Lisbon to prevent authorization by HICEM of the emigration of 500 refugees from Lithuania. The reason was that Lithuanian refugees were "now constituting tremendous burden Japan costing us about $500 daily. We cannot authorize further indiscriminate emigration from Lithuania without end visas and under no circumstances can HICEM Lisbon authorize such." JDC had no money. But the refugees came nevertheless, and JDC paid.[22]

Beckelman could not do much more to facilitate emigration than to intervene with the Soviets to allow people to leave once they had their foreign visas and to help with foreign currency. JDC-New York, however, which received his reports, came under pressure to extend more help. Many Jews and Jewish organizations in the United States received parallel reports from their refugee friends in Lithuania. American Orthodox rabbis organized in the Agudas Harabonim began pressuring JDC to give special consideration to the 2,800 rabbis and their students whom they estimated to be in Lithuania (actually, as we have seen, there were somewhat fewer). They demanded intervention with the State Department to obtain nonquota visas for them as students and rabbis.

JDC had always tried not to get involved in any political stand, normally leaving contact with the American government to its political alter ego, the AJC. It had not always successfully avoided a public stand, however, and in fact had always been loyal to State Department policies. In this case, JDC felt it "desirable" to consult leaders of Agudas Harabonim, the AJC, the American Jewish Congress, B'nai Brith, HIAS, HICEM, the Jewish Theological Seminary (representing Conservative Judaism), Agudat Israel, the NRS, and the Zionist Organization of America.[23] This major conference took place on August 15, 1940. The problem was real: would official representatives of American Jewry brave their countrymen's isolationist and antisemitic tendencies and demand the absorption of 2,800 religious people, most of whom would of course become a burden on the community, or would they leave them to their fate as refugees in the USSR, where obviously they would, at best, be unable to follow their calling?

The main speaker at the meeting, according to JDC sources, was Stephen S. Wise, the Zionist leader. He might perhaps have argued, as Saly Mayer was to do later in the war, that all Jews are equal and that no elite group could demand preference, but according to our admittedly biased source, he did not. Leavitt wrote:

> Rabbi Stephen S. Wise and others deemed it important to give consideration to the profound question as to the advisability of transferring so large a number of yeshivoth [sic] to the United States. It was his opinion that a few of them, perhaps three or five hundred, might be absorbed here. This, he felt, was an important contribution for American Jews to make to Jewish culture, but he did not feel it was feasible to think in terms of resettling a large number in this country, and he disadvised the use of pressure on the Administration in connection with the issuance of visas.[24]

JDC, well covered by the Zionist leader and AJC, wholeheartedly agreed. Even these "small symbolic groups" that were to be helped to come to the United States were to come for the duration of the war only; after that "it might be possible to reestablish them in Europe."[25]

The first waves of refugees arrived at Vladivostok, the terminus of the trans-Siberian railway, in the autumn of 1940. Only one Japanese ship was making the run to Japan, to the port of Tsuruga, once a week. Where should Jewish refugees with visas to nowhere go from there?

There was a Jewish community—if that is the right word for it—at Kobe, on the east coast, facing the Americas. It numbered fewer than 200 Jewish families, among whom there was one Japanese citizen. A local committee under a Mrs. Hochheimer had been set up there in September, 1940, to aid Jewish refugees from

Germany on their way to America.[26] A parallel committee had been set up at Yokohama by Ernest Baerwald, brother of the chairman of JDC, and himself a refugee from Germany.[27] Lithuanian and German refugees intermingled at first. Soon, however, there was no more room for Lithuanians, no money, and no hope of getting them out of Japan. Sephardic merchants, such as the Jerusalem-born Nissim Tawil, might help, but their means were limited. Most of the predominantly Sephardic community showed no interest, and the 26 Ashkenazi families were incapable of doing more than the great deal they were doing already. At this juncture another savior appeared, almost literally out of nowhere: Abraham Kutsuji, a Japanese biblical and Hebrew scholar who later converted to Judaism.[28]

Upon realizing the gravity of the situation, Kutsuji obtained a large sum of money as a personal gift from a rich uncle. Aided by a friend, a naval captain named Fugamuchi, he used it to bribe the police chief of Kobe, to whom he says he paid 300,000 yen ($50,000). This bribe ensured that the police would not bother the refugees as long as they kept to themselves and did not become too conspicuous. Kutsuji then used his contacts to obtain an audience with Foreign Minister Yosuke Matsuoka, explaining to him that these Jews were on their way to other destinations and that it would enhance the Japanese reputation to let them pass through for humanitarian reasons. Matsuoka agreed, Kutsuji says, provided the Jews undertook not to stay in Japan. In New York, in the meanwhile, the Japanese made overtures to JDC. Kozoh Tamura, a Japanese diplomat, suggested to Bernhard Kahn in November, 1940, that in return for American Jewish support for Japanese expansion, Japan would be benevolent toward Jewish refugees.[29] Obviously one does not have to take Matsuoka's agreement to tolerate the refugees and the reasons he gave for it at face value. Antisemitic propaganda about Jewish influence had been accepted in Japan as well as in other places where there were no or few Jews. Given the peculiarities of Japanese behavior in those years, however, one need not therefore completely discount humanitarian considerations.

Inevitably, problems arose concerning the relationship between the immigrants from Germany, who arrived fully equipped with passports, visas, and tickets for America, and their less fortunate brethren, who had neither money, visas, nor tickets. Charges of discrimination by the local committees representing the two groups of refugees, angry cables to New York, and accusations of various kinds followed the arrival in October, 1940, of the first Vilna groups. Inexplicably, JDC was surprised by the new development, even though Beckelman had both actively pushed the flight from Lithuania and had reported it to New York. These troubles were compounded by the erratic policy of the Japanese. The authorities regulated the flow from Vladivostok in accordance with the movement out of Japan of refugees who were already there. Tragedies occurred when refugees were stranded at Vladivostok, or when JDC, critically short of funds in 1940, refused to honor commitments made by the committees at Yokohama or Kobe. Yet these people had to be helped, and money was in the end borrowed. Between October, 1940, and May, 1941, refugees came to Kobe from the west, and money and exasperated cables from the east. It appears that the total number of refugees who came to the Far East from Lithuania was about 2,400. Among them were some of the Vilna leaders—generals without armies, Beckelman called them. One of them, Zerah Wahrhaftig, was instrumental in setting up a local committee in Kobe which put pressure on American organizations, including JDC, to solve the plight of the refugees in Japan as quickly as possible.[30]

It is impossible to estimate the number of those who had visas for Palestine. However, 186 people finally went there, paid for by JDC because the UPA was unable to make good on its promise to pay for transport. After an odyssey that took some of them via Burma and India, others via Australia and South Africa, and some even via the Dominican Republic, they finally reached their destination.[31] All the others either had to go to the Americas or finally ended up in Shanghai. A total of $350,000 was spent to save these refugees and feed them in Japan, of which over 75 percent came from JDC. Leavitt wrote at the time that "the sums are woefully inadequate." If JDC had had $12 million instead of roughly $6 million during 1940, the situation would of course have been improved.[32]

In January, 1941, the emergency in Lithuania became even worse. Refugees were given a choice of opting for Soviet citizenship by January 25—or else. Beckelman pleaded to get another 2,000 refugees out immediately, but there were no funds.[33] By March, 1941, JDC had quite simply run out of money. After it cabled on March 5 that it could not grant another $2,500, the Kobe committee resigned. JDC now had to tell its contributors that stranded refugees could not be helped. Fortunately, Beckelman arrived at Kobe at the end of March, and his angry siding with the local committee helped to make up the New York office's mind. More money was lent and, against Beckelman's advice, monthly rather than longer-term allocations were made available, which of course made any planning more difficult. The committee again resigned, "categorically and finally," but in fact work went on until late spring, when refugees stopped coming.[34] At that time there were still 1,200 refugees crowded in Kobe. The Japanese had declared repeatedly that they would only agree to the continuation of Jewish emigration through Japan if the Vilna refugees were taken out. After June, 1941, with the German invasion of the USSR, no further Jewish migration via Siberia was feasible in any case, and the problem was what to do with the residual refugees.

In the meantime, the problem of preferential treatment for rabbis and students again cropped up. In August, 1941, religious organizations led by Mizrahi, the Zionist religious party, attempted to emigrate rabbinical students as a special group, this time to Canada. Finally a rather reluctant JDC agreed that its Canadian affiliate, the United Jewish Refugee and War Relief Agencies, should give assurance to the Canadian government that the immigrants would not become public charges. In the end, JDC had to pay out $2,000 to support twenty-nine persons who came to Canada, because the other groups paid little or nothing towards their immigration and maintenance.[35]

More significantly, on November 13–14, 1939, Agudas Harabonim initiated a special agency called Va'ad Hahatzalah (VH; Emergency Committee for War-Torn Yeshivot). This agency applied itself first and foremost to the problem of saving the yeshivot that had fled into Lithuania. By early 1940, a fund-raising campaign was under way, and by the end of 1941 the organization had raised a total of $154,512.[36] How much of this was actually transferred to Lithuania is unclear. In 1940–41, $97,000 were spent on transporting yeshivot people and families to Japan. This sum apparently included $50,000 to bring the Mir yeshiva, some 300 persons in all, to Japan. The other religious people, who seem to have constituted about half of the total number of refugees in Japan, were mostly supported by JDC, and marginally by other agencies. The VH itself claimed to have resettled 1,302 persons, of whom only 750 left Japan—273 for the United States, 250 for Palestine, 29 for Canada, and the rest for other places. Its attempt to settle 300 rabbis and students from Lisbon and another 70 from

Kobe in Canada failed, apparently because Saul Hayes, the Canadian Jewish leader, thought there was no justification for saving rabbis in preference to other Jews.[37] All the figures quoted by VH are very doubtful, and according to the organization itself, over 500 of its 1,302 "resettlers" were people who were forcibly brought to Shanghai by the Japanese. JDC claimed that VH had managed to save no more than 150 people from Kobe.

The details of this particular altercation may seem unimportant, but in fact they were not. The VH very emphatically said that it was more important to save rabbis and rabbinical students than anyone else. It was of primary importance to save the bearers of tradition and Jewish scholarship, for without them there would be no Jewry, no future for the Jewish people. JDC was not dedicated to the same assumption. Its leadership entertained deep respect for the learning of the rabbis but could not see why their lives should take precedence over the lives of others. In Vilna, Beckelman had taken a similar position regarding the claims of the Bund group, but Orthodox Judaism in America was incomparably stronger than was the Bund, and that was the source of a practical problem. JDC argued: "If a separate drive were to be launched for every project which enjoys the interest and sympathy of special groups, it would cause untold confusion."[38] JDC's monopoly of fund-raising was threatened, and on this very mundane level a compromise was reached: VH would be permitted to approach religiously-minded people with its special appeal. If these people were prepared to make contributions over and above what they gave to general relief needs, JDC would not object. Because of the difficulty of determining just what the over-and-above clause meant, an ill-concealed guerilla warfare over the contributors' dollars started between the two organizations.

All through 1940, Moses Beckelman stayed on in Vilna—a lone American in a weak neutral state that was overrun by the Soviets halfway through the year. His job was to keep the refugee committee in business and himself out of prison. He solved the two problems in a truly brilliant way.

Until October, 1940, it may be remembered, the Lithuanian Soviet authorities granted 450,000 lits ($75,000) to the refugee committee on the strength of Beckelman's promise that, if the transfer of money became possible again, he would reimburse his hosts for that amount. On December 31, 1940, a decree was published which dissolved all refugee committees and terminated the activities of foreign relief organizations. It also provided for the right to work for refugees and gave them the choice between Soviet citizenship or statelessness. Beckelman had to liquidate JDC in Lithuania without losing face or harming the refugees.

In discussion with the authorities, Beckelman proved that only 400,000 of the promised 450,000 lits had actually been paid. Of these, 130,000 were paid without reference to JDC, so that JDC was obligated to repay only 270,000. However, as this amount was to be repaid in dollars, Beckelman argued that "there was no reason why the original arrangement that the government provide a 50% contribution on all foreign transmissions in dollars at the official rate of exchange should not apply in this case." JDC's liability was finally established at 160,000 lits, or $26,000. From this sum, Beckelman deducted the value of furniture and fixtures confiscated by the Soviets from the Vilna office. The debt now stood at less than 145,000 lits. JDC's last transfer from the United States, of $24,441, more or less covered the debt, but it had been blocked in a Kovno bank by the Soviets. In a grandiose gesture, Beckelman transferred all claims to the blocked money to the Soviets. JDC and the USSR were quits. He left Kovno on February 21, 1941, en route to Kobe, Shanghai, South America, and New York.[39]

From all accounts, Beckelman was probably the best-loved Jewish representative in Lithuania.[40] To the refugees there he was living proof that Jews abroad cared about them; his fights with the New York office and his superiors were well hidden from his clients, and through him hope penetrated into a ever-darkening reality. Beckelman was not simply energetic—he was independent, compassionate, and a man of impeccable integrity.

In August, 1941, only 1,007 refugees were left in Japan, and these obviously had nowhere to go. The Japanese decided to get rid of them by transferring them to Shanghai, and this was effected in September. The Lithuanian chapter of rescue—of 2,400 via Japan and of another 1,200 directly to Palestine, out of 14,000 refugees in Lithuania and 240,000 Lithuanian Jews—had come to an end.[41] The tremendous effort by the few that cared had paid off against enormous odds; every person emigrated was a person fewer to be murdered later by the Germans. And yet, so very few were saved.

5

Immigration to Palestine

Since 1936, the British government had increasingly limited Jewish immigration to Palestine.
Faced with an Arab rebellion whose aim it was
to establish an Arab-controlled Palestine under British tutelage,
Britain increasingly turned towards a policy of appeasing the
Arab national movement at the expense of the Jewish national
movement. The Jews would have no choice in the event of war
with the Axis powers; they would have to support the democracies even if Britain turned against them in Palestine. On the other
hand, it was deemed most important from a military and strategic
point of view to prevent the Arabs from joining the Axis. In the
light of Britain's military weakness in the Middle East and the
vulnerability of her long lines of communications to guerilla tactics, British leaders thought it imperative to stop, or almost stop,
Jewish immigration to Palestine. This was what the Arabs wanted
most of all, and it was essentially given to them when the British
White Paper of May, 1939, limited immigration to 50,000 persons
in the next five years, plus another 25,000 refugees from Europe.

In other words, just when the Jews of Europe most needed
the open gates of the Palestine refuge, those doors were shut to
them. Yet it seemed to most Jews that Britain had no moral right
to bar Palestine to Jewish immigrants. Palestine did not belong to
Britain; it was the birthright of the Jewish people, and Britain was
just a caretaker whose task it was to enable the Jewish National

Home to develop. A home made no sense if one was barred from it at a time of danger. There was in any case no democratic rule over Palestine, because the British administration ruled by edict, and the Jews claimed the right of entry whether the British thought that legal or not. The result was an increasing flow of illegal immigration, known as *Aliyah Bet* ("B Immigration," as distinct from legal, or "A Immigration"). JDC often referred to it, in a somewhat genteel way, as "irregular" immigration.

Aliyah Bet had begun as far back as 1934, when the ship *Velos* deposited the first organized group of halutzim on Palestine's shores, undetected by the British. The JA opposed the *Velos* venture, as did the Histadrut, the leftist and nationalist trade unions federation. David Ben Gurion, chairman of the JA Executive, for one, thought illegal immigration would only hamper legal entry, which in 1934–35 was still relatively easy. The right-wing Revisionist movement led by Jabotinsky, which opposed the Labor-led Executive, was not to be outdone. It also attempted a transport in September, 1934. The ship was caught, as was the *Velos* on its second attempt. With the exception of a few small boats organized by the Revisionists, Aliyah Bet more or less ceased until the second half of 1938, when illegal immigration began in earnest. Up to the outbreak of war in September, 1939, a total of 17,240 passengers arrived in Palestine illegally. Of these, the leftist groups associated with Hehalutz, the Histadrut's pioneer organization, claimed 7,780, whereas the Revisionists and private entrepreneurs claimed 9,460. Of the 17,240, 11,370 were seized by the British, put into a quarantine camp in Palestine, and later released. The remaining 5,861 were not seized and managed to mingle with the local Jewish population.[1]

The attitude of the British government to the problem of illegal immigration became more and more severe. After the publication of the White Paper it was obvious that the desired effect of the new pro-Arab policy could only be achieved if Jewish immigration were indeed stopped. Continued illegal immigration would not only bring into Palestine immigrants over whom Britain would have no control, but would also endanger the whole structure of British policy in the area. The British, however, were faced with a number of problems. To start with, they had no means by which to detect and deter ships arriving off the Palestine coast. A special police launch destined to fulfill this task was sunk on August 9, 1939, by Israel Norden, a member of Haganah. Police launches could not in any case prevent the ships, usually flying Panamanian flags, from approaching Palestine as long as they kept outside the territorial waters. Usually the ships sent small boats loaded with immigrants to the shore, and the British launches often came too late to stop them. Once the refugees were on the beaches, they could hardly be expelled even when they were caught, as they often were. They used to destroy their papers so that their citizenship could not be established and no country would take them back; furthermore, using British force to return Jewish refugees to Nazi Europe might outrage British public opinion. On top of everything else, there was a legal problem. The Palestine administration was engaged in a struggle with its high court, whose judges were not very sympathetic to the new policy. Ships seized outside the territorial waters would be released, and even crew members and immigrants would be set free on any more or less acceptable technical legal ground.

In effect, therefore, the British government had two choices: either intern the immigrants and deduct their numbers from the half-yearly quota under the White Paper provision of 75,000 in five years; or abolish the quotas altogether, deduct the numbers from the 75,000, and disallow any legal immigration. Neither policy was free of problems, and the government used both approaches in 1939 and 1940. On July 13, 1939, Colonial Secretary Malcolm MacDonald announced in the House of Commons that all further "illegals" would be deducted from the White Paper quota, and in October, all legal immigration was forbidden for the half-year from October through March.

In addition, the government exerted diplomatic pressure on the Balkan states to stop the flow of Jewish immigration and intervened with the Panamanian and Greek governments to prevent their protection of ships engaged in the transporting of illegal immigrants to Palestine. These attempts met with varying degrees of success. On December 13, 1939, Panama did abolish the registry of eleven ships which the British indicated had been involved in the illegal traffic,[2] but of course this did not prevent the Jews from using other ships of Panamanian registry. Even more disastrous was the attempt to protest in Paraguay against the granting, by the Paraguayan consul in Prague, of 675 Paraguayan visas to Jews obviously intending to go to Palestine. On February 1, 1940, the Paraguayan government told the British that it did not have a consul in Prague at all.[3] Protests to Rumania and Bulgaria, among others, did have some very limited effect. The *New York Times* reported on February 20, 1940, that the Rumanian government had

131

promised to lift its ban on Zionist activities if the Zionists promised to quit fostering illegal immigration from Rumania.

It appears, however, that there was some dissension between various British ministries regarding illegal entry to Palestine. The Foreign Office, while opposing it, did not want to soil its hands by forcing refugees back to Nazi Europe. When the *Hilda*, which had taken on illegals at a Bulgarian port, was caught on January 17, 1940, with 728 immigrants aboard, the Foreign Office refused to ask the Bulgarians to take it back. The venture had been organized by the Maccabi group, at whose head stood the British Lord Melchett, although the government was not aware of its involvement, and probably Melchett himself did not know what the organization had been doing. When the *Sakarya* was captured on February 13, with 2,228 refugees, the idea of forcing the ship back was brought up and rejected. Then the idea of returning those Jews who had kept their passports to their countries of origin was discussed. Six Jews were finally sent back to Europe. The odd case of two Hungarian Jews was also debated—that of Stephen and Gerhard Lux, who had been in Palestine since 1934. In the end, apart from the unfortunate six, the British high commissioner for Palestine, Sir Harold MacMichael, refused to deport the refugees. His decision was not taken out of humanitarian considerations, but because of "the importance of avoiding any measures which by inflaming Jewish opinion would tend to immoblize in Palestine the trained British troops who may be required for service elsewhere." In London, humanitarian arguments were advanced and accepted, but it was the high commissioner's dispatch of March 23 which apparently clinched the issue.[4]

Behind the increased drive of Aliyah Bet stood the terrible plight of the Jews and the cynical desire of the Nazis to drive out as many penniless Jews as possible; if at the same time an embarrassment could be caused to Britain, so much the better. Adolf Eichmann, as the SS officer in charge of the anti-Jewish measures in Austria, named Berthold Storfer, a Viennese businessman, as the sole Jew responsible for illegal transports in 1940. The first transports still took place under the aegis of the traditional organizers: Hehalutz, the Revisionists, and private entrepreneurs. In line with basic Nazi policy at that time—to get rid of the Jews by forced emigration and by the establishment of a Jewish "reservation" near Lublin—Eichmann even granted up to twelve dollars per head in foreign currency, taken out of confiscated Jewish property, for the illegal transports.[5] At the end of December this practice stopped. The Jews were so eager to escape from Nazi Germany that foreign currency inducements were no longer necessary. The details of this whole development were not known to the British authorities trying to fight Aliyah Bet.

The British government was no less concerned with the security problem created by the refugees than were Breckinridge Long and the American State Department. The JA was quite willing to subject any refugees arriving from Nazi Europe to investigations, but the British argued that it would be quite natural for the Gestapo to press refugees into their service or infiltrate their own agents among the immigrants. Britain simply preferred not to have the refugees and to run the risks. Jewish opinion tended to impute to the British the desire to cover up for their anti-Jewish policy by presenting the security argument. Stated thus simply, Jewish suspicions had no basis in fact. The British really were worried about security. MacMichael could write to Colonial Secretary MacDonald early in 1940 that the admission of a small number of adult German Jews on legal permits "would entail unjustifiable risk of introduction of German agents, notwithstanding safeguards proposed by [Moshe] Shertok [Sharett; JA's "foreign secretary"] and I am strongly opposed to waiving the general principle in their case"— the general principle being that Jews residing in Germany or in German-occupied territories no longer qualified for legal entry into Palestine. Yet in the same document, MacMichael declared that he had no objection to an equal number of German Jewish children entering Palestine legally. It therefore seems clear that the security argument was not just a pretext.[6]

The British of course knew in a general way that the Gestapo was furthering illegal immigration; it seemed logical to assume that the ships, the passports, and indeed the whole procedure was organized by the Nazis. Blissfully unaware of the real import of Nazi antisemitism, they could not realize that the idea of Nazis organizing Jewish escape would have been absolutely preposterous to a Nazi mind. They merely facilitated their expulsion. In their contempt of Jews, the Germans did not even think of using Jews as agents. But the British embassy in Ankara insisted that the organizers of the ships were Germans. Sir H. Michael Palairet in Athens thought likewise. But no Nazi could be found, and the Foreign Office commented plaintively: "It is a pity that we cannot find an authentic Nazi at the bottom of it; it would have helped the Palestine government." In Palestine itself, Jews were arrested on the suspicion of being Nazi agents. The government fed the

House of Commons with stories that such agents were being uncovered; MacDonald himself stated on March 20, 1940, that a few hundred were being detained (which was untrue) and that "some of the Jewish members of these parties are German agents." As late as January, 1941, Howard F. Downie of the Colonial Office maintained that there were strong suspicions of some detained Jews in this respect, but, he added, "in the nature of the case there is no definite evidence." In the nature of the case there could indeed be none. No agent was ever found.[7]

British attitudes, so important to the whole problem of escape from Europe at that early stage of the war, were complicated. The term "Jewish race" was in general use, though it was directed more to ethnic or national identity than to the German usage. British diplomats experienced extreme distaste when dealing with Jews. "This place swarms from morning till night with a scrofulous crowd of kaftanned, bearded and side-curled Jews," wrote a British diplomat after a visit to Lwów.[8] Jews were accused of being Bolshevik sympathizers; Jewish journalists were suspect, as is indicated in a British report written in Kovno, Lithuania, in November, 1939: "Incidentally Poleski is a Jew and may be inclined to take a somewhat favourable view of doings of the Soviets."[9] This in spite of the fact that the Soviets were expropriating Jewish businessmen and shopkeepers who formed the majority of Polish Jews, and that they were arresting Jewish leaders and suppressing all expressions of autonomous Jewish life.

As far as illegal immigration to Palestine was concerned, British officials tended to think in terms of conspiracies and worse. A memorandum of January 17, 1940, submitted to the government by both the Colonial and the Foreign offices, expresses the British attitude in a nutshell. "Illegal immigration into Palestine is not primarily a refugee movement. There are, of course, genuine refugees among the immigrants. . . . the problem is thus an organized invasion of Palestine for political motives, which exploits the facts of the refugee problem and unscrupulously uses the humanitarian appeal to the latter to justify itself." When Jabotinsky's associates in London devised some plans for money transfers to enable Jews to migrate legally, a high Foreign Office official wrote: "Mr. Jabotinsky and his associates among the Revisionists will surely devise with all the cunning and skill of their race" means of using money for illegal immigration. Illegal shipments of immigrants were "traffic" in a derogatory sense, as

134

when in February, 1940, another official commented: "This traffic is similar to the slave trade or rum running."[10]

Britain's position in the Middle East was very difficult in 1940. Their forces there were pitifully small, and there was woefully little military equipment available for even those troops which could be used. General Archibald Wavell was preparing his winter attack on the Italians with inadequate forces; the Italians were still in control of Abyssinia and Eritrea; and Iraq's allegiance to Britain was becoming most uncertain. Iran was swarming with Nazi agents; the Turks were beginning to waver; and anything that might disturb the delicate balance in the area was most unwelcome from the British point of view. Moreover, in addition to the Jewish refugees, the British had the problem of the Poles (and, marginally, the Czechs) who had fled into Rumania and Yugoslavia and wanted to join the Polish forces in the Middle East. Wavell opposed their coming to Palestine—the only staging area available—because he had no equipment to give them. He thought there might be as many as 20,000, and he was appalled at the prospect of feeding additional mouths. He was supported by the civilian and military authorities in Palestine. In the end, despite strong Colonial Office and local opposition, the Foreign Office managed to force the acceptance of a few thousand refugees and prospective soldiers onto unwilling authorities in Cairo, Cyprus, and Palestine. As Sir Reginald Hoare in Bucharest put it, it was inconceivable that the British should treat these Poles, who were Britain's only ally, shabbily.[11]

The way in which the Foreign Office forced the other British ministries into accepting Polish soldiers highlights its attitude towards Jewish refugees, whose immigration to Palestine clearly was against British interests as defined by the government. Nevertheless, the humanitarian concerns that prevented Britain from taking an even grimmer stand than it actually took are evident in the sources. One might say that the British were quite clear in their own minds that what they were doing was morally indefensible, but they did it nevertheless, because they put their alleged interest first. Yet one may sense, in the actions and even the words of some British officials, uneasiness caused by serious moral scruples. For instance, the British tried to find a legal way to confiscate the ships once they reached Palestine and to arrest their captains and crews. Attempts to capture ships outside territorial waters and then drag them into Haifa failed miserably, either because they evaded capture, or because, having been dragged into port, their captains maintained that they never had intended to land their passengers illegally. The Admiralty did not like its new role as persecutor of refugees fleeing from Nazism; it cabled the Colonial Office on March 14 that it refused to intercept all illegal ships, because the danger was "not serious enough in the case of ships carrying Jewish refugees from persecution to Jewish settlements in Palestine." MacDonald himself opposed the towing out to sea of the *Sakarya* with its 2,200 refugees in February; he feared that the Jews might jump into the sea rather than be returned to Europe, and "in that event our action would be open to serious misrepresentation." That is, everyone would understand that the British were sending helpless refugees back into the hell they had escaped from.[12] When on March 18, 1940, the government of Palestine finally published new edicts designed to enable the confiscation of ships dragged into harbor from outside the territorial waters and the arrest of their crews if they carried illegals, it did so after having realized that "the choice appears to be between allowing the provisions of the White Paper to break down and adopting preventive precautions which cannot be legally justified."[13]

It was Sir Harold MacMichael who first indicated in his dispatches that JA did not seem to favor illegal immigration very enthusiastically. Officials in London concurred. The JA's leadership, especially Haim Weizmann and Moshe Sharett, were hoping for a breakthrough on the political-military front of their relations with Britain. A plan for recruiting Jewish volunteers in neutral countries and in Palestine to form a Jewish division in the British army was being discussed in 1940–41 and was very near realization. It must have seemed to Weizmann that the future of Palestine was in the balance again, and that if a Jewish division fought for the liberation of Europe, the chances of a Jewish Palestine and of a Jewish say at the peace conference table would be considerably enhanced. The number of illegal immigrants could not change the balance of Jewish suffering materially, and the bad blood created between British and Jews would be a greater danger than JA's discouragement of Aliyah Bet. Thus Weizmann and Berl Locker submitted memoranda to the British government in November and December, 1940, which were thinly veiled disavowals of illegal immigration. They suggested that ships be caught before they reached Palestine, and that they should be exiled to some place of detention during the war. Rabbi Maurice Perlzweig of the World Jewish Congress expressed the same idea in a letter of

November 27.[14] They reasoned that JA and the Zionist movement should not add to Britain's difficulties when it stood alone in its great battle against the Nazis.

On the other hand, those Jews who shared Ben Gurion's brand of Zionism, and most Palestinian Jews, would certainly have rejected the attitude of JA's London office had it been widely known. Zionists had for years argued that the only moral solution was the political one, that the only way to save Jews was to establish Jewish autonomy in Palestine. When the British closed Palestine, Aliyah Bet had to be the answer, even though the only ships available were rickety old tubs into which bunks and sanitary arrangements were fitted at minimum cost and which had little coal and less water and food. Nevertheless, driving the Jews onto these boats and towards Palestine, Eichmann was unknowingly saving them from the gas chambers. The Gestapo literally forced the Jews to save themselves; the JA, Revisionists, and other organizers were apparently more aware of this irony than the Germans themselves. Many of the participants in the transports of late 1939 and early 1940 were released from concentration camps on the strength of places provided for them on the boats. They certainly had the feeling of having escaped with their lives from an indescribable hell. Thirteen voyages between September, 1939, and March, 1941, brought 10,628 people to Palestine (see table 14).[15]

JDC's attitude towards Aliyah Bet was ambivalent. On the one hand, no official help could be extended to an illegal operation, but on the other, it was recognized that this was a way of getting people out of Germany. In any case, when shiploads of people were stranded in some Rumanian harbor or on a Greek island, JDC could not possibly refuse to help. Furthermore, while large sums had to be expended to help such migrants, creating an unbudgeted extra burden on diminishing funds, illegal immigration to Palestine was still cheaper than many of the legal escape routes JDC supported.

JDC's official policy was enunciated by Bernhard Kahn, who had been JDC's European director throughout the twenties and the thirties, when he was asked to comment on the attempts of Revisionist leaders to collect money in America for this type of migration. In June, 1939, Kahn stated: "We do not stop the refugee committees [from supporting illegal immigration], for we give funds to them, which may be used for this purpose . . . but no direct JDC participation in this illegal immigration could be envisaged." Joseph Hyman added, also in June, 1939, that "JDC could

137

Table 14: Transports to Palestine, 1939-41

Ship	Arrival	Refugees	Comment
Rudnitchar	Sept. 16, 1939	368	Organized by Confino of Bulgaria
Noemi Julia	Sept. 19, 1939	1,123	
Rudnitchar	Nov. 14, 1939	457	Organized by Confino of Bulgaria
Rudnitchar	Jan. 8, 1940	505	Organized by Confino of Bulgaria; the British claimed the number was 519
Hilda (Aghios Nicholaos)	Jan. 17, 1940	728	Mossad ship
Sakarya	Feb. 13, 1940	2,228	According to Jewish sources, the number was 2,165; Revisionist ship
Libertad	July 18, 1940	343	According to Jewish sources, the number was 355
Pencho	Oct. 11, 1940	510	Date of wreck in the Aegean Sea
Pacific	Nov. 1, 1940	1,062	Some 250 more persons drowned; Storfer ship
Milos	Nov. 3, 1940	709	Storfer ship
Atlantic	Nov. 24, 1940	1,708	Of this number, 1,770 were deported to Mauritius on Dec. 9, 1940; 124 died there; Storfer ship
Salvador	Dec. 12, 1940	126	The number represents those saved of some 320 from wreck in the Sea of Marmara
Darien	Mar. 19, 1941	789	

not associate itself with a situation regarded as illegal by the British government."[16]

JDC's attitude was tinged with genuine naiveté. Kahn and others were sure that in 1939 British military and civilian authorities in Palestine viewed this immigration favorably, because though they could have, they "did not prevent illegal entry." In May, 1939, Kahn went so far as to indicate his belief that the British-based Council for German Jewry might be interested in supporting illegal immigration. Through its contacts with British authorities, the council might enlist British sympathies and cooperation.[17] In truth, of course, while the Council for German Jewry opposed the May, 1939, White Paper, it could not possibly approach the British government with appeals to defy its own laws.

Morris C. Troper, however, who had been responsible for JDC's affairs in Europe since late 1938, was much less inclined to take an illusory view of the situation. On July 26, 1939, he and James Bernstein of HIAS met with Sir Herbert Emerson of the IGCR. Emerson combined his international post with an influential position at the Foreign Office, and his statement on illegal immigration reflected British government policy: he was very worried, concerned, and confused. No help could be extended to illegal transports by IGCR, and no direct help should be extended by the "responsible organizations." But at the same time, the humanitarian concerns of the British government became clear when he added that there would be no objection to humanitarian relief for stranded victims. Troper understood this statement the way he wanted to understand it. At the Paris meeting of the Jewish social organizations in August, 1939, Saly Mayer learned from Troper that "out of those who immigrated into Palestine and other countries illegally, only a very few have returned; therefore, do not stop."[18]

When war broke out, it became clear that the Gestapo wanted the illegal transports to continue. A trustworthy report received by JDC at the end of September, 1939, indicated that JA's Mossad le'aliyah Bet (Institute of "B" Immigration), formed early that year, was actively supporting the movement. Originally planned and partly executed through Italian ports, illegal immigration from late 1939 concentrated on the Danube route.[19] Troper decided to support the move through two channels: first, through parts of the official budgets of the Central European communities, because these communities would devote unspecified sums to promote the migration; and second, through additional JDC allocations when the unseaworthiness of vessels, mishaps on the high seas, insufficient or inefficient funding and organization, corruption, and so on made them necessary to save the refugees. JDC's policy was to debit the local budgets for such help, but this course was not always possible. Increasingly, JDC had to bail out the refugees with supplemental funds. How this was done in the light of contracting resources, while no "direct" help could be given, is a very tragic story indeed.

The Prague community brought pressure to bear on Troper as early as November, 1939. They wanted to provide funds for seven or eight hundred illegal immigrants, provided JDC helped them on their way in Bratislava in Slovakia. This action would involve a slight but significant departure in JDC policy. JDC involvement would be direct, from a moral point of view at least, though technically JDC would continue merely to provide help at Bratislava and not pay for the actual transport—that would be done by the Prague committee out of its budget. Yet the fact that Prague had specifically asked for JDC approval was a new factor in the situation. Troper was in favor, feeling that the game of legality could no longer be played in the face of human suffering. The matter, he said, would "pass through good hands," by which he meant that Mossad was responsible rather than the Revisionists, whose militaristic methods had been the cause for complaints by immigrants earlier in the year. Hyman hesitated; the matter was submitted to the leadership of JDC on November 9, 1939, and he then informed Troper that New York approved, provided JDC funds would be used "explicitly for refugee assistance and relief and are included within your present appropriation."[20]

The Prague affair was the thin edge of a very large wedge. At the end of 1939, three groups of refugees arrived at Sulina and Balchik on the Black Sea: 720 persons in a transport organized by Maccabi, and 620 persons in two transports arranged by a private organizer, Dr. Willy Perl, and the Revisionists. Another Revisionist transport of 530 people arrived before the end of the month, so that there were 2,000 people or more at Sulina in the cold winter weather. The Balchik group was taken off on the *Hilda*. The *Sakarya*, under Revisionist auspices, finally took over 2,200 refugees in early February, 1940. Between the end of December and the final sailing, the refugees were at the mercy of the Rumanian Jewish community and its JDC liaisons, Moses Ussoskin and Israel Millstein. These two did whatever they could; they managed to raise $7,000 from the persecuted and impoverished Rumanian Jewish community. The remaining $15,000 necessary to pay for the immigrants had to come out of JDC central funds. In the meantime, however, another group of 1,000 persons was stranded on the way to the Black Sea at Kladovo, Yugoslavia, and yet another 1,000 were waiting at Bratislava, at the Patronka harbor. No wonder that the Revisionists were appealing for funds for immigration in the United States.[21]

Faced with this grim pressure, JDC reacted by retreating to its former stance. JDC could give relief, but it could not "participate in any form of illegal immigration." Costs of future transports would be charged to local committees "in order to discourage this type of activity." JDC's attitude was undoubtedly influenced by the treatment meted out to the refugees by the organizers of the transports. Berthold Storfer and Willy Perl appear responsible for the further suffering inflicted on the victims of Gestapo pressure. They indeed seemed to be "unscrupulous, private entrepreneurs," as a JDC report called them.[22] Other transports, such as those of Maccabi or Mossad, and indeed some of the later Storfer transports, were slightly better appointed. All of them, however, suffered from a lack of funds, unscrupulous shipowners and captains, and the brutalization of human relationships in the face of privations and suffering. The British did not help. On February 13, a government spokesman in the House of Lords, the marquess of Dufferin and Ava, probed the depths of human political wisdom when he said: "The situation of these Jews is the result of an attempt to escape from the consequences of a deliberate policy of the German government, and His Majesty's Government cannot accept responsibility for it." Indeed, governments of Allied countries accepted no responsibility, nor did anyone else. The result was creaky old Danube boats with cargoes of fortunate unfortunates escaping from Hitler. The really unfortunate ones were those that did not manage to get on the boats.

Soon the terrorized heads of the Jewish communities in Central Europe began to do what they wanted with the funds officially budgeted for them by JDC. This money was in any case emigrants' counterpart funds—that is, funds left behind by emigrants in local currency. JDC paid out their equivalent in the form of tickets, relief, landing money, and so on, and there was in practice little it could do to control expenditures in Berlin, Prague, or Vienna. Troper, whose sympathies with the situation of these leaders were markedly stronger than those of his colleagues in far-off New York, had no great wish to interfere. In America, Revisionist and JA efforts to pry loose some JDC funds for broadening the scope of the transports failed to produce a positive response. The Revisionists were trying to get JDC to influence the official Zionist organizations, especially the UPA, to support their efforts. But JDC refused to be involved in intra-Zionist fights. It also resisted pressures by some of its own contributors who wanted a more positive JDC policy regarding illegal immigration.

During the early summer of 1940, the Central European

141

communities became more insistent on allocating funds from their emigration reserves to Aliyah Bet. In July, the Berlin community wanted $42,000 of counterpart funds to be officially allocated for this purpose. On July 15, Troper in New York cabled to Joseph Schwartz in Lisbon: "After long meeting yesterday and overcoming with difficulty much reluctance part many our members succeeded securing approval transfer $42,000. . . . committee here agrees conclusion reached some time ago that JDC cannot continue this type of activity not only because lack of funds but also view disagreements among various groups." [23] There were similar problems with the Vienna and Prague communities, and similar pious resolutions by JDC to get out of Aliyah Bet activities. Necessity, however, was much stronger, and JDC involvement grew.

In July, 1940, another Revisionist ship, the *Pencho,* was moving along the Danube, with no money and less chance to cross the Mediterranean. The passengers had paid £13,000 ($42,000) to the organizers, who then abandoned them to their fate. Among the refugees were some of the leaders of Zionist organizations in Germany and Czechoslovakia. JDC was furious. Having agreed to the allocation of funds from the reserves of local committees, it was now faced with demands to support the suffering passengers of the *Pencho.* Although JDC-New York protested that "the strongest objections must be raised against this sort of transport," there was no choice; in order to induce the small Zagreb community to help, JDC had to spend more, and by September, $17,000 had been paid through the Yugoslav committee headed by Sime Spitzer in order to support those aboard the *Pencho.* Additional funds were sent to the indefatigable Ussoskin to help when, in the autumn, the ship finally arrived in the Black Sea. It sailed for Palestine early in October and sank on October 11 in the Aegean. Its 512 passengers were rescued by the Italians and interned at Rhodes. From there they were transported to the Italian detention camp at Ferramonti in the south of Italy; they survived the war, and most of them immigrated to Palestine after their liberation.[24]

Less lucky was the *Salvador,* which sailed out of Varna in Bulgaria in early December with 320 refugees. The *Salvador* reached the Sea of Marmara and sank. Only 126 people were saved, among them 20 children. The JA representative in Istanbul, Haim Barlas, cabled JDC for money, and of course money was sent.

In Vienna, Storfer was preparing for his major effort, the sending of three ships toward the end of 1940. In a report dated

July 10, he described to Troper how his organization worked.[25] The Jews were being transported down the Danube on river boats belonging to the German Danubian Steamship Company, while all his ships, which he was hiring through Greek agents, flew Spanish or Panamanian flags. What he did not mention was that about February, 1940, the Gestapo had named him to be the executive commissioner for all illegal transports. The more idealistic organizations, Revisionist or connected with Mossad, thus were reduced to a subsidiary role. Thousands of people were desperately clamoring for an opportunity, at any risk, to leave German-occupied Europe, and by early September close to 3,600 refugees from the areas included in Storfer's mandate—Germany, Austria, Danzig, and the Protectorate—arrived on the Danube and boarded four river boats which finally got them to Tulcea, Rumania, after almost two weeks of travel in extremely bad conditions. Three steamers were awaiting them on the Black Sea: the *Milos,* the *Atlantic,* and the *Pacific.* The shipowners had not been paid for making the adjustments necessary to accommodate such a large number of persons, and after some bitter negotiations with Storfer and his brother-in-law, the passengers had themselves to improve the conditions. In the end, the boats left without enough drinking water or food. A fourth boat which might have relieved the congestion was retained by Storfer for a later transport.

The *Milos* passed the Dardanelles in early October and reached Sigri in the Aegean Islands, where it appealed for water and food to the Athens community and JDC. The *Atlantic* and *Pacific* also passed the straits and reached Crete, where they too had to ask for help. On the way, the *Pacific* had to stop at Varna, where the Bulgarian police, with the aid apparently of one of the famous private organizers of illegal transports, Dr. Baruch Confino, forced some forty refugees onto the ship. JDC in 1940 sent $16,000 to the Athens committee, and it was this help which enabled the transports to proceed. The *Pacific* carried some of the leaders of the Hehalutz in Germany, the Protectorate, and Vienna, and by the time the *Milos* and the *Pacific* reached Palestine early in November, an orderly and well-organized regime prevailed aboard.[26]

Once the immigrants were in Haifa, High Commissioner MacMichael threatened them with expulsion to a British colony. The British government was at its wits' end as far as illegal transports were concerned. No longer as hard pressed in the western desert as it had been in the summer, and encouraged by the successes of General Wavell against the Italians, the Colonial Office was persuaded by its experts that it was better to risk the wrath of the Jews than an Arab rebellion. An example had to be set, and the Jews would be deported. A French ship sequestered by the British, the *Patria*, was in Haifa harbor, and the refugees were transferred to it to be transported to Mauritius.[27]

The expulsion order was issued on November 20, and both Haganah and the Irgun Zvai Leumi (National Military Organization, the Revisionist armed underground in Palestine), unknown to each other, prepared to prevent the *Patria* from sailing. Haganah got in first, on November 25, but miscalculated the amount of explosives needed to blow a hole large enough to prevent sailing but small enough to prevent a disaster. The *Patria* sank, with a loss of over 250 immigrants. Even though the rest were allowed to stay in Palestine as an act of mercy, the passengers of the *Atlantic*, which had arrived on November 24, were exiled to Mauritius. MacMichael, acting on instructions from the Colonial Office (and not, as has been suggested, on his own responsibility), incurred the somewhat belated wrath of Winston Churchill by announcing that the exiles would never be permitted to land in Palestine. (In fact, most of them immigrated to Palestine when the war was over.) Unknown to the Jews, General Wavell had opposed permission to stay even to the survivors of the *Patria*. The British were fearful of widespread Arab disorders in Palestine and of Arab guerilla activities on the desert route from Iraq to Haifa. The decision stood, however, without those results.[28]

British attitudes had hardened, partly because almost no illegal immigration had taken place throughout the summer of 1940, and the British thought that they had seen the end of it. But the Jews started coming again, and the British were determined to stop them. When the *Salvador* sank in the Marmara, Thomas M. Snow, head of the Refugee Section at the Foreign Office, commented: "There could have been no more opportune disaster from the point of view of stopping this traffic."[29] Opposition to Aliyah Bet, however, did not prevent the government of Palestine from advocating recruitment of illegal immigrants to the British army, in the light of "urgent need for rapid recruitment." It wanted the best of both worlds: it would fight the traffic and recruit the Jews when it needed them.[30]

"This traffic" included, among others, an organized and rather successful attempt at mass escape by a whole community—that of the former Free City of Danzig. An independent city under

League of Nations tutelage between the two world wars, Danzig had a predominately German population, although the Poles had harbor rights because the city stands on the estuary of the Vistula River, the main waterway of Poland. The Nazis had captured the city government in the thirties. Persecution of Jews developed only slowly, but the Jewish community saw the handwriting on the wall and began organizing a mass exodus of the close to 7,000 Jews who lived there. The Zionist faction was fairly strong, and among the Zionists there was a strong Revisionist minority. By August, 1939, only 1,666 Jews remained in Danzig, the others having left for Poland, the United States, Palestine, and other places. When war broke out, German units took over the city immediately. JDC felt a responsibility for this unique community, which exhibited a curious combination of East and West European Jewish traditions. Responding to the energetic local leadership of David Jonas, JDC intervened with the RVE in Germany to transfer some funds to Danzig. Some 250 visa-holders to the Americas were able to leave, but the rest were left the choice between staying in Danzig and illegal immigration to Palestine.

The Nazis were interested in pushing these Jews out. In December, 1939, Troper recommended a special appropriation for the purpose of emigration. JDC would not be directly involved, since the practical issues and the expenditures would be handled by a local committee. It is not clear how much money was finally transferred, via the RVE in Berlin, but it seems that up to $50,000 were used. Negotiations between Berthold Storfer and the Danzig people continued throughout the spring and the summer of 1940, and a Nazi commissar named Rudolph Bittner was responsible for ensuring that the Jews were expelled and their property expropriated. As it turned out, JDC, in its efforts to help, had come very close to negotiating directly with the Nazis—in fact, it was Gertrude van Tijn in Holland and JDC representatives in Belgium who had met with the Germans. The net result seems to have been a mass exodus of the remaining Jews of Danzig, most of whom reached Palestine in the transports at the end of 1940.[31]

The three-ship transport which resulted in the *Patria* disaster and the exile to Mauritius was the last big illegal transport to escape from Nazi Europe. Hitler was about to decide on the mass murder of European Jews, and only one more ship, the *Darien*, sailed from Rumania with 789 passengers, arriving in Haifa on March 19, 1941. Most of the passengers were Rumanian Jews. The Nazi decision in 1941 was implemented only in the German-occu-

145

pied areas of the USSR, and throughout the year a trickle of legal Jewish migration from the rest of Europe to the western hemisphere was still possible. In March, however, German troops began entering Rumania and Bulgaria, and after April 6, the invasion of Yugoslavia and Greece finally put an end to any rescue attempts via the Balkans and the Danube.

The number of Jews trying to come out by illegal migration was very small compared to those in danger. Yet it is not the large numbers that convey the urgency of the situation, but the individual stories within them. One such story was that of Mr. Steinhardt, a Czech Jew who was the Sofia representative of the British-owned Exchange Telegraphic Agency, a cover for British intelligence operations in Bulgaria. Without work and threatened with expulsion, he turned to the British embassy. George Rendel, the minister, wrote a letter to the Foreign Office on November 25, 1940, saying that the British government was under an obligation to Steinhardt for services rendered; besides, he was a Czechoslovak citizen. Could he be admitted to Palestine or elsewhere? No, said the Colonial Office; no, said the British embassy in Cairo; no, said the Home Office in London. Wrote Thomas M. Snow on December 1:

> The C. O. will turn him down as far as admission to Palestine goes, both because he is a Jew, and because of the general situation there. The Security Services and the Home Office concur in refusing, on security and social grounds, to admit a single further refugee here. In my humble judgment this attitude is exaggerated; however that may be, it enormously complicates the Foreign Office's task of satisfying the Czecho-Slovaks and others that their allies (ourselves) are willing to help them over the matter of their refugees. We are reduced to hoping that somebody else may be more reasonable than we are.

In the end, Steinhardt received a temporary permit for Palestine.[32]

There was one group of refugees whose fate exercised the minds of JA and JDC officials throughout a very long period, and whose tragic end clearly underscored the frightful problems which Aliyah Bet was meant to solve. The fate of millions was exemplified in the story of the Kladovo transport.

There was a refugee relief committee at Belgrade run by Sime Spitzer, the secretary of the Yugoslav Jewish communities. The committee had received aid from HICEM and JDC since 1934, and thousands of emigrants had passed through Yugoslavia. The numbers cared for officially were 11,200 in 1939, declining to 8,200 in 1940, and 3,100 in early 1941—a sure sign that the majority of refugees managed to escape before the Germans invaded the country in April, 1941. JDC's total expenditure in Yugoslavia for refugees from 1933 to 1941 amounted to some 21.6 million dinars (about $400,000); this figure represents about a third of the total cost. The Yugoslav government was becoming increasingly unhappy about the illegal crossings of its frontiers by Jews escaping from Nazism, but there was not much it could do regarding the passage of ships on the Danube, which was an international waterway. Ships flying other than Yugoslav flags could not legally be stopped.[33]

Towards the end of November, 1939, a group of 1,003 persons was organized in Vienna and Prague by Hehalutz and sent on the river boat *Uranus* to Rumania. Its captain refused to continue the journey after reaching the Iron Gate rapids on the Hungarian-Yugoslav border, and the passengers had to be transferred to Yugoslav boats. These then could not continue the journey because of ice on the river, and on December 30, the refugees were finally disembarked at the small Yugoslav township of Kladovo. The Yugoslav government had a choice: either get the refugees out as quickly as possible or prevent their departure on the grounds that they were illegals.

While the Yugoslavs were making up their minds, the first problem for the local Jewish community was to provide sustenance and aid. Spitzer's committee contributed food, and in the spring and summer of 1940 certain basic material needs were seen to. The small Yugoslav Jewish community numbered only 75,000, many of whom were very poor, and was quite unable to shoulder the burden. JDC was reluctant to enter into an open-ended engagement to provide for the Kladovo group unless a guarantee was given that they would be transported to some haven. The JA was eager to get them out. Yet the whole story of Kladovo shows quite clearly the difference between Storfer and the Jewish groups sponsoring Aliyah Bet. Storfer may have become an unscrupulous agent, terrorized by Eichmann, but he certainly got his clients away and on boats. The Hehalutz transport of Kladovo, on the other hand, was run humanely and responsibly, but Hehalutz and Mossad proved incapable of providing a ship and the means to get people to it. JDC correspondence with Spitzer, Storfer, JA, and Mossad revolved around the question of funds to be provided for Kladovo. After protracted negotitations, caused largely, one feels, by JDC's financial crisis, Troper and Schwartz arrived at

147

at agreement with representatives of JA and of the European communities at their meeting at Budapest in early June, 1940. An original sum of $50,000 promised by JDC as their half of the amount needed for emigration was first reduced, then increased. In the end, JDC sent $68,500 to Yugoslavia for all needs in 1940, including those of the Kladovo refugees and of the *Pencho* group who also spent some time in the country.[34]

Despite the constant bickering over funds, it soon became clear that the main problem was not money, but a ship to carry the Kladovo people to Rumania. JDC found itself pressing JA to move the people on—in effect, it was asking for the illegal journey to continue. Months were spent buying a suitable ship. The *Darien*, out of Piraeus in Greece, was found and bought, and Mossad requested money, through Haim Barlas in Istanbul, to provide it with coal. It stood in Istanbul for over a month, from September 27 to November 2, until $4,000 arrived and the coal was finally bought. Uncertain whether the people would actually come, Mossad sent an emissary to Sofia to meet with Spitzer, who undertook to get them to the Danube delta where the *Darien* would be waiting. On November 9, 1940, the *Darien* finally sailed to Constanta.

In the summer of 1940, Spitzer had already advised JDC that the *Darien* had been bought and could, he hoped, take the refugees to Palestine. But until this happened the refugees had to be fed, and Spitzer was dependent on outside funds to do that. Funds were also needed to get the refugees to the ship when it arrived in Rumania. These needs coincided with the worst crisis in JDC finances, and JDC refused to pay $15,000 which it had promised on a technicality (JA had not paid its share either). Spitzer threatened to stop relief to the refugees, who were blissfully unaware of what was going on. One suspects therefore that JDC has to share the blame for the long delays in organizing their departure. Storfer's offers to intervene and save the Kladovo group if he were paid more money were refused. Most of the financial burden was certainly borne by Spitzer's Yugoslav communities.

Lack of money was one reason for not finding boats to move the refugees, but the reluctance of Yugoslav authorities to provide Yugoslav river boats for the transport to Rumania seems to have been more important, though one source claims that Spitzer also hesitated to send the people to Constanta.[35] He demanded that the *Darien* sail up the Danube to Kladovo, which would have been more convenient for the Yugoslav government. The British ambassador at Belgrade, Ronald I. Campbell, tried to stop the Kladovo group from going through Yugoslvia on their way to Palestine. A strong British note of December 1, 1939, had been answered by the Yugoslavs on January 13, 1940; they claimed that because of the international character of the river, they could not stop Jews from traveling on it. Campbell did not despair. On January 29, and again on February 5, he presented notes asking the Yugoslav government to take steps to stop the "illegal traffic." He was not alone; Sir Reginald Hoare in Bucharest, George W. Rendel in Sofia, and Sir Hughe Knatchbull-Hugessen in Ankara also pestered local governments about boats bringing Jews to Palestine. Faced with demands from the Colonial Office for more action, the Foreign Office commented plaintively that it had protested to twelve governments in Europe. "In Roumania, Turkey, Greece, Bulgaria and Yugoslavia these representations have been carried to a point which has made the question of illegal immigration a factor constantly present in our relations with the governments of those countries."[36]

A letter by a Kladovo merchant, addressed to a relative in Jerusalem and intercepted by the censor, reached the Foreign Office and caused a stir by the hope it expressed that the journey would continue when the ice melted in the spring of 1940.[37] Another intercepted message, this time of a cable sent by JDC-New York asking Troper to aid the Kladovo refugees, occasioned in intervention with Sir Herbert Emerson of the IGCR, who was asked by the Foreign Office to warn Troper against helping. R. T. E. Latham of the Refugee Section wrote on January 22, 1940, that while Emerson's intervention should be sought, "the question whether we should try to stop the JDC succouring the suffering people on the Danube with food is quite another one. . . . This time the C[olonial] O[ffice] is really carrying too far its policy of calling upon other Departments to do its dirty work." On May 14, the then head of the Refugee Section, John E. M. Carvell, wrote to the Colonial Office that "it is probably no less important that this country should not appear to be vindictive towards marooned parties of Jews, whose predicament inevitably has a universal, humanitarian appeal, than that we should appear not to be encouraging the illegal immigration traffic itself." The Foreign Office was reluctantly working against the humanitarian instincts of at least some of its members. Others, and especially the ministers themselves, were determined not to let the Jews through. One can therefore conclude that British pressure was behind many of the problems bedeviling the Kladovo situation.[38]

The refugees were moved to the neighboring town of Sabac

on October 16, 1940, while JA offered Spitzer tugs to go up the river to haul the refugee boats down (the *Darien* could not negotiate the Danube). Spitzer declined, and one can only surmise that he did so at the behest of the authorities. Urgent cables came to JDC for more money, and after holding out for a time ("There was nothing more we could do about it," JDC-Lisbon answered on October 31), some money was again sent. On November 29, Spitzer cabled Schwartz that the Kladovo transport was leaving the next day on three Yugoslav boats. On December 3, Spitzer was certain the boats had already left and asked for more money to cover the deficits incurred by his committee, a request which was refused. Then, on December 4, a cable came: "Because weather conditions here and lower Danube particularly Sulina our authorities order immediate debarkation and return Sabac." In fact, the Danube did not freeze over until at least two weeks later. A last, unsuccessful attempt to travel by train was made on December 17. The *Darien* finally loaded other refugees and started her trip to Palestine. In the meantime, 111 children and a few adults from the Kladovo group received Palestine immigration certificates and reached Istanbul early in April. On April 6, the Germans overran Yugoslavia. The numbers at Sabac had grown to 1,200 by the addition of more illegal refugees.[39]

The Sabac refugees were included in the first German anti-partisan measures in the late summer of 1941. On September 8, Edmund Veesenmayer, special Reich Foreign Office representative in Serbia, asked Berlin to agree to the expulsion of all male Jews to Poland or to a Rumanian island in the Danube. But Franz Rademacher, also of the Reich Foreign Office, was opposed. Asked for his opinion, Adolf Eichmann commented on October 13 that they should all be shot. By the time Rademacher himself arrived in Belgrade, only 4,000 of the original 8,000 Serb and refugee Jews in the area were still alive. It appears that the Sabac-Kladovo refugees were all shot on October 4, in fulfillment of an order by the military commander, General Franz Boehme. The observance of British immigration laws regarding Palestine was no longer threatened by the so-called illegal traffic from Kladovo.[40]

JDC was just one of the partners in the Kladovo affair, as it was just one partner and not the main one in the whole issue of Aliyah Bet. It participated by contributing money for food, medicines, clothing, and other items, but in the case of Kladovo it was also called upon to pay for coal and probably part of the sums required to buy ships. The Kladovo affair cost about $75,000 and the total expenditures on Aliyah Bet through affiliated communities for shipwreck and relief (including Kladovo) came to approximately $550,000 in 1940. The work itself was done by JA and its Mossad organization, and by the Revisionists, Storfer, Confino, and others. The net result was that 10,600 Jews immigrated to Palestine, 1,770 were expelled to Mauritius, some 400 drowned in the *Patria* and *Salvador* disasters, and over 500 refugees on the *Pencho* spent the war years in Italian detention camps but survived. The 1,200 Kladovo-Sabac people were murdered.

6

The Jews of France

French Jewry was made up of a number of groups. Among the most established were the Jews of Sephardic origin, from Bordeaux and Avignon, and the Alsatian Ashkenazi Jews who had drifted into metropolitan France or remained in the Alsatian borderlands. These two groups increasingly considered themselves Frenchmen of the Jewish religion, and they tended to cut themselves off very distinctly from later arrivals, whom they considered not to be French, or not French enough. Prior to World War I, and even more in the 1920s, immigration from Eastern Europe brought Russian, Polish, and Rumanian Jews, who concentrated in the main in Paris, either around the Pletzl (Yiddish for "little square"), the area surrounding the Saint-Paul Métro station in the Fourth Arondissement, or in the Belleville area. As in America or Britain, these immigrants were divided into those who kept to their traditional religious observance (usually the older generation) and those who adopted left-wing political views. The latter tended to predominate, and the Communists in particular gained ground among them. Yet it was a very peculiar type of communism, because most of its adherents continued to speak Yiddish and were characterized by a very strong Jewish feeling which was to express itself in clearly nationalistic Jewish stances throughout the war.

The diversity of Jewish groups was reflected in the number

of organizations representing them. East European Jews of non-Communist persuasions had established their own organization, the Fédération des sociétés juives (FSJ) in 1928, and prior to World War II, Marc Jarblum, the general secretary and a moderate left-wing Zionist, was the most important single personality in it. The Communist-directed counterpart to the FSJ was the Union des sociétés juives (USJ), founded in 1938; it included a number of groups who did not identify with the Communist movement, but accepted Communist guidance because of a radical mood engendered by French xenophobia and the economic depression.[1] On the French Jewish side, the representative organization was undoubtedly the Consistoire central (CC), the chief religious organization of French Jewry. In the 1930s, about 6,000 families belonged to affiliated synagogues in Paris, practically all of them French Jews. The Rothschild family occupied a very prominent place in the circle of French Jews who supported the CC. Early in World War II, individuals such as Jacques Heilbronner or William Oualid, along with Chief Rabbi Isaie Schwartz, were influential in CC councils. Finally, the most prestigious French Jewish aid society was the Comité d'assistance aux réfugiés (CAR), which had grown out of the Comité national de secours, set up in 1933 to help the German refugees. This latter committee had had the support of the then French government, and CAR, as its successor, had about it the aura of an official body. CAR was supported by the Rothschilds and was led by the representatives of the so-called notables, respected citizens such as Albert Lévy, Raymond Raul Lambert, and Gaston Kahn.

JDC supported all of these groups, with the exception of the Communist-led USJ, but its main channel was CAR. Small groups on the fringes, such as vocational and medical aid societies, also received support. Toward the end of the thirties, one of the latter, the Oeuvre secours aux enfants (OSE) became increasingly important. OSE, founded in Russia in 1912, began as a general medical aid society, but as some of its leaders moved into France, its work shifted more and more to the support of refugee children. At the beginning of the war, it controlled six children's homes with some 1,200 children, and its leadership was made up partly of older Russian Jews (Drs. Simon Brutzkus, Lazar Gorevich, and Boris Tschlenoff) and partly of young people, either refugees from the east or local French Jews. Outstanding among these younger people were Drs. Joseph Milner, Eugene Minkowsky, and Joseph Weill. JDC had a special relationship with OSE dating back to the end of World War I, and it supported OSE in France as well as it could.

Among the youth organizations, as yet unknown to JDC in 1939, was the Jewish scouting movement, the Éclaireurs israélites de France (EIF), a religious, bourgeois, and patriotically French group. Its leader and founder, Robert Gamzon, was to play an important part in the history of French Jewry during the Holocaust.

In 1933, an estimated 240,000 Jews, or 0.57 percent of the population, were living in France. Despite attempts at emigrating the refugees who came in after that year, the Jewish population rose to about 300,000 in 1939; one source estimated the number of Jewish refugees from Germany, Austria, and Czechoslovakia at 57,500; about 13,000 more were added in 1939. In 1940, when the German armies caused a tremendous flood of refugees to enter France from Belgium, an estimated 310,000 Jews remained in France. Probably 20,000–30,000 others, mainly Central European and Belgian refugees, managed to flee beyond the Spanish frontier and were not included in that figure. At the end of 1940, it would probably be true to say that almost one-third of the Jews in France were refugees from Central Europe and Belgium, about one-third, or perhaps slightly more, were East European Jews, and less than a third were "old" French Jews. Furthermore, Jewish refugees and immigrants were by no means the only ones in France. In 1939, it was estimated that there were 3 million immigrants in the country, of whom 800,000 were Italians, 400,000 Poles, 300,000 Republican Spaniards who had fled France after Franco's victory in the Spanish Civil War, 300,000 who were former nationals of Balkan countries, 80,000 were Armenians, and so on.[2]

French attitudes to Jewish refugees had already hardened in 1938.[3] On September 5, 1939, two days after war broke out between France and Germany, 15,000 Jewish refugees from Germany and Austria were interned, and in November, the government decreed the internment of "undesirable strangers." The treatment of these people was little short of shocking; their wives and children were abandoned, and to JDC's surprise and chagrin, French Jews washed their hands of their coreligionists as a mark of their French patriotism. According to a CAR report:

> It is materially impossible to ask the Jews of France not to accomplish their national duty first of all. . . . A public appeal without a distinctly national aim would risk failure, misunderstanding, and

might even have a most deplorable effect. We do not know of a single French Jew who could place himself at the head of a campaign on behalf of foreigners, no matter what their situation may be.[4]

CAR offices in Paris were closed just as help was needed more than ever.

When the September arrests were made, Morris Troper decided to intervene energetically, ignoring CAR temporarily. He met with Minister of the Interior Maurice Sarraut, and with General Jouard, commander of the Paris region. While French Jewry "disassociated itself completely" from any activity in behalf of refugees and JDC claimed that "even French relatives of refugees from Germany and Austria seemed to have forgotten that they were relatives," JDC obtained official agreement to its aid efforts. Having first set up an emergency committee with the help of Jarblum's FSJ, Troper established the Commission des centres de rassemblement (Camps Commission). Now helped by Robert de Rothschild, the commission obtained the cooperation of the French Red Cross, the Quakers, and even the official Protestant and Catholic organizations, under the aegis of the French minister for health. Troper was to claim later that it was his pressure that produced the French decision of December 21, 1939, to allow male refugees of military age to volunteer for the Foreign Legion or auxiliary work battalions. The panic receded somewhat, and some releases were obtained. But at the end of 1939, about one-half of those originally interned remained behind barbed wire.[5]

The sudden collapse of France in June, 1940, and the division of the country into occupied and unoccupied zones were accompanied by the flight of millions of people, mainly from the north southward. Among the French and Belgians there were Jewish refugees, whether established French Jews, "naturalized Frenchmen," or recent arrivals from Nazi Europe. The numbers concentrating in the unoccupied areas controlled by Marshal Henri Pétain's government at Vichy were estimated at between 165,000 and 210,000. At first conditions were extremely chaotic; all of the aid organizations suffered a temporary eclipse. In New York, the American Red Cross announced that it would aid refugees in southern France, and as a result Moses Leavitt cabled Troper in Lisbon that JDC should pull out. There was no need for its services, because aid would be provided on a nonsectarian basis, and that was preferable.[6]

The illusion of help from the Red Cross did not last long. Reports from France indicated waste and the lack of essential supplies, while a Red Cross decision not to provide help in areas bordering the new demarcation line, for fear of supplies reaching the Germans, soon made it clear to JDC that it had to go in itself. Herbert Katzki of the Lisbon office was sent to France and arrived in the Vichy-controlled zone on July 23. He found that the only effective aid was given by the AFSC, under the leadership of people like Howard E. Kerschner. The AFSC, working on a non-sectarian basis, established small but effective aid programs in centers where there happened to be concentrations of Jewish refugees, such as Toulouse and Montauban. But even the Quakers shared the feeling that the Jews could take care of their own group. The nonsectarian approach clearly had its limits.[7]

However, supplying aid to the masses of refugees from the occupied zone was not as difficult as the problem of the many thousands of unfortunates who were put into French internment camps. This was JDC's main concern in France in 1940 and 1941. Jewish undesirable aliens had been interned in 1938, Spanish Republicans in 1939, and German and Austrian refugees, most of them Jews, in September, 1939. When the Germans attacked France in May, 1940, these Central European refugees were again interned, and they tended to be retained in the camps after the French defeat. Most camps were in the south, and the Vichy government used them as a dumping ground for all undesirables. Some 10,000–12,000 Belgian Jews were interned for a short while, mainly at Saint-Cyprien. The number of interned people was estimated at 55,000 at the end of 1940, of whom about one-third were thought to be Jewish, while one-half were Spanish.[8] Generally the treatment of prisoners was more callous than actively brutal, though conditions in some camps were really not much different from those in Nazi concentration camps. The camps at Gurs and La Vernet were among the worst, but those at Rivesaltes, Noe, Recebedou, Argeles, and Des Milles were not much better.

Both Gurs and La Vernet were situated in the inhospitable wind-swept plain north of the Pyrenees. At Gurs, men and women were separated, and the inmates divided into blocks (*ilots*). A report from February, 1941, indicates that only 18 out of the 1,200 persons in each block were allowed to leave the barracks each day for outdoor exercise. Inmates were allowed to receive no more than 800 francs (fr.; $15) per month from the outside; in La Vernet, only 350 fr. were allowed. People could receive no clothes, even though shoes, especially, were worn out quickly. Rags wrapped around the feet took their place. Bread was scarce, and inmates were given watery soup and some vegetables. In 1940–41 it was estimated that about 600–700 Jewish inmates died in the camps, most of them in Gurs. The situation at La Vernet, built for political and "dangerous" internees, was even worse. Of the 3,500 people there in early 1941, about 600 were Jews, the others being mainly Spaniards and anti-Nazi Germans and Austrians. People who had been arrested in September, 1939, were still in the camp in 1941; others had been sent there in May, 1940. Mere suspicion of anti-French sentiments by a minor official was enough to condemn an individual to La Vernet even before the fall of France.[9]

All inmates at La Vernet were shorn periodically, and heavy and absolutely senseless labor was required, regardless of an inmate's age and health. No work clothes were provided.

> If it pleased any subaltern officer, he called the whole camp for an inspection, chased all the inmates out of their barracks with sticks, in order to use them for picking up stones or tearing out small tufts of grass in the camp or between the barbed wire fences. . . . on rainy days the guards amused themselves by chasing the inmates detailed to carry the pails with excreta from the barracks through puddles and mud to the garbage area one kilometre away rather than allowing them to choose a drier way.[10]

People were beaten for no apparent reason and thrown in jail (where more beatings took place) when the doctor accused them of asking for medical help without sufficient cause. Sick people admitted to the camp hospital had to pay for their own medicines; those who could not were simply left lying without treatment. Food consisted, from October, 1940, of soup; meat disappeared, as did most fats. Inmates could obtain release if they arranged to emigrate, but since they were not allowed out of the camp, their only chance was to do so by mail, an almost impossible task. Some people were freed as a result of interventions with the minister of the interior by relatives or aid organizations, but for the vast majority, simple people caught up in the whirlwind of war, there was no escape. Crippled, aged, or incurably sick prisoners had no hope at all.

Ironically, after the fall of France, while the food situation deteriorated, treatment improved from a simple human point of view. The new commander at La Vernet, an officer by the name of Royle, stopped the senseless labor, tried to improve the leaking roofs, put in some stoves and electric lights, both of which had been completely lacking, and made various other improvements.

A similar development can be observed at Gurs and the other camps.

In the summer of 1940, JDC estimated that 37,300 Jews needed immediate help, of whom 8,000 were in the camps. The others included 8,000 German and Austrian Jews still at liberty, 1,300 OSE children, 15,000 East European Jewish refugees, and some 5,000 Alsatian Jews. These last were part of a group of 29,000, approximately 22,000 of whom were driven out by the Germans in the autumn of 1940 and settled around the town of Perigueux. There, under the leadership of Rabbi René Hirschler, they established a self-help organization, but they needed additional aid.

JDC Work in France in 1940

While Herbert Katzki was trying to get his bearings in Vichy France, the whole problem of aid for French Jewry was being discussed in New York. Voices were heard to the effect that "JDC should do nothing to circumvent regulations of our government and should avoid sending funds into France, since there was no assurance that such help would not tend to relieve the German government of meeting its responsibility to the population in the areas it now dominates"—surely as classic an expression of naiveté and miscomprehension of the times as was ever uttered by a misguided Jewish liberal.[11] But Edward Warburg and Moses Leavitt stood fast, probably influenced by the action of the Quakers; a first monthly sum of $25,000, which was soon to be increased, was approved for French JDC operations.[12] The method of funding was similar to that used in Poland. French francs were accepted from organizations or individuals; those from individuals were received mostly against promise of repayment after the war, but in fact people who claimed their money back before then were repaid. The exchange rates were usually set at the current unofficial price, which meant that neither JDC nor the depositors lost anything by the transaction. The depositors knew that their money was safe from German or French confiscation.

Local funding was carried out chiefly through the Jewish National Fund (JNF), whose very energetic head, Joseph Fischer (Joseph Ariel, after his emigration to Israel), used JA and Zionist money as well as funds from individuals and gave them to JDC and JDC-supported organizations. The understanding was that JDC would make repayment in pounds sterling at almost half of the official rates ($1 for 80–90 fr.) to JA in Palestine. In this way the money was not lost to the contributors: it was used to save Jews and then repaid in Palestine. Joseph Schwartz of JDC-Lisbon was the man who, after much effort, managed to persuade the New York office to enter into the arrangement. Joseph Hyman and Moses Leavitt were at first very reluctant, until they were assured by Joseph Chamberlain of the Presidential Advisory Committee on Political Refugees that this method of funding was quite legal. By July, 1941, the JNF had provided 20.4 million fr. ($210,000–250,000) to JDC and JDC-supported groups on instructions from Lisbon. Table 15 presents the total JDC expenditures in France from 1939 through 1942.[13]

Table 15: JDC Expenditures in France, 1939–42

Year	Total
1939	$698,760
1940	$620,661
1941	$793,384
1942	$872,682

It was Katzki's first impression that the old CAR group would still be the best channel for JDC help. In August, 1940, all the Jewish organizations resumed their operations in the south, but the discord which had characterized relations between the various groups before the defeat was even more apparent. JDC relations with FSJ were very reserved, partly because Katzki felt that the FSJ group had a "desire to spread themselves all over the map so to speak," and that they were too publicity-conscious. JDC also accepted the view expressed by George Picard, the secretary to the Rothschild interests, who said that social work should be done by French Jews, because "antisemitism in France will affect mostly the East European Jews and will not strike at all at the French Jews." He believed that few results could be expected from any efforts that the East Europeans might make with Vichy authorities on behalf of refugees. It would be a blunder to entrust the handling of refugee questions to any but French Jews.[14]

In August, Katzki still had no funds to work with, but he was already negotiating the acceptance of local donations and had decided, very wisely as it turned out, to work in the camps primarily through the AFSC rather than through a Jewish organization. A Christian group was better situated to help in the prevailing climate of antisemitism. The arrival of funds at the end of August eased the situation somewhat, though the Jewish organizations had by then been forced to close their doors for lack of money. After the money came, Katzki returned to Lisbon, but he soon came back to France to supervise expenditures. Continual visits established strong links with Lisbon until September, 1941.

JDC's policy in France was decisively influenced by the development of Vichy and Nazi measures against the Jews. The first anti-Jewish act came on September 27, 1940, when the authorities in the occupied zone decreed the registration of all Jews. On October 4, all alien Jews were declared subject to internment, and on October 8, the Statut des juifs appeared (predated to October 3), which removed Jews from public office, the press, radio, theater, agriculture, and most types of industry and wholesale trade. This statute was followed on October 18 by the registration of Jewish enterprises. Yet the illusion that all of these discriminatory measures ultimately would hit only alien Jews persisted among French Jews. The so-called foreign Jews, most of whom were French citizens of East European ancestry, deeply resented this attitude.[15]

On October 22–24, another blow fell. The Germans suddenly expelled into France a group of Jews from the Baden-Saarpfalz area (including Mannheim, Karlsruhe, and other cities) in western Germany. A total of 6,504 persons, many of them elderly, were sent to Gurs from Baden, and 1,150 from the Saarpfalz. The French objected; this was not part of the armistice agreement, and Pétain even registered a formal protest on November 19. It had no effect. The expulsion of these groups of Jews was the last clear indication of the German desire for a "Final Solution" of the Jewish problem by forced emigration. Since June–July, 1940, the term had been applied to the plan to turn Madagascar into a colony into which millions of European Jews would be shipped after peace was established. Then the decision to attack the Soviet Union was made, and the Final Solution became synonymous with mass murder.

The Nîmes Coordination Committee and the Internment Camps

In the autumn of 1940, Herbert Katzki was busy preparing the ground for a large-scale aid program. Joseph Schwartz himself visited France and succeeded in at least papering over the animosities between the different groups. A meeting, very energetically promoted by JDC, took place at Marseilles on October 30–31 of all the Jewish organizations, and yet another roof organization was established, this time under Chief Rabbi Isaie Schwartz, called the Commission central des organisations juives d'assistance (CCOJA). Subcommittees were set up and a rough division of tasks was arranged: FSJ was to look after the East European Jews, CAR after the internees in camps, OSE after the children, and so on. In fact, CCOJA was hardly set up when it became clear that it could not serve as a central committee to distribute JDC funds because of the continued interorganizational tensions.[16]

An effective solution to the organizational problem appeared from an unlikely quarter. One of the Americans moved by the plight of refugees and interned foreigners was the representative in France of the Young Men's Christian Association (YMCA), Donald A. Lowrie. It appears that his willingness to help was strengthened by a discussion with Katzki; in any case, he managed to assemble the representatives of all the major organizations trying to work for refugees for a preliminary meeting at Toulouse on November 5, 1940. His own YMCA served as a cover for the operations of the Polish Red Cross; the AFSC, which at first was rather reluctant to join, ultimately added its weight and contributed the chairperson to the group in the impressive personality of a real Baltic princess—Princess Lieven. Varian Fry, a Scarlet Pimpernel figure who headed a fictitious committee and was engaged in smuggling antifascists and intellectuals out of France, also became a member. JDC tried to keep away from him as much as possible, because it did not wish to be identified with any illegal activities which would have jeopardized its major, openly conducted operations. Katzki himself, described by Lowrie as a "young American, baffled and frightened by his first experience in a strange country and still more by the antisemitic atmosphere in which he had to work, yet with no idea of retiring, as he might have, to safer and more normal Lisbon," of course participated. The new committee was joined by OSE, FSJ, a CAR representative, and the Unitarians under Dr. Charles J. Joy. OSE in particular began to be an effective organization working in this framework. Joseph Weill, himself a refugee from Alsace, became active in child work in the camps. Julien Samuel, an OSE worker, arranged illegal shipments of foodstuffs into camps under various pretexts. A group of Catholics, led by Abbé Alexander Glasberg of the Lyons archdiocese, and a parallel group of Protestants under Pastor Marc Boegner, called the Comité intermouvement auprès des evacuées, also joined.[17]

A rough division of work was agreed upon by these twenty-five groups, of whom six were Jewish. The Unitarians, with a small grant of $1,500 a month from JDC, engaged in medical work and some schooling. At Gurs they installed windows and disinfected the housing blocks. AFSC provided medicines, and so on. From November 20, 1940, meetings were held, usually fortnightly, at Nîmes, and soon the group came to be known as the Nîmes Coordination Committee (or, in French, Comité des camps). It was officially recognized by the Vichy authorities, and through it the various organizations brought much-needed help.[18]

In spite of some alleviation of conditions for internees, for many of the Central European refugees especially, no effective help seemed possible except emigration. Vichy France was interested in Jewish emigration, but it was also tied to the armistice provisions which included Germany's right to prevent the escape of former German nationals. Exit permits were increasingly difficult to obtain. A Unitarian attempt to emigrate fifty children to the United States in the autumn of 1940 failed because the Vichy authorities procrastinated. The U.S. State Department did not help. Arguing that no orderly emigration procedures could be worked out with governments under German domination, it refused a French plea in November to take in "thousands of refugees of many races and nationalities now in France." Alluding to the contradictions in French policies on this question, the State Department suggested that the French might begin by giving exit permits to holders of U.S. visas in unoccupied France.[19] One clear point emerged from these mutual accusations, however: people belonging to these "many races" had no chance of leaving France legally, and despite efforts by Lowrie and Fry, the number of illegal immigrants was necessarily limited.

As 1940 drew to a close, JDC reestablished itself in France. Continuing the policy adopted by Morris Troper in late 1939, it intervened directly in interorganizational jealousies in order to establish a viable aid program. JDC, however, did more. In the persons of Herbert Katzki and Joseph J. Schwartz, it attempted to exert political influence to alleviate conditions in France, thus to a certain extent stepping out of its accustomed role. In January, 1941, Schwartz, together with representatives of other American organizations, went to see the French minister of the interior to try to obtain releases from the internment camps. The Vichy government was interested in maintaining diplomatic relations with the United States, and Schwartz apparently thought that in these circumstances his intervention might help. It appears that the French agreed to ease conditions somewhat, fixing 1,200 fr. as the sum that would have to be guaranteed monthly to obtain an internee's release; in addition, a residence permit would have to be granted by the regional prefect. The proposal became the subject of long discussions among JDC leaders. There was much soul-searching, but in the end JDC's financial problems were such that Leavitt wrote to Schwartz in August: "In the light of the situation as we know it in unoccupied France and in the light of our own financial resources and responsibilities at the moment, we will not be able to undertake the guarantee of internees in the camps, as you suggest."[20] At 1,200 fr. each, the liberation of 1,000 internees would have cost about $250,000 a year, or between a third and a half of the total amount JDC spent for France in 1941. Such an expenditure would have meant cutting down on supplies to the many thousands of internees remaining in the camps. Besides, as 1941 progressed, it appeared that the French were releasing internees in any case, and a host of ways and means were utilized to increase that number without resorting to a formal guarantee.

As may be seen in table 16, the numbers of Jewish internees diminished considerably throughout 1941.[21] This decrease was due in no small degree to the efforts of the Nîmes committee and its individual components, which drew upon the goodwill of local prefects, who had considerable administrative powers, in order to obtain agreements for internees to reside in the several prefectures. The whole problem of the camps was an embarrassment to many Frenchmen even in the Vichy administration, and in October, 1941, a new commissioner for the camps, André Jean-Faure, introduced a slightly easier regime and speeded up releases. This policy continued in early 1942, so that when, in July-August 1942, the Germans began looking around for victims to deport to the death camps, they could not find two-thirds of

Table 16: Populations of French Internment Camps, 1940–42

	end 1940	Jan., 1941	Apr., 1941	Dec., 1941	Feb., 1942	July, 1942
Gurs	14,000	12,000	11,000	4,600	4,050	
Rivesaltes		4,000	4,000	5,124	3,700	
La Vernet			588	1,900	1,900	
Argeles			3,000	100		
Noe			1,550	1,300	1,450	
Des Milles			1,100	1,680	1,500	
Saint-Cyprien	3,150					
Recebedou			1,800	1,450	1,500	
Jews	**35,000(?)**	**33,910**	**34,100**	**14,850**	**18,722**	**12,000-13,000**
Total Internees	**60,000**	**51,439**	**?**	**25,610**	**?**	

those who had been there in 1940. Those they did find were for the most part doomed—caged by the French and absolutely helpless, they were the first and main prey of the Nazis in unoccupied France.

The Establishment of a French Judenrat

The progressive worsening of the situation of the Jews overshadowed the releases from the camps. Most of French society seemed to pick on the Jews as scapegoats for the misery into which France had been thrown by her defeat. In letters addressed to the pope and later made public, the assembly of bishops and archbishops of France declared their complete loyalty to Vichy on January 15, 1941, for the occupied zone, and on February 16 for the unoccupied zone. On March 29, pressure by the Nazi ambassador, Otto Abetz, resulted in the establishment of the Commissariat aux questions juives (Commissariat for Jewish Affairs), headed by an old and trusted antisemite, Xavier Vallat. On April 26, a decree was published forbidding Jews to exercise professions that would bring them in touch with the public. On May 28, Jews were prohibited henceforth to dispose freely of their bank accounts. On June 14 (predated to June 2), a law was published forbidding Jews to engage in various commercial occupations,

164

such as banking and transactions in immovable property. Only 2 percent of all lawyers and doctors and 3 percent of all students could be Jewish. Finally, a law of July 22 expropriated the Jews by appointing Aryan commissars in their businesses, in accordance with German practice. The aim of the law was stated to be the elimination of all Jewish influence in the national economy.

It was of course important for the Vichy government to obtain the sanction, or at least the acquiescence, of the Vatican for its antisemitic policies. On July 16, 1940, Cardinal Pierre Marie Gerlier of Lyons, primate of Gaul and head of the French Catholic church, informed Pétain of his approval of the old marshal's program. But it was nonetheless Lyons that soon became the center of half-legal, and later illegal, actions to save the Jews. A senior Jesuit priest, Father Pierre Chaillet, began to publish his *Cahiers du témoignage chrétien* in November, 1941, defending the Jews against antisemitism. By 1942, the publication was selling 50,000 copies. Behind it stood an organization led by Abbé Glasberg and Father Chaillet, L'Amitié chrétienne, which aided Jews with Gerlier's express knowledge. Pétain must have been troubled by the possibility of the church turning against him on the Jewish issue, for in August, 1941, he asked his ambassador to the Vatican, Léon Bérard, to ascertain the Vatican's reaction to his policies. The answer he got was very reassuring. Measures had to be tempered with Christian charity, wrote Bérard, quoting a high Vatican source. No provisions against intermarriage should be introduced, but apart from that stipulation there was no tendency in the Vatican to quarrel with the Vichy government's antisemitism. Limiting Jews in the exercise of their professions and prescribing special dress for them had been recommended by Thomas of Aquinas, added Bérard. There was no need to worry.[22]

For a long time, the Germans had been pressing for the establishment of a French Jewish council on the model of the Polish Judenräte, intending to use it as the vehicle of their destruction policy. As early as September, 1940, they tried to establish a Judenrat in the occupied zone, but the Paris Consistoire, the local branch of the CC, declined to do so, despite German threats. However, in November the Consistoire had to appeal for funds to alleviate distress, and they had to obtain German approval; the Comité de bienfaisance, a long-established and respectable local welfare committee, therefore became the core around which a coordination committee was organized. Rabbi Marcel Sachs of the Consistoire was forced to report to the Gestapo in order to have this committee recognized; Theodor Dannecker, the Nazi in charge of Jewish affairs, reported its establishment on January 30, 1941, and the rabbinical authorities announced its existence in April. It was composed of the Comité de bienfaisance, the Paris OSE under Eugene Minkowski, the Association philanthropique de l'asile de nuit (Night Asylum of Rue Lamarck), and the Colonie scolaire, an institution connected with the central FSJ agency in Paris, which was known as the Rue Amelot and run by David Rappaport. Rue Amelot, which supported the FSJ clientele in various ways, had gone underground in 1940, so that in it one finds for the first time the peculiar and unique feature of French Jewish reaction to Nazi rule: utilization of legal forms, but maintenance of a parallel illegal operation. It is significant that the Communists tried to join the Comité de coordination but were refused on account of the Nazi-Soviet pact—that is, out of French patriotic motives! The Colonie scolaire, however, left the incipient Judenrat as soon as it was founded and began to wage a campaign against it, recognizing it as a possible German tool.

The Nazis brought in two Austrian Jews, Israel Israelowicz and Wilhelm Biberstein, to instruct the local Jews in the art of setting up a Judenrat. This was a tactic the Nazis used in other places: in 1941, Mordechai H. Rumkowski of Lodz was brought to Warsaw, and Jacob Edelstein of Prague to Amsterdam. In Paris, the two Austrian Jews began publishing an information bulletin whose aim was to advise Jews of, and accustom them to obeying, Nazi orders. Walking a very dangerous tightrope, the Austrians avoided any active participation in Nazi actions and were cleared of charges of collaboration in a postwar trial. OSE's Minkowski also resigned from the Comité de coordination, and by the summer of 1941, it was clear that a Judenrat had not been established in Paris, though the Consistoire had been forced to join, as well as other respectable groups.[23]

The Germans, angered by this failure, then pressured the French to establish a Judenrat. On August 29, they informed Vallat that if no Judenrat had been established in the occupied zone by September 25, they would do so themselves. Vallat thereupon decided to set up a Judenrat for all of France, with separate sections for the two zones. He hoped to preserve French dominance over the Jews and guard French interests in the occupied zone against German encroachments. For the north—in effect, for Paris—a respectable French Jew, André Baur, was chosen as head; but in the south, the proposed Judenrat soon ran into difficulties.

On September 24, Raul Lambert, associated with CAR and a senior representative of French Jewry, was asked to come to Vichy, where the plan of establishing a Union générale des israélites de France (UGIF) was conveyed to him. Vallat's aim was to nominate to the UGIF, especially in the south, respected and authoritative leaders of the community. Albert Lévy and Lambert saw no possibility of resisting the establishment of the new organization, but they sought to introduce some changes in Vallat's proposed law. Lambert was to claim later on that Vallat had been in touch with Jacques Heilbronner of the CC and had received counterproposals from him as well. Lévy and Lambert asked Vallat to limit UGIF to welfare activities and also raised objections to the use of the so-called Solidarity Funds (*Fonds de solidarité*), which was essentially Jewish money confiscated by the Vichy authorities, to finance UGIF. The final decree of November 29, 1941, establishing UGIF mentioned that its chief field of action would be welfare, but the wording was ambiguous enough to provide a legal basis for using it as a Judenrat. No concessions were gained on the financial side at all. Valiat promised not to use it politically—but this was a gentleman's agreement entered into by an individual upon whom such agreements were hardly binding.

Opposition to UGIF came from two separate and contradictory positions. The CC, under Jacques Heilbronner, met on December 7, 1941, and again on January 18, 1942, and declared its opposition to the organization of a secular political institution that would define the Jews as a race or a people. They were a religious group, and the French among them had nothing but their religion in common with East or Central European immigrants, whether naturalized or not. It was inadmissible for French Jews to sit together with non-French Jews and represent something called Jewry. The funds which were going to be used by UGIF were illegally confiscated private property, and it was morally wrong to participate in their use for any purpose. Finally, welfare was a matter for the synagogue and should not be secularized. In its January resolutions, the CC directly attacked Lambert, and through him Lévy, deplored his activities, rendered "homage to those personalities in the 'zone libre' who by their dignity and firmness of attitude safeguarded the honor of French Judaism," and confirmed that those named to UGIF did not represent "Frenchmen of the Jewish religion." In other words, the CC rejected any indentification with a Jewish peoplehood as distinct from a purely charitable approach based on a common religion. It was defending its position as a religious body of Frenchmen; a letter written by Rabbi Jacob Kaplan on July 31, 1941, and a petition by the CC to Marshal Pétain in the summer of 1942 amply bring out these points.[24]

The other type of opposition came from the FSJ, and the prime mover was Marc Jarblum. He asserted that all Jews, French or foreign, shared a common fate. They should, he thought, defend themselves against an attempt to set up a political organization which would be under the control of an antisemitic government. On October 22, the leadership of CCOJA met at Marseilles and suggested a nine-man presidency for UGIF, among whom were Jarblum, two CC stalwarts, William Oualid and David Olmer, and the head of HICEM in France, René Mayer. On December 18, after of the official decree establishing UGIF had been published and the Jewish leaders invited to take part, Jarblum managed to persuade Mayer, Oualid, and Olmer to refuse to join, both because of the funds that were to be used and the danger that UGIF might become a political weapon in antisemitic French or even German hands.

Neither Jarblum nor the CC, however, really grasped the full import of the UGIF. The CC was willing to nominate a rabbi to represent religious interests on the UGIF if conditions warranted it (they were never asked, and the problem never arose); Jarblum had also been willing to join if certain conditions were fulfilled. It was more a healthy political instinct than anything else that prevented the two groups from joining UGIF. In the end, both the CC and FSJ—and the Communists, who of course had not been considered in the first place—remained outside UGIF.

JDC involvement in these negotiations was indirect, but rather close. Lévy and Lambert were the main recipients of JDC funds and were considered to be reliable and serious persons, as were Heilbronner and Mayer. While JDC remained officially neutral, it seems that its sympathy by and large lay with those who saw no alternative but to cooperate with UGIF. This attitude was in line with JDC's main preoccupation, that of sending help to refugees both in and out of the camps, which obviously could not be done except through UGIF once that body was established. Yet JDC never limited its support only to UGIF; it also granted funds to FSJ and OSE, though it was always perfectly clear to Schwartz that at least part of the money would be used illegally. JDC was kept informed of every move that was made in the establishment of UGIF, and the different protagonists made sure that JDC was

aware of their positions. At least some of the time that the negotiations were taking place, either Katzki or Schwartz was on hand
to receive direct reports. JDC representatives unofficially expressed sympathy with embattled French Jews but did not advise
them what to do; JDC took no official position on UGIF.[25]

JDC's Policies in France, 1941–1942

JDC's attitude to the unfolding tragedy of French Jewry was
marked by contradictions stemming from conflicts between the
legalistic approach of the New York office and the more compassionate response of Joseph Schwartz in Lisbon. One of the problems troubling JDC-New York arose from the British blockade. It
did not wish to appear to be trying to help Jewish refugees at the
cost of violating British regulations which it thought were scrupu-
lously observed by the U.S. government. It did not even wish to
request shipments of foodstuffs to France, unless this were done
under the auspices of the Red Cross or some such impeccable
group and with full British agreement. The Quakers were much
less hesitant in this respect. In January, 1941, Schwartz participated with other American aid representatives in requesting the
State Department to induce the American Red Cross to make
shipments to refugees in the camps. The presence in France of
American organizations would guarantee that none of the supplies reached the Germans. John F. Rich of the AFSC supplemented this request in February by asking for an early reply and
indicating that the Quakers, JDC, and others would wish to send
shipments to France outside of Red Cross programs, for which of
course British approval would be essential. JDC's attitude was
different. JDC policy, Paul Baerwald said, was not to attempt
anything that might in the slightest degree embarrass or impair
the effectiveness of the British government in the conduct of the
war. JDC's own procedure was to secure francs from persons in
France approved by the Treasury Department, in return for dollars that were blocked in the United States for the duration.[26] In
the end, the American Red Cross did not send anything to the
camps.

The differences in attitude between Schwartz in Europe and
JDC in New York was fairly clear. Schwartz did not notify his
central office of certain financial arrangements he made in France,
nor did he have any compunction about pressing his points regarding general policy. In fact, he was getting rather impatient

with some of the New York policies. When JDC's financial crisis
was getting worse, he did not hesitate to use strong language and
biting sarcasm to get out of his colleagues what he wanted. On
February 25, 1941, for instance, he sent a cable demanding
$50,000 a month for France: "figure 50,000 monthly Herb [Katzki]
budget which I sent ex Marseille was not based on love round
figures but represented rockbottom minimum."[27] He got what he
asked for. Yet, on the other hand, he also knew how to handle
JDC-New York understandingly; no American Jewish organization could disregard the fact that the Roosevelt administration
stood between American Jewry and antisemitism, nor could it
disregard the overwhelming desire of American Jews to help Britain in its lonely struggle against the Nazis in early 1941.

JDC's trust in CAR as the main body dispensing aid to
needy refugees and, increasingly, to impoverished French Jews
was not misplaced. As 1941 progressed, CAR abandoned old dis-
tinctions and began helping Jews without regard to their origin or
status. The numbers, as can be seen in table 17, were considerable. As table 18 shows, CAR's budget almost doubled between
1940 and 1941, and a fair proportion of it was provided by JDC or
the JNF by arrangement with JDC.[28] FSJ was supporting a smaller
number of people, mainly intellectuals, rabbis, students, and
workmen of East European background not normally eligible
under CAR rules.

Close cooperation was maintained between FSJ and OSE,
which increasingly became the major child-care agency in France.
By 1942, OSE was maintaining fourteen homes with 1,350 children, and much of its money was coming from JDC. Together

Table 17: Refugees Aided in Unoccupied Zone, 1940–41

Organization	Date	Total
CAR	Aug., 1940	3,500
	Dec., 1940	9,500
	Feb., 1941	13,738
	Dec., 1941	10,100
FSJ	Jan., 1941	2,813
	June, 1941	3,892
	Aug., 1941	3,927
	Sept., 1941	4,502

Table 18: CAR and FSJ Budgets for Unoccupied Zone, 1940–41

Organization	Year	Total Budget	JDC Contribution	Percent of Budget
CAR	1940	19,500 fr. ($490,000)*	14,800 fr. ($370,000)	75
	1941	35,939 fr. ($450,000)	25,467 fr. ($320,000)	70.1
FSJ	1941	9,500 fr. ($120,000)	7,500 fr. ($94,000)	79

*The dollar figures are approximate. One dollar was worth about 40 fr. in 1940 and about 80 fr. in mid-1941.

with other organizations, OSE participated in the Nimes Coordination Committee's efforts to rescue children from the camps, and in that it began to register a great deal of success as 1941 progressed. Towards the end of 1941, the French authorities agreed to concentrate most of the children at Rivesaltes, where conditions were somewhat better than in other places. From December, 1941, to February, 1942, the number of children imprisoned at Rivesaltes decreased from 1,487 to 875. In the ensuing months, the numbers decreased still further, although in the summer of 1942 there were still hundreds of Jewish children in the camps who became easy victims of the Nazis. From its headquarters at Montpellier, OSE began to place children with local families, a system that apparently started when some local prefects accepted children in order to release them from the camps. In May, 1941, with the help of the Quakers, OSE chose 130 children who were lucky enough to receive U.S. visas and be accepted by the U.S. Committee for the Care of European Children. The children left France in June, and Morris Troper sent Eleanor Roosevelt an account of their departure.

> The train . . . stopped at the station of Oloron and the fathers and mothers interned at the Gurs camp were brought to the station under police escort and given a last three minutes with their children. . . . these kiddies . . . refused to eat their breakfasts on the train that morning but wrapped up bread and rolls and bits of sugar and handed them to their parents when they met. There is one tot in the group, a wan, undersized girl of seven whom we haven't been able to make smile. She had been separated from her mother for over a year. When they met at Oloron, for the last time, for it is most unlikely that they will ever meet again, they were

171

unable to converse, for the child had forgotten her native German
in the effort of learning French and English, and they had no common language except tears.[29]

In the occupied zone, CAR did not operate at all. Welfare
work was bound up much sooner with illegal activities and opposition to the Vichy regime and the Germans than was the case in
the south. FSJ, the Communists, and OSE were the main bodies
that attempted to deal with the problems of 140,000 or more Jews
who were living in Paris.[30] In fact, four canteens and two dispensaries run by FSJ affiliates continued to operate in the city after its
conquest. JDC supplied half a million francs to these through the
Quakers.

The situation of Parisian Jews, however, deteriorated much
more quickly than that of Jews in the occupied zone. As early as
May 15, 1941, 5,000 foreign Jews were arrested and placed in
camps at Beauné la Rolande (3,600 inmates) and Pithiviers. The
attitude of the Paris populace, among whom there had been hostile manifestations towards the foreign Jews, improved after the
October, 1940, discriminatory laws, and FSJ and Communist
groups managed to provide some aid. The Communist aid organization called Solidarité was of course not supported by JDC, instead collecting its funds from the Jewish working-class population of Paris. In early 1941, it consisted of about 400 active members, organized in cells, who were attempting to help the families
of those arrested among its membership. In August, the Germans
arrested some 7,500 intellectuals, among whom there were 1,602
Jews. These were put into the Drancy camp, while others were
sent to Beauné la Rolande and Pithiviers. On August 22, another
4,200 Jews were arrested by the Germans. By September, 1941,
Drancy had a population of 10,000, Pithiviers and Beauné 2,000
each, and another 1,000 were kept at Compiègne. Official help
was available from UGIF and clandestine aid from FSJ and
Solidarité. In December, 743 doctors and lawyers were sent to
Compiègne and, after an attack by Communists on German soldiers in Paris on December 14, the German military shot 100 Jews
and levied a huge fine of one billion francs. JDC provided only
minimal help in the Paris area during this period, limiting itself to
supporting FSJ and OSE, which ran a children's home under the
guidance of Eugene Minkowski.[31]

The reaction of French Jewry, "native" and "foreign," to the
persecution in France differed considerably from that of Jews in
other countries. The reason must be sought in the fact that French

society enabled Jews to find active outlets for their opposition to the antisemitic regime. We have seen the dispute surrounding UGIF, and the themes of those discussions can be seen in different forms in other manifestations of Jewish response. Thus, when the Vichy government announced that Jewish war veterans would be exempt from some of the antisemitic laws, the Ligue des anciens combattants juifs, the Jewish veterans' association, dispatched a letter to the government on August 11, 1941, proudly declining to be treated any differently from the rest of French Jewry. In Paris, Germany's attack on Soviet Russia released the Jewish Communists from their ideological constraints. The Main d'oeuvre immigré, a Communist front organization for recent immigrants led by Jews (L. Lerman and J. Kaminski), branched out into sabotage and guerilla activity. The first overt armed action against the Germans in Paris came on August 2, and was carried out by two young Jews. One of them, Samuel Tyszelman, was caught and executed on August 13. Other armed actions, in which a special Jewish unit took a prominent part, followed.[32]

Among the Zionists, an armed underground developed, somewhat grandiloquently called Armée juive (AJ). This group was founded in August, 1940, at Toulouse, by a Revisionist sympathizer, David Knout, a liberal Zionist, Abraham Polonsky, and a socialist-Zionist, Leo Lublin. After some changes and an interesting ideological development, AJ (also known as OJC; Organisation juive de combat) decided to fight for France, but as a distinctly Jewish group. At its greatest strength, toward the end of the war, it claimed some 900 adherents, yet its importance was far greater than its numbers. From the JDC point of view, AJ was important because Jules (Dyka) Jefroykin, who had been nominated by Joseph Schwartz in 1941 to be the French representative of JDC, was its treasurer. Jefroykin's father, Israel, was the venerated president of FSJ, and with Dyka's nomination as JDC representative, JDC had clearly somewhat changed direction. This shift in policy was to become more evident in 1942 and 1943: JDC became the ally of the more radical Jewish forces, FSJ, OSE, and AJ, though it is doubtful whether Schwartz knew of Jefroykin's involvement with AJ before 1943.[33]

JDC activities in France included not only work in the camps, with the refugees, in Paris, and with what was to become the Jewish underground, but also an attempt to help the foreign Jews who had either volunteered or been conscripted to the

Groupements des travailleurs étrangers. There were 15,000–18,000 of these persons in 1941, of whom 8,000–9,000 remained in the summer of 1942, out of a total, including Gentiles, of 55,000–60,000. Jews tended to be separated into companies popularly known as the "Palestiniens" and treated badly. Their work consisted of drying up swamps, repairing roads, and making charcoal; no clothing was provided, food was poor, and the sanitary and medical conditions were appalling. Some companies received pay of up to 35 fr. a day (about 50 cents), but some received only 50 centimes (less than 1 cent). JDC help of almost 100,000 fr. monthly was provided to these Jews through the Nîmes Coordination Committee and its individual components. Gaston Kahn of CAR appealed to foreign Jews to volunteer for this service in March, 1942, no doubt out of patriotic motives. Fortunately, not many followed his advice.[34]

Summer, 1942: Deportations

In the early spring of 1942, aid from any source seemed pitifully inadequate in the face of the murderous attack on the Jews of France. On March 27, 1942, the first deportation took place from Drancy to Auschwitz, sending 1,112 Jews on the road that so many thousands were about to travel. On May 5, Reinhardt Heydrich, head of the RSHA, came to Paris to discuss deportations, where he found the French police commander, René Bousquet, eager to provide all the help he could. As a first step, stateless Jews from the south would join stateless and foreign Jews from the north. On May 29, the yellow star was introduced to mark the Jews. On June 15 and 23, instructions from Berlin detailed the plans: 100,000 Jews would be deported from France in the first wave. On July 6, Prime Minister Pierre Laval proposed that, contrary to the German suggestion that children should not be deported, children under sixteen should be sent away. On July 20, Theodor Dannecker, the SS officer responsible for Jewish matters in Paris, received permission from Berlin to deport children. It should have been clear to the French officials that small children would not be used for forced labor in the east and that the purpose of the deportation was murder. Laval, of course, cannot have been under any misapprehension. In order to execute the new policy more efficiently, in June, 1942, he replaced Xavier Vallet with the more extreme Darquier de Pellepoix.[35]

There followed the horrible scenes of July 16, 1942, when

174

12,884 Jews, including 4,501 children, were arrested in Paris and taken to the Vel d'Hiver stadium in preparation for deportation. As a matter of fact, the Germans had planned to arrest between 22,000 and 28,000. Their relative failure seems to have been due to the fact that some French policemen warned Jews who spread the information; the Communist Jewish underground also quite plausibly claimed to have received prior information.[36]

It so happened that Joseph Schwartz arrived at Marseilles on one of his periodic visits to France on July 27. On July 29, Raphael Spanien of HICEM, who was visiting Vichy with Raymond Lambert, came down in a panic and informed Schwartz that the Vichy government was turning over 10,000 foreign Jews in the south to the Germans for deportation. Schwartz immediately mobilized all the help he could: he asked the American chargé in Vichy to intervene and arranged with the American agencies of the Nîmes Coordination Committee to go up to Vichy immediately in order to protest. It was learned that 3,600 Jews would be taken from the camps, others from the labor battalions, and the rest from the cities. On August 4, the arrests started with 70 women at a hotel in Marseilles. On August 5, 1,000 people were prepared for deportation at Gurs. Children five years old and up were taken, but they could be left behind if their mothers so wished.[37]

The U.S. chargé at Vichy was S. Pinkney Tuck. Schwartz saw him on July 31, but Tuck had not waited. Somewhat exceeding his government's instructions, he protested to the Vichy government against the deportations. He was reported by Schwartz to have said: "The French government considers the Jewish problem as of no importance and is going to use first the foreign Jews and later, if necessary, the French Jews to bargain with the Germans against the silly promise which Laval made to furnish 350,000 workers [to them]. How much longer the civilized world will continue to have anything to do with this, I do not know." Tuck added he could not intervene any further without instructions from his government, which had been kept fully informed. Asked by Schwartz what he thought could be done now, he answered: "I wish to God I could tell you something concrete but honestly I do not believe that anything can be done by anybody for the time being. The only language these people understand, is force." Schwartz concluded that Tuck undoubtedly had done and would continue to do everything he could, but unfortunately there did not seem much anyone could do.[38]

Tuck's feelings were translated into action by the American

and other representatives of member groups of the Nîmes Coordination Committee, who tried, unsuccessfully but valiantly, to change Vichy's mind. Donald Lowrie of the YMCA saw Pétain and his general secretary, Jean Jardel, on August 6, and Pétain tried to explain that the foreign Jews had been sacrificed instead of 10,000 French Jews the Germans had demanded. This statement was later repeated by Prime Minister Laval and by reputable historians, but there is no evidence to show that the Germans had insisted on French Jews. There is every reason to suppose that they asked for Jews and were offered foreign Jews in the first place. Lowrie tried to argue against the deportations as such, but Pétain said that nothing could be done. The AFSC representative, S. R. Noble, saw Laval on the same day; in that meeting Laval did not even mention German pressure, instead saying that he was glad that a change in German attitudes made it possible for him to get rid of the Jews. The papal nuncio also seems to have intervened, though the details are uncertain.[39]

On August 25, Tuck saw Laval and talked about the treatment of the Jews in very strong language. The occurrences in Paris "had shocked public opinion throughout the civilized world." Unfortunately, Tuck expressed disgust especially at the separation of children from parents, and the cunning French antisemite immediately picked this up: Tuck was right; there should be no separation, and he would see to it. Indeed, the French saw to it that children were deported with their parents to their deaths in Auschwitz. French Jews approached Cardinals Gerlier of Lyons and Emmanuel Suhard of Paris, and as early as July 22, the national assembly of cardinals and archbishops protested the deportations.[40] By the end of August, 5,000 Jews from the unoccupied zone had been delivered to the Germans, and 7,100 more arrested and held for future deportations. From JDC's point of view, a major departure had been made: Schwartz had tried to intervene directly in favor of these Jewish victims. He inevitably failed, but the important thing is that he tried his best.

The immediate effect of the deportations on Schwartz was to bring him to another direct intervention in French Jewish affairs. He visited the CC headquarters at Lyons and impressed upon them the need for a united Jewish front in France. He went away from meetings with Lambert and Lévy convinced that they were strongly opposed to the UGIF they were heading, but he concluded that the legal cover it afforded should not be given up. The agencies dealing with social work, such as HICEM, ORT,

OSE, and CAR, had maintained their independence despite their official absorption within UGIF. The Solidarity Funds, the money confiscated from Jews, had not in fact been touched so far by UGIF. Nevertheless, "Everybody agreed that it was necessary to keep as much of the program as possible outside the bounds of the Union." The CC was to get 1 million fr. monthly from JDC (about $15,000), because it was not included in UGIF and would be independent of government control. JDC was moving more and more into the shadow area of "grey" financing, supporting groups that were moving towards illegality. In this way, under the guidance of Schwartz, it was "not only financing but also to a certain extent guiding and motivating."[41]

The change in JDC's policies in France was apparently made plain at a meeting at Nice of the representatives of the major Jewish organizations, probably in the summer of 1942 (Jules Jefroykin places it in the spring, but this is unlikely). The aim of the meeting was to establish priorities in funding and expenditures. Despite a great deal of opposition, a move was made to give priority to funds to quasi-legal or illegal operations. JDC, it appears, gave Jefroykin carte blanche to spend the money in the interest of saving as many people as possible, but without explicitly authorizing its use for clandestine purposes. This decision was precisely in accord with Schwartz's policy; it was the only policy that JDC, as a legal and open American organization, could follow if it wanted both to save lives and yet to remain within the legal bounds necessary for the continuation of its work. It was Schwartz's leadership that made this policy possible.[42]

7

Facing the Reality of the Holocaust

America's entry into the war completely changed the conditions of JDC's work. Many JDC officers and workers were either recruited or volunteered for the army. More importantly, perhaps, JDC was swept along in the tide of patriotism that engulfed the American people. Aid to Jews in Europe was no longer hampered by considerations of neutrality or opposition by isolationist elements in the United States. On the other hand, military operations became all-important, and mere rescue of human lives appeared to become subordinate to the central task of winning the war.

Even before Pearl Harbor, JDC had been in effect split into three separate networks—in a sense luckily, because this division enabled the organization to overcome at least some of the problems caused by the deepening abyss between the relatively sheltered existence of the New York organization and the realities of life in Nazi-dominated Europe. These differences became more accentuated in 1942 and the following war years. The American center of the organization, the Lisbon European headquarters, and the several local committees in the individual countries were experiencing conditions so utterly different that the emergence of different philosophies as well as of widely diverging views on practical matters was quite natural. Yet it is surprising how little in-fighting and bitterness there was. The danger of severe clashes seems to have been lessened by, on the one hand, the terrible calamity in which all parts of the organization knew themselves to be involved and which demanded maximum forbearance and mutual understanding; and, on the other hand, by the fact that most of the individuals concerned knew each other from before the catastrophe, and there prevailed a sense of mutual reliance between people now living—or dying—in different worlds.

There was, first of all, the New York office, where since early 1941 Edward M. M. Warburg had been chairman and Paul Baerwald honorary chairman. When Edward Warburg joined the American army at the outbreak of hostilities as a private, Baerwald returned to be the lay leader of the organization. The Executive Committee, by now a fairly large body—it had thirty-three members in 1941—met for formal discussions; day-to-day work was carried on by the Emergency Administrative Committee, which had been elected at the Annual Meeting after America's entry into the war, on December 19, 1941. The secretary was Moses A. Leavitt, and his deputy was Louis H. Sobel.[1] The professional administrators within JDC increasingly determined policy, though in the purely financial sphere of fund-raising and allocation, the lay leadership was still prominent. But we shall again have occasion to see that policies accepted in theory in New York were by no means always followed in the field. The tendency of Joseph Schwartz and other overseas representatives of JDC to change, ignore, or reinterpret directives from New York increased as the war went on.

The second JDC operated in Europe, and to a lesser degree in Cuba and in Shanghai. Morris C. Troper, the European director, had been spending most of 1941 in New York, making only occasional visits to the European headquarters in Lisbon. Meanwhile, Schwartz, Troper's deputy, was growing in stature and experience. On February 18, 1942, Troper resigned his position, having accepted an important job in Washington's quickly developing wartime bureaucracy. Schwartz now became in name what he had already been in practice: JDC's chief overseas representative. Fiercely loyal to his organization, he nevertheless was unequivocal in the demands and opinions he expressed in his frequent consultations with the New York office. For most of the war he enjoyed the cooperation of a staff which included Herbert Katzki, Robert Pilpel, and others who were attuned to his leadership and were active participants in his ventures. On a different scale and to a lesser degree, the relationship, one marked by

179

loyalty tempered by independence, that developed between Schwartz in Lisbon and Leavitt in New York was duplicated in the cases of Charles Jordan in Cuba, Laura Margolis in Shanghai, and the New York office.

There was a third JDC as well. It consisted of the local committees and their leaders in the occupied countries of Europe, who were now cut off from both Lisbon and New York by the American entry into the war. They still spoke in the name of JDC, but they did not necessarily reflect the opinions of JDC-New York. Social aid and child care became for many communities the central problems of their existence. In some places, JDC committees began to occupy prominent positions in the struggle of the Jewish communities for survival. In Poland, JDC's "directors" became more, rather than less, influential. The Warsaw office became the center of an underground system that tried to keep Jews alive; it then became the hub of the educational, cultural, and political activities out of which developed the underground that finally rebelled in January and April, 1943. On the other hand, there were areas of Poland where JDC disappeared altogether, even before the final murder of the Jews. In Slovakia, a new leader appeared in the great personality of Gizi Fleischmann. In France, Jules Jefroykin caused the transference of JDC support from the assimilationist French Jewish group to the East European immigrants who stood behind various illegal activities—hiding Jews, smuggling refugees into Switzerland and Spain, and, finally, armed resistance. In Italy, Vittorio Lelio Valobra emerged as the head of the Delagazione Assistenza Emigranti e Profughi Ebrei (DELASEM), the Italian welfare group associated with JDC; Valobra did his share in rescuing the remnants of Yugoslav Jewry fleeing into the Italian zones of occupation. In Rumania, the old JDC committee under Wilhelm Filderman stood its ground, but changed its tactics and politics. The liaison between all of these local organizations and JDC-Lisbon was Saly Mayer in Switzerland. It was he who coordinated most of JDC's European work; his role became increasingly important, until in 1944 he was the central figure, though for a short time only, in all of JDC's work. We shall have occasion to return to him later.

JDC's basic attitudes did not change in 1942–44, despite the tremendous upheaval of world and Jewish history during that time. One cannot reasonably expect such changes, which usually take place over a longer period of time and after a crisis, not during it. Just as the American Zionist movement asserted the

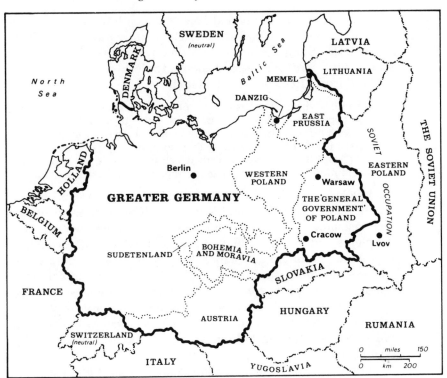

Nazi Europe in June, 1941. Reproduced by permission with some changes from Martin Gilbert, *Final Journey* (Tel Aviv: Steimatzky and *Jerusalem Post*, 1979).

right of Jews to an undivided Palestine as a Jewish state, basing their assertion on the presumed existence after the war of millions of homeless European Jews—at a time when these Jews were no longer alive—so JDC asserted the principles that it had espoused in the thirties. In 1943, Leavitt stated:

> The JDC makes the basic assumption that Jews have a right to live in countries of their birth or in countries of their adoption; they have a right, as human beings, to reside there with full rights; they have the right to emigrate if they so wish. . . . The success of the JDC will lie in the speed with which it can make Jews and Jewish communities self-supporting and thereby liquidate its activities.

He invoked the biblical concept of "social obligation and mercy" and declared that JDC would never "absolve governments of their responsibilities to their Jewish nationals."[2] These statements were supplemented by others that emphasized JDC's continued adherence to a "nonpolitical" stance. It was declared to be a purely welfare-oriented organization helping Jews abroad, and all political activities to protect Jewish rights were outside its scope. JDC-New York was trying to be very American, very loyal to the government generally and to the State Department in particular. We have seen this attitude in action in 1939–41, and it did not now change.[3]

In reality, however, the foundations for most of these beliefs and attitudes were being eroded. The right of Jews to live as equals had been denied in most of the countries of the globe, and, with the important exception of the great western democracies, was not to be reinstated. The hope of making European communities self-supporting after the war was based on the assumption that they would exist; in 1943, they no longer did. As a result, in a number of countries and through its office at Lisbon, JDC was in fact forced into adopting practical measures which could not but have a far-reaching political effect.

On the home front, JDC's main problem in 1941 was its continued competition with Zionism. While on the purely practical plane JDC demanded the lion's share of the dollars given for overseas causes, in theory—and JDC leaders did not refrain from theorizing—it had no quarrel with the desire to build a haven in Palestine for those who would want to go there. This was the traditional stand of the American non-Zionist leadership. Even the idea of a Jewish state did not particularly alarm them. Joseph Proskauer, the future head of AJC, might declare that such a state would be "a Jewish catastrophe," but most JDC leaders would have agreed with Morris D. Waldman, the secretary of AJC, and Cyrus Adler, who headed AJC until his death in 1940 and was also chairman of JDC's Cultural Committee. They were not opposed to a Jewish state because they did not think it endangered the status of Jews elsewhere. However, Waldman added, "We do reject Jewish nationalism, which means the organization of the scattered Jewry of the world into an international political unit or entity and we object to the existence of the World Jewish Congress as the Parliament of such an international political Jewry." When, in 1942, negotiations took place between AJC and David Ben Gurion of JA, AJC recognized JA's Palestinian program, but demanded that JA disassociate itself from WJC. Leaders in these discussions included Henry Ittleson and James H. Becker, who were among the most important lay leaders of JDC.[4]

To some of the more influential persons within JDC, non-Zionism meant a neutral, benevolent position. To others it meant opposition to anything but a purely philanthropic approach to the problems of Palestinian Jews. Given the often bitter competition between JDC and UPA for funds, this was hardly surprising. Thus Joseph Hyman argued in favor of organizing non-Zionists against the "clever manipulation" practiced by the Zionists.[5] Exception was taken to the very idea that Jews might have to leave Europe and seek homes elsewhere. Evelyn Morissey, JDC's administrative secretary, wrote to Leavitt in April, 1943: "One fundamental policy of the JDC is to help Jewish populations in the countries in which they reside and to adjust them to the conditions in their own countries." Only forced emigration from Germany made JDC, unwillingly, change this policy. Another leading member of JDC councils thought that, during the war especially, nothing should be done which would conflict with the thesis that the Jews were finding their destiny in being recognized as citizens of "their" countries.[6]

JDC usually refrained from airing its disagreements with the Zionists in public. It preferred to stand on its record, and in addition had to take into account the fact that a small group on its own Executive Committee, led by Morris Rothenberg, were identified with Zionism. The Zionists had no qualms, and tended to attack JDC in their publications for its alleged lack of vision and purely philanthropic approach. The September 1, 1942, issue of *Zionews*, for example, stated that while "it is quite possible" that JDC representatives had shown devotion and "perhaps" also exhibited "exceptional courage" amidst the trying war conditions in

Europe, its funds had been poured into a sieve. JDC had not realized that "Jewish suffering would reach dimensions that would dwarf and minimize the value of their millions." Attacks like this were actually not unwelcome to JDC. The American Jewish public could identify with the *Daily Forward*, which answered such onslaughts by commenting that it thanked God for having created the *Yahudim* ("up-town" German Jews), for "if the Zionists would have been the leaders of the JDC, the Jews of Europe would not have received a single cent; all the money would have gone for Zionist purposes."[7] While not denigrating the support of Palestine as a most important refuge, JDC could point to the necessity, whatever the prospects of Europe's Jews in their countries of residence, of supporting brethren in need. In fact, as we shall see, JDC actively assisted JA in many aspects of its work.

The real enemy—the word is not too strong—of JDC on the Jewish scene remained WJC. It embodied the claim of Zionists to represent a Jewish nation dispersed in the world, loyal to its host countries provided these kept faith with it, but quite distinct as an ethnic or national minority. Furthermore, it regarded material support and the demand for equal rights as part and parcel of the same basic idea and therefore did not define itself as a purely political organization. In attempting to support European Jews by relief activities, WJC competed directly with JDC and its claim to represent American Jewry in relief and rescue activities abroad. Schwartz in Lisbon did not share the opposition of some of JDC's lay leaders to Zionism; he did, however, fully agree with their opposition to WJC's often rather pathetic attempts to appear as a relief agency. Offers to cooperate with JDC in its overseas work, most probably prompted by WJC's desire to acquire a legitimate standing in relief work, were rejected by JDC throughout the war, on the grounds that WJC was a political organization and should not meddle in relief. When, at the end of 1942, a Joint Emergency Committee on European Jewish Affairs was set up by the major American Jewish groups, JDC only sent an observer because of WJC's participation. An American Jewish Conference was convened by all major Jewish organizations in September, 1943, in order to prepare postwar Jewish demands. This group established a rescue commission which also asked JDC to participate. But the AJC had abandoned the American Jewish Conference because of its outspoken Zionist platform, and both the Jewish Labor Committee and the General Jewish Council had doubts. JDC again refused to join, asserting that it would not associate with political organizations. Early in 1945, Nahum Goldmann, administrative chairman of WJC, suggested establishing yet another body of Jewish organizations to coordinate postwar rescue and rehabilitation plans, but again JDC replied that it "must adhere to its policy of avoiding affiliations with political organizations."[8]

On the whole, JDC managed to maintain its predominant position in the field of overseas work throughout the war. WJC's attempts to intervene—or interfere—were neither very effective nor very significant. The activities of the JA, which began to engage in large-scale relief and rescue in early 1943, were much more important. Its efforts were supported by the impressive sums of money raised in the Palestine Jewish community (only some 500,000 strong), mainly through the Recruitment and Rescue Fund, originally founded in June–July, 1942. In early 1943, emissaries of two left-wing kibbutz organizations, Menahem Bader and Wenja Pomerantz (Ze'ev Hadari), were sent to Istanbul to help Haim Barlas, the local JA representative. Funds from Palestine began reaching Geneva from Istanbul and found their way to France and other occupied countries. Istanbul also supplied funds to Rumania, Bulgaria, Hungary, and Slovakia, and the two emissaries, with the aid of citizens of neutral or enemy countries, tried to send help to Poland.

On the face of it, therefore, JA was meddling in JDC's proper sphere. Schwartz, however, recognized the importance of close cooperation between the two organizations. There were activities into which JDC could not enter because they were not entirely legal, whereas JA had a completely different attitude.[9] Schwartz found a kindred spirit in Eliezer Kaplan, the JA treasurer, who defined the division of labor between the organizations as "aid by JDC, rescue by the Jewish Agency." Schwartz let it rest at that, though the definition was incorrect. Practically speaking, JDC funds could be concentrated on projects approved by the legalistic New York office because Schwartz knew that JA would take care of situations where half-legal or illegal activities were called for. On the other hand, JDC bailed JA out in a number of more or less legal situations. Schwartz's actions were not always understood in New York, where even the offer of cooperation by the Jewish War Appeal of South Africa caused some concern. In the end, it was felt that "despite the fact that the South African War Appeal is strongly Zionistic, their offer to collaborate should be accepted."[10]

On the more practical plane of the battle for the philanthropic Jewish dollar, it was the Zionist side that was constantly endangering the very existence of the UJA. By early 1944, the Zionists were getting worried about what they considered the low proportion of funds they were getting from it. JDC insisted on an overall proportion, after deducting sums for the absorption of immigrants to the United States, of 60 percent for its own activities, as against 40 percent for all Zionist programs. The UPA wanted to equalize the proportions and, in addition, raise sums through activities that would not come under the UJA agreement, such as the JNF campaign for buying land in Palestine. Exactly the same struggle was repeated in 1945. In both cases it was the War Refugee Board, an American governmental agency established in January, 1944, which intervened, supporting the Council of Jewish Federations and Welfare Funds in its attempt to bring UPA and JDC to an agreement. In both cases, too, it was the UPA which broke off the negotiations but was finally forced back to accept a compromise which gave it 43 percent of the funds, with a ceiling fixed for additional JNF fund-raising ($900,000 in 1944 and $1.5 million in 1945). But whereas in 1944 the war situation and the immediate demands for rescue in Europe and North Africa forced UPA's hand early in the year, in 1945 it dissolved the UJA in March and did not come back before the beginning of June. It was only at that late date that the vast campaign for 1945–46 really got started.

By the end of the war, JDC's attitude toward Zionism was undergoing a change caused by a new political atmosphere among American Jews, the lessons many people thought had been taught by the war—and by the very practical fact that Zionism had become the predominant conviction among the large numbers of social workers and others whom JDC began to employ for its overseas operations. The old leadership muted its opposition, and, with its great gift of sensing changes in mood, kept its hold while adjusting to the new situation. As Moses told JDC fund-raisers in early 1945:

> Life-saving, keeping Jews alive, takes priority over all programs . . . but not in the sense of its being an anti-Zionist approach. It is not. It is a Zionist approach because if the Zionists do not want Jews to be alive to come to Palestine, what is the whole purpose and what does this whole movement amount to? We are not building a Jewish national home for the Jews of America. They don't need a Jewish national home. . . . Therefore we say we are not Zionist; we are not non-Zionist. We are for Jews and we must keep the Jews alive for the sake of Palestine.[11]

While the logic of this statement may not have been perfect, the desire for a compromise with the Zionist position was obvious. The legitimacy of Zionist arguments was not to be doubted; rather, it was Zionist fund-raising at the expense of rescue work in Europe that was questionable. One can see here the beginning of that process that would ultimately unite American Jewry behind a pro-Israeli, but not necessarily Zionist, position.

Information, Knowledge, and Reactions to Mass Murder in Europe

There can be no doubt that anyone who read the papers, listened to the radio, or read the daily reports by the Jewish Telegraphic Agency (JTA) had access to all the information about Europe's Jews that was needed to establish the fact that mass murder was occurring. Information did not mean knowledge, but the information at any rate was there. In England, the *Jewish Chronicle* and the *Zionist Review* knew of Soviet reports regarding the massacres of "Jews and other Soviet citizens"—as it was usually put—early in 1942. The JTA, which was received in New York, originated some of these reports and hammered away at them. Yiddish papers, and later non-Jewish papers as well, published accounts of mass murders in Vilna as early as March, 1942. Such reports can be found clipped and tucked away in JDC files, proof that JDC officers had access to them. By May, 1942, the *JDC Digest* had printed some of this information for its officers, staff, and fund-raisers.

Until June, 1942, all this information was admittedly scattered. Nobody imagined a campaign of mass annihilation, and the information was always presented in a form which allowed for doubts as to its veracity. Yet an article like that reporting Dr. Henry Shoskes's information regarding the Warsaw ghetto, which appeared in the *New York Times* on March 1, 1942, should have made people stop and think. Shoskes was well known and well thought of by JDC and other American Jewish groups, and he stated that, according to reliable information, "there will be no more Jews in Poland in five or six years." Americans, including Jews, regarded this and similar items sometimes as good propaganda, sometimes as exaggerations that might unfortunately have some grain of truth in them. In either case, while they indicated that persecution was occurring and Jewish lives were being lost, the situation was not perceived to be essentially different from what European Jewry experienced during World War I.

The first authoritative and exact report of a general plan to annihilate Polish and, by implication, European Jewry, was dated May, 1942, and was sent by the Bund to the Polish government-in-exile in London. It declared that the Germans had "embarked on the physical extermination of the Jewish population on Polish soil." It correctly related how the process of destruction had spread from the east to western Poland and from there to the GG. It estimated the number of murdered Jews at 700,000—rather an understatement. On June 2, 1942, the British Broadcasting Corporation broadcast the gist of this report to Europe. On June 10, the Polish National Council of the Polish government-in-exile sent a call which included the main points of the Bund report to all Allied parliaments to take steps to stop the murder. The *Daily Telegraph* carried the report on June 25 and referred to it repeatedly during the following week. On the twenty-sixth, the report was rebroadcast by the BBC, and a Polish White Book containing the information was circulated on June 27. When Britain and the United States failed to react, the Polish National Council, at the request of its two Jewish members (Ignacy Szwarcbart and Szmul Zygielbojm), repeated its June 10 call on July 8. A note incorporating the main points was handed to the American ambassador to the Poles in exile. Roman Catholic Cardinal Hinsley of London broadcast the information to Europe on July 7. A press conference was held on July 9 to disseminate the contents of the Bund report, and the Polish minister for home affairs, Stanislaw Mikolajczyk, as well as the British minister of information, Brendan Bracken, participated along with Jewish representatives. The London *Times* carried a garbled version of the July 9 press conference on the following day, July 10.[12]

JDC, along with the other Jewish organizations, was informed of all this. Like the others, its leadership simply did not grasp what the information meant. Schwartz had reported in April that the situation in Poland, according to Saly Mayer, was incredibly bad; the mortality was frightening. The one consolation was that JDC local committees were carrying on, doing whatever they could to alleviate suffering. His statement, obviously reflecting the situation in the GG before the mass murders of March–April, 1942, was interpreted by Hyman into an almost lyrical description of life in the ghettos and distributed all over the United States in the *JDC Digest* for May, 1942.[13] Completely unaware of

Major Concentration, Forced Labor, Transit, and Extermination Camps in Europe, World War II. Reproduced by permission from the *Encyclopaedia Judaica*, vol. 5 (Jerusalem, 1971).

the import of what he was saying, Hyman wrote to Harold F. Linder, who had joined the army: "The atmosphere in which you work is remote from our smaller problems in the JDC."[14]

One must constantly emphasize that JDC was not alone in its failure to comprehend the truth. The Zionists had held a conference at the New York Biltmore Hotel in May, proclaiming the need for a Jewish state in the whole of Palestine to absorb the millions of Jews uprooted from Europe. This plan was then adopted in Jerusalem by the Zionist Executive Council in November, after it had become well established that the millions were no more. Zionist papers in the United States reacted by stating that "the obvious aim of the Nazis is to bring about the destruction of the Jews," only to indicate after that that life for the Jews in Polish ghettos was going on.[15] Bundist publications were no different. *The Ghetto Speaks,* a periodical published in English in New York for the specific purpose of disseminating information about Poland, stated on August 1, 1942, that "the Jewish nation in Poland is being ruthlessly annihilated." In the very next sentence it declared, "Jewish life continues now behind ghetto walls." A mass meeting in Madison Square Garden in mid-July, 1942, protested the slaughter of the Jewish population in Nazi-occupied Europe. People were aware that something terrible was going on, did not dare to disbelieve openly, but could not bring themselves to lend credence to information that the total Jewish population of Nazi Europe was being murdered. The reason for this is not really difficult to understand. Jews were being killed in Europe for no other reason than that they had been born Jews (by Nazi definitions). The crime they were being accused of was one which quite literally had no precedent: they were accused of living, of having been born. This was stated repeatedly and openly in various Nazi documents: "criminals" were accused of various transgressions, but in the case of Jews, it was simply stated that they had been killed or punished because they were Jews. Raised and educated in an American society based on certain elemental values that originally derived from Jewish moral concepts, American Jews were singularly unprepared to adapt quickly to the thought that they were living in a different century from the one they had imagined.

On August 8, 1942, Dr. Gerhart Riegner, the WJC representative at Geneva, sent a cable to WJC in New York and London which has commonly been interpreted as breaking the silence regarding the mass murder of European Jews. Yet Riegner was unsure how accurate his information was. The cable said that he had received "alarming report that in Führer's headquarters plan discussed and under consideration" that all of Europe's Jews should be concentrated in the east and there "exterminated at one blow." The action was being planned for the autumn, and methods under discussion included "prussic acid." He added that he was transmitting the information "with all necessary reservation as exactitude cannot be confirmed." It is hardly surprising that government officials in Washington should have had doubts regarding reports that in Riegner's own eyes looked incredible; they decided not to hand the cable to Stephen S. Wise, the president of WJC, as Riegner had requested, until the reports had been checked. However, Wise received the information from Sidney Silverman, head of WJC's London branch, on August 28. Wise agreed not to make the information public; nevertheless, he did use it publicly, although he had not acted upon the much more detailed and unequivocal Bund report two months earlier.[16]

What happened between August and November in Switzerland, where Paul C. Squire of the American embassy was trying to find out whether Riegner's information had been correct, has been described in some detail in Arthur D. Morse's book, *While Six Million Died.*[17] What apparently convinced the Americans of its accuracy was, more than anything else, the testimony of Dr. Carl J. Burckhardt, former commissioner of the League of Nations in Danzig and in 1942 the most active personality in the International Red Cross (IRC). Squire interviewed Burckhardt on November 7, 1942, and was told that Hitler had signed an order early in 1941 that before the end of 1942 Germany must be free of all Jews. Burckhardt added that the term *Judenfrei*, as employed by his sources, meant "extermination."[18]

In the meantime, the Poles in London continued to receive similar information about mass murders apparently occurring according to a plan. From time to time they made their information available to the British and American ambassadors accredited to their government-in-exile, but no action seemed to result. As early as July, they had told themselves that if "Polish information from the homeland is not believed by the Anglo-Saxon nations because of its unlikelihood, surely they must believe their Jewish informants."[19] The Poles, and even the British, still believed in the great influence of Jews in America. The arrival in Palestine on November 13, 1942, of sixty-nine Jewish civilians who had been exchanged for Germans because they held Palestinian passports

191

confirmed the information to Palestinian Jewry. But it was not until the Polish government finally submitted an official note on December 9, 1942, that the Allied nations at last acted. On December 17, 1942, they published a condemnation of the massacre of the Jews, thus officially announcing that the Jews were actually being killed.[20] From then on, the facts were available in great detail everywhere in the Allied world. Whether they were believed is a different matter.

What is decisive for a history of JDC is the extent to which the information regarding the Holocaust became a guide to action. Even after the Allies had officially admitted that annihilation of the Jews had begun, there was no forceful, unequivocal response by American Jewry, including JDC. Instead, reactions varied among incredulity, hope that the reports might turn out to be a nightmare from which the Jewish people might one day mercifully awake, utter despair resulting from accurate appreciation of what was happening, desire for immediate action, feelings of helplessness, and even desire to escape responsibility and hide behind words or meaningless action. Typical perhaps of the muddle and disorientation of all sections of Jewry in the West was the declaration of the Bund in America in October, 1943: "The common sufferings in the present Nazi hell and the common fight of the Polish and Jewish underground Labor Movements will, certainly, strengthen the more the common bond of fate and struggle linking the Polish and Jewish masses."[21] *The Ghetto Speaks*, which carried this declaration, had itself told its readers throughout the preceding year that only a few Jews were still left alive in Poland. Zionists, including WJC leaders, were so absorbed in planning for after the war's end that they were paying little attention to what was happening in Europe—in direct contrast to their friends in Istanbul, whose letters and cables cried out for immediate action to save the remnants of European Jewry.[22]

JDC's leadership in New York reflected all the possible attitudes. Adolph Held, the veteran Labor leader, spoke of the tragedy of Polish Jews in February, 1943, obviously with a clear-headed understanding of the situation. Yet there was no practical plan of action he could propose. Schwartz, writing from Lisbon, did not want to cause even greater despair, and he tempered his information with hopeful phrases. The cumulative tragedy of Europe's Jews would have been far greater but for JDC, he said. This solace was reflected in JDC literature and pronouncements. Obviously fearing that too gloomy a picture might cause American

Jews to give less, JDC announced in March, 1943, that Europe's Jews "are not yet dead, not by far. Even in darkest Poland there is organized Jewish life—committees that still function and leadership that guides Jews through these difficult days. It is up to us to preserve as much of this as possible."[23] Expressing the certainty that a million and a quarter Jews had been saved from Nazi Europe, 50 percent of whom had fled into the Soviet Union, the *JDC Digest* of October, 1943, added: "Day after day, the tenuous process of escape continues, over the Pyrenees" and elsewhere. "Out of the rescued and the waiting ranks of those who have obstinately refused to die, the future of Europe's Jews will be built." In actual fact, no more than 400,000 had fled into Russia, but of these only some 250,000 survived. JDC hoped that two, three, or even more million Jews would survive (about a million did).

Thinking in terms of millions was one way to escape the reality of the murder of individual human beings, a way in which sanity could be preserved in the midst of unthinkable disaster. In Istanbul and Geneva, representatives of Jewish organizations were closer to reality; they could not understand why those in Palestine, or England, or America did not comprehend and did not act desperately and radically. The Palestinian emissaries in Istanbul reported that letters came from Nazi Europe containing "tears, and suffering, and despair, and madness and blood— much Jewish blood that will scream and boil and froth for thousands of years because it was spilt in vain."[24] Palestinian Jews did not understand this kind of language; American Jews would have to undergo a process of redefining their attitudes and rethinking before it became comprehensible.

JDC was hoping for results from the Bermuda Conference of British and U.S. officials called in early 1943, ostensibly to find some solution to the "refugee question." In actual fact, the two governments were trying to find a way of appeasing public opinion, which, especially in England, was demanding action to save the persecuted Jews of Europe. No nongovernmental agencies were permitted to participate at the meeting, which opened at Bermuda on April 19, 1943—the very day the Warsaw ghetto rebellion began. JDC followed the proceedings with great interest, and the reports to the British House of Commons and the debate that followed were carefully read in New York. Osbert Peake, British undersecretary for the Home Office, expressed the Allied view when he said, on May 19, 1943, that "these people" were "for the present mostly beyond the possibility of rescue. . . . We must, I think, recognize that the United Nations can do little or nothing in the immediate present for the vast numbers now under Hitler's control."[25]

The line taken by Britain and America, and accepted by most Jews at the time, was that there was nothing that could be done to help Jews under Nazi rule except to win the war quickly. As a result, nothing that might hamper the war effort, including any rescue plan that diverted means and manpower from the pursuit of victory, could be justified. Occasionally Jewish leaders might demand immediate action to rescue European Jewry—as, for instance, Henry Monsky did in his address at the American Jewish Conference on August 29, 1943—but he then went on to talk about postwar reconstruction. JDC-New York reflected this attitude. "The best assurance of rescue . . . is the success of the armies of the United Nations," wrote a staff member for a press release in September, 1943.[26] It sounded hopeful, almost cheerful. Very few, however, actually believed that something could be done immediately to help. Only the lonely people in Istanbul and Geneva seem to have realized what opportunities were being missed.

> It is not known in Palestine and perhaps they don't believe that it is still possible to help. The news that came from Geneva [that is, Riegner's information] did not convince; and just as before, the mind could not grasp that this is how they are murdering us, so now the mind doesn't grasp that there are nooks and paths through which help can be given.[27]

Even there, despair soon took hold. The Allies would not budge; there was no money. "On the whole I think that one can hardly do anything to extend help in the most crucial areas, all we are really doing is patchwork," wrote Richard Lichtheim, the JA man in Geneva.[28]

The Bermuda Conference ended with the decision to reactivate the IGCR and establish a camp in North Africa for persons who had managed to escape to Spain, which might also open the way for more refugees to cross the border. Beyond these half-hearted measures, nothing. No ships would be set apart to rescue those in need of it, no food would be allowed into Europe, no negotiations regarding civilians would take place with Germany. No warning to Nazis and their collaborators was issued, no approaches made to the Vatican, no guarantees for the upkeep of refugees and their care after the war were given to neutral countries. Moreover, all of these negative decisions were left unannounced and secret, while hope was held out for a time that more positive ones had been reached.

Jewish organizations in America were, on the whole, fairly well informed about the failures of the Bermuda Conference. But they did not respond with plans of their own. In addition to the formidable psychological hindrances to action hinted at already, there were certain objective circumstances that militated against "radical" demonstrations, hunger strikes, and the like. Any such actions would have had to be taken against the Roosevelt administration, which, for all its shortcomings, had stood between the Jews and American antisemitism. Any demonstration against the government would be perceived as a demonstration against the war. Jews in 1943 simply could not demonstrate against Roosevelt.

Some action was attempted, and might have been more successful if more representative groups had joined: the mission in the United States of the extremist underground Revisionist Irgun organized an Emergency Rescue Committee which roped in senators and congressmen and demanded action, such as sending funds to Nazi-controlled territory and creating a special governmental agency to deal with rescue plans. But their activity, aimed at maximum publicity and lobbying, went far beyond what JDC considered its proper line of approach.

Slowly, as 1943 came to an end and 1944 arrived, the tragedy was accepted as fact—not really grasped, not really understood, but accepted as a kind of verdict after which life had to go on. Luckily perhaps for the Jewish people, JDC was the type of organization that took no time to stop and reflect on what had happened. There was a job to be done. Those who could be helped had to be helped; those who had to move had to be moved. Had Joseph Schwartz and others had time to stop and ponder over the murder of the Jewish people, would they have had the strength to carry on? On November 15, 1943, the Jewish National Committee in underground Warsaw sent a message to London: "The blood of three million Jews will cry out for revenge not only against the Hitlerite beasts, but also against the indifferent groups that, words apart, did not do anything to rescue the nation that was sentenced to destruction by the Hitlerite murderers."[29] And, in the autumn of 1944, David Ben Gurion wrote an article called "Before the Tribunal of History," in which he asked:

What have you done to us, you freedom-loving peoples, guardians of justice, defenders of the high principles of democracy and of the brotherhood of man? What have you allowed to be perpetrated against a defenceless people while you stood aside and let it bleed to death, without offering help or succour, without calling on the fiends to stop, in the language of retribution which alone they would understand? Why do you profane our pain and wrath with empty expressions of sympathy which ring like a mockery in the ears of millions of the damned in the torture houses of Nazi Europe? Why have you not even supplied arms to our ghetto rebels, as you have done for the partisans and underground fighters of other nations? Why did you not help us to establish contacts with them, as you have done in the case of the partisans in Greece and Yugoslavia and the underground movements elsewhere? If, instead of Jews, thousands of English, American or Russian women, children and aged had been tortured every day, burnt to death, asphyxiated in gas chambers—would you have acted in the same way?[30]

That was the context within which JDC conducted its work.

8

JDC-Lisbon, 1942–1943

At first it seemed that the entry of the United States into the war might spell the end of direct JDC action in Europe. Americans were being evacuated from all over Europe, and on December 11, 1942, JDC-New York cabled to Joseph Schwartz: "Believe entire staff should be evacuated immediately."[1] Augusto d'Esaguy was leaving Lisbon, and, with the impending departure of Joseph Schwartz and the other Americans, the Commissão de Assistencia aos Judios Refugiados dissolved, leaving Moses B. Amzalak, the most powerful figure in the Portuguese Jewish community, in direct charge of refugee affairs. A three-months' budget was left behind, and Schwartz suggested that Saly Mayer in Switzerland be asked to establish a kind of clearinghouse for JDC work in Europe. Schwartz would stay a bit longer than his staff to settle all these matters. JDC work would continue to be carried out through U.S. diplomatic representatives stationed in Europe, and the fact of continued activity would have to be stressed. Jewish communities all over the United States had begun flooding the New York office with queries, which, on the whole, expressed the expectation that JDC would stop its activities overseas now that America was in the war. One could almost hear a sigh of relief that, for the duration at least, communities would no longer be required to support JDC's work.[2]

Schwartz himself seems to have agreed with the idea of abandoning the Lisbon office, at least at first. He thought that his main duty after Pearl Harbor was to get the hundreds of visa-holders out of Europe.[3] With ships booked weeks and months ahead for American citizens returning home, finding places for refugees was very difficult, but JDC's entire organization sprang into action to guarantee that not a single holder of a valid visa to the western hemisphere would be left behind. Fear that Spain and Portugal might be occupied by the Germans became stronger, and from January, 1942, Rommel's big victories in the western desert were coupled with expectations of a new German offensive in Russia. By about February, 500 visa-holders remained after Schwartz had succeeded, against tremendous odds, in shipping 1,400 to the Americas.

JDC originally thought that the organization of ships for visa-holders would be the only direct work the organization might still accomplish in Europe after Pearl Harbor. But soon Schwartz began to realize that there were great possibilities for doing good from Lisbon. One could work in France, in Spain, in Portugal itself, and in North Africa. In addition, one could reach Switzerland via Vichy France, with which the United States still maintained diplomatic ties. Parcels could be sent to Nazi Europe, and a listening post as well as a supervisory point for activities centered in Switzerland could be of great importance. The Treasury Department was willing to grant licenses to transfer funds raised in America to Lisbon, as long as proper controls were maintained. Furthermore, American Jews increased their giving for overseas causes. Contributions in 1941 had been very modest, amounting to a mere $6,078,769, the lowest total in the war. But in 1942 they were $7,385,725, and JDC spent $6.3 million as compared to $5.7 million in 1941. These figures do not show great improvement, perhaps, but they are remarkable as the first indication of a trend. Increased awareness of general issues, fostered by the war, was coupled with greater knowledge of the terrible facts and the beginning of a sense of obligation to European Jewry. The developing war economy also eliminated the last vestiges of the Depression and enabled people to give more. It is therefore not surprising that Schwartz began to consider staying in Lisbon after all. Initially JDC was reluctant and—until the first licenses were granted—unable to send money. JDC-New York was told in February, 1942, that Schwartz was "willing to stay if he could be helpful, but he was getting requests to help and all he could do was to say 'no' to these requests."[4] In the end the money came, and the work, which had in fact never stopped, continued.

The original estimates of "hundreds" of visa-holders proved widely off the mark. It turned out that between January and July, 1942, 4,058 Jewish refugees were transported to safety in eight JDC-organized sailings from the Iberian peninsula (as compared to 3,682 in nine sailings between June and the end of the year 1941).[5] The methods by which these sailings had to be organized were nerve-racking indeed. Berths on neutral ships had to be paid for, though the refugees, coming from a Spanish camp or from unoccupied France, might be prevented from arriving. However, JDC and HICEM managed to get out all of the people with papers enabling them to leave Europe. The saving of these thousands of people was not eased by the complications that many Latin American states, and the United States, put in the way of the potential escapees.

During the first months of 1942, when he still thought that help to such people was about the only thing he could do from Lisbon, Schwartz tried to create good relations with the Lisbon American legation by offering to pay for impecunious Americans returning from Europe after Pearl Harbor. In the end the State Department paid for these people, but some American Jews received JDC help in getting back, in order to counteract a feeling prevalent (Schwartz believed) at the legation that JDC was helping only aliens and that it should do something for American citizens too.[6] JDC-Lisbon depended on the legation for help, and reports from it to Washington might affect the granting of licenses and other essential items. Visas to the United States were almost out of reach for European Jews. They had to be near an American consulate; they had to prove they would not become a public liability in America and that none of their close relatives had remained under Nazi rule. As this was practicably impossible, except in a small number of cases, most Jews turned to Latin American countries. Cuba especially was a desired country of entry, because most people hoped they would be able to get an entry visa to the United States from Havana. In the end, most people did.

Settlement Schemes and Emigration to the Western Hemisphere

Settling Jews on the land in various parts of Latin America and in the Philippines was a dream that some of JDC's leaders had pursued in the wake of the Agro-Joint venture of settling Jews in the Crimea in the early thirties.[7] Joseph A. Rosen, the great agricultural expert and social engineer, had been responsible for that work, and when he was forced to abandon his Russian enterprise in 1938, he had turned his attention to the western hemisphere. Rosen's new activities coincided with the American and British interest in finding a haven for Jewish refugees outside the Middle East. An attempt to designate British Guiana for that purpose was made with Rosen's hesitating approval, but the scheme fell through for financial and political reasons. Agro-Joint received repayments on its Russian loans and investments from the Soviet government until 1940, so that some money was available.

Rafael L. Trujillo, the Dominican dictator, had expressed willingness to accept 100,000 Jewish refugees at the Evian Conference in 1938. It is hardly likely that he meant this figure to be taken seriously, but he certainly wanted to attract Jewish funds and agriculturalists who would develop a pilot scheme for the settlement of Jewish refugees. Trujillo's purposes were in tune with Roosevelt's dreams for vast areas of settlement for refugees, though hardly with the State Department's more cautious approach. James N. Rosenberg, head of Agro-Joint, founded the Dominican Republic Settlement Association (DORSA) on December 9, 1939. A survey indicated that some 28,000 people could be settled on land donated by Trujillo and in other areas. By March, 1940, DORSA, financed by JDC through Agro-Joint, appropriated $500,000, which grew to $855,000 by the end of 1941. By the end of 1944, $1,423,000 had been invested, with most of the money coming from JDC, and Rosenberg was asking for more money. He wanted to show that Jews could work on the land and succeed, even outside of Palestine. He thought that too much was spent on Palestine; rather, "from the point of view, both of the Dominican Republic and the State Department of the US it is, in my opinion, a matter of paramount importance" to allocate more money to DORSA.[8] A success at Sosua, the experimental settlement in the Dominican Republic, would open the way for large-scale settlement of Jews.

The scheme was beset with difficulties from the beginning. Rosen had to leave Sosua for health reasons, and his successors did not possess his skill, especially in the area of social and human relations. Most of the immigrants were German Jews who refused to adjust to their new environment and who transferred their yearning for German culture to the tropical island. A detailed and expert report written in late 1944 stated that, as far as the settlers were concerned, Sosua was only a transit point to greener pastures. "They told me not to convert them to Zionism. The cowbarn does not interest them. They do not want to be settled here and work on roads and fences is not for them."[9] About 1,000 other Jews escaped to Sosua from Europe, but many of these came from England or had reached Portugal and Spain on their own. The number of people who were actually saved from Nazi Europe by emigrating to the Dominican Republic was rather small. The end result was that a grand total of 159 Jews were settled on the land, and 285 had drifted away to an industrial area at Batey. Most of the work on the farms was done by hired Dominican labor. The rest of the refugees made their way to the capital, San Jose (now Ciudad Trujillo), and from there to the United States. With the growing security scare, American and British services vied with each other in ridiculous accusations against the settlers, whom they suspected of fifth-column activities.[10]

A similar venture was made in Bolivia, where in 1941 a company called Sociedad Colonizadora de Bolivia (SOCOBO) was founded to promote Jewish settlement. In that year 142 people were settled there, but they drifted away; experts sent from time to time created a muddle by proposing opposing and difficult schemes. No attempt was made to educate townspeople into agriculturalists, and by the end of 1944, only nine families remained on the farm.[11] Five hundred thousand dollars had been spent.

Other attempts, in the Phillippines and elsewhere, did not reach a practical stage. Money was invested for surveys, but nothing came of them. One must conclude that these settlement projects were ill-advised and proved absolute failures. The claim that at least some refugees were saved is not convincing; many more could probably have been saved with the money spent on these attempts. Why did they fail? It would seem, judging from the reports of Agro-Joint experts at Sosua, that the basic problem was the lack of purposeful commitment necessary if people who had lived in towns all their lives were to adjust to working on the land. The only permanent success in settling Jews on the land was in Palestine, where the national Jewish revival permitted a sense of purpose for which no substitute was found elsewhere. Sosua was not by the Jordan, and San Jose was not Jerusalem. It was as simple as that.

JDC also tried to save thousands by piecemeal immigration to Latin America. Immediately upon the American entry into the war, the S.S. *Cabo de Hornos,* carrying 107 refugees equipped with Brazilian visas, sailed for South America. While they were afloat, the Brazilians canceled the visas retroactively and then admitted the 20 Catholics among the boat's refugees when it arrived on December, 1941. In the end, through JDC intervention, 86 Jewish passengers were admitted to Curaçao in the Dutch West Indies, where they were put up in a special camp at JDC expense.[12]

In April, Cuba closed its doors to further Jewish immigration; Mexico followed suit. So did other countries in Latin America, and by mid-1942 the possibilities of escaping from Europe were very slender. Jamaica accepted 152 Polish refugees, all of whom were Jews; occasional individuals with special qualifications could enter Britain. All the new refugees arriving in American countries had to be supported. JDC spent large sums keeping the people fed and housed so that the countries concerned might have an incentive to accept more Jews. Especially important was Charles Jordan's job as JDC representative in Cuba, where $125,850 were spent in the first nine months of 1942 alone in looking after the refugees. JDC was spending about $750,000 a year in Latin America, and it was clearly that investment that made it possible for more Jews to escape there. By April, 1942, Cuba had accepted 6,000 refugees, of whom 5,600 had come during the preceding twelve months. By that time, about 30,000 Jewish refugees were being supported by relief committees subsidized by JDC, out of a total population of some 460,000 Jews in all the countries south of the Rio Grande.[13]

JDC's Involvement with North African Jewry

From 1940 on, JDC was increasingly involved in North Africa. Some 400,000 Jews lived there, most of them in primitive conditions, surrounded by a population which considered them inferior. In Morocco especially, Jews had a definitely subordinate role in Muslim society; they were infidels, to be protected, but having duties and no rights. Jewish property was always liable to be taken or destroyed by hostile mobs. In Algiers, the 125,000 Jews were considered French citizens, in line with the so-called Crémieux Law of 1870, and thus placed in a legal position that was superior to that of the Muslims. In Tunis, most of the 60,000–70,000 Jews, except for those who were foreign nationals, were considered the Bey's subjects and protected by local and French authorities, but again not equally with the Muslim population.

When France fell, alien Jews who had volunteered for the French Legion were transferred into what amounted to forced labor units; they were lodged in concentration camps and assigned the work of building a trans-Saharan railway. The Jews and the Spanish Republicans, who formed the majority among the 5,000 inmates of these French camps, were treated with great brutality. Of the Jews, 1,500 survived, but there is no exact accounting of the many who succumbed. The camp at Columb-Béchar in Algiers was especially notorious.

In addition to these forced laborers, approximately 5,000 civilian Jewish refugees managed to leave France for Algiers and Morocco by the end of 1941. Some arrived by ship, such as those aboard the S.S. *Alsina,* which was stopped at Dakar with 340 refugees, who were taken off and interned in January, 1941. Some sources estimate that, in the first chaotic months after the fall of France, 10,000 refugees, most of them Jewish, passed through Casablanca on their way to the Americas. This figure is probably exaggerated and in any case impossible to check. What is clear is that a Jewish refugee committee was established in Casablanca by Helen Benatar, which after some hesitation formed a working relationship with JDC. A HICEM representative, Raphael Spanien, arrived to help with emigration, and 1,500 of the 5,000 managed to leave North Africa again in 1941. Of the rest, the majority were interned in camps that resembled those at Gurs and Rivesaltes in France. The most infamous of these camps, as far as the Jews were concerned, was the one at Sidi el Ayachi, not far from Casablanca. There were probably 500 refugees of this type in Algeria, concentrated at Djelfa and Berroughia.

As 1941 passed into 1942, most Jewish civilians were released, especially in Morocco, thanks to the intervention of Mme. Benatar and some of her allies among the French officials. However, a residue of a few hundred people still remained in the camps, and of course all the forced laborers. JDC began supporting the Benatar committee in December, 1940. By the end of 1941, $15,500 had been spent, and the same amount was sent there in 1942. Local collections supplemented the JDC allocations. In Algiers, the Association d'étude d'assistance sociale of the local community began to be supported by JDC in 1941, and by the end of 1942, $36,000 had been sent. Smaller programs were started for Tangier, where 350 of the 1,000 refugees in a population of 8,000

Jews had to be aided, and in Tunisia, where an initial 200 Jewish families whom the Germans had expelled from Libya had to be supported.

This essentially was the picture when the Allies landed in North Africa on November 8, 1942. The Americans began working through Admiral Jean-François Darlan, Pétain's main supporter and minister, who happened to be in Algiers when the Americans conquered it. When Darlan was assassinated in December, their man was General Henri Giraud, an essentially antiliberal opponent of Pétain. They would not work through Charles de Gaulle and his supporters. Moreover, contrary to the hopes of opponents of the Vichy regime, at first no changes occurred, either in the persons running the area or in the Vichy laws, which remained in full force. These had included the whole gamut of discriminatory anti-Jewish legislation which in France had prepared the ground for the Final Solution. The forced labor units remained in their camps, as did the civilian internees. For good measure, they were joined by Italians who were now arrested as supporters of the Axis.

The Jews of Algiers had actively helped in the Allied landings. Led by the Aboulker family, they had risen against the Vichy French and aided in the capture of the town of Algiers. They were now in effect being abandoned to the mercies of the antisemitic Vichy officials. The Americans refused to intervene in "internal affairs" such as French concentration camps, though out of military and political convenience rather than malice. Intervention by Henry Morgenthau, secretary of the treasury, and a spate of press reports in the *New York Times* and *Washington Post* began to change the situation slowly. Roosevelt announced on November 18, 1942, that all vestiges of Nazi rule and laws would be removed. However, nothing much happened, and indeed the situation of the Jews grew worse. Some protested in the form of hunger strikes; some escaped from the camps but were picked up by the French and reinterned. Schwartz decided that the time had come to take part in the press campaign, and on February 10, 1943, an account appeared in the American press of an interview with him in New York in which he lambasted the treatment of the Jews and demanded the release of Jewish and Spanish internees.[14]

In the meantime, in January, the inmates of Sidi el Ayachi had been freed, and over a period of four months those at other sites were also set free. In Algiers, the releases were accomplished with the active participation of the local JDC-supported committee under Eli Gozlan, who used forceful methods in achieving his aim. By March, 1943, he had managed to get 1,600 internees of all kinds out of the camps, though another 600 remained in them. A Quaker representative described Gozlan as a man with "a great deal of ability. He cares for Jews and non-Jews, and is greatly idolized by his clients."[15]

General Giraud, prompted by a Gaullist representative who increasingly influenced his political stand, declared all Vichy laws, including the anti-Jewish ones, abolished on March 14, 1943. However, he also abolished the Crémieux Law for Algiers, leaving the Jews in a position worse than that they enjoyed in 1939. It took another energetic campaign, lasting until November, to restore the decree.

In 1943, JDC increased its involvement in North Africa, a decision made in response to new conditions. First, it appeared that for the time being there was little that JDC could do in Europe, except in France. Second, the Anglo-American invasion had suddenly uncovered a big Jewish population whose economic, social, and educational condition was appalling. An association now began that was to continue for more than twenty years and that was to make JDC into one of the chief forces behind change and modernization in the North African Jewish community. The first JDC representative, Max S. Perlman, arrived in North Africa in September, 1943; about the same time, Donald B. Hurwitz, who had represented JDC in London, was called upon to make a survey of conditions and needs in the vast area. There were then apparently 4,500 Jewish refugees in Algiers and Morocco, besides 1,000 in Tangier. Money was given to the committees in Algiers and Morocco to deal with the situation, and the total given to both countries in 1943 came to approximately $80,000. For the first time, JDC became involved with medical work and education in North Africa, after the elementary needs for clothing and emergency relief had been met.[16]

Another difficult situation arose in Tunisia, where direct German rule had hit the Jewish community for a few months. "The Jewish community was abandoned completely by the French authorities who neither could nor would do anything on their behalf. They were abandoned by the Moslem majority who saw an opportunity to acquire some of the possessions of the Jewish group."[17] Five thousand Jews had done forced labor and had to be paid by the Jewish community, and a fine imposed by the Nazis had forced the community to borrow 58 million fr. from local French banks. These banks had demanded repayment. With British agreement, it was postponed until after the war, though the U.S. Treasury Department representatives demanded outright cancellation. No less vexing were the problems of reinstating Jewish officials and returning Jewish property. Education was dealt with largely by the Alliance israélite universelle, the old French Jewish cultural and social welfare organization, but medical work and relief had to be provided by JDC. Especially important was the question of the refugees from Bizerta in Tunis, 1,800 of them, and of 700 Libyan Jews, all of whom had to be reestablished in the Tunisian communities. Even Libya received $4,000 from JDC after WJC intervened there by sending $2,000 to help the local Jews. A JDC representative commented that the money was not really needed because Jewish troops from Palestine had "adopted" the local community and helped it along before JDC and WJC could arrive.[18]

JDC soon redirected its efforts in Tunisia, Algeria, and Morocco, switching from immediate to long-term problems. Efficient local committees under the supervision of American staff took measures to look after the refugees and then try to ameliorate the situation in the indigenous communities. A disproportionately large amount of money was spent in Tangier, where Jews formed 10 percent of the population. A well-organized community committee under Jacob Laredo had to see to it that the Spanish government that had ruled the formerly international city since 1940 did not turn against them. Eighty thousand dollars were sent there in 1943 to deal with problems of emigration and support of refugees.[19]

The Refugee Problem in the Iberian Peninsula

The third main area of activities directed by JDC-Lisbon in 1942 and 1943 was in Spain and Portugal. In Spain, the tenuous link that had been maintained with refugees through Dorsey Stephens, the wife of the American military attaché, was breaking because Carlton J. H. Hayes, the new ambassador, was opposed to such activity. According to Hayes, he based his objections "entirely on instructions from Washington" that a distribution of private relief should not be made by the embassy.[20] Worse still, it was impossible to obtain American visas for Jewish stateless or other detainees in Spanish camps or prisons. The American consul refused to visit the camps, and the inmates were not allowed out. Schwartz clashed rather sharply with Hayes. In his view,

Hayes "was a good man, but he was interested primarily . . . in two things . . . : in getting American prisoners of war out of France and across Spain, and he thought that any activity of getting Jewish refugees out of France across Spain would be a hindrance." Hayes looked at JDC's activities "as a sort of nuisance." Moreover, Hayes was a devout Catholic, who "would not recognize that there was a problem of antisemitism in Spain, which there was." Hayes therefore did not intervene as rigorously as he might have on behalf of the Jewish refugees." And while he undoubtedly was a liberal, his attitude, in Schwartz's opinion, "was not the most sympathetic."[21]

Schwartz was not alone in having difficulties in Spain. The AFSC and the Unitarians were also having problems with a fascist government which did not allow non-Catholic organizations any foothold in its country. Once again, however, the close alliance of the Friends and JDC enabled both groups to find a solution. Through Philip Conard, the AFSC representative in Lisbon, Schwartz suggested to Hayes that a Quaker should represent both organizations working out of the embassy. The Spanish government agreed to this procedure, because it meant that there would still be no official representation of non-Catholic groups in the country. Accordingly, David J. Blickenstaff and his Spanish-born wife, Janine, arrived in Madrid on January 27, 1943, and began supervising the Madrid end of relief activities, which included the Miranda de Ebro camp (until then looked after by Samuel Sequerra from Barcelona). Blickenstaff's office was finally officially recognized by the Spanish government on April 10, 1943, as the representative in Spain of the American relief organizations. At first JDC and AFSC alone were represented, with JDC paying 75 percent of the costs. In September, the Unitarians also joined, and JDC then paid 40 percent.[22]

Table 19: JDC Expenditures, Spain and Portugal, 1941–42

	Year	Dollars	*Percent of Total JDC Expenditures*
Spain	1941	33,592	
	1942	481,722	7.6
Portugal	1941	221,276	
	1942	324,119	5.1

Spanish attitudes toward refugees were determined by the course of the war. In the summer of 1942, people crossing the border were not, as a rule, returned to France, but they were put into the Miranda camp or kept in prisons. One must realize that Jewish refugees did not constitute more than 15 or 20 percent of those who were crossing the Pyrenees. The major problems, as far as the Spanish government was concerned, were Allied prisoners of war escaping from German camps, airmen shot down over France making their way to Spain, and French and other potential soldiers crossing the border in order to join their national units fighting the Germans. Fortunately for the refugee Jews, their fate was closely linked to that of the others, in many of whom the Allied representatives were interested. A general closing of the border was therefore very much against the Allied interest, and as one did not know whether any particular party was Jewish, or stateless, or perhaps consisted of Jews who were Allied nationals and wanted to join the Allied forces, both closing the border to Jews and returning them to France was against Allied interests.

Frightened by the mass deportations from France in the summer of 1942, hundreds of Jews crossed the border, some with the help of the French Catholic priest, Pierre Marie-Benoit, and some through OSE, but most on their own initiative. In July, there seemed to be a real danger that the Spaniards would hand over 500 Jewish refugees to the Germans on the border. A WJC request in Washington caused Hayes to intervene in Spain, and on August 14, he could inform Washington that the danger of deportation had passed. In the early autumn, however, with the seemingly tremendous advances of the German armies in the east, Spanish attitudes suggested that Spain had decided to deport the Jews. "Situation refugees Spain including both new arrivals and old group extremely critical," Schwartz cabled on October 26. "In Barcelona arrests being made on mass scale with object return entire refugee population not in possession residence cards to France." On October 29, Schwartz advised JDC-New York that ten persons had actually been deported on the previous day, apparently to test the Allied reaction. Organized border crossings were becoming more frequent, and the number of refugees was steadily increasing. On November 6, Schwartz again insisted that the entire refugee population was in grave danger, though he indicated that the local authorities in Barcelona were especially antiforeign; those in Bilbao and Vigo were less so.[23]

The basic change in the situation occurred after the Allied landing in North Africa on November 8, 1942, the subsequent occupation of southern France by the Germans on November 11, and the consequent German occupation of the full length of the Franco-Spanish border. For a moment Spain wavered between neutrality and immediate intervention in the war on Germany's side, but moderate counsel prevailed. Indeed, the weight of the massive Allied force south of Spain and on the seas made the Spanish government more amenable to Allied pressure against deportations. On November 9, the first secretary to the American legation at Madrid intervened to prevent the deportation of the Jewish refugees, because it might serve as a precedent for similar treatment of Allied personnel. But what seems to have been decisive were the pleas of the Vichy ambassador to Spain, François Piétri, on November 14–17, not to return refugees to France now that the Germans had occupied all her territory. Spain decided to desist from deportations.

A similar situation arose in the early spring of 1943. The growing number of refugees, coupled with German pressure, led Spain, on March 23, to announce the closure of her border to any further unauthorized entry. JDC accounts indicate that at Barcelona and Pamplona especially, police headquarters were pressing for such a step to be taken. Immediate British and American interventions caused Spain to declare that Allied military personnel would not be prevented from crossing, but that Spain reserved her judgment as to all the others. Winston Churchill then decided to intervene personally, and on April 7, 1943, told the Spanish ambassador in London that closing the border to refugees would be considered an unfriendly act. The Americans, the papal nuncio in Washington, and the Argentinian embassy at Madrid also protested. In some cases refugees were handed over to the Germans, but Spain retreated from her March announcement and the border remained relatively open. It is very difficult to establish how many Jews managed to cross the border into Spain from early 1942 until the liberation of France, but the best estimate seems to be 7,500 for the period from August, 1942, to August, 1944, with a few hundred added for the early months of 1942.[24] Of these, about one-half were Jews holding French citizenship.

Probably the major burden in caring for the non-French, mainly stateless (ex-Polish, German, Austrian, or Czech), Jews was carried by Samuel Sequerra in Barcelona. Working out of a hotel and plagued by visits from the police, who on one occa-

sion simply took away all his files, he nevertheless managed to
create a kind of semiofficial position for himself in behalf of JDC
(officially he represented the Portuguese Red Cross). Sequerra
succeeded, sometimes by unorthodox methods, in thwarting the
police's desire to hamper his activities. He was helped by a
friendly British consul at Barcelona, who agreed to support stateless refugees with JDC funds on the general grounds that speed-
ing up emigration and assuring the maintenance of the refugees
would further the possibility of getting more potential soldiers
into Spain.

Nevertheless, in late 1942, Sequerra noted that at the Miranda camp he was able "to see their very desperate situation
despite the efforts which the Joint is making."[25] There was no
warm clothing and the barracks were practically open to the elements. JDC sent more help, but the problems were very grim,
especially between October, 1942, and July, 1943. At the end of
December, 1942, there were 3,500 internees at Miranda, instead of
the 1,400 who had been there in October. A "forced residence"
(confinement to a village or town) for women and children was
opened in December at Caldas de Malavella. In January, the authorities began to release people from Miranda to other forced
residences, especially people who were being supported by some
foreign legation. JDC intervention with the Spanish Red Cross
caused the inclusion of many JDC protégés among them.

For purely administrative reasons, the situation seemed to
take a turn for the worse in July, when most of those in forced
residences were rounded up and sent back to Miranda in cattle
cars. It is not quite clear what happened after that, but most
refugees were soon sent back to their residences. In August, 1943,
JDC was assisting about 1,500 people through the Barcelona and
Madrid offices. The subventions were large (650 pesetas—about
$60—per person per month) and equaled the salaries of Spanish
officials; there was some discontent over this fact, but JDC-Lisbon
thought, probably rightly, that if the subventions were reduced
these people might face Miranda or worse. The relief work that
went on through the Blickenstaff and Sequerra offices continued
through 1943 and into the spring of 1944.

While the Spanish government afforded grudging toleration
to Jewish refugees, its overall attitude toward Jews can only be
described as unfriendly. This can be clearly seen in its handling of
European Jews of Spanish extraction, who had been granted
Spanish citizenship or protection prior to the war and were now

trying to escape into Spain. Germany decided to give Spain and the other neutral countries until March 31, 1943, to repatriate Spanish nationals of the Jewish "race." Any Jews left behind after that date would be treated as all the Jews were.[26] Spain was not interested; the Spanish ambassador in Berlin suggested to the Germans on February 24, 1943, that all Spanish Jewish passport-holders be sent to Greece or Turkey, saying also that Spain would be willing to offer transit visas to the United States or Portugal. Those who could not go to these places because they had no end visas (which meant all of them) would be of no further interest to Spain. Pleas from Jewish holders of Spanish passports in Paris and from a local Spanish commercial society, coupled with memoranda from the Paris and Berlin Spanish embassies, caused Spanish Foreign Minister Francisco Gómez Jordana to soften this policy somewhat, and, on March 15, he advised the Germans that some Spanish nationals would be repatriated. This was followed on March 22 by a note declaring that bona fide Spanish nationals would be taken back.

The German ultimatum and the various Spanish responses to it occurred during preparations for the Bermuda Conference, and Blickenstaff told the Spaniards that JDC would support the Jewish Spanish nationals; that at least was what the authorities understood, though Blickenstaff's offer apparently was ambiguous.[27] The first of the repatriates came in May, and by the end of the war, a maximum of 800 had been saved in this way from France, Saloniki, and Athens. This was only a small portion of the several thousand holders of Spanish passports in Nazi Europe, in most of whom Spain declared its lack of interest and who were consequently deported and killed. We shall have occasion later to deal briefly with Hungarian Jews who received Spanish protection letters in late 1944; it seems that the total number of Jews saved through Spain or Spanish intervention of one kind or another in the latter part of the war was about 11,500 (7,500 who crossed the border, 800 who were repatriated, and 3,200 Hungarian Jews).[28]

Early in 1943, the facts regarding the destruction of European Jewry began to be realized in their full extent. When, therefore, Herbert Katzki asked JDC-New York in August, 1943, whether the organization would now guarantee to support any Balkan Jews who might be saved by Spain, the immediate reply was positive.[29] JDC did in fact maintain these people, some of whom later received certificates for Palestine. Furthermore, it be-

came clear immediately upon the arrival of the first of the repatriates that Spain had no intention of treating them as Spanish citizens. With a few exceptions, they had to leave and find homes
elsewhere. As the government informed Blickenstaff on August
16, 1943, that more repatriates would be allowed to come only if
those already in Spain left, JDC had to place a priority on emigrating these so-called Sephardics as quickly as possible.

The establishment of a transit camp in North Africa to relieve the pressure on Spain had been decided at the Bermuda
Conference. However, on April 26, 1943, the American chiefs of
staff who now bore the brunt of the responsibility for French
North Africa refused to allow it, both because it might create
opposition from the local Arabs and because it was superfluous
from a military point of view. The British tried to change the
American position but failed. In the end, the problem was
brought before President Roosevelt, who decided, on May 14,
that while it would be "extremely unwise" to bring too many
Jews to such a camp, it should nevertheless be established as a
kind of depot. When little progress was made, Winston Churchill,
pressed in Parliament for some kind of action to help Nazi victims, on June 30 asked Roosevelt to speed up action. As a result,
a camp was set up at Fedhalla (later moved to Philippeville),
which began to operate late in 1943. By the time France was
liberated, not more than 630 Jewish refugees had been moved to
Fedhalla from Spain, among them many of the Sephardics.[30]
Needless to say, JDC was involved in paying for transport to the
camp; Moses Beckelman volunteered to direct it for the United
Nations Relief and Rehabilitation Administration, established in
the autumn of 1943.

Cooperative Rescue Efforts in Portugal and Spain

JDC's work in the peninsula was strongly influenced by the
relationships it established with other Jewish organizations working there. Its affiliation with JA was especially close and cordial.
JA had discussed the question of representation in Lisbon as early
as 1942, but nothing came of it, largely because of administrative
muddle and sheer inefficiency at JA's Jerusalem center. JDC was
very interested in having someone come in and grant Palestine
certificates to as many stateless Jews as possible, but JA procrastinated in its search for the person to do this job.

The question of a JA representative was closely connected with another problem, that of Isaac Weissman, a Turkish-born refugee of Polish Jewish ancestry, aged fifty, who had been in Lisbon since June, 1940. Early in 1941, he became the unofficial representative of RELICO. Motivated by a burning desire to do something, regardless of diplomatic niceties and legal permits, Weissman clashed with the official Jewish community in Lisbon and its head, Moses Amzalak. On the other hand, he persuaded the Polish representative to grant him a Polish passport and established close relations with Charles Gorlier, the Free French representative, and with Sir John Hart of the British legation. He became, in fact, an Allied undercover agent, organizing courier services into occupied territory with the help of a double agent called "Alexander."

Weissman received most of his information from Alfred Silberschein in Switzerland, and he transmitted it to WJC in America and to his French and British friends. In 1942, he began looking after the some 200 illegal entrants into Portugal; there was no organization attempting to legalize them. Weissman asked for an authorization from WJC that he was its representative, but WJC was uncertain. HICEM and JDC, whose whole existence in Portugal was predicated on strict observance of Portuguese regulations, did not want to risk their work for many thousands of Jewish immigrants in order to bring additional illegal immigrants from Spain or from France, as Weissman was now trying to do. The only allies he had were the Unitarians under Dr. Robert C. Dexter, who, with his wife, was looking after precisely this type of person.

Weissman got permission from the Portuguese Alien Police, under Captain Catella, to liberate the illegal immigrants from their prisons and assign them to a residence at a place called Ericeira, outside Lisbon. He then approached JDC-Lisbon and asked it to support the people he had thus managed to release. He was at that time unknown to JDC, but known and disliked by the Lisbon Jewish community. JDC replied that it would support Weissman's group just as it supported all other Jews, but that it would not do so through his committee. Its suspicion of Weissman was strengthened when "Alexander" was exposed as a double agent by the British and JDC was warned against any contact with him or his associates. However, on the strength of a recommendation by a Palestinian Jewish journalist in Lisbon, JA in Jerusalem suggested Weissman as its representative for the purpose of distrib-

213

uting Palestine immigration certificates. When this was suggested to HICEM, which of course was kept informed by JDC and Amzalak, it declined vehemently. By that time Weissman had finally obtained recognition as RELICO's representative in Lisbon, and in June, 1943, he became WJC's representative too. The pattern, therefore, of JDC cooperation with JA and opposition to WJC's attempts at relief was repeated in Lisbon.

The person JA finally chose to handle the Palestine certificates was Wilfrid B. Israel, a Berlin-born member of an important British Jewish family and an ardent Zionist. Israel had been a close friend of the Warburg family and had many connections with influential Jews and non-Jews in Britain. On March 26, 1943, he left London for Lisbon, and stayed in the peninsula until May 31. He found up to 1,500 stateless Jews in Spain, and decided to grant Palestine certificates to approximately 200 of them. He also proposed to Sir Samuel Hoare, the British ambassador, that the rest either should be emigrated to various countries under existing procedures or recruited into the Allied forces; only some 15 percent would remain to be looked after locally. This proposal was submitted with Schwartz's concurrence, and when Israel left on June 1, it seemed that the efforts of these two men might go a long way toward improving the local situation. The aircraft that carried Israel back to England (and on which the actor Leslie Howard, a Hungarian Jew, also flew) was shot down by the Germans. The Jewish people had lost another remarkable personality.

The whole process of selection and preparation of those who were to receive certificates had to begin again. This time JA chose Peretz Lichtenstein (now Leshem), who arrived in Portugal in October, 1943. His direct dealings were with HICEM, which apparently did not much like JA's intrusion into emigration, feeling that it was their bailiwick. In any case, HICEM's attitude to Palestine was not particularly sympathetic, and Leshem complained that some of the candidates to whom HICEM promised Palestine certificates were quite unsuitable. On the other hand, later criticism of Leshem from Jerusalem was even more severe—on precisely the same grounds. HICEM and JDC and Leshem together finally obtained a ship to transport the emigrants, and on February 1, 1944, 757 people reached Haifa on the S.S. *Nyassa;* 425 more arrived on the S.S. *Guinee* on November 4. Leshem returned to London in January, 1944, leaving Lisbon without a JA representative.

In the meantime, Joseph Schwartz's relations with Weissman's WJC operation did not improve. Weissman tried to effect

more illegal entries, especially of children, into the Iberian peninsula, a parallel effort by Dr. Paul Block, a German Jewish refugee
working out of Blickenstaff's office in Madrid, having failed. In
early 1944, Weissman moved WJC to cause radio broadcasts from
Algeria to France that called on the French population to hide
Jewish children. At the same time he apparently also sent a Span-
iard, Manuel Alvez, to bring children from France into Spain. He
wanted to bring them into Portugal, and in the late spring obtained authority to establish a home for such children near Lisbon. Schwartz was very unhappy with these activities. Weissman
did not know, because Schwartz mistrusted him deeply, but by
the spring of 1944, JDC—or, rather, Schwartz—was also deeply
involved in bringing out children through its contacts with Jules
Jefroykin in France. Hundreds of these children did cross the
mountains, but they were taken to Barcelona, which made more
sense from JDC's point of view than taking them to Lisbon.
Weissman was left with twelve children for a house arranged for
eighty, and he was certain that JDC had not only taken the children away from him, but had also caused the death of Alvez,
who was caught by the Germans.

In June, 1944, Eliahu Dobkin, a member of the JA Executive
in Jerusalem, finally arrived in Lisbon to look after JA's interests.
He reported: "On my arrival I found a shameful situation. Both
parties [WJC and JDC] had been engaged for a long time in a
quarrel which hampered all activities."[31] JA, which maintained
cordial relations with both organizations, tried to mediate. In late
February, 1944, a JA Executive meeting in London under Haim
Weizmann's chairmanship decided, against Weizmann's advice,
to approach JDC with the idea of a body to be called Jewish World
Relief, in which all three organizations would participate. Moshe
Sharett was sent to talk to Schwartz about the proposal. On
March 15, he reported:

> As regards the WJC, Dr. Schwartz said that there could be no
> coordination on any account. Either, he said, the Congress carried
> on political work only which was its right sphere, and then there
> was no necessity of coordination with the Joint, which did no po-
> litical work; or the Congress would interfere in relief work which
> the Joint would never tolerate.[32]

JDC's attitude was brought out very clearly in a letter Joseph
Hyman wrote to Stephen S. Wise in his capacity as president of
the American Jewish Congress, on July 7, 1944, after a direct
confrontation at the JDC office in New York with WJC representa-

tives. Hyman said that he saw no reason for setting up separate, distinct, and competitive machinery for the care of children in Portugal or anywhere else. The scale on which Weissman could operate would hamper rather than further rescue. "We do not challenge the right of other competent organizations or the sincerity of their interest. . . . we do however believe that a centralized effort on the part of a single competent Jewish organization will bring the maximum number of Jews out of danger."[33] The message was clear. Schwartz did not think that WJC was competent to carry out relief and rescue work. Whatever his sympathies may have been with WJC's overall political aims, he had no quarrel with the New York office's attitude to WJC's activity, which was interpreted as meddlesome interference. The meager results of Weissman's efforts as compared with the commotion they caused seemed to justify Schwartz's attitude.

There can be little doubt that terrible consequences would have followed if JDC had succumbed to the temptation to abandon its overseas work after Pearl Harbor. Fortunately, wiser counsels prevailed; Schwartz in particular quickly realized that the organization must not shirk its obligations to suffering European Jewry. The result was an intensive effort to emigrate those who fled to Spain and Portugal to safe havens in the western hemisphere. Help was extended to Jews in North Africa before and after their liberation from the Vichy regime. The fact that more was not done seems traceable to three main causes: insufficient funds; the hostile indifference of the Spanish government and the indifferent neutrality in matters of Jewish rescue of the Anglo-Saxon powers; and inter-Jewish organizational squabbles. JDC did what it could regarding the first of these, stood helpless in the face of the second, and must bear its share of responsibility for the third.

9

"Uncle Saly": The JDC Outpost in Switzerland

After Pearl Harbor, the JDC office in Lisbon was no longer able to handle the task of aiding European Jewry single-handedly. When the United States entered the war, JDC became the agency of a belligerent country and could no longer send funds into enemy-occupied Europe, even to the limited extent that that had been possible while America was still neutral. The organization's central problem became that of loyally following U.S. government instructions forbidding transfer of funds to and human contacts with persons in Nazi-held territories and yet aiding such persons. There is no doubt that the New York office was very much concerned to keep its patriotic American image untarnished, and the lay leaders on its committees saw to it that every transaction should be strictly within the legally permitted framework.

Schwartz in Lisbon was no less a loyal American than his New York superiors, but his task was to bring maximum aid to people suffering what was gradually perceived to be an unprecedented catastrophe. Fortunately, he was not asked to report everything he did—with wartime communications being what they were, this would hardly have been possible even had he wanted to tell everything he knew or did. The result was that while he formally kept within his instructions, he interpreted them in a way which was consonant with European realities as he understood them. It quickly became clear to him, in early 1942, that JDC would have to develop a second center in Europe outside Portugal, which could serve as a conduit of funds and other aid. Such a center would have to be run by a citizen of a neutral country, and while JDC would be unofficially involved, it would have to rely on such a representative to do what he felt was in line with JDC policies without official supervision. Switzerland was the obvious choice for such a center. Unlike Portugal, which had no common frontier with Nazi Europe, Switzerland had been surrounded by Nazi-held territories since 1940. It was still economically viable, had a small but active Jewish community, and its conservative regime was solidly democratic and basically pro-Allies.

The establishment of JDC's base in Switzerland actually predated Pearl Harbor, thanks to the foresight of Morris Troper and Joseph Schwartz. But when the United States entered the war, its development became a matter of utmost urgency. In order to understand JDC's policies in all of Europe in the post-Pearl Harbor era, it is therefore of great importance to look at Switzerland and at the man who was to represent JDC there and thus acquire a central role in the JDC story.

The head of the Schweizerischer Israelitischer Gemeindebund (SIG), the federation of Jewish communities in Switzerland, was Saly Mayer. Mayer was born at Saint Gallen, Switzerland, on June 3, 1882, to a family of well-to-do Swiss Jews whose ancestors had emigrated from southern Germany. He made his living as a lace manufacturer until, in the thirties, he sold his business, invested the proceeds, and lived on the interest. Contrary to later legend, Saly Mayer was not a rich man, only comfortable and secure. He was married to Jeanne Ebstein of Basel, and they had one son, who developed a mental illness and eventually had to be permanently institutionalized. His fate became the private tragedy of Saly Mayer's life and probably explains much about his character and behavior. Apart from his brothers and sisters, with whom he maintained a loyal but not particularly close relationship, he had very few friends. As time went on, he devoted his whole life to the communal and welfare work he was engaged on.

Saly Mayer was a very observant Jew; though by East European standards his knowledge of Jewish law and tradition was superficial, by Swiss standards it was considerable. He used to walk about with the Pirke Avot, the homiletic Mishna tract which contains some of the basic Jewish moral teachings. He knew enough Hebrew to read and understand it, and he also knew some German Yiddish. He strictly observed the sabbath, the holy days, the dietary laws (*kashrut*), and attended the synagogue; yet he was surprisingly uninformed regarding the Jewish world, especially Zionism and Palestine, though he considered himself pro-Zionist.

Besides his religious convictions, Mayer's political and social activities before the war helped to prepare him for the role he later played. In 1921, he was elected to represent the liberal-democratic party in Saint Gallen and was engaged particularly in the financial side of municipal administration until his resignation in 1933. He belonged to the governing body of the local Jewish community, founded a modern welfare institution, and also became secretary of the SIG. In that post he was active in the fight against antisemitism, which, especially after 1933, became a strong force in Switzerland. When Jules Dreyfus-Brodsky resigned the presidency of SIG in 1936, Mayer was elected to fill the vacancy.

During Mayer's presidency, the SIG joined the WJC and was actively involved in the JA deliberations in 1936–37 over the future of Palestine. From early 1938 on, SIG had to take care of the stream of refugees coming from Austria, and Mayer was responsible for negotiating with the Swiss government, and particularly the Alien Police under Dr. Heinrich Rothmund, regarding them. He was later criticized for the restrictive policy regarding Jewish immigration that resulted from these negotiations. It is true that Mayer accepted the fiat of his government without public protest. The Swiss Jewish community numbered about 17,000; they had to look after 4,500 refugees. It is doubtful whether there was any alternative to accepting the government's position, especially as it was supported by public opinion. Mayer continued his presidency until the end of 1942. But as time went on, and the Swiss community found it increasingly difficult to find the funds it had promised to support Jewish refugees, Mayer had to rely more and more on JDC help. The ties that developed between him and Morris Troper were friendly and cordial. When war threatened to cut JDC off from Europe in the spring of 1940, Troper, accompanied by Joseph Schwartz, visited Mayer in Saint Gallen and asked him to accept the honorary post of JDC representative in Switzerland. Mayer agreed, and on May 30, 1940, Troper wrote to the Swiss government acquainting them with the appointment.[1]

Saly Mayer never became a paid official of JDC. He did his work on a voluntary basis and never even agreed to have his expenses reimbursed. Only secretarial help and other official out-lays were charged to JDC's account, because he thought that every penny should go to those who needed it. From 1940, this lonely, pedantic, and suspicious man began to develop a curious friendship with Schwartz, who thus became the third of the really close friends he had: the others were Marcus Wyler-Schmidt, his lawyer and confidant, and Pierre Bigar, his deputy caring for the refugees from Germany. To these three were later added Nathan Schwalb, the emissary of Hehalutz in Switzerland, and Roswell D. McClelland, an American who became an official at the Ameri-can embassy in Bern.

As it turned out, Mayer's intervention in other European countries was not needed in 1940. The JDC-Lisbon office was established, and throughout 1940 Mayer was called upon to trans-mit only 26,751 Swiss francs (sfr.; $6,370). In 1941 the total dwin-dled to 12,742 sfr. ($3,030). By then Schwartz was in touch with all the countries of Europe. Contact with Poland was maintained through Joseph Blum in Slovakia and Bertrand S. Jacobson, an American, in Rumania. In Italy, France, and Yugoslavia (until its conquest by the Nazis), JDC also worked directly, and this situa-tion did not change as long as the United States remained neutral. Mayer was responsible for the administration of JDC funds for local refugees, and he battled against decreases resulting from JDC's financial crisis. But he received his JDC education in those years, because he was kept informed by Schwartz of all the activi-ties in Europe.

It was in 1941 that Mayer was first approached by Nathan Schwalb, who was a Polish Jew, a member of a Palestinian kib-butz, and an ardent follower of the Tolstoyan philosopher and prophet of the kibbutz movement, Aharon David Gordon. In May, 1941, Schwalb asked Mayer for JDC subventions for agricul-tural training communes in Poland and child care in Croatia. Schwalb had become the center of a widespread net of contacts with occupied Europe. Members of the Zionist youth movements wrote to him, usually in coded language, from all over the suffer-ing continent, and at that stage he thought they should conserve their strength by preparing for a better day when they would have to lead an exodus to Palestine. Mayer was impressed by Schwalb's personality, his obvious enthusiasm, and his accurate and reliable reporting. He began to receive regularly whatever Schwalb received from occupied Europe, at first because Schwalb hoped to move Mayer to intervene with JDC on behalf of Hehalutz. Mayer did so, but with little result. Schwartz and Troper were facing smaller and smaller budgets, and they simply would not consider another venture, important though it might be. Under Mayer's continued pressure, they eventually made available, for Hehalutz activities all over Europe, a total of $5,900 up to January, 1942—not a very satisfactory solution for Schwalb.[2] Mayer, however, became very close to Schwalb, who sent him Gordon's work and soon converted him to a fervent and effusive Zionism, though this remained Mayer's private affair.[3] Mayer had still other sources of information in Alfred Silberschein of RELICO and Gerhart Riegner of the WJC in Geneva, although his relationships with these men tended to be strained. Silberschein, like Schwalb, passed on letters and reports. Mayer's contacts with Riegner were minimal and unfriendly, but, as a member himself of WJC, he could not share JDC's extreme stand against it.

Mayer's own philosophy regarding rescue and aid grew gradually out of his ever-increasing knowledge of the activities being carried out all over Europe. One finds his chief notion constantly repeated in his notebooks, letters, and records of conversation: the idea of klal, a Hebrew word meaning "all" or "the community," as opposed to sectional or ideological interests. It was Klal Yisroel ("the community of Israel," in Mayer's Ashkenazi pronunciation) that had the right to call on Jewish resources, rather than groups or sections or individuals. When, in the autumn of 1941, the ultraorthodox Agudat Israel demanded more representation for religious Jewry on Swiss Jewish bodies and the introduction of religious observance in refugee camps, the Orthodox Mayer replied very clearly: "Just now, the most important orthodox fact is—Help." Nor did he hesitate to say in his typically sardonic way that religion was about the last thing the refugees in Switzerland wanted. "Not one of our dear 'coreligionaires' has been asking for any religious supply. Their requests have been for more pay, more leave, more freedom and less work."[4]

Mayer's relatively inactive role in JDC undertakings changed dramatically when America entered the war. In New York, the idea immediately came up to ask him to serve as a conduit of funds into Europe; this was premature, as people quickly came to realize, because the Treasury Department would not allow the transfer of funds to a neutral country if they might reach Nazi Europe. Soon, however, JDC had to withdraw its American staff from everyplace but Lisbon. Laura Margolis was supposed to leave Shanghai (she did not, in the end), and Jacobson left Rumania. JDC used his arrival in New York in March, 1942, to press for more money from the American Jewish community. In the light of his experiences, Jacobson declared, he found it difficult to understand that the Jews of America should have to be persuaded to give more generously. It should have been obvious to every newspaper reader, he added, that the Jews in Europe had to have more help to survive.[5]

Schwartz in Lisbon still faced the dilemma of how to pass on funds to Jews in Nazi Europe and yet act "in full conformity with US government regulations and policies."[6] It was Saly Mayer who proposed the solution, in a telephone conversation on February 24, 1942. He suggested that JDC should double its allocation to Switzerland, thus paying a big share of the expenses of refugees there; the funds collected by the Swiss community would be released to pay for aid to Jews under Nazi rule. There was no other way Mayer could see, even though it was difficult to raise funds in Switzerland because people with money were leaving the country or were too frightened to part with it, even as a loan. Schwartz consulted New York. Was the arrangement feasible? There had been precedents. In 1941, Mayer had paid Fred M. Oberländer in Barcelona with Swiss money which was then reimbursed in the form of a JDC grant to SIG. Moses Leavitt in New York immediately saw the possibilities of such an approach and asked the Treasury Department whether it would grant a license embodying the Mayer proposal. He put this to the Treasury in rather vague terms—a larger JDC subvention to SIG would enable Swiss Jewry to extend "relief to needy Jews who cannot be helped by American organizations." On March 6, 1942, he received the signal to go ahead. The Treasury had apparently understood perfectly well what JDC had in mind; it was agreeing to a virtual reversal of its own and British policy regarding help to Jews in Europe.[7]

There was of course another problem. JDC had to be able quite honestly to say to the U.S. government that American dollars did not leave Switzerland and that it had no idea what the Swiss community did with its own funds. This was explained in a crucial telephone call by Schwartz to Mayer on March 13. He was to support Blum (Slovakia), Klein (Croatia), Spitzer (Serbia), Neustadt (Poland), Valobra (Italy), and Greece, but not RELICO. How he did that was his affair. There would and could be no control over him by Lisbon. Of course he knew what was expected; he should do nothing that might cause trouble for JDC.

He was, however, free to get so-called loans aprés, that is, loans for repayment after the war. Could he use false Paraguayan or Dominican visas to save Jews, asked Mayer on March 18? No, he could not.[8]

From the point of view of the Lisbon office, this situation was ideal: Schwartz could always truthfully claim that he did not know what Mayer was up to. Many years later, Schwartz described the situation vividly.

> Saly Mayer, because he was Swiss, was able to do a lot of things that we couldn't do and we were always able to say—look, we can't control the Swiss.[9]

> I did a lot of things that the JDC didn't know and Saly Mayer did a lot of things that I didn't know. . . . The man on the spot had to make decisions and if he couldn't make decisions he was no good: and the telephone lines were always open [that is, censored].[10]

One must understand Mayer's situation clearly. He was being asked to act in JDC's name towards the Jews under Nazi rule, but he was not actually to receive funds for that purpose. These were to come from Swiss sources. He was not to present any accounts, and he was allowed consultation with the Lisbon office to a limited extent only. If he succeeded, he would be an unsung hero, and all the glory would go to JDC in Lisbon or New York; if he failed, he could be disowned by JDC or attacked by rival organizations. One thing was obvious to him from the start: he could not let anyone know that he was not really a representative of JDC, but only a confidant who was to act on his own responsibility. What happened was, of course, precisely what he had foreseen. As he could not possibly endanger his work by telling people that he had no JDC authority beyond a general injunction to go and do good, he had to be secretive and largely negative, because he simply did not have the money he needed. "We desist from calculating how much would be needed really to help the hundreds of thousands of poor Jews sufficiently," is the way Mayer put it.[11] In actual fact, he received a grand total of $235,000 in 1942, of which he spent $229,910; $105,295 were spent in Switzerland, and the rest, or the equivalent in Swiss francs, was used for help outside it. In 1943, he received $1,588,000, of which he spent $590,190 in Switzerland for local needs. The funds at his disposal for these two years from JDC sources which he could use outside Switzerland was therefore $129,705 in 1942 and $997,810 in 1943, or a total of $1,127,515. Of that money, some of which arrived very late in 1943, he spent \$169,490 in 1942 and \$564,275 in 1943, or a total of \$733,765.[12]

As Mayer got into touch with Jewish leaders in the occupied countries, many of whom of course knew him from before the war, the story began to spread of the rich "uncle" in Switzerland. All over underground, dying Jewish Europe, word was passed, and those who dealt with him, through Schwalb's or Silberschein's or his own couriers, referred to him as "Uncle Saly," even when they spoke to him over the telephone. Uncle Saly was supposed to be able to help with sums that were commensurate with the need. Saly did not destroy that illusion, knowing very well that it helped maintain morale. What he could not tell Gizi Fleischmann in Bratislava, or Wilhelm Filderman in Rumania, was that he had pitifully little money, that he was struggling desperately to get more, and that he would not abandon them, even though it meant lying to them, postponing answers from one week to the next, and, in the end, incurring their wrath. This little, lonely man of rigid principles and abrupt, abrasive behavior, who wrote his letters himself in antiquated German or atrocious English or French, quite consciously decided to do what was almost impossible—create hope where there was none.

Other aid organizations, made suspicious by Mayer's secretiveness and persuaded by the fable of the immensely rich "Joint," blamed Mayer for his miserliness and obsession regarding exact accounting when the lives of millions were at stake. With the exception of Schwalb and the French OSE, Mayer soon ceased to have friends among the many organizations in Switzerland engaged in rescue work. He could not come out and deny the stories, so he withdrew into a shell of increasing bitterness and loneliness. It was only in his conversations with Schwartz that Mayer occasionally let the bitterness come out. Why could JDC not do more? "If it would not go against my feelings [of loyalty to JDC]," he said during a telephone conversation with Schwartz on April 1, 1942, "I would join the RELICO or the WJC this next minute. Though it is true they are making nothing but noise, they at least make themselves heard. The Joint has not yet grasped the enormous responsibility resting with American Jewry. I know that at present they are helpless, but I have warned in good time and nothing has been done." Schwartz responded, "I quite agree."[13]

One must of course ask how it was that Mayer did not get more money in the crucial two years of 1942 and 1943, when

JDC's expenditure stood at $6.3 million and $8.4 million respectively. JDC-New York allocated $610,000 in 1942, and $940,000 in 1943, or 10–11 percent of its budget, to Mayer, but even these funds did not reach him in time. It was not until September, 1943, that he began to receive the funds he had been promised for 1942.[14] The reason was that the United States wanted to pay in dollars for Swiss francs which the Swiss would give to Mayer in Switzerland. But the Swiss had too many dollars already and did not want to buy more; they wanted blocked Swiss francs controlled by the U.S. government to be used instead. The Treasury Department did not agree, a deadlock ensued, and no money could be transferred. In May, 1942, the last transfer of dollars had been effected, and from then on, Leavitt pestered the Treasury and the Swiss diplomatic representatives in the United States to permit transfers of money without achieving anything at all. Mayer's idea of paying dollars in America to the IRC and getting the equivalent in Swiss francs paid out in Switzerland was rejected. According to Leavitt, the U.S. government would not permit such transfers.[15] Mayer was using the small amount of loans he could get from Swiss sources, but he really had no money to go on. The SIG fund-raising campaign, which in 1942 had yielded 900,000 sfr. ($246,000), was down to 700,000 sfr. in 1943 ($191,000).[16] Mayer did receive some loans après, but these were not enough to tide him over. In September, 1943, he finally suggested a solution that was adopted—buying Swiss bonds with dollars and selling them in Switzerland for francs at a discount. After November, 1943, transfers could again be effected.

In a sense, insult was added to injury when Mayer's demand that JDC give him an official letter recognizing him as their representative was refused. Such a letter, used discreetly, might enable him to receive large credits from private persons against promises of repayment by JDC after the war. "Mr. Leavitt's reaction was definitely that Dr. Schwartz could not give him such a letter since we have absolutely no control from here over Mr. Mayer's actions, and whatever he did he would have to do on his own responsibility."[17] Mayer accepted the verdict, but he returned to his demand almost a year later, when no money was forthcoming from New York and he had to borrow locally; he could not do it without an authorization. Officially, the New York office argued in March, 1943, only an American citizen could be a JDC representative. But this time Schwartz prevailed, and Mayer got his letter of recognition at long last.[18]

In the meantime, Mayer's position in his own community deteriorated. He complained that people no longer trusted him—which, considering his own growing secretiveness, was not really surprising. He told Schwartz in September, 1942, that he would soon be giving up the presidency of SIG (his resignation actually took effect on March 28, 1943). His usefuless to JDC had lain in his position as president, and he was therefore willing to resign from JDC.[19] He repeated this offer several times, until Schwartz told him that JDC would not accept it. The organization had faith in him and wanted him to continue. In fact, there seems to be no trace in the New York files of Mayer's offer of resignation. Apparently Schwartz did not transmit it; he had his reasons, no doubt.

Switzerland the Lifeboat

When World War II began, there were some 5,000 Jewish refugees in Switzerland, over half of whom had to be supported by the local Jewish community. They were living in a small country which, after June, 1940, was surrounded by Nazi or pro-Nazi regimes. When the Nazis occupied southern France in November, 1942, Switzerland became even more tightly encircled. Although the Swiss remained neutral, their economy suffered: the tourist trade disappeared, imports were severely curtailed, rationing was introduced from October, 1939, and per capita caloric intake declined from around 3,000 per day to 2,160 in 1943. A large proportion of the national budget had to be spent on keeping the Swiss army prepared and watchful. The Nazis, in fact, weighed the possible conquest of Switzerland a number of times before they finally abandoned all such plans in 1943, when it became clear that the venture would be too difficult and the advantages small.

The attitude of the Swiss government towards refugees generally was determined by three considerations: the overwhelming might of the Nazi neighbor; the country's precarious economy, which kept the population reasonably well provided but which might be upset by large numbers of additional refugees; and a xenophobia which was particularly prevalent in the conservative, predominantly Catholic autonomous cantons making up the Swiss federation. This latter factor was particularly obvious when it was a matter of accepting Jewish refugees. Nevertheless, there was also a deep humanitarian strand in Swiss society, which found expression in demands to accept Jewish—and other—victims of Nazism. For all of these reasons, Alfred Häsler's reference to Switzerland as a lifeboat is particularly appropriate.[20]

For the government, the power of Nazi Germany especially was a determining factor. Afraid that Switzerland might be regarded as an anti-Nazi Jewish center, the government had no intention of endangering the country for the sake of Jewish refugees; in fact, the Nazi press had made some bitter attacks, terming Switzerland "the last paradise of the sons of Judas."[21] The traditional right of asylum was conferred by the Swiss, not exercised by the refugee. In any case, it applied to politically endangered individuals and not to people persecuted for their race. A good deal of antisemitism, usually unconscious, or an antisemitism directed against "eastern" Jews, entered into these considerations. Eastern Jews were essentially foreign (wesensfremd) to the Swiss and therefore often branded undesirable. In November, 1939, the Ministry of Justice and Police declared its fear of the entry of such undesirables, primarily immigrants, and "especially Jews." The government differentiated between emigrants in transit (those who received visas of entry into Switzerland) and refugees (those without visas who had been allowed to stay out of humanitarian considerations). Both groups were liable to be interned and had strictly limited freedom of movement. Occasionally, those admitted as refugees might be pushed back over the frontier by individual cantons, against the wishes of the Alien Police and its head, Heinrich Rothmund. Early in 1940, labor camps were established, which were supported by SIG and its special branches for the care of refugees, the Verband Schweizerischer Israelitischer Armenpflegen (VSIA) and the Schweizerische Jüdische Flüchtlingshilfe. As refugees were not allowed to find jobs, the camps, providing work, food, and some pocket money, were on the whole welcomed by everyone concerned.

A basic police instruction of June 18, 1940, issued during the fall of France, regulated the entry of military and civilian refugees into Switzerland. Military personnel seeking asylum were to be disarmed and interned, while civilian men of military age were to be denied admission. Women, children under sixteen, and men over sixty were to be admitted. People trying to cross the border surreptitiously were to be returned (a process known as refoulement). Over 30,000 French soldiers who crossed the border at that time were returned to France early in 1941, but 10,000 Poles were allowed to remain. Between the summer of 1940 and April, 1942, however, there were relatively few Jewish refugees trying to cross into Switzerland; 8,325 emigrants and 1,235 refugees were accepted between September, 1939, and July 31, 1942. Of the latter, probably 90 percent were Jews. Of course, refoulement of Jews did take place, and these unfortunates were returned to France at night so they would not fall into the hands of the Vichy police. In April–July, 1942, the number of civilian refugees increased, and by midsummer, 1942, Switzerland found itself torn between a traditional humanitarian attitude and political considerations, including fear of Germany. The decisions regarding the refugee problem finally taken by the Swiss were heavily influenced by the degree of their awareness of the fate of Jews under Nazi rule.

A report submitted by a senior police officer to the Swiss Alien Police at the end of July, 1942, after the first wave of mass arrests in Paris and after the first reports about the mass murder in the east had begun to circulate, related to the fact that since April, 1941, all Jews had been declared undesirable and had to be refused admission. In accordance with this general policy, the initial wave of Jewish refugees from France in July, 1942, had to be turned back. The report continued:

> Lately, however, we could no longer take the decision to effect such refusals. The unanimous and reliable reports regarding the ways and means used in these deportations [to the east] and the conditions in the Jew-districts [*Judenbezirke*] in the East are so frightful, that one must show understanding for the desperate attempts of the refugees to escape such a fate, and one can hardly undertake responsibility for refoulement any more.[22]

On the same day, Rothmund wrote to his minister, Eduard von Steiger, that he had ceased to deport French Jews and was taking full responsibility for his action. What could the minister instruct him to do now? Von Steiger told Rothmund to resume refoulement, and the other ministers approved his action on August 4. In accordance with this policy, a circular of August 13 instructed the frontier police to admit political refugees only, pointing out, "Refugees for racial reasons only, for instance Jews, do not count as political refugees."[23]

But reports of Nazi treatment of European Jews reaching Switzerland multiplied, and though Rothmund defended his government's policy in a meeting with the SIG leadership on August 20, attacks on von Steiger and the police mounted. Socialists and evangelical churches, acting on information fed to them by WJC and SIG, were especially critical. On August 24, 1942, von Steiger had a stormy meeting with the central Swiss roof organization for refugees, and on August 25 he had to instruct the police to "ease" the admittance of refugees. Local police officials had in any case not always observed the previous instructions, though many refugees were refused admission. From April to mid-September, 1942, 2,380 had been admitted, and a new circular of September 26 repeated the principle that Jews as such should not be allowed in. But the principle was rendered almost meaningless when it was added that the sick, pregnant women, those over sixty-five years old, close relatives of people already in Switzerland, children under sixteen, and parents of such children should be admitted. The very next sentence then said that French Jews should be refused admission because they were not endangered in their homeland. The contradictory orders reflected contradictory pressures on von Steiger, exerted by liberals on the one hand, and by conservatives and the army on the other. Frontier police also practiced a more humane policy than their instructions warranted, though many Jews were still refused admission. Nevertheless, in September, 3,800 entered; and in October, 1,904. The restrictions were slowly eased, and on November 11, 1942, the order not to admit French Jews was rescinded. From August 1 to the end of December, 8,467 refugees arrived.

There is fairly conclusive proof that specific testimonies by Swiss citizens regarding the fate of European Jews reached the government; at any rate, proofs exist that they were submitted. Rothmund visited Berlin in October, but his impression tended to counteract earlier reports. The police chief saw the concentration camp in Oranienburg, and while he got the impression of harsh treatment, he did not see any murder going on. Stories about mass murders proliferated in liberal and liberal-Protestant newspapers during September and October, but Swiss censors tended to forbid publication of such reports on the grounds that they were "foreign rumor propaganda of the worst type" (December, 1942).[24] The government considered the Allied proclamation of December 17, 1942, denouncing the mass murder of the Jews to be pure propaganda, despite its corroboration in large parts of the Swiss press. This attitude persisted through most of 1943, even in the face of official church protests such as that of the Synod of the Evangelical Reformed Church of May 5, 1943. The result was that, while the orders and instructions emanating from Bern strike one as harsh, and while the higher police officers' behavior was characterized by a local Jewish reporter as "odious in most cases" (*odieux dans la plupart des cas*),[25] the lower officials and ordinary policemen overwhelmingly treated the refugees humanely.

With the fall of Mussolini and the capitulation of Italy in August–September, 1943, the same pattern of behavior repeated itself on the Swiss-Italian border as had been evident on the French side. The Swiss army objected to a new massive influx of civilians, while grudgingly admitting Italian military formations who were then disarmed and interned. The government in its regulations followed suit, but under the pressure of churchmen and liberals, as well as in the light of the sympathetic approach of local police, it was found necessary to ease the restrictive instructions. These at first decreed that only especially endangered civilians should be accepted, but in fact fairly large numbers were admitted. On December 3, 1943, an instruction was finally given to accept all Jews. Between August, 1943, and the end of the year, 10,708 civilians were accepted into Switzerland. Throughout 1943, 16,379 had been admitted, but 3,344 were rejected at the borders.

The process of liberalization continued in 1943 for non-Italian refugees as well, despite repeated protests by the army. Civilians of military age were still rejected, but an order of February 29, 1944, which allowed for the entry of all those whose lives were "really" threatened, provided in practice for the admittance of all Jewish persons. By then even the Swiss government had accepted the idea that all Jews were in mortal danger. By the end of the war, 59,800 civilian and 46,670 military refugees had been allowed to enter and stay on in the country; of these, 28,512 were Jewish "emigrants" and "refugees" by Swiss definition. If one deducts from these figures those Jewish refugees who had been resident in the country before the war, but takes account of over 1,000 Jews who managed to emigrate during that period, one arrives at a grand total of about 21,000 Jews for whom Switzerland was indeed a lifeboat. For at least 5,000 more who suffered refoulement at the Swiss border, it was a death trap. For the many thousands who did not try to reach it because they were uncertain whether they would be admitted, it was no more than a forlorn hope. Von Steiger had declared in the Swiss parliament on September 22, 1942, that 6,000–7,000 refugees was the most Switzerland could accept. In the end, 295,381 people entered the country after 1939, including military personnel.

As early as the first half of 1942, it became obvious that SIG would not be able to pay for all the new Jewish refugees that were coming in. The government turned to the public for a general voluntary effort for all refugees and also taxed the wealthier refugees in a kind of equalizing taxation process. These measures had netted 2.4 million sfr. ($570,000) by 1947, of which a part was paid out to the private aid organizations as the money came in: thus, in 1942, some 1.2 million sfr. ($285,000) reached these private bodies, including SIG. The government itself began spending really considerable sums from about 1942. In 1939–41, it spent 2.8 million sfr ($666,000); by 1943–45 this sum jumped to 79.9 million sfr. ($19 million). Private organizations spent a total of 87 million sfr. ($20.5 million) during the war years. Conditions for the refugees were by no means luxurious, and often not even comfortable, and there was, inevitably perhaps, some unnecessarily harsh treatment. But on the whole, the situation was bearable and later on became fairly comfortable. Labor camps accounted for 20–25 percent of the refugees; the rest were accommodated with individual farmers, in homes for internees, and in private homes; there was also a tiny minority (286 refugees in early 1944) in punitive camps established to deal with troublesome or criminal elements. Table 20 illustrates the total funds from various sources expended as aid to refugees by the Swiss Jewish community throughout the war.[26]

Table 20: SIG Funding of Jewish Refugees, 1939–45

	Local (sfr.)	JDC($)	JDC(sfr.)	HICEM(sfr.)	Total(sfr.)
1939	1,331,289	432,000	1,916,461	131,407	3,379,157
1940	696,845	187,000	744,409	418,961	2,400,000
1941		92,000	391,177	132,841	2,202,716
1942	900,000		282,864	94,045	2,522,939
1943	750,000		1,500,000		
1944	700,000		3,355,244		6,041,959*
1945			6,855,980		9,033,485*

*These totals include government funds. The exact proportion of direct government funding and other funds is not clear.

This survey of Swiss policies towards refugees seems to indicate that while acceptance into Switzerland meant escape from certain death, the overall Swiss attitude left a great deal to be desired. After the war, the major criticism of Swiss policy came from the Swiss themselves. Characteristic of the general attitude is von Steiger's untruthful postwar statement: "Had one known what was happening over there in the Reich, one would have enlarged the possibilities" of refugee admittance. And the aid organization of the evangelical churches admitted in 1954: "When the synagogues went up in flames in Germany and the Jews were stripped and beaten, the priests and Levites saw it and passed by. When the refugees ran for their lives and begged for admittance at our borders, we Swiss saw their predicament and we passed it by."[27]

JDC Work in Switzerland

Saly Mayer occupied a central place in the care of Jewish refugees in Switzerland. Until March, 1943, he was actually president of the SIG; after that date, as the representative of JDC, he channeled funds to the SIG, which in turn gave them to VSIA. Mayer's own organization, the Schweizerischer Jüdischer Unterstützungsfond für Flüchtlinge (SJUF), was created solely to accept the funds and distribute them. It was run by a committee composed of Mayer, Pierre Bigar, and Silvain S. Guggenheim, which rarely, if ever, held formal meetings. From the correspondence, it appears that Mayer sometimes informally consulted the committee members and his lawyer, Marcus Wyler-Schmidt, when major decisions were to be made. Usually he did not consult even them. Bigar and Guggenheim helped whenever they were asked to and whenever they could. They left it at that.

Mayer's problem was to find the funds to support needy Jewish refugees who had arrived prior to 1942; after 1942, the Swiss government accepted financial responsibility for newcomers, but the Swiss Jewish community continued to look after the "old" refugees. Many of them were supporting themselves, sometimes with the aid of their Swiss Jewish relatives. A residue of 2,200 to 2,500 people had to be supported by VSIA and Mayer. The community also tried to help ease the lot of those who were under government care. Especially important was the care of children, of students, and of many of the female refugees. A committee headed by Marie Ginzberg cared for some 100 intellectuals and received Mayer's support even after it had run foul of the Swiss authorities for encouraging illegal border crossings by endangered intellectuals and well-known public figures. In the field of child care, six children's homes were operating by the latter half of 1943, where about 300 children were looked after. Another 900 children were placed with families and supervised by OSE and the Swiss community. Tubercular and other patients were cared for in homes such as the Pro-Leysin at Lausanne and in a home at Davos.[28] Refugees under government care received supplementary food, medicines, clothing, and cultural amenities of various kinds, as required. Food supplements, however, were limited to special cases in order to avoid bad feeling between Jews and non-Jews.

In order to do his work successfully, Mayer had to keep up his contacts with Heinrich Rothmund, the Swiss official most concerned with Jewish affairs, and representatives of other government agencies and try to get out of them as much as he could. Rothmund was an enigmatic figure, torn between a desire to be helpful and an anti-Jewish tendency which he would have denied strenuously, but which nevertheless was very apparent. In July, 1940, he told Troper that he should tell his "New York people" that though he, Rothmund, would demand the funds that the Swiss community had promised in order to keep the refugees, "no German refugee will ever starve in Switzerland."[29] He was to be as good as his word when the 1942 influx came and the Swiss Jews could not pay. But in 1941, he had threatened JDC that Swiss Jewry was in danger unless emigration possibilities were kept open. "Switzerland is among the very few countries in Europe which have not adopted anti-Jewish laws," he told Schwartz, "and in order to maintain that record, it would be far better if the refugee population were diminished."[30]

Rothmund also did not hesitate to try to affect American policies. Like most Europeans, he believed that American Jews had a decisive influence on the U.S. government. Was it right, he wrote to Troper in August, 1941, that America should close its gates to the Jews? Switzerland had been defending its independence for 650 years, and now it was saddled with this potentially dangerous Jewish refugee problem. Shouldn't America distribute these Jews in its vast land so that none of them could cause damage? He knew that Troper could discuss such basic problems with the leaders of his country. In the meantime, he was doing all he could, and so was Saly Mayer, "the untiring optimist and philosopher and good friend."[31] Rothmund's letter was followed by similar warnings, both by Saly Mayer and by independent agencies. In a letter to Eleanor Roosevelt, Pierre Ceresole, a Swiss Quaker leader, stated in October, 1941, that the position of Jewish refugees was "very precarious." If the Germans exerted real pressure to hand them over, the Swiss would be hard put to resist it.[32]

Mayer was in constant touch with Rothmund, but precisely what happened between them is difficult to establish. Some indication of Mayer's own policy can be gleaned from his statement to the SIG in May, 1941, when he insisted on what he called *Minhag Suisse* (customary Jewish policy as practiced in Switzerland): a low public profile, inner unity, and cooperation with the government, but intervention when necessary to protect Jewish interests and the interests of the refugees. Very significantly, he added that he would be willing to talk to anyone to save Jews. His draft speech contained the words "from the Third Reich"—he was willing to talk to the Nazis if that could save Jews—but he struck the words out and left them unsaid.[33] Mayer also defended the refugees' claim to a Swiss standard of living, characteristically basing himself on the biblical injunction that commands equality toward the "stranger that lives in your midst."[34] It is clear, however, that when Swiss governmental policies came under pressure from liberal public opinion in 1942, Mayer's relations with Rothmund became strained. The multitude of clippings and some coded notes in Mayer's papers seem to indicate that he supplied the newspapers with some of the materials they used to demand a more liberal treatment or that he used intermediaries to do so. When, late in 1943, Rothmund asked Mayer to indicate where the Swiss should draw the line in accepting Jewish refugees, he refused. He had to leave such decisions to the government, "since from his standpoint, he could only stop where the need stopped."[35]

Rothmund had appealed to Mayer as a Swiss citizen, and it is true that he was a loyal one. Swiss neutrality must not be endangered, since it formed the basis for preserving the lives of Jews in Switzerland, local citizens and refugees alike. Mayer thought that Jewish public pressure would be counterproductive, but liberal demands for easing restrictions were to be supported discreetly. External interventions would be welcome, and in private discussions with government authorities, strong arguments should be used to save as many as possible. But an open clash had to be avoided at all costs. We shall see that Mayer used these tactics to some good effect later on, when the conservative tendency was weakening in Switzerland. Was Mayer's policy the best possible? No alternative was suggested, and after his resignation essentially the same policy was followed. Considering the actual strength at Mayer's disposal in those difficult years up to 1944, with a tiny Swiss community and little money, it seems that he did not do badly.

10

Under the Threat of Drancy: French Jewry, 1942–1944

When the first tens of thousands of non-French Jews were rounded up in Paris in giant hunts, many thousands of small and very small children remained behind in apartments and on the streets. Before they could be tended by kind neighbors, 4,000 of them were collected and put into the sports stadium of the Velodrome d'Hiver. Children from the age of three up were torn away from their mothers, thrown on trucks. . . . Through the main thoroughfares of the city one could hear the screaming and the crying of the children and the long reverberating despairing cry: mummy, mummy . . . several days after the deportation of the adults, the four thousand children were loaded into cattle cars. Sixty children of all ages were thrown into each wagon. One pail with water was the whole furniture. No bench, no straw, no provisions were put at their disposal, and the children were sent away without any supervision. Then the doors and openings were hermetically sealed and after many more hours the trains slowly moved away. . . . A nurse, who alone among the many French officials present protested against this procedure and against the conditions in this transport, was given the following reply by the responsible doctor: "we normally expect about thirty percent loss during the journey."[1]

This was the fate the Germans had in store for French Jews. From July, 1942, on, manhunts of increasing severity and brutality were organized by the Paris branch of Adolf Eichmann's special Gestapo branch for Jewish affairs, under HSSPF-Höherer SS und Polizei-

235

Führer Karl A. Oberg, and the "experts," Alois Brunner and Heinz Röthke. The problem for the SS, however, was that it had at its disposal only very small specialized Gestapo staffs and the German police numbering 3,000, and it could not always rely on the German army, despite the army's positive attitude to the anti-Jewish measures. It therefore depended greatly on the 47,000 French policemen, among them the dreaded profascist Garde mobile militia, in its anti-Jewish operations in France, the aim of which was quite clearly the deportation of French Jews to the death camps in Poland. The first deportation from France to Poland took place on March 27, 1942, and the last in July, 1944. The figures for deportations from the main Nazi deportation center at Drancy in 1942, 1943, and 1944 were 41,792, 21,856, and 14,263 respectively, or 77,911 altogether. When one adds the numbers deported from places other than Drancy, the total is probably somewhere between 86,000 and 90,000. Thousands more were murdered by the Germans in France. Nevertheless, the fact is that about two-thirds of the Jews in France either fled or survived in the country.[2]

There was very little actual resistance to the Germans in France before 1943. The single most important factor changing this attitude was the agreement of the Vichy government on February 16, 1943, under heavy German pressure, to publish a law supplying French labor to Germany. It was the attempt of many workers to escape deportation to German factories that furnished recruits for the French resistance. Early in 1943, French freedom fighters—*maquis*—began to gather in the mountains of the Massif Central. Their number grew slowly; as late as early 1944, there were not more than 30,000 maquis in France. After the Allies landed in Normandy in June, 1944, however, some 350,000 Frenchmen formed the united Forces françaises de l'intérieur (FFI), an internal army rebelling against German rule. There was little the armed underground could offer persecuted Jews in the form either of shelter or of an opportunity to fight.

French Jewish Leadership, 1942–1944

The reactions of Jewish leadership to the unfolding Nazi anti-Jewish terror mirrored the general situation in France. The CC's struggle to prevent the establishment of UGIF, the French Judenrat, in 1941 had failed, and in early 1942 it seemed as though UGIF would gain unchallenged ascendancy among French Jews. But in August, 1942, the authority of UGIF began to be shaken. In fact, one can see that in the peculiar conditions of France, the German terror tactics regarding UGIF were probably mistaken. It drove UGIF leaders to support clandestine work, even if they did not engage in it themselves. It did not take long to discover that German promises were worthless. UGIF never became what the Joodse Raad (Jewish Council) became in Holland: a completely subservient organization engaged in what has been aptly called "anticipatory compliance."[3] Instead, the brutal persecution practiced by both the Germans and the Vichy French caused some of the organizations that had been transformed into sections of the UGIF to set up parallel illegal bodies. UGIF in the south had seven sections. Of these, the second (vocational training) was in effect the old ORT organization; the third (health) was OSE; the fourth (youth) was identical with the EIF, the Jewish scouts; the fifth (foreign Jews) included CAR and the FSJ; the sixth (emigration) was HICEM; and the seventh (education) was identical with the Alliance Israélite Universelle. Parallel clandestine organizations sprang up in the third, fourth, and fifth sections (though in the latter only the FSJ developed an illegal setup). These illegal groups were mainly concerned with hiding foreign-born Jews and supplying them with money, often using the official UGIF premises, personnel, and funds for that purpose.

However, while parts of the UGIF became more radical, the CC moved in the opposite direction. In September, 1942, it requested local consistories to obey the anti-Jewish laws without accepting them—whatever that meant. The consistories could not really engage in illegal activities, and they became correspondingly less important as centers of Jewish endeavor. The UGIF, meanwhile, underwent several changes in leadership. Albert Lévy remained president until he resigned because of ill health in February, 1943, though Raymond Raul Lambert in the south and André Baur in the north carried on their functions until the summer of 1943. On July 21, 1943, Baur was arrested because he refused to organize a search for two escapees from Drancy. Jacques Heilbronner, president of the CC, protested against Baur's arrest on August 2, and was himself arrested and sent to Drancy on October 23. Lambert was arrested in July, 1943, and it was only towards the end of 1943 that UGIF was reorganized. On October 25, George Edinger was appointed chairman, but in actual fact it was Raymond Geissmann, formerly head of the

Entr'aide français israélite (EFI), the mutual aid organization of French Jews, who now took over to become the real head of the organization.

The disappearance of the old leadership—Lévy, Lambert, Baur, and Heilbronner—was of course the result of German policies. In June, 1943, the Germans began to deport French Jews in increasing numbers, primarily from the more outlying provinces and smaller towns and villages. In 1943, the Germans were trying to get a more compliant leadership, because the old UGIF had shown disturbing signs of independence. In February, 1943, it had refused to hand over to the Gestapo lists of foreign Jews employed in the organization, and in April the southern section refused a demand to take its funds from the money confiscated from Jews. But Edinger and Geissman were no more compliant than their predecessors. Nevertheless, bitterness and controversy grew between the different organizations and UGIF, because UGIF, especially on the local level, fell into a Nazi trap by repeatedly opening offices, only to have its officials arrested, together with anyone who happened to be present at the time. The UGIF leadership reasoned that there were still large numbers of Jews who could not hide and were completely dependent on UGIF aid, and that therefore UGIF had to maintain its services, even knowing that its personnel would be easy prey to the Nazis and the Garde mobile. The opposition group, however, argued ever more forcefully that it was irresponsible to cling to the legal front. In December, 1943, when a whole department of the southern UGIF at Sisteron, the Service social aux étrangers, was arrested with a large number of its clients, Marc Jarblum, leader of the FSJ, commented bitterly on the UGIF leaders: "On est homme de parole . . . mais surtout, on est imbécile, et surtout criminel" ("They keep their word . . . but above all, they are idiots, and above all, criminals").[4]

The Nazi attack on UGIF was part of an overall strategy of energetic action which, as we have just seen, culminated in arrests and the removal of the old leadership. It also coincided with the deposition of Mussolini in Italy on July 25, 1943, and the subsequent occupation of the formerly Italian sector of southern France. Alois Brunner, one of Eichmann's most trusted murderers, was sent to Drancy, which he organized, making the UGIF responsible for much of the feeding and clothing of the deportees and instituting a reign of terror, torture, and humiliation. Small mobile striking groups of Gestapo officials under his control then

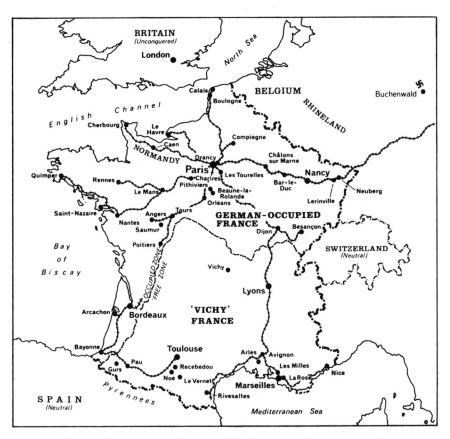

France and French Concentration Camps in 1942. Reproduced by permission from Martin Gilbert, *Final Journey* (Tel Aviv: Steimatzky and *Jerusalem Post*, 1979).

made arrests and deportation an acute danger for every Jew in France.

On August 3, the UGIF offices in Paris in the rue de Bienfaisance were raided, and seventy-one officials and visitors were taken to Drancy, of whom only a few were later released. Armand Katz and other central figures of the northern UGIF were among those arrested, and Juliette Stern, head of the Paris branch of the Women's International Zionist Organization (WIZO), who was responsible for UGIF children's homes in Paris and was in the process of transferring her children to illegal hiding places, escaped by a near miracle. Raids in towns and villages followed. On August 23, 1943, all prefectures were ordered to recruit for forced labor all male French Jews between the ages of twenty and thirty, and all male foreign Jews between eighteen and fifty. On September 9, finally, the complete occupation of the Italian sector enabled the Nazis to institute a reign of unparalleled terror. Donald Lowrie of the YMCA, who had gone to Switzerland from France and continued to work for aid to victims of German persecution, cabled to Herbert Katzki in Lisbon: "A systematic campaign for exterminating all Jews in France has reached a new climax using all the methods of persecution already known in Germany, Holland and Belgium."[5] It was this attack on the Jews in the summer of 1943 that was a turning point in JDC's policy towards French Jewry.[6]

JDC and French Jewry, 1942–1944

The first question facing JDC in France after Pearl Harbor was whether to operate there at all. The New York office had been in two minds about continuing to work abroad; as late as July, 1942, Paul Baerwald doubted whether Schwartz should go into France. "Perhaps we have come to the point where we must admit that our activities have been curtailed. If we admit this to ourselves only, the next question which should logically come up is the building down of the campaign organization."[7]

The next problem Schwartz had to face in France was what policy to follow in relation to UGIF. JDC's attitude to UGIF had been cool from the beginning of the latter's existence in 1941. JDC had subsidized the CC during and after its quarrel with UGIF, and through the Nîmes Coordinating Committee it had worked in a quasi-legal group comprised of a number of JDC-supported agencies, among them the AFSC, the Unitarians, and L'Amitié chrétienne, the Catholic organization headed by Abbé Alexander Glasberg. JDC did not refuse help to UGIF, especially as the chief component of UGIF was CAR, with whom JDC had a long-standing association, but Schwartz more and more came to the support of opposition tendencies. Even though FSJ was suspect because of radical leanings and ties with WJC, it began to get more JDC funds.

This process of moving away from what had been regarded as the more "respectable" agencies can be followed in the policies of JDC, with the summer, 1942, deportations as an obvious dividing line. In June, 1942, Jules Jefroykin had been named JDC's representative at Marseilles. Soon afterwards, Maurice Brenner, Lambert's secretary, became Jefroykin's adjutant. Jefroykin's association with JDC dated from 1941, and as early as December, 1941, he had been picked by Schwartz to represent JDC in France in case JDC pulled out of Lisbon, and he had been given wide powers to borrow funds against repayment after the war.

Jefroykin at first fully supported the JDC line regarding UGIF. It had to be given financial support. CAR was maintaining about 13,000 foreign Jews in early 1942, and the EIF was funded through it, as well as the Memorial Relief Committee at Marseilles, a small hassidic group, a group of Lubavitcher Hassidim, and a Czech aid center. Provided the funds were remitted according to their detailed appropriation, Jefroykin said, there was no reason JDC should refuse to cooperate with anyone; if JDC stopped aid to UGIF, it would turn to the Solidarity Funds of confiscated Jewish property and thus be an accomplice to the robbery from Jews. (The UGIF did of course later use these funds.)[8]

German policy, however, tended to make UGIF less and less effective. Late in 1942, the main UGIF departments were dispersed in small townships or villages in the south of France: CAR was in Gap, HICEM in Brive, and OSE in Vif. A raid on the UGIF center at Lyons followed in February, 1943, and at the end of the month, Lowrie reported from Geneva that Jefroykin and Brenner were in hiding. By March 1, all foreign Jews were supposed to be interned. The situation continued to worsen, until the August persecutions made it clear that UGIF was a trap for French Jews. Lambert, who thought he could still speak in JDC's name, was told in June that as long as he was "holding his present position in UGIF, he could not act as Joint's representative."[9] Gaston Kahn, another CAR stalwart, carried on after Lambert's arrest in

July, 1943, until December, when he too narrowly escaped arrest. JDC's financial support of UGIF dwindled after that.

New forms of organization of French Jewry developed in 1943, reflecting new political tendencies. The Communists became a dominant force and could no longer be ignored. Main d'oeuvre immigré (MOI) units in Paris engaged in armed anti-Nazi actions in the spring of 1942 and continued until May, 1943; after a short pause they resumed. The first armed group of MOI members in the south, made up chiefly of Jews, was organized at Lyons in late 1942. This developed in 1943 into four predominantly Jewish units. As early as summer, 1942, a specifically Jewish group was organized: the Union de la jeunesse juive under Jacques Kot and Francis Chapochnik. For the older age group, the Union des juifs pour la résistance et l'entr'aide (UJRE) was set up in the spring of 1943, with the help of some members of the FSJ, whose Zionist-socialist and Bundist components were in sympathy with the Communist call for radical resistance. UJRE and FSJ then set up a roof organization for resistance to the Germans, the Comité général de défense (CGD) in the summer of 1943. This trend of uniting anti-German forces ran parallel to similar developments in the French underground, where a united command was created for the first time by Jean Moulin in May, 1943. For political purposes, UJRE had contacted the CC in January and, in line with the Communist "Popular Front" alliances with "bourgeois" elements struggling against the Germans, set up the Conseil représentatif des israélites de France (CRIF) under Léon Meiss, who had succeeded Jacques Heilbronner as president of the CC. The Jewish Communists themselves underwent a change which was not perhaps sufficiently noted at the time. Contrary to prevalent Communist doctrine, Jewish national traditions were emphasized, and in May, 1943, MOI even brought out a booklet extolling the Jewish national hero Bar-Kochba, who had led a rebellion against the Romans in 135 c.e.[10]

JDC never supported either the CRIF or the other leftist underground organizations directly. It did, however, maintain close liaisons with the other Jewish groups who gradually descended into illegality: the FSJ, whose head, Marc Jarblum, had opposed the UGIF from its founding; the CC, whose importance waned somewhat in 1943, but which would have a significant role to play after the war; the EIF, whose chief, Robert Gamzon, was a member of UGIF, but which was moving into illegal action; the Mouvement de la jeunesse sioniste (MJS), which was closely al-

lied with EIF; ORT and HICEM, whose activities were less important as they, too became underground organizations; CAR; and,
above all, OSE, whose task of saving children became the activity
which received the greatest financial support by JDC. OSE, EIF,
and MJS operated entirely independently from Communist activity, whereas FSJ and the CC were in touch with it. EIF and MJS
developed the AJ as their own armed underground.

Until the German occupation of the southern zone in November, 1942, JDC could supply funds from Lisbon straight to
Jefroykin, or at least supervise local borrowings, but this of course
became impossible later. For a period of six or seven months,
until May-June, 1943, funds were supplied through local borrowing against promises of repayment, in what had become the traditional JDC manner. Joseph Fischer, collecting for the JNF, was
part of the system: he received money which he gave to Jefroykin
to distribute according to JDC policies, and the money was returned in dollars or sterling to JA in Palestine by JDC. During this
stage, Jefroykin and Fischer managed between them to raise
enough funds to keep the various agencies going. However, in
the late spring of 1943, this method gradually became more difficult, and, towards the end of the year, practically impossible.
Wealthy individuals either needed their own money or were
willing to part with it only at rates Schwartz and his Lisbon office
considered too high.

Up to May-June, 1943, Saly Mayer had not been involved in
the French operations, although he was kept informed through
the Geneva OSE office, headed at first by Boris Tschlenoff, who
was joined in early 1943 by Lazar Gourvic and then by Joseph
Weill. Jarblum arrived in Geneva in March, 1943, and opened his
FSJ office, where much of the information regarding French Jewry
was received. He too began his contact with Mayer only in the
summer of 1943. In fact, Mayer was told by Schwartz to keep off
French affairs. But when OSE approached him in June, 1943,
because Jefroykin had been unable to raise enough money in
France, he responded and gave a one-time subsidy. He was then
told by JDC-Lisbon that he should subsidize France if necessary,
but very carefully, to avoid double budgeting through him and
Jefroykin.[11] The trouble, of course, was that Mayer did not have
the money, which he carefully avoided telling OSE and FSJ. Some
anxious months passed, until in November and December, 1943,
the Swiss transfer tangle was solved and larger sums could be
transmitted. The problem was that during these months of 1943,

243

money was urgently needed, because this was the critical moment when the first group of UGIF leaders was arrested and the agencies were turning to illegal work. Jarblum, especially, bitterly accused Mayer and JDC of lack of support. Mayer simply did not reply. Balancing carefully on the verge of the legal, Mayer began to make his first contributions to France, with Lisbon's agreement. In a parallel effort, Jefroykin managed to raise 28,380,000 fr. ($280,000–300,000) up to July 1, but this sum was reduced to 13,355,000 fr. ($140,000) during the second half of the year.[12]

During this time, about February, 1943, Jefroykin set up a kind of central committee of JDC in France to allocate the funds he raised. This committee obviously was a compromise between the centralized administration of funds as practiced by Lisbon and, later on, by Mayer, and a direct local response to changing needs. No minutes of the committee's meetings have survived, but we do know that they were held at irregular though fairly frequent intervals. Mayer, however, began to allocate to individual agencies; OSE especially began to turn to him, which created some bad blood between OSE and the others, especially FSJ, who were largely dependent on Jefroykin's committee.[13] Table 21 lists JDC's expenditures in France for the period 1941–44.[14]

Table 21: JDC Expenditures in France, 1941–44

	Official($)	Of which Mayer($)	Total JDC Expenditure	Percent of Total Budget
1941	793,384		5,716,908	13.8
1942	872,682		6,318,206	13.8
1943	1,748,500*	149,935	8,470,538	31.7
1944	1,657,223	1,056,930	15,216,643	10.9

*$789,599 also were unofficially appropriated for Jefroykin's loans.

The Rescue of Children

In 1942, JDC moved from the provision of aid to persecuted Jews to supporting groups engaged in physical rescue. Such clandestine rescue operations in France could succeed only with some measure of public tolerance, if not overt support. While it was true that many Frenchmen sympathized with the Vichy regime, they did not necessarily love the Germans, and they felt that the German treatment of French Jews was an insult to France. Even those who were antisemitic shared this feeling: they did not want the Germans to tell them how to deal with their Jews. Moreover, the brutal mass deportations of July-August, 1942, disgusted many Frenchmen, including large parts of the Catholic clergy. It would therefore seem that while a considerable part of the French population still supported the Vichy government in 1942–43, growing numbers of them were opposed to its anti-Jewish policy and its cooperation with the Germans in the persecution of the Jews. The result was readiness on the part of many Frenchmen to help Jews.

Apart from this willingness, and the German difficulties regarding their own manpower, there were two other essentials if significant numbers of Jews were to be saved: leadership and money. Leaders did arise—typically, as in other places in Europe—not primarily among the old leaders, but among the younger generation or among people who had never before been involved in Jewish affairs. Yet leadership was useless without money. Even the neighboring borders of neutral Switzerland and Spain were inaccessible if no funds were available. French peasants, and even Protestant or Catholic institutions, wanted money to pay for those whom they hid, and *passeurs*, the border smugglers, demanded payment for the dangers they were incurring. The organizers of rescue operations had to eat and sleep and wear clothes. Somebody had to pay the price, in cash. This was JDC's role.

The major rescue action undertaken in France was undoubtedly that of OSE, which originally had its headquarters at Montpellier.[15] In summer, 1942, the organization was led by Joseph Millner, head of the health section of UGIF, and had 1,200 children in twelve homes. In addition, and with the active cooperation of the AFSC, it was engaged in taking children from internment camps, with increasing help from French prefects. A transit camp for children at Palavas-les-Flots near Montpellier looked after children who had been taken out of the camps, first from Agde, and then from Gurs and other places, especially Rivesaltes. OSE also ran nine health centers, of which perhaps the most interesting was that run by Julien Samuel at Marseilles, opened in June, 1941. Two young social workers there, Nicole Salon-Weill and Huguette Wahl, later were to become heroines of OSE. Charles Lederman and Elizabeth Hirsch were at Lyons, Joseph Weill and Gaston Levy were in charge at Limoges, and Eugene

Minkowsky held the fort in Paris. Apart from the homes and the dispensaries, OSE supported children who were living with their families, usually providing partial relief in the form of medical care, and occasionally food or clothes.

Important as these activities were, they dwindled into insignificance when the deportations came. Some of OSE's leaders realized immediately that children must be saved, which could be done either by hiding them or by emigration. I shall deal with attempts at legal emigration separately, but the other alternatives, involving hiding and illegal crossings into neighboring neutral countries, meant that this purely social welfare agency had to become an underground organization. Nowhere does one find a clear statement of what exactly OSE thought was happening to the deportees. Stories circulated regarding Poland and Auschwitz that pictured these places as ghettos where Jewish councils governed: "The old people do not work. The children go to Jewish schools. Men and women capable of working are put to hard labor in factories and mines. Nourishment and lodging are reasonable."[16] But OSE's—and others'—actions showed clearly that they believed their charges' lives to be in acute danger. Deportation meant death; they knew it, though they occasionally denied it. It was this deep feeling of danger that made OSE act. Occasionally, very rarely, they tried to explain why it was that the Germans were killing Jewish children (one just has to accept as fact that such explanations contradicted rosier pictures of Poland and Silesia). The reason, they thought quite correctly, was that the Germans wanted to uproot and destroy "Judaism": "The extirpation of Jewry is finally to be accomplished by methodical extermination of the children ("Die Ausrottung des Judentums aber soll durch die methodische Vernichtung der Kinder besiegelt werden").[17]

It was Joseph Weill who decided to look for someone to organize the hiding of children. It had to be someone completely unknown who could easily pass for a non-Jew, a French Jew with an innocuous occupation, young, energetic, and completely devoted to his task. He found such a man in George Garel, the owner of a small electrical appliance shop in Lyons. His name was impeccably French; he had never been connected with any Jewish causes; he was completely unknown; and he had all the human qualities essential for such an undertaking. Garel established contact with Abbé Glasberg and decided to try his hand at smuggling out a group of children at a camp at Vénissieux near

Lyons, who were on the point of being carried off to Drancy and Poland. On August 26, 1942, Garel and a few others cut the fence of the camp, persuaded the surprised parents to part from their children, and took 108 of them away on trucks to be dispersed among Christian homes and institutions. On September 2, the Gestapo came to Cardinal Gerlier to demand the return of the children. But Gerlier did not know where they were.

The "Circuit Garel," as it was called, was swiftly organized. By mid-1943, Garel had four subregions with their own commands, with at least twenty-nine full-time workers. He used a system of small cells which ensured that workers did not even know that they were hiding Jewish children. At first he obtained help from Catholic and Protestant institutions, but soon he concentrated on hiding children with families, preferably peasants. He obtained the active help of Archbishop Jules-Gérard Saliège of Toulouse, who gave him a letter to all Catholics asking them to help his work. Similar aid was obtained from Pierre-Marie Theas, bishop of Montauban, and the Protestant church. Of course, the main problem was money. It soon became established that families or institutions hiding Jewish children received 600 fr. (about $6–8) monthly to defray their expenses, which mounted to a large sum for the 1,600 children hidden by Garel's group by mid-1943.

The children were selected on the basis of the danger they were in. First chosen were children of deported parents, who would be deported themselves in order "to reunite the families"; children whose parents had German, Czech, or Polish citizenship; children above the age of fourteen, who were liable to be seized and deported without further ado; and so on. Gradually, all Jews were threatened and all had to be hidden, including those in OSE's own children's homes, which of course were under UGIF surveillance. Fortunately, perhaps, the problem of hiding these groups only came at a stage when Garel was already organized to receive them. During the first months, children were accepted for hiding who were either smuggled out of internment camps or handed over by endangered parents.

It appears that the Circuit Garel underwent a number of reorganizations, and our documentation is not always clear about who did what and when. By the autumn of 1943, Garel's work had been split between "sector Garel," with headquarters in Lyons, and "sector Limoges," where Julien Samuel took over until he was arrested. Independent of both was the Paris sector, where Minkowsky was responsible. The same system was used in all three sectors, and all of them were responsible to a central group consisting of Joseph Millner ("Jomi"), Andrée Salomon, Dr. Jean Cremer, René Borel, and Alain Mosse. Mrs. Salomon took part in Samuel's work at Limoges and also became responsible for the transfer of children to Spain. Mosse was the last OSE representative at the UGIF. From an account given of OSE's activities in August, 1944, it appears that when liberation came, 1,260 children were hiding out with Garel's sector and 850 were in the Limoges sector where, after Samuel's arrest, Mrs. Salomon was responsible.

The danger to children in Paris was, if anything, greater than that in the south. In the frightful summer of 1942, 4,000 children had been deported, and 800 more followed by early 1943. As far as is known, not a single child survived these deportations—all were eaten up by the Nazi Moloch. In mid-1943, there were estimated to be some 2,000 children in Paris who had to be hidden, of whom approximately 1,000 were in official UGIF homes. With the help of French social workers, Minkowsky had hidden 550 children by August, 1943, while still maintaining a legal front. He then took over 100 children who had been cared for by the FSJ, and he sent about 200 more into southern France, where they were taken over by Garel. Of the UGIF children, 600 were under FSJ care, and FSJ was looking for a way to rescue them.[18]

OSE was not the only group trying to help, especially in Paris. The Communists, through the Mouvement national contre le racisme, led by Alex Chertok, Suzanna Spaatz, and Thérèse Pierre, organized their own commission for saving children and, with the help of a Protestant pastor, managed to save 63 children from a UGIF home on rue Lamarck by a really brilliant stroke. On February 16, 1943, their social workers visited the home and "promenaded" with the children in the fresh air, bringing them to the pastor, whence they were whisked to the countryside to sympathizers.[19] In about May, the EIF and the MJS established a branch of their own illegal organization in Paris, called, in the north as in the south, *la sixième* ("the sixth"); it was so named because EIF believed that only five departments of UGIF were doing any work. It therefore activated a sixth, illegal, one to produce forged documents and hide children. The Paris sixième cooperated both with the Communists and with Minkowsky and FSJ. By the summer of 1943, child-saving operations in Paris were more or less coordinated, and while FSJ played a smaller part after the deportation of David Rappaport, head of the rue Amelot group of FSJ, a new figure emerged who, in alliance with Min-kowsky, took over much of the work: Juliette Stern of WIZO. She remained with the Paris UGIF and at the same time engaged in illegal activities. With her help and that of other groups, at least 1,000 children were hidden and saved in Paris and then dispersed in the northern departments.[20]

The dispersal of children from OSE's own homes presented the organization with very considerable difficulties. These chil-dren were under strict surveillance, and it was not easy to smuggle them out gradually while maintaining the legal facade and avoiding German reaction. OSE persuaded some prefects to requisition its homes for local reasons and thus force dispersals. Elsewhere other subterfuges were used. On November 12, 1943, Millner reported that an OSE council had been held at Limoges devoted to finding ways to rescue the children; it decided upon immediate dispersal. By December, only two official homes re-mained: Masgelier and Poulouzat, with 450 inmates, while 850 had been taken out. By March, 1944, only some babies remained in a home at Limoges, where their identities were changed and they were left under IRC protection as non-Jewish children; at Chaumont, the last 50 children were similarly left under the offi-cial French social service.[21]

It was the express wish of OSE not only to save the chil-dren's bodies, but to see to it that they were not deprived either of affection or of education. It is in the carrying out of this com-mitment that one can see the tremendous effort made by indi-viduals: by administrators and by the social workers, who were often simply youngsters who volunteered to visit the children in their foster homes and in some cases form a link between them and their parents or other relatives who were in hiding or in other places in the country. Special efforts were made to keep the chil-dren within the Jewish faith and attached to their people. Occa-sionally one finds that Catholic institutions attempted to convert Jewish children. Over 100 proven cases exist, and there must have been more that we do not know of; very few of these, however, occurred within OSE's sphere of activity. On the whole, the Catholic church did not misuse its opportunity.[22]

In addition to hiding children with non-Jewish families, OSE cared for many who were living with their families, some of them in hiding, and most of them in a shadowy semilegal existence. There seem to have been about 1,000 such children. OSE also looked after 500 more, who were being cared for by the Amitié

249

chrétienne and the Service social d'aide aux émigrés of Marie Chevally. Higher numbers have been claimed, but it would appear that OSE had, under its direct or indirect care in France, about 4,600 children just before the liberation in August, 1944.

OSE work cost lives—not of the children, but of many of the brave workers. Of the children hidden in the north, eight were caught by the Germans by pure accident. No record exists of any children caught in the south, a testimonial to the Frenchmen who hid the children. Of the adults who sacrificed their lives to save them, one should mention Alain Mosse, who kept the official OSE offices open because he wanted to hide all the children in OSE homes; had he closed them, the Germans might have descended on the homes and deported the children. In early 1943, Chambéry, in the zone occupied by the Italians since November, 1942, had become the center of OSE activities. As long as the Italians were there, OSE was relatively safe, but conditions changed after the German occupation of the region, and on February 8, 1944, the Germans raided its headquarters at Chambéry and took Mosse and some of his fellow workers to Drancy and Auschwitz. Charles Lederman and Julien Samuel were also caught, though Samuel managed to survive and lived to occupy important positions in postwar French Jewry.

The EIF numbered between 1,700 and 1,800 members in 1940. They too, under their founder and leader Robert Gamzon, entered the child-care field in 1940, looking after 300 to 400 children. In a meeting at Clermont-Ferrand in July, 1940, they adopted the idea of a return to the soil, and founded an agricultural training center at Moissac in the unoccupied zone which soon became the center for EIF as a whole. EIF was a religiously oriented, patriotically French group, representing tendencies close to those of the CC. It interpreted religion in a liberal rather than orthodox sense. Under the impact of the war, a more orthodox tendency developed, refugee and immigrant youths joined, and Zionist tendencies began to influence the movement, without, however, transforming it completely. Gamzon was also one of the founder-members of UGIF, and he remained in charge of its youth section until it was abolished in early 1943. His rather conservative tendencies enabled him to convince Vichy officials to help him in the establishment of nine agricultural centers for Jewish youth in addition to that at Moissac, where 200 youths found homes and a way of life in 1941 and 1942.

The EIF widened its scope in early 1942 by engaging in educational activities in Gurs and other camps under the aegis of the

AFSC, thus becoming indirectly involved in JDC-subsidized activities. Among its leaders, Dr. Simeon Hammel and Rabbi Leo Cohen represented a deeply religious, even neo-hassidic trend, centered especially around the farm at Taluyer. At the Lautrec farm, another leader, Marc Haguenau, of old French Jewish origin, was pressing for immediate anti-German action. Two EIF members, Simon Levitte and Andrée Solomon, formed contacts with Zionist groups and the OSE. In August, 1942, an underground group was founded at Moissac, the sixième which we have already seen in action with OSE in Paris. Eighty-eight individuals working with the sixième in the south, and another thirty in the north, created an organization which exactly parallelled the Circuit Garel. The sixième was in touch with the Gaullist underground, whom it also supplied with false papers. In January, 1943, the EIF united with MJS, the Zionist youth group which had been founded in May, 1942, as a unification of left-wing movements. MJS was in touch with the Communist MOI and FSJ, and when Levitte caused it to unite with EIF, these links continued. It is of course very difficult to estimate the numerical strength of the united movement, because many EIF members were cut off from their groups for a variety of reasons and many MJS members were caught by the Germans in Paris. The united EIF probably numbered several hundred active members. In Paris, they were largely connected with Juliette Stern and did not engage in independent activities. In the south, under Henri Wahl, the sixième hid about 850 children, mainly in the Tarn et Garonne area, under the noses of the SS Das Reich division, which was stationed there.[23]

All three organizations—OSE, EIF, and MJS—engaged in illegal border crossings into Switzerland. From the summer of 1942, children were smuggled into neutral Swiss territory by George Loinger, who had been OSE's sports organizer, Mila Racine of MJS, and Marianne Cohen of EIF. At first these crossings took place chiefly from Italian-controlled French territory. Those involved quickly learned that the Swiss would not refuse admittance to children under sixteen or to families with small children, and this knowledge governed the transfers. After September, 1943, children were usually brought to the French border town of Annemasse, where a friendly mayor helped with arrangements, until the crossing could be effected. A total of about 1,300 children were transferred to Switzerland. There was one case of treachery: Mila Racine and Marianne Cohen were caught and died in Auschwitz.

251

The Italian Sector in Southern France

While JDC's main effort in France was directed toward saving children, other situations arose which had to be dealt with. One such case was in the Nice area, which was held by the Italians from November, 1942, to September, 1943. The Italians were never very convinced racists or antisemites. Increasingly disenchanted with the war and with Germany, Italian military and civilian authorities assumed the task of protecting Jews from Germans wherever they ruled—in Greece, in parts of Yugoslavia, and around Nice. (In fact, an Italian Jew, Angelo Donati, was the most influential personality in Nice in Jewish matters.) At first the Italian army had the responsibility for Jewish affairs, and in early December, 1942, they assured the Germans all Jews would be interned. Nothing of the sort happened, however, and repeated interventions at Rome by Hans G. Mackensen, the German ambassador, were met with prevarications on the Italian side. In February, 1943, the Italians even forced Vichyite police who had arrested some Jews to release their captives, and a French report to that effect became the subject of a talk between the German foreign minister, Ribbentrop, and Mussolini on February 25. Early in March, more Jews were released by the Italians from French clutches. On March 18, Mussolini intervened as if to solve the problem in accordance with German wishes. An Italian commander of the gendarmes named Guido Lospinoso was put at the head of the "racial police" and in charge of the Jewish question. His deputy, however, turned out to be no other than Donati. The Italians then proceeded to intern several thousand "foreign" Jews in mountain resorts, including Saint-Gervais, Mégève, and Saint-Martin where they had to be taken care of by Jewish organizations (in this case, largely by the FSJ). Jewish sources estimated that during the year of the Italian occupation, 18,000 Jews fled into the zone from German-occupied France, joining 5,000 who were already there.[24]

FSJ had warned other Jewish groups that the Italians would ultimately leave. In fact, after the fall of Mussolini on July 25, 1943, German troops began to occupy the Italian zone under a number of pretexts, and Jews tended to concentrate in Nice, still under Italian control. They were moving into a trap. The Italians promised that if they had to retreat, they would take at least those Jews that were most immediately threatened with them. On September 6 and 7, eighty-four Italian trucks appeared in the mountain resorts and brought some 3,000 Jews into Nice, where they were lodged in hotels. On September 8, Italy capitulated, and on the following day the Germans entered the city. The Italians had not kept their promise. They withdrew, and no more than 1,000 Jews managed to escape with them. Even those did not fare well; a few hundred people from Saint-Martin who crossed into Italy were interned at Voldieri and then handed over to the Germans. The Germans themselves, under Brunner who arrived from Drancy, pounced on the hotels, taking 3,000 or more Jews away to their deaths in the first few days. The railway stations were blocked, and a large number of those who tried to get away were caught. In the town, French fascists—adherents of Jacques Doriot—and members of the criminal underworld helped the Germans to identify Jews, and there were some Jewish traitors. UGIF opened its offices, but after a while all those who came there were caught in a raid and deported. Then the offices reopened and the Germans repeated their tactic. It was simply impossible to hide 22,000 people in a town like Nice. Yet, when all these events are taken into account, it is surprising that the Germans did not catch more victims that they did. Though exact figures are impossible to come by, it is unlikely that more than 5,000 people were caught and deported.[25]

The Jewish organizations reacted immediately to meet the new emergency. A young MJS member, Jacques Weintraub, organized the crossing of 120 especially endangered children into Switzerland and managed to set up an apparatus for forged papers before he was caught by the Germans and shipped to Drancy. Nicole Salon-Weill and Huguette Wahl, the OSE social workers, were caught hiding children and organizing their transfer back to the former unoccupied zone. Many hundreds of children who had been with local families were nevertheless taken out of the danger zone. Locally, Dr. Moses Abadie, a resident of Nice who up till then had had no contact with rescue work, organized a network to hide some 200 children, in coordination with OSE and with the help of two Catholic priests. Help was also received from the Protestants, while the Gaullist underground gave some food and other material help. The Communists published leaflets calling on the population to oppose the deportation of Jews. A defense committee in which all the organizations participated aided mass evasion.

It is quite clear, then, that without the help of many French people, it would have been impossible to save such a high proportion of the Jews trapped at Nice. That Brunner received the help of some additional German police did not materially change the situation. For some reason the German army does not seem to have been used, and, working in a situation with relatively small forces and facing an increasingly hostile local population, the Gestapo and other SS units did not manage to achieve their murderous aim. Of course, had the Jews remained passive, they would have been caught nevertheless, but we know that they did not. The funds for most of the activities were supplied by JDC. The Nice crisis occurred at the end of 1943, when Mayer already had some funds at his disposal; he was in a position to help, and as the saving of lives became primarily a question of money, JDC supplied it.

Escape to Spain

The organized crossings into Switzerland were paralleled by crossings into Spain, but in these cases it was AJ (also known as the Organisation juive de combat; OJC) that coordinated them. Dedicated to the preparation of armed action against the Germans, AJ became, after September, 1943, a group in which the active elements of EIF, MJS, and even OSE workers participated. AJ had its contacts mainly with the Armée secrete of General Charles Délestraint, a supporter of de Gaulle. Towards the end of 1943, it established three maquis groups, in the Montagne Noire and the Tarn and Loire districts. Members were recruited largely from EIF, and in fact the most important of these groups ultimately came under Robert Gamzon's command.

Small groups of Jews began crossing the Pyrenees in the summer of 1942, usually with Frenchmen. Some of these were helped by the Catholic priest, Marie Benoit; others apparently organized independently. One of the sources indicates that, out of 154 candidates for immigration into Palestine from Spain in 1943, 55 crossed into Spain in 1942 up to November, and 50 after November, when the Germans occupied the south of France.[26] Many others came with French parties that intended to join the Gaullist forces. In October, the sixième got a party of youngsters across, but unfortunately two of the boys were caught by the Germans. A second party crossed in early 1943, and more followed. The numbers smuggled across through Jewish efforts were very small by comparison with the large numbers of Frenchmen—including a proportion of Jews—who came across in organized French groups, and this was especially true after the law of February, 1943, which intended to force French workers to labor in Germany. Throughout 1943, about 16,000 Frenchmen crossed the border into Spain, and 10 or 12 percent of these were Jews. But the majority of Jews came across in privately organized groups. At the end of 1943, there were approximately 6,000 Jews in Spain, of whom two-thirds must have come in such groups.

In 1944, up to the liberation of southern France in August, 1,500 more Jews went to Spain, and during this period the influence of Jewish organizations was much greater. Even before it was joined by EIF in September, 1943, AJ was interested in the border crossings, because it gave its members the option of staying on and fighting the Germans in France or getting out into Spain and joining either the Free French forces or the Palestine Jewish units in the British army. After September, the crossings were better organized and conducted more professionally. Special branches—the Service d'evacuation et rassemblement for adults and, later, the Service d'evacuation et de regroupement d'enfants for children—were set up. Simeon Hammel, and later Jacques Roitman and Rabbi Leo Cohen of the AJ-EIF, were involved in the organization. In 1943–44, 500 members of the united AJ and 100 children crossed into Spain.[27] A number of the organizers fell into German hands, including Cohen and Roitman. Difficulties with the professional passeurs at the borders, some of whom paid with their lives for their work and a few of whom betrayed the refugees, lack of money, and the sheer physical hardship of climbing in the snow-capped Pyrenees contributed to the relatively modest results.

The AJ had hoped for more. In May, 1943, a committee of which Jefroykin was a member sent emissaries to contact JDC and get help organizing a large-scale transfer of people out of France. Joseph Croustillon and Shlomo Steinhorn, East European immigrants and AJ members, were entrusted with the task. Croustillon tried to establish contact with Samuel Sequerra in Barcelona, or Paul Block of David Blickenstaff's Madrid office. Unfortunately, their stories of an armed Jewish resistance movement that needed immediate help and that wanted to smuggle Jews into Spain so they could join Allied armies seemed wild and irresponsible. Croustillon especially, the older and more articulate of the two, was a man of rather inflexible and difficult bearing, and his insistent demands made Sequerra and Block even more suspicious of him. Croustillon also contacted Isaac Weissman, the WJC representative in Lisbon, which did not endear him to JDC's Lisbon office. Steinhorn was the first to give up; from Barcelona he wrote to Jefroykin in France: "Here we have Sequerra, which is something you cannot imagine . . . nobody wants to understand us or to help us."[28] Croustillon vegetated in Madrid, completely helpless. In 1944, he finally managed to meet Schwartz, from whom he then received help and recognition. But it was too late. The opportunity of organizing a large-scale evacuation to Spain had passed, if indeed it had ever existed.

It is now clear that the JDC operations responsible for France—Lisbon-Switzerland and Jefroykin-Brenner—were pursuing contradictory policies in 1943–44. Jefroykin later said that JDC-Lisbon had in effect let him write his own check for rescue work, though without explicitly authorizing clandestine channels, and above all without ever agreeing to finance the armed resistance.[29] In May, 1944, Schwartz did explicitly authorize 10 million fr., which were given to FSJ for Spanish border crossings and which must have been handed by FSJ to the AJ-EIF groups. Fischer and AJ functionaries testified after the war that they had received their funds from JDC and that they had never lacked money for their work.[30] In a report of August, 1944, Jefroykin claimed that 30 million fr. ($360,000, or about one-eighth of the total JDC budget in 1943) had been spent on illegal work, presumably including the Spanish and Swiss border crossings.

These statements stand in stark contradiction to instructions which Mayer received from Lisbon. In July, 1943, Mayer was told that JDC did not want "this job" (the crossings into Spain) "to be financed through us," and he was instructed to tell FSJ, who acted as a go-between with the AJ, to find other sources.[31] Both statements were repeated several times throughout the year, but never by Schwartz personally, who seems to have been content to let Jefroykin assume responsibility for these actions in France. In fact, therefore, JDC pursued a double policy. It could not afford to be caught organizing a smuggling operation and remain a respectable, legal American body in Spain, Portugal, and Switzerland. On the other hand, Schwartz seems to have been determined not to allow anything to tie Jefroykin's hands. He could rely on Jefroykin to do what was necessary without asking too much of Lisbon or Mayer. Lives had to be saved, and one had to be judicious and walk the tightrope between a head office which did not always understand the exigencies of the European situation, suspicious neutral governments whose cooperation was essential for saving Jews, and the cries of anguish from France. The money was given and the regulations obeyed, all at the same time.

Nowhere does Schwartz's policy appear more clearly than with relation to FSJ. Jarblum came to Geneva in March, 1943. By July, Jarblum told Mayer, FSJ was supporting 7,700 people in France, and 75 had already crossed into Spain. Of these, 850 were internees at Saint-Gervais in the Nice area. The situation was catastrophic. He needed 4 million fr. (about $30,000) monthly, as against only 1.7 million ($17,000) a year earlier. "Tante Feder" (the code name for FSJ) was "up to her neck" in debts. Could Mayer help? Mayer, of course, had no money, but he did give some very small amounts, carefully checking with JDC-Lisbon what should be done. Jarblum concluded that Mayer was a hard-hearted bureaucrat and turned to Schwartz himself. In many cases, he wrote in October, one could not save human beings because of lack of money. Luckily, he said, he had other resources and was not entirely dependent on JDC. "Saly Mayer, who knows the situation, helps me a little, but this is all insufficient." To Mayer, a month later, he protested against not receiving any answer to his pleas. "Should I write to my friends frankly, in response to their many letters, that they cannot count on serious help from you?"[32]

At the end of 1943, after the debacle at Nice, FSJ was supporting 6,582 people monthly, at a cost of 2.3 million fr. ($19,000). But by then Mayer had some money, and while Jarblum's letters to him remained cold and formal, Jarblum was getting funds. Mayer was apparently suspicious of Jarblum's many contacts outside of JDC, not knowing how much money he was receiving from them. In any case, FSJ operations, while important, only dealt with relatively small groups, whereas OSE dealt with children—who obviously had a first claim on JDC resources. By May, 1944, Mayer thought FSJ was receiving its due share of JDC resources. When Jarblum continued to complain, especially regarding funds for border crossings into Spain, even Schwartz stated that he had given Jarblum enough money. What infuriated Jarblum more than anything else was the fact that in the spring of 1944, Mayer began transmitting money directly to France through his own couriers, even to the FSJ center at Lyons, rather than through Jarblum's office in Geneva. And, of course, both JDC-Lisbon and Mayer simply refused to answer his pleas regarding Spain; to react to appeals for funds for illegal frontier crossing in censored cables, letters, or telephone calls would have been most unwise.[33]

Nevertheless, in the spring of 1944, children's transports did begin going even into Spain. The Germans were hunting down the last legal homes; French non-Jews working for Jewish organizations were beginning to "show a tendency to decrease their involvement." The indomitable Andrée Solomon, acting in conjunction with AJ, organized two transports, later followed by others, which got a hundred children across into Spain under very difficult conditions. The money for this venture, and apparently part of the money for AJ generally, came through the Quakers, who had received $100,000 from JDC "to help children out of France to Spain and possibly Switzerland."[34] Helga Holbeck, the Quaker representative at Marseilles, paid out the funds in accordance with instructions she received orally from Schwartz and, possibly, Jefroykin.

"Dyka" Jefroykin himself crossed into Spain and arrived at Barcelona on May 8, 1944. There was nothing further he thought he could do in France. He could no longer obtain loans against repayment after the war, and his job was to try to repair the damage caused by the failure of Croustillon and Steinhorn's mission. In a very difficult crossing, during which he lost his father-in-law, Jefroykin, now as an AJ member, made the journey. Immediately after arriving, he set up an organization that provided a hotel and guides in Andorra, the tiny neutral republic in the Pyrenees which could be reached from the French side. He met with Schwartz and opened the way for larger sums to reach the AJ via FSJ.

Jarblum, however, still did not rely only on JDC funds. He was suspicious of JDC's slow and legalistic methods, and he did have contacts with Palestine and WJC. As soon as he got to Geneva, he contacted JA representatives in Istanbul, demanding money for armed resistance and flight into neutral countries. At first there was no money, and it seemed there would have been no way of transferring the funds to Switzerland in any case. But both obstacles were surmounted, and in June, 1943, Istanbul approved a budget of £2,200 (approximately $8,800) monthly for these purposes, and especially for the flight of children. It is unclear how much money Jarblum received from that source, but the total must have been considerable. In December, 1943, and again in 1944, $25,000 were obtained under a U. S. Treasury license through Riegner of the WJC for evacuating refugees to Spain or Switzerland, and $10,000 from Istanbul in response to Jarblum's complaint that Schwartz "still refuses his help to this

258

activity." It is uncertain whether this money actually reached Jarblum, but it is clear that funds did reach FSJ from both Palestinian
and WJC sources and, through it, AJ and other groups.[35]

An Official Rescue Plan

JDC was involved in yet another attempt to rescue children
from France. The State Department hinted to JDC as early as
June, 1942, that there might be a possibility of emigrating 2,000 to
3,000 children, but nothing happened about this proposal until
August.[36] When the deportations in the south began, Schwartz
could not get in touch with his New York office. He had to get
out of France first, and it was not until the third week in August
that he contacted New York. In the meantime, AFSC inquired of
Moses Leavitt whether he thought it a good idea to try to bring
7,000 children to the United States. Leavitt replied that, if no free
homes were found, it would cost $500 a year to maintain one
child. JDC would have to find $3.5 million; he would have to
weigh the proposal carefully, because it would cost half of JDC's
annual budget. Inevitably, the plan implied drastic cuts in funding for everything else JDC was doing.

On August 14, Boris Tschlenoff in Geneva called a conference of aid organizations at which he recommended an identical
scheme; this was approved by Donald Lowrie for the Nîmes Coordinating Committee, and endorsed by Schwartz in France.
When Schwartz finally cabled New York on August 26, 1942, he
asked for immediate U.S. visas for 1,000 children. "Literally thousands of fathers and mothers are leaving their children behind in
unoccupied France rather than take them along on their journey
eastwards which can have but one conclusion."[37] The JDC leadership in New York tried to weigh the proposal. Could not Spain
and Portugal be persuaded to serve as temporary havens? Could
not Switzerland be persuaded? No, said Schwartz. Spain and Portugal were not that friendly to Jews, and Switzerland was already
carrying a heavy burden of refugees. Baerwald, however, still
hesitated. He was concerned "with respect to large commitments
for these children's projects and although desirous of doing maximum . . . we must now take stock before incurring additional
commitments."[38] But Schwartz insisted. In cables sent on September 4 and 5, he reported that children were being shipped off to
Poland. Every minute counted.

Leavitt turned to the State Department. Would they help? The American press was full of the French deportations. But Washington also had its own information, from S. Pinkney Tuck at Vichy. On September 11, he cabled to Secretary of State Cordell Hull that he was "greatly disturbed as to the fate of foreign Jewish children in the unoccupied zone who have been and are still being separated from their parents. I am convinced that it is useless to expect any moderation" from the French. He suggested that Washington should enable him to approach Pierre Laval to allow as many children as the United States would be willing to accept to emigrate from France. Laval might agree, in order somewhat to calm the storm of criticism which his "inhumane policy has aroused throughout the country." It was obvious that the Nazis did not intend the children's parents to survive, and therefore those whose parents had been deported "may already be considered as orphans."[39]

JDC now acted swiftly. On September 16, its Executive Committee appropriated $400,000 towards an estimated cost of $950,000 for the transport of 1,000 children and their upkeep in America for the first year. On September 21, the U.S. Committee for the Care of Children, under Eleanor Roosevelt's chairmanship, decided to adopt the program, provided JDC subscribed another $400,000. On September 28, Hull cabled to Tuck that the visas were approved, the Quakers would choose the children, and would he get the French to give them exit visas? Tuck reported on October 3 that Laval had agreed "en principe" to grant the exit visas. He had obviously been taken by surprise, not really expecting that the United States would actually grant visas. But Krug von Nidda, the German envoy at Vichy, had called on September 29 and told the French that the Germans would want to be consulted. The children might be used against Germany for propaganda. "I had difficulty in restraining my anger," reported Tuck. "To suggest that the US wanted anything else but to make a humanitarian gesture was a base and contemptible suggestion." On October 9, Laval agreed to give the exit permits, provided the United States gave an official assurance that no propaganda use would be made of the children.[40] Nevertheless, Laval retreated later in the month. There had been adverse publicity in the United States, and he would not give the visas. Very strong pressure by Tuck finally caused him to relent and grant 500 of them.

In the meantime, however, Schwartz and other American social workers in Europe were well aware that 1,000 visas were not enough. While the negotiations for them went on, other countries reacted in different ways to the situation in France. At the end of August, the Dominican dictator Trujillo inquired of the British, and than of the American, envoys in San Domingo whether a gesture on his part would be appreciated. He had no intention of accepting any more adult Jews from Europe, having promised to accept 100,000 in 1938, but he would do something regarding children. Gestures were always appreciated, he was told. On August 27, the Dominican government announced that it would accept 3,500 Jewish refugee children. "He repeated his government intended to make a gesture and contemplated no practical arrangements."[41] The Jews, of course, were unaware of the tragicomic aspects of the Dominican offer: they took it very seriously.

Canadian Jewry, always closely associated with JDC, tried to get whatever it could from its government. Canada asked the Americans whether it was true that they were accepting 1,000 Jewish children, and when the information proved to be correct, Canada had to do something. On October 2, the government informed Canadian Jewish leader Saul Hayes that it would accept 500 children. In response, the U.S. Committee for the Care of Children then decided to ask the U.S. government to accept more children. Sumner Welles of the State Department wrote to James MacDonald of the President's Advisory Committee for Refugees that the United States would admit a total of 5,000 children, provided there was no publicity as to the numbers. JDC then pledged $400,000 for each 1,000 children, or $2 million for the 5,000—a sum which would have somehow to be raised. The Roosevelt committee would pay the balance from the general war appeals conducted throughout America.

Other countries now joined in the offers. Britain could not very well stand aside. The Anglican and Roman Catholic churches, especially, began pressing the government to admit refugee children. Yielding unwillingly and slowly to public pressure, Home Secretary Herbert Morrison provided for a number of children who had close relatives already living in Britain. Canada then increased her offer to 1,000, and Argentina joined in with another 1,000. Other Latin American countries offered smaller numbers of visas.

What is interesting in this development is the snowballing effect of public pressure on rather unwilling governments. It would not "look good" if others acted and one's own government did not. One could no longer hide behind "after you, sir." A real chance of saving thousands of children suddenly opened up, prompted by aroused public opinion, the public press, and individuals and organizations such as Schwartz, Lowrie, the Quakers, OSE—and, in a crucially important position, the American chargé at Vichy, S. Pinkney Tuck.

But fate decreed against the mass rescue. Twenty-eight escorts for the first 500 children chosen by the Quakers left New York on November 7, 1942, for Lisbon. While they were on the high seas, an armada of Allied ships approached the shores of North Africa, landing on November 8. On November 9, Germans began occupying what had until then been the unoccupied zone in France, and exit visas were canceled. With diplomatic relations broken, the American chargé left Vichy. The children were trapped.

There was one hope left. Lowrie and most of the other Americans managed to escape to Geneva, where they tried to persuade the Swiss government to accept the children officially into Switzerland. The Secours Suisse aux enfants, a child-care society connected with the Swiss Red Cross, was concerned because the French had forcefully taken some Jewish children to their deaths from the organization's homes in France. The Swiss minister and IRC representative at Vichy, Walter Stucki, had an audience with Marshall Pétain in late September. Afterwards he told a friend that it was "probably the first time in history that a Swiss Minister in order to drive home a point has pounded a table before the Chief of a Foreign State."[42] Stucki's effort was in vain, and children were again taken away from the homes. But now the Swiss were angry, and Lowrie hoped he could do something.

The Swiss were actually willing to take children in, but they wanted an assurance that after the war they would be taken away again. In January, 1943, Lowrie cabled the U.S. State Department to that effect, but the department refused to obligate a subsequent administration for the issuance of visas to children who might be adults by the end of the war. In London, Sir Herbert Emerson of the IGCR approached the British government; it also refused to guarantee that the children could to to Palestine after the war. In any case, the 1939 White Paper provided that Jewish immigration to Palestine would cease after five years, in 1944. Yet, while the great U.S. and British powers would not promise to save 5,000 children's lives, Switzerland, despite its refusal, approached the Vichy government and demanded the release of the children, offering to accept them. Vichy refused. A cable by Philip Conard of the Quakers' Lisbon office on January 19, 1943, said: "Vichy advised Swiss Foreign Office impossible at present envisage departure children. Our legation Berne interprets this as definite refusal."[43] It was.

The matter, however, did not end there. On November 11, 1943, the British colonial secretary announced that the unused portion of the Palestine immigration certificates, although due to expire in 1944, could still be used after that date. On the strength of his announcement, JDC turned to the British, asking them to guarantee the children's visas for postwar emigration from Switzerland to Palestine. The suggestion, made on November 23, was answered on December 31. It took the British government five weeks to decide on a negative answer: there would be difficulty in reserving the certificates until after the war. The Allies were working on a general assurance to neutrals that all refugees from Allied countries—which did not include German or Austrian Jews—would be repatriated after the war. Only in 1944 did a declaration of this sort reach them.[44]

Fortunately, most Jewish children that could be saved were saved. From all accounts it would appear that between 5,500 and 6,000 children were hidden and kept alive throughout the occupation, not counting about 1,000 more who were helped (largely by OSE) while staying with their families. In addition to some hundreds saved by the Communists, there were 4,600 under OSE, 850 under EIF, and 1,400 who were rescued and transferred into Switzerland and Spain. JDC, through the organizations it supported, played a significant role, not only indirectly as a funding agency, but directly through people like Jefroykin and Brenner. Jefroykin claimed in July, 1944, that JDC "encouraged, inspired and directed the various organizations in the rescue of the children in France."[45] There was a dark side to the story, too. Many thousands of children were deported, together with their little brothers and sisters from all the other Nazi-controlled countries. Probably no less than 8,000 to 10,000 children up to the age of sixteen fell into Nazi hands even in France. The ovens of Auschwitz solved the problem.

JDC and the Holocaust in France

One can observe differences in the behavior of the major actors on the Jewish side of the events in France: the burning zeal of Jarblum, Millner, or Jefroykin; the deft handling of the possible by Schwartz; the courage and self-sacrifice of workers in the OSE, EIF, FSJ, and other agencies; and the secretive actions of Mayer, pedantic, remote, and yet passionate in his own peculiar way. Mayer gave money when he had it and when it was needed. He demanded accounting, and he was full of praise when he got OSE's exact reports or even when a furious and disgusted Jarblum practically threw the FSJ reports at him. He insisted on Jefroykin stopping to borrow money at rates that were lower than those he could get in Switzerland. Why waste public money? He got the same amount, after all, and it got into France. Above his desk at Saint Gallen there was a plaque with the letters O. P. M., for "Other People's Money."

What makes France and JDC's work in France such an important subject for study and reflection is the clear way in which the problem of the general awareness of the Holocaust presents itself. Tuck in his memoranda to the State Department, Schwartz and Lowrie in their cables and reports, the OSE in its desperate pleas for funds to save lives—these hardly leave any doubt that they knew what they were talking about. Yet we find a wealth of documentation that tends to deny it. An OSE report of July 25, 1943, speaks of the time after liberation, when "the veterans of Drancy, of Silesia and Poland will have the word. And we, you [OSE in Switzerland] and the Herberts [Katzki; that is, JDC] will have to be very modest indeed." Reports circulated about Auschwitz as a place of work, where children went to Jewish schools. Deportees from Drancy in their last letters expressed certainty that they would survive because they were young and strong, and they took care of abandoned children on the trains so these children would have someone to look after them in Poland. Perhaps one of the most amazing pieces of evidence is a letter written by Jules Jefroykin himself to Leavitt on November 24, 1944, after the liberation of France, in which he reports that he is arranging for an index system of all deportees, "which will make it possible to bring together the various members of the families when we shall be able to take up our work in Eastern Europe."[46]

Information regarding mass murder simply was not enough. Instincts of self-preservation and psychological mechanisms to defend against the knowledge of destruction of one's self or one's world militated against the internalization of this information. If it was not internalized into "knowledge" it could not become knowledge—a basis for reaction and action. It is not impossible that remarks such as Jefroykin's might have had unconscious magical significance, as though the expression of confidence in the victims' return would make wishful thinking into reality. It was therefore perfectly possible for people to act on two levels: as though the danger were real; and as though it were not.

One must not underestimate the tremendous psychological advantage which the Germans enjoyed in planning the murder of all the members of a people for no other reason than that they had been born. There were no mechanisms of defense prepared against such a course of action. The amazing thing about French Jewry was the speed with which, without information necessarily becoming knowledge, it created defensive measures suited to the situation. JDC could not claim to have originated or guided this process. But it did help, and not only, as Jefroykin rightly said, as a funding agency, but as a full and important partner.

11

Rescue Attempts in Western and Southern Europe

JDC rescue operations in Belgium, Holland, Italy, and Yugoslavia between 1941 and 1945 had a number of characteristics in common. They were mostly directed by Saly Mayer in Switzerland rather than by JDC-Lisbon, and they consisted largely of funding rather than direct involvement such as we have seen in France. This meant that while large numbers of people were helped, JDC had no central role in organizing the aid that it funded. Rescue and aid were dependent on Jewish bodies and individuals, and in none of these countries did Mayer initiate activities. All he could do was find ways to help the initiators—when he had the money. Despite the geographical and political differences between the four countries and their Jewish populations, JDC's methods were similar: when no local Jewish activists appeared, JDC was as powerless as the rest of the Jewish world to save Jewish lives.

Rescue in Belgium

The available statistics regarding Jews in Belgium during the war years are contradictory and problematic, but it appears that there were about 85,000–90,000 Jews in that country when the

Germans attacked it on May 10, 1940. Large numbers of Belgian Jews fled south into France, but many of them returned to their homes in the summer and autumn. In October, 1940, 46,652 Jews above the age of fifteen registered with the Germans, while a postwar inquiry elicited an index of 57,313 names of Jews who were in Belgium in late 1940 and 1941. Some hundreds were shot during the war, and 31,416 Jews were deported, of whom about 3,000 returned or survived deportation. The number of Jewish survivors in Belgium would therefore be about 26,000: with the addition of the camp survivors, the total reaches 29,000, or over half of Belgian Jewry.[1]

Actually, it is misleading to speak of "Belgian Jewry" because only 7 percent of the Jews in Belgium were Belgian nationals. Most of the country's Jews were newcomers from Eastern or Central Europe, many of them still speaking Yiddish or German or some Slavonic language and rather bad French. There was a sizable proletariat in Brussels—tailors, furriers, and other representatives of "typically Jewish" trades; there were diamond cutters in Antwerp. Strong leftist tendencies were felt, especially in Brussels, whose prewar Jewish population of 30,000 had a variety of communist, Trotskyite, or left-wing Zionist groups. Antwerp, with 55,000 Jews, had tended to become the haven of the more tradition-minded elements, from liberal to ultraorthodox. However, many members of the Jewish prewar leadership fled the country in May, 1940, and as the occupying Germans tightened their grip, this relative lack of leadership became apparent.

Occupied Belgium was under German military rule, and the highest SS officer was an SS und Polizei-Führer, a district officer of the SS and security services, of the relatively low rank of Obersturmbannführer, the equivalent of a lieutenant colonel. The number of SS-commanded police was not very great, and the SS had to rely, as in France, on the cooperation of the military and of the local Belgian police and antisemitic volunteers. Such antisemites were stronger in the Flemish than in the Walloon part of Belgium, and especially in the city of Antwerp, where a pogrom was organized by Nazi sympathizers in April, 1941.

While there were many similarities between conditions in Belgium and in France under German rule, there were significant differences as well. Belgium had no collaborationist government. As in Holland, civilian government was largely in the hands of secretaries-general of Belgian ministries, who maintained various degrees of loyalty to the Belgian government-in-exile in London.

Belgian parliamentary committees had some say in restraining German policies, and a rather undefined influence was wielded by the prisoner-king, Leopold III, and the queen mother, Elizabeth. In the autumn of 1940, when the Germans registered the Jews and their property, the secretary-general of the Ministry of the Interior refused to legislate against the Jews. The University of Brussels declared that it could not "participate in the execution of these orders."[2] A local initiative in Flanders sent 3,284 Jews for labor in the Limburg province, but there was no work for them and they drifted back. The most important countermeasure was taken in London: on January 10, 1941, the government-in-exile issued an injunction (*arrêté-loi*) which declared all German laws or orders against religion, race, or language inoperative and illegal. This meant that anyone profiting from Aryanization procedures was profiting from an illegal act, and his action was therefore punishable.[3] German laws and ordinances proceeded parallel to those instituted in France: progressively, they removed Jews from everyday economic life and deprived them of their property, reducing most of them to penury. The Belgian Judenrat, the Association des Juifs de Belgique (AJB), was established on November 25, 1941, at the same time as UGIF in France. The head of AJB was the chief rabbi of the Belgian army, Solomon Ullman, who took the precaution of inquiring of the Belgian authorities whether they approved of his accepting the post. They did.

In the spring of 1942, Belgian Jews were taken by the Germans for forced labor in northern France; these laborers were mostly deported later on. In May, again as in France, the yellow star was introduced. On June 22, Eichmann's order declaring that he wanted 10,000 Belgian Jews (along with 40,000 each from France and Holland) deported to their deaths was passed on to the SS in Belgium. The AJB had created problems for the Germans by refusing to distribute the yellow star, and it was in two minds about the deportations "for work in Germany," explained to it by a deceptively mild SS officer. A local Judenrat leader at Charleroi gave the Germans a false list, enabled many Jews to escape, and made a getaway himself. But the other local Judenrat members and the central AJB sent people to the houses of candidates for deportation to advise them to present themselves. The quota was filled.

After the deportations had been effected, the AJB had second thoughts. Disquieting news arrived from the east of what was happening to the Jews, and nothing was heard from those who had been deported. A Communist underground group, led by Jacques Gutfreund, burned the new index of Jewish names. An AJB member named Holzinger who had cooperated with the Germans, was killed by that same group. In September, 1942, the AJB refused to send any more notices for deportation. Ullman was arrested on September 24, but Queen Elizabeth intervened. The German military did not want trouble over some rabbi, and Ullman was released. He promptly resigned as head of AJB, thus rendering that body useless as far as the Germans were concerned. Months later a second AJB was finally established, with Marcel Blum as its head. But it limited itself to social work. Deportation remained in German hands.

There is some doubt about exact dates, but apparently it was in July, 1942, that certain Jews took a decisive step: under the leadership of the Communist Jewish leader Joseph Jospa, the Comité de défense des juifs (CDJ) was established in Brussels to coordinate illegal Jewish activities as part of the Front d'indépendance. Jospa succeeded in obtaining the adherence of a broad political spectrum. The CDJ included some of the members of AJB (Charles Perelman, Maurice Heiber, and Eugene Hellendael), some of the Communist Solidarité group, members of the LPZ, other Zionists, Bundists, and respected independents, including the former president of the Brussels Jewish community, Maurice Rothkehl, who refused to join the AJB. For about a year and a half, the Brussels committee acted on its own, but in November, 1943, it became the Comité national de défense des juifs (CNDJ), with local branches in Antwerp, Brussels, Liège, and Charleroi. Its aim was opposition to the Germans, and it was not going to "degenerate into simple social work."[4]

After a period of time, two non-Jews joined the CNDJ— Emile Allard, who became its president, and Yvonne Nevejean, the director of the Belgian child-care society, the Oeuvre national d'enfance (ONE). Active in both official and underground work, she became involved in CNDJ's main activity, the saving of Jewish children. The hiding of children was triggered by the Germans' brutal seizure of children in AJB's home at Wezembeck on October 30, 1942. By May, 1943, 1,300 children had been hidden, some in Catholic and Protestant institutions and some with private individuals, mostly in the Walloon region. Working with twenty Jewish social workers and nurses, a system was developed that was similar to the Circuit Garel in France. Despite both German and Belgian Nazis, the local population responded positively. More children were placed, until at the liberation, 2,104 CNDJ protégés were in hiding, about 60 percent of them in Catholic institutions. In addition, 200 children were placed privately but with CNDJ's knowledge, and 500 more were under the direct care of ONE.[5]

The problem of the adults was again parallel to that in France. From about the middle of 1943, 7,500 adults were hiding and in contact with CNDJ. The costs were considerable, because very few Jews could earn anything and CNDJ also had to provide people with false papers and ration cards. Children cost 350 Belgian francs (bfr.) ($8.70) per month in institutions and double that sum in private homes. Adults had to be given money for lodging, clothes, and medicines, amounting to about 1,000 bfr. ($25) per person. But the sums simply could not be paid, and the real budget was in the neighborhood of 2.1 million bfr. ($50,250) monthly.

Continued assistance by the government-in-exile and CNDJ's involvement with the Belgian underground help to explain the success and intensity of the rescue operations. One ought to add that the Catholic church, and the Walloons especially, saw protecting Jews as part of the national struggle against the Germans, despite the fact that about 65 percent of those in hiding were Polish Jews and that among the others there were many German-speaking Jews. Other Belgian groups and societies also extended their help, including the Belgian Red Cross, welfare societies, and even banks. It is this massive help, which seems to be explicable mainly in the context of anti-German sentiment and horror at deportations, that made the rescue of so large a percentage of the Jews in Belgium possible. It has been noted that despite the seemingly uncompromising German policy towards the Jews, that policy was nevertheless influenced by the general attitude of the conquered populations.[6] In Belgium, the distinctly negative reaction to the deportations, coupled with the continued interventions of the royal family, protected in some measure even the AJB. In early 1944, there were still six AJB children's homes and three old-age homes. Four hundred children survived the war in these AJB homes, and most of the aged did as well; it appears that the Germans hesitated to deport these groups, though they were entirely in their grasp.[7]

Queen Elizabeth intervened several times with various German authorities, making good her promise to a delegation of Belgian Jews on August 1, 1942, to do everything in her power to help them. King Leopold protested against the deportation of foreign Jews. Cardinal Joseph-Ernest Van Roey of Antwerp protested against the deportation of Belgian Jews, Catholic converts, pregnant women, and young girls. When his protest was ineffective, he demanded that the mayor of Antwerp deny the Germans the help of the city's police in rounding up the Jews. Writing about all this to Cardinal Luigi Maglione at the Vatican on August 4, 1942, he said that the German attitude was truly inhuman and had caused general indignation. He called on his clergy to hide Jews and "recommended" not to baptize them while they were in hiding. More exhortations and anti-German statements by Van Roey and other high clergy followed, and the general result was that many Catholic clergymen and institutions were willing to harbor Jews, though Van Roey's "recommendation" was not always observed. Bishop Kerhofs of Liège also asked his flock to aid the Jews. The large Belgian fascist movement and many people who were frightened into collaboration with the Nazis by German threats did make efforts to discover the hidden Jews; 300 bfr. ($7.50) per head were offered for Jews denounced to the Germans, and many took advantage of the offer. On the other hand, many Belgians were arrested for hiding Jews, and quite a number paid with their lives.[8]

Jewish efforts to escape, to hide, and to fight should not be overlooked, of course. Many of the organizers and workers in the CNDJ were arrested and deported, among them Joseph Jospa. Armed action also took place, not only by the many individual Jews fighting in various Belgian underground formations, but also in Jacques Gutfreund's battalion. Other Jews, in alliance with the general resistance, managed, on April 19, 1943, to engineer the only derailment of a deportation train to Auschwitz during the Holocaust. Unwittingly, they did it on the day the uprising began in the Warsaw ghetto. Several hundred Jews escaped.

JDC's Rescue Activities in Belgium

JDC's trusted representative in prewar Belgium was Max Gottschalk. Gottschalk got away in 1940, emigrated to America, and became the president of HICEM. There was nobody to take his place, and JDC did no work in Belgium until the CDJ was founded. After that, however, two separate channels opened: one through Switzerland and the other through the government-in-exile in London.

Early in 1943, CDJ delegated one of its young Zionist activists, Benjamin Nieuwkerk, to try to get into Switzerland and obtain funds for hiding children. Nieuwkerk got in touch with Nathan Schwalb, arrived in Switzerland, and contacted "Uncle Saly." Mayer was most impressed, and though this was the time when he had very little money indeed, he promised to help. From Mayer's accounts, it would seem that he transferred to Belgium 150,000 sfr. ($35,700) up to February, 1944, or about 1.4 million bfr. After February, 1944, he provided a regular subsidy of 30,000 sfr. ($7,100; 285,000 bfr.) monthly. The money was paid to a Swiss businessman whose brother in Belgium paid out the funds in Belgian money. The total direct subsidy by Mayer eventually came to 360,000 sfr. ($85,700). Benjamin Nieuwkerk went to Switzerland three times; on his third journey he was caught by the Germans and killed. His brother Adolf continued in his stead.

When the CNDJ rendered its accounts at the end of the German occupation, it thought that it had received about one quarter of its total budget of 4.5 million bfr. monthly from Mayer. This budget provided only bare subsistence, especially for the hidden adults, but it was therefore essential that at least that sum be covered somehow. Part of the funds were obtained through a loan by the Bank société générale in Louvain, which, in early 1944, accounted for about 250,000 bfr. ($6,200) monthly. Some money was also obtained through AJB's official welfare society, with which CNDJ continued to be in touch, but most of the difference was made up by what CNDJ thought were Belgian government funds, given either directly through underground channels from London or through a government credit via Cardinal Van Roey. However, these were not really Belgian funds at all. In the summer of 1943, Ernest de Selliers of the Belgian embassy in Washington contacted Joseph Hyman at JDC and asked for a subsidy of 750,000 bfr. ($18,700) monthly for helping Belgian Jews. JDC agreed, giving the Belgians $90,000 for May to October, and then settling on a $15,000 monthly subsidy which continued to be paid to the end of the war. The JDC funds equaled about 600,000 bfr., which covered most of CNDJ's deficit. It is therefore correct to say that the work done by CNDJ and its cooperating groups in saving Jewish lives was largely accomplished with JDC funds, totaling some $680,000 in 1943 and 1944,[9] though JDC neither intervened directly nor exercised direct control as it did in France.

Rescue Attempts in Holland

JDC involvement in rescue attempts in Holland was sporadic and unsystematic. This was the result of a situation that differed considerably from those in Belgium and France. The 140,000 Jews living in Holland in 1940 (including recent refugees) were well integrated into the larger society, but, while Dutch Jewry had no central body, it did maintain strong communal organizations around the Ashkenazi and Sephardi synagogues. A minority group of Zionists was also well organized. In 1933, a strong refugee committee had been created to aid persons fleeing from Greater Germany. This committee, under David Cohen, a prominent classics scholar and a lifelong Zionist, had received considerable JDC support, throughout the thirties, primarily through Gertrude van Tijn, a German Jew who had settled in Holland during World War I.

Following the conquest of Holland in May, 1940, German administration of the country was in the hands of the Nazi party: the Reich commissar, Artur Seyss-Inquart, was not really controlled by the military or the German Foreign Office, and he welcomed the establishment of SS control over Jewish affairs. A sharp struggle within the Jewish community between Lodewijk Ernest Visser, the Jewish president of the Dutch High Court, who opposed all contacts between Jews and Germans, and David Cohen, who agreed to head a Dutch Judenrat in February, 1941, ended with a victory for Cohen. Most of the Zionists opposed Cohen and their representative finally resigned from the Judenrat, but with the SS supporting it, the Judenrat had little trouble in establishing its supremacy within the community.

Dutch reaction to German persecutions of local Jews was strong, but by no means unanimous. The Dutch Nazi party had a rather considerable following, and Dutch society was deeply split on the Jewish issue. The majority was willing to protect the Jews, but the difficulties of hiding anyone in the well-ordered and organized Dutch towns and villages and the complete surrender of the Judenrat, led by Cohen and his collaborator, Abraham Asscher, militated against effective action. The Catholic church tried at first to protect mainly Jewish converts to Catholicism, although some of the Protestant churches were very outspoken against the Nazi measures from the start. Dutch socialists and Communists declared a strike against the Germans in February, 1941, as a result of a German attempt to have a pogrom in the Jewish prole-

273

tarian quarter in Amsterdam. The strike was broken, partly because of German measures and partly also because the newly established Judenrat requested the strikers to desist, fearing Nazi reprisals. Dutch officialdom which, as in Belgium, was responsible for everyday civilian administration, refused to protect the Jews beyond a few ineffectual verbal protests. It obeyed German orders and facilitated Nazi measures. The Dutch government-in-exile in London never followed the Belgian example of publicly disavowing the legality of all the Nazi anti-Jewish measures.

When the deportations began, people were confused about what was happening to the deportees; indeed, Jews in Holland never really knew what was going on in Poland. We find the same mixture of information and disbelief or repression as we find in Belgium and France. Following publication in England of the May Bund report from Poland, Radio Orange, broadcasting to Holland from London, declared on July 29, 1942, that Polish Jews were being done away with in gas chambers. An underground paper, *De Waarheid*, warned the Dutch police on August 3, 1942, not to cooperate with the Germans because all the Jews would be deported to their deaths. An authentic eyewitness account by Kurt Gerstein, the controversial SS man who tried to warn the world regarding the murder of the Jews (and whose report formed the background to Rolf Hochhuth's play, *The Deputy*), was written up in Dutch and transmitted to Holland. As it was not believed, however, it remained hidden on a farm until the end of the war and was never used. Another eyewitness account was published in an underground Dutch newspaper on September 3, 1943, and six Dutch women of the Jehovah's Witnesses sect who returned from Auschwitz between February and April, 1943, also told their stories; again, nobody would believe them.[10]

This mixture of information and disbelief could have caused complete disorientation and blind obedience to the Judenrat and the Germans, which indeed is what happened in some other places in Europe. Yet Dutch Jews asked to appear for deportation ceased to do so as early as the summer of 1942, as a worried SS official cabled to Berlin.[11] Dutch Jews definitely felt that deportations entailed mortal danger and were to be avoided at all costs. This surprising gap between a compliant leadership and a reluctant following trying desperately and largely unsuccessfully to evade regulations is hard to explain. One of the factors in the situation was the Amsterdam Jewish proletariat—some 40,000 stevedores, boatmen, and factory workers—who were not represented on the Judenrat and were suspicious of its doings. Among the Jewish middle class, too, the attempted rebellion of Visser and his Zionist-oriented group against Cohen's submissive line in the Judenrat shows that Dutch Jewry was deeply suspicious of Nazi intentions. The fact that 24,000 to 25,000 Jews tried to hide among the Dutch people (which, given the topography of Holland and the strict German supervision, was very difficult) goes to prove that Jews tried to evade deportation. The tragedy was that the majority could not.

In the end, 103,000 Dutch Jews were deported; the Nazis sent 4,000 additional people out of Holland to German concentration camps before the deportations to Poland began. One thousand emigrated legally and 2,700 illegally; 900 were eventually liberated at the notorious Westerbork camp, from which the deportations had taken place during the war. Of the 28,400 unaccounted for, about 9,500 were living in mixed marriages, and 3,000 had been declared "Aryan" by Hans G. Calmeyer, a German doctor who wanted to save Jewish lives. After the war, 16,000 emerged from hiding. It is estimated that about 9,000 more shared the fate of Anne Frank—they were caught while hiding and deported to their deaths.[12]

Van Tijn's work for emigration, first of foreign Jews and then of anyone who could escape, continued after the German conquest. Small groups of Jews managed to get out, but no new allocations of JDC funds for that purpose were made in 1940 or 1941. In April, 1941, van Tijn was allowed by the Germans to go to Lisbon, where she met with Morris Troper and made a simple clearing arrangement—JDC would leave funds in neutral countries for Jews emigrating from Holland, who would leave their money behind with the Jewish community. When she returned to Holland, however, she was told that the Germans had changed their minds. No large-scale emigration could take place, though Jews were still allowed to leave in groups up to August, 1941, and then occasionally as individuals. This emigration required the deposit of considerable sums of foreign currency, which were then used by German interests. In other words, it was a ransom arrangement. Two Nazi agents in Zürich, a Dr. A. Wiederkehr and an Anna Hochberg, served as intermediaries between those who paid the ransom outside Europe and the trapped Jews in Holland whom it saved. The sums involved were never disclosed. It appears that the Dutch Warburgs and several other wealthy Jewish families took this way out of Holland. They left behind sums in guilders which were used by van Tijn—who never asked, and was never told, how the German exit permits were obtained.[13]

Van Tijn claims that she used the money obtained from these emigrants in order to pay for hiding other people. Exactly how many were hidden and with whom was never exactly stated; perhaps it could not have been, as no records would have been kept. In order to get more money, she also approached the Swiss vice-consul, Ernst Prodillet, when the Swiss consulate was closed by the Germans in November, 1942, and obtained a large sum. "He left the guilders with me. Then he concocted an address-book, in which names, telephone numbers, all sorts of figures, were written down in fantastic disorder. Somewhere in this mess I wrote down a figure and signed it." The figure was 57,500 sfr. Prodillet showed the signature to Mayer in Switzerland, who promptly paid the money.[14]

Van Tijn's next exploit was to follow the initiative of Helmuth Mainz, a friend who had worked at the Swiss consulate. He suggested that the people should try to obtain Palestinian immigration certificates, be registered by the Germans on exchange lists, and thereby be saved. In October, 1942, fourteen more or less real Palestinian Jewish citizens or their nearest relatives were actually sent to Palestine, which pointed to the potential of the scheme. Van Tijn established a small commission of Zionists and then registered persons who could claim close relatives in Palestine or who had long been active in the Zionist movement. With the cooperation of the IRC in Amsterdam, cables were sent to Switzerland and even to Palestine, and the Zionist offices were alerted to this new possibility, while the names were sent to the Swiss legation in Berlin and the persons affected were informed. Feverish activity then began in Switzerland, where JA representatives Haim Posner and Richard Lichtheim and others did what they could to speed things up. Confirmation of the availability of Palestine certificates began to arrive in the spring of 1943, and, by early 1944, 2,500 had been given out. They did not always protect their holders against deportation; according to van Tijn's own account, 710 people were deported anyway. But 550 heads of families with their dependents were sent to Bergen-Belsen exchange camp, and 221 of these were actually sent to Palestine in July, 1944.[15] Van Tijn used some of her JDC funds in this venture.

JDC, through Saly Mayer, contributed indirectly to other rescue efforts as well. A Joodsche Coordinatie Commissie (Jewish Coordination Committee) was founded in Switzerland by Mozes

H. Gans, a Dutch Jew who was working with the aid of the Dutch embassy to try to transfer funds to Jews in Holland. Gans was helped by a Dr. Polak Daniels, who emerged from Holland in October, 1943, having obviously been released by the Germans in return for a considerable ransom. The whole affair seemed rather peculiar to Mayer, but he did not want to be accused of not using every means to aid Jews, and he gave the committee funds in 1943–44. The Gans group does not seem to have achieved much through its own work, but it gained some credence in Mayer's eyes because it was recognized for the purposes of aid by the World Council of Churches, whose leading personality at that time was Dr. Willem Visser t'Hooft. Mayer transmitted 200,000 sfr. ($47,000) through the council to Holland, apparently to pay Dutch Protestants hiding Jews. He also spent more money to support Jewish refugees from Holland who had reached Switzerland and who were aided by a committee headed by the Dutch General Aleid G. van Tricht.[16]

No independent operation was conducted in Holland by JDC during the Holocaust; no large efforts at rescue were supported by it. Dutch Jewry, led by a submissive leadership, went to its doom despite the willingness of large numbers of Dutch Jews to take any escape route that offered itself. Helped by individual Dutch people, a relatively large number hid, though nothing like the percentage hiding in Belgium or France. Some were discovered; some must have died in hiding; others survived the war. JDC had very little to do with any of this.

Aid to Zagreb

In Yugoslavia, the situation was quite different from that in Holland. A community of 75,000 Jews there had shown great self-sacrifice in trying to look after thousands of refugees who reached the country from Austria and Germany in the 1930s. The chief figure was Simon (Sime) Spitzer, who has already been mentioned in connection with the Kladovo transport. Yugoslav Jewry was organized in two communities: a general one comprising 110 congregations and a smaller Orthodox one with 15. There were wealthy people and intellectuals, mainly in Zagreb and Belgrade, but there were also thousands of very poor Jewish traders, peddlers, artisans, and manual workers. These were concentrated mainly in the south and in parts of Croatia, among the country's long-established Sephardi Jews.

When the Germans overran the country in April, 1941, 34,000 Jews found themselves in the newly created "independent" Croatian state under the "leader" *(poglavnik)* Ante Pavelić, who established a regime on the Nazi model and with German advisers. Serbia, where the Germans tried to create a puppet state under Milan Nedić, a well-known Serbian general, had 14,000 Jews. The others were in areas occupied by the Hungarians (the Voivodina and the Banat) and the Bulgarians (Macedonia). The Germans made short work of the Serbian Jews. In a series of murder campaigns, they were shot or thrown, bound so that they could not swim, into rivers. Those who could escaped into the mountains and eventually joined the partisan detachments that formed there in late 1941–42. Macedonian Jews were eventually deported to their deaths in March, 1943.

The main remnant of Yugoslav Jewry that survived for some time and could still perhaps be reached from the outside was that in Croatia. Parts of Croatia were occupied by the Italians, and there the writ of the Ustasha, the political murder gangs who became the official armed force of the Pavelić regime, did not run. These included areas of Slovenia (with Ljubljana, the capital) and Dalmatia and some other neighboring areas. Croatian Jews tried to reach these parts, and it is estimated that about 12,000 Jews finally managed to escape there. The rest, mainly in the communities of Zagreb, Sarajevo, and Osijek, were trapped by the Croatians and Germans.[17]

The Ustasha were a mixture of extreme nationalistic and blatantly criminal elements. There was none of the cold efficiency of the SS murderers about them—they were messy, inefficient, and brutal. The old SA storm troopers and the Ustasha had much in common. Ironically, the founder of the Croatian chauvinist movement was one Dr. Josef Frankel, a "full" Jew. His daughter, half Jewish, was married to Pavelić's war minister, Slavko Kvaternik, who was the father of the head of the security branch of the Ustasha, Eugen Kvaternik. Pavelić's own wife was also half Jewish. This meant that the Croatian fascists had to prove by their behavior that their Jewish family connections had not influenced them and that they could still be true allies of Nazi Germany. Their antisemitic laws were drastic, detailed, and obviously influenced by a special Gestapo mission which advised them on Jewish matters. Confiscation of property through "Aryanization," marking of Jews, and expulsion of Jews from apartments in cer-

Yugoslavia under Axis Rule.

279

tain sections of the towns followed in quick succession after the entry of the Germans into Zagreb.

The Jewish community at Zagreb was largely middle class and predominantly Zionist-oriented. The Croats at first tried to bypass the better-known leaders by nominating an ad hoc committee of rich men, some of them of suspect character, in order to collect a huge fine which was imposed on the Jews. But in May, 1941, a respected lawyer with Zionist leanings, Dr. Hugo Kon, was elected to head the community. Kon's deputy was Dr. Dragutin Rosenberg and the secretary was Dr. Alexander Klein, both well-known community servants. Klein, however, was arrested in August and not released until November, 1941, and effective leadership at Zagreb rested with Rosenberg.

Jewish matters soon came under the Jewish section of the Ustasha security service, headed by Vilko Kühnel, who was half German and half Croatian. Kühnel, though he at all times carried out the anti-Jewish orders he received, nevertheless developed a human relationship with the Jewish leaders and slowly came around to trying to protect the Jewish community rather than harass it. Arrests started soon, and camps were established for lawyers and young men, and later for members of B'nai B'rith lodges, in the inhospitable mountain districts, at Kerestinec, Koprivnica, and Gospić, and on the island of Pag. But when a readjustment of occupation zones in late 1941 was about to transfer these places to Italian administration, internees were imprisoned at Jasenovac and Kruščica; in the latter camp, mainly women were interned. The young men and the lodge members were murdered. Another camp for men was opened in the autumn at Stara Gradiśka.

All of these camps were under the jurisdiction of the younger Kvaternik, but directly supervised by a sadist named Vjekoslav Luburić. Conditions were appalling: internees were inadequately clothed, made to work under impossible conditions, starved, and even beaten to death. Dragutin Rosenberg, who found it impossible to reach any higher official, tried to persuade Luburić to allow the sending of food and clothing, though because of the chaotic arrests and the isolation of the camps, it was impossible to estimate the number of the inmates or establish their identities. Luburić would only agree to bulk consignments, obviously intending to keep the Jews in the dark about the names of the internees who were still alive. It was also clear that most of any shipments would go to improve the standard of living of the brutal and dehumanized guards. Nevertheless, as long as the community had evidence that at least part of the consignments actually reached the internees, it continued sending parcels, from September to December, 1941. Rosenberg estimated that 15,000 Jewish males were arrested up to the summer of 1942. Of these, despite desperate attempts by the Jewish community, only 1,200–1,500 were still alive that summer. Thousands were persuaded to convert to Catholicism in order to save themselves, but even this action, which was encouraged by many of the Catholic priesthood, did not help. They were all killed in the end.[18]

Conditions at Kruščica were perhaps even more frightful than at Jasenovac, for there were many children at the camp. Rosenberg managed to convince Kühnel that he should establish another camp at Lobor-grad, an abandoned castle, which would come under the administration of the Jewish community rather than under the Ustasha. Eventually 1,600 women and children, among them 300–350 Serbs who were also persecuted under the Pavelić regime, were sent to Lobor-grad, but they were put under a guard of Croatian ethnic Germans. Still, the Germans could be bribed, and there was little physical maltreatment. From October, 1941, the community cared for these women and children although a typhoid epidemic killed 150 inmates before it was overcome. There was very little food, but at least no mass murder took place.

Continuing arrests necessitated further accommodation in the camps. In December, 1941, Rosenberg and Klein managed to persuade Kühnel to establish another camp at Djakovo, to which women and children at Jasenovac and Stara Gradiška were then sent. The population soon numbered some 3,000, of whom 500–600 died of typhoid fever in the winter. Conditions were primitive, although the communities at Osijek and Zagreb did their best to supply food. Unfortunately, the Ustasha took over the camp in May, 1942, administering it until August, 1942.

Until the late summer of 1942, JDC help to the Croatian community was minimal. Mayer was not really responsible for Zagreb; Joseph Schwartz thought that aid to the city could be better handled from Budapest. It is not clear, however, what means Joseph Blum and Bertrand Jacobson in Budapest had at their disposal at the time. It is obvious to us—but it was not obvious to the Zagreb Jews—that no money could actually be transferred from Lisbon to Hungary. At first the Zagreb Jews, through some intelligent maneuvering of taxes and other funds, managed to cover their swiftly increasing costs from their own resources. Soon, however, no further taxation of Jews was possible because all Jewish property was confiscated. With the Croatian government's permission, Klein went to Budapest in July, 1941, and Rosenberg and Klein went again in January and April, 1942, in order to persuade Blum and the Hungarian Jews to help Zagreb. These trips have been represented as a "procurement mission" on behalf of the Croatian Gestapo.[19] Nothing could have been further from the truth. The Croats hoped for some foreign currency, and therefore Klein was permitted to ask for outside help.

Hungarian Jewry did not respond with money, despite some promises that apparently were made. Blum wrote to Zagreb on November 25 that some funds would be made available, provided that at least two-thirds of the budget was covered by "local funds"—"if you wish the JDC to help you."[20] The Zagreb leadership did not apparently think much of this letter, but it used it as proof that in principle JDC was willing to help it. It showed the letter to the Croatian finance minister, Vladimir Košak, who finally condescended to receive Rosenberg and Klein in January, 1942. Košak agreed to supply the community with 2 million kuna (dinars) monthly out of the confiscated Jewish property. (In 1942, 100 kuna equaled 1 sfr., or 20.7 U.S. cents.) Originally Rosenberg had to promise that JDC would cover two-thirds of the budget, but this later became one-third, because the Croats were desperate for foreign currency, even Hungarian pengö. However, the Budapest JDC office could only send Rosenberg the equivalent of $2,000 and some small sums in the late summer of 1942. It all amounted to much less than a third of the budget, and the Zagreb community was in deep trouble.[21]

In the meantime, however, these budgetary problems were completely overshadowed by the existential ones: apart from the slow, sadistic killing in the camps, the Germans now demanded that the Croats hand the Jews over to them for deportation to Auschwitz. The Croats, like the Slovaks, paid the Germans for each deported Jew, and in August, 1942, most of them were sent to Poland, where they disappeared into the ovens of Auschwitz. Nobody has yet been able to give exact figures, and nobody knows how many were killed before or after in the camps. Djakovo and Lobor-grad were liquidated, but at Jasenovac and Stara Gradiśka a few hundred inmates remained. In Zagreb, some "privileged" Jews remained behind, and also the Jewish halves of mixed marriages. There was nothing much that Rosenberg or Klein could do. Rosenberg fled to Italy and then to Switzerland in September; Klein had got out even earlier. Two Jews who were protected by their non-Jewish wives, Oskar Kiŝicky and Dr. Robert Glücksthal, slowly assumed leadership of the remnants of the community; they became responsible when old Dr. Kon and the rest of the "unprotected" Jews were sent off in early May, 1943. Just as in other countries, however, the knowledge of what was happening to the deported Jews was a curious mixture of realism and repression. Writing as late as April, 1944, when details of the mass murder had long since been publicized, Rosenberg said that one could get no authentic information regarding the place of deportation. "These were all state secrets of the first order; I do not want, however, to express in words that which I was told, because perhaps there is still some small hope that the reports are not completely authentic."[22]

A tiny, dwindling group of Jews remained behind, apparently a total of 1,250 people in camps and old-age homes; in June, 1944, Kiŝicky in Zagreb was reporting 850–900 people in the two camps, and another 350 scattered in detention places. In Zagreb itself, 70 aged individuals were left, and perhaps 120 to 150 "free-living" Jews.[23]

Apparently Rosenberg and Klein approached Alfred Silberschein of RELICO before they reached Mayer. Mayer, of course, was much less averse to contacts with RELICO than was Schwartz in Lisbon, and he developed a reasonably good relationship with Silberschein. Mayer realized that while Silberschein was unable to help the Croatian Jews financially, he had contacts which could effectively shield JDC from the necessity of engaging in half-legal arrangements itself. Silberschein found a Swiss businessman named Hockey, who was paid Swiss francs in Switzerland and who then paid out kuna in Zagreb. When this arrangement came into force is unclear, but it appears that in the second half of 1942, 8,700 sfr. were transferred monthly to Zagreb via RELICO and Hockey, with Mayer in the background demanding detailed accounts. At the same time, Mayer was trying to activate the IRC and send parcels to Zagreb under its supervision. This would have the advantage of leading to IRC supervision in the camps and the provision of Swiss food to the remnant of Croatian Jewry. He only began to succeed in this in 1943. Until then, Kiŝicky kept appealing for more money, not only through Silberschein, but also through Vittorio L. Valobra in Italy and through

Nathan Schwalb of the Hehalutz, who received accurate information regarding the situation in Croatia.

We already know what extremely limited means Mayer had at his disposal. Valobra, furious at Mayer's apparent lack of understanding, wrote him a letter rejecting any responsibility for what was happening at Zagreb. Mayer replied in October, 1942:

> We acknowledge receipt of your relevant correspondence and cables and ask you to take notice that there is in our view no reason why you should cable us in this manner. It is illogical [*unzulässig*] for you to reject a responsibility which cannot, in our view, be thrown upon you or any other Jewish organization.

Having thus placed the burden of responsibility on the criminals rather than on the victims and their organizations, Mayer proceeded:

> There is a simple duty to help each other to the limit of the circumstances and conditions. Our last aid was delivered on September 30. Now we shall send a double amount.[24]

Late in 1943, the IRC finally sent a representative named Julius Schmidlin to Zagreb at Mayer's insistent urging. He appeared to the few Zagreb Jews as a real savior. After his arrival, JDC assistance usually took the form of parcels supplemented by grants of money, sent increasingly through IRC. Kišicky and Glücksthal were arrested in October, 1944, but released at Schmidlin's insistence. The small number of Jews at Zagreb, probably around 1,500, were literally kept alive by JDC until their liberation in April, 1945.[25]

Italians to the Rescue in Yugoslavia

JDC aid to Jews who fled from Croatia into Italian-controlled territory was provided through Vittorio Valobra. These were largely foreign Jews from Germany, Austria, and Czechoslovakia who had been lodged in camps under the old Yugoslav regime and had escaped early in the German occupation. Zagreb Jews joined them, and there must have been between 10,00 and 20,000 persons spread over a large area, although some groups concentrated in places like Kraljevica and Split. As long as the Italian general Mario Roatta was in charge, they were relatively safe. Roatta adamantly refused to hand them over to either the Germans or the Ustasha. On the collapse of Italy, Tito's partisans overran parts of the region, with the Germans coming in from another side. Some of the Jews were caught by the Nazis; others managed to escape into Italy; others again joined the partisans. There was very little that Jewish organizations could do for any of these. One particular group of some 2,700 people, who had been interned at Kraljevica, were transferred to the island of Rab by the Italians. When the Italians capitulated in September, 1943, 600 of them escaped to Bari, which was already in Allied hands. Tito's partisans captured the island and held it for a time; when they withdrew, 200 people had to remain behind and were promptly murdered by the Germans. The rest retreated with the Yugoslavs to the mainland, where those capable of bearing arms joined the partisans as a Jewish unit and suffered severe losses in a number of engagements. About 1,000–2,000 noncombatants were left to fend for themselves in the Glina-Topusko area during the most bitter struggle between the partisans and the Germans. Frantic appeals to Palestine and JDC from these beleaguered people were of no avail. JDC-New York intervened with the British and the Americans to try to get the civilians out, but there were no airplanes to be spared for such a mission, and only a few people were flown to Bari. JDC sent some aid to the area, and many of the Jews survived to the liberation of Yugoslavia in early 1945.[26]

A special episode, an almost unbelievable odyssey of a number of children, took place within the larger terrible tragedy of Croatian Jews. In May, 1940, Recha Freier, the founder of Youth Aliyah, an organization dealing with the immigration of children and youth to Palestine, had escaped from Germany and arrived in Zagreb with a number of her charges. She stayed until just before the German attack, and when she left, a group of Youth Aliyah children who had entered Yugoslavia illegally left with her. Another group of 43 illegal children was left behind under the care of a young leader, Josef (Joshko) Indig of Zagreb. They were joined by 18 girls who had crossed to Maribor in Slovenia from their Austrian home, also just before the German attack. All were housed in Croatia, where they were when the Germans came. By a stroke of good luck and with a great deal of courage, Indig managed to get his children, aged from ten to sixteen, to Ljubljana in June, 1941. From there he appealed for money to Schwalb in Zürich, who agreed to send 1,000 dinars weekly. Indig got a house with a farm at Lesno Brdo in July, and had to spend 3,000 dinars a week for food. His support was paid out to him by Valobra, and he not only managed to keep his children's home intact, but also accepted more refugee waifs. Studies were ar-

ranged, examinations held, and morale kept up in the most impossible conditions, until on July 18, 1942, he moved his group to
Nonantola in northern Italy, because Slovenia was clearly becoming more dangerous. In October, 1943, helped by local people, he
fled with all his children to the Swiss border, where they were
admitted as refugees. His group, now numbering 167, was kept,
mainly at Bex and Versoix, under Mayer's special care until the
end of the war. Their survival was a happy exception to a sad rule
and a testimony to the initiative and daring of a member of a
Zionist youth movement.[27]

JDC and Italian Jews

The story of the Jews in Italy falls naturally into the periods
before and after the Italian surrender of September 8, 1943. In the
early part of the war, the Jews were under the rule of the Italian
racial law which affected their property rights, freedom of movement and marriage, and professional status. Forced labor was
instituted for Jews in Rome, Bologna, Milan, and Tripoli on a
number of occasions, although many evaded it with various
ruses. Moreover, about 10 percent of the Jewish population had
converted to Catholicism; these individuals were generally treated
better than their brethren who had remained Jewish. Some 6,000
Jews emigrated up to the end of 1941, leaving 40,000 Italian Jews
in Italy. On the whole, those who remained managed to carry on
reasonably well until the Italian surrender.

The story of the foreign Jews in Italy was quite different.
They lived under a constant threat of internment and persecution.
Most had come because it was easy to obtain Italian tourist visas
up to 1939; some also arrived on their way to Palestine, but could
not continue their journey. It has been estimated that 7,000 foreign Jews were in Italy at the end of 1939.[28] An assistance committee which had provided some aid was dissolved by the government in August, 1939, but the Italian authorities soon realized
that such an organization would serve their own interests. They
therefore allowed the Unione delle Communità Israelitiche Ital-
iane, the roof organization of the Italian Jewish communities, to
establish DELASEM in November. Its head was the Unione's
vice-president, Vittorio Valobra, and its secretary was Enrico Luzzatto. It maintained close contact with Raffaele Cantoni, the leading personality in the Unione at the time. Most of the funds
required to maintain the refugees in Italy and to speed their emi-

gration were provided by the Italian Jews, but outside resources had increasingly to be tapped. A total of up to 4,500 refugees was mentioned by JDC in 1940, but the Unione's official count in April, 1940, was 2,987, while the Italian government in late 1941 knew of 3,674. The difference can probably be explained by the arrival in Italy of refugees from Yugoslavia. In 1942, the 500 passengers of the *Pencho* arrived from Rhodes.[29]

Among this not very large number of refugees there were a number of groups with different fates. There were between 2,000 and 3,000 Polish Jewish students, mostly at Bologna, who were cut off—luckily for them—from their families. In early 1941, 2,000 refugees were in internment camps, largely in Ferramonti in southern Italy; about 1,100 more were living in assigned residences. DELASEM could give those in assigned residences up to 100 lire a month (about $4), which obviously was completely inadequate, although the Italian welfare agencies helped somewhat and parcels could be received. In addition to all these, there were converted Jews, Italian and refugee, who were being cared for partly by the Quakers, represented in Italy by Roswell D. Mac-Clelland before he and his wife moved to France and Switzerland, and by the Catholic Pallottini Fathers under Father Otto Weber.[30] It seems that several hundred of the Christian Jews escaped to South America, chiefly to Brazil, and their fares were paid by the Vatican out of JDC funds contributed for that purpose to Catholic aid organizations in America.[31]

When Italy entered the war, JDC authorized Valobra to borrow money against repayment après. But it was very difficult to raise such loans in Italy, which was not an occupied country, but rather a well-organized community at war. In March, 1941, Valobra was again authorized to borrow; both times JDC-Lisbon mentioned $10,000. Lichtheim of the JA in Geneva and Schwartz also arrived at an arrangement, parallel to that in France, whereby JNF funds were used by JDC-DELASEM in return for repayment in Palestine. This arrangement was more important than borrowing money, and Lichtheim, reporting to Schwartz in late 1941, remarked: "It can only be to the good if our executives in New York, who have a tendency to quarrel with each other, are occasionally informed that there is friendly collaboration between our organizations" in Europe.[32]

In spite of these efforts, the situation slowly worsened. Ferramonti received some of the illegal immigrants who had tried to reach Palestine but were stranded on the way, among them the

Pencho group and another that was caught at Benghazi while waiting for a ship that was to have been sent by Baruch Confino, the Bulgarian organizer of illegal transports. As we have seen already, Valobra was also forced to extend some aid to Italian-occupied Yugoslavia. He turned to Saly Mayer. As early as March, 1942, Mayer was sending stopgap help, which in April became a regular subsidy. Mayer paid into a Swiss bank, and Valobra received the money in lire in Italy. Schwartz was not very happy about this arrangement, but, in line with his general policy, he did not interfere. Mayer himself hesitated, but he could not abandon Valobra. He refused *en principe* to give Valobra vast sums (which he did not have anyway) when Valobra visited him in July, 1942. But Valobra again received the permission to borrow; by then more people were willing to give lire for the promise of postwar dollars.[33]

In 1943, the number of refugees grew to between 10,000 and 13,000, of whom an increasing proportion were Yugoslav Jews. It was almost impossible to keep these people even minimally supplied. About 3,000 foreign Jews were in internment camps in Italy by then, and most of the Yugoslav Jews were interned at Rab or on the island of Korcula.[34] The Italians gave them some food, though barely enough to keep body and soul together. Then came the Italian surrender, and the situation changed completely.

Jews under DELASEM's care were now divided into four sections which had no contact with each other. The refugees in northern Italy, which was occupied by German troops, were joined by local Jews who found themselves being hunted down for deportation to their deaths. The Jews still in the former Italian occupation zone in Yugoslavia were cut off from Italy. The Jews of Rome were cut off from the north and underwent a terrible period of trial until the city was liberated in June, 1944. Finally, the 2,500–3,000 Jews in the southern part of the country, including those in the main internment camp at Ferramonti, remained there until they were liberated by the Allies. Each of these groups experienced its own unique ordeal before the war ended.

We have dealt already with the Jews trapped in the former Italian zone in Yugoslavia. The Jewish internees in the south were saved by the Allied armies. There remained the Jews caught by the Germans who, after September, 1943, occupied all of Italy down to and including Rome. It is generally assumed that when the Germans entered Rome in September, 1943, there were about 8,000 Jews there. In addition, there were probably well over 1,000 foreign refugees who had left their places of internment to hide in the big city. Of these, up to a third were Yugoslavs, and some 400 had formerly been interned in the Nice area and had accompanied the Italian army retreating from France. A vanguard of 110 such persons reached Rome as early as September. A parochial quarrel soon developed between a group of these refugees and the Rome DELASEM, but the majority of foreign Jews, including an increasing number of Italian and Roman Jews, came to rely on it for help.

By March, 1944, 2,500 Jews had been cared for, of whom 1,100 were Italian and Roman. In October, 1943, on Hitler's direct orders, the Germans tried to deport all Roman Jews. Most hid, however, and the Nazis caught only 1,007 out of the 8,000, shipping them to Auschwitz on October 18. The Vatican offered a loan of gold to help pay a sum which was extorted from the Jews as a forced payment by the Germans, and some Jews found refuge within Vatican City. Others were hidden by Catholic institutions, though the number is not known. The pope, as the German ambassador remarked with a sigh of relief, did not comment publicly on the Germans' action and thus did not burden the already strained relations between the Catholic church and Germany.[35]

Those who were deported could not be saved. But a precondition for escaping the Germans' clutches was to be able to hide, eat, and have false identity documents. DELASEM in Rome played a central part in providing these things. Under its president, Dante Almansi, and its secretary, Settimio Sorani, it organized aid with the help of local Italians and some of the Catholic priesthood. Rising inflation made the problems worse, and by March, 1944, DELASEM had borrowed some 2 million lire (about $20,000), probably against dollars après. JDC-New York tried to help, but because of American regulations had to be satisfied with promising repayment after the war. Starting with $20,000 in January, 1944, it had increased its promise to $100,000 by June. Some additional loans were obtained against this specific sum, but not enough; most, if not all, of the money came from non-Jewish sources, and they did not want to risk their money for promises. After much searching, Saly Mayer, with Valobra's help, found a way of transferring funds through the papal nuncio in Switzerland and the Red Cross. He began to do so in April, 1944, but Rome was liberated in June and his help came too late. However, additional funds did come from the central DELASEM office at Genoa, and all these sources together enabled Rome DELASEM to make ends meet.[36] Roman Jews also received help from the

Polish representatives at the Vatican, who apparently supported mainly the small dissident group from Nice.

In March, 1944, the Nazis executed—again on direct orders from Hitler—335 hostages in the Ardeatine caves in retaliation for the killing of some German soldiers. Among them were 57 Jews. Otherwise, losses among Roman Jewry between the October deportations and the liberation of the city were few.

The situation was different in the north of Italy. The neo-fascist republic set up after the German conquest was too weak to exert any influence, and a direct SS terror regime began. A wave of arrests and the deportation of Italian Jews to Auschwitz commenced in April, 1944. Nevertheless, the relatively long delay between the German conquest in September, 1943, and the beginning of deportations and the ineffectiveness of the Italian law of December, 1943, providing for the arrest of all Jews enabled the majority of Jews to escape, despite intensive German and Italian search operations.

The hiding or conveying to the Swiss border of as many as 30,000 people meant that organized help was not only important but essential. Many Italian Jews were helped by neighbors or villagers, protected by partisans, or even warned by fascist mayors or policemen. Catholics, too, especially individuals such as Cardinal Elia della Costa of Florence and the Franciscans, became increasingly involved in rescue work with Jews. In fact, it was through Catholic dignitaries that DELASEM's work could be continued in northern Italy in the first place. Valobra and Luzzatto contacted Cardinal Pietro Boetto, archbishop of Genoa, who assumed the responsibility of distributing funds through his secretary, Francesco Repetto. The bookkeeping was done by Giuseppe Ariccio, a layman banker trusted by the clergy. During the first two months of the German occupation, Luzzatto went around northern Italy and obtained loans, bringing them to the Genoese archbishopric which then distributed them, with his help, in thirty-five places. During the first few months, 3 million lire (about $30,000) were handled in this way.

In the meantime, DELASEM offices were closed and the archives hidden. On November 18, 1943, Enrico Luzzatto and his wife were arrested and later deported to Auschwitz, but they did not betray their connection with Repetto. Valobra managed to escape, arriving in Switzerland on November 23.[37] In Genoa, Massimo Teglio, a friend of Valobra's who had no previous connection with DELASEM, took over. With his help, funds were distributed to the increasing number of Italian Jews and former refugees who were now in hiding. Two thousand such people managed to cross into Switzerland, but it became more and more difficult to approach the border. DELASEM's committees were dissolved, and in Florence, as a result of betrayal by a fascist, all the members who had hidden were arrested. Teglio was helped by a few Italians, among whom another Catholic priest, Giuseppe Biccherai of Milan, was perhaps the most important. Repetto was arrested in 1944, but the work went on with the help of the other members of the archbishop's entourage.

In the one year between September, 1943, and September, 1944, Saly Mayer transmitted 32.5 million lire (about $320,000) to northern Italy. He used Valobra's contacts and the transfers were largely done through two Italian Jewish businessmen, Carlo Schapira and Sally Mayer of Milan (the close similarity of the latter's name with that of Saly Mayer in Saint Gallen caused unending confusion).[38] This was the time of the arrests and deportations, and the sums were spent on literally saving the lives of a large, though necessarily unknown, number of Jews. On the other hand, the period from about October, 1944, to the liberation of northern Italy in April–May, 1945, was one of intense suffering for the remaining Jews, whose number Valobra estimated at about 15,000. The deportations had all but terminated in October, but the neo-fascists received up to 5,000 lire ($50) per head for every Jew they delivered to the Germans. Jews who were caught were often summarily murdered. People were starving; they had to have forged food ration cards as well as false identity documents in order to exist, or else they had to stay hidden. One example may perhaps suffice: a well-known Parisian children's doctor had fled from the Nice area, escaped arrest after the German occupation, and arrived in the Turin area. A rescue worker identified only as "Sylvio" reported:

> In the small town where he lives, he spends the nights in the office of a lawyer who allowed him to do this but on the understanding that he pretends not to know about it. During the daytime, however, the refugee is forced to stay outside in the fields, in any weather, where he has been observed eating grass because of his complete lack of means. Finally I managed to approach this person, who impresses one as a noble character. After some hesitation he accepted the help I offered him with alacrity.

This same physician after a while accepted responsibility for treating some hidden children in the neighborhood.[39]

Teglio carried on his work in Genoa, but the chaotic transportation conditions, as well as Repetto's arrest, meant that help
had to be provided in a different way for the Turin, Milan, and
Venezia areas. Valobra was in touch with the Italian freedom
movement, the Comitato di Liberazione Nazionale (CLN), which
directed the maquis of northern Italy. As it turned out, Valobra's
great contribution to rescue efforts lay not only in his work for
DELASEM in Switzerland and his very good relations with Saly
Mayer, but also in his success in convincing the CLN in January,
1945, to characterize help to Jews as one of the central tasks of
Italian partisans. He achieved this despite the fact that Mayer was
reluctant to get involved with the CLN because of JDC's policy of
abstaining from political work, but Valobra convinced him that
the CLN was the future government of Italy and that Mayer was
not going to identify himself with any of the political groups that
made it up. "Sylvio" crossed and recrossed the Swiss border and
brought JDC money into Italy, where he distributed it to his
agents, both Jews and others (including priests). In April, 1945,
Mayer made an allocation to the CLN for its work with Jews. A

Table 22: JDC Expenditures in Belgium, Holland, Yugoslavia, and Italy, 1941–44

	Year	Official JDC Figures	Mayer's Accounts
Belgium	1941	———	———
	1942	———	
	1943	$140,818	$37,100
	1944	$540,000	$85,950
Holland	1941	———	
	1942	———	$ 2,345
	1943	$ 36,140	$ 6,900
	1944	———	$59,800
Yugoslavia	1941	$109,700	———
	1942	$ 63,000	$16,315
	1943	$ 40,000	$34,570
	1944	$ 1,745	$56,160
Italy	1941	$ 99,725	———
	1942	$ 60,000	$ 5,595
	1943	$ 41,000	$24,740
	1944	$347,534	$97,850

total of 85,000 sfr. ($20,000) was paid out, probably fetching 9 to 10 million lire, between November, 1944, and May, 1945.[40]

The rescue of most of the Jews living in northern Italy was undoubtedly primarily due to the sympathetic attitude of the Italian population. But in Italy, as for instance in Belgium, self-help was also important; JDC played an indirect, minor, but essential role in providing a minimum of funds without which nothing could have been achieved. Table 22 presents both the official JDC figures and Saly Mayer's expenditures in western and southern Europe from 1941 until 1944, and this requires some explanation.[41] The New York office was dealing with only those accounts that had reached it by the end of any given year. Allocations for repayment of funds borrowed in Europe were also included in their figures, and these must have been adjusted against actual payments in later years. The New York figures are hardly more than provisional estimates and may be misleading. Mayer, however, recorded what he actually spent, and his figures are certainly reliable.

12

Rescue outside Europe

The eruption of the Holocaust in Europe caused direct repercussions outside the countries occupied by Nazi Germany. Jewish refugees fled the Nazi hordes into the Soviet Union, and especially into Soviet Central Asia. The Soviet government did not have sufficient food for its own civilian population and simply left the refugees from the enemy-occupied areas in the west, whether Polish or Jewish, to their own devices. This often meant starvation and a slow death. The problem of saving Jews from the combined effects of starvation, Soviet lack of interest, and the anti-Jewish attitude of the Polish officials in the Soviet Union under whose wings they were posed a challenge to the Jewish organizations. The only gateway to the Soviet Union for the Jewish organizations was Iran, which was conquered in 1941 by combined Anglo-Soviet forces.

Other waves of refugees, mainly from Germany, had reached Shanghai before the war and in its early phase. Stranded in a huge and strange country, without the means to support themselves, the Jewish refugees, though few in number compared to the Polish and Baltic Jews in Russia, posed a similar problem. They had managed to escape the direct rule of the Nazis, but they were still far from safe.

Aid to Jews in Russia

Hundreds of thousands of Jews escaped into Russia when the Germans invaded the eastern parts of Poland annexed and ruled by the Russians. Many thousands more were deported into Russian concentration camps from those regions between 1939 and 1941. Nobody really knew, or knows now, exactly how many. The Polish government calculated the number of their citizens in Russia in 1941 at about 1.8 million, but this was just a vague estimate. About 250,000 Jews left the Soviet Union after the war to return to Poland, and there may have been another 50,000 at the most who either came out in the 1950s or remained in Russia. It is therefore probable that there were between 400,000 and 450,000 Polish Jews in Russia, of whom up to 300,000 were alive after the war.

JDC, of course, had a long history of aid to Russian Jews. It had settled about 60,000 Jews in the Crimea up to the early thirties, but after the organization had to leave the Soviet Union in 1938, most of them left their settlements. Those who remained were destroyed by the Germans. Very few were to come back after the war.[1] In American Jewish circles, the Crimean venture had left a deep mark—the Zionists opposed it vehemently, whereas some of the old leaders of JDC, especially James N. Rosenberg, saw in it an answer to Zionist claims and were eager to renew JDC's efforts in Russia. The opportunity seemed to come when Germany attacked the Soviets in June, 1941, but nothing really was done before the Polish government-in-exile, under Premier Wladyslaw Sikorski, signed an agreement with Russia on July 30, 1941, which appeared to usher in a new era in the two countries' relationship. As a result of this agreement, Polish citizens were released from Russian camps, and the men began to gravitate toward the Polish army that was being organized at Buzuluk in Soviet Asia by General Wladyslaw Anders.

A head count, probably made early in 1942, produced a figure of 245,175 Polish citizens released from the Russian concentration and internment camps, but it probably came nowhere near the real total. Jews constituted 30 to 40 percent of this number, which means either that most Polish Jews were still in the camps (some of them continued to languish there throughout most of the war) or that many had not registered with Polish delegates distributing relief. The situation became more complicated when the Russians claimed on December 1, 1941, that all former Polish citizens who were not ethnic Poles—that is, Jews, Ukranians, and White Russians—who were in Soviet-controlled territory in November, 1939, were Soviet citizens.[2] Many such Jews nevertheless managed to become charges of Polish relief officers, especially in the regions around Tashkent.

The situation of the Jews, already suffering from mass hunger and the spread of typhoid and other diseases, was aggravated by the antisemitism of at least some of the Polish officials. The Polish army was not eager to accept Jews; this attitude was strengthened by the extreme reluctance of the British, once they had agreed to accept part of Anders's forces into their Mideast armies, to allow a significant percentage of Jewish soldiers to come there. The Poles were of course very concerned about the fate of their women and children, who, like the Jews, were being decimated by hunger and disease. They wanted these civilians to be taken out of Russia, but the British resisted. They would not know what to do with the Poles or how to feed them (a figure of 50,000 children was mentioned), and it was better that they should remain in Russia—presumably to continue to die there.

Lord Halifax, the British ambassador to Washington, did approach Roosevelt about accepting some of these women and children, but the president was worried about raising the matter with a Congress that was still nervous about immigration, especially as he imagined that there would be many Jews among the Poles. He "admitted that what [the] administration feared was antisemitic agitation." Halifax assured him that there would be no more than 5 percent Jews among the refugees, although almost half of the needy in Russia were Jewish. But nothing came of the American idea. While two Indian maharajahs agreed to accept 5,000 Polish children, there were no takers for them apart from Palestine. But of course Palestine was out for political reasons.[3]

Eventually, as a result of agreements reached between the Poles, Soviets, and British, two groups of Polish soldiers came out of Russia in April and August, 1942, each accompanied by numbers of civilians. The first batch of 43,808 included 12,619 civilians, of whom probably about 800 were Jews. There were some 26,000 civilians in the second batch of over 70,000; a slightly larger number of Jews were among them than were in the first group.[4] From these refugees, Poles as well as Jews, Jewish organizations such as the JA, WJC, and JDC learned of the conditions of those who had remained behind in Russia. What was even more important, addresses were obtained. Postcards also began to arrive in Palestine from Russia, and in these Jews in the USSR were asking for help in the form of parcels. When it became clear during 1942 that the opportunities of leaving the Soviet Union were to be strictly limited, the best alternative appeared to be shipping help into Central Asia, where most of the Jewish refugees were now concentrated.

In New York, JDC had no clear idea of the situation until Jews came out of Russia in 1942. But even vague reports that reached the West before that showed that starvation was rampant. JDC quite naturally thought that with a new era in Polish-Russian relations seemingly in the offing, the best way to approach the problem of Polish Jews stranded in Russia would be through the Polish government-in-exile. The Polish Red Cross and the delegates sent out by the Polish embassy in Kuibyshev to administer relief in places where there were Polish citizens in the USSR were obvious conduits for such help. Negotiations with Ambassador Jan Ciechanowski began in Washington early in December, 1941. JDC budgeted $100,000 (and actually spent $83,345) for distribution of relief in areas of heavy Jewish concentration.[5]

JDC also tried to reach Russian Jewry. The obvious way was through the Soviet ambassador in Washington. Joseph Rosen spoke with Konstantin Oumansky in September, 1941, and in February, 1942, Maxim Litvinoff, the new ambassador, was approached. JDC offered help in resettling Jews in Uzbekistan. Litvinoff asked Moscow, and gave a final negative answer to all such approaches on March 2, 1942.[6] Nevertheless, JDC set up a nonsectarian committee to send medicine and medical equipment to Russia, and James Rosenberg participated in the Russian War Relief committee (RWR), an American organization established by private citizens, though with government approval, in 1941. After much argument, a Jewish section was set up in the RWR, which of course inevitably competed with JDC's own fund-raising efforts. In June, 1943, Rosenberg tried to get JDC to contribute a large sum to the RWR but failed. JDC leaders argued that Soviet goodwill could not be secured by the modest contribution which was all JDC could make. Moreover, Jews had given their money to help other Jews, and that was how JDC should spend it.[7] However, in September, the actor Shlomo Mikhoels and the writer Itzik Feffer arrived from Moscow. They were members of a Jewish antifascist committee which the Soviet government had set up in order to organize help for the Soviet Union from Jews all over the free world. Mikhoels and Feffer appealed to JDC, and on October 27, 1943, JDC appropriated $500,000 for general supplies to the Soviets, stipulating only that there would be no discrimination against Jews in the distribution of them. One senses JDC's hesitation: the action was clearly taken against the better judgment of a number of its stalwarts. The money represented a large chunk of JDC's resources, and it did not go to Jews. Saly Mayer had solved the difficulty of transferring dollars to Switzerland in September, and there were places where these half-million dollars could have been used better than as part of America's contribution to Russia's war effort, which amounted in that year to $33 million.

Part of the reason for JDC's action, however, was the hope held out by Mikhoels and Feffer that JDC might be allowed to resume its settlement operations in the Crimea. The hope was futile, though communications with Soviet officials were continued until April, 1945.[8] What is most interesting in this episode, however, is the evidence it affords of the continuing attachment of the most conservative JDC leaders to a completely outdated policy. They collaborated with the Soviet regime in pursuit of an archaic agricultural settlement plan whose attraction seems to have been both its inherent anti-Zionism and an ill-defined mixture of sentimental desires to "return to nature" and to regain contact with that reservoir of real or supposed Jewish virtues, Russian Jewry.

Since late 1941, the American Federation of Polish Jews had been sending parcels to Russia through a Polish bank in America. In Palestine, *Landsmannschaftn*, groups of Jews originating from the same town or village in Eastern Europe, collected names and addresses in Russia from the postcards that were arriving. On April 16, 1942, JDC inquired of Judah L. Magnes, its representative in Palestine, whether parcels could be sent from there and how many refugees there were in Teheran. On June 11, Magnes cabled that the situation in Iran was bad and that the possibility of parcels was being investigated. He also thought that a JDC representative should be sent to Turkestan, and that JA plans for help via Teheran should be supported. JA in fact sent Raphael Szafar to Teheran, and JDC sent him a first allocation of $3,000.

The JA treasurer, Eliezer Kaplan, who happened to be in New York, also appealed to JDC for help in June. On his suggestion, JDC protested to the Polish representatives in America against the alleged antisemitism of Poles in Russia, but nevertheless in July made an allocation of $144,500 for medical supplies for the Polish Red Cross. Originally the money was intended to supply the Poles with six complete hospitals in the Central Asian region; this idea, however, was quietly dropped, and the more modest but practical way was adopted of sending medical supplies, which the Poles distributed in the areas of Russia where most of the Jews were concentrated. By the time Russia broke off her relations with the London Poles in April, 1943, about two-thirds of this money had been spent. The rest, some $36,000, was given to the Polish Red Cross for use in the Polish refugee settlement in East Africa—where there were next to no Jews.[9]

Szafar's reports indicated that there was a real chance that parcels sent to individual addresses in Russia would actually get there, and JDC therefore allocated $18,000 for the project in October. The conditions were not clear, however, and in November JDC decided to send Harry Viteles, an American living in Palestine and an expert banking manager and general troubleshooter, to Teheran to investigate. He found 26,000 refugess (the figure almost agreed with the official British-Polish statistics), among whom there were 2,200 Jews—1,000 children and 1,200 adults. Of the children, 834 were dispatched in January, 1943, to Palestine. They arrived by ship, having sailed around the Arabian peninsula because the British refused to press the Iraqis, who objected to Jewish children going to Palestine, to permit the transport to use the short Iran-Palestine route via Iraq. Once in Palestine, the children caused great dissension between the religious and nonreligious segments of the Jewish population: both sides wanted to get the children into their own schools. JDC paid for transportation but adamantly refused to be drawn into the controversy. Palestinian Jewry would have to sort it out itself.[10]

More important was the question of the parcels. Viteles reported that by November, 1942, 2,400 parcels had been sent from Palestine and had been organized for JA by a private company, Peltours. He recommended that this practice be stopped and JDC take over. The JA parcel system was not bad, but the Polish Red Cross had been charged with "dishonesty, unfairness, inefficiency, waste and extreme selfishness" by the American Red Cross at Teheran. Viteles tended to agree, and suggested that the Polish organization should not be helped any longer.[11] The advice was not accepted. Ultimately JDC did send in Charles Passman, another Palestinian-based American citizen whom it occasionally employed, but it continued its involvement in the parcel scheme through the Polish Red Cross and JA, and in fact increased it considerably. An arrangement was arrived at with Intourist, the official Russian tourist agency, whereby 1,000 parcels could be sent into Russia monthly; at first 200 of these were arranged for by JDC, and the rest by JA and by private individuals, especially in Palestine. The number increased to 2,000 monthly after Passman, who arrived in Teheran in June, 1943, intervened with Intourist. Each parcel, however, cost the considerable sum of $28, and 800 of the 2,000 were paid and arranged for by JDC.[12]

In the spring of 1943, a special consignment of 3,279 cases of matzot was sent through the Polish Red Cross. Of these, 2,002 cases were lost in the Caspian Sea; the rest were salvaged, but most of them did not reach their destination. "It is common knowledge that the Polish soldiers in Iran have been enjoying the matzot sent from America for the Jewish refugees in Russia," as Passman put it.[13] But generally, despite many difficulties, most of the parcels did get to Russia and saved lives of people who otherwise might have perished of starvation. Not taking into account the matzot episode, 6,827 parcels were sent up to the end of 1943; in other words, the Russian permit was not exploited fully, partly because of difficulties in obtaining the foodstuffs and partly because of various petty regulations.

After the break in Russo-Polish relations in early 1943, the Polish Red Cross handed over some 150 tons of the JDC-subsidized foodstuffs it had been using for its own parcel system. Half was sent to Jews and half to Poles through the JDC-JA scheme. As time went on, Soviet attitudes toward such operations eased, and in 1944 customs were at first reduced and then to a large degree waived. However, in June, 1944, the Soviets forbade the sending of packages to Polish non-Jews, and began to press JDC and JA to get involved with the emerging leftist Polski Komitet Wyzwolenia Narodowego (Polish National Committee of Liberation), which had created a new Polish army on Soviet territory that was admitting fairly large numbers of Jews. In Teheran, representatives of the leftist Poles were willing to get all parcels in without duty provided the shipments were made through them. Rosenberg in New York was all in favor of working through a quasi government subject to Soviet rule.[14] As his colleagues on JDC committees considered Rosenberg an expert on Russia, his advice was followed, though with some misgivings.

From about mid-1943, the parcels included not only food, but also clothing, shoes, yarn, and needles. As a result of quick action by Magnes, JDC bought 252.5 tons of U.S.-owned lend-lease materials, though it did so rather reluctantly because it had to borrow the $474,000 purchase price. The packages, however, reached an increasing number of persons: a first list of 1,500 grew to 20,000 early in 1944, and 36,000 at the end of the year. The Russians also lifted all restrictions on the number of parcels in early 1944, so that 99,666 could be sent in that year—at a cost of $2.5 million, of which $1.7 million came from JDC. The same rate was maintained in early 1945, but then the volume began to taper off, and in August, 1946, the Teheran office was finally closed.[15]

JDC saw the Teheran operation as an offshoot of its representation in Palestine. It did not particularly want Judah Magnes to dominate there, but it had not much choice—Magnes had been on the scene since 1914 and could not easily be brushed aside. Unfortunately, his opposition to Jewish statehood made him persona non grata with JA. While many members of the JDC Executive Committee sympathized with his views, they had to work with a Zionist JA to whom Magnes's involvement in any Palestinian affair was unwelcome. JDC, and especially Joseph Schwartz, who visited Palestine in the summer of 1943, tried to establish a committee there which would include Passman and a few other persons. The plan did not work out, however, and Magnes remained a force to be reckoned with.

JDC's wartime work in Palestine fell into two main categories. One was economic, and accomplished through the PEC. Investments were maintained and profits reinvested in ventures such as the Cooperative Bank and other institutions in which the PEC had an interest. In the summer of 1942, JDC decided, after much internal argument, to help JA with its soldiers' fund, and allocated $200,000 for that purpose. The money, under full JA control, went into building projects and the support of soldiers' families.[16]

The other category was support of the yeshivot. This effort remained in JDC hands and was, in fact, controlled by Magnes. However, the funds appropriated for yeshivot everywhere were channeled through the cultural-religious committee which, after Cyrus Adler's death in 1940, was chaired by Rabbi Dr. Leo Jung. The amounts were of course dependent on JDC's general financial situation, but a great deal was done to preserve the traditional forms of Jewish learning with relatively little money. During the war JDC could act only in Palestine and Shanghai, which had received some of the yeshivot that had fled from Poland to Lithuania. Those who had reached American shores did not of course need JDC's help. Palestine had begun to absorb some of the European yeshivot before the outbreak of war, and some of the Lithuanian refugees who arrived in 1941 were rabbis and yeshiva students. The main burden of JDC's work in Palestine was to provide a minimum that would maintain the various schools and communities. Its task was not made easier by the fierce partisanship of the different rabbinical authorities and the hassidic rabbis, and because yeshiva students were dependent on outside funds to maintain themselves, competition was strong for the small amount of available money. Nevertheless, it was due largely to Jung's committee that the yeshivot were kept going throughout the war.

Shanghai

The story of the roughly 18,000 Jewish refugees in Shanghai and JDC's involvement with them differs in many ways from that of the other rescue attempts during the Holocaust.[17] For one thing, the attitude of the Japanese, who had occupied most of Shanghai in 1937 when the "incident" (as they called their war against China) began, was not racially based like that of the Germans. Rather, their view of Jews arose from the way they perceived their interests in their struggle for the domination of East Asia. Moreover, there was no organized Jewish community at Shanghai, but rather a number of warring factions. Consequently, JDC had to rely on Americans rather than local people to direct its welfare activities—a situation quite unlike that in any of the European countries. Even the cases of Lithuania and Hungary-Rumania, where JDC had local American representatives, were different in that these places had active and responsible committees which simply needed the backing of a Jewish representative from neutral America. On top of everything else, the sudden Japanese attack on Pearl Harbor forced JDC's representatives to stay in Shanghai far longer than had originally been intended. The result was that, relative to its resources and the number of refugees involved, JDC spent a vast amount of money there. In other areas it usually managed to raise significant sums of money locally, but again Shanghai was the most important exception to the rule.

The factionalism of Shanghai Jewry had its roots in prewar settlement patterns. Early in the twentieth century, the Jewish community there was largely Sephardi; it originated with a number of Iraqi and Iranian Jews who had mostly become British citizens. They numbered about 600 and became very wealthy as traders, real estate owners, and bankers. Among them, the Sassoon, Kadoorie, Hardoon, and Abraham families showed a certain minimal interest in the local community. The Beth Aharon synagogue, built by S. A. Hardoon in 1927, was to become important during the war by serving as the center of the Mir Yeshiva group, who came from Kobe in 1941.

In the twenties and thirties, Russian and Polish Jews, including those who had begun to enter Manchuria in the early years of the century and refugees from the Bolshevik Revolution, began to come to Shanghai. In 1932, the Shanghai Ashkenazic Jewish Communal Association was established, and it acquired a spiritual leader of some eminence in Rabbi Meir Ashkenazi, a saintly personality and an adherent of the Lubavitcher hassidic sect. The 4,000 Russian and Polish Jews had certain other basic institutions, including a shelter for the poor which could provide up to 400 meals a day; a Jewish Club for the well-to-do; a Talmud-Torah (traditional elementary schooling facility); a free loan society; and a day school, founded in 1930. Also in the thirties, 200–250 volunteers made up the Shanghai Jewish Volunteer Corps, a part of Shanghai's International Municipal Police.

The Japanese invasion caused an occupation of the city by 20,000 Japanese, on the one hand, and, on the other, the flight into it of up to 800,000 Chinese trying to escape from the war zone. The International Settlement area of the city, where practically all of the Jews were living and part of which was also occupied by the Japanese in 1938, was in effect a separate neutral state. It was an enclave ruled by a council of fourteen, five of whom were Japanese, representing the foreign powers with economic interests in China. Outside of it was the vast Chinese city under Japanese rule and another small separate area, the French Concession. Japanese influence in China generally, and in Shanghai specifically, was wielded by three main branches of the Japanese power structure: the navy, the army, and the consulate general, to which latter the gendarmerie later became attached in all matters concerning Jews. The Japanese Naval Landing Party—the official name of the invading forces subordinate to the navy—was represented from 1938 by Captain Koreshige Inuzuka. The three Japanese institutions were constantly at odds, and anyone dealing with them had to walk a tightrope between them.

After encountering a small but important Jewish community in Manchuria, which they had occupied in 1931, the Japanese were groping for an understanding of the Jews. The *Protocols of the Elders of Zion* was available in Japanese and appears to have influenced Japanese thinking. Some saw the Jews as competitors in the Japanese bid for world power, but others concluded from the same material and from personal contacts with Russian Jews in Harbin (Manchuria) that precisely because they were powerful and well connected internationally, the Jews should be cultivated or pressured into cooperation. A lecture in October, 1938, by an important Japanese "expert" on Jewish affairs urged that the Jews be forced to come over on Japan's side, influencing their brethren in America and elsewhere to do the same.[18] The Japanese government tried to follow this policy of pressure and threats. However, even when Japanese power ruled supreme, diplomatic niceties were observed, and civilian refugees especially were treated with a certain amount of consideration. There was undoubtedly a Nazi influence in Japan, but it was not deep enough to shape Japanese attitudes to Jews decisively. One finds a certain amount of lipservice to the Nazi characterization of Jews, but it was too foreign to the Japanese mind to be accepted. Japanese policy towards Shanghai Jews, including the refugees, was therefore a mixture of German influence, of the way Japanese interests were interpreted by the various elements in the Japanese power structure, of the avariciousness and desire for personal aggrandizement of some individuals, and of a type of idealistic humanitarianism among the Japanese.

The relatively placid life of the Jews of Shanghai was interrupted in the spring of 1938 by the first influx of Jewish refugees from Austria and Germany. JDC had been involved in Shanghai since February, when the first signs of trouble appeared. Shanghai was important to the United States, and State Department pressure caused JDC to join the London-based Council for German Jewry in sending money there. The situation took a decisive turn for the worse with the Crystal Night pogrom in November, after which escape from Germany to anywhere at all was preferable to Nazi concentration camps. Shanghai happened to be the only place in the world for which no entry visas were required, because of the peculiar governmental structure of the International Settlement.[19] By early February, 1939, there were 2,500 new refugees there; by the end of March, there were 4,000; by May, there were 9,000. At the end of 1939, some 17,000 German and Austrian Jewish refugees had come to Shanghai.[20]

The Japanese tried to influence Jewish and German representatives to stop the flow into Shanghai, but with no success.[21] On August 21, 1939, the Japanese forbade the entry of any more

Jewish refugees, and the Shanghai Municipal Council followed suit the next day. Jewish organizations had been forewarned by the fact that various governments and their local representatives had been asking for such an action for over a year; in fact, Jewish groups, including JDC, had tried to convince German Jewry to stop the migrations to Shanghai, but Gestapo pressure and the threat of concentration camps were much more potent than legal niceties or even the threat of starvation.[22] Immigration did not cease, and it was typical of the cautious Japanese attitude that still no decisive action was taken. A Municipal Council committee deliberated for two months how to apply the new policy of non-admittance, and on October 22, the full council relaxed the prohibition by allowing refugees with $400 cash ($100 for children) or with close relatives in Shanghai to enter. Herman Dicker theorizes that Inuzuka, who was responsible for Jewish affairs in Shanghai, wanted more Jews in the city because of their value as hostages in Japan's game with the western powers.[23]

Two relief committees were active in Shanghai at that point: the International Committee (IC), set up by Sir Victor Sassoon in July, 1938; and the Relief Committee for German Jews, established by a German Jew named Dr. Karl Marx in October, 1938. Marx left Shanghai in 1939, and his organization became the Committee for the Assistance of European Jewish Refugees in Shanghai (CFA), headed by Michael Speelman, a Dutch Jewish banker. In January, 1940, Sassoon resigned from the chairmanship of the IC, but entrusted it to his close collaborator, a Hungarian Jew named Paul Komor. The IC looked after legal problems, passport affairs, and migration, but its chief activities were to supply milk for children and mothers and individual support for people who wanted to establish themselves independently. CFA was to look after the mass feeding and medical program. IC was financed largely by Sassoon, whereas CFA received the bulk of its funds from JDC.

The basic problem of the German refugees in their unwanted exile was that Shanghai was already overcrowded with people accustomed to a very low standard of living. The Chinese standard would have meant starvation for these Europeans, and they found the climate unbearable: hot and humid in the summer and very cold—but still humid—in the winter. The refugees came from all walks of life, had no common bond except that of being refugees, and were struggling for individual survival and for escape from Shanghai. By the end of 1939, 15,030 of them had registered with CFA, of whom 603 were Protestants, 420 Catholics, 80 "others," and the rest Jewish.[24] There never was an exact head count, and Dicker estimates that in 1940 and 1941 another 4,000–6,000 Jews came in with the $400 landing money provided by relatives, mainly in the United States, who transferred it to a bank in Shanghai. Five camps were organized in Hongkew, a part of the city which had been partly destroyed during the fighting in 1937. At the end of 1939 and in early 1940, the 2,500 camp inmates and an equal number of others were receiving a monthly allowance of $7.50 to keep body and soul together.[25]

Surprisingly, thousands of others managed to find some kind of gainful occupation. Women made dresses or underwear; men traded with all kinds of articles or took over agencies for foreign companies; artisans opened shops for shoemaking, metalworking, and tailoring. Even artists and musicians somehow eked out a pittance. The IC gave aid to individuals who then founded businesses that developed a whole area in Hongkew, especially along Chusan Road. It was perhaps not entirely accidental that that was precisely the area where whole streets belonged to Sir Victor Sassoon.[26] JDC estimated that 11,000 lived in Hongkew, 4,000 in the French Concession, 1,500 in the International Settlement, and the rest elsewhere in the city. Those who could rented rooms and then sublet part of them to others. The camps in Hongkew provided dormitory housing, but some of them were not only filthy and lice-ridden, but also conducive to passivity, lethargy, and disease.

The local leadership, whether of the IC or the CFA, was quite unfit for the task it undertook. The CFA was guided by a steering committee which included, besides Speelman, some of the established Sephardi aristocracy—Ellis Hayim, Horace Kadoorie, and others. They treated the refugees very high-handedly. "They had been totally and completely humiliated and deprived of every remnant of self-respect as adult human beings."[27] Actual day-to-day administration was left in the hands of Captain A. Herzberg of the Shanghai Jewish Volunteer Corps, a rigid, insensitive person who was unsuited to the job. Furthermore, while the CFA employed about 500 refugees, their pay was totally inadequate, amounting to one U.S. dollar a month. The result was that the CFA staff had to steal and engage in corrupt practices in order to exist at all. Some had to put themselves on the relief roll and pay themselves.

The refugee camps and the individual families scattered in the vast city had no effective representative body of their own.

There was indeed a Jüdische Gemeinde representing the German refugees, but by all accounts it was ineffective and weak. It won some kind of representation on the CFA, but was quite incapable of influencing CFA's policies. On the other hand, schooling was one of the brighter spots in the picture. From November, 1939, some 700 pupils were studying at the Horace Kadoorie Shanghai Jewish Youth Association, and another 150 at the Freysinger School. There were some Jewish students at the city's two universities, and with the influx of the Polish Jews from Lithuania in 1941, traditional Talmud-Torah and yeshiva studies began to flourish.

The Polish Jews escaping from Lithuania began arriving in Shanghai in early 1941. They tended to rely on the well-established Ashkenazi community and were reluctant to identify with the German refugees and the Sephardi-led CFA. JDC recognized the potential difficulties and sent a small initial sum of $3,500 to CFA to provide for the Lithuanian contingent. The problem, however, became much bigger than originally expected. Not only did people come from Kobe, but also straight from Vladivostok, because they had no valid Japanese transit visas. By August, 1941, more than 1,000 Polish refugees from Lithuania, mostly rabbis and their students, arrived in Shanghai, among them the whole Mir Yeshiva group of over 300 persons. In May, 1941, Russian and Polish Jews in Shanghai organized a committee for East European Jewish refugees, known as Eastjewcom and chaired by Alfred Oppenheim; the vice-chairman and treasurer was Joseph Bitker. Eastjewcom was ostensibly a subcommittee of CFA, but the two groups quarreled. The new arrivals insisted on strict kashrut, and kosher food was much more expensive than non-kosher. Furthermore, they felt that there was no point in preservation of life if Torah studies were not to be pursued. Rooms had to be found for study, books had to be provided, and the yeshivot were extremely reluctant to share their living quarters with other refugees.

JDC in New York was sufficiently alarmed at the worsening situation to decide to send an American representative to Shanghai. The choice fell on Laura L. Margolis, who had a first-class social work background from Cleveland and was at the time JDC's representative at Havana. She arrived in Shanghai on May 12, 1941, charged with investigating and advising on reorganization, if necessary. She had scarcely had time to get acquainted with the situation when the German attack on Russia on June 22 caused the American government to advise its nationals to evacuate the area. In July, therefore, Margolis went to Manila, from where she reported to Moses Leavitt that she had tried to mediate between CFA and Eastjewcom, but that matters were grave. The relationship between CFA and the refugees was hostile and the wealthy and powerful Jewish families in Shanghai were unwilling to pull their weight. Leavitt had absolute confidence in Margolis, and by October she was back in Shanghai, fully empowered by JDC-New York to do whatever she felt was right. Faced with a tremendously complex situation, she demanded help, and Leavitt made another excellent choice, sending Manuel Siegel, who arrived in Shanghai in late November, 1941, as Laura Margolis's codirector.

Margolis supported Eastjewcom in its fight with CFA. Contrary to Japanese wishes, Herzberg wanted to house the new arrivals from Kobe in Hongkew. Eastjewcom refused to participate in such an unnecessary defiance of the Japanese, but as CFA was utterly unprepared to meet the influx, despite the fact that ample warning had been given, Eastjewcom undertook to register the refugees and generally care for them. (The result was a very sharp reprimand to Herzberg by Inuzuka on September 17, before Margolis's own return from Manila.)[28] Rabbi Ashkenazi and some of the Eastjewcom members found housing, on the floor of Beth Aharon synagogue and other places, for the new arrivals. The 409 actual rabbinical students were then lodged separately. Margolis supported their claim for larger allowances, and a compromise with CFA was patched up. Later on, in 1942 and 1943, these student groups provided some leadership for the more traditionalist elements among the Jews. The local Ashkenazi community arranged for the photo-offset printing of the Talmud, and the VH in America, whose chief activist at the time, Rabbi Abraham Kalmanowitz, was head of the Mir Yeshiva, also supported the Shanghai rabbinical group.[29]

Laura Margolis was just settling down to examine the workings of CFA when the Japanese forced her hand. In fact, she had called a meeting for December 8, 1941, to discuss reorganization: due to time differences, the attack on Pearl Harbor took place simultaneously with the attack by the Japanese on the American and British gunboats in Shanghai harbor on that day. Margolis and Siegel had very little money with which to meet the suddenly changed conditions. Their December allocation had not yet arrived, and while JDC had authorized Margolis to borrow money against repayment après should hostilities break out, there was no certainty that this plan would work in Shanghai. Herzberg decided immediately to reduce allocations to the mass feeding program. Bread rations were cut from twelve to six ounces, and 8,000 people who had been receiving two stew soups a day were now receiving only one.

There was enough money to continue the program on that basis till the end of December. Speelman, Hayim, and Abraham turned to Inuzuka to find out what could be done to help the refugees. All three were of course enemy nationals, but that was not why Inuzuka practically threw them out of his office. Rather, his reaction stemmed from dissatisfaction with CFA. The two Americans thereupon decided to take the bull by the horns and went to Inuzuka themselves—which, apparently, was exactly what he wanted. They asked for his approval to contract for loans in accordance with the permission they had from New York and he agreed, provided they took the money from neutral nationals only. He also agreed to free some frozen funds which remained in CFA's name at the bank and gave them 5,000 sacks of cracked wheat which the American Red Cross had stored and was willing to hand over to the Jews. Inuzuka's condition was that CFA should be reorganized and Herzberg dismissed.

Margolis and Siegel got to work. Early in January they had Speelman call a meeting of the Ashkenazi community, the Jüdische Gemeinde, and some wealthy individuals to reorganize the committee and underwrite the loans. The meeting, unfortunately, was a disaster. The wealthy people refused to underwrite the loans, thereby putting off a Siberian Jew who had been prepared to lend 1.5 million local dollars (about $80,000 at the time).[30] No money was forthcoming except some small sums from the wealthier refugees themselves; the soup kitchens kept going, but at an even more reduced rate. On January 10, Margolis informed the refugees that from now on only 4,000 persons—only children and some women—would be getting one soup daily. She and Siegel decided to take the refugees into their confidence. All 500 staff members were asked to work on a voluntary basis. They would get IOU's repayable after the war for January, but afterwards their salaries would depend on the availability of money. Only one resigned. Meetings were held in the five camps, and the inmates began to plant vegetables, organize cultural activities, provide for the equitable distribution of their meager food and goods, and so on. Of all that Laura Margolis and Manuel Siegel accomplished during their stay in Shanghai, bringing about constructive cooperation was probably the greatest achievement—though it did not, unfortunately, last very long.

On the CFA battlefront, they fired Herzberg and in effect dissolved the committee, taking upon themselves direct responsibility for the administration of relief to the refugees. But the loans were still not forthcoming. In desperation, they had the story published in the *Shanghai Times* on January 16, 1942: they were out of funds and the refugees would starve if help were not offered. Inuzuka was furious about the newspaper campaign, but he did not stop the stories and they did have an effect. On January 20, the first break came when a German Jew gave $10,000. Russian Jews then also came forward. Finally, a shrewd Jewish businessman, Joseph Shriro, lent $138,500; soon the entire $180,000 for six months which JDC-New York had authorized Margolis to raise were subscribed, and the feeding could proceed at a rate somewhere between the original 8,000 and the reduced number of 4,000.

The two JDC delegates next, in late February, called a final meeting of the old CFA leaders at Speelman's office and there accused CFA of having been responsible for the demoralization of the refugees and the maladministration of funds. Speelman was the only person who accepted the criticism and the blame. The others walked out. Early in March, a new CFA was formed, with Speelman at the head, but with Margolis and Siegel still in full control. Eastjewcom now demanded that one-sixth of the funds go to support the refugees from Lithuania. Margolis and Siegel found this claim for special consideration quite outrageous in the new situation that had developed, but they had no choice—future loans would depend largely on the goodwill of Russian and Polish Jews. Eastjewcom's conditions were accepted, provided that the contributions from the Ashkenazi community flowed into the common kitty in the first place, and that the one-sixth for the "Lithuanians" would be deducted after that.

Slowly the two Americans set up an administration they could trust. They found a close ally in Joseph Bitker, the vice-chairman of Eastjewcom, who became their confidant for the duration. They found a first-class bookkeeper, a social secretary, and a man to be responsible for housing matters—all of them from among the refugees. The Quakers, here as everywhere they operated, were again JDC's most natural allies: they took over the supply of some badly needed clothing, as well as the social organization of one of the camps. But probably the most significant decision in that period of 1942 was made when Laura Margolis accepted an offer of voluntary help from Avraham Levenspiel, a Polish Jew and an engineer by profession, who took upon himself the organization of the feeding venture.[31] The basic question was technical: the committee had been spending sixty cents (local) on each meal, fifty cents of which went to pay for the coal that was used in a most inefficient boiler system. The real problem was how to rebuild the kitchen and install different boilers. Usable boilers were owned by the Cathay Land Company, which belonged to Sir Victor Sassoon, and though they were lying unused in storage, the company refused to lend them. Japanese help was obtained, and a requisition order for the duration brought the boilers to the kitchen. At a cost of $5,000 a new kitchen to serve up to 10,000 meals was completed by Levenspiel in September, 1942.

All these details tend to show the peculiarities of the Shanghai situation and the sometimes rather odd role played by the Japanese. This role was highlighted by the increasing involvement in refugee affairs of Carl Brahn, a Jew who had lived in Shanghai for at least twenty years, and whose main asset was a liaison with a Mrs. Nogami. She worked for the Japanese gendarmerie (which was allied to the consulate general and opposed to the navy), and it was she, for instance, who requisitioned the boilers. Passes and permits of various kinds could also be obtained through her. It was therefore essential to keep Brahn in the picture, without, however, antagonizing Inuzuka and the navy. Throughout 1942, that was one of the Americans' main tasks.

JDC-New York was in touch with Laura Margolis through the JDC office in South America, where Moses Beckelman was stationed at the time. Soon, however, American regulations put an end to this contact. JDC had to be careful if it wanted governmental help in vital matters, and Leavitt informed Margolis on May 21, 1942, that henceforth all contact must cease. Margolis's problem, however, was that she had been given only a very general understanding that loans après might continue, and her attempt to elicit an explicit authorization failed. By the time JDC's Administrative Committee got around to discussing the matter, contact was cut.[32] It was not until December, 1942, that Leavitt asked the IRC to instruct its representative in Shanghai, Eduard Egle, to tell Margolis that she could borrow 100,000 sfr. (about $30,000) monthly for another year.

Meanwhile, the money was running out. The two refugee

hospitals had to close in June, the patients being gradually transferred to the municipal hospital, which was under an understanding Italian doctor. One of the refugees apparently conceived the idea of "patronages" (*Patenschaften*), whereby a Shanghai Jew would pay 50 (later on, 100) local dollars a month to keep a refugee alive. Into the picture came Robert Peritz, who now filled Paul Komor's place as secretary of the IC, and who worked as an official on Inuzuka's staff. He was deeply mistrusted by the two Americans as well as by most of the Jews, yet he did manage to obtain a number of such patronages for the refugees. By 1943, 500 refugee children were receiving regular patronage money each month.

The problem of how to obtain loans remained insoluble. Margolis and Siegel, expecting to be interned at any moment, wanted to arrange for them as quickly as possible. They could not promise repayment after the war because they had no authorization to do so, and as time went on and contacts were cut off, they began to wonder whether JDC would honor any undertakings they made, or, indeed, whether JDC was still operating at all. They could only say that they personally were convinced that the money would be repaid, which simply was not good enough. Money came in only in small driblets, from loans or from very limited voluntary contributions. The situation was made worse by the continued intercommunity hostility between Eastjewcom and the German refugees. Eastjewcom, for example, refused to undertake patronage of German Jews. Nevertheless, Margolis and Siegel resigned in July, 1942, and handed the administration over to Speelman and the efficient refugee administrators.

Just at that point, apparently in July, a dramatic incident occurred which threatened to nullify all of the work already done. Three Nazis—Robert Meisinger, Adolf von Puttkammer, and Hans Neumann—arrived at Shanghai.[33] According to our sources, they suggested radical measures against the Jews. Some rumors spoke of ghettoization, others of concentration on an island off Shanghai, and still others of mass murder. What does seem clear is that a friendly Japanese on the staff of the consulate general and Peritz informed the Jewish leaders meeting at Speelman's office of some Japanese ghettoization plans. The secret of the meeting leaked out, and all the participants were arrested, including the Japanese official. The Japanese were again very angry, especially the Captain Saneyoshi who had taken Inuzuka's place in June. Nevertheless, the fact that the Nazi plans had been divulged prevented the Japanese from taking immediate action, and it was possibly one of the reasons why ghettoization was postponed for several months.

As a result of this episode, however, Speelman and the others were interned and CFA ceased to exist. Margolis and Siegel were due to sail for America on a civilian exchange program on September 6, 1942, and action had to be taken very quickly. A JDC committee was therefore established, with Brahn at the head and Bitker as treasurer. Other members included Margolis's secretary and other refugee representatives. A so-called Kitchen Fund was organized to look after feeding, and when the Jüdische Gemeinde refused to administer housing, the Kitchen Fund took that over as well. It was nominally headed by Dr. David Berglass, but the actual leaders were some Polish Jews who reinstituted the old CFA management and dismissed the refugee administrators appointed by the JDC delegates. There was nothing Margolis and Siegel could do. The refugees themselves were dependent on the funds that would be collected, and the Kitchen Fund leaders were in charge. It seems that Margolis later regretted having put Brahn at the head of the JDC committee, because his collaborationist attitude toward the Japanese caused friction between him and the other committee members, especially Bitker.

As it happened, Margolis and Siegel did not sail in September after all. With the help of an American lawyer, they drew up a very peculiar kind of contract which stated that any loans given to the JDC committee would, in their judgment, be repaid in America, but that neither they nor JDC had any legal obligation. Bitker was then limited to $30,000 monthly from November, 1942. After tremendous difficulties which it is not necessary to detail, most of the $30,000 monthly was obtained by Bitker, largely (and indirectly) from the same Joseph Shriro who had lent the first substantial amounts. In January, 1943, Siegel was interned, and Laura Margolis on February 25.[34]

The Japanese finally announced their ghettoization plan on February 18, 1943. Stateless refugees were to be concentrated at Hongkew, in an area of about one-half to three-fourths square miles, embracing the five established camps. Other Jews were told this would not apply to them, but the panic was understandably great among all Jews. Ghettoization was to take effect in May, and all the refugees who had managed to move out of the ruined Hongkew district and establish themselves economically outside would be forced to move back and in effect deprived of their livelihoods. A Shanghai Judenrat was established for the purpose, called the Shanghai Ashkenazi Collaborating Relief Association (SACRA). This organization was subordinate to the Office of Stateless Refugee Affairs, headed by Tsutomu Kubota. At the head of SACRA stood a hitherto unknown Rumanian Jew, Dr. J. A. Cohn; Bitker became treasurer. SACRA's tasks were to transmit Japanese orders and channel the funds raised in Shanghai by the JDC committee of the Ashkenazi community to the Kitchen Fund, which remained responsible for the actual administration of them. Typical Nazi ghetto features were introduced, including the marking of stateless Jewish refugees (outside the ghetto area by a yellow star, inside by a yellow stripe) and a Jewish ghetto police called the Vigilance Corps. It is not quite clear how many people the ghetto contained, but most probably up to 15,000 Jews were concentrated there. Hunger and disease became rampant, and in 1944 about 10,000 people were being fed by the Kitchen Fund. Most of the money necessary for these feeding programs was raised by the JDC committee—about 8,000 sfr. ($1,900) monthly by August, 1943, and similar sums up to the end of 1943. By the end of 1943, however, local funds were definitely drying up, and SACRA was reduced to being nothing more than a small taxation program of the Ashkenazi community. An increase in the patronages to 900 did not make much dent in the situation either.

Finally a way was found for JDC-New York to transmit money. Margolis, feigning illness, met with Bitker while she was hospitalized in Shanghai in July and August, 1943, and Bitker proposed that money be channeled to him from Switzerland through the IRC. In September, 1943, Laura Margolis left Shanghai on the exchange ship *Gripsholm* for the United States, where she arrived in early December. JDC-New York had thought of the IRC idea previously, but now they knew who to send the money to, and Treasury Department approval was obtained. A first 100,000 sfr. ($23,000) had been sent to the Polish-Lithuanian group by the IRC in September, 1943, and another 30,00 ($7,000) entrusted to Egle at Shanghai in November.

In January, 1944, Saly Mayer began transmitting money through the IRC to Bitker and Brahn, simultaneously receiving Egle's reports about the bitter arguments inside the JDC committee. Throughout 1944, he sent 1,886,652 sfr. (about $517,000) to Bitker, which appear to have constituted roughly 90 percent of the Kitchen Fund's expenditures. Even that rather massive (by

JDC standards) amount did not provide for more than about 1,300 calories daily for each of those fed.[35] The same rate of funding was maintained in 1945, until liberation on August 10, 1945, despite the fact that both Mayer and JDC-New York were fully informed of the unsatisfactory internal situation in Shanghai. According to official JDC figures, the numbers supported rose from 7,395 in early 1944 through the 10,000 mentioned earlier to approximately 11,500 at the end of the year.[36] The VH continued to send separate support for the rabbinical group through the IRC, and an enraged Leavitt calculated that each yeshiva student in Shanghai was getting $200 a year, as against the $36 a year worth of food that JDC provided for the roughly 10,000 persons it fed. JDC opposed an attempt to try to get special treatment for the rabbinical group in emigration, because it felt that singling out the students might make the position of all the others more difficult.

The Japanese named a certain Ghoya to be responsible for the administration of the ghetto. A petty tyrant, he was the central object of hatred by the oppressed Jewish population, though some reports claim that he actually was an American spy. Whatever the facts, Ghoya did no more than make life miserable on a low level—he did not kill, nor did any of the other Japanese officials or military men. Lives were lost only when the Americans bombed the city. Yet without JDC help, conditions would have been very grim, though probably not grimmer than the situation of the hundreds of thousands of Chinese refugees, who died by the thousands throughout the war years. From every point of view, theirs was a much more depressed, dangerous, and indeed tragic situation, and they had no Chinese JDC to help them.

JDC's financial investment in Shanghai was very considerable: $60,000 in 1938; $190,000 in 1939; $241,026 in 1940; $355,166 in 1941; $361,807 in 1942; $98,192 in 1943; $340,000 in 1944; and $1,210,617 in 1945. But the organization did achieve its aim: the Jews of Shanghai survived the war, largely through JDC's efforts. Borrowed money was repaid to those who lent it. Shriro got his first loan of $138,500 back in October, 1944, in America, by a special Treasury license. Moreover, he had made a good profit, for the exchange rates at which he gave his Chinese dollars were far below the current ones.[37] JDC could also be proud of its two delegates, who had guided the refugees through misfortune and dangers, and it could be thankful to the few individuals, such as

315

Bitker and Levenspiel, who proved to be the righteous men in a Sodom of no mean magnitude. When liberation came, Manuel Siegel escaped from the internment camp even before the official release. The first thing he did was to fire Brahn, the SACRA administrators, and the entire leadership of the Kitchen Fund. Avraham Levenspiel became the chairman of the new committee, and Bitker the treasurer. But that was another story.

13

Amid the Tide of Destruction: Polish Jewry, 1942–1944

The entry of the United States into the war in December, 1941, was a turning point in the martyrdom of Polish Jewry. European Jews were cut off from the one neutral power whose very neutrality seemed to have put at least a minimal restraint on Nazi policies. It is true that the murder program was already going on in the conquered Russian areas where no Americans could penetrate, but the fact that the first Polish death camps came into existence about the time of America's entry into the war seems to have convinced some writers that Pearl Harbor was one of the causes for the beginning of the mass murder in the non-Soviet areas under German control. There is, however, no evidence of this. The Japanese did not inform Hitler of their intention to attack on that day. Chelmno, the first death camp, began to operate about December 8—but surely this must have been prepared before, so that the fact that the two events occurred on the same day is purely accidental. Besides, Heinrich Himmler, the leader of the SS, seems in fact to have informed Rudolf Hoess, the commander of Auschwitz, about the plans to have Auschwitz serve as a major killing center as early as July or August, 1941. The first gassing of Soviet prisoners of war took place there on September 3. Yet one cannot deny that the raid on Pearl Harbor facilitated the Nazi's task after the event and enabled them to proceed with the lightning speed that made their action so "successful."

JDC-Warsaw, as an American agency, was shut down by the Germans on December 21, 1941. JDC, which had controlled all the social work in the GG through JSS, lost that control completely and became a Warsaw organization which was only very occasionally able to provide some help outside the capital. And, of course, any tenuous contacts that JDC-Warsaw may have had with areas outside the GG were automatically cut off. Furthermore, JDC could no longer control the JSS in Kraków; Michael Weichert, orignally a JDC-nominated director of a JDC front, thus became independent. We do not know what happened to Isaac Borinstein; he disappeared in the maelstrom that engulfed all of Polish Jewry. In Warsaw, Isaac Giterman, David Guzik, Leib Neustadt, and Emmanuel Ringelblum carried on, but Weichert was now free from supervision and could carry out whatever he planned, if the Germans permitted. What he did or tried to do we know from some of his office files and from two books which he published after the war in order to defend himself against the accusation that, by keeping up his Kraków-based office under SS supervision, he had knowingly misled Jewish organizations abroad into thinking that Jews were still living in Poland and into misinterpreting the murderous policy of the Nazis.[1]

At the end of 1941, JSS was ordered by the Germans to take over responsibility for all foreign aid that might arrive through the IRC or by other means. It seems that Weichert at first continued his operations with the help of allocations received from NRO, the all-Polish aid committee of which JSS was the Jewish section. The termination of JDC help of course meant that Weichert had to look elsewhere for money to supplement the Polish allocation. Borinstein had in fact suggested that he follow JDC's example and borrow Jewish money for repayment après. Weichert refused—he was, at that stage at least, wedded to the concept of legality. When in March, 1942, deportations to the death camp of Belzec began from the Lublin ghetto, Weichert tried to find out where the deportees had been taken and to organize some help for them. He was kept informed of the developments, as we know from the surviving documents of the Lublin ghetto, because the head of the Lublin Judenrat, Mark Alten, was also Weichert's representative. In fact, in May, 1942, Alten wrote to Weichert that he would send 10,000 zl. to the deportees once he knew where they were, and why did the Germans not tell him? Surely they knew, and surely it was their interest to have Jewish organizations look after them.[2] At that stage, Alten and Weichert may still have been in the dark regarding German intentions. It is probable that the deportations from Kraków in May and June, 1942, opened Weichert's eyes to what was really happening.

Weichert delighted in detailed statistics, and we learn from him that in early 1942 he had contact with 412 local departments; 56 were in Eastern Galicia, which had been added to the GG after its conquest from the Russians in the summer of 1941. In early July, he made a list of 321 institutions all over the GG that he recorded as looking after 58,483 children (the very exactness of the figure makes it suspect). His statistics included Warsaw, though, as has been noted, his writ did not run there. Despite his detailed figures, however, it is impossible to find out what his expenditures were in 1942, or exactly how they were distributed.[3] But there seems little doubt that Weichert tried his best to find funds, distribute them, and save lives—while preserving his position as the sole arbiter of social welfare. He tried to provide constructive help by supplying raw materials for Jewish artisans; he was in touch with Gruppe Handwerk, the relevant government department, and he sent money to Lwów for that purpose. In most places he managed to maintain a semblance of independence from the Judenräte, though in Lwów, for instance, he failed singularly, and his nominee, Leib Landau, had to give way to the head of the local Judenrat.

One can almost physically feel the increasing despair and aimlessness of Weichert's JSS. Slowly his influence became limited to the Kraków area. On June 3, 1942, he was notified that, by Governor Hans Frank's decree, all Jewish matters in the GG were henceforth to be handled by the SS. He could no longer use the weak and ineffectual BuF, which the SS treated with some condescension and even contempt, as a buffer. Weichert became quite friendly with BuF, especially with an official named Lothar Weihrauch, who ultimately was to save Weichert's own life, but neither BuF nor any of the other economic departments could stop the SS.[4]

The very existence of JSS was endangered. In May, Weichert had changed his organization's name to Jüdische Soziale Hilfe (JSH; Jewish Social Help) in order to be less offensive, but the gesture did no good. At the end of July, the SS gave orders for a slow dissolution. In August, NRO was dissolved by the German

authorities, and its Polish constituent, the Rada Glowna Opiekuncza (RGO; Chief Aid Committee) and the JSS were left without a roof organization. Nevertheless, Weichert managed to hang
on, and on October 16, BuF handed down a decision recognizing
a Jüdische Unterstützungsstelle (JUS; Jewish Aid Center) which
would be permitted to supply Jewish labor camps (but not ghettos, which were being liquidated) with whatever aid came from
abroad through the IRC or other groups.

Weichert claims he was in touch with thirty-six camps until
the end of 1942. Like all his other figures, this one is suspect.
Twelve camps were near or in Kraków and they were often not
more than small workplaces for Jewish slaves. The only large
camp to which he appears to have had access was Plaszów,
where he apparently did distribute some materials. The end
seemed to have come on December 1, 1942, when BuF closed the
organization on the express demand of the SS. Weichert claims to
have stolen the last twenty-one boxes he received of medicines
from abroad and to have hidden them, together with his main
archives, with RGO.[5]

In March, 1943, however, JUS reopened just as the final
liquidation of the Kraków ghetto was proceeding. Weichert was
now operating with a skeleton staff, including the well-respected
Dr. Haim Hilfstein and a few others. According to Weichert, the
IRC informed the Germans that if their consignments to Poland
were not also distributed to Jews by Jews, there might be measures taken against German internees in Allied countries. This is
most unlikely, at least in the form that Weichert presents it. The
IRC in 1942 showed a very marked disinclination to get involved
in protecting Jews, and a threat regarding the treatment of Germans would be almost impossibly out of character. What probably happened is that it indicated to the German Red Cross that
Jews should have a share in whatever was sent to Poland; if they
did not, difficulties with sending help to non-Jewish civilians
might ensue. The German Red Cross was one of those organizations that tried to ameliorate some of the worst aspects of Nazi
rule without endangering itself, and it may have transmitted what
it heard in language that persuaded the SS there would be no
harm in maintaining a Jewish front to receive aid from abroad and
silence questioning.

Weichert therefore operated solely as a receiving and distributing agent for medicines, foodstuffs, and clothes received from
abroad, supplying such Jewish slave labor camps as the SS per-

mitted him to have access to. The only cash he received was 11,000 zl. (about $100) from Rabbi Marcus Ehrenpreis, head of a WJC aid group in Stockholm, but he also got a Red Cross consignment of 245 boxes (fifteen tons) of medicines from the CPR and 24 more boxes from Saint Gallen. This aid was supplemented by what he claimed were "thousands" of small parcels from Lisbon and Switzerland. He sold the contents of these, buying flour and medicines with the proceeds. Despite the seeming accuracy of his figures, they are by no means clear, but it appears that he received and distributed some 30,000 sfr. ($7,000) worth of medicines and foodstuffs in 1942. He gave no exact figures for 1943; for 1944 he mentions a figure of close to thirty-five tons of materials, whose worth he estimates at 250,000 sfr.[6]

In August, 1943, after only a few months, JUS was closed down again, but Weichert was not deported. He apparently continued working in RGO, sending shipments to camps, until he was allowed to reopen his organization in February, 1944. JUS remained in operation until July, 1944, and then Weichert went into hiding, aided by his German friend Weihrauch. Throughout the whole period that JUS existed, most of the consignments it received from abroad originated with JDC and WJC. Some of these were sent through the IRC or through fictitious addresses in Lisbon, some by Saly Mayer, and some by OSE through the IRC after Mayer's approval.

However, Weichert's activities were looked upon with increasing distrust by the Jewish underground movement, especially by the Żydowski Komitet Koordynacyjnj (Jewish Coordination Committee), organized in October, 1942, as the political body of the Żydowska Organizacja Bojowa (ŻOB; Jewish Fighting Organization) which was preparing the Warsaw ghetto rebellion. Repeated appeals were sent by the ŻOB leaders in the summer of 1943 and then again and again in 1943–44, and by the JDC in Poland, to stop sending parcels and medicines to the JUS from Jews outside Nazi Europe, because Weichert was a German stooge and the materials would never reach the Jewish inmates of the camps.[7] However, although they wavered occasionally, both Joseph Schwartz and Mayer took the line that if a reasonable proportion of the shipments reached Jews, they should be sent, even if the rest were confiscated by the SS. Furthermore, the relations between Weichert and the SS were irrelevant. As for JUS: by the summer of 1943, nobody was being deceived by them. Responding to continuous Polish pressure in this matter,

Schwartz finally informed the Polish Social Welfare Ministry in London in July, 1944, that in JDC's opinion relations with the Nazis did not necessarily disqualify Weichert, because how else could one send aid to Nazi camps? JDC would not stop sending parcels to JUS despite the protests from the Jewish underground.[8]

Weichert survived the war, and so did the leaders of the Jewish underground. Weichert produced large numbers of receipts, letters of thanks, and so on to prove that the goods sent to him had reached the camps. But the main evidence in his favor was given by Hilfstein, who claimed that lives were saved at Plaszów thanks to the help from JUS.[9] On balance it is probable that at least a part of the shipments did reach Jewish inmates; another part was certainly used by the SS. Little aid came to camps outside the Kraków district, but perhaps some came to the camps in the Radom area. In any case, it was only a drop in the sea. But was not a drop in the sea infinitely better than nothing at all?

JDC's own sphere of activity was therefore limited to Warsaw, with its 350,000–400,000 inhabitants.[10] JDC went underground in December, 1941, but in fact nothing much changed. It is clear that the "directors" continued to borrow money against repayment après and that they continued to control ŻETOS, the Jewish self-help organization in the ghetto. Through Emmanuel Ringelblum, the house committees were run with the aid of a committee representing the political parties and bodies. CENTOS, TOZ, and TOPOROL existed under different guises, but run by the same people. Moreover, despite Ringelblum's extreme hostility to the Judenrat, it emerges even from his own diary notes that Adam Czerniakow and the Judenrat were increasingly active in the social aid work in the ghetto. Ringelblum felt that they were interested solely in gaining power over the independent ŻETOS,[11] but both Czerniakow's diary and the testimony of survivors indicate that the Judenrat was honestly trying to do some good, especially with regard to children. For instance, Czerniakow says that he met with Giterman in April, 1942, in connection with programs for them.[12] It seems that legal and semilegal operations in the ghetto were closer than Ringelblum would have us believe.

We have no statistical details regarding JDC operations in Warsaw in the half year of 1942 until the great deportation. We do know that the situation continued to be appalling, while JDC's resources were steadily diminishing. But we also know that, as the spring of 1942 advanced, the typhoid epidemic began to be conquered. TOZ activities and the tremendous self-sacrifice of the doctors and nurses of Luba Bilecka's school were beginning to pay off. Deaths went down from 5,123 in January to 3,636 in May, the lowest figure for over a year. About 100,000 people had perished, mainly from starvation and starvation-connected causes since 1939, but those left alive had more stamina and better chances of finding work. In July, 1942, the labor office of the Judenrat, which was of course under German control, found that there were 70,000 persons gainfully employed in the ghetto—that is, excluding those in illegal shops and smugglers. A Judenrat official estimated at the same time that there were 20,000–30,000 people who were reasonably to very well off; about 200,000 who were not suffering visibly from hunger (though their situation was dangerous, and they were near descent into life-endangering poverty); the rest, whom the writer estimated at a quarter of a million (the figures do not correspond to the population figures) were suffering and dying. Yet, from all accounts, the situation was actually improved over what it had been in 1941. Employment was increasing; there was less hunger. Governor Frank said in August, 1942: "One does not have to talk about the fact that we have condemned to death by starvation 1.2 million Jews. That is clear, and if the Jews do not die of starvation it will be necessary to increase the severity of anti-Jewish measures."[13] But with the aid of smugglers, a tremendous will to live, and, finally, the self-help organizations, the Jews were actually on the point of defeating the murder-by-starvation plan when the Nazis turned to more immediate methods.

JDC's struggle against starvation created very serious moral dilemmas. Ringelblum, who was himself responsible in large measure for the administration of relief, wrote:

> Relief doesn't solve the problem; it only keeps people going a little longer. But they have to die in the end anyway. Relief only lengthens the period of suffering, but is no solution; for in order really to accomplish anything, the relief organization would have to have millions of zlotys a month at its disposal—and it has no such sums. The well-established fact is that the people who are fed in the public kitchens are all dying out, subsisting as they do only on soup and dry rationed bread. So the question arises whether it might not be more rational to set aside the money that is available for the sole use of certain select individuals, who are socially productive, the intellectual élite, and the like. However, the situation is that, in the first place, the élite themselves constitute a considerable group and there wouldn't be enough to go around even for

them; and in the second place, why should laborers and artisans, perfectly deserving people, who were productive in their home towns, and whom only the war and the Ghetto experience have deprived of their productive capacity, why should they be judged worthless, the dregs of society, candidates for mass graves? One is left with the tragic dilemma: What are we to do? Are we to dole out spoonfuls to everyone, the result being that no one will survive? Or are we to give full measure to a few—with only a handful having enough to survive?[14]

Despite Ringelblum's misgivings, ŻETOS-JDC did play a central role in saving those that were saved, only to be murdered later. Children, especially, were cared for by the Judenrat, through homes run by Abraham Gepner, by CENTOS, and by the house committees. There were still thousands that did not receive any care and were sentenced to a slow and horrible death. The Judenrat and CENTOS declared two months—October, 1941, and April, 1942—to be devoted to fund-raising and organizing projects for children; these efforts alleviated some of the suffering, but could not solve the problem. Ringelblum claimed that they were held at the expense of the parents. "The worst parents," he said, "are better than the best home."[15] But some food was better than none.

No less important than the outright self-aid program were the activities by the directors in other fields. It is clear both from postwar testimonies and from contemporary diaries that JDC-Warsaw was very much involved in illegal publishing, political activities, youth movements, and clandestine education. The underground high school organized by the youth movement Dror was financed by JDC, as were many of the study circles and seminars held by the different movements. During the period of the ghetto, forty-nine clandestine journals, weeklies, monthlies, bulletins, and news sheets were published by the different illegal political bodies. Though no figures are available, funds for many of these were provided by JDC. In fact, from early in 1942, Giterman's policy of encouraging all and every sign of independent anti-German action is quite clear. We have a direct testimony bearing on this in Haika Grossman's memoirs. On January 21, 1942, the Farainikte Partisaner Organizacje (FPO; United Partisans Organization) was founded in Vilna to fight the Germans. It embraced all the Jewish underground bodies, from the Communists to right-wing Zionists. Grossman was sent to Bialystok to help organize a local fighting group; from there she came to Warsaw, apparently in the early spring, to establish contacts and to get funds for buying arms. She met with Giterman and Guzik and told them of the mass murders at Ponary, of the call of Abba Kovner, the Vilna ghetto poet and leader, to armed resistance, and of the need for money. Giterman, she says, listened carefully, and then: "He gave us a budget the size of which I do not recall, but I do remember that it was not at all small in our estimation." This was important, "not only because of the money that was received, but because it was Giterman who gave it, specifically for armed rebellion, to buy arms."[16]

As time went on, Giterman, Guzik, and Ringelblum drew closer to the left-wing Zionist youth movements, who became cofounders, with the resuscitated Jewish section of the Polish Communist party, of the first Jewish underground fighting group in Warsaw, the Anti-Faszistisher Blok (Antifascist Bloc), founded in March, 1942. They had no weapons, but they began with a propaganda campaign and the organization of cells. On April 18, the Germans reacted. Something of what was going on must have reached them, because they murdered fifty-two people that night in the ghetto, some of them connected with illegal publishing. The leaders of Dror, Yitzhak Zuckerman ("Antek") and his wife, Zivia Lubetkin, were also on the list, but were forewarned and hid. On May 30, some of the Communist leaders, including the main military expert, Andrzei Szmidt, were arrested and murdered, and the Bloc in effect broke up. Czerniakow knew whom to turn to to try to prevent the publication of illegal sheets. On the morrow of the April 18 murders, he called Ringelblum and told him to tell the political underground to stop publishing.[17] He turned to Maurycy Orzech of the Bund with the same request. The publications continued.

On July 22, the great deportation from the Warsaw ghetto began. We need not concern ourselves here with its antecedents; suffice it to say that some attempts had been made by German officials dealing with labor supply to postpone or stop the deportations, and indeed continued to be made throughout that period. But all these feeble attempts were brushed aside and the Jews of Warsaw deported, almost all of them to the Treblinka death camp. On July 23, Adam Czerniakow, head of the Warsaw Judenrat, committed suicide rather than carry on supplying the Germans with Jewish victims.

It was some time before the Jews of Warsaw fully understood that deportation meant certain death. Despite detailed reports from Vilna, Chelmno, and the eastern provinces, despite the Lublin deportations in March, despite the BBC broadcasts in

July which had in effect transmitted to Poland the contents of the Bund report of May—and which were heard in the Warsaw ghetto[18]—despite all this information, the Jews still did not know, because knowledge would have meant the end of hope. This central fact cannot be overstressed, because it is vital to understanding the victims' reaction. Alexander Donat observes in *Holocaust Kingdom* that it was not until the famous orphanage of Janusz Korczak was led away for "resettlement in the East" that he (and others) fully realized that the Germans had decided on mass murder.[19] Between July 22 and September 21 (the deportations officially ended on September 13, but there was another on September 21), about 265,000 Jews were sent to their deaths, 10,380 died or were killed during the action, 11,580 were deported to slave labor camps, about 55,000 remained in the ghetto, and some 8,000 remained hidden in Aryan Warsaw.[20]

On July 23 or thereabouts, there was a meeting of a so-called public committee (in fact, of the ŻETOS political committee, composed of representatives of the political groups in the ghetto). There are a number of accounts of this meeting, which discussed possible reactions of the ghetto to the deportations. Among the sixteen participants were Giterman, Guzik, and Ringelblum, and the leaders of Dror and Hashomer Hatzair participated for the first time as equal partners. The youth leaders called for armed resistance, supported by the left-wing parties and the JDC representatives and opposed by the Agudat Israel leader, Zishe Friedman, and the secularist intellectual Isaac Schipper. The political parties were unable to arrive at a policy at this meeting; this inaction of the political parties led to the creation of the first ŻOB organization. Dror, Hashomer Hatzair, and Akiva, a small youth movement associated with the General Zionist liberal wing, set up ŻOB on July 28. The Bund was waiting for its Polish socialist comrades in the Aryan part of the city to send arms. Nothing came. ŻOB tried to smuggle arms into the ghetto during the deportations themselves, but it succeeded in getting only a few pistols and some explosives. Betrayed by a member who broke down under Gestapo torture, the leader of ŻOB, Josef Kaplan of Hashomer Hatzair, was caught and killed. By pure accident, the Germans caught a girl who was carrying the newly acquired weapons to a hiding place, and the ŻOB was disarmed, in despair, and leaderless. The Communists were disorganized; the Bund was disillusioned and hit hard by the deportations. There is very little evidence of any action by JDC-Warsaw during that critical time.[21]

When the great deportation was over and the remaining 55,000 Jews tried to see what could be done, the mood was such that ŻOB members were seriously considering a mass suicide. It was only through the great effort of Zuckerman, Lubetkin, and Mordechai Anielewicz, who had been on a mission outside of Warsaw until early September, that spirits rose again. At the end of October, the ŻOB was refounded with the participation of the left-wing parties, to which later were added all of the others except the Revisionists. The latter established their own organization, the Żydowski Związek Wojskowy (Jewish Military Organization). ŻOB's political wing was the Żydowski Komitet Narodowy (Jewish National Committee), which united all of the parties and movements except for the Bund. This committee and the Bund together established the Żydowski Komitet Koordynacyjnyj (Jewish Coordination Committee). The Coordination Committee was quite clearly under the influence of the new military leadership, with Mordechai Anielewicz as the commander. A civilian committee was also established, whose main task was to make nonmilitary preparations for the armed rebellion, including finding the necessary money and materials and building underground bunkers. This committee had seven members, among them Isaac Giterman and David Guzik.

We do not know the details of Giterman's and Guzik's actions between October, 1942, and January, 1943, nor what Guzik did between January and April, when the great rebellion broke out. But we do know that JDC abandoned its traditional fund-raising methods. The ŻOB resorted more and more to forcible expropriation, and as Giterman and Guzik were responsible for monetary affairs, one must assume that they were estimating how much a person could afford to give and then pressuring him to give it. The prestige of JDC was thus used to extort money for an anti-Nazi Jewish rebellion—a far cry indeed from the policies and tactics pursued even at that time by JDC in America or neutral Europe.

On January 18, 1943, a second Nazi "action" (*Aktion*) against the ghetto began. The Germans wanted to deport another group of thousands of Jews. But this time they met resistance, and for a few days shots were heard in the ghetto. One of the victims was Isaac Giterman.

> At dawn on Monday, January 18, 1943, the ghetto was surrounded by gendarmerie, SS and Ukrainians. Giterman lived on Mila 69 where the inhabitants had just completed building a hideout in the

cellar. Giterman had not yet managed to learn the location of the hideout. At dawn he left his room to find out where it was located. On the stairs he met the director of the Tarbuth School [Hebrew-language school], Rosenblum, and the secretary of the kehillah, [Leo] Bornstein, and engaged them in conversation about the news in town. Giterman was standing in a corner of the stairs, a step away from his own residence. Suddenly a shot was heard and Giterman fell dead on the spot. It turned out that the SS men had occupied the house and, seeing a group of three Jews standing, they shot and killed Giterman without a moment's hesitation.[22]

Leib Neustadt was shot at about the same time at the Pawiak prison, where he had been interned after trying to get out of the ghetto on the strength of a Latin American passport which had been sent to him, apparently by Silberschein in Switzerland. Borinstein disappeared, probably killed during one of the expulsions from Kraków. Of the original directors, only David Guzik remained. Apparently he was responsible, after Giterman's death, for financing the rebellion which finally broke out on April 19, 1943. Guzik himself managed to flee to the Aryan side of Warsaw. For a short time he was involved with a scheme to rescue people who had access to Latin American passports or promises of passports or visas sent from Switzerland, and afterwards we find him, together with Yitzhak Zuckerman and Adolf Berman, signing messages sent from the Jewish National Committee to London. (Guzik signed *Kaftor*, which is Hebrew for "button"; his surname means "button" in Polish.)[23] He was arrested, got out again, lived on the Aryan side, participated in the work of the Jewish National and Coordination committees, and continued to be responsible for financial matters until the liberation. Unfortunately, Guzik died in an airplane accident shortly afterwards, and we have no direct evidence of his activities during the last year and a half of German rule in Poland.

What emerges from the sketchy descriptions and bits of information is that JDC's leaders in Poland, to the extent they could, carried on their work of aiding the Jewish population and moved towards a determined support of armed rebellion. Guzik continued to try to find funds for armed action and the hiding of Jewish people in Aryan quarters until the end of the war. Ringelblum, who may not formally have been a director but was certainly a leader of JDC, was deported from Warsaw, but brought back in a daring escape operation by Polish friends of the ŻOB. Tragically, his hideout was discovered in March, 1944, and he and his family were murdered immediately. That was the end of

JDC's work in Poland during the war. The tremendous effort to save the many failed. The people who gave JDC their money in return for promises of postwar repayment never claimed it. They and their heirs turned into ashes along with the notes they had, scattered on Polish soil.

JDC-New York's Attempts to Help

The response—or lack of it—of American Jewry to the plight of Polish Jews has presented a bitter problem for post-Holocaust commentators. JDC, as American Jewry's instrument for aiding Jews abroad, was faced with an American policy that made effective aid difficult, because it denied direct help through the British blockade and opposed any idea of negotiating with the enemy to protect civilians. In addition, it postulated that only quick victory might save people's lives, whereas efforts to help civilians under Nazi rule would prolong the war and with it the suffering of the very people that were to be helped. American Jewry was not prepared, politically, organizationally, or in any other way, to challenge these attitudes.

In light of this situation, there was not a great deal that could be done to aid Polish Jews on a small, practical scale from New York, and Allied policies precluded any large-scale action. In early 1942, JDC-New York discussed the additional loans which the Warsaw committee obviously was taking on for postwar repayment, all of the New York office's warnings notwithstanding. Just before America's entry into the war, Josef Blum of Budapest had actually met a JDC representative on the Polish-Slavak border, probably either Borinstein or Neustadt. Blum said that Jewish children were dying of diseases and hunger, and food was needed for 1.5 million Jews. Could New York help?

On March 11, 1942, the WJC, in the person of Dr. Arieh Tartakower, came to JDC and suggested a joint approach with the Labor Committee and JDC to the U.S. State Department to ask permission to ship food to Poland on a basis analogous to that of shipments to the Greek islands, where the British had sent food in the winter of 1941–42, despite their own blockade regulations, because of starvation there. The reason was not purely humanitarian. The British appear to have been afraid of a mass movement of Greeks into Turkey if hunger persisted, and they might well clog all the routes as the refugees in France had done during the May–June campaign in 1940. Rather than having the Greeks on their lines of communications, the British preferred to send food to them. When, on the other hand, the British at the same time received detailed information regarding the starving Polish children in Russia, they did their best to prevent them from coming out to Iran. JDC and the other Jewish groups tried to use the Greek case as a precedent for shipping food to starving Jews in Nazi Europe.[24]

The sending of food to Polish Jews was another matter altogether, because no direct British (or American) political or military interest was involved, but this the Jews did not realize. WJC, the Jewish Labor Committee, and JDC went to the General Jewish Council, the weak and ineffectual coordinating body of the major Jewish groups in the United States, and there the whole problem was discussed. It was decided that Polish and other general non-Jewish aid groups should be contacted before approaching the State Department in order to present a united front. The practical proposal was to send $24,000 worth of food parcels from Lisbon to Poland, one-half to Poles, and one-half to Jews. April and May passed, and slowly the various organizations were roped in. But the Polish organizations were still not quite ready to join, and so the summer passed too. WJC was represented on the General Jewish Council by its American group, the American Jewish Congress; occasionally even Stephen S. Wise himself, the founder of WJC, participated in the deliberations. On September 1, Rabbi Maurice Perlzweig of WJC wrote to Isaiah Minkoff of the Jewish Labor Committee that it was a scandal to wait any longer, and that the Jews should act on their own. WJC was in fact sending some parcels through RELICO, and Agudat Israel was also active. Joseph Hyman wrote to Morris Waldman of the American Jewish Committee that JDC could not follow that example; it had to have State Department approval.

In the meantime, Jewish relief organizations in Britain, under local WJC prodding, managed to get British agreement for a similar scheme, financed locally and activated through the IRC. This was reported by JTA in July, and when a surprised JDC inquired, British Jews confirmed the information on September 23, 1942. In America, Dr. Nahum Goldmann, a member of the JA leadership and of WJC, thought that enough time had been wasted. He cut through the Gordian knot and approached the State Department for a license without bothering to inform the other organizations, which had just prepared a memo for submission in Washington with the knowledge of a WJC representative.

JDC was very angry and announced it would also approach Washington separately. Herbert B. Sussman, director of the United Galician Jews of America, commented on November 9 that he "thought $12,000's worth of food for the Polish ghettoes (only God knows how much of it will be taken away by the Hitlerites) is very little, even if the entire amount gets there. I feel there should be no quibbles as to who gets the license and who should get the credit."[25] The deep animosity between JDC and WJC is evident in this unhappy episode. Letters were exchanged and positions stated, and JDC declared once again that it would not coalesce with "what was essentially a political international organization and that it must limit its participation in this matter to contacts with American agencies."[26] WJC had acted in breach of a gentleman's agreement and behind the backs of everybody else. JDC approached the State Department, and Assistant Secretary of State Long gave it the desired license in December, nine months after the original idea had been proposed.

Some parcels were sent from Lisbon. Early in March, 1943, however, IRC informed Herbert Katzki in Lisbon that the Germans no longer accepted parcels for JUS; there were few other addresses to which parcels could be sent. The Portuguese also put obstacles in the way of exporting food from their neutral but not very rich land.[27] Yet these obstacles were overcome, and JUS was also allowed to resume operations later in March. In February–April, 1943, 12,559 parcels were sent from a fictitious address in Lisbon through the IRC, partly to JUS and partly to other addresses in Poland. Of these, 925 were ackowledged, 849 by Judenräte and 76 by individuals. Later in 1943, 7,226 more parcels were sent, but only 42 receipts received. Nevertheless, the sending of parcels continued.[28]

JDC acted very late. Its tardiness even within the very narrow confines of the practical possibilities cannot be explained by lack of awareness of what was happening in Poland. It was clear to JDC leaders that the London-based Polish government-in-exile was not only receiving reliable information from Poland, but that it had means of transmitting funds which could help the Jewish remnant there. The urgency of the situation was put to JDC (and others) in letters from Szmul Zygielbojm in London, which were sent in by the American Bund leader, Jacob Pat. In January, 1943, Zygielbojm wrote that only immediate punitive measures against the Germans could help, yet he was afraid that by the time people realized that that was the case, it might well be too late. There was not much JDC could do about that, but in February he stated the simple truth when he wrote: "The world is hiding behind a convenient cloak of disbelief and does nothing to rescue those who may yet be alive."[29] Pat also transmitted desperate appeals from the Polish Jewish National Committee and Jewish Coordination Committee. "The remaining Jews of Poland now realize that you did not aid us in our most tragic moment of need. Act now at least, in the last days of our lives."[30] The JTA also provided very detailed reporting of the Warsaw ghetto rebellion as it was unfolding in April and May, 1943. JDC, it is clear, was fully informed.

The course of action JDC took followed that of the Labor Committee, which from 1942 had been sending small amounts of money to Poland via the London Poles. Pat reported to Hyman in March, 1943, that they had already sent $45,000 in that manner.[31] Carefully, JDC inquired of the Polish representatives whether such funds actually reached Poland. Having been assured that they did, JDC then proceeded to build up goodwill with the Polish government-in-exile. In the process, funds were donated to the Polish refugees then housed in East Africa. With Treasury Department agreement, the first $100,000 were transferred to London as late as September 14, 1943, to be sent to Poland to the Jewish underground groups. Similar amounts followed on December 9, 1943, and March 30, 1944. On July 19, 1944, a further $125,000 were sent, of which $25,000 were sent by the Labor Committee for the Bund. Finally, $200,000 were sent on September 13, making a grand total of $650,000 in a year.[32]

Reports from Poland dated late in 1943 and early in 1944 tell us something of the amounts received by Jews there. By October, 1943, the Jews had received Polish governmental aid in the amount of 4,750,000 zl. through the Rada Pomocy Żydom (Commission of Help for Jews), known as Żegota, which had been founded in Warsaw in December, 1942 (after a false start in October). In November and December, an additional 1.5 million zl. were spent, and from January, 1944, the sum increased to 1 million zl. monthly. Some funds also were received in dollar notes from London and handed over to the Jewish organizations, which then used them independently of Żegota. The dollar was worth 100–150 zl. in Warsaw in 1943 and 1944, so that it is possible to argue that Żegota got the entire JDC contribution and some Polish funds as well.

This money enabled fairly large numbers of Jews to stay alive.

In the summer of 1943, after the rebellion, 15,000 were estimated to be hiding in Warsaw alone, and of these well over half were in some way connected with either Żegota or the Jewish organizations. In fact, there was not much difference, as Adolf Berman of the Jewish National Committee was also secretary of Żegota. A combined special branch in which the two groups cooperated looked after stray children who were maintaining themselves on the Aryan side of Warsaw by selling matches and cigarettes or by begging. Most of these children were ultimately caught by the Polish and German police and killed as though they were vermin, but some survived, thanks to the help they received.[33] Aid was supplied fairly regularly through these agencies up until the Polish rebellion of Warsaw in August, 1944. During the rebellion, in which about 1,000 Jews participated as fighters, numerous Jews in hiding lost their lives, many at the hands of antisemitic rebels. After the rebellion was crushed, many Jews again were caught because they had to leave their hiding places when all the Poles were evacuated from Warsaw by the Germans. Not more than 2,000 survived in the area until liberation. Committees at Kraków and Lwów were established as branches of Żegota, but they were weak, and only a few hundred people received help from them.

Saly Mayer's activities relative to Poland were simply a follow-up on the lead by Schwartz in Lisbon, not because Mayer was unaware of what was happening, but because the control of action for Poland remained in Schwartz's hands. Mayer was responsible for the negotiations with the IRC, and it was he who persuaded it to take over the delivery of parcels to JUS. It was Mayer, too, who sent parcels directly labeled "St. Gall" and helped OSE to send more under its own name. In fact, most of the medicines sent from Switzerland to Weichert came from Saly Mayer through various intermediaries. He also sent funds to Bratislava in 1943, and the Slovak Jewish leadership sent parcels to individual deported Slovak Jews in southern Poland until news from these places ceased. In the summer of 1943, prompted by Nathan Schwalb, Mayer sent money which helped to save a few dozen survivors of the anti-German Jewish underground movement in the Upper Silesian region of Bendin and Sosnowice; helped with these funds, they made their way into Slovakia.

By the time JDC again had money and had found ways of transmitting it to Poland, there were few Jews there. Nevertheless, JDC made funds available to IRC for general distribution in Poland, on the understanding that part of it would reach Jews;

the IRC, early in 1944, was not prepared to receive the funds on any other terms.[34] By the summer of 1944, Schwartz realized that little more could be done. "What we have been witnessing as Jews is the systematic extermination of a people—an extermination policy which in a very large measure succeeded, and the remnant [surviving] that extermination policy will need emergency assistance, not only at the present time, but for a considerable time in the future."[35]

All in all, the story of JDC aid from outside Poland to Polish Jews does not make happy reading. The Red Cross, the Allies, and the neutral countries were unwilling to get involved and help, but Jewish agencies must also bear part of the blame. The machinery of these organizations, including that of JDC, moved too slowly; it did not adapt in time to the radical changes in the Polish situation. Internecine fights that now seem so trivial also impeded swift response. But when all is said, it is the viciousness and speed of the murderer that holds the key to understanding what happened to the greatest Jewish community in the world. Polish Jewry was destroyed in a manner that cannot be called "bestial," because the term would be an unbearable insult to the animal world.

14

Rumania

At the end of World War I, Rumania acquired territories from its neighbors which contained considerable Jewish populations, especially Transylvania (taken from Hungary), Bukovina (from Austria), and Bessarabia (from Russia). According to a government census of 1930, there were 756,000 Jews in what was then Rumania. Northern Translyvania, which was to be transferred to Hungary at the bidding of the Germans in 1940, had a Jewish population of 148,294, while 307,340 Jews were counted in Bukovina and Bessarabia. The rest lived in the "Regat," or Old Rumania.[1]

The attitude of the Rumanian governments to their Jewish subjects ranged from grudging acceptance of their equality before the law, under pressure from foreign powers, to overt antisemitism. The minimum program of most Rumanian governments was the eviction of Rumanian Jews from Rumania. Despite the paper protection of the post-World War I treaties, there were continual rumblings regarding the denaturalization of Jews in Transylvania, Bukovina, and Bessarabia under the pretext of supposed recent immigation into these areas from Russia or Poland.[2] A brief but very dangerous interlude in late 1937 and early 1938, when a violently antisemitic government tried to execute anti-Jewish measures on the Nazi model, clearly indicated which way things were developing. In 1938, King Carol instituted a dictatorship which, while avoiding any drastic antisemitic legislation, still pandered to

335

the many antisemitic intellectuals. However, the power of the Iron Guard, the local brand of fascism whose trademark was extreme hatred of Jews, was temporarily curbed.

Rumanian Jewry was basically divided into a Jewish national movement, which was under Zionist leadership, and liberal non-Zionist groups. An Orthodox group faded into insignificance in 1940, when Northern Transylvania, its main stronghold, was given up. The rabbinate, especially the more important Ashkenazi group under the leadership of Dr. Alexander Safran, took a middle position, but tended towards the non-Zionists.

The Zionist group originally coalesced around the most important Jewish national newspaper to appear between the wars, the *Renasterea Noastra*. In line with similar developments in Poland and in Czechoslovakia, a Jewish National party was founded in the late twenties, which not very successfully tried to find non-Jewish allies that would protect Jewish interests in return for political support. One of the main figures in this party was Abraham L. Zissu, a writer and thinker whose ideas gradually veered towards those of the Revisionists, though he never joined them officially. Zissu was also a wealthy industrialist and head of the Sugar Trust, a government-supported monopoly; he had many important connections in the government. The Zionist Federation was an organization separate from the Jewish National party, orienting itself towards preparing people for immigration to Palestine and doing educational work. It also included Zionist groups who were not identified with the Jewish Nationalists. Shortly after the war broke out in 1939, Leon A. Mizrahi became the federation's president, but he left Rumania in early 1941. For the rest of the war Mishu Benvenisti, one of the younger men in the movement, assumed the presidency. The Zionist movement in Rumania was closely allied to the WJC branch there, at whose head stood Wilhelm Fischer.

The acknowledged leader of Rumanian Jewry, however, was Dr. Wilhelm Filderman, a wealthy lawyer, head of the Union of Rumanian Jews, the non-Zionist political organization, and chairman of the Union of Jewish Communities. Filderman was a non-Zionist in the Warburg mold—he was not opposed to Zionism, and in fact was a member of JA as a non-Zionist. He supported its work in Palestine, and, unlike many American non-Zionists, he was also in close touch with WJC. It was one of JDC's achievements in the community that Filderman, in a rather ill-defined way, also accepted the position of chief collaborator of JDC and its spokesman in Rumania. His attitude was typical of that of Rumanian Jewry in general: Zionists and non-Zionists worked well together. In 1936, a Consiliul Centrala Evreilor din România (Central Committee of Rumanian Jews) was formed, under WJC's influence, to defend Jews against antisemitism. The leaders of Zionist and non-Zionist groups were in close contact and were to form a united front when Rumanian Jewry's existence was threatened. Zionists were members of Filderman's organizations, and JDC's chief contacts were drawn from both groups. A central position under Filderman was held by Fred Saraga, head of the JDC-subsidized low interest loan banks, the kassas. JDC was officially represented in the Regat by Moses Ussoskin, but Ussoskin left Rumania in early 1941, and one of JDC's problems throughout the war period was whom to entrust, under Filderman, with its work.

Despite the serious economic situation of Rumania—largely caused by inefficient and corrupt administration in a very wealthy country—and despite antisemitic tendencies, parts of Rumanian Jewry, especially in the Regat, were relatively affluent. Jews had a large share of the development of industry and commerce, and Jewish craftsmen and artisans were prominent in trades. An increasing number of lawyers, doctors, engineers, and architects had graduated in the twenties and early thirties, and although this trend was cut short by university antagonism to Jews in the later thirties, these Jewish intellectuals were prominent in the cultural and intellectual life of the country.

In the summer of 1940, however, external events brought on a precipitous decline in the position of Rumanian Jewry. A sharp Russian ultimatum on June 26 demanded the immediate surrender of Bessarabia and northern Bukovina; the Germans advised the Rumanians to yield, and on June 27 and 28, the Russians marched into the two provinces. Hungary demanded the return of Transylvania, which Rumania had taken from her after World War I. The Germans, who wanted to control both countries, pronounced their verdict, and on August 30 Northern Transylvania was awarded to Hungary. A small section of southern Dobrudja, an area on the bank of the Danube, was also lost to Bulgaria. The government of Ion Gigurtu, who had been named premier by King Carol, had to take the blame. The outlawed Iron Guard now conspired with disaffected army generals and, on September 4, Carol had to yield and appoint General Ion Antonescu premier. On September 6, he abdicated and left the country, leaving Michael, a minor, nominally king.

On August 8, the Gigurtu government had published a series of anti-Jewish decrees in order to curry favor with Germany and with local nationalistic opinion. Jews were ousted from government employment and forbidden to own agricultural land. All Jewish trade in villages was forbidden. Jewish lawyers were severely restricted; access to universities and high schools was in effect denied, and permits for Jewish schools were withdrawn. Following the establishment of the Antonescu-Iron Guard regime in September, further restrictions followed in rapid succession until January, 1941. Sales of certain products, which until then had been permitted to Jewish war veterans and war widows or orphans, were forbidden; first attempts were made at the "Romanization" of Jewish property—that is, it was virtually confiscated, and Rumanian custodians were named for it. This last step, however, was not very successful, because few Rumanians were competent to take over Jewish enterprises. Furthermore, bribery was rampant and softened the impact of the blow: confiscations were sometimes prevented or postponed through bribes, or an arrangement was made with the custodians which left Jewish owners in virtual control of their establishments. Such methods of course were not universal, and it is at present impossible to say what percentage of Jewish firms effectively remained in Jewish hands. More immediately dangerous was the ouster of Jews from trade associations and trade unions, which affected electricians, butchers, chemical engineers, journalists, engineers, writers, and others. Teachers were thrown out of schools, and Jewish religious establishments were denied recognition as representing a "historic religion." Historic religions—defined as Roman Catholicism and Greek Orthodoxy—were entitled to government funds, and the Jews were now excluded. Even the pigeon-raisers' association solemnly passed a regulation forbidding Jews to breed pigeons.

The Iron Guard, in its ideology and social complexion, was somewhat akin to the early Sturm Abteilung (SA) in Germany. It was a band of lower-middle-class toughs out for plunder and destruction, led by a disgruntled and embittered intelligentsia reveling in extreme nationalism and hatred, both of the socialist workers and of the capitalist and land-owning upper crust. It was not much concerned with legal arrangements, which therefore lagged behind Iron Guard initiatives. The situation in Rumania was swiftly approaching a mass pogrom. After five months, Antonescu quarreled with his unruly Guardist allies. The Guardists, engaged in a struggle for power with the military, had counted on

German support. But Hitler allowed Antonescu to provoke a Guardist uprising (January 20–23, 1941), which ended in a complete victory for the military and banishment of the Iron Guard chiefs to Germany. During the rebellion, a brutal pogrom was organized in Bucharest by the Legionnaries, as the militant Guardists were known, in which 116 Jews are definitely known to have been killed, and Jewish apartments and personal property as well as synagogues and Torah scrolls were pillaged and burnt. After the Bucharest pogrom, conditions eased somewhat until the outbreak of the German-Russian war, which Rumania joined in order to regain her lost provinces of Bessarabia and Bukovina.

The Transnistrian Deportations

All the frustrations of a violent nationalism were let loose on the helpless Jewish minority when Rumanian forces joined in the attack on Russia in June, 1941. Despised by their German allies, insecure and vengeful, Rumanian soldiers and gendarmerie vented their dehumanized instincts on the Jews. In a mass murder action in Iasi, probably close to 8,000 victims were shot, beaten, choked, and clubbed to death between June 28 and July 1, 1941. Two trains were loaded with 3,300 Jews and sent, without water or food, to travel from place to place for days on end. When they finally stopped, 2,645 victims were counted.[3] An order of June 21, 1941, paralleling Reinhardt Heydrich's famous letter of September 21, 1939, in Poland, ordered the expulsion of some 50,000 Jews from villages in a wide area in the Regat. Small pogroms occurred in a number of places, and individual Jews were thrown out of moving trains, people were robbed without redress, expelled from the villages, and sometimes murdered.

Mass murder of Jews by the Rumanian fascist regime was committed chiefly against the Jewish population of Bukovina and Bessarabia, the two provinces reconquered in July, 1941, from the Soviets. During July and August, German murder columns (*Einsatzkommandos*) belonging to Einsatzgruppe D and, with their help and guidance, Rumanian military and police units, engaged in wholesale murder actions. These were committed partly by shooting and partly by aimless forced marches during which laggards, sick, and old people were shot as the hapless columns of evicted Jews were hustled backwards and forwards through Bessarabia.

In the meantime, German and Rumanian troops conquered

parts of the Ukraine. In a speech on July 8, Antonescu said that the Jews of Bukovina and Bessarabia would be expelled into the newly conquered areas. As the area between the Dniester River, the old Bessarabia-Ukrainian border, and the River Bug, running more or less parallel to it in the north, would soon be handed over to Rumanian rule, the Jews were to be shipped right across the Bug into German-held territory. For a start, 15,000 Jews were pushed across the Dniester into German hands before the Rumanians took over the area. But this action went against the German grain—destruction should be orderly, not haphazard. The Germans therefore pushed the Jews back, though the Rumanians tried to refuse to accept them. At the same time in August, Antonescu wanted to expel another 60,000 Jews from the Regat to Bessarabia; it was clear that the problem was getting out of hand and needed rearrangement.

In late August, 1941, an agreement was signed at Tighina in Bessarabia between German and Rumanian military commanders which specified that Jews from Bukovina and Bessarabia would be expelled into the Rumanian-administered area between the Dniester and the Bug now called Transnistria, but not beyond the Bug into German-held territory.[4] From September, 1941, deportations to Transnistria proceeded vigorously. According to the available statistics, 146,555 persons were so deported (including 10,358 Jews from the Dorohoi district in the Regat). Of the other roughly 150,000 Jews who had lived in Bessarabia and northern Bukovina, the overwhelming majority were either killed on the spot or perished on their way to exile. About 17,000 remained in Cernauti, the capital of Bukovina.

During this period of disasters the Rumanian Jewish community organized as best it could to fight for survival. There began a most peculiar struggle, waged largely by Wilhelm Filderman, of memoranda and personal interventions. Such tactics were rarely successful elsewhere in Europe, but in Rumania they had some effect. Filderman had been a schoolmate of Antonescu's and he had friends and acquaintances among many Rumanian intellectuals whose support the regime valued. Through friends or personally, Filderman could reach Greek Orthodox and Roman Catholic dignitaries, though Rabbi Safran often took the initiative in this field. The Rumanian dictatorship never completely muzzled the press nor entirely suppressed its political opponents, and Filderman was able to make use of groups such as Juliu Maniu's Peasant party and Constantin (Dinu) Bratianu's Liberals. Nevertheless, Filderman displayed tremendous courage when influential Rumanians were cowed into submission.

Early in September, 1941, the Rumanians wanted to introduce a yellow badge for Jews, obviously at the instigation of the Germans, who sent a special adviser on Jewish affairs named Gustav Richter to their embassy in Bucharest. Ghettoization was also threatened. In a dramatic interview with Antonescu, Filderman managed to convince him to rescind the decree (September 8, 1941). When the first news regarding the Transnistrian deportations filtered through to Bucharest, Filderman tried a variety of means to stop them. Apart from the usual bombardment by memoranda, he attempted to enlist the support of the papal nuncio, Andreas Cassulo, and of the Greek Orthodox patriarch, Nikodem. The Roman Catholic church was at that point interested mainly in Jewish converts, and many Jews did convert, at least on paper, in order to escape persecution. However, we do not know the exact details. Cassulo's later actions may possibly indicate that even at that early stage he went beyond simply protecting converts. Nikodem enlisted the help of Elena, the queen mother, but they seemed to accomplish little. The antisemitic Orthodox Metropolitan Tit Simedrea was also persuaded to intervene, but again the effect seemed small. What probably helped influence Antonescu to halt the deportations was the presence of the American minister, Franklin M. Gunther, though in November, 1941, Gunther opposed a major intervention by the neutral diplomatic corps in Bucharest on the grounds that he did not have conclusive proof of the brutalities alleged by the Jews. An initiative by the very helpful Turkish representative to have 300,000 Rumanian Jews emigrate to Palestine, at least temporarily, was rejected.

On October 14, 1941, Filderman met with Mihai Antonescu, the deputy prime minister (not related to the dictator), and was promised that certain privileged categories of Jews in Bukovina and Bessarabia would be exempt from deportation. However, five days later, Ion Antonescu himself published his reply to one of Filderman's impassioned pleas and accused the Jews of being Communists and of murdering Rumanians. The publication of such a letter by the dictator was of course an incitement to pogroms, but it was also a sign of weakness in that an antisemitic dictator found it necessary to debate with the despised Jews. The deportations in fact ceased in late November, without the threats to the Jews of the Regat having materialized. Antonescu declared at a cabinet meeting on December 16, 1941, that as far as he was

341

concerned the Jews could be thrown into the Black Sea, but he and the other members of his clique apparently were influenced by Filderman's arguments: it was inconsistent with Rumanian national interests to go beyond the measures taken by Germany's other allies; and it would be harmful to the Rumanian economy to push out the Jews. Filderman did not explicitly make use of the common antisemitic belief in Jewish power over the western democracies, but the existence of this belief was certainly working in his favor also.

Throughout these first stages of war, finding money to aid Rumanian Jewry was becoming more and more difficult. A social aid committee, established by Ussoskin and part of the Union of Communities, brought together the leaders of the different Jewish organizations. JDC was represented by Bertrand S. Jacobson, though his residence was in Budapest and he visited Bucharest only as occasion demanded. From about June, 1941, he seems to have stayed in Bucharest on a more permanent basis, until he was recalled when the United States entered the war.

Funds were obtained first of all from JDC's investments in the kassas, which had to be liquidated at government command in 1941. There were 85 such kassas, of which 44 were in Bukovina and Bessarabia, and these latter had to be written off as total losses when the Russians came. The rest were dissolved, with the funds realized being transferred to JDC activities. The social aid committee dealt in 1940 with 6,000 totally destitute people, and through the Union of Communities kept up feeding stations for 3,000 children, 15 hospitals, and 24 schools and kindergartens with close to 7,000 children. Its major effort therefore was children's programs, for which Mala Jancu was responsible. However, though JDC appropriated $98,000 for Rumania in 1940, the financial crisis that hit JDC midway through that year meant that JDC could actually provide only $52,500. In 1941, another year of great financial stringency for JDC, the situation did not materially change. Total spending was $61,000. Money was again directed to children's programs. But the social aid committee now had to look after increasing numbers of people who had been robbed and pillaged or whose family members had been murdered, and there had to be organized help for people who had suffered from the denationalization decrees and lost their professional licenses. JDC could do little except lend its name to Filderman's committee, although this was of course important. The actual funds came largely from local sources rather than from America.

342

An additional problem arose which Filderman tried to use as a pivot for his negotiations with the goverment. There had been no way to transfer actual dollars to Rumania since it had come under German control in the latter half of 1940. JDC funds were made available through an emigration transfer on the same lines as in Germany; the dollars that JDC actually paid were converted into a much larger number of Rumanian lei, which the emigrants were required to deposit in Bucharest. But about $100,000 were blocked in America in Rumanian accounts, and Filderman tried, perhaps rather naively, to persuade both the Rumanians and the Americans to use them for Jewish emigration, mainly to the United States. Antonescu's regime wanted to use the same funds to repatriate Rumanians in America. Nothing could possibly have come of this totally unrealistic project, but it did provide Filderman with leverage for maintaining contacts with government officials and for seeking postponements of anti-Jewish measures.

The Rumanian Judenrat and the Threat of Deportation in 1942

On December 17, Filderman's Union of Communities was closed down. On January 31, 1942, a Rumanian Judenrat, the Centrala Evreilor din România, was established under a Catholic convert named Nandor Ghingold. The Rumanian supervisor was Radu Lecca, a close collaborator of the Germans. The idea was to create a streamlined organization which would expropriate the Jews, abolish communal autonomy by establishing the communities as branches of the Centrala, and prepare the ground for eventual deportations to the death camps. It did not work. Not only were the Rumanian officials corrupt and inefficient, much to the disgust of Richter, the German adviser, but Ghingold was also ineffective in the Jewish sphere. He had no authority and his measures were disobeyed and undercut. When he tried to abolish the autonomy of the communities, one of his collaborators, a man named Heinrich Stefan Streitman, resigned. More importantly, both the Zionists and Filderman's men infiltrated the Centrala. They persuaded its treasurer, Adolf Grosman-Grozea, to present false accounts in order to conceal funds from Lecca and his ilk; money was diverted for social aid, bribing officials, and so on.

In the summer of 1942, the Nazis decided to deport all of Rumanian Jewry to Polish death camps. On July 26, Eichmann reported that there were no obstacles to such deportations, and on August 17, the German Foreign Office was informed of Antonescu's agreement. A week later, Lecca arrived in Berlin, but was treated rather disdainfully as a troublesome and minor official from a statellite country. The German ambassador in Bucharest, Manfred von Killinger, told Berlin that this cavalier treatment had backfired, and that the Rumanians were now not prepared to go through with the original plans, according to which deportations were scheduled to begin on September 10. It would be rather naive to suppose that the insult to Lecca was a very important factor; interventions by Filderman and by the papal nuncio and other church dignitaries were doubtless more important, but they came after the crucial weeks of late August and early September. What is clear is that the Rumanians changed their minds and the deportations did not take place. It might well have been the great losses sustained by the Rumanian troops during the German summer offensive in Russia and the German refusal—or incapability—of providing the Rumanians with promised war materials that made Antonescu waver. Also, by deporting the Jews he would be on a par with Slovakia and Croatia, rather than with Italy or Hungary. In any case, by the end of 1942, the Germans themselves had despaired of deporting Rumanian Jewry.[5]

Organization of Aid to Transnistria

Filderman had asked for permission to send help to the deportees in Transnistria as early as October, 1941, and in December, Antonescu agreed to give the permit. By that time, massacres of both deportees and local Jews were taking place all over Transnistria: in the Golta region alone some 70,000 Jews were murdered. The Transnistrian deportees who escaped the massacres were threatened with a slow death from hunger and disease, for what few rations were allocated were further decreased by officials who stole the food. Labor was demanded, but no money or food given in return. A typhoid epidemic in the winter of 1941–42, which came at a time when the deportees had not yet learned how to organize in the new conditions, caused thousands of deaths. Hungry orphans were roaming the ghettos established by the Rumanians or the countryside. Gheorghe Alexeianu, the Rumanian governor of Transnistria, was a virulent antisemite and wanted to kill all the Jews. Both Filderman's friends and the Zionists, but especially the latter, established illegal contacts with Transnistria, and received first incoherent reports of the conditions there late in 1941. The first help they sent arrived in February, 1942, but the process was complicated by the fact that the money used in Transnistria was the German RKKS mark (*Reichskassenkreditschein*), which was officially bought for 60 lei in Bucharest. In Transnistria it was considerably cheaper, so that money transfers were hardly worth the trouble. By November, 1943, the united aid committee in Bucharest had sent 79,462,000 lei in cash (about $160,000; the dollar was worth about 180 lei in 1940, but climbed to about 800 in 1943), or 1,324,000 RKKS marks. More important were the 653 boxes of clothes worth 119,663,000 lei (about $240,000); 13 railway wagons of medicines and clothing for children valued at 11,267,473 lei (about $22,000), 3,000 tons of coal, 4 wagons of glass, 5 tons of soda for manufacturing soap, and 180 tons of salt. The total value of all these goods was over 500 million lei (or about $700,000 in early 1943). In addition, relatives in the Regat began to send individual parcels in 1943, and small sums were sent by bodies such as the Hehalutz.[6]

Not all of this aid arrived, and not everything that did was handed to the Jews, but enough got through to justify the tremendous efforts made to send it. A good example is that of the ghetto of Shargorod, not far from Mogilev-Podolski, which contained some 7,000 deported Jews. Early in 1942, they began to receive about 4,000–5,000 RKKS marks (roughly $1,400–$1,500) monthly out of the 30,000 they needed to keep body and soul together. But soon they began to receive supply shipments that helped considerably. A wagon of salt, which cost 30,000 lei (about $150, or 500 RKKS marks) in Bucharest was sold to the local people for 25,000 marks ($7,500), and the Jews could buy the food essential to stopping the hunger-cum-typhoid epidemic that was decimating the ghetto.[7] Unfortunately, only a minority of the Transnistrian camps and ghettos were reached by these shipments. Wherever the aid did arrive, it improved the situation considerably, though by the time it came many had already perished.

Sending help was not enough, and Filderman attempted to get permission to have his people see the conditions at first hand. The very fact of an official visit might put an end to murder actions. As early as January, 1942, the Jewish representatives tried to get permission to visit the ghettos and camps in Transnistria. Alexeianu objected, but after much pressure, including publication in the West of stories regarding Transnistria, the government finally agreed. The Jewish mission was led by Fred Saraga and started off on December 31, 1942. On January 14, 1943, it came back, having succeeded in visiting not only some of the main ghettos, but also the remnants of the local Ukrainian Jews. In February, 1943, Mihai Antonescu promised to have the 8,000 orphans in Transnistria returned, but no action ensued.

A second mission left on December 10, 1943, and split into two, one part being led by Saraga and the other by an equally undaunted young lawyer, Dadu Rosenkrantz. This second mission, which in any case took place after it had become clear to the Rumanians that the war was lost, was intended to prepare the ground for an evacuation. On December 20, part of the Dorohoi contingent, who had been deported "by mistake," returned from Transnistria. They were followed by others, until by early 1944, 6,430 Dorohoi deportees had returned. In February, 1944, after many false starts, 1,884 orphans were finally rescued. Two further missions, mainly led and organized by Rosenkrantz, saved another 2,538 people in the midst of a German and Rumanian retreat during which thousands of Jews were murdered.

At the end of 1943, Charles Kolb, IRC representative in Bucharest, counted 47,378 survivors from among the deportees in Transnistria. But of these not more than a certain proportion survived until the end of the war. Some were killed by the German and Rumanian armies during their retreat, and some were deported by the Russian liberators to work in the mines of the Donbas or near Arkhangelsk. Slowly, those who could drifted back to their former homes or crossed the border into Rumania. A recent estimate is that there were 62,000 survivors, including the returnees in early 1944 and the Jews of Cernauti who were not deported, but we have no exact figures.[8]

Rumanian Jewry's Struggle for Existence, 1942–1944

Parallel with the struggle for the lives of the deportees in Transnistria went Rumanian Jewry's fight for the survival of the Jews in Old Rumania itself. In May, 1941, a forced labor law for Jews of the Regat had been promulgated, and while the middle and upper classes could buy themselves free, the full weight of Rumanian antisemitism now descended on the poorer sections of the Jewish population. Men were taken away and their families had to be supported. Many were also arrested for infringing one or the other of the draconic regulations and put into detention camps. Their families, too, had to be fed. With the progressive deterioration of the situation of the Regat Jews, one possible solution seemed to be emigration. This was the avowed aim of the Zionists, but it was opposed by the Germans, who wanted to prevent the Jews from leaving the country so that they should be able to destroy all of them. Early in 1942, Gustav Richter informed the Zionist leadership that they should give up their struggle to get Jews to Palestine, because the Germans had promised Haj Amin el-Husseini, the mufti of Jerusalem, that Palestine would become Arab. But the Zionists did not heed Richter's threats, although the Zionist Federation was officially dissolved in August, 1942. Undeterred by such legalistic considerations, Radu Lecca floated a trial balloon on December 3, 1942, in a talk with Mishu Benvenisti, head of the now illegal federation. He suggested that 70,000 Jews might go from Transnistria via Odessa. Apparently the idea was that 100,000–200,000 lei ($500–$1,000) per head and an additional lump sum of 3 billion lei ($1,500,000) should be paid to let the Jews out. Lecca obviously thought that JA, which he believed to be identical with the world Jewish government ruling the West, would pay these sums. What the intention was in making this fantastic offer is unclear, but it is doubtful whether Lecca meant more than to put out feelers at that stage. He himself informed the Germans, and they reacted quickly: there was to be no emigration.

The negative German response was not known in the West. As a result, the news of the Rumanian offer was carried by the *New York Times* on February 13, 1943, as though it still held good, whereas in fact it had already been killed. In America, the WJC and a body called the Emergency Committee to Rescue the Jewish People (founded by emissaries from right-wing underground military organization in Palestine, the Irgun Zvai Leumi) pressed the State Department to do something about it. In the end, the State Department agreed to send $170,000 to WJC in Switzerland for transfer to Rumania. Because of British objections, however, this was whittled down to $25,000 by December, 1943. The transfer was effected, but it no longer had anything to do with emigration.

Zionist attempts to emigrate small numbers of Rumanian Jews, with or without official Rumanian and British permission, via neutral Turkey to Palestine met with very little success. In December, 1941, the *Struma*, a small, unseaworthy tug with 769 Jews on board, was not permitted to land its passengers in Istan-

347

bul because the British had refused them visas to Palestine. On the other hand, the British at the last moment asked the Turks to permit the landing of the children, to whom they were willing to grant entry permits to Palestine. The Turks refused, the ship was sent away, and it sank on February 24, 1942. There was one survivor. After that tragedy, illegal immigration from Rumania came in very small driblets, though large schemes were being discussed between Zionist leaders and Rumanian officials. The Palestine Office in Bucharest, which was not supposed to exist at all, was nevertheless active in a very thin disguise. It dealt largely with attempts to obtain legal permits for the emigration of children. Some groups managed to reach Istanbul, but even that journey was fraught with danger. When a group of seventy-three children who had been notified that Palestine certificates would await them in Istanbul left Rumania at the end of March, 1943, three among them who had Polish passports were stopped by the Germans at the Bulgarian border, taken away from the rest, and murdered.

The attempts at emigration by the Zionists, Filderman's political struggle, and the need to pull together all those who worked for the rescue of Rumanian Jews—all led to the setting up of an illegal Jewish coordinating council in early 1943. Filderman, Benvenisti, and Wilhelm Fischer of the WJC participated, and an aid committee with Fischer, Moshe Zimmer, Arnold Schwefelberg, and Fred Saraga was established. It was largely this group of individuals which was responsible for Jewish communal work during the last year or so of the Antonescu regime. The underground leadership had to overcome a severe crisis soon after its establishment, when Filderman was himself deported to Transnistria. This arose out of the imposition of a 4 billion lei tax on Jews (about $5 million at the time). With his typical audacity, Filderman protested against the tax in a memorandum addressed to Ghingold but obviously intended for the government. Antonescu, perhaps in order to pacify the Jewish leader, told him that he had stopped all plans for deportations from the Regat. But Filderman was not to be sidetracked, and on May 20, 1943, he again attacked the tax. That proved too much for Antonescu. On May 26, Filderman and his wife were deported to Mogilev in Transnistria. German newspapers, even the *Völkischer Beobachter* in Berlin, paid him the honor of writing articles about his arrest and publishing his picture. But Filderman had many friends, and some of the Rumanian newspapers supported him. He set about organizing life in Mogilev, and on June 22 wrote a memo from there demanding the return to Rumania of the deportees! By August, he was back in Bucharest with firsthand knowledge of the situation in Transnistria. After his return, the underground coordinating council again worked under his leadership.

One of the most important political activities of the council was the transmittal to Switzerland of the information that reached it from areas outside Rumania. This was made possible by refugees from Poland, largely from the Lwów region, who infiltrated Rumania throughout the war. Coming via Cernauti into the Regat and Bucharest, some of them in German uniforms, they brought with them authentic reports regarding the death camps of Belzec and Treblinka. The influx became most significant late in 1942 and early in 1943, and some at least of the most detailed accounts sent out from the Swiss offices of JA, WJC, and by Mayer to JDC reached Switzerland from Fischer in Bucharest, who collected the testimonies from the Polish refugees. The council had to provide the refugees with papers. Polish interests in Rumania were taken care of by the diplomatic representative of Chile, and the Jewish leadership managed to convince the Chileans (though only after much argument and intervention by the Sephardi chief rabbi, who had connections with Chilean Jews) to give Polish papers to these refugees. However, in March, 1943, Chile severed diplomatic relations with Rumania, and other means had to be found. These were very largely false papers manufactured by the Zionist youth movements. Occasionally Filderman and Benvenisti had to intervene to see some of these refugees through. Mayer arranged through Schwalb to provide half of the $2,500 that were needed monthly to support them, the other half being paid by JA in Istanbul and local funds. At the end of 1942, there seem to have been 800–1,000 such refugees, and hundreds more came in 1943.[9]

The members of the council realized that the more the neutral governments and the IRC were involved in what was happening to Rumanian Jews, the greater was their chance to survive. Throughout 1942, attempts were made by WJC in Geneva to involve the IRC, but without result, despite the great friendliness displayed by the Swiss representative in Rumania, René de Weck. Early in 1943, Fischer of WJC and Filderman again wrote to Gerhart Riegner in Geneva, and Riegner asked the IRC to send a delegate to Rumania. Mayer made the same request, but it was really in response to WJC pressure that the IRC finally sent a delegation to Bucharest in May, 1943. When they came back in

June, they reported that Antonescu was not only willing to discuss the Jewish problem, but even interested in having an IRC delegation to help him revive the Palestine emigration scheme of December, 1942. The delegates had the "definite impression that Rumania is trying to establish a bridge to the enemy and that the Jewish question appears to them suitable to be such a bridge."[10] In August, 1943, Charles Kolb of IRC arrived in Bucharest and plunged into a most important activity. Supported by JDC funds, he did his best to protect the Jewish population from the wavering policies of a brutal dictatorship in decline. The influence of the IRC delegation was central, not only in the day-to-day interventions with various Rumanian ministries designed to mitigate or stop anti-Jewish actions, but also as a natural and relatively easy conduit for JDC funds, which could now be transmitted in larger quantities in order to help Rumanian Jews.

JDC Work in Rumania

JDC's influence in Rumania had become very tenuous in 1941. In 1942, Saly Mayer began to seek ways to reach embattled Rumanian Jewry. He was in touch with Nathan Schwalb on Rumanian matters, and he also contacted Alfred Silberschein of RELICO. He was looking for a reliable courier to transmit information and money. Everything would have to be done without involving JDC, and in line with his instructions from Lisbon, all transfers of funds would have to be effected under his own name. Schwalb soon found a man who seemed admirably suited for the job: Hans Welti, a Swiss journalist who also traveled to Bucharest as a businessman. Towards the end of 1942, Filderman and Moshe Zimmer began reporting to Mayer via Schwalb and Silberschein. They had well over 4,000 orphans to look after in the Regat, they were now spending 25 to 35 million lei monthly ($35,000–50,000), including help to Transnistria, and all they had managed to collect locally was 50 million lei. They were working out of the Centrala offices but had complete control of the aid effort. Could JDC help?[11]

During the first half of 1943, Mayer sent 28,570,000 lei ($35,000) to Rumania, part in Swiss francs by a transfer arrangement and part by asking Welti to arrange for local loans against repayment après. All this was done in RELICO's name. But Mayer did not particularly like Silberschein, a sentiment that seems to have been reciprocated, and when the IRC appeared on the scene in May, with a first delegation to Bucharest, Mayer used it to transfer money to the aid committee there. Again most of the funds were obtained against repayment après; the total came to 61,286,000 lei worth of Swiss and American currency (about $65,000). The transfer through IRC was made in Mayer's name.[12] In November, 1943, Mayer received Filderman's report on expenditures: since the beginning of 1942, 537.8 million lei (about $670,000 in 1943) had been spent, mostly for Transnistria. But he was now also supporting soup kitchens in the Regat for 45,000 people and raising as much money as he could locally. Dr. Baruch Costiner and Samuel Singher, two former JDC workers, had been added to the aid committee, and IRC was a great help.[13]

JDC maintained its contact with Rumania through Wilhelm Fischer, except when Filderman himself wrote. Willy-nilly, WJC and JDC found themselves in close cooperation over Rumania. JDC-New York was not happy about this situation, but WJC saw it as an opportunity to break into the JDC monopoly of aid and rescue. When their plan to send food to Poland bogged down, Nahum Goldmann suggested, in the summer of 1943, a grandiose plan for raising $10 million and buying food for the ghettos and camps of Eastern Europe, on the model of food for Greece. Joseph Schwartz proposed instead that 250 tons of food should be bought in Turkey and shipped to Transnistria. Moses Leavitt thought the idea was excellent and turned to Washington to obtain a license for $100,000 to ship the food. The Treasury Department, stipulating that the shipments must be made through IRC, issued a license on November 17, 1943, and the money was remitted on November 29. Schwartz also got in touch with Mayer and asked him to consult Rumania about what to send. Mayer did so, and suggested that every effort should be made to buy mutton. But, Mayer added, should that prove impossible and the alternative was starvation, pork should be bought. For Mayer, an Orthodox Jew, it was clear that human life had precedence over dietary laws.[14] But despite all the efforts that were made in Turkey early in 1944, few bulk shipments got to Rumania. Instead, the $100,000 intended for the meat paid for 10,000 parcels; some of these reached Transnistria, while the rest were used for feeding in Bucharest. It is almost impossible to compute how much was spent in Rumania in 1944 until Rumania changed sides in the war on August 23, but the sum for the whole year was $846,439, of which probably three-fifths were spent after liberation. The total included 750,000 sfr. ($200,000) from Switzerland.[15]

351

Hans Welti transmitted most of the letters and messages between Switzerland and Rumania. Mayer, ever suspicious and cautious in financial matters, did not entrust him with money. As it turned out, Mayer's caution was fortunate. Welti came under German influence and allowed the Germans to make copies of all the correspondence he had from both countries. By the end of the year, Mayer had definite suspicions. Welti was supposed to be a journalist, but he had not even visited "his" newspaper in Saint Gallen. Unfortunately, it was too late. Mayer had met Welti on December 1, 1943, and had discussed all the matters pertaining to Hungary and Rumania with which Welti had been connected: the escape of Jews from Poland to Rumania; their internment; the aid they were receiving; and Filderman's negotiations for the return of Transnistrian deportees. In December, 1943, when some youth movement members were caught with false papers connected with the smuggling of Polish Jews into Rumania, the Germans decided to spring their trap.

From January 26, 1944, until February 18, leaders of the Zionist youth movements, other important Zionists, and members of the aid committee were arrested in Bucharest. Among those arrested were Benvenisti and Fischer, who were beaten and tortured in an attempt to make them reveal their contacts with JA and other "Jewish international" groups. In actual fact, the secret police already held most of the correspondence. What saved the arrested leaders was the fact that Rumania by that time was looking for a way out of the war. The Rumanian representative in Spain had contacted the Allies in December, 1943, and declared his nation's willingness to surrender immediately upon an Anglo-American landing in the Balkans. Filderman's memoranda also helped in the rescue of the Jewish leaders, because he pointed out that they had acted more against the Germans than against Rumanian interests. The very accusation against them, that they had contacts with the West, was used in their favor. Kolb also intervened, and by this time the IRC carried a great deal of weight in Bucharest.[16]

Silberschein tried to help from Switzerland, because the arrests endangered the whole structure of the aid program. Without asking Mayer, he committed 45,000 sfr. ($10,500) to the defense of the youth leaders. Mayer would not answer Silberschein's urgent requests for help to free the Rumanian Jewish leaders, preferring to work through IRC, and then refused to reimburse Silberschein for the money he advanced, believing that his own way of handling the matter was correct. The whole affair generated a feud between the two that was not settled until 1947, when Mayer requested of JDC that, if it wanted to pay Silberschein, it should do so directly from New York and not through him. Mayer did not forget easily.[17]

The Final Stage: The Collapse of the Antonescu Regime

When it became clear towards the end of 1943 that Benvenisti and his group of Zionist leaders were likely to be in serious trouble, an alternative leadership was already waiting in the wings. Abraham Zissu, the intellectual industrialist, had not been inactive. He had connections with groups opposed to the Antonescu regime and had been jailed for six months in 1942 for his political activities. Towards the end of 1943, he organized a small group of devoted followers and, when Benvenisti was arrested, he took over, to all intents and purposes, the leadership of the Zionist movement. Unlike Benvenisti's, his relations with the youth movements were not very good, and his authoritarian manner alienated Filderman as well. Zissu took over the immigration work from Shlomo Entzer, who was among the arrested leaders, and on June 19, 1944, Haim Barlas in Istanbul named him the JA representative in Bucharest.

Playing on the dictatorship's fear of the advancing Allied armies, Zissu introduced a Jewish factor into the negotiations that the Rumanians were conducting at Cairo in March and May with the Allies. Filderman was also involved, but this time there was no united front. Zissu managed to restart emigration from Rumania because the Rumanians saw in it a gesture towards the Allies and a partial alibi for their crimes against the Jews. On April 9, 1944, the S.S. *Maritza* landed 246 refugees at Istanbul. The S.S. *Kazbek* arrived at Istanbul on July 9, with 759 Jewish refugees on board, some of them Polish, some Hungarian, and some Rumanian. Two other small vessels, the *Marina* and the *Mefkure*, were also plying the Black Sea; the *Marina* landed 308 people at Istanbul on August 5, but on the same day the *Mefkure* was torpedoed, apparently by a Russian submarine, with 379 refugees on board. Only 5 were saved.[18] Even after this disaster, JDC and the American diplomats in Turkey involved in the rescue attempts agreed that emigration should continue, despite the fact that the Turkish rupture of relations with Germany on August 2 had increased the dangers.

JDC was involved in all these operations because it supplied part of the funds necessary to pay for ships, acting through and with the War Refugee Board. It was marginally involved in the row that broke out when Zissu tried to control decisions about who should go on the ships. The Jews had been cheated and squeezed by an unscrupulous Greek shipowner called "Fat" (Jean D.) Pandelis, who had been connected with Mossad, JA's organization for illegal immigration to Palestine, since before the war. By late 1943, his company, Societatea Official Roman Anonima de Transporturi (ORAT), had a virtual monopoly of emigration from Rumania, thanks to Radu Lecca, who got a kickback from it. In June, 1944, Filderman and Zissu managed to get this company out of the picture, but they disagreed about how migration should then be organized. For a short time Zissu controlled the operation and tried to send only members of Zionist groups, but then Filderman claimed that as a member of JA he should have the right to send non-Zionists on the ship as well. The matter was still pending when Rumania surrendered on August 23, 1944.[19]

Another major activity, which was financed chiefly by Palestinian funds but which also received some support from JDC, was the smuggling into Rumania of Hungarian Jews when the deportations to Auschwitz began in that country in May, 1944. It is not quite clear just how many Hungarian Jews managed to get across, but the number was in the neighborhood of 4,000. Most of them came by a route organized by the youth movements, though some paid individual smugglers on the border. In Istanbul, Alexander Cretianu, the Rumanian minister, agreed that these Jews should be let into his country. Filderman and Zissu obtained similar assurances in Bucharest, despite heavy German pressure.[20]

The Rumanian chapter of the Holocaust has so far received very little of the attention it deserves. On the whole, Rumanian Jewry stood the test: it provided aid to its brethren in exile, produced a proud and intelligent leadership, and maintained internal unity, at least until Benvenisti's arrest. It showed no lack of courage and determination. The Zionist youth movements were, in Rumania as in other places, of great importance in the aid programs as well as in the fight for Jewish survival. Help was received or organized from Bucharest by IRC, by some of the representatives of neutral countries, and by the Palestinian emissaries in Istanbul. The sending of Palestinian parachutists to organize the Jews for a possible armed stand against the Germans and the parallel attempts at arming the Jewish youth of Bucharest belong to the same picture, but they cannot be treated as part of a history of JDC.[21]

An estimated 342,890 Jews survived in Rumania in 1944, including the Transnistrian deportees. While the vacillations of Rumanian governmental policies tipped the balance against mass destruction in the Regat, effective organization by the Jews themselves, including the aid extended and organized by the JDC committee, was an important contributory factor. A major role was undoubtedly played by Wilhelm Filderman, a Jewish leader of the highest stature. The aid he received from JDC was significant, and it enabled him and others to save many Jews. He did not succeed in saving more than a remnant of the 300,000 Jews of Bukovina and Bessarabia; the vast majority of these people-and a considerable number of Jews in the Regat, despite the efforts of individuals, groups, and organizations—including JDC—perished.

15

Slovakia: Can One Ransom Jews?

In 1942 and 1943, negotiations took place in Slovakia between the Nazis and their Jewish victims. These led, in 1943, to a grand ransom scheme which the Jewish negotiators called the "Europa Plan." Conducted by a group of Slovak Jews who united, despite deep ideological differences, to try to save their brethren, these talks highlight one of the central questions of the Holocaust: whether rescue by ransom negotiations was possible. JDC had a central role in these proceedings.

Slovakia, the eastern part of the former Czechoslovak republic which was in effect destroyed by the Munich agreement of 1938, became an autonomous state under German "protection" on March 14, 1939. The president was a Catholic priest, Josef Tiso, and effective power was in the hands of the Slovak Hlinka People's Party (SLS), a fascist and clerical nationalist group founded by another Catholic priest, Andrej Hlinka. Prime Minister Vojtěch Tuka and Interior Minister Alexander (Šaňo) Mach were the chief figures in an increasingly corrupt and terrorist regime.

Among the 2.6 million Slovaks there were, according to a head count in December, 1940, 88,951 Jews. There had been 136,737 Jews in prewar Slovakia, but about 40,000 lived in areas ceded to Hungary in 1938, and some managed to emigrate before the end of 1940.[1] About two-thirds of this Jewish population were

356

Orthodox; some inclined towards religious Zionism; but most, especially in the poorer eastern parts of the country, were strictly observant and extremely anti-Zionist. The spiritual leader of this large section of Slovak Jewry was Rabbi Shmuel David Halevi Ungar of Nitra, a respected sage. There was an organization of Orthodox communities; its leader, Isidor Pappenheim, died in the second year of the war, and because other members of the organization's committee had by that time fled the country, leadership of Slovak Orthodoxy passed, almost by default, into the hands of Ungar's young son-in-law, Rabbi Michael Dov-Ber Weissmandel. Weissmandel was to become one of the great figures in the history of the Holocaust.

Opposed to the anti-Zionist Orthodoxy stood the Zionist movement with its many factions, led by people such as Dr. Eugen Winterstein and Dr. Oskar Neumann. Some Zionists were secularists, others were members of the Liberal (Neologue) communities, and still others belonged to the so-called status-quo-ante communities—conservative groups that stood between Liberal and Orthodox interpretations of Judaism. Their spiritual leader was undoubtedly Rabbi Armin (Avraham Abba Hacohen) Frieder. JDC interests were taken care of by a committee with an overwhelmingly Zionist composition, in effect headed by Mrs. Gizi Fleischmann, president of the Slovak WIZO, who also represented WJC and HICEM. Her unique position was partly due to her personality and partly to the fact that she was Ungar's first cousin. Despite being a Zionist and a woman, therefore, she was respected by the Orthodox community.[2]

Slovak Jewry had developed in the years of the Czechoslovak republic from an economically backward branch of Eastern and Central European Jewry into a relatively prosperous one. Bratislava, the capital and the home of one of the greatest figures in premodern Jewry, Rabbi (Moshe) Hatam Sofer, had traditionally been a seat of learning. Slovakia had become a flourishing center of Jewish culture, both Orthodox and Zionist, in the interwar period.

During the first two years of World War II, Slovak Jewry underwent an ordeal similar to those endured by Jews in other European countries. After a period during which anti-Jewish measures were passed on a religious basis rather than a racial one, the German ambassador to Slovakia, Manfred von Killinger, asked Heinrich Himmler to appoint an adviser on Jewish questions. The man chosen was Dieter Wisliceny, apparently a former journalist,

357

who arrived on September 1, 1940. Anti-Jewish measures had started in April, 1939, and became increasingly severe as Jews were pushed out of jobs, forbidden to pursue professions, and dispossessed. A specially created central economic office, the Ústredný Hospodársky Úrad (ÚHÚ), headed by Augustín Morávek, was responsible for carrying out the expropriations. The general idea was to put SLS members in controlling positions in the formerly Jewish businesses and shops.[3] This was a slow process, partly because the fact that about one-fourth of Jewish property was invested in land caused legal complications, and partly because Slovak officialdom was corrupt and the "Aryan" commissars that were put into Jewish enterprises were inefficient. Slovak officials were often bribed to appoint commissars who in effect left the old Jewish owners in control.

On September 26, 1940, the Slovaks nominated a Judenrat on the Nazi model. Once the rumor had spread that this would happen, a bitter struggle developed between the Orthodox and Zionist factions over who should control it. The former seem to have intervened with some of the Slovak officials, and as a result an Orthodox-controlled Judenrat, called the Ústredna Židov (ÚŽ), was set up under Heinrich Schwarz, secretary of the Orthodox organization of communities. The Zionists decided to join nevertheless, and the struggle for control continued. It was interrupted by the removal of Schwarz in April, 1941, because he was alleged to have offered a minor bribe to a Slovak official. To everyone's surprise, the authorities nominated as his successor a completely unknown person, an Orthodox school principal named Arpád Sebestyén, who turned out to be a weak and pliant tool of the Slovak and German Nazis.

All of the various anti-Jewish laws were included in a comprehensive "Jewish Code" published on September 9, 1941, following a meeting at Salzburg on July 28 of the Slovak leaders with Hitler and his chief aides. Another meeting with Hitler, specifically on the Jewish question, was held in November. Apparently some of the guidelines were arranged at the July meeting, for Slovakia enacted racial laws, speeded up "Aryanization" procedures, and began introducing the yellow star. The period between October, 1941, and March, 1942, thus was characterized by a swift deterioration of the Jewish position. An order for the evacuation of 10,000 of Bratislava's 15,000 Jews to the eastern parts of the country and growing harshness of the expropriation measures led up to the final blow of deportations early in 1942.

Throughout the whole period of war, there were basically three persecuting organs in Slovakia as far as the Jews were concerned: the Germans, represented mainly by Wisliceny; the ÚHÚ; and the so-called Section XIV of the Ministry of the Interior, established in the autumn of 1941 and headed, from April, 1942, by Dr. Anton Vašek, a violent but corrupt antisemite.[4] Dr. Izidor Koso, the head of Tiso's and Mach's chancelleries, also influenced decisions affecting the Jewish communities.

Jewish Reactions to Nazi Persecutions, 1939–1942

JDC activities in Slovakia in late 1939 and throughout 1940 were strictly limited by its lack of funds. It appropriated $122,000 for the country in 1940, most of which was spent feeding refugees. In the autumn of 1939, the Slovaks demanded that 20 percent of the JDC funds come in in foreign currency. JDC yielded, and for a time at least actual dollars were transferred to Bratislava—a unique arrangement which the organization was careful not to repeat elsewhere.[5] The number of refugees, which had been 6,900 in early 1940, rose to 7,400 at the end of the year, and stood at 7,600 in June, 1941. All illegal immigrants to Palestine passed through Bratislava, and some stayed for long periods; other refugees came from Poland, including about 100 young Zionists who came in early 1941 and were to be important later in armed resistance. The numbers of those fed in kitchens organized by the JDC committee rose to 2,000 in September, 1941; 4,600 children were receiving additional milk; there were three hospitals and eighteen homes for the aged.[6]

All of these welfare activities were organized by the JDC committee, but until the end of 1941, JDC was officially represented by Josef Blum and Bertrand S. Jacobson, who were responsible for the whole of Southeastern Europe. Blum was a Slovak Jew and had offices at both Bratislava and Budapest; he seems to have controlled JDC operations in Slovakia rather closely, although with Jacobson's full support. Blum was also responsible for help to Poland from Slovakia and Rumania. However, as an Orthodox Jew closely connected to the Orthodox leaders, he was constantly in conflict with the Zionist-dominated JDC committee. A report written in late 1940 and signed by both Blum and Jacobson castigated the committee as inefficient. They pointed out—

quite correctly—that Robert K. Füredi, Gizi Fleischmann, and Ernst Abeles, the three Zionist committee members, were opposed to Schwarz, head of the ÚŽ. They were seeking direct contact with JDC-New York "to hinder and obstruct the heavy job that had been placed on President Heinrich Schwarz by the authorities."[7] But what is interesting is that the committee felt responsible for their brethren outside Slovakia, though their own situation was far from rosy. Emigration seemed to be the only way out, especially for the refugees, but while Gizi Fleischmann, who was responsible for the emigration work, tried hard to facilitate the flight of as many people as possible to the United States, San Domingo, or anywhere else, she had very limited success. As American regulations were tightened, emigration became increasingly difficult, and America's entry into the war stopped all such attempts. Jacobson left Europe, and soon afterwards Blum went to Budapest and did not return. Füredi became less active, and in effect Fleischmann came to represent JDC in Slovakia, though her contact with Mayer in Switzerland and with the Lisbon office was tenuous.

The committee did have one resounding success: early in 1940, it obtained Slovak agreement to admit into their country all of the inmates of a small concentration camp at Sosnowice in Poland, where 326 men from Prague had been held. The committee paid a sum of money and promised that the people would emigrate. Most of them did, to Palestine and elsewhere. Their odyssey, an unusual story of self-discipline and organization, has yet to be told.[8] The committee tried its hand at rescuing deportees to Nisko (the so-called Lublin reservation) on a similar principle. Also early in 1940, they asked the Slovaks to agree to the entry of 300 men from Moravaská Ostrava who were at Nisko, promising money and that the people would be emigrated. This time the plan did not work.[9]

The Slovak Deportations and the First Ransom Negotiations

The idea of expelling all Slovak Jews was broached as early as May, 1941, by Morávek. In a way, this plan was connected with an agreement of May 29, 1940, according to which the Germans received 120,000 Slovak workers for the Reich's industries and fields. Why should not the Jews be required to work there? When, in late

1941, the Germans asked for 20,000 workers, Koso suggested that Jews might be sent. The suggestion of course coincided with the German desire to murder European Jewry, and in fact while the first feelers were being extended by the Slovaks, the Wannsee Conference of top officials of various ministries of January 20, 1942, discussed with the SS chiefs which Jewish communities would be the first to be engulfed in the Final Solution. Slovakia was included in the list of the satellite countries where deportations could be organized immediately because no political impediments were foreseen. In mid-February, Adolf Eichmann asked the German Foreign Ministry to instruct German ambassador Hans Ludin in Bratislava to approach the Slovaks for 20,000 young Jews. The rest would come later. Ludin was told on February 16, and he informed Martin Luther of the Foreign Ministry on February 20 that the Slovaks were eager to deport their Jews. They would profit from the acquisition of Jewish property and would not have to send Slovak workers. However, they insisted on sending all the others Jews after the first 20,000, because with the expulsion of the young and strong, they were afraid they would have to care for the old people and the children. Eichmann at first opposed the idea, because it did not fit in with his timetable. On March 27, a day after the first deportation began, he relented and agreed to take all the Jews, or, as Martin Luther put it: "As a consequence of this enthusiastic consent [of the Slovaks to deport the 20,000], the Reichsführer-SS proposed to deport also the remainder of the Slovakian Jews and thus to free Slovakia of Jews." However, Luther added: "As the Slovak Episcopate had meanwhile protested to the Slovak government against the deportation of the Jews, it was explicitly emphasized that internal political difficulties because of the evacuation of the Jews in Slovakia must, by all means, be avoided."[10] The Germans demanded 500 marks per head for each Jew they took into Poland, supposedly for food, lodging, and retraining. On June 23, the Slovaks agreed to this payment, after having been assured that the rest of the property left behind by the Jews would not be claimed by Germany. The tax amounted to 45 million marks if all the 90,000 Jews had been deported, which was 80 percent of the tax the Slovaks had levied on Jewish property.[11]

On March 3, 1942, the Slovak government decided to start the deportations by shipping off girls of sixteen, to be followed by boys of sixteen, and then the rest. The children were supposed to prepare living accommodations for their parents; in fact, they were sent to Auschwitz. The first deportation train on March 26 was therefore filled with young girls who had been torn from their families in nocturnal raids by the Hlinka Guards, the Slovak fascists' counterpart to the SS. Beaten, starved, tortured, and abused for a few days in makeshift prisons, they were then marched to the train. Suddenly they began singing. A very few of the girls survived the war—probably not more than two score.

The Jewish leaders reacted first to the deportations by trying to influence President Tiso. Armin Frieder, who knew him, went to Tiso's parish at Banovce and submitted a strongly worded memorandum, but to no effect. Two memoranda were also dispatched to the Vatican—one jointly by representatives of the Orthodox, Neologue, and "status quo," and one by the Orthodox alone, written by Michael Weissmandel. Neither of the full texts is now available, but Weissmandel later wrote that the joint memorandum committed the fatal mistake of complaining about the separation of families, and Ungar called it "a criminal stupidity" (*verbrecherische Dummheit*), intimating that little else could be expected from community leaders who were not observant Jews. Apparently Weissmandel's own appeal was humble and suppliant. What is clear, however, is that the Slovak ambasssador to the Vatican, Karol Sidor, was bribed with 30,000 Slovaks crowns (about $1,000) to take the messages to the Vatican. In response, Luigi Maglione, the Vatican's political secretary, called Sidor on March 14.

> The political secretariat [of the Vatican] would like to hope that this information does not correspond to the truth, because it cannot bring itself to believe that in a country that wishes to conduct itself according to Catholic principles, grave steps should be possible that would have such painful effects on many families.

As the separation of families was mentioned in preceding paragraphs of Maglione's message as one of the things that had been brought to the Vatican's attention, and because "grave steps" could mean any or all of those things listed by the Vatican, the Slovak government felt free to interpret the Vatican protest as being directed only against the separation of families. There was no problem about that: the families would be reunited in Poland—in death.[12] On April 4, Ludin reported that despite the Catholic protests, Tiso was prepared to carry on with the deportations.

As the deportations proceeded, large numbers of Jews turned to the Hungarian frontier to escape from a terrible, though as yet uncertain, fate. Members of the Orthodox group in Hungary, including Josef Blum of JDC, rallied to facilitate the refugees' entry. Blum claims to have tried to enlist Hungarian Primate Cardinal Justinian Seredi to intervene against the deportations and in favor of the admittance of Slovak Jews, but he says Seredi refused. Otto Komoly, head of the Zionist group in Budapest, apparently contacted General Delera of the Italian military delegation there at the end of March. The Zionists hoped to influence the Germans through Galeazzo Ciano, the Italian foreign affairs minister, to stop the deportations. With his expenses paid by the Zionists, Delera went to Rome, but he had to report that Ciano thought any intervention with the Germans on the Jewish problem would be hopeless. According to his own account, Blum concentrated on smuggling Slovak Jews across the border and then having them legalized. Again both the Orthodox and the Zionist groups participated. The Orthodox effort was made largely through Aron Grünhut, a courageous Bratislavan merchant; on the Zionist side, the smuggling was done chiefly by the youth movements. Simcha Hunwald, leader of the Hashomer Hatzair group in Hungary, was most responsible until he was finally caught and put into a labor battalion by the Hungarians. It was estimated that about 7,000 people managed to cross the border by stealth.[13]

For Blum, the problem was how to support the illegal immigrants, and he reports that he received 50,000 Hungarian pengö (about $4,000–5,000) from Saly Mayer for that purpose. People were at first kept in living quarters that had to be changed every three months, because after that period police registration had to be proved. The official Hungarian Jewish community, headed by the Neologues under the aristocratic Court Councillor (*Hofrat*) Samu Stern, refused to help, and indeed threatened to cooperate with the police in finding the refugees. The Zionists, who also received a JDC subsidy for their part in finding havens for the illegals, were too weak to influence Jewish opinion in Hungary. As it happened, some of the police officers charged with hunting down the illegal immigrants actually helped them. In the end, the situation was changed by the Allied landing in North Africa in November, 1942, and the victory at El Alamein. After those successes, Jews who were discovered with forged documents or with none at all were put into camps, but they were not returned to Slovakia.[14]

Although the accounts of participants and survivors are often contradictory, it seems that the divisions in Slovak Jewry at first militated against concerted action. Apparently it took two or three months of deportations before an emergent underground leadership began to formulate a concrete plan to stop them. Until then, uncoordinated attempts were made to bribe Slovak officials, to help people escape to Hungary, to help people to hide, and to alleviate the suffering of those who had been caught and were being deported. In June, 1942, however, Weissmandel apparently conceived the idea of approaching Dieter Wisliceny, the Slovaks' German adviser, and offering him a bribe. He was moved to do this, he says, because of two events. The first occurred in August, 1941, when Solomon Gross, a well-known Orthodox merchant, had approached Wisliceny with emigration proposals. To his utter amazement, Wisliceny had suggested in his own and in Eichmann's name, to emigrate 1,000 Hungarian Jews a day from Budapest to Spain. Gross must have objected on practical grounds, and Wisliceny suggested that the Jews should be transported in cattle wagons. Weissmandel claims Wisliceny said, "If you do not go abroad in cattle wagons, you will travel in cattle wagons to the slaughter house" ("Wenn Sie nicht in Viehwagen ins Übersee fahren, so werden Sie in Viehwagen ins Schlachthaus fahren").[15] In light of what followed and his general reliability, Weissmandel's testimony must be taken very seriously; however, no other proof of the date or the details of this contact with the Nazis, which allegedly took place in the summer and autumn of 1941, has come to light.

The second, relatively minor, case was that of a Jew who bribed Wisliceny and avoided deportation. Weissmandel concluded that if Wisliceny accepted bribes for individuals, he could be approached with an offer made for the generality. The intermediary for all such approaches had to be Karl Hochberg, a Jewish engineer from either Vienna or Prague, who had risen in the ÚŽ's statistical department and come to Wisliceny's attention because of his submissive devotion to his Nazi masters. He was made head of a section for special tasks set up by the Nazis and thus became another important element in the situation, an alternative center of power in the community to the ÚŽ itself. Weissmandel says he approached Hochberg after "a Friday in Tammuz, 5702," which would correspond to June 16–July 14, 1942. Other accounts leave open to doubt whether Weissmandel went alone or with others, and whether he asked others to establish an underground committee after speaking to Hochberg, as he says, or before.

Whatever the exact sequence, Weissmandel went to Gizi

Fleischmann and also to his own friends, such as Solomon Gross and Aron Grünhut. A committee was established in which Fleischmann and a few other individuals participated, though the exact composition of it is not clear and may have been rather elastic in any case. Rabbi Armin Frieder was part of it, as were a young architect named Andre Steiner, Dr. Tibor Kovac, and Eugen Winterstein; others knew of its existence and occasionally participated, such as Ernst Abeles, Grünhut, and Oskar Neumann. Weissmandel, with or without another person being present, received Wisliceny's answer through Hochberg: yes, the deportations would stop if a bribe were paid. According to Grünhut, Eichmann agreed to the cancellation of the deportations in a telephone conversation to Bratislava. "You have a swine's luck. Eichmann agrees," Wisliceny said ("Sie haben ein Sauglück. Eichmann ist einverstanden"). Weissmandel says that the bribe was $50,000, to be paid in dollars in two installments. Deportations would stop immediately; the first installment was to be paid within ten days, and the second one seven weeks after that. Neumann and Frieder mention $40,000 and claim that Hochberg appropriated half of the sum; they do not refer to two installments. Wisliceny, on the other hand, claimed in his testimony before the People's Court in Bratislava which tried him in 1946 that he only received $20,000, and that he wrote a memorandum on the subject for Himmler. No trace of this memorandum has been found, but if Wisliceny's story is true, it would indicate that Himmler himself was behind these peculiar negotiations. This is likely, though it is difficult to prove because we do not know the exact date on which the money was paid.[16]

Weissmandel says that after the first installment had been paid, the deportations ceased immediately. The real bait, as he points out, was not the bribe itself, but the fact that when he offered it he claimed to represent the world's rabbis—who had never taken an active anti-German stand, as Hochberg was to explain to Wisliceny—and of JDC. For, Weissmandel says, it had already become clear in the Gross negotiations that "the Germans always insisted that the money come from abroad, from American Jews—which meant that, apart from the money, they inclined to and favored such an approach to contacts with Jews in the U.S. for some political purpose which was more important to them than the destruction of Israel."[17]

Weissmandel had no doubt but that JDC would pay the money. It was, after all, such a relatively puny sum. However, there was no possibility of obtaining the first installment within ten days, and the money had to be found locally. An Orthodox banker, or rather former banker, Benjamin Solomon Stern, borrowed and collected the first $25,000 in dollar bills—by itself no mean achievement. The money was duly handed over to Wisliceny, or rather to him through Hochberg, supposedly having come from a Swiss-based emissary of American Jewry named Ferdinand Roth. This Roth was entirely invented by Weissmandel, who even obtained blank paper from Switzerland and wrote letters addressed to himself and signed by "Roth" on an ancient Underwood typewriter.

Wisliceny had told the Jews that he would see to it that the Germans did not demand further deportations, but that the Jews would have to prevent the Slovaks from doing so. The committee, increasingly known to itself and others as "the Working Committee" (*pracovná skupina*), detailed Kovac to bribe Vašek, head of Section XIV, and Steiner and Grünhut to contact Koso. Letters were sent to Switzerland, to Nathan Schwalb and to the Orthodox group's contact there, Bela (Baruch Meshulam) Leibowitz. JDC was to be asked to supply the money. In the meantime, Grünhut, and later Gizi Fleischmann, went to Budapest to obtain the help of Hungarian Jewry.

The different accounts of what happened next are again contradictory in details, yet the general outline is clear. Grünhut contacted Hungarian Jewish bodies and was refused money both by Samu Stern and by the official Zionist representative. Josef Blum tried to help, but when he turned to Baroness Edith Weiss, head of the aristocratic family whose industrial empire supplied much of Hungary's war-making capacity, she demanded that JDC guarantee any money she might lend. She had recently converted to Catholicism and apparently did not want to endanger herself, though it seems she was willing to help on a local scale. In the end, $10,000 were given by Gyula Link, an Orthodox merchant and philanthropist, but the loan of another $20,000 was again dependent on a JDC guarantee. Grünhut claims that Mayer refused to give it. Blum does not mention the incident, but says that the $20,000 were in the end obtained from Link.[18]

In Switzerland, Saly Mayer had been kept informed as the situation developed, both by Riegner of WJC and by Schwalb, but there was tragically little he could do. His total income for 1942 was only $235,000, of which $105,295 were preempted by the Swiss government's demands relative to Jewish refugees in the country. There therefore remained $130,000 for the year of mass murders throughout Europe for Rumania, Hungary, Slovakia, Croatia, Italy, and France. Yet Mayer had to bear the burden of this knowledge virtually alone. He could not admit how inadequate his funds were, even to Schwalb, and JDC-Lisbon would not hear his reports because it could not afford to receive them.

In these circumstances, Mayer received the first detailed reports from Blum in May. Until September, he had no personal contact with Bratislava; instead, Blum transmitted the demands of the committee: retribution should be threatened against the 300,000 Slovaks in the United States; the BBC and U.S. radio should report the deportations; Mayer should try to influence the Vatican to intervene with the Hungarian government to accept refugees from Slovakia. Not only were these demands unrealistic, but they were not accompanied by detailed requests for money or by a budget. Mayer did tell Schwalb what the committee wanted, and Schwalb informed Riegner and Richard Lichtheim of JA, but they could do nothing more than send censored reports to the free countries. Mayer also contacted the IRC to find out what had happened to the deportees in Poland. On July 27, Fleischmann wrote to Mayer saying that the committee had received some news from families who had been deported to the Lublin region, but that they had no idea what had happened to the people in Silesia (Auschwitz). On August 15, a Polish Jewish diplomat informed Mayer that the Jews were being murdered. On August 27, Fleischmann wrote that they knew that deportation was synonymous with death.[19]

In her letter of July 27, Fleischmann also for the first time made clear what the committee's monetary demands were. About the same time, Weissmandel approached Leibowitz, who contacted Schwalb. The immediate request was for $10,000 in dollars and large sums in Swiss currency to be placed in a Swiss bank, against which the committee would receive money in Slovakia. The request obviously reflected complete despair, because the committee must have doubted whether large sums clearly designated for bribery would be made available. Mayer must have responded immediately, though we have no proof of this, that dollar bills were unobtainable. The committee's demands then crystallized to include 100,00 sfr. ($23,000; "for Willy"—that is, for Wisliceny) plus a budget of 1 sfr. a day per Jew in labor camps. This last item meant 1.8 million sfr. ($420,000) yearly.[20] Even if Mayer had been a more flexible person, it was simply impossible for him to meet these demands. Dollar transfers had ceased in April, and he did not know whether and when they would recommence. Nor did Fleischmann and the committee stick to the original figures. On September 1, she wrote that she needed $100,000 for bribes. She hoped she would get 80,000 sfr. ($18,700) from Hungary, plus a large sum in pengö. Even so, she would still need 90,000 sfr. ($21,000) immediately. This amount, in fact, seems to have been the second installment for "Willy" which Weissmandel had promised.[21]

On August 28, 1942, a day after receiving Fleischmann's report, Mayer decided to do something. He would give $5,000 immediately and another $5,000 in September. That would mean, however, that Hehalutz would receive nothing more that year. Schwalb, with Leibowitz's help, saw to it that the money, ostensibly available in a Swiss bank against local payment, was in fact transferred in Swiss bank notes and American dollars to Slovakia. At a meeting on September 9, Mayer told Schwalb that he would give another 5,000 sfr. ($1,165) monthly from September on, if he could, for the labor camps. For local needs, he was giving 10,000 sfr. ($2,300) for September; the rest was budgeted, but the money was not there yet. "Unfortunately, we still have no possibility to make definite arrangements regarding further payments; we have talked to the various decision-making organs today, and as in the past we depend on what they say."[22] These "organs"—that is, JDC-Lisbon—had no way to transfer money. In November, Schwalb, in Mayer's name, persuaded a very angry and reluctant committee in Slovakia to accept the suggestion of borrowing locally against repayment après, and 40,000 sfr. ($9,300) were thus obtained. The total amount that actually reached Slovakia cannot have been large; it was probably not more than a few thousand dollars worth of Swiss francs and the 40,000 sfr. just mentioned.[23]

JDC's reputation among the Orthodox in Slovakia suffered badly as a result of all this. Fleischmann, however, despite her bitterness, did not accuse Mayer personally; rather, she blamed the western democracies who had instituted inhuman currency regulations which prevented the saving of lives. From what we can reconstruct, Mayer never doubted the seriousness of the situation. He could not respond because he simply did not have the money. What he did have, he carefully spread out, trying to keep up the illusion that JDC was a rich organization which would help with large sums when the time came. There was indeed little more he could do.

Weissmandel says that the second installment of the bribe

for Wisliceny came late, only after Yom Kippur (September 21, 1942), and that this was the reason the Nazis sent away a further four trainloads of Jews. In fact, however, only two of these went before Yom Kippur, on September 18; one went on September 23; the last left on October 20, a month after the second installment had been paid. Deportations did not resume until the summer of 1944. It might therefore appear that Weissmandel's claim that the bribes stopped the deportations is highly doubtful. Yet there are a number of facts that make it plausible. On June 25, 1942, Wisliceny and Ambassador Hans Ludin met with the Slovak leaders and, to the great surprise of the Slovaks, announced that the Germans would not carry on with the deportations because the Slovaks had allegedly granted 35,000 exemptions to the Jews. Ludin repeated this claim the next day in a cable to Berlin.[24] Prompted by the BBC's broadcast of the contents of the May Bund report regarding the murder of Polish Jewry, Ludin tied this in with a supposed increase in English propaganda. On the Slovak side, Prime Minister Tuka asked the Germans to support him in his demand for further deportations, which has usually been interpreted as a request to be supported against fellow Slovaks who were weakening on the issue. I would suggest instead that this might have been a way to overcome Wisliceny's opposition. Yet we also know that Eichmann continued to demand deportations from Slovakia. Why then Wisliceny's very sudden change of heart and the ridiculous excuse of 35,000 exemptions if the bribes are not taken into account?

Tentatively, then, the following picture emerges. Himmler decided to postpone the deportations in order to establish contact with JDC and some nebulous "world Jewry"—in which he quite sincerely believed[25]—through the fictitious Ferdinand Roth. The $50,000 were just a means of establishing such contacts. Eichmann and others demanded that the deportations continue, and a few more trains were dispatched, but not too many, so that the contacts could be developed. A total of 57,837 Jews had been sent to Poland in fifty-seven trains, 39,006 of whom were sent to the Lublin region, whence they were soon transported to the Belzec, Auschwitz, or Maidanek death camps. The rest were sent directly to Auschwitz. About 25,000 Jews remained in Slovakia. Some of them were living in towns because they were economically important to the regime; others lived in labor camps at Nováky, Sered, and Vyhně, which were maintained by the ÚŽ. These camps soon became independent factories and plants producing goods which were very useful to the Slovak economy. The profit derived from them played an important part in averting further deportations that were suggested from time to time by Slovak fascists.

The Europa Plan

On the morrow of Yom Kippur, probably September 22, 1942, Michael Weissmandel was arrested after evidence was found in his office that he had received reports from Poland on the fate of the deported Jews. In the midst of the Sukkot festival, or about the end of the month, he was released. He says that it was while he was in prison that he made up his mind to attempt the seemingly impossible—to negotiate with Wislicery for the end of deportations all over Europe. His idea met with some opposition from the Working Committee; they did not believe it was possible, and, if the negotiations were fruitless, their failure might actually trigger more deportations. Even the little that had been achieved might be lost. But, says Weissmandel, after some initial hesitation, Gizi Fleischmann joined him in his proposal, and the others followed. Ernst Abeles had been on his side from the beginning.[26]

Fleischman asked Andre Steiner, who by now had access to Wisliceny, to pave the way, while Weissmandel let Hochberg have another letter from "Ferdinand Roth" which "proved" that the money received to date had come from JDC and some nebulous world rabbinical authority, and that future negotiations in Slovakia would lead the Germans to these same authorities. Wisliceny rose to the bait, agreeing to ask his superiors what their conditions would be for stopping all deportations of European Jews. It appears that the answer was given about the end of November, 1942. Versions of it have been preserved in two letters, one by Fleischmann, written in German and sent to Silberschein and Schwalb, and the other signed with Frieder's name by Weissmandel (who forged the signature because Frieder was away at the time, though Frieder agreed fully to the proceedings when he returned). Weissmandel's letter was sent to Istanbul and to Switzerland, was written in rabbinical Hebrew, and was much fuller than Fleischmann's letter, which had been sent somewhat earlier. Fleischmann's letter actually reached Mayer on December 4, whereas Weissmandel's letter was dated December 5, 1942.[27]

Fleischmann's version reported that the Germans were offer-

370

ing such small concessions for deported Slovak Jews in Poland as permission to receive letters and parcels, but the centerpiece of this first proposal was the undertaking to cease deportations *from* the GG and *from* Auschwitz. What this wording probably meant was the cessation of the mass murder. Further, the Germans explicitly offered "cessation of the European deportation except for Old Germany, Austria, and the Bohemian-Moravian Protectorate." Weissmandel's version differed slightly, speaking of an alleviation or possibly cessation of deportation procedures. It then repeated the German offers as reported by Fleischmann, adding that they would come into force fifteen days after an agreement was reached. No sum of money was mentioned, but the Jews were asked what sums they would offer.

Weissmandel says that even in the preliminary stage Hochberg had suggested offering some contact to the western powers, but that he had immediately squashed the idea, believing that the Jews should not enter into any such political problems. However, the fact that Wisliceny did not make any specific demands, but instead left it to the Jews to offer something, indicates that the Nazis—whichever of them were behind these negotiations—were eager to know what the actual power of the Jews was. Schwalb and Mayer were of course completely taken by surprise by the contents of Fleischmann's letter, and the unidentifiable foreign diplomat who brought the messages did not carry any response back to Bratislava. On December 19, Fleischmann wrote bitterly to Mayer that she "must therefore conclude that the will to help is not present." On January 14, she reported that she had also met with an absolute rebuff in Budapest, where she visited during the Christmas period. "Hungary's Jews have neither feeling of Jewish solidarity nor any sense of social responsibility; nor do they know how to give." Again she turned to Mayer, saying that the mere desire to help was not enough. "It is humanly unbearable to think that American, Swiss and Hungarian Jews should be unable to avert our tragedy. I can never be convinced of this, and the accusation is against all those who did not fulfill their most primitive human responsibility."[28]

Despite the wealth of documentation available, there are some links missing in this story of the "Europa Plan," as it came to be called. We know that Schwalb tried to convince Mayer from the very beginning to take positive action on it, and Mayer, or Schwalb in Mayer's name, must have given some noncommittal answer late in December or early in January to justify Fleischmann's harsh words on January 14.[29] Mayer, however, was obviously waiting for some response from Lisbon and New York to the demands as summarized in Weissmandel's first communication, which he now had and fifty copies of which he sent to various parts of the globe. Clearly he considered the proposal very important, though he was not sure whether the Nazis were serious. Mayer consulted with leaders of the Swiss community, and, in the meantime, on January 29, he advised Fleischmann of another 20,000 sfr. ($4,600) clearing arrangement. On February 24, he asked Herbert Katzki outright about the proposal but received no answer. Finally, on March 1, Katzki told him that nothing could be done. Richard Lichtheim of JA also thought "that this proposal is a lie and a deception."[30]

Late in February, Mayer decided to take action at least on some aspects of help to Slovakia that he did not have to clear with the Lisbon office, and he promised Fleischmann a 100,000 sfr. ($23,000) clearing arrangement in dollars après in addition to the monthly 20,000. He then allowed Schwalb to tell the committee in Bratislava that their big proposal was being carefully considered and that means were being prepared to meet German demands. This information was conveyed to Wisliceny, who showed "tremendous interest."[31] By then it was evident that the Germans would want at least $2 million, and that a first payment would have to be made. Who suggested the price tag is unknown, but it was probably Wisliceny, who got tired of waiting for a Jewish proposal. Mayer responded ambiguously. In a letter to Fleischmann of March 4, 1943, he explained that he had to consider the needs of other countries, but at the same time he held out the prospect of meeting "Willy's" demands. On March 31, he wrote that he was trying to place $100,000 for "Willy" in America, hinting that any money offered would only be available after the war.

In his quaint English, Mayer explained his tactics in a conversation with Katzki on April 2. He would try to "avoid that the negotiations snap and the blame is being put on our shoulders. I wrote somewhat vaguely to continue the negotiations and I on my part shall try to create a deposit of Maiah Elef [100,000] dollars in USA. You will understand that I have not definitely promised but only said that there is a chance of prospect."[32] In the meantime, he increased the amounts in the clearing arrangement for Slovakia, which by then had been accepted by the committee, and tried hard to convince the IRC to send a delegate there, which would give him some measure of control over events.[33] Mayer had moved from a clear stand against the negotiations to a position of careful procrastination.[34] Schwalb and (possibly) Silberschein were the only representatives of the Jewish organizations to take the proposal seriously, but it was quite obvious that any payment in dollars was completely out of the question. Mayer could not even get Swiss francs for dollars paid in by his own JDC in New York; even if he could, it was impossible to send them to Slovakia. His account was controlled, and any large-scale illegality was bound to be discovered, with disastrous results for JDC's work all over Europe. On the other hand, he wanted to see whether there was anything behind these particular negotiations.

In America, the WJC received Weissmandel's Europa Plan letter in April. A meeting apparently was held to discuss it, but nothing resulted. Obviously WJC did not believe much in such offers.[35] In Istanbul, Haim Barlas of JA was not quite sure what to do, and it was not until February, 1943, that two new and energetic Palestinian emissaries, Wenja Pomerantz and Menahem Bader, who had been sent to try to contact Jews under Nazi control, became active. Bader was also in doubt; on March 10, he and Pomerantz wrote to Tel Aviv, saying that it was of course very difficult to gauge the seriousness of the proposal. Yet it was clear that the deportation of the last 20,000 Slovak Jews had been averted "by these means."[36] Bader met with Nuncio Angelo Roncalli (later John XXIII) on March 9, but apparently did not even mention the proposal.

Wisliceny was very busy elsewhere, and the German side was in no real hurry. But on May 5, a meeting took place between Steiner, Fleischmann, and Wisliceny. Wisliceny had just returned from Saloniki, where he was active in deporting the local Jews to their deaths. Unfortunately, he said, he could not prevent it; other Germans had been involved, and the Jews had shown no understanding of the need to establish labor camps like those in Slovakia. Moreover, while he would meet his chief in Prague and return with an answer about the Europa Plan, the problem was that Hitler was now quite adamant regarding the destruction of the Jews. Then matters took a surprising turn: "Willy" reported in his chief's name that the price for stopping deportations would be $2–3 million and that there would be no deportation until June 10, when he expected a reply to his proposal. If $200,000 were paid on June 10, there would be another stay of deportations for two months. The arrangement would not include Greater Germany or Poland.[37]

373

Mayer had to consider the new German proposals in light of the amount of money he had at his disposal in May-June, 1943. He eventually had a total of $997,810 in francs at his disposal in 1943, but practically all of this money arrived after September. He therefore had to borrow from his Swiss organizations, using the money for deposits in Swiss banks for the Slovak clearing arrangement. From the Bratislava committee's point of view, JDC money was preferable despite the small amounts, because the money of Weissmandel's Orthodox friends, used to pay for bribes to Slovak officials, for the upkeep of the camps, and for refugees who managed to filter through from Poland, was lent, whereas JDC funds were grants. By June, Mayer had made available 180,000 sfr. ($42,000) and $10,000 had been given to the Hehalutz, apparently with Mayer's tacit knowledge that the money would find its way illegally into Slovakia. The Swiss francs were paid into the account of the representative of Orthodox Jews in Switzerland, Hugo Donnebaum. Much of that money, and some $16,000 received in April from Istanbul, was used to avert two more Slovak threats of deportation that arose in April and in early June.

Early in June, Mayer was again pressed by Fleischmann for an answer regarding the Europa Plan. On June 8, he told Schwalb by telephone that by then responsible people in the United States and Palestine knew all about the proposal, but he "had not received any encouragement from any side to do something positive in this affair, and therefore I say to-day No!!"[38] But on the very next day, one day before the final answer was due in Bratislava, Fleischmann telephoned Schwalb and Mayer began to waver, saying that at the moment he could not promise anything. On June 10, he again asked Katzki whether he was right in saying "nothing doing" to a proposal which would put money into German hands.

On June 11, Fleischmann called again. Because she had no answer, she had asked Wisliceny to extend the time limit to July 1. Wisliceny had agreed, but had changed the German conditions: cessation of deportations was promised only as far as France was concerned; Belgium and Holland were excluded. The money—$2 million—could be paid in fourteen installments. She now had to have an answer: were the Jews outside of the Nazi hell prepared to pay a ransom?

Mayer decided to call a meeting at Bern on June 17, at which Silberschein, Schwalb, and Pierre Bigar participated. Silberschein and Schwalb impressed on him that the responsibility for refusing to help was too large; there was no way to save the Jews except by somehow making the first $200,000 available for payment après. Mayer agreed. On June 18 he wrote to Fleischmann that he would try to have $200,000 deposited in the United States. His own conditions were that the negotiations should be expanded to include Poland; that all murder actions must cease; and that emigration must be made possible by transit through countries controlled by Germany. On June 20, he told JDC-Lisbon of his action, explaining it in terms of his reluctance to assume responsibility for saying no.

Mayer also made larger sums available on a clearing basis, amounting to 100,000 sfr. ($23,000) for the period July-December, 1943, and an additional $45,000 in the United States for payments après. The dollars were part of the budget he now had, though he was still waiting for the actual dollar transfer from America. He was giving the money for bribes, for maintaining the camps, and, chiefly perhaps, for enabling the committee in Bratislava to smuggle Jews from Poland, a most dangerous activity in light of the situation of Slovak Jews, and one which had already brought some 300 Jews into the country. Fleischmann's response was an outflow of gratitude which cannot be explained simply as a desire to humor the JDC representative in Saint Gallen. "Dear, good uncle, many, many thanks for your goodness and helpfulness, may God preserve your health for all of us."[39] In the meantime, Wisliceny should have met with the group in Bratislava, but he did not come. The decisive meeting with him was postponed, and finally the date was fixed for August 5. They were desperate in Bratislava, because neither JDC nor JA really gave them anything in cash to offer. "The unique event in history will have taken place, that there was a possibility to save the lives of doomed people, and that this chance was passed by."[40]

Mayer's reply of August 4 was intended to be reassuring. "With a child-like conviction and undeviating patience I am trying to work for future happiness."[41] He would make money available for Wisliceny in the United States or Britain after the war. But the Slovak Jewish leadership continued to ask for cash. Fleischmann telephoned Schwalb on August 5 to say that if the Nazis were not paid a first installment, they would kill all of the remaining Jews. At that point, however, JDC no longer bore the sole responsibility. Joseph Schwartz was in Palestine and had met Moshe Shertok, head of the political department of JA. Pomerantz and Bader

375

in Istanbul were pressing hard for a positive reply to Weissman-del's and Fleischmann's appeals. There was a decision in Tel Aviv to keep £25,000 ($100,000) in readiness—this, of course, would have to be smuggled out in contravention of blockade regulations. Istanbul cautioned Tel Aviv regarding JDC: its attitude was "known," and its promise to pay $200,000 was suspect. But Tel Aviv was not actually ready to send money. On August 3, Pomerantz and Bader wrote to the Histadrut in Tel Aviv comparing Fleischmann's appeals for help to those from Poland. "We are desperate that we did not convince you in time. . . . Leave now all your work and help to rescue, before the curtain falls on everything." They asked the Histadrut to provide the bulk of the funds to be sent to Bratislava.[42]

On July 21, Fleischmann wrote to Istanbul that "Willy" had refused the offer of postwar payment. On August 1, the Istanbul people decided, without authorization from Tel Aviv, to send $50,000. In fact, £15,000 ($60,000) were sent in cash and acknowledged from Bratislava on September 9. The Istanbul action was approved by Shertok after the event; in his talks with Schwartz, the agreement was to share the responsibility between the two agencies. A cable went to Mayer from Shertok in Istanbul on August 10, 1943, in which Mayer was asked to "provide immediately 150 [thousand dollars] shall back you utmost in shouldering responsibility."[43] Schwartz must have known of this cable, which stood in glaring contradiction to JDC's official policy. But Mayer, unknown to Schwartz, had already acted. Fleischmann had insisted that an immediate transfer of 70,000 sfr. (about $16,000) was needed, and on August 5, Mayer sent the money in cash through an emissary—not in JDC's name, but in his own, though the money was afterwards budgeted to JDC. Gizi Fleischmann acknowledge it on August 9.[44] In his answer to Shertok, Mayer expressed satisfaction that everyone understood that immediate help was needed. The problem now was what Wisliceny would say. To Lichtheim Mayer said that he could only pay what he himself had; "one cannot discuss this with the Joint."[45] But in a telephone talk with Barlas and Shertok on August 13, Mayer had indicated that while he thought Fleischmann should receive every help, Wisliceny's promises were not as serious as she believed. The Nazis had undertaken to stop deportations while the negotiations were in progress, but deportations had proceeded from France. Nevertheless, despite his serious doubts, he sent another

90,000 sfr. in cash on the same day and 70,000 more on September 22.[46] Weissmandel's charge that Mayer and the JA men in Istanbul, by insisting on the après arrangement, had left him and Fleischmann without means with which to negotiate therefore is not quite accurate. In August and September, Mayer sent a grant total of 230,000 sfr. ($53,600) to Slovakia.

On August 27, another meeting took place in Bratislava between Wisliceny and the members of the committee. Wisliceny said that he would have to get new powers from his chief, but he thought that the deportations from Western Europe would cease in any case. Poland had only recently become his chief's responsibility (which was a blatant lie), and he could not say much about it, but probably no murder would occur there either, once an agreement was reached. As to Bohemia, that was a separate problem. There would be no more deportations from Germany (by that time there were no more Jews there). Fleischmann, however, could not prove to Wisliceny that she had the necessary money. On September 3, Wisliceny finally came back and announced that the Germans had withdrawn their offer. He did not think the deportations would recommence, but he was not sure; the general atmosphere was not conducive to negotiations, but the Germans might return to them. In the meantime, there was a plan to send children to the West in order to counteract Allied propaganda. Perhaps 2,000, or ultimately 5,000, would be sent from Poland via Theresienstadt. Ways would be open for aiding Polish Jews, and there would be no deportations from Theresienstadt. A new exchange camp at Bergen-Belsen would house important Jews who could be exchanged to the West. At a last meeting on September 12, he repeated most of these points, and Fleischmann paid him $10,000 in cash. She says that he put it away and said he considered it a deposit. The negotiations for the Europa Plan were at an end.[47]

What is one to make of these tortured exchanges of information, these desperate demands for money, and the embittered memoirs of survivors? Was the Europa Plan just a ruse to get money out of the Jews, as had been the case so often, especially in Eastern Europe? There is no doubt that the Nazis were motivated, among other things, by greed. But the very sums mentioned must surely militate against such a facile conclusion. A paltry $200,000, or even $2 million dollars, was of little consequence for the Nazi war machine. Weissmandel seems to assume that the money went to the pockets of individual Nazis. Perhaps some of it did, but it is clear that Wisliceny did report to Himmler and that most of the money went to the SS.

The promise that deportations from Western Europe would end was not kept. There were four trains to Sobibor from Holland between May 10 and June 10, and two more between June 10 and July 10. There were no trains from France and Belgium during the first of these two periods. But whether or not German promises to stop deportations were kept seems to be less important than the fact that Wisliceny was insisting on negotiations with the West, and the money he demanded would be tangible proof of contacts leading to such negotiations. For Himmler, who stood behind these talks in Bratislava, contact through Wisliceny with "World Jewry" must have had central importance. After all, in his eyes, these were the real, demonic enemies of the Reich, the real rulers of the anti-Nazi coalition. Even after the talks failed, possibly because no cash was offered, the Nazis seem to have considered "goodwill" gestures. A trainload of children, complete with nurses, was actually sent from Bialystok to Theresienstadt for an unknown reason, and kept there for some time before the children were sent to Auschwitz to be murdered, like the rest of the children of Polish Jewry. The question must be posed whether a chance of negotiating the rescue of Jews was not missed in the failure of the Europa Plan. No documentary proof can be offered, but the circumstantial evidence provided by the story just told points to the answer that a chance was indeed missed.

JDC's policy was of course tied to that of the United States government. JDC's purpose was to rescue endangered Jews so long as its efforts did not run counter to America's wartime policies. This purpose was based on the double assumption that what was good for Allied victory was good for the Jews, and that in any case JDC was in no position to question, and even less to act counter to, governmental policies. JA's attitude differed mainly in degree, not principle. A specifically Jewish "foreign policy" simply had not yet emerged. Had JDC articulated such a policy, it might well have defined the saving of Jewish lives as a priority, while yet not denying the first necessity of winning the war. This indeed was what Weissmandel demanded in his letters. But the time was not yet ripe for such a revolution in political outlook.

Mayer's policy changed under the impact of the Europa Plan. He really had neither the financial means nor the political base from which to help. He was bound hand and foot by Swiss regulations, and his escapades in sending money to Slovakia might have cost him and JDC very dearly indeed. Contrary to what Weissmandel, and probably Gizi Fleischmann as well, thought about him, he was moving from a strictly legalistic stance to an attempt to help through any route available. He kept his changed attitude strictly to himself, however, playing his cards very close to his chest. Having begun by disbelieving the whole story of the bribery plan, he ended up doing everything he could to enable Fleischmann to conduct the negotiations. He did not want to be accused of missing chances. He kept Weissmandel's Hebrew epistles in his files; he must have studied them carefully. Uncle Saly began to realize that he could not ask others what to do. He had to make some frightful decisions, and he had to make them on his own.

16

The German Ransom Proposal and the Destruction of Hungarian Jewry

On May 19, 1944, two Hungarian Jews alighted from a German courier plane that had flown them from Vienna to Istanbul: Joel Brand, a Zionist rescue worker from Budapest, and Andor Grosz, a smuggler and espionage agent. Brand brought with him a Nazi ransom proposal of mind-boggling implications: in exchange for war material and goods, they would release one million Jews from Nazi Europe. This ransom proposal, which developed from the Europa Plan but was much more concrete and wide-ranging, became the subject of intense international negotiations despite the Allied preoccupation with the Normandy landings on June 6. Its repercussions can be followed to the end of the war and beyond. Parallel with it occurred the mass murder of Hungarian Jewry, which the ransom proposal was to have prevented. The intertwined stories of the mass murder and of the ransom proposal are most complex, and only some of the ramifications can be dealt with here.[1]

There were 725,007 Jews in Hungary in 1941. These included 400,980 in what was known as Trianon Hungary, the area of Hungarian sovereignty before the annexation in 1938–41 of Southern Slovakia, Subcarpathian Russia (PKR), Northern Transylvania, and the northeastern corner of Yugoslavia. Jews in Trianon Hungary had numbered 473,355 in 1920 and 440,567 in 1930; the decrease was due partly to a steep decline in the birthrate, typical of a community in deep cultural trouble, and partly to a wave of conversions, especially among the middle and upper classes. In 1941, 61,548 "Christian Jews" were counted. By Nazi racial definitions, therefore, the total was probably well over 800,000.

Hungarian Jewry was divided into Orthodox and Neologue communities. The former represented a deeply traditional, overwhelmingly anti-Zionist element, whereas the latter, consisting of the majority of Jews in Trianon Hungary, represented the middle classes who were seeking entrance into Hungarian society. An attempt in 1868–69 to unify the two groups having failed, they had become incapable not only of cooperation, but even of any kind of personal contact with each other. In 1930, 65.5 percent of the Jews belonged to Neologue, 29.2 percent to Orthodox, and 5.3 percent to conservative, or "status quo," communities. The relative strength of the communities was changed, however, with annexations, because the Orthodox element was much stronger in the new areas. The Zionist element was very small and lacking influence, but it too gained some strength from the newly acquired territories after 1940–41.

Politically, Hungarian Jewry was overwhelmingly magyarized and patriotic; even the Orthodox community had assimilated in speech and secular culture in a way that was not dissimilar to that of German Jewish Orthodoxy. The leadership of Hungarian Jewry was firmly vested in the aristocratic banking and industrialist families, whose representatives were Court Councillor Samu Stern, Dr. Karl Wilhelm, and members of the Chorin and Weiss families, many of whom were Christian converts. The Orthodox leaders included Fülop von Freudiger, head of the organization of Orthodox communities (and son of another head), Gyula Link, and other wealthy and respected men. From before the war, welfare and social work was done largely through the Országos Magyar Zsido Segitö Akcio (OMZSA), a fund-raising agency attached to the Neologue community, and the Magyar Izraeliták Pártfogo Irodája, which was largely concerned with distributing welfare. This latter office was guided by Dr. Sandor (Alexander) Eppler, secretary of the Neologue community and JDC's chief contact in Hungary until his death in 1941.[2]

In spite of their assimilationist and loyalist tendencies, Hungarian Jews were subject to discriminatory legislation long before World War II. Admiral Nicholas Horthy's regime, in the wake of nationalist and antisemitic propaganda which culminated in pogroms throughout Hungary, in 1919 accepted the demand of a largely economically motivated middle class to enact anti-Jewish legislation. In 1920, Jews were admitted to universities to a total of 6 percent of the student body. Furthermore, in order to prevent the admission of converted Jews, a first clearly racial definition was made—thirteen years before Hitler came to power—and the Jews defined as a nationality. After years of campaigning at the League of Nations and direct pressure on the Hungarians by Jewish organizations abroad, the racialist clauses were abolished in 1928. However, with the advent of the Hitler regime and the deepening economic crisis, antisemitism grew, and the pro-Nazi Arrow Cross party under former Hungarian army major Ferenc Szálasi gained 49 out of 226 parliamentary seats in 1935. In May, 1938, a law was enacted limiting Jews in most branches of the professions and business to 20 percent. A second law of May, 1939, limited them to 6 percent. Jews who had converted to Christianity after 1919 were counted as Jews, and while Catholic and Protestant dignitaries tried to protect some of the converts, they apparently found nothing repugnant to their religious consciences in the antisemitic laws themselves.

During the first period of the war, legal restrictions multiplied: marriages between Christians and Jews were forbidden in August, 1941; the official status and rights of the Jewish religion were denied by decree; and in 1942, Jewish-owned land and forests were made subject to expropriation. Worse yet, Jews and other minorities were denied the right to army service and Jewish officers of all ranks were expelled. Instead, Jews were recruited into labor units under Hungarian officers; they wore their own civilian clothes and yellow armbands and only military caps distinguished them from prisoners. They were put to work, often doing completely senseless labor, and were subject to ill-treatment and humiliation. From July, 1939, to November, 1940, some 52,000 Jews were thus recruited. After Hungary entered the war, the call-up was intensified, and the Jews were sent to the Ukrainian front. Some 40,000 went, of whom 5,000 returned in late 1943, and a few thousand more survived Soviet prisoner of war camps. The rest were starved or beaten to death, massacred, or simply abandoned to freeze in the Russian winter. OMZSA used funds emanating in part from JDC in order to send parcels to these unfortunates. Most were stolen, some were burned during the Hungarian retreat in Russia in 1943, and only a few got through to the intended recipients. During the 1944 deportations, some labor units were deported to Auschwitz, but others afforded protection from the death camps.[3]

During the first two years of the war, however, JDC's major concern in Hungary was with the approximately 3,000 Polish and 3,000 German Jewish refugees who had managed to get there. In addition, abysmal poverty reigned in the PKR region and the welfare office was feeding 5,000 adults and 1,000 children there daily, partly with JDC funds.[4] There were also about 30,000–35,000 Jews who had been born in Hungarian-controlled territories, especially the PKR, but who did not have papers to prove it and therefore had to register with the dreaded Küföldieket Ellenörzö Oországos Központi Hatoság (KEOKH; Central Alien Control Office). Other threatened individuals were a few thousand Polish and Russian Jews who had entered after the first world war.

Immediately after Hungary's entry into the war on June 27, 1941, the government decided on the deportation of all these "aliens" from the PKR to the new territories in the Ukraine. A decree of July 12 settled the details: they could take with them thirty pengö and food for three days. By the end of August, 18,000 Jews had been deported, first into Hungarian-occupied territories in eastern Poland and then to Kamenets Podolskiy in the Ukraine. The Germans objected at first—this again was an "untidy" approach. But on August 25, at a conference at Vinnitsa, SS Obergruppenführer Franz Jaeckeln agreed to accept the Jews and dispose of them by September 1. He was as good as his word: on August 27–28, 14,000–16,000 Hungarian Jews, in addition to several thousand local ones, were machine-gunned by the SS, Ukrainian collaborators, and a Hungarian sapper unit. About 2,000 escaped, largely through bribery. When Hungarian Interior Minister Ferenc Keresztes-Fischer was informed of the details, he ordered a stop to the deportations. Another massacre on a smaller scale took place in January, 1942, in the newly occupied Novi Sad area in Yugoslavia, where 3,309 civilians were murdered. These victims were mostly Serbs, but about 700 Jews also died.[5]

These events were followed by the flight into Hungarian territory of the Slovak Jews after mid-March, 1942, and, in the summer of that year, Polish Jews from the ghettos in southeastern Poland that were then being liquidated also began escaping over the frontier. I have already noted that some 700 Polish Jews entered Slovakia in 1943, mainly from the Bochnia-Sosnowice-Bendin area in southwestern Poland. On the other hand, many of the original Polish refugees from the 1939–40 influx had managed to move on to Rumania.[6] Support of the poverty-stricken Jews in the PKR and the refugees from Slovakia and Poland called for JDC's intervention. However, the sums it spent in Hungary up to 1944 were not large. According to the official figures, JDC spent $157,215 in 1940; $23,935 in 1941, $9,879 in 1942; $100,000 in 1943; and the much larger sum of $884,786 in 1944. To these official amounts should be added the funds transmitted by Saly Mayer, which amounted to only $2,170 in 1942, but $812,690 in 1944. Had the official Orthodox and Neologue leadership of Hungarian Jewry done its duty by its unfortunate brethren, no JDC funds at all would have been necessary, but as the situation was, they were an important contribution. The only other outside aid was money that began to come in from Istanbul in 1943, after Wenja Pomerantz and Menahem Bader, the emissaries from Palestine, arrived there.

Most of the funding for Hungary from 1941 to 1944 was effected by a clearing arrangement whereby forty-one (later fifty-three) Hungarian Jewish students from wealthy families were sent to study in Switzerland, their expenses being paid by Saly Mayer, and their parents gave pengö to Josef Blum in return.[7] The sums were not large, but they contributed materially to the possibilities of the undercover groups aiding refugees in Budapest, faced not only by Hungarian police but also by a Neologue leadership that was unwilling to help. Those who did help were either Zionist or Orthodox groups.

JDC and the Emergence of a Zionist Rescue Group

The Zionists gradually came to dominate the clandestine operations in Hungary; the respected and energetic figure of Otto Komoly provided them with a necessary rallying point. Prominent among Komoly's group was Reszoe (Israel) Kasztner, a brilliant journalist from Cluj in Transylvania, who came to Budapest after the annexation of his home district by Hungary in 1940. Another such expatriate, but of a different kind, was Joel Brand, the man who was to bring the Nazi ransom proposal to the West in 1944. Born in 1906 in Transylvania, educated in Germany, Brand became a Communist agent, working as a sailor and an odd-jobs man in the United States, the South Seas, the Far East, and South America. His cousin claims that Brand even became a member of the Party executive in Thuringia. Wounded in one of the skirmishes with the Nazis, he was arrested by the Gestapo after the Nazi takeover, but freed in 1934. He left Germany and returned to Transylvania, but he failed to establish himself there, possibly because of his restless nature and his propensity for drinking. He then moved to Budapest and joined a training center of Gordonia, a moderate left-wing Zionist group. He married, left the training center, and with his wife established a glove factory that flourished until the war.[8] Brand himself says he liked the life in cafés, and, one can probably safely add, in nightclubs and other such places. He there made the acquaintance of one Josef Krem, a Hungarian espionage agent who was not averse to making some money on the side. When his wife's sister and her husband were deported to Kamenets Podolskiy in 1941, the Brands paid Krem to bring them back. Krem succeeded and brought in other Jews as well, for which he was of course paid by their relatives. Krem's activities opened up the border to Poland, and from 1941 on Brand became increasingly involved with border-smuggling and support work for refugees, joining Kasztner and Shmuel Springmann, another left-wing Zionist who had been dealing with other aspects of this work since 1941.

In December, 1941, Kasztner tried to organize a Jewish rescue and aid committee with the help of Social-Democratic and liberal Jewish public figures. This attempt ended in failure, but a small group began to crystallize around him and Komoly. In addition to Kasztner, Springmann, and Brand, it included Ernst (Zwi) Szilagyi of the left-wing Hashomer Hatzair, Eugen Frankel of the religious Mizrahi group, and Moshe Krausz, the Mizrahi head of the Palestine Office, who was responsible for the allocation of Palestine immigration certificates.[9] Polish Jewish refugees established a parallel committee, headed by Bronislaw Teichholz, which supported Polish Jews in Budapest. It received its funds largely from the Zionist group, though it also maintained contacts with the Polish mission in Hungary. Teichholz was a member of the Lwów Judenrat who had fled to the border forests and then crossed into Hungary. Having almost been deported back to Poland, he did his best to help others avoid that fate.

In October, 1942, Springmann contacted a quadruple agent, a

petty criminal named Andor ("Bandi") Grosz, who had converted (or who had acquired a conversion certificate) and passed under the names of "Andreas Gyorgy" or "Greiner." He was recruited successively by the Abwehr (the counterespionage branch of the German military), the Gestapo, the Hungarian counterespionage organization, the Americans, and the British. In February, 1943, the JA men in Istanbul asked the Zionists in Budapest to organize a proper aid and rescue committee and establish a courier service; starting in March, Grosz constituted a large part of that service.[10]

In the meantime, at the end of January, 1943, the Va'adat Ezra Vehatzala (Aid and Rescue Committee—Va'adah for short) was established in Budapest, with Komoly as chairman, Kasztner as his deputy, and Springmann as the treasurer and one responsible for contacts with the German and Hungarian secret services. Springmann reached the Abwehr not only through Grosz, but also through Josef Winninger (alias Duftel), another converted Jew, and other members of the Budapest Abwehr group who accepted money for courier services to the Polish ghettos. The Abwehr of course had its own aim: it wanted to establish contact with the Allies in order to prepare for eventual negotiations with the West. Brand even claims that it gave him a list of anti-Nazi Germans to transmit to JA which proved to be identical with much of the list of participants in the anti-Hitler attempt in July, 1944.[11] An Orthodox rescue group under Fülop von Freudiger also was founded, apparently in 1943.

All of these activities required help from JDC. In August, 1942, Joseph Schwartz explicitly told Mayer not to do anything beyond the Hungarian students' clearance, apparently because he thought the Hungarian Jews should be moved to provide the help themselves,[12] but in late 1942 and early 1943, Mayer became much more independent. The money he could use was Swiss money in any case, until the dollars came from America, and JDC-Lisbon was insisting all the time that he should do what he thought fit without reporting. Aroused by the fact that the Va'adah and Orthodox groups were helping Polish Jews cross into Hungary, Mayer offered help for the illegal action. He also offered a clearing arrangement to the welfare office and Samu Stern. It soon became clear in Budapest that JDC help would not be effective as long as there were competing committees, and on November 16, 1943, the Orthodox and the Zionists established a coordinating group to receive and administer the funds. Stern, however, refused to do anything that was not strictly legal and insisted on getting the permission of the Hungarian National Bank for any clearing arrangement. On March 2, 1944, Mayer wrote to Kasztner, Brand, and Teichholz that they could take on loans for 100,00 sfr. immediately and another 100,000 sfr. later; he would negotiate with Stern through Jean de Bavier, the IRC delegate in Budapest. He was prepared to give any additional sum for saving children, saying, "The whole Hungarian Klal [generality] is responsible for their welfare."[13] Stern finally did receive permission from the Hungarian authorities to get pengoš for welfare against promise of repayment after the war, but by that time it was too late. On March 19, 1944, the Germans marched into Hungary.[14]

The Deportation of Hungarian Jews and the Nazi Ransom Proposal

On March 14, Josef Winninger of the Abwehr told the Va'adah that Hungary was to be occupied by the Germans. A courier brought the information to Istanbul on March 17. The Abwehr people, obviously afraid that the Jews would reveal their contacts with the Allies to their SS competitors, took Brand, the documents in his possession, and some money, and spirited him away into the private apartment of one of the Abwehr men when the German army entered Budapest.[15] They could not prevent Grosz's arrest by the SS, though he was quickly released. Immediately upon the entry of the Germans, Dieter Wisliceny and Hermann Krumey, another of Eichmann's men, called upon the Jews to keep calm and promised that nothing untoward would happen. In personal meetings with Jewish representatives, these assurances were repeated. It is clear that Eichmann was trying to avoid a rebellion like that in Warsaw. A Judenrat was established on March 31 which was allowed to assume certain functions and laws were published, creating the impression that long-term regulations were aimed at. Samu Stern, the loyal Hungarian citizen, turned to the Hungarian government and asked whether he should obey the Nazi orders. The answer was yes.

The German invasion was also followed by Prime Minister Miklos Kallay's flight to the Turkish legation and by an interregnum that lasted until March 25, when a new, pro-German government, headed by Döme Sztojay, the erstwhile ambassador to Berlin and a rabid antisemite, was forced on Horthy. Interior Minister Andor Jaross and two Hungarian Nazi undersecretaries, Lászlo

Baky and László Endre, began preparing for the immediate elimination of Jews from Hungarian life. Adolf Eichmann arrived with his special squad (*Sondereinsatzkommando*) immediately following the occupation, and an understanding on the deportation of Hungarian Jews was speedily reached. On March 29, Jaross suggested introducing the yellow badge for Jews, and this became law on April 7. On April 4, ghettoization procedures were prepared by Endre and appropriate instructions sent to the provinces, also on April 7. German documentation shows that while the new German ambassador was discussing the transportation into the Reich of 50,000, and later 100,000, Jews for labor, Eichmann was busy organizing deportations quite independently; in the end the RSHA agreed to ship the slave labor from Auschwitz after "selection" (that is, after murdering all those incapable of working). Ghettoization began in mid-April, and the first Hungarian train to Auschwitz left the camp at Kistarcsa, not far from Budapest, on April 28. Large-scale deportations started on May 14, after the prisoners had endured a period of the most frightful mistreatment in temporary, open-air detention places. Crammed into cattle cars, Jews of the provinces, starting from the PKR and continuing through the other Hungarian regions, were deported to their deaths. Only those transferred to slave labor were spared—temporarily.[16]

For the historian, one of the basic questions regarding the destruction of Hungarian Jewry is whether the Jews knew what was in store for them. Those who have commented on this crucial theme seem sometimes to have mistaken information for knowledge or understanding.[17] There is no doubt that both the leadership and the general Jewish population had fairly accurate information regarding was was happening in Poland. The basic facts of the mass murder were established by BBC broadcasts heard in Hungary and by reports from Slovakia, Rumania, and Yugoslavia, while the massacre of 14,000–16,000 Jews at Kamenets Podolskiy was known to large numbers of Hungarian Jews. At the end of 1943, 5,000 members of the labor battalions returned from the Ukraine and told their relatives all over the country what had happened. Thousands of Polish refugees arrived, and many of those that at first congregated in Budapest were afterwards dispersed for security reasons in other places, carrying their first-hand knowledge with them. The argument that Hungarian Jews were unaware of what had been happening in Poland, and, had they been informed "in time," would have taken precautionary measures, simply cannot be taken seriously. In fact, recent research has established that a special department for provincial matters within the central Judenrat in Budapest was handed over to the Zionists in the knowledge that they would use it to convey information to the provincial ghettos as quickly as possible. Members of Zionist youth movements tried to warn local Judenräte that they were going to be deported to their deaths. They were not listened to; they were chased out of the ghettos. It could not happen here. Until the very last, Hungarian Jews chose to believe they were being transported to labor camps within Hungary.

JA had tried to persuade the Va'adah of the need to prepare armed resistance early in 1944, and had even nominated the Va'adah's Moshe Schweiger to serve as commander. Some arms were collected, but the committee entertained grave doubts as to the possibility of any armed action. The youth movements had few members; the Jewish population was not concentrated; the Jewish men were in labor battalions; no help could be expected from the non-Jewish population; there was no base from which to start operations; and the majority of Hungarian Jews would be entirely opposed to such action. Besides, there simply was not enough time for preparations. Immediately upon the entry of the Germans, Schweiger was arrested and ultimately sent to Mauthausen, to be liberated towards the end of the war by Kasztner's intervention.[18]

Having rejected the possibilty of preparing an armed uprising, the Va'adah turned to other possibilities. Apparently it was Moshe Krausz's task to try to mobilize the help of the neutral countries, and Otto Komoly tried, largely in vain, to influence right-wing Hungarian politicians to exercise a moderating influence. Brand and Kasztner were to contact the Germans, on the assumption that if a bribe had worked in Slovakia it might again. Meanwhile, the youth movements, while working in coordination with the Va'adah, relied on it less. Under an ad hoc leadership of their own—Peretz Revesz of Makabi Hatzair, Moshe Alpan and Rafi Friedel of Hashomer Hatzair, Zvi Goldfarb of Dror, and members of the Noar Zioni and Bnei Akiva groups—they also established an illegal network to produce forged papers and organize escape routes. Menahem Klein was in charge of these routes. Probably 3,000–4,000 Hungarian Jews escaped into Rumania and about 2,500 into Slovakia, mostly Slovak Jews.[19]

JDC was involved as a funding agency in all these activities, but its participation in the German negotiations was especially important. Shortly after the occupation of Budapest, Wisliceny went back to Bratislava, where he talked to Gizi Fleischmann and Michael Weissmandel, receiving letters of recommendation from them to leaders of Hungarian Orthodoxy and to the Zionists. Armed with these letters, Wisliceny contacted Fülop von Freudiger, but Freudiger seems to have been more interested in saving the members of his own Orthodox group than in a general rescue effort. On March 24, Kasztner and Brand met with the Abwehr people, who had arranged the contact with the SS, and with Wisliceny. Their proposal to the Nazis closely followed the Europa Plan negotiations in Slovakia: they offered $2 million for a guarantee that Hungarian Jews would not be ghettoized or deported, and $200,000 were to be paid as an immediate down payment. In his answer, Wisliceny seems to have promised that there would be no deportations, but said that he doubted whether the $2 million would suffice. He would accept the down payment. What seems to have been the basic inducement was Kasztner's statement that the money had to be obtained from abroad. Even in his postwar testimony, Wisliceny still referred to Kasztner as JDC's representative, and it was this connection which was uppermost in the minds of the Nazis.[20] Other details were also discussed. The Abwehr was promised $20,000 out of the first $200,000, with $2,000 going directly to Winninger. It is clear that this was simply another case of extortion, but Wisliceny must have reported it to Eichmann, and it formed an introduction to the negotiations that were to follow. A request for emigration to Palestine was rejected, but, according to Kasztner, negotiations regarding the emigration of a large number of people nevertheless could be entered into.

The first payment of 3 million ($92,000) of the 6.5 million pengö (the equivalent of $200,000) was received by Hermann Krumey and Otto Hunsche for Eichmann on April 9. Wisliceny was out of the running; it seems that Eichmann thought him too soft. For the Jews, the appearance of additional SS men was a sign that the money was indeed going to the organization rather than into private pockets. Some members of the Va'adah who had been arrested were set free, and the Germans promised further meetings. At a third meeting with the Nazis on April 21, the Jews could pay only 2.5 ($77,000) instead of the 3.5 million pengö ($107,000) still outstanding, and Hunsche especially was most indignant about this breach of promise. The Nazis, after all, were gentlemen. However, Dr. Josef Schmidt, the Abwehr chief, said that while deportations were unavoidable, 600 Jews with Palestine immigration certificates might be allowed to emigrate.

While these negotiations were going on, and while the youth movements were increasing their illegal activities, Eichmann intervened personally. On April 25, he summoned Joel Brand and offered to send him wherever he wanted to go outside of Nazi Europe in order to negotiate for payment in kind for the release of one million Jews, who could be taken from anywhere in Nazi-controlled territory. Trucks were mentioned as possible objects to be bartered for Jews, but no firm statement was made by Eichmann on the subject. In effect, Brand was asked to formulate an offer. Brand's answer was noncommittal on the payment, but he agreed to go, choosing Istanbul, where he said he hoped to negotiate with the JA representatives. Why Eichmann should have picked Brand for the mission is unclear. Kasztner, the moving spirit in the Va'adah, objected to Brand's going, but the fact that Eichmann had made his choice gave the Va'adah no option but to yield on this point. Kasztner and other members of the organization thought that Brand had neither the diplomatic experience nor the strength of character for a mission of that magnitude. Kasztner stated in his report that "the question whether the sending of another person might not have influenced the outcome of the Istanbul negotiations will remain unanswered [here]."[21]

A second meeting between Eichmann and Brand took place a few days after the first (the exact date is unclear), and it appears that Edmund Veesenmayer, a high SS officer and the German ambassador in Budapest, was present. This indicates that the Eichmann offer was backed by important Nazi interests.[22] "Some days after these events"—probably around May 8—Eichmann again summoned Brand. At that meeting he gave him, according to Brand's account, 270,000 sfr. ($61,000) and over $50,000 in cash and a bunch of letters from Switzerland. The whole bundle had been sent by Mayer to the Swedish embassy in Budapest for Brand, but the SS, with the help of Grosz, managed to get hold of it. They decided to hand it over to the Jews. Eichmann talked in the presence of Otto Klages, the SD commander in Budapest, which might indicate that Himmler was checking on Eichmann's conduct of the negotiations. Eichmann offered to blow up Auschwitz and deliver the first 100,000 Jews immediately after receiving information from Istanbul that agreement had been reached regarding the sending of trucks (one truck per hundred Jews). The trucks, he promised, would not be used against the West. In addition, an unspecified quantity of coffee, tea, chocolate, and other foodstuffs would be required. Brand agreed to try to obtain these goods in exchange for Jews' lives.[23]

Brand's report is peculiar in one important respect. We know from other sources that Mayer paid out to Schwalb and to a courier the sums of 50,000 sfr. ($11,000) on April 11, 1944, 150,000 sfr. ($33,000) on April 30, and 200,000 sfr. ($45,000) on May 2. Brand quotes from a letter by Mayer dated May 4, so one must assume that Eichmann handed the money to Brand after that date; even assuming that all three sums were in the same parcel, they still do not amount to 270,000 sfr. plus $50,000 (there were about 4.39 sfr. per dollar at that time). Eichmann's motives in handing over this money—and, more important, the accompanying letters—to Brand are equally unclear. Was it a contemptuous gesture, a typical game played by the cat with the mouse that is about to be destroyed? Did he want to show the Jews that all their contacts were in his hands and thereby assure himself of their full cooperation? Was it part of a power game between himself and other SS groups?

In early May, the rivalry between the Abwehr and the SS in Budapest came to a head. This is the more peculiar because in February the Abwehr was actually abolished as an independent organization. It was removed from Admiral Wilhelm Canaris's hands and taken over by Walter Schellenberg, head of the SD. Schellenberg was later to try to extricate Himmler and Germany from the war by making contacts with the West; it is likely that in early 1944, while taking over the Abwehr's contacts with Allied intelligence services, he saw the possibility of using them for the SS for the same purpose as that intended by the Abwehr: preparation of a separate peace with the West. It is not at all clear to whom the Budapest Abwehr bureau owed allegiance between March and May, 1944, yet it was important because it controlled the routes to Istanbul. There are hints that it had some connections with the opposition groups within the German army who attempted to assassinate Hitler on July 20, 1944.[24] In any case, it seems obvious that the Schellenberg group, represented in Budapest by Otto Klages, would want to maintain the Istanbul contacts and at the same time remove them from the control of the rather unreliable group that had formed around Schmidt, head of the Budapest Abwehr. Bandi Grosz, the chief courier to Istanbul, realized that the Abwehr people in Budapest were now in trouble. He was arrested by the SS twice and allowed himself to be persuaded to betray his former Abwehr friends; Joel Brand, who was at the time friends with Grosz, also implicates himself in the betrayal of the Abwehr group in his own account of the episode. The group was arrested and confronted with Brand, who then told the SS what they wanted to know, mainly regarding money matters.[25]

Klages and Eichmann thereupon sent Brand and Grosz to Istanbul. Brand, of course, was to present the Nazi offer of trading Jewish lives for goods. Grosz, on the other hand, was instructed by Klages directly to "arrange a meeting in any neutral country between two or three senior German security officers and two or three American officers of equivalent rank, or 'as a last resort,' British officers, in order to negotiate for a 'separate peace' between the Sicherheitsdienst and the Western Allies." If that failed, a meeting was to be arranged with the British through the mediation of the Zionists in Istanbul.[26]

Brand certainly had a general idea of what the Grosz proposals contained. Yet he obviously thought his mission was the more important one from the German point of view; that was the impression he conveyed to the Istanbul Zionists and it was transmitted to the Allies. Whether he was right is more than doubtful. Klages told Grosz that his orders came from Himmler—nor could it have been otherwise, considering the implications of the SD offer. Himmler may well have thought that the Jewish part of the mission was a good way of opening negotiations with the West because the West was controlled by the Jews and was likely to exert itself to save a million Jewish lives. Certainly, for obvious political reasons, Grosz was the core of the mission, though Brand could serve to provide a good reason for negotiations that might start with the Jews and lead to other matters.

Nevertheless, considering that the Allies were eager to maintain their wartime alliance with Russia, that they had decided to see the utter destruction of Nazi Germany, that they were reluctant to accept large numbers of refugees for whom they would have no places of refuge, and that the Allied landing in Normandy occured on the very day Brand left Istanbul for Palestine, Himmler's peace feelers were obviously doomed to failure. In British eyes, Brand was a terrorized instrument of the Nazis and Grosz a Gestapo agent. The proposals were designed to split the Allied front and either lead to inadmissible negotiations with the SS or provide an alibi for continued German murder of the Jews. The situation looked somewhat different in American eyes, but in any case it was soon clear to both governments that the Grosz proposals emanated from Himmler and that they were serious. But while that seemed to the British a good reason to caution against any negotiations whatsoever, the Americans thought that the door must be kept open.

The Mission of Brand and Grosz

Joel Brand and Bandi Grosz arrived in Istanbul on May 19 without Turkish visas, and the Turks did not want their neutrality put in jeopardy by emissaries with fantastic proposals from a belligerent area. The two Jews were arrested and threatened with deportation. Brand could not understand why the powerful Jewish influence could not even assure him of a Turkish visa. Although it was one of the main elements in Nazi antisemitism, Jewish power was simply an illusion, and the JA representatives could do no more than postpone the deportation of Brand and Grosz for a few days. In an eerie, emotion-charged atmosphere, aware of the awful responsibilities involved, these men discussed Brand's proposals. At first Brand did not mention the fact that the 10,000 trucks were destined for the eastern front only—this came out later, under interrogation. On May 27, when the deportation of Brand was to take place the following night, Bader wrote that they hoped Brand would not be executed immediately upon crossing into German-held territory. Brand gave Bader his personal last will. He thought that he, his family, the Va'adah, and Hungarian Jews generally were doomed. An attempt to have him deported to Palestine instead seemed to have failed. Bader managed to convince an unwilling Brand that there was no other alternative but a return to Hungary. Grosz objected, saying that he had failed to make contact with those for whom he had messages, and that without his success, both of them were doomed. At that, Brand refused categorically to return to Hungary without Grosz. Whatever their personal preferences, the situation on May 30 was that both men were to be deported back to German-held territory.

On May 31, the British suddenly decided to enable the two to leave for British-held territory, and on June 1, Grosz left for Cairo, followed by Brand on June 6. By now Brand was doubtful regarding the journey, but the JA people believed a British promise that he would be interrogated, his proposal transmitted to London, and that he would then be permitted to return to Hungary. In fact, both men were arrested and kept in Cairo for months. After the war, Brand was to accuse JA of having betrayed him by forcing him to surrender to the British. This false accusation was intended to present JA as a kind of Judenrat organization: the Hungarian Judenrat cooperated with the Nazis, and JA collaborated with Britain in foiling Brand's rescue mission. Nothing could be further from the truth.[27]

The details of the German ransom proposals, the reason for all of this activity, apparently were not very clear in Brand's mind. A comparison between his statements in Istanbul, in Cairo, his interview with Moshe Shertok of JA on June 11, and his statements to Ira A. Hirschmann some days later reveals several inconsistencies and differences. However, three basic facts emerge: the Nazis wished to exchange trucks for Jews; they were willing to send a first batch of Jews to neutral countries as a sign of goodwill if the Allies agreed in principle to their offer; and Grosz's mission was to put out feelers for a separate peace. The Brand proposals in their general outline were cabled to the War Refugee Board (WRB), the U.S. agency that had been dealing with rescue problems since January, 1944, by the American ambassador to Ankara, Laurence A. Steinhardt, on May 25. On the preceding day, Pomerantz had arrived in Palestine from Istanbul and repeated the story to Shertok, who immediately tried, with the help of Sir Harold MacMichael, the high commissioner for Palestine, to get a Turkish visa in order to prevent Brand's coming into Allied territory, whence it would be difficult to allow him to return to Hungary. But the Turks objected. Brand finally arrived at the Syrian border, and Shertok was there and interviewed him on June 11. MacMichael cabled the gist of the Brand proposals, as presented to him by Shertok and Ben Gurion, to London on June 26, a day before Shertok came there to try to save Brand's mission by negotiating with the British government.[28]

There now began a complicated exchange of cables and hurried consultations between the three major Allies. The views and policies as they evolved can perhaps be summarized by saying that the Russians categorically rejected any negotiations regarding Jews; that the British were looking for a way out of an unpleasant business without clashing openly with either the Americans or their own public opinion; and that the Americans, split between the WRB on the one hand and everyone else of any consequence on the other, were trying to keep the door open.[29] Basically, JA wanted to "dangle a carrot," in Shertok's phrase, before the Nazis' eyes, though he knew that sending any war materials to Germany was out of the question. But he also knew, and said with great force, that negotiations were in themselves a way to keep human beings alive. The WRB held a similar view; other American agencies opposed it.[30] The demand was also put forward—by Itzhak Gruenbaum of JA and by Isaac Sternbuch of VH, both on June 2—to bomb Auschwitz and/or the railway lines leading up to it. Others picked up the idea and it was presented to the western governments. The Americans rejected it on July 4 and the British followed on September 1, both arguing that there would be technical difficulties and that the diversion of the war effort to that particular mission could not be justified. That the Americans nevertheless bombed part of the Auschwitz complex in September, and flew over or attacked other targets in the general area of Upper Silesia in July, August, and September, was due to the presence there of the Buna artificial rubber factory and other military targets. It was very important to destroy the German capacity for making war goods; it was apparently less important to hamper their capacity for producing corpses.[31]

In Hungary, in the meantime, the mass deportations proceeded without letup. The provinces and the suburbs of Budapest were "cleared" of Jews; 437,402 were deported to Auschwitz.[32] The WRB, with the help of WJC, tried to counteract the murder policy by enlisting the aid of neutral governments, the IRC, and the Vatican. Prompted by the WRB, President Roosevelt issued a declaration on March 24 announcing that the United States would support those Jews who got out, and he warned the Hungarians not to lend a hand in the persecution of Jews, threatening retribution to those who did. While the British government refused to join in the appeal, pressure on the pope did result in a protest on May 15 by Angelo Rotta, the papal nuncio in Budapest. There was a vast difference between the papal protest and a pastoral letter by Cardinal Justinian Seredi, which agreed with all the antisemitic measures except the deportations. Nevertheless, the letter was suppressed (though it was read out in some of the churches on July 1, 1944) after the Hungarian government promised the cardinal that Jewish converts to Catholicism would in future be protected.

Towards the end of June, interventions against the deportations multiplied. The Swiss ambassador, Maximilien Jaeger, transmitted a stern American warning against continued deportations on June 26, and the Swiss legation announced on June 29 that Switzerland would accept 10,000 Jewish children. The IRC brought to the attention of the Hungarians a WRB proposal to feed the Jews in Hungary. On June 25, a few weeks after the conquest of Rome by the Allies, the pope implored Horthy to prevent further suffering and pain to the Jews, while on June 30, King Carl of Sweden cabled him "in the name of humanity" to save the remnant of Hungarian Jewry and Hungary's good name among nations. What appears finally to have made up Horthy's mind, however, were threats to destroy Budapest and the railways leading to Auschwitz. These were contained in reports sent from Switzerland to Washington and London and intercepted by—or perhaps intentionally leaked to—Hungarian military intelligence. Budapest was bombed on July 2; on July 6, Edmund Veesenmayer, the German ambassador to Hungary, reported to Berlin on a conversation he had had with Horthy two days previously, in which Horthy obviously was preparing the ground for a change of policy regarding the Jews. Döme Sztojay had seen Veesenmayer on July 5 and read out to him three intercepted cables, in one of which (on June 24) Roswell McClelland had outlined the proposal to bomb railway lines in Hungary and Slovakia. It is perhaps not uninteresting to note that these proposals had reached McClelland via Schwalb from Weissmandel in Slovakia, who sent them to Switzerland on May 18; by this complex network of persons working toward the mutual goal of saving Jews, the Hungarian ruler was influenced to modify his actions. He was also afraid of a possible takeover of his government by the fascist-dominated gendarmerie who had perpetrated the deportations, and he ordered loyal army units into Budapest to forestall such a move. With the Budapest situation firmly in his hands, Horthy stopped the deportations temporarily on July 9, while assuring the Germans that the Jews would soon be deported from the capital nevertheless.[33] Eichmann managed to deport just one more trainload of Jews already interned at Kistarcsa camp, but against Horthy's wishes.

As these events occurred on the international scene, JDC was a passive observer. However, JDC leaders were very well informed. Reuben Resnik in Istanbul was actually the first American to interview Brand in depth, and his report to Ambassador Steinhardt in Ankara of June 4 was the first detailed description of Brand's and Grosz's missions to reach the United States. It was also Resnik who pointed out to the WRB the far-reaching implications of the Grosz message.[34] The interventions by neutral governments in Hungary were also done with JDC's knowledge. Mayer in particular was kept in the picture, and his involvement in the

Va'adah's further attempts to negotiate with the Nazis grew slowly. From March 21 on, he began to send money to Hungary in bank notes as well as through clearance arrangements. By May 24, he had sent 539,000 sfr. ($122,000), largely through Schwalb's couriers; some of this went to the Orthodox group around Freudiger and Link, but most went to the Va'adah.

But JDC's involvement was purely financial, though the Nazis thought Kasztner represented JDC in his talks with them, and he did nothing to disabuse them of this notion. Brand, too, was supposed by the Nazis to negotiate with "World Jewry," by which the Nazis meant both JA and JDC. Brand was to have returned from these negotiations after a few weeks.

Bader in Istanbul tried to defuse the dangerous situation that was bound to arise in Budapest when Brand and Grosz did not return; they had been warned that if that happened, all Hungarian and other Jews would be killed. He sent a report to Kasztner saying that the Allies had accepted the Brand proposals in principle.[35] Eichmann of course charged Kasztner and his group with faithlessness and demanded Brand's return. But it was indicative of the mood inside the SS that Eichmann—clearly on orders from above—nevertheless continued the talks, not only with Kasztner, but even with Brand's wife Hansi, a member of the Va'adah. However, Himmler sent a new emissary, SS Obersturmbannführer Kurt Becher. Apparently Becher was a confidant of Himmler, a devout Nazi, and an adroit businessman. His first major job was to negotiate for the takeover of the Jewish-owned Manfred Weiss enterprises, Hungary's largest industrial concern. The Weiss family itself initiated the arrangement; they collected a large sum of their foreign currency holdings and were allowed to leave to Lisbon, while the SS received the right of disposal over their 51 percent share in the vast complex of industrial and war-equipment enterprises.

Towards the middle of June Kasztner got to know Becher, whom Himmler had ordered to supervise and then take over the economic and political negotiations with the Jews. Throughout June, these negotiations concentrated on permission for certain privileged Jews to escape to the neutral countries, the idea being to deliver them to the Spanish frontier.

As a result of these talks, a transport with 1,684 people actually left Budapest on July 1, but it was directed, not to the Spanish frontier as promised, but to Bergen-Belsen, which was then a transit camp for potential candidates for exchange with the

Allies. Eichmann stated in his memoirs that he had agreed to this transport in order not to be disturbed in his wholesale destruction of Hungarian Jews.[36] On the other hand, Kasztner in his postwar report argued that this was an attempt to break the principle of murder by committing the Germans to letting some Jews out—a breach that would then be widened. After the war Kasztner was accused of having tried to save his relatives and friends on the train and of having avoided warning the rest of Hungarian Jewry of the threat to their lives. However, it would appear that the motives behind the "Kasztner train" were rather close to those he stated. The train, which carried persons such as the rabbi of Satmar, Joel Teitelbaum, and representatives of practically all political and religious groups in Hungarian Jewry, could of course have been directed to Auschwitz instead of the promised neutral country, but the fact that Kasztner's own family were also on it can be seen as a demonstration of his faith that this time the Germans would indeed keep their word. Apart from Kasztner, other members of the Va'adah, especially its head, Komoly, as well as von Freudiger and his Orthodox group, were very much involved in the preparations for the train's departure. As it was, Himmler apparently forced a reluctant Eichmann to send the Jews to Bergen-Belsen. The liberation of France soon afterwards made the journey to Spain illusory in any case.[37] In the end, we shall see, the train's passengers were saved into Switzerland.

Kasztner's negotiations with the SS dealt not only with the major ransom proposal inherited from the unsuccesful Brand mission and with the so-called Kasztner train, but also with other groups of Jews. An action that resulted in the saving of lives came when the mayor of Vienna, on June 7, 1944, asked the SS to send him Jews to work in the area's factories. Eichmann presented this request to Kasztner as a great opportunity for the Jews, and he demanded more money and tractors. The tractors were promised, some coffee was delivered, and somewhere between 12,000 and 18,000 Jews were sent. Ernst Kaltenbrunner, head of the RSHA, told the mayor on June 30 that the women and children were to be held ready for a "special action"—that is, for murder—when the time came. It did not come, and we shall soon see why.[38]

17

JDC and the War Refugee Board

JDC's attitude to the Brand negotiations was largely determined by the dramatic change that occurred in the policies of the United States towards the Jews under Nazi rule. This change found expression, early in 1944, in the establishment of the WRB which, in the remaining months of World War II, was to become JDC's main partner in its attempts to extend aid to Europe's Jewish population.

The WRB originated in the Rumanian feelers of December, 1942, regarding the emigration of 70,000 Jews, described in chapter 14. The WJC and the Emergency Committee to Rescue the Jewish People pressed the State Department to do something about the supposed Rumanian offer. After protracted negotiations, $25,000 were finally permitted to be transferred to Switzerland in order to facilitate the exit of Rumanian Jews (December 23, 1943). By that time, of course, the idea of a mass Jewish exodus from Rumania had become obsolete. German objections, Rumanian hesitations, and the fact that by the end of 1943 the Russians were already on the threshold of Transnistria—all contributed to the abandonment of the emigration idea by the Rumanians. However, this fact was unknown in the West, and liberals as well as Jews in the United States saw the whole affair as a blatant case of another missed opportunity; they accused the State Department of being responsible for the delays and the opposition to the

400

scheme. The negative results of the Anglo-American conference on refugees at Bermuda in April, 1943, also reverberated throughout the year. There, too, the State Department had been responsible for the acceptance of the British policy of not doing anything to save victims of Nazism while the war was in progress.

These developments were carefully watched by a group of young New Dealers who were working at the Treasury Department, under Secretary Henry Morgenthau, Jr. They were liberals and not Jewish: John W. Pehle, Josiah E. DuBois, Jr., and Randolph Paul were the chief figures. They were alarmed at the obviously antisemitic antics of Assistant Secretary of State Breckinridge Long, and their ire was aroused by the fact that the State Department had actually ordered Minister Leland Harrison in Bern not to transmit any further reports by WJC's Gerhart Riegner at Geneva on the mass murder of Jews. This instruction was sent after a particularly harrowing account had been transmitted by Riegner through the American legation on January 21, 1943. Throughout 1943, Long and some other officials at the State Department did all they could to prevent information regarding the fate of European Jews from reaching the American policy-making bodies. A dossier on the attitude of the State Department was assembled by the Treasury officials, and a reluctant Morgenthau was slowly convinced that drastic measures were needed if any help were to be extended by the U.S. government to the Jews. A meeting between Secretaries Morgenthau and Cordell Hull on December 10, 1943, proved to Morgenthau that his State Department colleague was tired, inattentive, and not really in command. Attempts of State Department officials to hide cables from Bern that might be inconvenient to them brought about action. On January 17, 1944, Morgenthau, Pehle, and DuBois went to see President Roosevelt and confronted him with a memorandum prepared at the Treasury, originally entitled "Report to the Secretary on the Acquiescence of this Government in the Murder of Jews," but changed by Morgenthau to "Personal Report to the President."[1]

Roosevelt readily agreed with the main recommendation of this report, which was to establish a special government agency to deal with the problem of Nazi victims. His reasons were, as so often with him, a combination of humanitarian impulses and very strong political reasons. A storm had been brewing in Congress and in the press for some time. A War Crimes Declaration issued after the inter-Allied conference at Moscow on November 1, 1943,

401

failed to indict the Nazis for the murder of the Jews, though all the other peoples who were in any way harmed by the Germans were duly listed. Attacks on the government's attitude appeared in the press, and the Emergency Committee to Save the Jewish People and the American Jewish Congress were especially active. The Emergency Committee triggered congressional hearings in November dealing with the administration's stance toward refugees, and Long's testimony on November 26 was self-incriminating. He said that the IGCR was empowered to negotiate with Germany to alleviate Jewish suffering (which was not at all the case), and he quoted figures of Jews who had been admitted to the United States since 1933 which were wildly wrong and were promptly refuted. In the State Department itself, Edward Stettinius took the place of Sumner Welles in September as undersecretary, and Roosevelt could make the department a scapegoat for the lack of action in the past without changing conditions in the present.

The creation of the WRB was therefore not pure humanitarianism by any means. The president yielded to a combination of public pressure, organized largely by the Emergency Committee of the Irgun and, quite independently, by a small group of non-Jewish Treasury officials exercising constant pressure on Secretary Morgenthau. On January 22, 1944, Presidential Executive Order No. 9417 established a War Refugee Board to deal with attempts to rescue victims of the Nazis. The amazing thing about the WRB was the extent to which it was permitted to ride roughshod over the laws and regulations of a United States at war. It was to "take all measures" "consistent with the successful prosecution of the war" to "rescue the victims of enemy oppression." It was to deal with rescue, transportation, maintenance, and relief; it was to engage in negotiations with foreign governments to the end of establishing havens; it could employ personnel without regard to the civil service laws and the Classification Act; it was to appoint special attachés to U.S. representatives abroad. In addition, the secretary of the treasury, with Roosevelt's concurrence, "vested in the WRB . . . full authority to communicate with enemy territory to carry out the purpose of the order" establishing the WRB. Other agencies could be authorized by WRB's local representative to act similarly. Heads of all government agencies had the duty to extend shipping, supplies, and any other assistance needed to the board. In effect, WRB executives told the attachés they sent abroad that under special circumstances they could engage in negotiations with enemy agents.[2]

The presidential press release which accompanied the executive order mentioned "the plan to exterminate all the Jews and other persecuted minorities in Europe," though the order itself did not. The addition of the "other persecuted minorities" in the sentence dealing with "extermination" showed two things: that Nazi verbiage (the word "extermination" was previously used only about vermin) was seeping into civilized usage; and that it was still unacceptable, or perhaps unbearable, to talk of the specific and unique position of the Jews in the Nazi universe. In order to make the new policy palatable, "other" had to be added.[3] Yet what made WRB such a unique body is that it was officially permitted to break practically every important law of a nation at war in the name of outraged humanity. True, its inception was politically motivated, and the execution of its designs was often beset with difficulties. The saving of Jews would be a good point in every future political campaign of the Roosevelt administration and its successor. But Jews, while important, were not *that* important; and in the case of their Palestine ambitions, the United States showed a markedly more reluctant attitude. The Jews themselves did not really press very hard for rescue, and their propaganda for Palestine often seemed stronger than their concern for immediate steps to save their brethren. There is at least a case for arguing that the establishment of WRB was a rare occasion, on which moral imperatives broke through into practical politics, and the complicated web of a wartime policy was cut in the name of a lifesaving mission. Even if it had accomplished nothing else, this fact would have given the WRB an important place in contemporary history.

JDC not only had nothing to do with these developments, but indeed was largely unaware of what was going on. The establishment of WRB caused Leavitt to hurry to Washington in order to find out what JDC's position would be in the new situation. Yet it was JDC funds that were to sustain WRB's work in the coming crucial months, and it was JDC personnel all over the world that were to prove WRB's staunchest allies.

The heads of WRB were, nominally, the secretaries of the State, Treasury, and War departments. But in fact it was John Pehle, the former Treasury Department official responsible for licensing transmittals of funds abroad, who as acting director ran the show, with the loyal support of Morgenthau. The original idea was that a permanent director with political clout be found to replace him. It is not quite clear whether this idea was abandoned because the WRB was not considered important enough by prospective candidates or because Pehle proved to be an efficient and very active head of the new organization. In any case, he eventually became executive director. Pehle placed a number of talented men as attachés in Europe. There was Iver Olsen in Stockholm and James Mann in London. The choice of Ira A. Hirschmann, an executive of Bloomingdale's department store, as WRB representative in Turkey seems to have been more or less forced on him. But for Switzerland, the other important spot, he chose Roswell McClelland, who had behind him close to four years' experience in Italy, France and Switzerland as a relief worker for the Quakers. He was to become the key man in WRB's attempts to help Jews in Hungary and elsewhere.

With the establishment of WRB, licenses for the transfer of funds no longer presented a problem. The question was, how could the board best pursue the task with which it had been entrusted? Pehle's general attitude was that, while small groups of Jews or others should certainly be taken out of Nazi territory whenever possible, emphasis should be laid on exerting pressure on the satellite and the neutral countries, and on international agencies, to prevent the deportation and murder of Jews. This policy was pursued, for instance, in the case of the IRC, when Harrison was asked by Pehle, on March 27, 1944, and again on May 25, to press the Red Cross to send effective representatives to Budapest who could then try to protect the Jews. The Swiss government was also asked to increase the number of its representatives in Hungary, at the same time and for the same purpose.[4] Gerhart Riegner of WJC and Saly Mayer of JDC made parallel efforts. Both the IRC and the Swiss government gradually increased the number of their representatives and also equipped them with greater powers, but this was a slow process which culminated in energetic action only towards the end of 1944. Friendly pressure was also exerted by WRB on neutral countries other than Switzerland, such as Sweden and Turkey. In the end it was the combined pressure of Sweden, Switzerland, the Vatican, IRC, and the United States—but mainly direct U.S. threats as transmitted to Admiral Nicholas Horthy by the Swiss legation in Budapest (together with the bombing of the city)—that influenced the Hungarian government to stop the deportations to Auschwitz early in July, 1944.

JDC was involved with WRB in several ways. First, there was the funding of JDC's own operations in Europe, which now proceeded smoothly, thanks to Pehle's wholehearted cooperation in issuing licenses. Second, there was the financing of WRB operations, which were not necessarily concerned with rescuing or aiding only Jewish victims of Nazism. JDC was the main source of money for such operations, which were then credited to WRB. These included, for instance, the financing of a small, democratically oriented German underground group, the financing of subversive pro-Allied activities in northern Italy, and similar undertakings.

But the third and most significant area involved ventures where JDC and WRB cooperated, not just on the financial level, but in actual operations. These took place in Lisbon, where Schwartz was in direct contact with Pehle, thus ensuring overall coordination between the two agencies, and where problems of transferring Jews from France via Spain to North Africa were dealt with; in Istanbul, where attempts were made to get Jews out of the Balkan countries; and in Switzerland, where a special relationship began to develop between Roswell McClelland and Saly Mayer regarding problems in Central Europe.

Cooperation in Lisbon was smooth. Ira Hirschmann was appointed to the WRB post in Turkey on February 12, 1944, and his main task was to find one or more ships that could transport Rumanian, or Transnistrian, Polish, and Hungarian Jews from Rumanian ports to Istanbul. For three months, Hirschmann tried to get a ship from the reluctant Turks or from Sweden. The Turks, however, were not willing to send one of their few commercial vessels into the Black Sea without guarantees from all the belligerents and without being assured that they would get a full replacement if the ship were lost. The WRB in Washington obtained such an assurance and sent it to Hirschmann. After a series of negotiations, the S.S. *Tari* was bought and fitted. But the Germans refused to give a safe conduct, and the vessel could not set out. Hirschmann, a rather flamboyant figure with a flair for publicity and dramatization, denigrated the small-scale efforts of JA's illegal immigration representatives (from the Mossad organization) and made a lot of enemies. He was severely criticized to JA and to JDC by the group of Jewish emissaries in Istanbul. But the major problem simply was his failure to get the ship.[5]

Hirschmann's negotiations with the Rumanian minister in Ankara, Alexander Cretzianu, were another case of self-dramatization. The talks took place early in August, 1944, at a time when Transnistria was already overrun by Russian armies and whatever

remnant was left of the Jewish deportees there was already stream-
ing back to Rumania. Undoubtedly the talks made clear to the
Rumanians that they would have to continue with their more le-
nient policies towards the Jews, but they agreed to the exit of Jews
and to their protection against German designs at the last moment
before the collapse of the Axis. Hirschmann had not yet appeared
on the scene: his efforts only strengthened an already existing
tendency.

JDC was in constant contact with Hirschmann, and with
Ambassador Laurence A. Steinhardt, a Jew of German ancestry
who belonged to the same social circles as most of the JDC leadership. Steinhardt had been rather hesitant on Jewish matters before 1944, but he had become a staunch supporter of any serious
rescue plan put forward by WRB, JDC, or anyone else. Nevertheless, it was clearly in JDC's interest to have a representative at
Istanbul, and in February, Reuben B. Resnik was sent from America to the Mediterranean. Problems soon developed between him
and the JDC's Middle East Advisory Committee, whose head was
Judah L. Magnes in Jerusalem. The area was much too large, and
Resnik did not really manage to control it. His work in Istanbul
got into difficulties rather early on, when he got little cooperation
from Hirschmann, and his overbearing attitude toward JA personnel, including a demand that the supremacy in policy making
should be conceded to JDC, made him unpopular. Resnik's notion was to send a number of American JDC executives to the
various European countries and take over all rescue and aid work.
But this was quite unrealistic—JDC had to work through the established agencies, and its attempt to enter the Istanbul center
must be judged to have been a failure. Neither Resnik nor Hirschmann made much headway in Istanbul. In the end, both WRB
and JDC were satisfied to support and strengthen JA's existing
rescue machinery.

The relative failure of WRB in Istanbul was an exception to
the rule. WRB support considerably strengthened both JDC and
WJC, which now entered the lists much more effectively, concentrating on political interventions with the neutral countries, IRC,
the World Council of Churches, and the Vatican. The lack of
coordination between the two Jewish groups—due very largely to
JDC's conservatism—probably prevented greater success, however. JDC could and did call upon WRB's political support in
financing its work from Shanghai through Rumania and France,
and Mayer's efforts in Switzerland gained a great deal from the

fact that he now knew he had, in his talks with Swiss banks and government officials, the backing of the U.S. government. On the other hand, WRB, while supporting Jewish organizations who tried to help, was given no American government or private non-Jewish funds of any importance to initiate actions. The WRB received an appropriation from the U.S. government of $1,150,000, of which it returned $603,000 at the end of the war, but it received $15 million from JDC directly; $5 million were obtained from other groups, most of whom were also subsidized by JDC.[6] The WRB acted courageously and imaginatively to save non-Jews as well as Jews, presumably with money from Jewish organizations. The conclusion, inevitably, is that the WRB was an expression of moral and political support by the administration to save Jews with Jewish means.

This conclusion does not detract in any way from the efforts of the men who represented WRB to save lives. Foremost among them was Roswell D. McClelland, who stood together with Saly Mayer to pick up the thread of the attempt to rescue Jews by negotiating with the Nazis which had been left dangling in a vacuum when the Brand mission failed.

18

JDC's Swiss Negotiations

By mid-July, 1944, it had become clear that the Allies would not consider the proposals advanced by Joel Brand and Bandi Grosz in the form in which they had been brought from Nazi Europe. The Russians, eager to prevent any separate negotiations with Germany, were deeply suspicious of the humanitarian motives and saw in any move to save Nazi victims a subterfuge for separate peace talks and a betrayal of the common cause. Their sentiments were shared to some extent by the British. Chief Rabbi J. H. Hertz had suggested to Foreign Secretary Anthony Eden on June 6, 1944, that all European Jews should be declared to be under British protection, arguing that such a declaration would have no practical consequences because these Jews would not claim British citizenship after the war. However, in the meantime it might protect them against murder. But Eden demurred. "To offer Jews, and Jews only, priority of escape as British-protected persons would overlook the fact that German brutality has been directed very extensively, above all in Poland, against non-Jews."[1]

Eden's statement was of course true, but his insensitivity to the Jews' unique position as victims of a total rather than a selective annihilation was indicative of a more general attitude he shared with many British officials. When faced with a request to discuss the Hungarian situation and the Brand mission with Haim Weizmann and Moshe Shertok of JA, Eden minuted: "What do you say? Must I? Which of my colleagues looks after this? At least one of them should be there if I have to see those two Jews."[2] It is therefore not surprising that, at a meeting of the British Cabinet Committee on Refugees on May 31, 1944, general apprehension was articulated concerning WRB and all it meant. The WRB had "committed itself to the 'rescue' of Jews," and ransom schemes might unfortunately get support in the United States. Negotiations with the Germans were opposed, among other reasons, on the grounds that "there seemed to be some danger that an indication we might negotiate . . . might . . . lead to an offer to unload an even greater number of Jews on our hands."[3] At first the British agreed to the WRB suggestion that Switzerland should be asked to tell the Germans that the Allies would agree to take certain categories of Jews, but that no ransom would be paid. But on July 13, Eden informed the committee that Churchill had vetoed the suggestion. Grosz's interrogation had reached London that morning, and it had become clear that Brand's mission had been a cover for German peace feelers. Therefore no negotiations of any kind could be entered into for fear of Russian reactions. Brand would be allowed to return to Hungary, but he could say nothing to the Germans.[4]

American attitudes varied much more, and the WRB had a much greater impact on thinking in the American government than had the pro-Jewish groups in Britain. While the British accused the Americans of succumbing to political considerations connected with the Jewish vote, against the best interests of the common war effort, in fact, WRB was firmly controlled by a group of non-Jews with humanitarian motives. A way had to be found to save Jewish lives without impeding the war effort. On June 9, John Pehle informed Undersecretary of State Stettinius that President Roosevelt had "agreed with our thought that we should keep the negotiations open if possible." Negotiations could gain time, "in the hope that meanwhile the lives of many intended victims will be spared."[5] In other words, while no goods or money would be delivered, and certainly no separate peace made, the very fact of negotiations might save the Jews until final victory delivered them from Nazi hands. This was precisely the attitude of JA also.

The difference between the attitudes of the two western governments became clear after the deportations stopped in early July, 1944. For one thing, the details of the Brand proposals were apparently leaked to the British press, and on July 20, all the major London dailies published and commented on them—negatively, of course. But continued British resistance to large-scale rescue operations was particularly evident in the government's response to plans for emigrating at least some Hungarian Jews to Palestine. As early as June 24, Moshe Krausz, the head of the Budapest Palestine Office, who was hiding in the Swiss legation, had asked for British citizenship to be conferred on as many Budapest Jews as possible.[6] This idea was rejected, but the British promised that they would issue a few thousand Palestine certificates. The Hungarians were eager to repair the damage done to their image in western eyes by the deportations. With the increasing Russian threat to their borders, they were preparing to sue for a separate peace. Frightened by the heavy bombardment of Budapest on July 2 by American bombers, they offered to release certain categories of Jews, mainly the Palestine certificate holders. The offer, which included 8,700 persons and another 1,000 orphans, was communicated to WRB by the IRC representative in Washington on July 25.[7]

The British then stated that the 8,700 permits would be to individuals, not families, but they were too late—the Hungarians were willing to let out 40,000 souls. The British were "perturbed." Palestine could not accept anything like that number; the White Paper policy had to be maintained. Negotiations regarding smaller Jewish emigration from Hungary should be conducted through Sir Herbert Emerson's IGCR, which was firmly under British control. "Urgent action should be taken to stop this movement" out of Hungary, which the United States had agreed to only because of "political motives." One can almost feel the sigh of relief when the British learned that the Germans would not allow the Jews to leave anyway. Eichmann reiterated the new position of the SS to Kasztner: "To extract necessary labor from Hungarian Jewry and sell the balance of valueless human material against valuable goods."[8]

German documentation seems to indicate that the idea of either selling or giving the Jews to the West, or of using them for labor instead of murdering all of them, was at that stage present in Nazi minds. On April 4, 1944, Veesenmayer asked Nazi Foreign Minister Ribbentrop whether anything had come of the idea the minister had suggested to the Führer of offering all the Jews as a present to Roosevelt and Churchill. On the other hand, the Jägerstab, the German agency in charge of economic warfare, was finding itself desperately short of labor. It asked for 100,000 Hungarian Jews on April 14. The Hungarian prime minister, Döme Sztojay, had already promised 50,000 for that month, but the SS told the Jägerstab that it would receive its Jewish slaves from Auschwitz only. Most Hungarian Jewish males were of course in labor battalions, so that the majority of the laborers sent from Auschwitz to Germany after selection and the murder of those unfit to work were women. When the Hungarians began to respond to the various pressures to release some Jews, the German reaction was at first negative, despite the April exchange of cables. On July 6, the Foreign Office in Berlin said the proposals should be shelved, and by the time an answer was given there would no longer be any Jews in Hungary. But Hitler decided differently: Ribbentrop informed Veesenmayer that the Führer had accepted his proposal to allow the Hungarians to release Jews to Sweden, Switzerland, and the United States, but not to Palestine, because of the Nazi alliance with the Palestinian Arabs.[9] The decision to murder the Jews en masse was not, or not any longer, the only course possible in Nazi eyes.

One must not forget that these events were unknown, or at least not known with certainty, in the free countries. Yet it must have been obvious that the Germans were very interested in continuing the negotiations. Bader in Istanbul received hints of another offer to negotiate in the second half of June. On July 8, Colonel Stiller of the German consulate in Istanbul approached him directly and offered to fly him to Berlin the same evening. He spoke in the name of the German Foreign Office, though it is more likely that Walter Schellenberg and the SS stood behind this initiative, because he spoke in the name of "Direktor Schroeder," an alias of Fritz Laufer, one of Otto Klages's confidants in the Budapest SD. Laufer represented the SS, which was interested in the separate peace negotiations, whereas the German Foreign Office supported the unyielding Hitler line against any talks with the Allies. Menahem Bader asked Ben Gurion for instructions, and was told on July 9 that he should wait. The British immediately refused their permission, and Bader did not go. However, the Germans tried again. This time, on Kasztner's suggestion, they tried to meet with Joseph Schwartz, head of JDC-Lisbon. The suggestion reached Pehle on July 26, and the next day he informed Stettinius about it, proposing that the idea should be turned down.[10] Schwartz was told accordingly the next day, and the British were also made acquainted with the development.

The First Stage: The Bridge at Saint Margarethen

With the receipt by Kasztner and the Budapest SS of the American refusal to allow Schwartz to negotiate with the Nazis, the name of Saly Mayer cropped up as a possible negotiator. On August 1, Kasztner, who did not know that Schwartz would not be allowed to negotiate, mentioned the desirability of meeting at the Swiss border and asked that Mayer and Schwalb attend the talks with Schwartz. JDC informed WRB of the proposal and WRB asked Roswell McClelland what he thought of Mayer as a negotiator. On August 11, McClelland suggested to Washington that the WRB agree to the negotiations, provided that Mayer managed to get Swiss approval. The aim, he said, obviously reflecting Mayer's suggestions, was "to draw out the negotiations and gain as much time as possible without, if feasible, making any commitments."[11]

Acting on the assumption that he would be asked to negotiate with the Nazis, Mayer prepared himself for the talks during the first days of August. His initial task was to find out what JDC thought he could offer and what he should demand. On August 6, Mayer talked to Schwartz.

> One thing has been made quite clear to us . . . if nothing is being done all Jews are lost. We [shall] adopt the policy of gaining time and then everything [will be] OK on account of the already changed political situation in Hungary and elsewhere. We shall deceive them of being quite serious, of entertaining all their demands regarding merchandise. . . . do you agree to negotiations on basis of food if they insist on merchandise being made available?

But on the very next day, a cable from Schwartz instructed him in clear language not to offer goods as ransom without express prior approval from JDC-New York. He was now in a quandary, because Kasztner cabled him on the same day that the only possible basis for the negotiations would be the supply of goods.[12]

The next question was whether he could offer ransom money. The answer was not at first quite clear, but in any case his resources were strictly limited. He received $6,467,000 in 1944, and was to receive another $4,600,000 between January and May, 1945. These sums far exceeded those he could dispose of in previous years, but it is immediately clear that they also fell very much short of the needs of 1944, even without the ransom negotiations. He had to spend $1,913,000 for refugees in Switzerland in 1944, and another $1,850,000 went to Rumania and France. That left him with $2.7 million for everything else, including Shanghai, parcels to Poland, Zagreb, Italy, and Slovakia.[13] It must be made clear once more that the fable about a rich "Uncle Saly" who hesitated to spend his millions was just that—a fable.

Mayer did not act completely on his own. He relied on a few trusted friends: Pierre Bigar, one of the SIG leaders, and, chiefly, Marcus Wyler-Schmidt, his lawyer and sole intimate friend. The only representative of a Jewish organization who was to be at least partially consulted was Nathan Schwalb; no other Jewish representative was let into the secret, although he also trusted Roswell McClelland. Nevertheless, he did not much like the idea of complete control by the WRB. He complained to Schwartz: "We are appointing them as our nurses, governesses, all will be controlled and checked." Schwartz answered: "You are quite right, they are not even nice-looking nurses, but it cannot be helped."[14]

Mayer, a loyal Swiss citizen, had to obtain the agreement of his government to the delicate negotiations ahead. On August 8 he met with Heinrich Rothmund, the chief of the Alien Police, and asked for an advance agreement to receive immediately 500 people from the Kasztner train interned at Bergen-Belsen, if the Nazis released them, and 1,700 later (he did not realize that the total number of this group was less than 1,700). Mayer had heard that 15,000 Hungarian Jews had been deported to Austria, and he asked that these be admitted too. Rothmund replied that only children and adults with relatives in Switzerland would be allowed to enter. The main point in his reply was that the Swiss government would not permit ransom to be offered, and people released against ransom would be forbidden entry into Switzerland. On August 10, these restrictions were repeated to Mayer, and he was told that nothing could be done that would endanger Swiss neutrality.[15]

Mayer also approached the IRC. The answer—we do not know the exact date of it—was clear. "It was definitely declared by the International Red Cross Committee that it could on no account associate with people who would use illegal means for rescuing Jews."[16]

These preliminary inquiries with JDC, the Swiss, and IRC showed Mayer that his task would be far from easy. While waiting for the decisive American instructions, he decided that he had to make a first clear demand of the Nazis, and in a letter to Budapest on August 10, he demanded the release of 500 internees from Bergen-Belsen, despite the unsatisfactory answer he had received from Rothmund on their eventual entry into Switzerland. But his main problem was what he could use to lure the Germans with, and there even McClelland abandoned him. Asked by WRB what he thought Mayer should offer, McClelland answered on August 11: "It is impossible to embark upon a program of buying Jews out of Nazi hands, especially in exchange for goods which might enable the enemy to prolong the war."[17]

On August 21, the WRB replied to McClelland's queries in no uncertain terms, sending the following instructions over Cordell Hull's signature:

> While the Government of the United States still intends to pursue all practicable means with a view to relieving the desperate plight of the Jews in Hungary, it cannot enter into or authorize ransom transactions of the nature indicated by the German authorities. If it is believed that a meeting between Saly Mayer and the German authorities will result in gaining time the Board has no objections to such a meeting. In the event that a meeting should take place Saly Mayer should participate as a Swiss citizen and as a leader of the Swiss Jewish Community, and not (repeat not) as representative of any American organization.

This cable, received by McClelland on August 22, reached Mayer only after his first meeting with the Nazis. But McClelland already had informed him about the probable American answer, and Mayer decided he had to follow the guidance of "Hanukka" (as he called McClelland in his own private code). He could offer no goods, no money, and no appearance in the name of JDC.[18]

By now he had no choice. He had accepted the assignment, and on August 21, the day that the WRB cable was sent off, he met with three Nazis and a Jew in the middle of the bridge between Switzerland and Austria at Saint Margarethen, because the Swiss authorities refused the Nazis' request to enter Switzerland. His partners in the conversation were Obersturmbannführer Kurt A. Becher, Hauptsturmbannführers Max Grüson and Hermann Krumey, and Dr. Reszoe Kasztner, while he supposedly represented the Schweizerischer Unterstützungsfonds für Flüchtlinge, the Swiss counterpart of JDC for the maintenance of Jewish refugees in Switzerland. (Afterwards Mayer always used the Hebrew word *Arba*, "Four," to describe his meetings with the Nazis.) The first German proposal was that the Jews should find 10,000 trucks and other machines for agricultural purposes. German counterpayment would be effected by letting Jews leave for the United

States. The trucks would be delivered in Europe from the United States on American ships, and the exchanged Jews would be able to depart on those very ships. According to Mayer's reports, Becher desired contact regarding this plan between the so-called Sonderstab Max Grüson and JDC. Mayer says that he replied that, though he was a JDC representative, he was negotiating on behalf of his Swiss organization. He would refuse to negotiate under pressure and would not do anything that was opposed to morals. Becher replied that there was nothing immoral in his suggestions. The first train from Bergen-Belsen with 318 people from Kasztner's group had come that very day to the Swiss border to show the seriousness of German intentions. Mayer asked for some time to consult his superiors and provide an answer.

Becher reported on the meeting to Himmler on August 25 and claimed that from that moment on, because of the delivery of 300 Jews (the expression he used was "300 pieces") from Bergen-Belsen, the Jewish side was convinced of the seriousness of the German negotiators. He also declared that Mayer had expressed doubts as to the practicality of payment by trucks, and Becher suggested that Himmler should ask for minerals and industrial goods that were in short supply in Germany and unobtainable from other sources because of Allied pressure. Mayer had promised, according to Becher, to try to get an American agreement for the supply of these goods by neutral countries. Mayer had also promised to say how much money would be available for the purchases and to submit a list of materials that could be supplied immediately.[19] Himmler responded on the same day, approving Becher's line in the negotiations and instructing him to proceed with it. According to Kasztner, Becher had promised that gassings would cease, but it is extremely difficult to believe this story. It is more likely that Becher tried to prevent the deportation of the Jews of Budapest; he suggested as much in his report. Apparently in expectation of the results of the Becher-Mayer meeting, Himmler did in fact issue a definite order against it which reached Budapest on the night between August 24 and August 25, as Veesenmayer reported to Ribbentrop on the latter day.[20] This order stood after Himmler received Becher's cable. It seems, therefore, that in return for nothing more than Mayer's promise to see whether the Germans' demands would be met, Himmler was ready to desist from the deportation of Budapest Jewry.

The day after the first meeting, Mayer received the American

415

instructions. In return, after McClelland reported on the meeting, WRB enthusiastically praised Mayer's conduct. He was asked both to continue the negotiations and to draw them out as long as possible. On September 1, McClelland informed him that $2 million had been set aside in the United States for the purpose of the talks. However, no payments could be effected from this fund without WRB approval.[21] Mayer had the feeling that his position was not really understood by those who wanted him to carry on. In his own quaint English, he wrote down what he told JDC-Lisbon on September 10.

> Wherever I have a chance, in all high quarters of diplomacy and politics, I draw attention to danger at last minute . . . unless intervention is taking place, up to 800,000 Jews still in hands of 'Nasty' are in immediate danger of losing their lives. Please do take careful note of this SM message. Myself being after all also only a mortal human being, I insist on having put on record 11h59 [that is, "one minute to twelve"; this was Mayer's code for the idea of immediate danger]. From all sides I am by now well informed about 'don't' and 'noes'. But what about *do it* and *yes*? USA says, no money for ransom and no goods for 'Nasty,' but do not let negotiations break down. Well, there is not much margin to go on with. . . . Jewish question to us, to me, is of foremost and vital interest and this is being recognized and appreciated from all sides concerned and approached. But generaliter and totaliter it is only a sector. . . . Please tell me if I have left anything undone, is there anything else I might do?[22]

There was no answer.

Three more meetings followed on the bridge, on September 3, 4, and 5. Becher preferred to remain in the background, but a new person participated: Dr. Wilhelm Billitz, a converted Jew who was a director of the Weiss heavy industry trust in Budapest and who was apparently sent to represent a more moderate line than the Nazi Max Grüson. For the meeting of September 5, Mayer brought Pierre Bigar.

Unmoved by Grüson's bluster and threats, Mayer steered the negotiations away from trucks and other goods towards money, though he was not supposed to offer that either. He was in principle ready, he said, to open a bank account amounting to 5 million sfr. for the negotiations on behalf of his Swiss organization, adding that he would do his best to convince the Swiss government to permit the SS to buy goods in Switzerland, provided that the Jews under Nazi rule, including the Jews of Hungary, were kept safe. The goods, he said, would not include war matériel. Mayer was hoping for a long discussion of the kinds of goods that might be made available, and demanded of Grüson that Becher delay his report to Himmler, while he would in the meantime consult with an individual who would keep him in touch with the United States (Mayer was thinking of Joseph Schwartz).[23]

One can say that with the meeting of September 5, the first stage of the negotiations terminated. Mayer clearly far exceeded his brief, thus endangering his position vis-à-vis both the Americans and the Swiss. Yet, without actually promising the Germans anything, he had succeeded in creating the impression that it would be worth their while to continue the bargaining. Mayer reported the truth to the Americans, but apparently not the whole truth; McClelland's report to the State Department spoke only of Mayer's dilatory tactics and did not mention his declaration that a Swiss bank account for the purchasing of goods in Switzerland would be at Germany's disposal.[24]

The prospect of getting goods from Switzerland when Ribbentrop's Foreign Ministry had failed to achieve similar results probably affected Becher's attitude, and of course that of Himmler who supported him. But one must note Grüson's decisive demand in his last conversation with Mayer: he wanted to negotiate with a political representative (someone with "full political powers"). Here apparently Himmler's real aim becomes clear: Bandi Grosz's mission had failed, but possibly the Swiss JDC representative might lead Himmler's emissaries to the Americans, while the negotiations continued to be camouflaged towards the outside world, as well as towards Ribbentrop, Hitler, and even Ernst Kaltenbrunner, as a deal for goods or money in return for Jews. On September 26, in a cable to Budapest, Mayer reiterated his agreement in principle to put an account in a Swiss bank at the disposal of the Nazis. Andreas Biss, Kasztner's second in charge in Budapest, went to Otto Klages with it, and Kasztner took it to Becher. Despite Mayer's ambivalent answer and the fact that three weeks had gone by with no signs of life from him, Biss later wrote: "It was surprising with what relief, even joy, Klages and Becher received the cable and promised to transmit its contents immediately to Himmler."[25]

In the meantime Grüson lost his position, as a result, according to Kasztner and Biss, of his having joined them in an attempt to prevent the expulsion of Slovak Jews. In his stead another SS man, Herbert Kettlitz, arrived at the Swiss border on September 29 with

Billitz and Kasztner. Becher again did not appear. Kasztner tells us that Mayer complained that the Nazis were trying to make him do things he did not wish to do because "of this damned Slovak affair." After much negotiating, he again agreed to promise Becher some money. Kasztner, Billitz, and Kettlitz then composed a report to Becher according to which Mayer was prepared to pay 15 million sfr. in three monthly installments. In return, three conditions were postulated, which Kasztner claims he put into the document: an end to the deportation of Slovakian Jews; no expulsion of the Jews of Budapest; and liberation of the group in Bergen-Belsen.[26]

Mayer's and Wyler-Schmidt's account is different. According to them, Becher asked through his representatives for a visa to Zürich and demanded goods. Mayer answered that he could not deal with the matter of goods because he had not received a definitive German "shopping list." He in turn demanded the liberation of the Bergen-Belsen group. He also declared that $2 million would be at his disposal, with which the Germans would be able to buy Swiss goods on two conditions: that they stopped all anti-Jewish measures; and that they improved the lot of all foreign slave workers in Germany. He noted Becher's statement that there had been no further anti-Jewish actions lately. McClelland reported this meeting on October 5, and emphasized that Mayer had demanded the cessation of deportations from Slovakia. One is inclined to believe McClelland rather than Kasztner, whose postwar account tried to prove to the world that Mayer was a useless old pedant. It seems quite clear, moreover, that Mayer never mentioned a payment of 15 million sfr. in three monthly installments, as Kasztner claimed. Mayer wrote in his notebook that he told Kasztner *Emess* ("the truth"): "have only five million of which 100,000 already spent, another 2m in USA. Hull: no goods, no ransom money, but keep negotiations going."[27]

Himmler's Other Negotiations

Saly Mayer was also involved in other negotiations on behalf of Jews under Nazi rule. The entrance of the Nazis into Hungary on March 19, 1944, stimulated feverish activity by various Jewish individuals and groups in Switzerland. Among them was the Comité pro Ungarn, headed by Mihály Bányai and including the consul of San Salvador, George Mantello. Mantello was very active in disseminating information about the developing Hungarian situation to the Swiss press and in providing Jews in Hungary with fictitious Latin American visas and even passports, which would protect them from deportation. This committee was in contact with the Sternbuch brothers in Montreaux, the representatives of the American Orthodox Va'ad Hahatzalah Committee, as well as with the representatives of the Orthodox community in Hungary, Gyula Link and Pinchas (Phillip) Fülop von Freudiger. In Switzerland they established connections with some Swiss who were well known for their good relations with the Nazis, such as Max Otto Boden (or Bodenschatz), a merchant who smuggled diamonds from Belgium and was perhaps a relative of the Dr. Boden who was the economic adviser at the German embassy in Budapest, and Otto Brindlinger, the representative in Switzerland of the Messerschmidt aircraft builders. Through these intermediaries they established contact with a man named Curt Trümpy, who was also a Messerschmidt representative and a commercial agent from Glarus.

On July 13, Trümpy tried on behalf of Bányai's committee to negotiate with the SS in Vienna regarding the emigration of 20,000 Hungarian Jews to Rumania. He and Max Otto Boden examined similar and even more presumptuous schemes at the end of July and the beginning of August. On August 12, the committee sent Trümpy, according to his own testimony, to Germany. He says he conducted negotiations in Bregenz with the local chief of the SD, Hauptsturmführer Gottlob Wandel, in order to clarify what the Nazis would demand in return for saving Jews. The Nazis sent Wilhelm Haster, a high SS officer from Verona, to see what kind of man Trümpy was. Haster told Trümpy that a part of the people of Bergen-Belsen would be released in exchange for further payments. Around the beginning of September, Trümpy contacted Saly Mayer, who instructed him to find out on whose behalf Becher was speaking. Mayer was absorbed with the questions of who Becher really was, for whom he spoke, and whether the sums which might be paid to him would actually help to save Jews. Mayer also used Trümpy to forward a memorandum to the Nazis in which he asked for a statement from Himmler with a clear definition of the German policy. We do not know whether this memorandum ever reached Himmler's hands.[28]

Another element in the picture was VH in Montreaux. Through Trümpy, Isaac Sternbuch hoped to achieve the liberation of a group of Orthodox Jews from Bergen-Belsen, among them the rabbi of Satmar (Satu Mare), Joel Teitelbaum. The fact that Sternbuch's group was wedded to an extreme particularism came out clearly when his representative, Leo Rubinfeld, informed Trümpy: "The aid organization to which I belong is not interested in the [other] people who came with the Hungarian transport to Bergen-Belsen."[29]

From the beginning of the Nazi occupation, the Freudiger-Link Orthodox group in Hungary had maintained contact with Isaac Sternbuch: it wanted him to pay for some hundred tractors which it had promised the Nazis for saving some Orthodox Jews. But Sternbuch, who had to pay Trümpy and others, did not have the money. Despite a mutual and total lack of confidence, Isaac Sternbuch approached Mayer and asked him to finance his Budapest rescue operations through the Orthodox group. Mayer put 260,000 sfr. at Sternbuch's disposal on September 13, apparently before he knew anything about the tractors. When Sternbuch asked specifically for money for tractors, Mayer first asked McClelland, who of course gave him an official no. Yet, amazingly, Mayer paid for the forty tractors, and documents in his files show that some of them went to Germany. Questioned after the war, McClelland said that while he recalled talk of a tractor demand by the Nazis, he did not think that Mayer had ever gone along with it, which would indicate that Mayer, having first asked him, had subsequently acted contrary to his instructions without telling him. Were it not for the receipts, it would indeed be hard to believe that the conservative Swiss Jew flew in the face of all his instructions. But he apparently thought he was not entitled to neglect any opportunity of saving lives.[30]

As it became known in Swiss ruling circles that Mayer was negotiating for lives, a climate of opinion developed that enabled other initiatives to be taken. One of these concerned Jean-Marie Musy, a former president of Switzerland (in 1925 and 1930) and a right-wing politician who had been in sympathy with the Nazi movement and was now seeking a political alibi. In April, 1944, a Jewish family applied to him and he managed to free some of its members from Drancy before they could be deported to Auschwitz and bring them to Switzerland. Having heard of this episode, Sternbuch contacted Musy and asked him to go to Himmler to negotiate over the liberation of the Jews under German rule. In October—the exact date is not clear—Musy left with his son for Germany, and reached Himmler through Walter Schellenberg. Sternbuch had given him a document allegedly proving that the

Americans were ready to let Jews into the United States and pay for their transportation and maintenance. Schellenberg and Himmler estimated that there were 600,000 Jews under their rule, and Himmler could free them without asking Hitler. But he needed goods, and especially trucks. Musy said that he proposed medicines to Himmler, who refused them. In his postwar report to WRB, Musy claimed that he had approached the Swiss for permission to ship trucks and other goods to Germany, and that the Swiss did not refuse out of hand.[31]

At any rate, it appears that Himmler said identical things, either directly or through his emissaries, to Mayer, Trümpy, and Musy. Until the fall of 1944, the SS held to its demand for trucks and tractors or at least other important or rare goods. In October, the rivalry became clear between Becher, Grüson, Kettlitz, and their Jewish partners on the one hand, Schellenberg and Musy on the other, and Kaltenbrunner and Eichmann against them all, while Himmler maneuvered with and against these partners of his. Himmler did not know with certainty who in the end would bring him the sought-for negotiations with the West, and he acted simultaneously on several fronts, including that of mass murder, to which Kaltenbrunner, Gestapo Chief Heinrich Müller, and Eichmann continued to be as committed as before.

Meanwhile, parallel negotiations were developing in Sweden, although they were not as important as those in Switzerland. On June 28, 1944, Iver Olsen, the WRB man at the American embassy in Stockholm, cabled that a three-man Nazi delegation, headed by Peter Kleist, who apparently was an SS representative, had proposed to release 2,000 Latvian Jews in exchange for $2 million, or, in a later version of the story, 2 million Swedish crowns. This money was supposed to be used by the Nazis to buy medicines and nonmilitary goods in Sweden. However, in the negotiations which started with Kleist, money was emphasized less than the more friendly atmosphere which would be created for Germany. This tentative approach brought no result, but Kleist returned to Stockholm in October, and Olsen wrote on October 14 that the German had actually come to negotiate the evacuation of 100,000 Estonians from Oesel to Sweden. Kleist had said that it was impossible to free the Jews from Germany in exchange for money, but he would advocate good treatment for the Jews who survived so that they would be pro-German after the war. Others had argued for murdering them, but this argument had been rejected, and Berlin was now inclined to adopt a middle way of using the Jews as hostages. This was why the last Lithuanian Jews were not killed.[32] Until the beginning of March, 1945, there were no further significant developments in Sweden, but Mayer knew about the contacts with Kleist and his partners, and the impression he had was that these tentative approaches paralleled his own with the SS.

The Second Stage: A German-American Encounter in Zürich

In October, 1944, Mayer concentrated his thoughts and activities on certain central points. First of all, as he jotted in his notebooks, he had to try to shift the negotiations from goods and money, which he did not possess and had not the right to promise, to an operation through the Red Cross, the purpose of which would be to keep the Jews under German rule alive. Second, he had to see to it that the negotiations applied to *all* Jews under Nazi rule, whereas Kasztner stressed the fate of the Jews in Budapest. Yet Mayer sometimes played with the thought of resigning his impossible task. Had he not already promised things that he could not carry out and had been forbidden to promise? He was criticized and resented by the Jewish organizations because of the mystery which surrounded the negotiations, and he could not defend himself by revealing that he actually was carrying out a deceit on a colossal scale—he, the honorable businessman, the well-known and incorruptible Saly Mayer. Furthermore, the help JDC extended to him was very small. He felt he stood quite alone, representing a nonexistent Jewish power against the dark forces of Nazism. Despite serious misgivings, Mayer decided to carry the negotiations one step further. McClelland and he managed to obtain visas to Switzerland for Kettliz, the Nazi purchasing agent, and for Becher, Billitz, and Kasztner. A cable to this effect reached Budapest on October 25, ten days after Horthy's removal by the Germans and the rise to power of Ferenc Szálasi and his Nazi Arrow Cross party.

On October 29, and again on November 2 and 4, negotiations proceeded between Mayer and the foursome from the other side of the frontier. Mayer jealously guarded his negotiating monopoly—he was furious because Kasztner had informed Schwalb of the resumption of the talks. We have two quite different versions of what transpired. Mayer's and Wyler-Schmidt's notes tell of a suggestion by Billitz that the Jews should use an existent Hungarian-Swiss commercial treaty, to which the Allies had given their agreement, to make their payment to the Nazis; nothing came of this idea. Becher understood that he would not get trucks, but because other goods would spare German blood, the Germans were ready to give "Jewish blood" in return for them. Hundreds of thousands of Jews would be able to leave for any place except Palestine (which was prohibited because of the Reich's obligations to the Arab leaders), provided that 20 million sfr. were made available within two or three weeks which could be converted into goods. Kasztner tells a different story. Becher, he says, justified on military grounds the deportations of the remnants of Slovak Jewry which were then taking place in the wake of a Slovak uprising against the Nazis. The Jews of Budapest, he threatened, would be deported to the Reich. Mayer's answer, Kasztner reports, was unrealistic and ineffectual. He spoke about Swiss neutrality and said that human beings should not be discussed as though they were lifeless objects of commercial transactions.[33] Kasztner's description raises many doubts; but so does that of Mayer and Wyler-Schmidt, and it is therefore impossible to find out what exactly transpired at these meetings.

On November 5 (November 6, according to Wyler-Schmidt), Mayer finally produced the WRB representative, McClelland, who met with Becher that evening at the Hotel Baur in Zürich. Both Wyler-Schmidt and Kasztner wrote reports of the meeting, though neither was actually present, and McClelland also gave an account of it to WRB.[34] An analysis of these sources leads to the conclusion that the central part of the meeting was a long, stern lesson, read to Becher by Mayer, built around the theme of the Nazis' inevitable defeat and buttressed by translated excerpts from an article by Dorothy Thompson in the *Reader's Digest*. McClelland and Mayer had previously agreed on a strategy to take advantage of the increasing Nazi military reversals. They hoped to divert the SS men's attention from the advantages they might gain for the German war effort to the more elemental and personal level of saving their own hides through leniency toward the Jews. (Becher, who regarded himself as an officer and gentleman whose hands were unsoiled by Eichmann's bloody doings, might be especially susceptible to such an approach.)

The specific demands Mayer put forward at this meeting were an end to the killing of civilians, both Jews and non-Jews, the transfer of orphan children to Switzerland, and permission for IRC to look after the inmates of concentration camps. In return,

Mayer and McClelland were able to show Becher a WRB cable of October 29, signed by American Secretary of State Cordell Hull, agreeing to the opening of a credit of 20 million sfr. ($5 million) in Mayer's favor. This credit could be used under conditions to be determined in due course by the American government. Kasztner claims that he, not Mayer, demanded that the Jews of Budapest not be deported. After a lengthy argument, Becher agreed only that children and old sick people would be spared. As for IRC protection, Becher conceded only that the international organization would be permitted to examine the different categories of Jews.

The Third Stage: Deceiving the SS, November, 1944–January, 1945

Herbert Kettlitz, the Nazi purchasing agent, remained in Switzerland after the Zürich meeting. McClelland sent a cable to WRB on November 16, in which the meeting with Becher was invoked and the transfer of the money proposed, but on November 21, a WRB telegram from the State Department arrived which put Mayer in a most difficult position. Over Stettinius's signature, the message stated that the transfer to Mayer of $5 million proposed by McClelland and Mayer "cannot (repeat not) be supported by the Board in any way, and further it is the Board's opinion that no (repeat no) funds from any source should be used to carry out such a proposal." With this the possibility of using money from the United States and local funds from other sources for the payment of ransom came to an end. Yet the WRB nonetheless expected to continue negotiating. "The Board is confident that you will take into consideration the fact that because of recent military developments, each day that can be gained is of increasing importance."[35] Mayer's position had become untenable. A new blow was dealt when he was informed on November 30 that Joseph Schwartz would indeed come to Switzerland, but that he would not be allowed to intervene in the negotiations because he was a U.S. citizen.

In the meantime, on November 8, Eichmann began deporting Jews to be used for forced labor from Budapest. By the end of November, thousands of Jews had been forced to walk toward the Austrian border, and many had perished. Kasztner was desperately pressing Mayer to pay ransom, but Mayer could not help. On

November 18, Kettlitz cabled that Mayer had no money and probably would not have any in the forseeable future. On the other hand, he had contacted Sternbuch's organization, and it seemed to him that better results could be obtained from it. Sternbuch himself saw the Kettlitz contacts and the Musy affair as part of the same approach, and he accordingly cabled to the VH to appeal to the U.S. government for funds for a ransom deal. Sternbuch thought he should receive 10 to 20 million sfr. The WRB in turn sent a cable to McClelland asking him to express his opinion on the Sternbuch proposals. In a cable of December 9, McClelland opposed sending funds and expressed suspicion of the Musy plan. In a postwar statement, McClelland recollected that Sternbuch was a genuine, sincere, but very impressionable and fanciful man who had to be held firmly in check. In 1944, he thought Sternbuch's ideas were full of "vagueness and unreliability."[36]

When Becher in Budapest received Kettlitz's cable that there was no money, he went to see Himmler in Berlin. To counteract the possible effects of such a report on Himmler, Kasztner, without consulting Switzerland, on November 20 sent Becher a cable saying that 20 million sfr. were in fact ready; Mayer, he said, was working night and day to remove the technical obstacles, and Kettlitz's assumption that the payment was not certain was incorrect.[37] The way Kasztner tells his story is, however, not very plausible. Becher would hardly have been influenced by a Jew caged in Budapest as against his own man's report from the scene. By that time, too, there must have been some kind of an understanding between Becher and Kasztner: Becher would save Kasztner's life in return for Kasztner's defense of Becher after the war. It is possible that the two had arranged beforehand that Kasztner should send a cable that would reach Becher while he was reporting to his chief.

At the same time, the Rumanian government, which was by then fighting on the side of the Allies, declared that it was ready to receive Jews from Northern Transylvania who had been deported to Auschwitz and were considered Rumanian citizens in exchange for Germans from Transylvania. This proposal made a strong impression on the Nazis; apparently it became clear to them that keeping Jews alive was worthwhile for the sake of "German blood." According to Becher, Himmler gave him (probably in November) a copy of written instructions to stop the extermination, after similar instructions had already been given orally in October and perhaps before. (However, gassings in Auschwitz continued until early November.) Even the death march from Budapest was stopped at the end of November, apparently by a similar instruction.

On November 27, Kettlitz cabled again that for ten days he had been unable to reach Mayer and that he wanted to leave. Actually, he had been expelled from Switzerland. Eichmann, Becher, Kasztner, and Billitz met in Budapest, and Billitz proposed a new journey to the border. In the meantime the Nazis issued a deadline—first set for November 24, but then postponed to December 2—for a clear and positive answer from Switzerland regarding the ransom money. The release of the remaining deportees in Bergen-Belsen would depend on a positive answer, as would the cessation of persecution of the Jews of Hungary in particular and the Jews under German rule in general. In a parallel action, Trümpy sent a telegram to Mayer and to the president of Switzerland, Eduard von Steiger, to inform them of the Nazis' ultimatum and to demand payment.[38]

On November 29, Billitz, Kasztner, and Becher's new representative, Hauptsturmführer Erich Krell, met with Kettlitz and Leo Rubinfeld from Sternbuch's group. Rubinfeld said that his group indeed had only 1 million sfr., but that he would get more. The next day, Kasztner met with Schwalb and Wyler-Schmidt and told them that Becher was angry with Mayer. He was "being led around by the nose by an old Jew."[39]

On December 1, Kasztner first met with Mayer alone. During this meeting, Mayer told Kasztner the whole truth. He could possibly collect 4 million sfr., but it would be better to transfer the money to the Red Cross. He thought he could not go on negotiating because he had nothing to offer. When Krell joined the meeting he also heard that Mayer had scarcely 4 million francs.[40] Any payment, even one made from the sums at his disposal, contravened the Americans' instructions, yet Mayer had been making such payments all along. Secretly, without "Hannukah" McClelland knowing about it, 260,000 sfr. ($59,000) had been paid to Sternbuch on September 13 for the tractors that Sternbuch had agreed to, and on the same day Mayer paid 64,750 sfr. ($14,700) more to Sternbuch for 3,500 kilograms of coffee. On November 30, on December 19, and at the beginning of January, Mayer paid considerable sums directly to Swiss producers for tractors which were conveyed to Germany.[41]

Increasingly, however, Mayer found himself in a cul-de-sac. The sums with which he could maneuver were small, and the demands of the Nazis large. It was at this point that Kasztner's decisive and positive intervention came. On the night of December 1, he convinced Krell and Kettlitz to send a completely untruthful telegram to Becher. It said, first, that there were 5 million sfr. available, and, second, that the continued imprisonment of the last people of Bergen-Belsen was causing many difficulties. On this point one may safely accept Kasztner's version; Saly Mayer's deeds and words reveal a state of despair which at that moment endangered the negotiations. Kasztner's intervention appears to have saved the situation. In his answer of December 4, Becher promised that no evil would befall the Jews of Budapest who were then gathered in a ghetto, but he demanded payment of the remaining 15 million sfr.

At a next meeting on December 5, Mayer was again strong and energetic. He explained to Krell, who represented the Nazi side, that the delays resulted from Nazi persecutions. The American party could not consider the German proposals serious when death marches were organized and the people in Bergen-Belsen were not set free. Mayer again proposed that the Jews under Nazi rule be kept alive through the Red Cross.[42] On the night between December 6 and December 7, the train with the remaining 1,368 Jews of Kasztner's transport arrived in Switzerland—as Kasztner said, after a stormy discussion between Krell and Kettlitz.

On December 10–11, Becher again demanded payment of the further 15 million sfr., for he thought that the first 5 million were already assured. But Joseph Schwartz, on a visit to Switzerland, explained to Mayer that JDC was unable to pay such large sums even if the American government permitted it: its total annual income in 1944 would only reach $15,095,000, all of which was already committed. In any case, $6,500,000 had been transferred to Mayer, or nearly 43 percent of the entire budget. Mayer nevertheless proposed to Schwartz the transfer of $5 million, which would be given to the IRC in exchange for "board and lodging," as he called the provision of minimum living conditions to the Jews who remained under Nazi rule. Schwartz accepted this proposal. McClelland was surprised by Mayer's opinion that the Germans also would be ready to accept it, but he forwarded the proposal in a cable to WRB dated December 13, 1944, and asked for the 20 million sfr., "or if not in cash, its equivalent in foodstuffs, clothing, shoes and medicines." He admitted that the Jews receiving Allied aid could be exploited as forced labor for the Reich's benefit, but he asked for "all possible support" for Mayer's plan, citing the arrival in Switzerland of the transport from Bergen-Belsen as evidence of the Nazis' serious intentions. The WRB hesitated; it questioned the chances of getting suitable goods in Switzerland. McClelland transmitted Schwartz's response that if there were difficulties in getting the foodstuffs, so much the better. But, he added, it was nevertheless imperative to send the 20 million sfr. immediately. Jewish sources in the United States would provide the money, the use of which would of course have to be under suitable control.[43]

On January 7, 1945, more than a month after the Nazis' extended deadline, the much-desired WRB telegram signed by Stettinius arrived, confirming the transfer of 20 million sfr. to Mayer by JDC. However, none could be spent without governmental approval. The transfer was carried out "solely in order that Saly Mayer may have something tangible with which to hold open the negotiations and for the gaining of more precious time." On January 26, Mayer was further informed that in any case the money could not be drawn without both his signature and McClelland's. Mayer believed the money was to be used to pay IRC for keeping Jews alive under Nazi rule, and while he was waiting for it, he obtained IRC's agreement in principle to this plan.[44]

Mayer's tactics in December and January impressed Becher enough, according to Kasztner's testimony, to protect the Budapest ghetto against the Arrow Cross regime. His behavior strongly suggests that he continued to consult Himmler and that his opposition to the Hungarian Nazis' murderous designs received Himmler's approval. This did not mean that Becher refrained from extorting money and goods from the hapless Jews, but Kasztner is probably right in claiming that Becher was instrumental in preventing further murders.[45]

One week after the cable confirming the transfer of the 20 million sfr., between January 13 and January 16, Pest was liberated by the Soviets. A month later, Buda too was freed. With this the third stage of the negotiations ended.

The End of the Negotiations: Himmler's Search for a Reprieve

The last stage in the history of the ransom negotiations started on January 1, 1945, when Jean-Marie Musy met again with Himmler at Wildbad in southern Germany. Musy reported that this time Himmler demanded that 5 million sfr. be put at Musy's disposal. The idea was that the money should be paid to the Red Cross, which in turn would supply medicine and food to the suffering German population. According to Musy, Sternbuch told him that the only organization fit to conduct those negotiations was VH, for JDC was not a political organization and dealt only with charities. Saly Mayer, Sternbuch said, was an obstacle to Musy's mission. When Musy came back to Switzerland on January 17, Sternbuch sent a cable to VH saying that he was able to bring about the liberation of 30,000 Jews in exchange for $5 million. The Jews would be set free at the rate of 1,400 a month, and $250,000 should be paid for each convoy. The sum of $250,000 which the organization had previously sent to Sternbuch, and which was then deposited in a Swiss bank, would serve as payment for the first convoy. On January 25, the WRB sent a telegram to McClelland asking what the truth was regarding this story. Clearly it wanted to know whether ransom was contemplated or had already been paid. On January 28, McClelland answered that Sternbuch denied any payment to Himmler, but that Musy had received 50,000 fr. ($11,000) from Sternbuch "for expenses" and had extorted 10,000 more ($2,200) from a private person whose relative he had brought out of Germany. In other words, Musy was suspected of acting counter to U. S. policies.[46]

On January 21, Musy went back to Germany, where his contact was Walter Schellenberg; on February 7, a train with 1,210 Jews from the Theresienstadt ghetto came to Switzerland, apparently as the result of these negotiations. On February 6, McClelland, Musy, and Sternbuch had a meeting during which Musy again wanted ransom money, this time 5 million sfr. ($1 million) for the liberation of all Jews under Nazi rule. Behind that proposal, McClelland thought, was Himmler's desire for negotiations with the West. "The release of the Jews may be the forerunner of proposals of much greater importance to the Germans."[47]

Sternbuch obviously fell into a Nazi trap. First he obtained a temporary credit of 5 million sfr. from private sources (on February 16), and then he requested $937,000 from VH in New York— all for ransom payments to Musy, which were in addition to those promised by Mayer. Musy, in Himmler's name, now also demanded that the Swiss and American press react positively to the humanitarian step Himmler had taken in liberating the 1,200 inmates of Theresienstadt.[48] In the United States, JDC lent the $937,000 to the VH, and on February 28, WRB confirmed the transfer to McClelland, but stipulated that the money could not be used for ransom. Expenditure was possible only with the explicit sanction of WRB and after a joint signature by Sternbuch and McClelland. The net result was that $6 million were now dangled before Nazi eyes—Mayer's $5 million and Sternbuch's $1 million—but in reality the money could not be used.

The facts of the money transfers could not be kept secret in Berlin, and the arrival of the Theresienstadt train in Switzerland embroiled Himmler with the SS faction that opposed the negotiations. Hitler was indignant at Himmler, and Ernst Kaltenbrunner obtained a definite interdiction against letting any more Jews leave the territory of the steadily diminishing Reich. The competition between the Schellenberg and Becher factions, supporting negotiations with Musy and Mayer respectively, brought Himmler to ask on January 15: "Who is really the one with whom the American government actually maintains contact? Is it a rabbinical Jew or is it the Joint?" ("Wer ist derjenige mit dem die amerikanische Regierung wirklich in Verbindung ist. Ist es ein Rabbiner-Jude oder ist es die Jioint [*sic*]?").[49] On January 29, Becher, Kasztner, Krell, and Kettlitz met in Vienna to try to provide proof that Mayer was the person Himmler was looking for.

The Becher group spent the next fortnight in desperate attempts to get their hands on actual cash in order to prove to Himmler that they were getting results or, even better, to meet again with McClelland. Meetings were held between Mayer and members of the Becher group on February 1, 7, and 11, with Mayer steering the discussions toward using the sums at his disposal, with Becher's consent, to pay for IRC support of Jewish inmates of Nazi camps. On February 11, Mayer promised to let Becher meet McClelland a second time, but the meeting never materialized. The Becher negotiations were at an end.[50]

Mayer's attempts to bring the Jews under the protection of the Red Cross were in line with the efforts made in February-March in Scandinavia, and even with the new approach of the IRC. Saly Mayer reported to Carl Burckhardt, president of the IRC, about the whole process of the negotiations and asked for his intervention. At that late stage, Burckhardt, in a move perhaps related to Mayer's negotiations, as well as to WJC pressure, indeed tried to intervene in Germany in favor of the inmates. Mayer took advantage of the situation. He was partly instrumental in getting George Dunant of the IRC to visit Bratislava and through him supplied Jews in hiding with funds. In Vienna, another IRC man, Dr. Lutz Thudicum, was given JDC funds to provide food for the Viennese and Hungarian Jews in and near the city.

In the light of the Mayer-Becher talks, it is easier to interpret the negotiations conducted by Himmler or his henchmen during the last two or three months of the Reich. Himmler was making desperate attempts to save part of his authority and possibly himself from the ruins of the collapsing Reich. Apart from the Mayer and Musy negotiations, and occasional contacts such as those through Trümpy, new attempts to save Jewish lives were made through Sweden. These were the work largely of Felix Kersten, Himmler's osteopath, a German of Finnish citizenship who was trying to create an image of himself as a humanitarian. He managed to convince Himmler to have a private meeting with Norbert Masur, one of Hillel Storch's colleagues in the WJC office at Stockholm. On April 21, Masur met Himmler with the object of saving the lives of Jews in Nazi camps. As a result, Himmler agreed to release 4,500 Jewish women from Ravensbruck.

The rivalry among the different groups of SS chiefs looking for an easy Jewish alibi now came to a climax. Under Schellenberg's aegis, Benoit Musy, Jean-Marie's son, visited Buchenwald on April 9, on the eve of its liberation, and Bergen-Belsen two days later, and claimed that he saw to it that Himmler's promises to transfer the concentration camps with their inmates intact to the Allies and to free the women in Ravensbruck were kept. Becher in turn brought Kasztner to Bergen-Belsen on April 11, and to Neuengamme, another concentration camp, a day later. On April 16 he was in Theresienstadt. This was meant to prove that Becher and Himmler were seeing to it that no harm befell the Jews.[51]

Consequences and Conclusions

Musy, with Schellenberg's help and Sternbuch's support, accused Saly Mayer after the war of having made public in the Swiss press the arrival of the Theresienstadt train in February, 1945; he also declared that Mayer spread reports that he had promised Himmler that 250 high-ranking Nazis would be rescued in return for the liberation of Jews. These developments supposedly had brought about Kaltenbrunner's intervention with Hitler in the middle of February, after which any further exchange of Jews was forbidden.[52] Musy and Schellenberg claimed that Mayer had been an agent of Becher and even Kaltenbrunner. All these assertions were of course groundless. There is no doubt that the Nazis, who felt the noose tightening around their necks, were frantically engaged in intrigues, competition, and accusations. After the war was over, Sternbuch and his friends repeated those accusations and gave Schellenberg the alibi for which he had been striving all the time. On the other hand, Kasztner too discharged his personal debt to Becher, whom in his report he described as a faithful antisemitic Nazi, by giving him a clearance letter (*Persilschein*) for the Allied authorities.

The controversy regarding Mayer's role in the negotiations raged and still rages. Some have maintained that while there was no doubt about Mayer's goodwill and devotion to the cause of saving Jews, he was totally incapable of a mission such as the one he undertook. He could not concentrate on any given point, he obfuscated any discussion in which he took part, and he was pedantic and unyielding.

Mayer was a very distrustful man. His attitude toward Kasztner was at first one of mutual respect and even sympathy. But as he discovered inaccuracies in accounts presented by Kasztner, he became angry and adopted an increasingly hostile attitude toward him. Kasztner apologized and even abased himself in his attempts to restore good relations, but later he did not refrain from taking revenge upon Mayer in his report. Yet he praised Schwartz, McClelland, and the Swiss administration, as though he did not understand that the latter were no more than ancillary to the actions Mayer conducted. By 1947, he was calling Mayer "a philanthropic gangster."[53]

McClelland's personal opinion of Mayer is far less harsh. In the warm atmosphere of McClelland's home in Bern, together with his wife, Marjorie, and their three small children, the lonely old man relaxed and became really the "Onkel Saly" of the Jewish underground correspondence. With respect to Mayer's conduct of the negotiations, McClelland says: "Perhaps, had you picked more of a diplomat, a man with greater political background and *savoir faire*, more could possibly have been achieved. Yet, this man succeeded in doing precisely what Becher once told Saly he, Becher, was accused of by his opponents, namely of 'being led around by a ring in your nose by an old Jew.' " This was exactly what happened. Mayer conducted a masterful holding operation for six months. In retrospect, it seems incredible that he could have sustained it for so long, particularly when he had so little of real substance to bargain with.[54]

From other accounts it seems that Mayer could be a taciturn and secretive person. He was highly intelligent, very nervous, and given to outbursts of violent temper. One gets the definite impression that Mayer recognized the value of putting on an act. The quiet man became suddenly talkative and overwhelmed his interlocutors with long speeches. He "led by the nose" not only Becher, but even his friends. Wyler-Schmidt, his only close friend, apparently did not know that Mayer paid for Sternbuch's tractors, for Wyler-Schmidt denied that such a payment had occurred.

Mayer took advantage of the growing weakness of the Nazis in the summer of 1944, redirecting the negotiations from Eichmann's initial demand for trucks to money, and then from money to the notion of supporting Jews through the Red Cross. The negotiations in themselves contributed to the relative softening of the Nazis' attitude towards the Jews, including the cessation of gassings, although the main factor in this change was certainly the constant worsening of Germany's military situation. But this worsening could instead have brought about the mass murder of the Jewish remnant, for which Hitler, Kaltenbrunner, Müller, and Eichmann had striven. It seems that the negotiations in Switzerland were among the influences which strengthened the less murderous tendency.

In any case, the August 25 order preventing the deportation of the Jews of Budapest was almost certainly a consequence of the negotiations on the Swiss border. The sometimes problematic though largely positive interventions of Becher would have been inconceivable without Mayer's dilatory tactics, although the contributions of Kasztner and Biss are not negligible, for they knew well how to take advantage of each opening. The entry of Kasztner's train into Switzerland is also undoubtedly a direct consequence of the negotiations.

It is difficult to know whether the negotations helped the survival of the 12,000–17,000 Hungarian Jews who had been deported to Strasshof, but it seems that this was the case. Mayer's negotiations, furthermore, helped other initiatives—such as Musy's, Kersten's, Storch's and Masur's—to occur and partly to succeed. One can assume that all these negotiations contributed to the transfer of the concentration camps of Buchenwald and Bergen-Belsen to Allied control, though some other factors may have been even more important.

Saly Mayer was far from an angel, but he acted successfully under well-nigh impossible conditions, bound from all sides by instructions and restrictions, and still rendered a great and faithful service to the last remnants of European Jewry. Quite instinctively, he tried to counteract the very basis of Nazi attitudes towards Jews: the Nazis saw in Jews not human beings, but commodities to be exchanged for other commodities. It was the dehumanization of themselves which produced in the Nazis the urge to dehumanize the Jews. Mayer's whole negotiation process was diametrically opposed to this assumption—which, because of the tremendous pressure, had even been accepted by Kasztner. Mayer tried to place the negotiations regarding Jews into a human framework again.

The disunity of the Jewish effort, which was partly a cause of Mayer's way of negotiating, was at the same time also an effect of his negotiations. In this he, and the organization he represented, must take a measure of blame, though the other Jewish groups, and especially Sternbuch's VH, were at least equally guilty. On the whole, though, Mayer's efforts succeeded beyond the wildest hopes. Walking a very dangerous tightrope, he conducted the only sustained talks with Nazis from the Allied side during World War II. He managed to bring about the only actual meeting between a representative of the Nazis (and of Himmler at that!) and an American diplomat (McClelland, on November 5, 1944, in Zürich). All this in order to save the remnant of the Jewish people in Europe. Would anyone else have done better?

19

"11:59": Saving the Remnants

The approaching collapse of the Nazi Reich endangered the last remnants of European Jewry in Nazi-controlled areas, namely those Jews in labor and concentration camps that still survived in the summer and autumn of 1944. Saly Mayer and Joseph Schwartz were among those who feared that the Nazis might annihilate Jewish inmates in an effort to eliminate witnesses to their crimes. They were not far wrong. Ever since June, 1942, a group of SS men under Paul Blobel ("Kommando 1005") were using Jewish slaves to burn bodies from Jewish mass graves in an attempt to do away with the physical evidence of the Holocaust.[1] In late 1944 and early 1945, the tendency to kill all those who had seen too much gained ground. Ernst Kaltenbrunner and Adolf Eichmann were examples of hard-liners who supported such a policy and were to claim after the war that Hitler was behind it. Rumors of such tendencies reached Mayer and Schwartz, and their actions during the last months of the war were designed to forestall such a threat and save as many Jews as possible.

Apart from their powers of persuasion, money was the only weapon they could use. With it, they could send parcels or pay others to send them or bring food into Germany; they also could—and did—bait Nazi officials with ransom offers. But the money came from America, and the problem was whether the information regarding the Holocaust that reached American Jewry in 1944–45 would be comprehended and cause the Jewish community to provide JDC with enough funds to do its rescue work. Indeed, American Jewry's eventual acceptance of the fact that European Jewish communities were being systematically murdered was probably the main reason for the decisive change in JDC's financial position during the latter part of the war. Between 1943 and 1944, JDC's income rose by 50 percent, from about $10 million to over $15 million, and reached $20.5 million in 1945. American Jews were coming to see the elementary truth that with more money more could be done to save lives. Undoubtedly the changed attitude of the U.S. government, which found its expression in the establishment of the WRB, also played a significant role. Too late, and with still too limited funds, JDC could increase its rescue efforts.

As 1944 proceeded, more and more funds were directed towards the liberated areas—a story which will not be dealt with here. Rome was freed in June, France was liberated in August, 1944, and Belgium followed. Rumania surrendered and joined the Allies in August, and Bulgaria in September. Yugoslavia was largely cleared of Nazis in October. In the second half of 1944, however, German power was still exercised in Hungary, western Poland up to the Vistula River, Holland, Denmark, Norway, northern Italy, Czechoslovakia, and the German-Austrian heartland. It was unclear to Jewish organizations how many Jews survived in those areas, and only some of the centers of Jewish population were known. Theresienstadt ghetto in Bohemia was one of them; Bergen-Belsen and Vittel became known because the Germans at various times sent people there who might be exchanged for civilian Germans in Allied countries. There were some 180,000 Jews in Budapest; there was a remnant of 20,000 in Slovakia, but their numbers diminished as a result of the deportations following the Slovak uprising of late August, 1944. There were Jews in Auschwitz until the camp was taken by the Russians in January, 1945, but most of its inmates were marched off beforehand and dispersed among the hundreds of labor and concentration camps in Germany and Austria. Figures as high as 600,000 were mentioned late in 1944 for the surviving Jews in Nazi-controlled Europe.[2]

During the second half of 1944, and until the end of the war in May, 1945, JDC was organized purely pragmatically by areas. The New York office was in direct contact with South America and Cuba; Shanghai was serviced through Mayer in Switzerland. The whole of the Middle East—including the relationship with JA via Istanbul and the parcel services in Teheran, North African Jewry, refugees in Italy, Spain, and Portugal, and the Jewish remnant in Tito's territory—were the direct responsibility of the Lisbon office. With the liberation of France and Belgium, those countries passed from Saly Mayer's care to that of JDC-Lisbon as well. All of the European areas still held by the Nazis were Mayer's concern, though there was a certain amount of overlapping in Rumania, for instance, where questions of emigration to Palestine were dealt with by Schwartz in Lisbon. Poland could not really be reached, but we have seen that JDC-New York took upon itself to transfer funds to the London Poles for sending on to Warsaw.

After the liberation of France, Switzerland was no longer isolated, and Schwartz supervised Mayer's work much more closely. Ultimate responsibility no longer rested solely on Mayer's shoulders, and he welcomed this development. In any case, Schwartz and Mayer agreed on the direction that JDC work should take. What is perhaps of central importance is that Mayer in effect represented JDC in the IRC councils at Geneva, acting under definite instructions from Lisbon and New York. Contacts with the WRB were of course in the hands of Paul Baerwald, Joseph Hyman, and Moses Leavitt, JDC's chief officers in New York, while contacts with the British government and the IGCR were handled by Schwartz, as was the growing involvement of JDC with the Allied armies.

JDC and International Organizations in 1944–1945

As the war began to draw to an end, JDC increasingly received help from the IGCR, which was in effect controlled by the British. The British government was moved to act by public pressure, with Eleanor Rathbone, M.P., and her Committee against Nazi Terror taking pride of place. The Foreign Office was apt to feel that American efforts to aid refugees had been overpublicized, while the British efforts to help victims of Nazism were not always sufficiently appreciated. It pointed out that a proportionately very considerable number of Jewish and other refugees had been taken into the small British Isles, and that the colonial empire had provided refuge for 40,000 Poles, 23,000 Greeks, 25,000

Yugoslavs, and many thousands of Jews.[3] Stung by growing criticism of the Bermuda Conference, the British began to support ideas to activate the IGCR which they had earlier opposed. Two main caveats, however, separated the British from the American effort in 1944. One was that the transfer of hard currency would help the Nazis and was therefore not permissible; the second was that any large-scale effort to rescue Jews from Nazi control was objectionable because the problem was not specifically Jewish. Jews were to be treated as nationals of their countries of origin and not as a separate group.

As time went on, British attitudes mellowed somewhat, largely because they thought that the U.S. government was more pro-Jewish than it was, and, while the British continued to think that this support was solely due to Jewish electoral pressure, the American alliance was too important for them to continue to insist on their point of view. When, therefore, Sir Herbert Emerson suggested at the end of 1943 that Britain offer the United States a governmental fund for IGCR, his government agreed. The United Kingdom would give up to £1.5 million if the United States gave an equivalent sum, and additional funds could surely be raised from the other members of the newly reconstituted IGCR. But the Americans had problems with this proposal. The WRB, which was being set up just at that time (January, 1944), was financed largely by private contributions—which in fact meant JDC—and the administration was reluctant to commit large sums which would have to be justified to Congress. A compromise was therefore reached in the early summer of 1944, whereby the contributions to IGCR proposed by Emerson were to be used to aid victims of Nazism, largely in liberated areas, and mainly people who were not citizens of Allied countries. The WRB would carry on its rescue work in Nazi-held areas, whereas the United National Relief and Rehabilitation Administration (UNRRA), set up in 1943, would look after Allied nationals displaced by the war. Of the £1 million that the two governments finally agreed to provide between them immediately, IGCR was to use £900,000 for actual work in the field.[4]

The IGCR, however, had no machinery for welfare work or any other form of aid. It was a political agency which had suddenly become a funding agency, and it needed someone to spend its money. When Joseph Schwartz visited London early in 1944, he and Emerson arranged that most, if not all, of the IGCR money should be channeled through JDC. On July 20, 1944, Emerson cabled JDC that he would allocate $930,000 as a first installment to be used in the Balkans, Italy, and the Iberian peninsula. Another $650,000 were allocated in February, 1945. Outlays were made by JDC, which was then reimbursed by IGCR. For Hungary and Rumania alone, for example, IGCR in 1945 reimbursed JDC $1.2 million for its wartime expenses.[5]

The main international organization through whom all Jewish groups had to work, however, was the IRC and its special committee, the so-called Commission Mixte, through which parcels and victuals could be sent to certain destinations in Nazi Europe. WJC and JDC in Switzerland were particularly eager to have the IRC send its representatives to Nazi Europe, because their presence might both prevent murder and raise the morale of the endangered Jewish population. Acting parallel to Gerhart Riegner's efforts, Saly Mayer met with Max Huber, president of IRC, on February 26, 1943, and asked for IRC representation in Bucharest, Budapest, and Bratislava; the request was granted only for Bucharest. But there was a price for this concession. On November 11, 1943, Huber in effect told Mayer that if he wanted IRC to act in favor of Jews, the Jews would not only have to pay for the actual help, but also contribute to administrative costs. Mayer's comment was bitter, but the message was clear. On November 24, he sent a contribution of five thousand sfr. (about $1,200).[6] In May, 1944, the IRC finally decided to send a delegate to Budapest. They sent Friedrich Born, who worked closely with the Swiss legation and with the Jewish bodies in the Hungarian capital.

IRC representatives might help, but what was urgently needed was IRC's direct intervention in Germany to supervise the treatment of Jews in Nazi labor and concentration camps. Ever since 1942, Jewish groups had been pressuring IRC to intervene, but until October, 1944, it refused to approach the Germans on this issue, arguing that it had no standing vis-à-vis the Germans on anyone but prisoners of war and certain categories of Allied nonmilitary personnel. It could not regard the Jews as "assimilated" to Allied civilian internees. The change in IRC's attitude came after the establishment of the WRB. Mayer could now speak with some assurance of American backing. On February 16, 1944, he asked Huber to establish a control over all matters pertaining to aid to civilians, and soon afterwards an Austrian nobleman, Josef Schwartzenberg, with whom Mayer and the other Jewish groups enjoyed cordial relations, was named head of a special department for civilian affairs. From February, the Americans began notifying IRC of arrangements whereby Mayer would pay the Red Cross for parcels or other help in the various countries.

Mayer's efforts, however, paralleled those of WJC. The WJC would have welcomed coordination with JDC, but JDC's attitude precluded such an arrangment. Although Riegner did not know it, Mayer was pro-WJC, but his loyalty to his organization prevented him from cooperating effectively with Riegner. Thus, at a meeting on July 21, 1944, between Carl Burckhardt of IRC and the WJC representative, the issue of IRC intervention on behalf of Jews interned by the Nazis was discussed; on August 8, Mayer had more or less the same conversation, telling Burckhardt that IRC "had done very little for the Jews . . . all the money which had been transmitted for Jewish purposes had come from Jewish sources, notably from the Joint."[7] Jews were considered citizens of their several countries of origin, but when it came to helping them, Jewish organizations were called upon to pay the bill.

Mayer's interventions contributed to the gradual, though very late, change in IRC's attitude. On October 2, 1944, IRC at long last asked the Germans to permit inspection of the conditions under which Jews lived in Nazi camps. On December 21, it finally set up a department dealing with Jewish problems. However, the establishment of this department did not solve the problem of IRC's failure to intervene vigorously in German concentration camps. JDC, through Mayer, therefore participated in a group of governments and organizations mobilized in November, 1944, by Riegner and the Czechoslovak envoy in Switzerland, Jaromir Kopecký, to pressure IRC to do more. It was asked to demand that Jews be treated as civilian internees, which implied that they should not be treated according to their citizenship. In February, the suggestion was made to the IRC that Jewish inmates should be separated from the others (except for prisoners of war, for whom separation would mean harsher treatment). In March, it was suggested that IRC accept a German proposal to have delegates live in the camps until the end of the war, and some camps did receive a resident IRC delegate during the last days of German rule.[8]

Apart from IGCR and IRC, the WRB and its local representative, McClelland, also contributed to rescue activities. Unknown to Mayer, even McClelland's discretionary fund for underground activities in Nazi Europe ($260,000) came from JDC. Through "Hanukka" McClelland, Swiss diplomats, Hehalutz couriers, and credit transactions of all kinds, Mayer sent money to various places in the German-held territories. Mayer's object in his negotiations with these non-Jewish organizations was, first and foremost, "Klal." As time went on, his opposition grew both to Kasztner's special work with his Bergen-Belsen transport and to Sternbuch's efforts for his Orthodox clients (especially as, in the case of the transport, Sternbuch supported the Orthodox element and Kasztner the others). He was not even primarily concerned with Hungarian Jews, but with attempts to save all Jews under the Nazis. By combining attempts to put all Jews under IRC protection with protection for all foreigners, Jews and non-Jews, in Germany, he hoped to put the saving of Jewish lives on a basis that would be more acceptable to the Allies. Yet he also tried to provide help to groups and individuals when necessary. Nevertheless, it must be admitted that despite his attempts to deal with the Klal, he in fact failed. His concrete work was piecemeal. The areas of his activity were Budapest, Vienna, Bratislava, and the German concentration camps, largely Theresienstadt, Bergen-Belsen, and Landsberg.

The Jews of Budapest: The Last Stage

The situation for Jews in Budapest improved after the order by Nicholas Horthy, the Hungarian head of state, to stop the deportations on July 9, 1944. A sizable emigration, to Palestine or elsewhere, appeared possible when the Hungarian government on July 18 declared its willingness to allow certain groups of Jews to leave Hungary, including 7,800 people to whom Moshe Krausz of JA's Palestine Office in Budapest had distributed Palestine immigration permits. The 7,800 visas soon became 8,700, and children would be accepted to Tangier. The Spanish government then agreed to take 1,500 more if they could get out of Hungary. The Portuguese legation joined in, offering 3 visas in August, but 700 in November.[9] The Swiss were prepared to take children, and a figure of 10,000 was mentioned. The Germans were prepared to release all those who had been accepted to neutral or Allied countries—provided that they could deport all the others. That was what the Germans intimated to the Hungarians. The Hungarians, now under a new government clandestinely trying to arrange a separate peace with the Allies, were not eager to anger public opinion in the West by further deportations of Jews. In the autumn it gradually became clear to the neutral representatives in Budapest that in fact the Germans would not allow anyone out.[10]

441

After the scare of August 25–26, when the Budapest Jews thought another deportation was coming, the situation became calmer, despite the fact that the Jews were concentrated in Jewish houses, were marked with a yellow star, and were in fact living in ghetto conditions. There were 2,168 such houses to start with, but the effect of Allied bombardment of Budapest was to reduce the number to 1,840.[11] Two were converted into hospitals, and children's homes were established in some.

On October 15, 1944, Horthy prematurely announced the Hungarian decision to seek a separate peace with the Allies. But the Germans were prepared: a fascist putsch with German backing swept away the old Hungarian ruler and the remnants of legitimate government on the very same day. The Hungarian Nazis under Ferenc Szálasi took power—a violent minority recruited from the dregs of society. The Jews, who only hours previously had joyfully greeted the Hungarian exit from the war, had torn off the yellow badges and left their ghetto houses, were the immediate objects of brutal revenge by the Nyilas, the Arrow Cross fascist militia. However, the new authorities were not eager to hand over the Jews to the Germans; they wanted to keep them for themselves. Mass arrests were made and large numbers of Jews brought into brick factories on the east side of the Danube to dig trenches against the approaching Russians.

By this time, of course, the Jews of Budapest had heard about the gassings, and they were afraid that they would be led to mass destruction of the kind that had befallen the Jews of the provinces in the spring. But in the meantime, unknown to them, Himmler had given his order to stop the gassings; on the other hand, Hitler had agreed to the reintroduction of Jews into the Reich as labor slaves in April, 1944.[12] When, therefore, labor was required to build defense lines on the Austrian border with Hungary, Jews were recruited. The first people taken were those whom the Hungarians had concentrated for building their own fortifications, but others were then forcibly taken from the city. Ostensibly only the able-bodied were to be recruited and marched on foot to the border, but in fact, from November 8–15, the first terrible week of the marches, very young boys and girls and people well above their fifties were also marched off. They received no food for a march of eight to nine days of over 200 kilometers, and they were forbidden by their Hungarian guards to seek food from the population. Thousands died, though it is impossible to say exactly how many; the most probable figure seems to be 7,000–10,000 people. "Not even the Germans deported so brutally," was the comment of a young Jewish observer.[13]

The IRC and the neutral missions in Budapest tried to defend the Jews as best they could. On October 21, the IRC intervened with the German embassy, because it was obvious that it was there that the real power lay. The Nazis said that Germany needed more workers, and the Hungarians had kindly agreed to supply them in order to defend both countries from bolshevism. In any case, the Germans said, 1,500 Jews had been caught with weapons in hand, and they deserved to be punished. They would all be evacuated in due course. Born of the IRC also met with the Hungarian foreign minister, protesting to him on October 19 against the brutalities committed by the Arrow Cross militia. In those first days of Arrow Cross rule, about 600 Jews were murdered and their bodies thrown into the Danube. On October 23, after the first Jews had been taken to the brick factories, Born addressed an official protest to the Hungarian government. The Hungarians did not hurry with their reply. When it came on November 11, it declared they had not deported any Jews, but merely sent them to work.[14]

Reszoe Kasztner and the Va'adah also entered the lists in an attempt to influence the Szálasi regime to cease persecuting the Jews. Kasztner tried to avoid excesses by pressing Kurt Becher to intervene in the name of overriding Nazi interests. Becher apparently did so, and the result was a Hungarian order published on November 15 that henceforth only men between the ages of fifteen and sixty, and women between fifteen and forty, were to be taken. Two days later, women were no longer marched off, and on November 27 the marches stopped. Men in labor companies, who were under Hungarian military command, were at first deported on foot along with the other Jews, and on November 28–29, trains were made available to deport more of them. From a German point of view—expressed by Rudolf Hoess, commander of Auschwitz—the foot marches were of no use. Even the Germans on the Austrian border refused to take many of the Jews because they were in no condition to do any work, and this time the Himmler command was clear: they were actually to work. With the same coldness and efficiency with which mass murder was accomplished, sick and exhausted people were refused admittance to Austria. Some of them returned to Budapest; some died on the spot, at Hegyeshalom. Eichmann, who tried his worst to get more Jews, failed. In the end, according to Hehalutz estimates, 25,000 civilians and 13,000 members of labor battalions were involved in these marches.[15]

From November 27, after the end of the foot marches, Jews were forced to move into a small area in the city set aside as a ghetto. A makeshift wooden fence was erected around it. Thousands of persons were taken out of their houses or kidnapped in the streets by Arrow Cross militiamen and were indiscriminately murdered, their bodies usually being disposed of into the Danube. There was no way of earning a living, and the people had to be fed, because there was very little possibility of buying food as the Russians began to invade Budapest. By December 26, the ring around the city was closed. Until the liberation of Buda on January 18, 1945, and of Pest three weeks later, the situation of the Jews was much worse even than that of the rest of the starving population. Further casualties were caused by aerial and artillery bombardment by the Russians.

What was unique in the Budapest situation was the way in which gradually, from July, 1944, to the end of the year, representatives of neutral countries and of IRC, as well as Jewish groups, developed means of saving Jewish lives in the face of a deteriorating situation. The starting point was the Palestinian certificates provided through Moshe Krausz, who was living at the Swiss legation. The man in charge there was Consul Charles Lutz, who had represented Switzerland in a similar capacity in Palestine earlier in the war. Lutz was friendly towards Jewish aspirations, and he allowed Zionist youth movements to use Swiss consular emblems to protect the house from which the distribution of the Palestine certificates was organized and in which a number of the holders of these papers lived. The Swedish legation was also engaged in rescue work. After King Carl intervened against the deportations in late June, it was decided that Raoul Wallenberg, scion of a well-known family of bankers and soldiers who had important social connections with Jews, should join the Swedish minister, Carl I. Danielsson, as a third secretary. Their objective was to save as many Jews as possible. The WRB equipped Wallenberg with up-to-date information about Hungary, and JDC gave him $100,000, of which he took one-half (200,000 Swedish crowns) and went to Budapest in July, 1944. Four Hungarian Jews with business connections, who had been given protection by Danielsson and promised that Sweden would admit them if they managed to reach it, served as a precedent. Wallenberg began issuing similar protection certificates.[16]

After the takeover by the Szálasi regime in October, Lutz and Wallenberg enlarged their activities considerably. A close relationship developed between them and leaders of the Zionist youth movements, especially the contact man with the foreign missions, Rafi Benshalom. The youth groups established an efficient workshop producing forged papers of all kinds, and Lutz and Wallenberg tacitly agreed to the large-scale forgery of Swiss and Swedish papers. Soon there were at least 14,000 instead of the 8,700 authorized holders of Swiss certificates, though Lutz's own estimates of the numbers ranged between 15,000 and 30,000. Many of the holders of these papers were concentrated by the youth groups in some forty houses that were placed under Swiss consular protection. Lutz established a Jewish department at his consulate to deal with the problems arising from the need to protect the houses and their inhabitants, which was run by Otto Komoly, head of the Va'adah. The Swedes had a similar set-up, and while officially 4,500 protection papers were issued by Wallenberg, probably thousands more such papers were in circulation. Wallenberg's personal style differed from that of Lutz: he intervened personally wherever he could and saved people from columns marching to the Austrian border or from the hands of the militia whenever he could find a pretext to grant them Swedish protection.[17]

The period after October, 1944, also saw a dramatic increase in IRC activities in behalf of Jews. The IRC specialized in the protection of children, primarily orphans or children of deported parents. The numbers varied from 2,000–5,000, and they were organized in up to twenty-four homes run by the youth movements. In addition, many hundreds of adults were given certificates as working with these children; again the youth movement members forged papers. Born also used JDC funds to open public kitchens that operated from late October until close to liberation. The numbers of these kitchens and the numbers of people served in them was never quite clear. Early in November, 18,000–20,000 people were reported to be receiving meals, while late in the month the number was claimed to be 40,000—surely an exaggeration. At any rate, it is fairly well established that basic feeding was provided on a considerable scale. Apart from the IRC kitchens, funds were supplied to the various groups, from the still functioning Judenrat to the Zionist Va'adah, to feed people.[18]

The Spanish and Portuguese legations followed the example of the Swiss and the Swedes. The Portuguese acting consul, Jules

Gulden, not only offered several hundred visas to Portugal, but handed out an additional 1,200 papers of protection. The papal nuncio followed suit, and 5,000 protection papers supposedly from that source circulated, though how many of these were genuine is not clear.[19]

What made the granting of protection papers a mass phenomenon was the activity of the Zionist youth movements. There were not more than 300–400 young men and women between the ages of seventeen to twenty-two or twenty-three, most of them refugees from Slovakia, who by a deliberate decision opted for an attempt at mass rescue by forgery rather than an armed rebellion on the model of the Warsaw ghetto. As a result of their forging of protection certificates, probably no fewer than 50,000 such papers were in circulation in Budapest in November–December, 1944. In addition, Benshalom and his friends engaged in daring exploits. Dressed in Arrow Cross uniforms and pretending to lead children—and occasionally adults—to places of execution, they saved them from prisons and makeshift camps or execution squads. Their close contacts with whatever Hungarian antifascist underground there was increased their possibilities of saving Jews by hiding them in non-Jewish areas.[20] As a result of all these efforts, about 119,000 Jews survived in Budapest: 69,000 in the ghetto area, 25,000 in hiding places in the city, and 25,000 in the protected houses. Many thousands of those who survived outside these houses were saved by the protection certificates.[21] All of these activities required money. Some was sent from Istanbul, but the bulk came from Mayer in Switzerland or from après arrangements. Direct transmissions by Mayer, usually in foreign currency notes, for the Judenrat and the Va'adah were effected through Schwalb's Hehalutz contacts or through IRC. Kasztner also received cash transmissions, which he brought from the Swiss border to Hungary; the IRC and Lutz received direct subsidies from Mayer. The youth movements received their funds either from the Va'adah or from IRC, whereas Wallenberg was largely financed from Sweden, where WRB sources paid him JDC funds. Because of the nature of these arrangements, it is extremely difficult to estimate how much JDC help was given.[22] However, IRC appears to have received for Hungary at least 1.25 million sfr. ($280,000) between July, 1944, and February, 1945. Over 1 million sfr. ($227,000) were transferred in cash to the Judenrat and the Va'adah, and Lutz received direct subsidies of about 81,000 sfr. ($18,000). Some of these sums were lost, stolen in transit or confiscated by the Germans, but, on the other hand, additional sums were made available locally through credit arrangements. Food was also sent, but some wagons from Switzerland never arrived, sugar and flour bought by Born in Budapest was damaged by bombs, and the rest presumably was stolen by Hungarians. The conclusion is that JDC financed most of the rescue activities in Budapest—the direct feeding, the upkeep of the children's homes, the protection papers, and, unknowingly, even the youth movements' underground activities. Again, as in some of the other areas we have discussed, JDC acted solely as a financing operation; the results were achieved through the self-sacrifice of Swiss people like Born and Lutz, Swedes like Wallenberg and his staff, and Jews such as Komoly, Kasztner, and the youth leaders.

The End in Slovakia

Another area where Mayer tried to help was Slovakia. The outbreak of the Slovak national uprising on August 29, 1944, triggered a series of events that spelled the end of Slovak Jewry. Thousands of Jews participated in the uprising, including a special Jewish unit formed out of the inmates of the Jewish camp at Nováky. The German reaction was swift. SS units crossed the border, and after two months of fighting, the rebellion was defeated. The three Czech generals in charge were captured and murdered at Mauthausen; the remnants of the rebel forces were either caught by the Germans or dispersed. Some of these latter, including 2,000 Jews, retreated into the Tatra mountains and continued to live and occasionally fight there until liberation. The rest of the Jews, probably over 20,000 with their numbers swelled by those who had returned from Hungary, became the objects of Nazi revenge. Towards the end of September, Alois Brunner, one of Eichmann's chief henchmen, arrived in Bratislava in order to deport the Jews to Poland. On September 28, 1,800 Jews were arrested in one mass action in that city. On November 16, the remaining Jews in the city were asked to report to the Slovak Judenrat building, but only 500 did. Thousands were caught in police raids, in Bratislava and in the province; some were murdered on the spot, while others were brought to the camp of Sered, from where 13,500 were deported to Germany—the first five trains to Auschwitz and the rest to other camps. The leaders of the ÚŽ, who remained at their post to the end, were included. A Gestapo agent caught Gizi Fleischmann while she was writing a

447

letter, probably to Schwalb or Mayer, and she too was brought to Sered, probably on October 20. The Nazis intended to let her stay there if she gave the names and addresses of Jews hidden in Bratislava, but when she refused, she was deported to Auschwitz with the remark that her return was undesirable. Michael Weissmandel was also deported, but he managed to jump from the train and returned to Bratislava, while his pregnant wife and five children went on to be murdered at Auschwitz.[23]

In Slovakia, just as in Budapest, attempts were made to move the neutral countries and the Vatican to intervene. But there were no neutral legations in Slovakia; the Swiss had a consul there, but they did not have diplomatic relations with the Slovak state. Nevertheless, they protested against the deportations, and the Vatican also sent a protest note on September 20. They were of no avail. The IRC, which also intervened, was told that the Germans were responsible and that one could not talk to the Germans on Jewish matters—this line of argument had been suggested by German ambassador Hans Ludin himself in order to make things easier for the Slovak government. On November 26, the IRC's attempt to approach Ottamar Kubala, the chief of the Slovak special police force charged with rooting out opponents and Jews, also failed. A special German murder squad, commanded by a Dr. Josef Witiska, reported at the end of 1944 that it had killed 2,257 Jews and deported over 7,000 others.

Up to the last, Reszoe Kasztner and his friends in Bratislava and Budapest believed that the deportations from Slovakia could be stopped by bribes, whereas Mayer, in his negotiations with Kurt Becher, demanded an immediate end to the Slovak deportations as a condition for any steps undertaken to satisfy German demands. But it was Becher himself who said that, because the Jews had participated in the Slovak rebellion, he could do nothing about them. Bratislava certainly was the last place where Eichmann had a free hand.

Mayer tried to help on two different planes. Unknown to Kasztner and Fleischmann, he provided some funds for the ransom arrangements Orthodox leaders made with Becher, though he did not believe in them. He paid a total of 537,900 sfr. (about $128,000) for goods supposedly supplied locally to the Nazis in fulfillment of their demands between September, 1944, and the end of the German rule in Slovakia and Hungary. More effective was the 200,000 sfr. (about $47,000) he provided through the IRC delegate to Slovakia, Georges Dunant, who reached Bratislava at the end of October. Five hundred Jews who were hiding in Bratislava were helped. Dunant's attempt to create a home for orphaned children in Liptovský Svätý Mikuláš, a town in central Slovakia, failed, however, and the children were deported. In January, Mayer sent him another 200,000 sfr. Through Becher's efforts—although Musy was to claim it as his achievement—a group of 69 people, most of them from Bratislava, left the city on March 31, reached Vienna on April 3, and then traveled to the Swiss border. Among them was Rabbi Weissmandel.[24]

The Final Months in Austria

Another area of Mayer's concern was Vienna. A pitiful remnant of 229 "full" Jews were still there in early 1945, including Josef Löwenherz, head of the community since 1938, as well as a few thousand half-Jews and Jews in mixed marriages. Life centered largely around the hospital, where an energetic but controversial young doctor, Emil Tuchmann, tried to save lives with practically no medical supplies.

In June, 1944, about 17,000 Jewish deportees from Hungary, including women and children, arrived at nine camps in the Strasshof area near Vienna. Of these, 1,500 were sent to Auschwitz or died locally in the summer of 1944. By the end of the year, many of those remaining in the camps were drifting into Vienna, where they were employed by Nazi industries; their women and children were still with them, and though there were losses from disease and aerial bombardment, there were still 6,000 of them in Vienna, and another 6,000 nearby, in early 1945. Approximately 2,500 people (it is unclear whether these were included in the 12,000 just mentioned) were sent to Bergen-Belsen early in 1945; many of them were to die of starvation in the camp in March-April, 1945. However, it is clear that a majority of the original transport survived.

That so many of the Jews in the Vienna area did survive was at least partly due to the work undertaken by Dr. Lutz Thudichum of IRC, who went there at the end of 1944. Mayer sent no less than 400,000 sfr. ($91,000) to Thudichum, who bought food and clothing, mainly in Bratislava, where some goods could still be obtained. When contact between Slovakia and Vienna became more difficult—though Bratislava is just across the Danube from the Austrian capital—Austrian food was also bought, and some was imported from Switzerland.[25] Thudichum, however, like his colleague Dunant in Bratislava, was liable to be fooled by the Nazis. For example, he thought that Hermann Krumey, Eichmann's henchman in Vienna and now responsible for a "just but strict" supervision of the Jews' well-being, was a gentleman. Dunant, visiting Theresienstadt on April 6, 1945, gained a favorable impression of it—the Nazis managed to hide the atrocities. The last 10,000 people who had been sent to Auschwitz in the preceding autumn, he reported, were sent "in order to be utilized as laborers or in order to supervise the administration of the camps."[26] In fact, of course, they were gassed.

Rescue at the Last Moment

Mayer's main concern, besides the ransom talks and the Hungarian situation, was his fear that the Germans would murder the last of their Jewish captives before they were finally defeated. This was the fear he called "11:59." He tried to persuade Becher to agree to the provision by IRC of food to the camps; he joined general and specifically Jewish efforts to persuade IRC to take a strong stand in the matter of keeping the camp inmates alive; and he of course provided funds and pressed IRC to do whatever it could. Up to the very end, he supplied money for parcels to Jewish inmates of the camps. Most of the $265,000 he spent through IRC in 1944, and the $587,000 he spent in 1945, went into parcels and truckloads of food. He knew quite well that it was never certain that Jews would get this food, but, as IRC wrote to him in early December, 1944, parcels were of very little importance from the "alimentation point of view, but very important psychologically."[27]

In July, 1944, the IRC had ceased sending parcels to Birkenau (Auschwitz), having realized that they were not received by Jews. Instead, it supplied Theresienstadt and Bergen-Belsen; probably a proportion at least of these packages were delivered to their intended destinations at Theresienstadt, and certainly at Bergen-Belsen to those privileged groups intended by the Nazis for exchange. Early in 1945, Mayer increased his efforts in this regard. He gave large sums to the IRC in order to get parcels to these two camps; on January 1, he sent 10,000 packages. The IRC was helped in this by a general agreement of November 20, 1944, by the German Red Cross to have packages sent to Jews.

As time went on, Mayer persuaded IRC to send convoys of trucks into Germany, despite the dangers from air attacks by the

450

Allies and the shortage of trucks in Switzerland. He gave money for ten trucks and a first convoy went off late in March, 1945, bound for Germany. In April, another convoy went to Landsberg and Kauffering concentration camps, where 12,000 Jews were reputed to be interned. The 14,000 parcels sent there were largely used after liberation, because no distribution of any size could take place in the chaos that reigned at the time. These large transports of parcels were apparently the basis of the rumors spread in America that Mayer had visited Germany before liberation and distributed help to the camps. Mayer was unhappy about these rumors, because he had avoided personal publicity; of course, the fact that he had never actually crossed the Swiss border was well known to his Jewish opponents, who then made great play with denying the hero-making image that JDC-New York was clearly trying to create.[28]

Joseph Schwartz involved Mayer with another venture after the Swedish government agreed, late in 1944, to the sending of parcels from Sweden to Jews in concentration camps in Germany. At first there were to be 20,000, amounting to 100 tons of foodstuffs. The WJC allocated $25,000 for this program, which was channeled through its representative in Stockholm, Hillel Storch. But Storch had no experience in this kind of work, and there were technical difficulties. When JDC was asked to help, Schwartz at first insisted on its taking over the whole program, though in the end he relented. An additional $75,000 were required, and Laura Margolis, the JDC representative in Sweden, was told to go ahead. The money was transferred largely from Switzerland. But most of the parcels came too late. Of a total of close to 40,000 that were prepared, 7,500 were sent to Bergen-Belsen, 7,500 to Ravensbrück, and 2,259 to other places. The rest remained in Sweden and were ultimately distributed among the survivors of German camps whom the Swedes took in during April–June, 1945.[29]

As the war drew to a close, Schwartz worried more and more about what he would find when the Germans were defeated. Some of the ideas occasionally heard from New York showed how little people had really learned in America. There they talked of a "reconstruction of Jewish life, restoring Jews to their economic position," and of retraining "those who cannot return to their former homes."[30] Schwartz knew it would be more complicated than that. The main problem was that the enormity of the Holocaust had not had time to sink in. Jewry acted in a state of shock.

451

JDC was no more prepared for the problems of liberation than it had been for the problems of mass murder. Nor were the other Jewish organizations. The Jewish public did not really believe that there would be many survivors, and yet on the other hand it had not internalized the loss of millions. In April, 1945, the big German camps began to be uncovered. Normal human beings had never before visited hell, nor had they seen the devil incarnate. What the Allies found was disbelieved, misunderstood, or trivialized in cheap statements. Probably some 200,000 Jews were liberated from the camps on the collapse of Hitler's Reich. Probably that number again had lost their lives in the last months of the Nazi regime, when untold thousands of prisoners were marched backward and forward through the ruined landscape of the crumbling Nazi empire. These victims were not gassed or shot en masse, but marches without food and with stragglers shot by SS guards did the job just as well. Nobody helped the Jews or any of the other persecuted groups in this last frightfulness of the Nazi regime. One by one, what was left of the marching columns was liberated by the Allied armies. The war ended on May 8. On May 9, Theresienstadt was liberated. The war against the Jews had started before the war on anyone else—it ended after everything else was finished. JDC had struggled against the horror as best it could. Now, after five-and-a-half terrible years, the vast graveyard could be surveyed.

20

Some Afterthoughts

The Nazis did not treat the Jews in the same way as all the other peoples they oppressed.

This qualitative difference was misunderstood at the time, and it is very difficult to grasp now. "What happened to the Jews, happened to others, Catholics, communists, liberals, socialists—all were persecuted. Their sole desire was liberty to express a point of view." This evidence of absolute miscomprehension was published in the London *Daily Mirror* on August 3, 1945, and it is representative of views widely held then and later. The fact of the matter is that in National Socialist ideology, the Jews were centrally important as a negative force.[1] They were an antirace, or a hybrid race with satanic qualities, and intent on ruling the world—in fact, ruling it already. Nazi imagery in, for instance, books for Nazi kindergartens and primary schools, contained the identification of the Jew with Satan, for which there were long-standing precedents in Christian antisemitic teaching, and the modern, quasi-scientific identification of the Jew with microbes, viruses, dangerous bacilli, or with repulsive insects.[2] What the Nazis were after was what they imputed to the Jews: the control of the world. This could only be achieved if Jewish world-domination was broken, and the demonic Jewish element removed. Hitler's planned invasion of Russia was motivated not only by strategic and political considerations, but also quite explicitly by his desire to destroy the Jewish enemy lurking behind

453

the Soviet regime.³ The Nazi regime thus rested on two foundations: the desire for German world domination and the need to destroy the imaginary Jewish power.

Nazi attitudes to the other European nations were never very clearly defined; the Nazi leaders held various views. One may, however, generalize by saying that apart from the Jews and, possibly, the Gypsies, all the other European nations were considered Aryan. By and large, West Europeans were considered either as possible allies (this was true of the Germanic nations), or as subject peoples to be treated, on the whole, firmly but kindly. The Slav nations were to be the slaves of the Nazi empire, and were often termed subhuman. There was never a clear plan for total physical annihilation of any of these nationalities—the Nazis would need their muscles—but there were both plans and actions designed to destroy them as autonomous ethnic groups, constituting what was afterwards called "genocide."⁴ It involved selective but massive murder (for instance of the Polish intelligentsia), the destruction of independent, nationally linked religious life (for instance the mass murder of the Polish Catholic priesthood in western Poland), the destruction of national culture and its symbols, the elimination of universities, and the plan to abolish all secondary and most primary school education.

But only in the case of the Jews did the Nazis intend the total physical annihilation of a people whom in their imagination they had identified with a demonic force. Their anti-Jewish attitude resulted from the combination of an age-old hatred fostered by the other monotheistic religions against the father religion and those who adhered to it and the secularist rebellion of a technologically oriented nationalistic civilization against the Judeo-Christian ethical tradition. It was that deadly pseudoreligious combination that produced Nazism and the Holocaust. The Nazis, in light of their quasi religion, could not and did not see the Jews as human at all. This well-documented fact is hard to grasp, but it must underlie any evaluation of Nazi policies towards Jews and the Jewish reaction to them.

Once the Nazi political mythology had denied the human qualities of Jews, the way was open to mass murder. Nevertheless, it was not the only option open to the Nazi regime. The Jews were not solely an anti-Germanic power, they were also parasites feeding on the body politic of the nations they controlled. While ultimately Jewish power had to be destroyed globally—presumably by mass murder—this was not necessarily the best short-term policy. The export of Jews in return for real political and material advantages might rid the Nazi empire of the Jews, and at the same time introduce their destructive influence into the societies of Germany's adversaries. Antisemitism would spread because everyone would hate the Jews fleeing from German rule—which would create a pro-German atmosphere among those nations. Furthermore, the enemy societies would be weakened by disruption caused by Jewish influence.[5] The sale of Jews was made possible by the same irrationality that had made mass murder possible: the identification of Jews as nonhuman beings made it feasible to barter them for other objects of trade.

These were at least some of the considerations that led the Nazis to their offers to release Jews against ransom, the payment to be made in money, goods, political advantages, or a combination of these elements. It appears that at times the Nazis were really expecting to sell at least some Jews for their own advantage. But the negotiations had no chance of success because the Allies were not willing to buy. The West, conducting a bitter war against the enslavement of nations and threats to its civilization, did not understand the Nazis' attitude to the Jews at all. Psychologically hemmed in by ancient anti-Jewish prejudices and laboring under the immense stress of a world war, the western powers failed to grasp that the Nazis' war against the Jews was different from their war against other peoples and yet was an essential part of their struggle for world domination. In the interests of the aims for which they fought the war, the western Allies might have decided that the total annihilation—from sacral, quasi-religious motives—of a people was too dangerous a precedent. That was the real or the only chance that the ransom negotiations had, but the western powers rejected it. The Soviet Union, fighting a nationalistic war, was in any case no partner for political actions ultimately based on ethical foundations. But, for the span of time between May, 1944, and the autumn of that year, ransoming Jews became a topic for top-level Allied consultations. The rejection of the proposals was anything but haphazard. It was the result of careful consideration. Brand, and later Saly Mayer and JDC's role in the negotiations, became a matter of world politics, and the fate of many Jews hung in the balance. The upshot of the ransom negotiations was, however, that the Nazis were willing to sell lives and nobody bought them.

Against this general background, Jewish options were very limited. During World War I the Jews could choose to support the liberal western powers or the conservative German-led coalition; the Germans fought a war against the archenemy of the Jews, tsarist Russia, while the Allied powers fought for a democratic world in which the Jews might hope to find their place. There was no such choice for the Jews in World War II. Jewish influence in the United States counted for little, contrary to the popular imagination, and for nothing in the United Kingdom.[6] Palestine Jewry was threatened with the extinction of its hope for national existence and could exercise no influence over what was happening in wartime Europe. The Jewish people had no armed might and little economic leverage; they were almost completely powerless. In that situation, aid, rescue, hiding, bribery, ransom, or, in special circumstances, desperate armed rebellion, were the kinds of reactions that could be expected.

JDC's involvement throughout the war was that of the body set up by American Jewry to extend help to Jews abroad. Despite attempts by some other groups to enter the field of aid and rescue, JDC remained American Jewry's representative in that area. Aid and rescue could be achieved by a combination of money and political pressure on those who could facilitate its work. The funds available, however, depended on American Jews' awareness of the Holocaust, and the concrete problem of money was therefore very much tied in with the seemingly abstract epistemological problem of the relationship between information and knowledge. We have noted in the preceding pages that at all stages of the war there was no lack of information regarding the fate of European Jewry, though it is true that explicit news items regarding the total mass murder reached Britain and America only in the late spring of 1942, or about a year after the beginning of the Nazi murder actions on German-occupied Soviet soil. But even without that specific information, enough was known of ghettos and camps to justify a rethinking of Allied and Jewish policy regarding the Jews in Europe. On the other hand, in the late spring and summer of 1942, when the facts of the Holocaust became known, millions of Jews were still alive who could be helped. The seeping in of knowledge was, however, a slow process, and was not completed even by the end of the war. JDC's leadership, not only in New York but even in Lisbon, did not grasp the full impact of what was occurring to Europe's Jews. In a sense, JDC's response was the reaction of sanity: had the organization grasped what was happening, it might well have lost its capacity to do anything at all. But it is clear that with the excep-

Some Afterthoughts

tion of a few individuals, JDC leaders in the free world were acting out what may be called "normal" reactions to "normal" disasters, whereas what was happening was an "alpine event" (to use Franklin H. Littell's terminology) calling for "not normal" reactions. "Not normal" would, in this context, refer to actions leading to the breaking of norms of ordinary warfare in the interest of Europe's Jews.

JDC acted in the way it understood best: energetically, spending its funds to help a maximum number of people. History was, in a way, kind to JDC. A conservative, antinationalistic agency of American Jewish philanthropists was suddenly faced with forces that were beyond its comprehension, and contrary to its creed, its very basis, it became, in country after country, in situation after situation, the embodiment of an embattled Jewish people. To the adversary, JDC became the representative of an imaginary Jewish world government; to many victims, it became a hope, a symbol of Jewish unity and Jewish compassion.

In beleaguered Europe, JDC was in most cases represented by a group of individuals who became leaders of the suffering Jewish communities and often rose to heights of heroism. This was true of the JDC group in Warsaw, who tried to save masses of starving people as long as there was any hope. JDC-Warsaw financed many of the preparations for the Warsaw ghetto rebellion and then, most probably, the rebellion itself. There were leaders such as Gizi Fleischmann in Slovakia or Wilhelm Filderman in Rumania, who were representative of large groups of Jews, and not only of JDC. To them JDC, personalized by Saly Mayer in Switzerland, tried to provide the wherewithal for their desperate fight against destruction. In other places, such as France, there was no unified Jewish representation, but JDC supported those groups and individuals who were involved in rescue; occasionally, usually indirectly, JDC supported armed activities.

Generally, one can divide JDC activities into three main types: direct involvement of American emissaries in local activities; direct involvement of local JDC groups in aid, rescue, and sometimes political activities; and funding of local initiatives. We have seen examples of the first of these with Moses Beckelman's work in Lithuania and Laura Margolis's work in Shanghai. The second type is exemplified in Warsaw and in Jules Jefroykin's group in France. The third we have seen in Slovakia, Rumania, Zagreb, Italy, Belgium, and Holland. The involvement of Americans was necessarily transitory; with America's entry into the

457

war, this kind of activity had to cease. It is hard to assess the relative effectiveness of the other two kinds of JDC involvement. No planning of these activities was possible; they arose out of desperate necessities and were adjusted to the concrete situation.

The link between JDC-Lisbon and the Jewish communities in most of Europe and Shanghai after 1942 was Saly Mayer in Switzerland. Our inquiry has shown the unique importance of this man in the JDC story. A more flexible, less complicated individual might have been a better choice, but Mayer did surprisingly well, his opponents' claims notwithstanding. Above all, he grasped the situation better than many others, managing to supply, with the little money he had to give, not merely help but hope.

The terrible question is often asked whether more could have been done to save lives. Michael Weissmandel wrote that the Jews of the West were asked to shed not blood—*dam* in Hebrew—but money—*damim*. If all the money in the world had bought the life of just one child, it would have been cheaply bought. American Jewry gave JDC very little money until 1944 ($37,909,323 in 1939–43) and somewhat more in 1944 and 1945 ($35,551,365). The $194,332,033 it raised in 1945–48 showed how late the reaction to the disaster of the Holocaust was. Some of the expenditures of scarce JDC dollars were, to judge with the benefit of hindsight, less than judicious. Hundreds of thousands were poured into the fiasco that was the Sosua venture in the Dominican Republic. Hundreds of thousands of dollars were given to the Russians, in addition to the millions that the American people as a whole gave. Had they been allocated to Gizi Fleischmann or Reszoe Kasztner, they might have made a real difference. Yet the bulk of JDC's limited funds went where it was needed most. The results achieved were in many areas and cases just what had been hoped for. Without JDC funds, the hiding of the children in France, the rescue from starvation in the Transnistrian ghettos, the feeding of the Jews beleaguered in the Swiss and Swedish houses in Budapest—these and many more ventures would have been impossible.

JDC's limitations lay in its very legalistic approach to rescue, its limited funds, and an Allied policy that aimed exclusively at military victory rather than at both victory and the saving of lives. Within those limitations, JDC did a great deal of good. It was basically an organization of volunteers. Its workers, from the lay leadership in New York who gave of their time without hesitation and often without limit, to the heroes of the Holocaust—Gizi

Fleischmann, Emmanuel Ringelblum, Isaac Giterman, and all the others—were united in a typically Jewish endeavor. It was perhaps best expressed by Saly Mayer in one of his notebooks: "Stop this Rezeach!" "Rezach," in Hebrew, means "murder." Jewish tradition says that he who saves one soul is likened to one who has saved the whole world.

Notes

Note on Archival Sources

Archives of the JDC (New York, New York). Unless otherwise stated, all archival material used in this book derives from the JDC archives. The following methods of citation have been used:

1. Where the cabinet and the file are numbered (or were numbered at the time the research for this book was done), citation is made by cabinet number followed by file number.

2. Where the files were not numbered, citation is made by the original file marking: e.g., 51-Lithuania, Administration—U.S. State Dept., Conf.-41 ("Confidential"), and so forth. Some of these files bear the addition "General and Emergency," which has been omitted in the notes.

3. Agro-Joint files are cited as AJ, followed by the file number.

4. The Saly Mayer Archive is kept separately; these files are cited as SM, followed by the file number.

5. Executive Committee minutes are cited as Excom, followed by the date of the meeting; Administrative Committee minutes are cited as AC, followed by the date; Board of Directors' and annual meetings are cited by full name, followed by the date.

6. Reports sent in from various countries or written by JDC staff members in New York are cited as R, followed by the number of the reports file.

7. Morris C. Troper's special file is cited as Troper File.

8. JDC material from Kraków and Warsaw preserved on microfilm is cited as WR, followed by the number of the reel.

9. Some typewritten manuscripts of conferences of JDC workers and some reports are kept in the JDC Library, which is part of the JDC archives. These materials are identified by a descriptive title and location.

Central Zionist Archive (Jerusalem, Israel). Cited as CZA, followed by the group symbol, file number, and date.

Moreshet Archive (Giv'at Haviva, Israel). Cited as MA, followed by the file number.

Nuremberg Trial Documents. In quoting documents submitted to the Allied military court trying the Nazi war criminals at Nuremberg after the war, the customary procedure has been followed by quoting the documents submitted to the court as NG or PS, followed by the number. Complete sets of these documents can be found in the Library of Congress and the Columbia Law Library, among others.

Oral History Documentation Center (Institute of Contemporary Jewry, Hebrew

University, Jerusalem, Israel). Cited as OHD, followed by the name of the person interviewed and the date of the interview.

Public Records Office (London, England). Material quoted from the General Correspondence section of the Foreign Office is cited as PRO-FO 371 or FO 371, followed by the file number, number of the paper, and date. Material quoted from the Cabinet file dealing with refugee matters is cited as CAB 95/15, followed by the number of the paper and the date.

War Refugee Board Papers (Franklin D. Roosevelt Library, Hyde Park, New York). Cited as WRB, followed by the number of the cable and the date.

World Jewish Congress material (Geneva, Switzerland). These files are still awaiting organization; papers are cited as WJC, followed by the date of the correspondence.

Yad Vashem Archives (Jerusalem, Israel). Cited as YV, followed by the file symbol. The Ringelblum Archive is cited as YVRA, followed by the file symbol.

Yiddish Scientific Institution Archives (New York, New York). Cited as YIVO, followed by the file symbol.

Introduction

1. See Joshua Trachtenberg, *The Devil and the Jews* (New York, 1943); Franklin H. Littell, *The Crucifixion of the Jews* (New York, 1975).
2. Norman Cohn, *Warrant for Genocide* (London, 1967). The *Protocols* were a forgery produced by the Russian tsarist police which purported to prove that there was a Jewish conspiracy to control and rule the world.
3. See Telford Taylor, ed., *Hitler's Secret Book* (New York: Grove Press, 1962).
4. See, for example, George Mosse, *Germans and Jews* (London, 1971), esp. pp. 34–76; George Mosse, *The Nationalization of the Masses* (New York, 1975).
5. Translated from Wilhelm Treue, "Hitlers Denkschrift zum Vierjahresplan in 1936," *Vierteljahreshefte für Zeitgeschichte* 3 (1955):184–210.
6. See, for example, Hitler's Reichstag speech of January 30, 1939, in Lucy S. Dawidowicz, ed., *A Holocaust Reader* (New York, 1976), pp. 32–33; see also Hermann Göring's remarks at the conference following the Crystal Night pogrom of November, 1938 (PS-1816).
7. Historians who grasp the centrality of antisemitism in the Nazi world view nevertheless shy away from drawing the logical conclusion. For a rare exception, see Andreas Hillgruber, "Die Endlösung und das deutsche Ostimperium," *Vierteljahreshefte für Zeitgeschichte* 20 (1972):133–53.
8. Walter Buch, quoted in Helmut Krausnick and Martin Broszat, *Anatomy of the SS State*, p. 309, n. 16. There the term *Fäulniserscheinung* is translated as "sign of rottenness." I believe the translation in the text is more accurate.
9. Cf. Lucy S. Dawidowicz, *The War against the Jews* (London, 1975), p. 17. She seems to infer from one word in a September, 1919, letter by Hitler that he had by that time made up his mind to murder the Jews. This seems to be a totally mistaken interpretation.
10. Heinrich Himmler, quoted in *Vierteljahreshefte für Zeitgeschichte* 5 (1957): 196–98.
11. PS-3358, Jan. 25, 1939.
12. See Krausnick and Broszat, *Anatomy of the SS State*, pp. 77–85; Uwe D. Adam, *Judenpolitik im Dritten Reich* (Dusseldorf, 1972), pp. 303–16. Adam says that the final order was not given until November, 1941.
13. Tables 1 and 2 are based on 3-1; 9-18; 14-6; 28-3; R-9; R-43. The RVE's 522,700 seems to refer to all Jews by Nazi definition, including Christians. The other 100,000 were therefore "half" or "quarter" Jews by Nazi definition. R-43

estimates that 262,000 persons left Germany in 1933–39, including 14,000 from the Sudeten area. The RVE says 281,000, and specifically relates this figure to the 522,700 in 1933. There was also an excess of 38,400 deaths over births in that period, so that the number of Jews had decreased by 320,300. Estimates of the number of Jews in Germany in 1939 made by different RVE officials vary between 202,400 and 240,000 (including the Sudeten area). R-43 also estimates that 146,000 left Austria in 1938–39 (presumably including "nonprofessing" Jews), and 29,000 left Bohemia and Moravia. The discrepancies between these figures explain the difference between the 404,800 emigrants cited in table 1 and the 429,000 immigrants cited in table 3.

14. Yehuda Bauer, *My Brother's Keeper*, pp. 138–79. Table 3 is based on 15-1 and 31-German Refugees, 1939–42.

15. 39-Germany, Reports, 1937–44; 28-3, Arbeitsbericht der RVE, 1939.

16. Bauer, *My Brother's Keeper*, pp. 278–80.

17. JDC claimed to have emigrated, directly or indirectly, 177,500 out of 450,000 emigrants from Greater Germany (R-9, Apr. 25, 1940). In 1939, it provided 38 percent of HICEM's budget; this support increased to 51 percent in 1941.

18. Morris D. Waldman, *Nor by Power*, p. 82.

19. Bauer, *My Brother's Keeper*, pp. 180–209, 243–50, 292–301.

20. Troper File, M. C. Troper-J. C. Hyman, June 10, 1939.

21. 44-4, Troper and Hyman-Baerwald, Aug. 29, 1939. There is a considerable discrepancy between the New York records, which indicate that $215,000 were transferred to Warsaw in early September, and JDC records salvaged in Poland, which speak of a transfer of close to 4,500,000 zl. (over $440,000).

Chapter One

1. Administration-U.S. State Dept., 1933-45, J. N. Rosenberg-J. C. Hyman, Sept. 9, 1939.

2. Excom, Sept. 7, 1939; 8-2, M. D. Waldman-J. B. Wise, Sept. 13, 1939.

3. Excom, Nov. 1, 1939; Sept. 27, 1939; Nov. 29, 1939.

4. Excom, Jan. 24, 1940; R-6, Outline of 1940 Report, Apr. 23, 1941; 14-68, Memo by I. Rosen, Nov. 23, 1940.

5. Excom, Feb. 11, 1941; Board of Directors, Mar. 19, 1941.

6. Cf. Saul S. Friedman, *No Haven for the Oppressed*. I have preferred to rely on his original Ph.D. dissertation, "Official U.S. Policy toward Jewish Refugees, 1938–1945" (Ohio State University, 1969). See also David S. Wyman, *Paper Walls*, pp. 14–23.

7. Conf.-3, Joseph Willen-Hyman, Nov., 1940; R-8, Isaac W. Bernstein-J. B. Wise; on April 15, 1941, Annette R. Saber of San Francisco cabled that she and her group objected to the "futility of aiding European Relief program thereby creating a preferred class in controlled area."

8. Excom, June 19, 1940. But an obviously exasperated Hyman wrote to Albert H. Lieberman on July 5, 1940: "I cannot understand the type of thinking which selects the most desperate, the most emergent period in the history of the Jewish communities of the world as the time when relief assistance, the extending of a word of hope, to these persecuted, harassed people should be denied."

9. Board of Directors, Sept. 9, 1940.

10. Excom, July 8, 1940.

11. YV, Chassidei Umot Ha'olam, file 264, containing letters and testimonies by Chaim H. Kruger, Joana de Sousa-Mendes, Fred Zimmerman, Marguerite Rollin, Harry A. Ezraty, and others.

12. Private information from Ilya Dijour, 1964; OHD, Interview with Joseph J. Schwartz, May 24, 1968, p. 2.

13. Ibid., and source cited in chap. 1, n. 11.

14. Haim Avni, *Sfarad Vehayehudim,* pp. 87–95; Troper report to Excom, July 8, 1940.

15. Avni, *Sfarad Vehayehudim,* pp. 107–10, deals very carefully with these figures, quoting a HICEM report claiming that HICEM had aided 10,500 refugees leaving Portugal in 1940–42. He suggests that the number of refugees in Spain and of those that did not require HICEM aid be added to give the number of refugees rescued. However, detailed JDC lists of sailings from Lisbon show that about 10,700 refugees sailed on JDC-sponsored ships from July, 1941 to January, 1942, alone. I could not find similar lists for all of the other months; another partial JDC list, however, covers the period July–September, 1940, and has 5,547 passengers, at a time when non-JDC or HICEM emigration was considerable. At the end of December, 1940, there were still 8,000 refugees in Portugal (*New York Times,* Dec. 15, 1940). D'Esaguy's figure of 32,000 is not the exaggeration that it might seem, and the figure of 25,000 is rather conservative. This indeed would tally with other JDC reports quoted but discounted by Avni. For 1941, he shows that JDC claimed some 9,000 refugees in the first five months. If we add the 10,700 listed above for the rest of the year, we arrive at about 20,000. But these must have included most of the 8,000 already taken into account for 1940, because early in 1942 there were only 1,000 refugees left in Lisbon. We therefore arrive at a figure of 13,000. Fewer people made private arrangements during that second period, and a conservative estimate would therefore be 15,000 for 1941.

16. See Krausnick and Broszat, *Anatomy of the SS State,* pp. 77–85.

17. Avni, *Sfarad Vehayehudim,* pp. 89–91.

18. Ibid., p. 92; 48-Portugal, Refugees, Troper cable, July 1, 1941; 51-Spain, 1941–42, esp. summary by F. R. Alderstein, Apr. 15, 1942.

19. 48-Portugal, 1933–42, Lisbon-New York, May 15, 1941; Hyman-de Bianchi, May 16, 1941; and Schwartz's cable of July 12, 1941. Schwartz had a very distinctive style; the July 12 cable reads: "Badge boys have established definite rule turndown without appeal all applications transvisas where applicant born Agrojoint territory."

20. See Henry L. Feingold, *Politics of Rescue,* esp. pp. 115–37.

21. Friedman, "Official U.S. Policy," p. 180.

22. 51-Spain, 1941–42, Lisbon-New York, Feb. 2, 1941. See also Wyman, *Paper Walls,* pp. 171–305; Feingold, *Politics of Rescue,* pp. 126–66.

23. 44-30, Feb.–Mar., 1940, correspondence between JDC and U.S. State Dept.

24. 45-Poland, Refugees, 1939–45, "A Polish Story," initialed M. C. T., Jan. 31, 1941.

25. 42-Luxemburg, 1938–44.

26. Ibid.

27. This account of the Luxemburg episode is based partly on Mrs. Ruth Zariz's paper, "Yahadut Luxemburg Ba'sho'ah" [Luxemburg Jewry during the holocaust], Institute of Contemporary Jewry, Jerusalem, 1975; and Luxemburg, Emigration 1941–42; Conf.-43; Excom and Board of Directors, Sept. 29, 1940; Nov. 27, 1940; Oct. 22, 1941; and scattered materials in R-5, R-41, and R-42. See also Paul Cerf, *Longtemps j'aurai mémoire.* D'Esaguy's accusation is contained in his letter to Nussbaum of September 20, 1941, in R-38.

28. Troper File.

Chapter Two

1. 14-55, van Tijn's memo on a visit to Berlin, Sept. 20, 1939; K. J. Ball-Kaduri, "Berlin Metoheret Miyehudeha" [Berlin emptied of its Jews], *Yad Vashem Studies* 5 (1963):215–59; Raul Hilberg, *The Destruction of the European Jews,* pp. 284–

93; Helmut Eschwege, "Resistance of German Jews," *Leo Baeck Institute Year Book* 15 (1970):171.

2. *Leo Baeck Institute Year Book* 2 (1957):302–13.

3. Herbert Rosenkranz, "The Anschluss and the Tragedy of Austrian Jewry, 1938–1945," in *The Jews of Austria*, ed. Josef Fraenkel, pp. 479–545.

4. Ibid.; also R-41; 10–12; 14–45.

5. Table 4 is based on 14-45, report of Feb. 6, 1940; 39-Germany, Reports 1937–44; R-9, 1939 Report; R-9, Apr. 25, 1940, circular. Other figures may be found in R-6; R-38; R-41; 14-66. The Austrian figures are partly based on Rosenkranz, "Anschluss and the Tragedy of Austrian Jewry." Estimates of Jewish populations varied widely, depending on the definition of Jew adopted. The figure for Germany at the end of 1939 probably includes some 30,000 "non-Aryans" (see table 3). The figure for 1940 is much in doubt, though even lower figures have been given. Paul Meyerheim estimated that there were 170,000 Jews in Germany at the beginning of 1941. The 35,000–45,000 difference between the 1939 and 1940 figures cannot really be explained. It is unlikely that more than 16,000 emigrated; the rest would have to be accounted for by deaths and the early deportation, and these figures do not tally out to the difference indicated. The figures for Austria are no less puzzling. Rosenkranz suggests 53,604 for the end of 1940. There seems to be no disagreement that 46,300 is correct for the end of 1941, when many Jews had already been deported and mortality was high. The only possible conclusion is that in 1939 there were in fact fewer Jews in Germany than was estimated, while in Austria there were more. In both cases, the error must have been due to mistaken calculations of the number of "non-Aryans."

6. 14-61, Report of July 11, 1941; Baerwald-George L. Warren, Oct. 25, 1939.

7. R-10, Berlin Conference of Sept. 30–Oct. 2, 1939. This conference is memorable because it was attended by Pastor Heinrich Gruber, representing Protestants trying to help Jews, and some Catholics with the same purpose. All such Christian groups, however, saw their main task as that of aiding the "non-Aryans."

8. 11-11, Jan., 1941, and Feb. 12, 1941. Even in 1939, not all German Jews were trying to escape. A small group of veterans of World War I offered their services to the Reich, but of course there was no response (see 39-9, Reports, 1937–44, and Oct. 4, 1939, report by a Dutch non-Jew).

9. AC, Apr. 28, 1940.

10. 25-9, HICEM 1940–41.

11. Troper File, Lisbon 428, report by Katzki, Jan. 23, 1941. Wyman, *Paper Walls*, pp. 171–72, 176, gives the following figures for direct emigration from Germany into the United States: 20,000 for fiscal 1939; 21,000 for fiscal 1940; and 4,000 for fiscal 1941. It must be assumed that these figures include Greater Germany. They cover "Hebrew" immigrants; "non-Aryans" and even some Jews would not describe themselves by that term. The figures therefore must be regarded as approximations; they also do not include tourists, of whom there were 2,800 in calendar 1941. The true emigration figures are probably somewhat higher.

12. Troper File, Lisbon 428, Dec. 19, 1940, cable from Vienna and report by Katzki, Jan. 23, 1941.

13. Ibid.

14. 14-66, Aug. 1, 1941; 25-Germany, International Committee for Securing Employment, 1933–44.

15. R-41, Jan. 20, 1941. The issuance of visas of course depended on the consuls, and a cable from Vienna on March 6, 1941, complained of difficulties there (File 9-1). See also 14-45, Mar. 11, 1941: "Reliable firsthand information G-men paid prolonged visit Deer [Hirsch] office taking away half staff for labor service. Deer himself now confined past week due unfounded suspicion he initiated protest Lionheart expulsions [Vienna deportations]."

16. 14-68, Mar. 21, 1941; 14-61, Apr. 24, 1941, and May 25, 1941; R-41, Aug. 5, 1941; 9-26, Sept. 4, 1941, for McDonald's talk with Roosevelt.

17. Evidence of these last attempts to leave Germany may be found in 14-66.

18. File Germany-Floersheimsche Stiftung, Frankfurt.

19. Table 5 is based on Rosenkranz, "Anschluss and the Tragedy of Austrian Jewry"; 14-45 (Sept., 1939); R-38; R-6.

20. Table 6 is based on Rosenkranz, "Anschluss and the Tragedy of Austrian Jewry." These figures account for 174,800 Austrian Jews: 128,500 emigrants plus 46,300 that remained in Vienna at the end of 1941. As there were about 200,000 Jews and "non-Aryans" in Austria at the time of the Anschluss, some 25,000 persons are missing from these statistics. Rosenkranz (p. 513) calculates an excess of 7,400 deaths over births. About 11,000 persons had been deported to Poland by the end of 1941. A residual 6,500 persons remain unaccounted for, unless deaths in concentration camps were not included in the 7,400. Of the total of 128,500 emigrants, 17,779 were caught by the Germans in European countries and were mostly killed. The total of emigrants who either reached safety or survived the war in Europe was 110,229, or about 55 percent of Austrian Jewry. To this number must be added the roughly 7,000 survivors in Austria itself, who included 1,700 persons who returned from the camps and ghettos of Poland.

Chapter Three

1. Raphael Mahler, *Yehudei Polin bein shtei Milhamot Olam* [Jews in Poland between the two world wars] (Tel Aviv, 1968), pp. 189–95; Jacob Lestschinsky, *The Jews in Contemporary Poland* (Paris, 1937), esp. pp. 103–11.

2. Michael Weichert, *Zikhrones*, 3:17–20; WR 1; cf. Marian Drozdowski, *Alarm dla Warszawy*, p. 217.

3. 44-21, Oct. 11, 1940, Committee on Poland; ibid., Jan. 10, 1940, Report by Alex Kahn. The Polish municipality gave the KK 340 tons of bread and 170,000 zl.

4. Emmanuel Ringelblum, *Ktavim fun Getto*, 1:28. A survivor who managed to flee to the United States (Szoszkes, in 44-21 above, n. 3) estimated that 16,000 Jews were killed during the siege of Warsaw. The figure seems high.

5. WR 1. A different estimate may be found in 44-3, Report of Jan. 20, 1940, according to which 1,780,000 Jews were then living in German-occupied Poland, 1,329,000 in the Russian sector, 80,000 in Vilna, and 70,000 in the Suwalki region. This report estimated that half a million Jews fled eastward, which would put the original total Jewish population of the German areas at 2,280,000. If only 200,000–250,000 actually stayed in the east, more than 2.5 million would have remained in the west, whereas the estimate based on JDC material from Poland itself is slightly under 2 million. This latter figure is close to that in a report by Joseph Blum to JDC from Budapest (R-6, Oct. 25, 1940), who estimates the number of Jews in German-occupied Poland at 1.9 million.

6. WR 1.

7. Szymon Datner, "Dzialaność Warszawskiej 'Gminy Wyznaniowej Żydowskiej' [Material of the Warsaw Jewish community], *Biuletyn Żydowskiego Instytutu Historycznego* [Bulletin of the Jewish historical institute in Warsaw; hereafter *BZIH*], no. 73 (1970), pp. 101–32.

8. Yisrael Gutman, *Yehudei Warsha*, esp. pp. 19–146. I am greatly indebted to Dr. Gutman for his help in preparing this chapter. See also Tatiana Berenstein, Aron Eisenbach, and Adam Rutkowski, eds., *Eksterminacja Zydow na ziemiach polskich, Zbior Dokumentow*, pp. 154–58.

9. Berenstein, Eisenbach, and Rutkowski, *Eksterminacja Zydow*, pp. 161–62.

10. Karol M. Pospieszalski, ed., *Documenta Occupationis*, 6:560.

11. Tatiana Berenstein, "Żydzi warszawczy w hitlerowskich obozach pracy przymusowej" [Warsaw Jews in Hitlerite forced labor camps], *BZIH*, no. 67 (1968), pp. 33–65.

12. Table 7 is based on YV, 378-270 Financial Report; WR 1; 46-Poland, Reports. For September–December, 1939, there are variations from 2.9 million zl. to $368,000 (3.68 million zl.?). Transfers to Poland ceased in October, 1941. Tables 8–13 are based largely on YV, M-28, files 264, 378, and WR.

13. On the other hand, there was the infamous group of Abraham Gancwajch, known as "the 13," who were both smugglers and collaborators with the Gestapo. See Abraham Rosenberg (Adam Rutkowski), "Dos Drayzentl" [The thirteen], *Bleter far Geszichte*, vol. 5 (1952), nos. 1–2, pp. 187–225; no. 3, pp. 116–48 [hereafter *BG*]. Rosenberg's account, however, is exaggerated, in line with tendencies prevailing in Poland in the early 1950s.

14. Tatiana Berenstein, "Ceny produktów żywnościowych w Warszawie. . . ." [Prices of food products in Warsaw. . . .], *BZIH*, no. 70 (1969), pp. 3–19.

15. Chaim A. Kaplan, *The Diary of Chaim A. Kaplan*, ed. and trans. Abraham I. Katsh, p. 140.

16. Quoted in Gutman, *Yehudei Warsha*, chap. 1, n. 94. In 1941, different groups of Jews in the Warsaw ghetto had the following average daily calorie intakes: Judenrat officials, 1,665; unemployed but supported intellectuals, 1,395; independent artisans, 1,407; workers in official shops, 1,229; small shopkeepers, 1,429; street peddlers, 1,277; horse and cart owners, 1,544; janitors, 1,300; refugees in shelters, 807; street beggars, 784. The average for the ghetto was estimated as 1,125 (ibid., chap. 2, n. 21, citing material gathered by Oneg Shabbat and published in *BG*, vol. 2, nos. 1–4 (1949), pp. 273–87. The figures are somewhat questionable.

17. See, for example, Peretz Opoczynski, *Reshimot*, pp. 58–84; Kaplan, *Diary*, pp. 270–71.

18. Michael Weichert, *Yiddishe Alleinhilf*, p. 34. Gutman quotes a table by Rut Sakowska in *BZIH*, nos. 45–46 (1963), according to which 490,068 parcels arrived in the ghetto in January–June, 1941. The peak month was June, with 113,006. There is no indication of how many were confiscated by the Nazis. Between August, 1941, and July 21, 1942, another 435,028 parcels arrived, of which 31,159 (7.1 percent) were confiscated (*Yehudei Warsha*, p. 155).

19. Gutman, *Yehudei Warsha*, p. 81, quoting *BG*, vol. 8, nos. 3–4 (1955); ibid., p. 83. The population of the Warsaw ghetto fluctuated because of new arrivals and high mortality. In January, 1941, there were 380,740 Jews officially registered; in May, 442,337; in August, 420,116; and 368,902 in February, 1942.

20. Kaplan, *Diary*, p. 61.

21. Krausnick and Broszat, *Anatomy of the SS State*, pp. 77, 80.

22. A detailed description of the evolution of the Madagascar project may be found in Leni Yahil, "Madagascar, chazon ta'atuim shel pitron hashe'ela hayehudit" [Madagascar, an illusory solution of the Jewish question], *Yalkut Moreshet* [hereafter *YM*], 19 (1975):159–78. The official stand was formulated by Rademacher of the German Foreign Office on July 3, 1940. Heydrich asked Ribbentrop on June 24, 1940, for a "final territorial solution" to the Jewish question, and Eichmann then cooperated with Office DIII of the Foreign Office to work out a detailed plan. See also Christopher R. Browning, "Referat DIII of Abteilung Deutschland and the Jewish Policy of the German Foreign Office, 1940–43" (Ph.D. diss., University of Wisconsin, 1975), pp. 120–22.

23. Most of the political parties continued to function underground, from the extremely well-organized left-wing parties (especially the Bund, and to a lesser degree the LPZ, PZ, and Hitahdut) to the loosely organized General Zionists, Revisionists, and Agudat Israel (the latter's activities were hardly evident).

Mizrahi and Hapoel Hamizrahi and their youth movements (with one exception) practically ceased to operate. See also Gutman, *Yehudei Warsha*, pp. 61–64.

24. See Yonas Turkow, *Hayo hayta Warsha hayehudit*, p. 20.

25. Most of Opoczynski's *Reshimot* are devoted to descriptions of house committees.

26. Gutman, *Yehudei Warsha*, p. 141. The head of the team was Dr. Israel Milejkowski; the research was edited by Emil Apfelbaum and published as *Choroba glodowa; badanie kliniczne nad glodem wykonane w getcie warszawskim z roku 1942*. Cf. Leon Poliakov, *Bréviaire de la Haine*, p. 112.

27. Gutman, *Yehudei Warsha*, pp. 130–31; Nathan Eck, *Ha'toim Bedarkei Hamavet* [Lost wanderers on the roads of death] (Jerusalem, 1960), pp. 27–28, 33–34.

28. Kaplan, *Diary*, pp. 141–44. Kaplan does not seem to have been well informed about JDC. On January 5, 1940, he lamented the "fact" that "to compound our tragedy, the Joint's official representatives have all left us . . . the Joint's administration is in the hands of unemployed teachers, idle actors, and loafers" (p. 97). The "unemployed teacher" may refer to Neustadt; the "idle actor" almost certainly refers to Michael Weichert. In any case, the only "director" to flee Warsaw was Giterman, and he was about to return. This entry shows clearly that Kaplan is not always a reliable source.

29. Weichert, *Zikhrones*, pp. 70–71. The other members of the committee were Stanislaw Szereszewski, a banker and longtime JDC supporter, Zisha Friedman, secretary-general of Agudat Israel, and Menahem Kirschenbaum of the General Zionists.

30. Kaplan, *Diary*, p. 237.

31. Using the figures in table 12, the total number of children cared for in Warsaw would, in theory, be 49,332 (29,516 plus 15,425 plus 4,391). But there were many overlaps, and the food often consisted of a piece of bread and some watery soup. The drastic reduction in the number of TOZ hospitals reflects the ghettoization that took place in November, 1940. 52-Medical, Poland, TOZ (2) 1941, one of the sources quoted in table 12, defined the problem as follows: when a TOZ team of 11 doctors and 12 nurses examined 12,063 children in the ghetto, it found that 13 percent had an adequate diet, 52 percent were undernourished, and 35 percent suffered from "absolute infirmity" as a result of hunger.

32. 45-Poland, Pogroms, 1940, Summary of Advice from Abroad, Jan. 10, 1940; 46-Poland, Reports 1939-Oct. 27, 1940.

33. The corresponding initials for the Polish (ŻSS; Żydowska Samopomoc Spo\łeczna) and the Yiddish (ISA; Iddishe Soziale Alleinhilf) names were also used. JDC made sure that the Germans knew it was an American agency. U.S. Consul General George H. Hearing in Warsaw made this clear (46-Poland, 1939–40).

34. NRO was headed by Prince Adam Ronikier. The Polish constituent was the Rada Glowna Opiekuncza (RGO). Cf. Czeslaw Madajczyk, *Politika III Rzeszy w okupowanej Polsce*, pp. 112–15. Referring to the CPR as the Polish Food Commission, he suggests that the Germans let it operate because they thought this would strengthen Herbert Hoover as against Roosevelt.

35. Weichert, *Zikhrones*, pp. 49–51. The participants were Czerniakow, Jozef Jaszunski, Abraham Sztolcman, Dr. Israel Milejkowski, Borinstein, and Weichert.

36. The "advisers" were Dr. Gamzej Wielekowski for Warsaw, Dr. Yehuda Zimmermann (later Jacob Sternberg) for Kraków, Dr. Marek Alten for Lublin, and Josef Diamant for Radom. Diamant was head of the local Judenrat; Alten was deputy head and actual chief in Lublin.

37. WR 1, Summary of Conversations in Lisbon, Jan., 1941, Lisbon-Troper, Jan. 25, 1941.

38. Weichert, *Zikhrones*, pp. 79–80.

39. Isaiah Trunk, *Judenrat*, p. 139, says that 32 tons of matzot were received

in April, 1941; however, JDC records show that a wagon from Slovakia brought an additional 3.71 tons.

40. Weichert, *Zikhrones,* p. 98.
41. Ibid., pp. 23–78.
42. See, for instance, his own discussion of the problem in *Zikhrones,* pp. 104–9.
43. Weichert, *Yiddishe Alleinhilf,* p. 89.
44. Quite apart from the struggle of TOZ and CENTOS over funds and over their independence from Weichert, the Germans also fought over who should control the Jewish organizations. The Health Department of Frank's government fought the BuF over controlling TOZ.
45. Weichert, *Zikhrones,* p. 168.
46. Ibid., p. 187.
47. Ibid., pp. 189–90.
48. Ibid., p. 241.
49. Ibid., pp. 241–43.
50. Ibid., p. 261.
51. There were thirteen of these communities: Sosnowice, Bedzin, Chrzanów, Trzebinia, Sczakow, Jaworzno, Wadowice, Zawiercie, Andrychow, Kobucko, Sucha, Olkusz, and Oswiecim. The last-named, called Auschwitz in German, was cleared of Jews in April, 1941, because of its proximity to the big concentration camp.
52. Hilberg, *Destruction of the European Jews,* p. 153.
53. R-8, Blum reports, based on discussions with Dr. Bohrer (Borinstein?) of Warsaw, sent by Joseph Schwartz, Oct. 25, 1940.
54. Ibid. for the first quotation; for the second, R-39, Oct. 2, 1940.
55. WR 1, Jan. 24, 1941, Summary of Conversations in Lisbon, Jan., 1941.
56. Ibid., no date and signature, but probably a direct report by Meyerheim, Jan., 1941. The two Warsaw visitors in Berlin were Giterman and Borinstein. See also WR 1, Krakau, Aufklärungen zu den Berichtstabellen, Jan. 1–Sept. 30, 1940.
57. Some flour and 50,000 zl. were received from the Polish municipality during the siege of Warsaw (Weichert, *Zikhrones,* pp. 19, 23).
58. Excom, Feb. 28, 1940.
59. Excom, Dec. 27, 1939.
60. R-9, cables, Feb. 1–7, 1940, and cable by Katzki, Mar. 14, 1940. The first clearance went through on June 24, 1940 (see 4-41).
61. WR 1, Kraków cable 1762/n to Lisbon, Nov. 4, 1941.
62. Excom, Mar. 13, 1940.
63. R-38, telephone conversations, June 7, 1940. This followed constant appeals from Warsaw. According to the material in WR 1: on April 1, 1940, a telegram signed by Giterman, Gepner, Guzik, Neustadt, and Szereszewski asked for immediate help as there was no money left; on May 10 a cable informed Troper that kitchens and children's homes were closing for lack of funds; on May 15 Czerniakow cabled Troper supporting Giterman's and Neustadt's appeals; on May 28 Troper wired New York that he was "receiving continuous stream wires from Neustadt regarding impossibility continuing work with present allotments and absence large shipments products. Neustadt advises needs until end month three million zloty and suggests securing loan from Hirsch [German Jewry]. Advised him categorically cannot exceed amounts officially authorized his disposal" (which were being transferred from Germany).
64. 46-Poland, Reports, 1941–44, Report for 1940; Excom, Mar. 15, 1940. JDC-New York reserved $2.5 million for repayment of Polish loans. Cf. Trunk, *Judenrat,* p. 140, n. 61.
65. YV, AJDC Kraków, File 378, Feb. 20, 1941; see also Trunk, *Judenrat,* p.

140, n. 61. On February 20, 1941, the Polish JDC sent a letter to the appropriate German official suggesting a clearing arrangement that would enable relatives to transfer money to Polish Jews, with 1 to 15 percent being taken off to support JSS. JDC-Lisbon agreed to the plan and wanted HIAS to operate it (WR 2). I have not found the German reply, which seems to have been negative.

66. 46-Poland, Reports, 1941–44, Report for 1940.

67. YV, AJDC Kraków, File 304-112, May 4, 1941.

68. Ibid., File 364-145, Erstes Halbjahr, 1942, Kraków, no date, no signature. At a conference between Giterman and Weichert in 1941, a monthly budget of 900,000 zl. was agreed upon, of which 50 percent would go to Warsaw (WR 2, May 20, 1941).

69. WR 1, Summary, Poland, 1941–47. The six shipments accounted for 9.2 tons of condensed milk, about 7 tons of cheese, and about 1 ton of medicines and medicinal aids. Some small packages were sent directly from RELICO, though Silberschein said in a letter to Czerniakow in October, 1940, that he would clear this action with JDC, because he did not wish to compete with it (ibid., frame 83, Oct. 11, 1940).

70. Kaplan's response was thus exceptional; see *Diary*, pp. 122, 129, 141–42, 143–44. He complained of ineffective distribution and favoritism. His personal resentment against Leib Neustadt, whom he regarded as an upstart schoolteacher, played a part. Neustadt, born in Gorki, Russia, in 1883, though an agronomist, also worked as a teacher.

71. 44-19, James T. Nicholson-Ernest J. Swift of American Red Cross, Apr. 26, 1940.

72. WR 1, esp. frames 145, 294, 384; Excom, July 17, 1940.

73. 44-3, cable New York-Lisbon, Nov. 9, 1940; Lisbon-New York, Nov. 22, 1940; memo Morissey-Buchman, Dec. 12, 1940; WR 1, Dec. 20, 1940, exchange between Jacobson and Blum and Joseph Schwartz (see AC, Dec. 16, 1940; Apr. 7, 1941). On September 24, 1940, Jacobson and Blum met with Merin, who wanted food shipments.

74. 44-21, Report by A. Kahn, Jan. 10, 1940; Madajczyk, *Politika III Rzeszy w okupowanej Polsce*, pp. 83–123.

75. WR 1, Kraków cable 1762/n to Lisbon, Nov. 4, 1941; Trunk, *Judenrat*, p. 139.

76. YVRA, M-10/PH/8-1-7a. This is a partially deciphered German-language analysis of the economic and social conditions in the ghetto (no signature, no date, but obviously written in November, 1941); WR 1, Sept., 1939–Oct., 1940.

77. YVRA, 4-4-3, "Wie azoi lebn die Heimloze oif di punktn?" [How do the homeless live in the shelters?], no signature, no date, but probably winter, 1941–42.

78. YVRA, 5-1-2, Report by Jan Kaptshan, Apr., 1941.

79. YVRA, 3-1-1 (1942 report).

80. YVRA, 1-3-2, Peretz Opoczynski, "Kinder oifn bruck" [Children on the wall], 1941.

81. YV, 364-184, Erstes Quartal, 1941.

82. YV, 364-145, Erstes Halbjahr, 1942, no date, no signature.

83. Opoczynski, "Kinder oifn bruck."

84. Ibid.

85. Interview with Mrs. Abrasha Blum (Luba Bilecka), New York, 1967. The TOZ protest mentioned in the text may be found in 52-Medical TOZ (2) 1941, Dec. 4, 1940.

86. R-6, Jan. 30, 1941, Alderstein-Coons.

87. R-8, Blum report of a conversation with Dr. Bohrer (Borinstein?), just out of the GG (Oct. 25, 1940). Bohrer said of the Jews: "Their faith in a better future remains unshaken." See also Kaplan, *Diary*, p. 383, entry for July 26, 1942, during the actual deportations from Warsaw to the death camp at Treblinka: he

was sorry he would not "witness the downfall of the Nazis, which in the end will surely come to pass."

88. YVRA, 24-3-4, "Notatka o rolnictwie u Zydow w 1941 r." [A note on agriculture of Jews in 1941], no signature; YVRA, 5-3-3, report for Dec. 1, 1940–May 31, 1941.

Chapter Four

1. Dov Levin, "Bekaf Hakela" [In the grip of fate], in Raphael Chasmon et al., eds., *Sefer Yahadut Lita* [Lithuanian Jewry], 2:349–53, who claims that the Jewish self-defense groups prevented more deaths; Yitzhak Arad, "Concentration of Refugees in Vilna," *Yad Vashem Studies* 9 (1973):201–14; Yehuda Bauer, "Rescue Operations through Vilna," ibid., pp. 215–23; Dina Porat, "Nessibot Vesibot Lematan Visot Ma'avar Sovyetiyot Liflitei Polin" [Conditions and reasons for the granting of Soviet transit visas to refugees from Poland], *Shvut* 6 (1979):54–67.

2. PS-3363, Reinhardt Heydrich's Schnellbrief of Sept. 21, 1939.

3. 45-Poland, Refugees, 1937–39, memo of Nov. 8, 1939, by Beckelman.

4. Ibid.; also ibid., report by a doctor on the condition of the Suwalki refugees, translated in Amsterdam, Nov. 15, 1939; Zvi Barak (Brick), "Plitei Polin be-Lita bashanim 1939–1941" [Polish refugees in Lithuania in 1939–1941], in Chasmon, *Sefer Yahadut Lita*, pp. 353–70.

5. Barak, "Plitei Polin," p. 354; 41-Lithuania, 1927–41, Troper's cable to New York, received Nov. 6, 1939.

6. Bauer, "Rescue Operations through Vilna," pp. 217–19.

7. Troper at Board of Directors, Sept. 29, 1940 (Excom Files).

8. The paragraph is based on Barak, "Plitei Polin"; R-6, Outline Report of Apr. 23, 1941; JDC VH-File; and Troper at Board of Directors, Mar. 21, 1941 (Excom Files). It is not clear whether the $717,000 represent appropriations or expenditures, which might be a meaningful differentiation because no more dollars could be sent to Lithuania after June, 1940. However, local funds were used against promises of later repayment by Beckelman (see Barak, "Plitei Polin," pp. 291–304), and thus the quoted sum serves as a rough indication.

9. 45-Lithuania, JDC Report by the Kehillah Refugee Committee, Vilnius; AC, Nov. 7, 1939.

10. 41-Lithuania, 1927–41, Beckelman-Troper, Feb. 18, 1940. Beckelman actually knew of only 123 Bundists, but they claimed 325 members and 100 dependents.

11. Bauer, "Rescue Operations through Vilna," pp. 216–17; Levin, "Bekaf Hakela," p. 349.

12. 45-Lithuania, JDC Report by the Kehillah Refugee Committee. In June the committee claimed that 1,069 refugees had been transferred out of Vilna; this figure seems too low. Beckelman quotes the figures in the text in his May 25, 1941, report to the Executive Committee (Excom File). See also, in the same file, a report by Beckelman and Chasmon, chairman of the Kovno Ezra committee, on a journey of May 6–7, 1940, to visit the Suwalki refugees in a number of places.

13. Zvi Barak, "Hamisrad Ha'eretsyisraeli be'Lita" [The Palestine office in Lithuania], MS, Institute of Contemporary Jewry, Jerusalem.

14. R-6, Outline Report of Apr. 23, 1941; 41-Lithuania, 1940–44, Beckelman and Anderson-Gen. J. Sutkus, June 13, 1940.

15. Levin, "Bekaf Hakela," p. 351.

16. 41-Lithuania, 1940–44, Leavitt memo of Aug. 22, 1940.

17. Ibid., Beckelman's cable of Dec. 12, 1940; see also his cable of Nov. 9, 1940. Leavitt stated: "We had taken the position that we could not evade the government regulations in this respect" (Excom, Sept. 18, 1940).

18. YV, Hassidei Umot Haolam, File 1054.
19. Ibid., Benjamin Grey's letter to Sugihara's son, July 5, 1963. Sugihara apparently said that the Dutch consul had issued 1,600 papers for Curaçao. It should be noted that Sugihara's testimony was originally given to a Polish historian who asked him about Polish refugees, not to Yad Vashem. It appears that there were 1,600 Curaçao papers, 500 Palestinian papers, and probably some 1,400 others, genuine or forged. Some of them must have gone to Polish non-Jews. See also Barak, "Hamisrad Ha'eretsyisraeli," pp. 17–23; Bauer, "Rescue Operations through Vilna," pp. 219–20.
20. Porat, "Nessibot Vesibot," for the estimates of JDC expenditures; Israel Sheib, *Ma'asser Rishon*, p. 32; Barak, "Hamisrad Ha'eretsyisraeli," pp. 20–23.
21. Barak, "Hamisrad Ha'eretsyisraeli," pp. 20–23.
22. Moses W. Beckelman, "Polish Refugees Eastward Bound," *Jewish Social Service Quarterly* 18 (Sept., 1941):50–55.
23. 40-2, May 28, 1942, Leavitt-Joseph Talamo; JDC VH File, 1940–42, Leavitt-Samuel A. Goldsmith, Jan. 27, 1941.
24. JDC VH File, 1940–42, Leavitt-Samuel A. Goldsmith, Jan. 27, 1941.
25. 40-2, May 28, 1942, Leavitt-Joseph Talamo.
26. 41-Japan, 1931–41, letter by H. Hochheimer, Sept. 8, 1940.
27. Ibid., Aug. 22, 1940, letter by E. Baerwald.
28. Abraham Kotsuji, *From Tokyo to Jerusalem*, pp. 158–67; Baruch Oren, "Mi'Vilna Derech Yapan el haolam hachofshi" [From Vilna via Japan to the free world], *YM*, no. 11 (1969), pp. 34–54.
29. 41-Japan, 1939–41, memo by B. Kahn, Nov. 19, 1940.
30. Porat, "Nessibot Vesibot," pp. 60–67. Simon Bergmann was the Jewish representative in the negotiations with the Japanese. See also YV, Hassidei Umot Haolam, File 3043.
31. 42-Lithuania, Emigration, Jan.–Mar., 1941, Leavitt-Sobeloff, Jan. 23, 1941; 45-Poland, JDC Publicity Release, "A Story within a Story," May 12, 1942.
32. JDC VH File, 1940–42, circular letter of Henrietta K. Buchman, Sept. 3, 1941.
33. AC, Jan. 13, 1941.
34. 41-Japan, 1939–41; 41-Japan, June, 1941–44. See esp. the correspondence of March, 1941.
35. 40-2, Leavitt-Talamo, May 28, 1942. The VH and a group of Habad Hassidim contributed $900 each.
36. Ibid., Memo of the Council of Jewish Federations and Welfare Funds, Jan. 14, 1942.
37. AC, May 19, 1941; source cited in chap. 4, n. 32.
38. JDC VH File, 1940–42, Jan. 27, 1941.
39. 41-Lithuania, 1940–44, Beckelman's final report, May 27, 1941.
40. Zalman Segalovitch, *Gebrennte Tritt*, p. 205.
41. It is very difficult to arrive at exact figures. Porat says in "Nessibot Vesibot," mainly on the basis of JDC documentation, that 2,178 refugees reached Kobe from Lithuania, and 300 more went directly from Vladivostok to Shanghai. From Kobe, 1,015 were sent to Shanghai by the Japanese, 532 went to the United States, 186 went to Palestine, and so forth. She also quotes 41-Japan, 1939–41, summary made in Kobe, Oct., 1941, which has figures of 2,074 "Poles," 2,203 "Germans," and 331 "others." It seems to me that 2,400 is as close an approximation as it is possible to get.

Chapter Five

1. 42-Palestine, Emigration-Immigration, 1938-47, B. Kahn Memorandum, Nov. 29, 1939.

2. FO 371-25238.
3. FO 371-25239/27 and 55.
4. FO 371-25241/12.
5. 42-Palestine, Emigration-Immigration, 1938–47, B. Kahn Memorandum, Feb. 2, 1940, p. 2.
6. FO 371-25238/217.
7. FO 371-25239/135; 25241/2, Sir M. Palairet; 25239/252, R. T. E. Latham; 25242/283, Downie, Jan. 3, 1941.
8. FO 371-24471/185, J. W. Russel, Feb. 26, 1940.
9. FO 371-23610, report by Thomas Preston from Kovno, Nov. 7, 1939.
10. FO 371-25241/253, Jan. 17, 1940; 25237, Feb. 15, 1940, minute by J. E. M. Carvell; 25239/150, minute, Feb. 8, 1940.
11. FO 371-25243/299, July 11, 1940.
12. FO 371-25241/97, Mar. 19, 1940; 25239/105.
13. FO 371-25239/146-7, Feb. 8, 1940. In fact, the *Noemi Julia* had been boarded by the police in September, 1939, and the refugees had thrown their water and provisions into the sea.
14. FO 371-25242/250, Memorandum by Weizmann, Nov. 27, 1940; 25242/276, Memorandum by Berl Locker, Nov. 27, 1940.
15. FO 371-25241/335; Haim Barlas, *Hatzalah Bi'ymei Ha'shoah*, p. 197; *Sefer Toldot Hahaganah*, 3:149–59.
16. 42-Emigration to Palestine, 1937–39, B. Kahn Memorandum, June, 1939; 9-23, Hyman Memorandum, June 16, 1939.
17. 15-2, Memorandum July 24, 1939; R-10, Kahn-Baerwald, May 29, 1939.
18. 15-2, July 26, 1939, meeting with Emerson; SM-518, Mayer comment.
19. 15-2, van Tijn-Baerwald, Sept. 20, 1939.
20. R-10, Hyman-Troper telephone, Nov. 6, 1939; 11-2, Troper-Hyman, Nov. 8 and 9, 1939.
21. German Immigration to Palestine, 1940, Feb. 1, 1940; Excom, Feb. 7, 1940; 42-Emigration to Palestine, 1940, letters by Millstein and Ussoskin, Dec. 14, 23, and 30, 1940.
22. R-9, Katzki, Mar. 14, 1940. Current research by Dalia Ofer at Hebrew University ("Aliyah Bet, 1939–1942," dissertation under my direction) seems to point to a partial vindication of Storfer.
23. 15-1, July, 1940 cables.
24. 15-32 contains material on the *Pencho* and the *Salvador;* see also Bruce Lorens, "Sipura shel haOniya 'Pencho' " [The story of the ship *Pencho*], *YM*, no. 20 (1975), pp. 35–50.
25. 9-2, Storfer-Troper, July 10, 1940.
26. 15-32, Oct. 16, 1940, E. Braun (on the *Milos*)-Athens Relief Committee; see also 42-Palestine, Emigration-Immigration, 1941–44, E. Frank and H. Rabl (on the *Pacific*)-Athens Relief Committee, Oct. 27, 1940; ibid., Oct. 18, 1940.
27. FO 371-25242.
28. See Meir Meridor, *Shlikhut Aluma* [Secret mission] (Tel Aviv, 1957), pp. 53–77 for an account of the Haganah sabotage of the *Patria*. The ship was to have deposited some of the immigrants in Trinidad because Mauritius was able to accept only a limited number. At a time when the British were having great difficulties with their shipping, they were nevertheless prepared to transport a few hundred Jews to the West Indies in order to avoid having them in the Middle East (FO 371-25242/172, Wavell-War Office, Nov. 30, 1940).
29. FO 371-25242/229, Dec. 16, 1940.
30. FO 371-25241/364, July 9, 1940.
31. 12-14; Excom, Mar. 13, 1940; R-9; Troper File.
32. FO 371-24865/593.
33. 15-32; R-38.

34. 15-32; R-38; 42-Palestine Immigration, 1938–47.
35. 42-Palestine, Emigration and Immigration, 1941–44, Spitzer-Weiss, Dec. 3, 1940, and Barlas-Spitzer, Feb. 13, 1941.
36. FO 371-25239/153, minute by J. E. M. Carvell; FO 371-25239/106. An interesting note verbale from the Yugoslav Foreign Ministry of February 19, 1940 (FO 371-25240/68) promises strict control over the passports of all Jews, "taking particular care that the passports are labelled with the necessary letter 'J'. This decision has been taken with the sole object of responding to the urgent requests made by the British Government."
37. FO 371-25241/155, Franz Steiner to Ezra Steiner in Jerusalem, Feb. 25, 1940.
38. FO 371-25238/287, Latham; 25241/181, Carvell.
39. R-38 (Lisbon), Oct. 31, 1940; 15-32 (Spitzer), Dec. 4, 1940.
40. Browning, "Referat DIII of Abteilung Deutschland," pp. 175–80.

Chapter Six

1. Cf. David H. Weinberg, *Les Juifs à Paris de 1933 à 1939*, pp. 11–13, 53–55.
2. Jacques Ravine, *La Résistance organisée des juifs en France*, pp. 45–48.
3. See Bauer, *My Brother's Keeper*, pp. 237–42, 264–66.
4. 13-11, Report of CAR for 1939; see also R-9, Troper to Board of Directors, Mar. 21, 1940 (Excom File). The figure of 15,000 internees is the lowest estimate. R-9 mentions 18,000, stating that 8,000 were still interned at the end of 1939.
5. R-9, Katzki memo of Mar. 14, 1940. Troper made his claim in "France's Jewish Veterans Today," *Jewish Veteran*, Aug. 5, 1941; cf. *New York Times*, Nov. 5, 1939; Excom, Oct. 10, 1939; 13-11.
6. The 210,000 figure comes from R-6, Outline of 1940 Report; see also Excom, June 19, 1940.
7. R-38, Aug. 9, 1940, from Lisbon.
8. JDC estimated the number of Jewish internees at 35,000 at the end of 1940; the one-third mentioned in the text is the lowest estimate (R-6).
9. 13-30; German report, n.d.; reports on Gurs, Feb., 1941 and Apr. 2, 1941; 13-31; 14-2.
10. 13-30, Mar., 1941 report.
11. AC, Aug. 14, 1940.
12. A conversation with John Rich of AFSC made clear to Leavitt that the Quakers, "with every desire to respect American regulations, nevertheless will insist in a dignified way on getting the support of the government to enable them as American citizens and as an American organization, to do everything that is legally permissible in connection with their relief undertaking" (12-43, conversation of Aug. 9, 1940). Leavitt contrasted this attitude with that of JDC, which was still doing all it could to accommodate what it thought were the wishes of the State Department.
13. 12-41 for Chamberlain's correspondence with Leavitt; see also ibid., Schwartz's cable of Feb. 8, 1941, in which he says that all the other American groups in France were doing "thriving business and encountering no difficulties their American headquarters—consequently our people asking whether Washington grinding out regulations applicable us only." In April, 1940, Katzki suggested that JDC accept as gifts balances held in France by French emigrants to the United States, but what happened to his suggestion is unclear.
14. 12-43, Katzki's report on his visit to France, Aug. 31, 1940; 12-42, Aug. 3, 1940.

15. The survey of French anti-Jewish measures follows in the main the description in Zosa Szajkowski, *Analytical Franco-Jewish Gazetteer, 1939–1945.*

16. 12-42; R-6, 1940 Outline Report; Board of Directors, Sept. 29, 1940.

17. Donald A. Lowrie, *The Hunted Children,* pp. 82–85. Parallel material may be found in JDC files.

18. The World Jewish Congress material, made available to me through the kindness of Dr. Gerhart Riegner, exposes some of the jealousies involved. WJC sent some funds to FSJ, especially in the Nice area, mainly through RELICO. Jarblum knew that any WJC help would be insignificant compared to what he might get from JDC, but he used his close contacts with WJC to exert pressure for more JDC funds. He did not much like the "notables" of CAR, who did not distinguish themselves at the Nîmes meetings ("messieurs les notables brillaient par leur absence"; "messieurs the notables shone by their absence" [WJC, Jarblum-RELICO, Dec. 5, 1941]). He emphasized that he was working with the "rabbis" (the CC) because he believed JDC looked favorably on the CC. In November, 1940, he wrote to the American Jewish Congress, indicating that JDC was limiting itself to officially recognized activities, and yet emphasizing JDC's help. The congress published his reports, thus exerting pressure on JDC to provide aid to him. Early in 1941, Katzki and Jefroykin wrote to Jarblum asking him to contact Nahum Goldmann to ask WJC to stay away from relief in France (13-30, Feb. 16, 1941); Jarblum did nothing of the sort. Schwartz also knew how to appeal to the JDC aversion to WJC for his own purposes. When JDC-New York could not allocate money to ship matzot to France because of its financial problems in 1940–41, Schwartz cabled: "Our failure furnish Easterbread here will provide golden opportunity Nahumboys make hay cheap price" (12-41, Jan. 20, 1941). It is not known whether Schwartz had his way.

19. *New York Times,* Jan. 9, 1941; 12-44, Nov. 18, 1941, Hyman-Lisbon, mentioning Guy de Rothchild's proposal to send 100 children to the United States; Lowrie, *Hunted Children,* pp. 96–98.

20. 13-14, exchanges of Feb. 25 and Sept. 18, 1941; 12-41, Feb. 10, 1941; 13-30, Katzki's report of Mar. 22, 1941. Katzki was particularly eager to obtain a special allocation for this purpose, but he did not succeed.

21. Table 16 is based largely on 13-29; 12-41; R-41; 14-2; R-6; and WJC material, Geneva. The table includes only the lowest estimates; there was a general tendency to inflate figures because the purpose of collecting statistics was to seek financial support. Nevertheless, the general trend is clear, and the figures for late 1941 and early 1942 seem to be fairly reliable.

22. Hilberg, *Destruction of the European Jews,* pp. 399–400.

23. This and the following paragraphs are based largely on the work of Zosa Szajkowski: *Analytical Franco-Jewish Gazetteer;* "The General Union of the Jews of France, UGIF," paper delivered at a YIVO colloquium, New York, Dec. 2–5, 1967; "The French Central Jewish Consistory during the Second World War," *Yad Vashem Studies* 3 (1959):187–202.

24. The quotations are from 14-2, Aug. 6, 1942, Katzki's report; Kaplan's letter is in R-5, May, 1942, and is discussed by Hilberg, *Destruction of the European Jews,* pp. 398–99.

25. JDC's neutral stance in the internal discussions of French Jewry is explicitly stated in 13-21, Schwartz-New York, June 17, 1942; Schwartz continued: "Our sole function is to see to it that the work of relief and of assistance to internees as well as to those outside the camps goes on with the maximum efficiency and effectiveness." In early 1942, this of course meant supporting UGIF.

26. R-6, Jan. 9, 1941, Nîmes memo to Hull; 13-30, Apr. 1, 1941, Hull-Rich; ibid., Apr. 10, 1941, Hyman-Rich; ibid., Apr. 18, 1941, Baerwald-Hull.

27. 12-41.

28. Tables 17 and 18 are based on material in 14-2; 14-3; 13-29; 13-11.

29. The quotation is from R-6, June 19, 1941. OSE's view that children should be removed from the camps at almost any cost was not uncontested. AFSC's Howard Kerschner wrote in January, 1941: "It is better to ameliorate the conditions of children in the camps rather than try to provide housing for them outside" (Szajkowski, *Analytical Franco-Jewish Gazetteer*, p. 34). The reasons were of course financial.

30. R-41 for material on Paris.

31. 12-42, Aug. 1, 1940, FSJ report; 13-25, Oct., 1940, report; 14-3, Dec. 31, 1940, report by Katzki. Actually, the Parisian Jews paid 1,289 million fr. as a fine.

32. Cf. Ravine, *Résistance organisée des juifs*.

33. Mordechai Kefir, "La Resistance juive en France" (Ph.D. diss., Sorbonne, 1969).

34. 14-2, undated report.

35. Hilberg, *Destruction of the European Jews*, pp. 405–9.

36. Ibid.; R-4, statement by E. Rosen, Sept. 2, 1942.

37. 12-40, Schwartz-New York, Aug. 11, 1942.

38. 14-2, Schwartz-New York on talk with Tuck, Aug. 11, 1942.

39. 13-28, Schwartz cable, Aug. 13, 1942.

40. *Foreign Relations of the United States, Diplomatic Correspondence* [hereafter FRUS], 1942, 2:710; see also ibid., p. 708; ibid., 1:463–64.

41. 12-40, Schwartz-New York, Aug. 15, 1942.

42. Jules Jefroykin, "Le Refus," *Le Nouveaux Cahiers*, no. 37 (1974), pp. 18–24.

Chapter Seven

1. Members of the committee were Paul Baerwald, James H. Becker, I. Edwin Goldwasser, Solomon Lowenstein, William Rosenwald, Irving H. Sherman, Jonah B. Wise, and Edward M. M. Warburg; Ralph F. Colin was added soon afterwards. Alexander Kahn, David H. Sulzberger, David N. Dattelbaum, and Isaac H. Levy were added in early 1943.

2. Nathan Reich, *JDC Primer—Principles* (New York, 1945), p. 1.

3. See, for example, 45-Poland, JSS, H. Buchman-Z. G. Weisman (Mexico), June 30, 1941; Buchman declared that the overwhelming number of contributors wanted to adhere strictly to the British blockade regulations. A representative of the British Press Service had discussed the question of sending food to German-occupied areas with JDC representatives, and he "indicated that his Government views all such transmissions . . . as in violation of the blockade." JDC, acting on the assumption that the U. S. State Department would in every case follow the British line, was thus having its policy laid down by a journalist. See also R-1, Dec. 15, 1943, Baerwald's comments at the annual meeting.

4. Waldman, *Nor by Power*, pp. 207, 227, 240.

5. Conf.-3, Hyman-Joseph Willen, Nov. 11, 1941.

6. R-2, Apr. 23, 1943, E. M. Morissey-Leavitt; 43-Palestine, Jan. 29, 1943, W. Rosenwald-Lt. Cmdr. S. J. Stabins.

7. Feb. 27, 1943, article by Dr. B. Hoffman. Competition with the Zionists occasionally led JDC staff members into somewhat futile exercises, such as trying to show that even in early 1942 in Poland there were opportunities for "constructive" aid, out of fear that the Zionists might publish articles stressing "the great opportunities for rehabilitation made possible by support of work in [Palestine]" (R-4, May 26, 1942, H. Buchman-F. Alderstein).

8. AC, Mar. 30, 1943; Excom, Apr. 28, 1943; R-1, Apr. 6, 1944, note by Hyman; Excom, Feb. 21, 1945.

9. MA, D.1.732, June 10, 1943, letter to Barlas from Tel Aviv.

10. AC, Apr. 21, 1943.

11. Conference of JDC fund-raisers, Feb. 17, 1945, manuscript notes in JDC Library.
12. Yehuda Bauer, "When Did They Know?," *Midstream,* Apr., 1968, p. 51; Ernest Hearst, "The British and the Slaughter of the Jews," *Wiener Library Bulletin* 21, no. 1 (Winter, 1966–67). A summary of the Polish notes may be found in the *Polish Fortnightly Review,* July 15, 1943.
13. "When the Warsaw ghetto walls were completed, all 'Aryans' left; Jews became watchmen, house workers, street cleaners, policemen. In some cities, workers' cooperatives have been organized for tailors, shoemakers, hosiery producers, cap-makers, glove makers. The German labor office supplies the cooperatives with raw materials. All members are punished severely if the order is not filled satisfactorily or on time. Probably the most heartrending news to come out of Warsaw are the reports of an active, developing cultural life." For more in that vein, see R-26, *JDC Digest,* May, 1942.
14. R-24, Apr. 4, 1942, Hyman-Linder.
15. "Life in the Polish Ghetto," *Jewish Frontier,* May, 1942. Information regarding the mass murders in the Baltic states, which had reached the West some time before but had not been published, was made public under the impact of the Bund report; see the British *Evening Standard,* June 16, 1942.
16. Arthur D. Morse, *While Six Million Died,* p. 8. Riegner's cable originated in information received from a German industrialist whose name he has kept secret; another source shortly afterwards (in September) was Artur Sommer, a famous German economist who was a German army liaison officer to the Abwehr. He was a member of the German delegation to the Swiss-German economic negotiations in 1942. He left the information regarding Hitler's plans with Edgar Salin, a Jewish scholar in Switzerland, who then gave it to Haim Pozner of the JA office in Geneva and to an American businessman. Pozner gave it to Benjamin Segalowitz, a well-known Swiss Jewish journalist. Segalowitz also gave Riegner the original decisive information from the industrialist. Riegner checked it for a week before handing it over to the U.S. and British embassies.
17. Pp. 8–22.
18. WJC, P. C. Squire on his conversation with C. J. Burckhardt, Nov. 7, 1942.
19. Sikorski Institute, London, *Sprawozdanie* [Information], Aug. 5, 1942.
20. PRO-FO 688-29-ERD/7147, Dec. 9, 1942, note by Polish Ambassador Edward Raczynski to Anthony Eden.
21. *The Ghetto Speaks,* no. 16, Oct. 1, 1943.
22. Menahem Bader did not write only to his chiefs in Palestine. On January 20, 1943, he submitted a memorandum to the papal nuncio in Istanbul, Angelo G. Roncalli (later Pope John XXIII), which Roncalli promised to send to Pius XII, in which he reported the massacres very directly: "The situation of the Jews in the occupied countries is a terrible one. The numbers of the massacred reach millions. It is impossible to repeat the details regarding the massacre of defenseless people—aged, sick, women, children—without crying or freezing into terrorized immobility" (MA, D.1.698).
23. Excom, Feb., 15, 1943; R-2, Feb. 8, 1943; R-26, *JDC Digest,* March, 1943.
24. MA, D.1.705, Bader-Palestine, Oct. 23, 1943.
25. Peake in *Parliamentary Debates,* Commons, 5th ser. (1942–43), vol. 389, cols. 1117–1204 (May 19, 1943). On May 28 Baerwald wrote to Sumner Welles at the State Department, offering JDC's help, either directly or as a member of the Inter-Governmental Committee on Refugees, in any steps the government might wish to take to rescue or relieve distressed Jews in Axis-occupied territories (JDC File, Administration and U. S. State Dept., 1939–45). But there were no plans for any steps. JDC was also involved in postwar planning (see, for example, R-2, Nov. 5, 1943, Hyman-Jacob Pat).

26. R-2, Sept. 7, 1943.
27. MA, D.1.730, Mar. 9, 1943, Bader-Bornstein.
28. MA, D.1.814, Apr. 12, 1953, Lichtheim-Bader.
29. MA, D.1.913.
30. *Zionist Review*, Sept. 22, 1944.

Chapter Eight

1. 44-18, Dec. 11, 1941.
2. R-5, May 4, 1942, memo of conversation.
3. R-26, *JDC Digest*, May, 1942.
4. R-30, Feb. 10, 1942.
5. 25-HICEM, Aug., 1941, list prepared by Dorothy Speiser.
6. R-36, May 25 and 29, 1942; June 5, 1942.
7. Bauer, *My Brother's Keeper*, pp. 57–104.
8. AJ, File 25, Nov. 7, 1940, Rosenberg-Baerwald.
9. 34-Germany, Refugees in Santo Domingo, Sept. 3, 1944, David Stern report.
10. 33-Agro-Joint, DORSA, 1939–43, Statistical Information, End 1942. According to this list, 571 refugees came as settlers and 549 as refugees admitted by the Dominican Republic. As to the security scare: Feingold in *Politics of Rescue*, p. 121, relates that the Federal Bureau of Investigation thought it had discovered that the settlers were conducting espionage with the aid of shore-to-sea signals. These were later found to be flashlights used by settlers doing their farm chores after dark. Equally silly stories came from an individual named Paterson, who served as His Majesty's minister on the island (see FO 371-29195/W4925, W49171, and W13277). The British Foreign Office was so agitated that it asked Emerson of the IGCR to write to Rosenberg about the accusations. It appears that 98 of the actual settlers came from Switzerland, 55 from Britain, and 7 from the United States. After mid-1941, people in Germany who had received visas for the Sosua scheme were no longer admitted. There must have been hundreds of them, because the total number of visas issued for Sosua was 1,079, whereas fewer than 600 actually got there.
11. Bolivia-SOCOBO, Dec. 27, 1944, report by David Stern. In 1941, a scheme pursued by the World Maccabi organization to settle some 4,800 Austrian Jews in Bolivia was discussed with JDC by the World Maccabi organization through a delegate in Zürich. The Maccabi people had been trying to get the scheme moving since 1939, but JDC had doubts about agricultural qualifications and the size of the scheme. In 1941, German agreement to large-scale emigration could no longer be obtained. The young people who had been interested in the plan probably shared the fate of the rest of Austrian Jewry. For some of the details, see R-9.
12. R-26, Nov. 19, 1941; R-36, Dec. 20, 1941, report from Beckelman.
13. South America-Gen., "Central and South America at a Glance, September, 1942."
14. *Washington Post*, Feb. 10, 1943. The material on North Africa may be found in JDC files 8-3 to 8-11; see also André Kaspi, *La Mission de Jean Monnet à Alger*, esp. pp. 61–63; Kaspi, "Hageneral Giraud Vehayehudim" [General Giraud and the Jews], *YM* 11 (November, 1969):143–56. Marcel Aboulker described his and Henri Aboulker's part in the liberation of Algiers in *Alger et ses complots*; see also Feingold, *Politics of Rescue*; Henry Morgenthau, *The Morgenthau Diaries*, ed. John M. Blum, 3:147–52.
15. 8-3, Apr. 21, 1943, Eric Johnson-AFSC.
16. 8-3, Hurwitz reports, July 8, 1943 (Casablanca) and Nov., 1943.

17. 8-8, Apr. 12, 1943.
18. 8-3, Hurwitz report, July 8, 1943, p. 3.
19. 8-11.
20. 51-Spain, 1941–42, Hayes-Schwartz, June 2, 1942.
21. OHD, Interview with J. J. Schwartz, Oct. 24, 1967, pp. 4–5.
22. 51-Spain, 1941–42, James Vail-Hyman, Dec. 14, 1942. Table 19 is based on the figures published in the JDC annual reports for 1941 and 1942.
23. Ibid.; 51-Spain, 1943-May, 1944. The general description closely follows Avni, *Sfarad Vehayehudim*, esp. pp. 108–35.
24. Avni, *Sfarad Vehayehudim*, pp. 146–48.
25. 51-Spain, 1941–42, memo by Sequerra attached to report of Oct. 2, 1942.
26. Luther (German Foreign Office) memo, Jan. 22, 1943, in Browning, "Referat DIII of Abteilung Deutschland," p. 412.
27. "Our representative made no commitments but pointed out that if these people did come to Spain, they would be considered candidates for refugee assistance the same as any other refugees there and as the circumstances may warrant. While there may be some question as to why, if the Spanish authorities were interested in these refugees by bringing them into Spain, the private relief organizations should be called upon to care for their maintenance, it was thought expedient at that time not to make an issue of this point because of the desirability of rescuing these people from German territory" (14-66, June 7, 1943, Lisbon-New York). One can see that the misunderstanding of the real situation had still not been dispelled. Use of terms such as "interest" of Spain in rescue and "desirability" of rescue from German control indicate that the Spanish attitude was misread and the knowledge of the facts regarding the murder had not yet been translated into drastic action.
28. Browning, "Referat DIII of Abteilung Deutschland," pp. 414–15; Avni, *Sfarad Vehayehudim*, pp. 149–215.
29. 51-Spain, 1943-May, 1944, Aug. 21, 1943, Leavitt-Katzki. "We prepared to give general assurance also do utmost reemigrate them." The change in tone as compared with communication such as that quoted in chap. 8, n. 27 is unmistakable.
30. Avni, *Sfarad Vehayehudim*, pp. 138–42.
31. Haim Avni, "Hahatzalah Derech Sfarad U'Portugal Bitkufat Hasho'ah" [Rescue through Spain and Portugal during the holocaust period], MS, Hebrew University, p. 226. I am grateful to Dr. Avni for permission to use this work, on which my description of the interplay of JA and WJC in Portugal is based. See also 48-Portugal, 1943–44, Aug. 22, 1944, memo by Louis H. Sobel on relations with Isaac Weissman; 51-Spain, Refugees, Apr. 1943–45, Israel-Hoare memoir, May 21, 1943.
32. Avni, "Hahatzalah Derech Sfarad U'Portugal," p. 190.
33. 48-Portugal, 1943–44.

Chapter Nine

1. SIG, *Festschrift zum 50 Jährigen Bestehen*, esp. Leo Littman, "50 Jahre Gemeindebund," pp. 7–51; see also *Israelitisches Wochenblatt*, Aug. 11, 1950; Bauer, *My Brother's Keeper*, pp. 239–42, 267–69. I am also indebted to the late Martin Mayer for personal documentation regarding Saly Mayer.
2. SM-24, July 29, 1941, Schwalb-Mayer; May 13, 1941, record of conversation between Schwalb and Mayer; June 13, 1941, Mayer-Schwalb.
3. Ibid., Sept. 9, 1941, Mayer-Schwalb. The following is an approximate translation from Mayer's peculiar German: "My dear Chawer Nathan, your letter of September 8 has made me very happy. It is a new proof for me that you have the

fullest understanding for the peculiar situation of an SIG president. Also that you have not the slightest doubt regarding my honest feelings, my admiration and my enthusiastic appreciation for country and population in my dearest Eretz [Jewish Palestine]. We are very happy to read words such as those expressed in your letter. They are a full compensation and have a calming effect after all that open and secret criticism which one must endure. It would perhaps be easier to use another tactic, but it is out of the question for me to prefer a position of 'Not Only But Also' [*Nicht Nur Sondern Auch*]. I share your belief in Eretz, and just as throughout this year, so at the end of this terrible year, my thoughts are in Eretz and with the men who are working for it, with Mr. Waizmann [sic], Shertok, Locker, Grunbaum, Gurion [sic] and last but not least with my dear Nathan Schwalb and all his protégées in the old and new land [*im Alt und Neuland*, an allusion to Theodor Herzl's book *Altneuland*]. Schalom—President [signature]." The letter was written just before the Jewish New Year, hence the allusion to the end of the terrible year. The phrase 'Not Only But Also' seems to refer to his uncompromising stand in helping Jews under Nazi rule. Schwalb's letter of September 8 is not in the file. The Schwalb archive in Israel was closed when this book went to press, despite repeated requests from various quarters for Nathan Drori (Schwalb) to open it to researchers.

4. 51-Switzerland, 1940–41, Nov. 14, 1941, Mayer-Bernhard Kahn. The letter of complaint was from Moritz Pappenheim (51-Switzerland, 1942–43, Oct. 8, 1941).

5. Excom, Mar. 18, 1942.

6. Excom, Dec. 10, 1941.

7. SM-7, telephone conversations with Lisbon, Mar., 1942.

8. Ibid.

9. OHD, Interview with J. S. Schwartz, Oct. 24, 1967, p. 16.

10. Ibid., June 14, 1968, p. 10.

11. SM-554, May 4, 1945, "Saldo." Mayer himself noted down the conditions under which he had to operate (SM-615, n.d., coded memo signed "these are notes about chronol. development of $ Frs transfers").

12. SM-554, May 4, 1945, "Saldo"; 51-Switzerland, 1944, Expenditures and Irrevocable Commitments during 1942 through 1945, as of Oct. 31, 1945.

13. SM-7, telephone with Lisbon, Apr. 1, 1942.

14. SM, note of Oct., 1942. "Nor does one at all have the means to give any substantial aid." ("Man hatte auch gar nicht die Mittel um irgendwelche substantielle Hilfe zu leisten.") See SM-615, where Mayer describes his and Schwartz's attempts to overcome the impasse by interventions with Swiss banks and the Swiss government. Schwartz visited Switzerland for this purpose in October, 1942. Mayer had a talk with Professor Bachmann, president of the Swiss National Bank. In his inimitable German, Mayer reports that Bachmann "meinte man hätte ja als Jude gute Beziehungen zu Morgenthau. Ich lehnte solches stricte ab bez. der Beziehungen." ("He thought one had, after all, being a Jew, good relations with Morgenthau. I rejected this decidedly, regarding the relations"; SM-4, Sept. 25, 1942.)

15. R-36, Feb. 19, 1942 ("Impossible under present circumstances to remit any funds to the IRC for use in enemy-occupied countries").

16. 51-Switzerland, 1942–43, Sept. 14, 1943.

17. R-36, Apr. 16, 1942.

18. AC, Mar. 16, 1943.

19. SM-7, telephone to Lisbon, Sept. 6, 1942.

20. This is the term used by Häsler in *Das Boot ist Voll.*

21. This account of Swiss policy towards the refugees closely follows Carl Ludwig, *Die Flüchtlingspolitik in der Schweiz*, p. 173.

22. Ibid., p. 199.

23. Ibid., p. 205.

24. Ibid., p. 247.

25. Ibid., p. 251.
26. Table 20 is based on SM-2, SM-3.
27. Ibid., p. 376.
28. 51-Switzerland, Refugees, ISS Report, Sept. 23, 1943; SM-25, report on the Comité international pour le placement des intellectuels refugiés; SM-31, Report on Pro-Leysin. The Ginzberg committee received 55,429 sfr. from JDC in 1942–43, out of its total budget of 218,068 sfr.
29. Excom, July 17, 1940.
30. Excom, May 21, 1941.
31. 51-Refugees in Switzerland 1938–42, Aug. 10, 1941, Rothmund-Troper.
32. 51-Switzerland, 1942–43.
33. SM-50, SIG General Convention, May, 1941.
34. SM-50, 1941 and Nov. 12, 1943, Wyler-Schmidt memo.
35. Ibid., Dec. 7–8, 1943, SM-Wyler-Schmidt on Rothmund.

Chapter Ten

1. SM-35a, OSE, Oct. 8, 1943, no signature ("Um die tieferen Motive des Kinderfeldzuges zu verstehen").
2. George Wellers, "Trentième Anniversaire du declenchement de la 'Solution Finale' en France," *Le Monde juif*, no. 67 (Sept., 1972), pp. 29–37.
3. The term appears in Hilberg, *Destruction of the European Jews*, p. 664. The general description of the UGIF is based on Hilberg's book, the previously cited works of Szajkowski and Ravine, and Alexander Werth, *France, 1940-1955*.
4. SM-32, Aug. 5, 1943, FSJ report ("Feder," or "Tante Feder," stands for FSJ); see also ibid., Aug. 4, 1943, and other material submitted to Mayer by OSE and FSJ.
5. 12-45, Lowrie-Katzki, Sept. 9, 1943.
6. Ibid., see also SM-32.
7. 48-Portugal, Refugees, Baerwald memo, July 13, 1942; also Excom, June 17, 1942. L'Amitié chrétienne received 1,020,000 fr. in August, 1942 (12-40, Aug. 10, 1942). Regarding Jefroykin's authorization to borrow funds, see R-36, Dec. 13, 1941, Schwartz cable.
8. 13-21, May 6, 1942, Jefroykin memo; 12-40, CAR report, Jan. 15, 1942.
9. SM-8, June 16, 1943, telephone Mayer-Lisbon.
10. Ravine, *La Résistance organisée*, pp. 133–35.
11. July, 1943, reports to Mayer indicate that Jefroykin was trying to obtain frozen funds of the Alliance Israélite Universelle in France (about 15 million fr.; $150,000), but nothing came of his efforts (SM-34(1), report for July 29, 1943). Millner wrote on July 8 that Jefroykin could no longer cope with the problem and was trying to absolve himself of responsibility. On August 17, Weill and Gourvic told Saly Braunschweig, the president of SIG, that no JDC help had been needed until recently. But now, in response to their urgent request, Mayer had sent money to France and thereby prevented a catastrophe. See also SM-35a, June 7, 1943, OSE-Mayer.
12. 14-1, May, 1944, Jefroykin report. On the other hand, Robert Pilpel reported on May 15, 1944, that Jefroykin had borrowed a total of 180 million fr. (about $2 million) over his two years of work for JDC (Conf.-50). The two statements are not necessarily contradictory: the larger sum must include Fischer's borrowings. Cf. table 21, which illustrates that JDC appropriated a total of about $4.2 million for France in 1942–44. Mayer says that he spent $1,206,865 in France in 1943–44 and nothing in 1942 (51-Switzerland, 1944–). As there could have been only very minor direct JDC outlays in France, Jefroykin must have borrowed the difference of about $2 million.

13. 14-1, May, 1944, Jefroykin report; cf. Jarblum's material of August 3, 1944, from which it would appear that the "conseil du Joint" was founded in May, 1943. This report says that "Lazare's family" ("Lazare" was Lazar Gourvic, that is, OSE) refused to tell how much they received from Switzerland. Jefroykin seems to be a better authority on this issue.

14. Mayer paid OSE 275,000 fr. in 1943 and 610,000 fr. up to April, 1944. OSE's monthly budget in May, 1943, was 3.6 million fr., and it stayed near that level until liberation. A typical budget for France in February, 1944, was 17,450,000 fr., of which OSE got 3.5 million and all of the operations connected with UGIF got 5 million. FSJ received a total of 22 million fr. from 1943 to liberation. The amounts borrowed and spent by Jefroykin, Fischer, and Brenner are in dispute. Brenner mentions 238,290,000 fr. (74.2 in 1942, 144.1 in 1943, and 19,990,000 in 1944); Jefroykin claims 260 million. At an average exchange rate of 100 fr. per dollar, this figure still would not tally with the $789,599 appropriated for loans. It is today impossible to straighten out these discrepancies. Table 21 is based largely on SM-32.

15. I am indebted to Mrs. Nili Keren-Patkin for allowing me to use her "Hatzalat Yeladim Betsarfat Bitkufat Hakibbush Hagermani (1940–1944) Al-yedei Irgunim Yehudiyim" [The rescue of children in France during the German occupation (1940–1944) by Jewish organizations] (M.A. thesis, Institute of Contemporary Jewry, Hebrew University, 1975), which gives an accurate picture of the work of OSE, including the Circuit Garel. See also SM-35a, "Auszug aus einem Bericht ueber die Methodik des Kinderschutzes des OSE in Frankreich," Geneva, Jan., 1944; "Jomi" reports, Feb. 20–26, 1944.

16. SM-35a, Report "Drancy," n.d. (end 1943), no signature.

17. Ibid., OSE report, Oct. 8, 1943.

18. Ibid., Weill report, Aug. 9, 1943.

19. Keren-Patkin, "Hatzalat Yeladim," pp. 97–99; Ravine, *La Résistance organisée,* pp. 111–12.

20. 12-45, May 22, 1944; other material on Paris may be found in the OSE and FSJ reports that reached Mayer throughout 1943 and early 1944 (SM-32, SM-33).

21. 12-45, May 22, 1944.

22. The subject of forced conversions by French Catholics of Jewish children and even of old people is still very much disputed. There is no doubt that they did occur, but it is very difficult to give a numerical estimate or even an evaluation of the relative importance of such conversions in the overall aid extended by Catholic institutions.

23. SM-35a, "Rapport sur l'activité . . ."; see also Keren-Patkin, "Hatzalat Yeladim," pp. 10–75; Anny Latour, *La Résistance juive en France,* pp. 58–89; Robert Gamzon, testimony, YV033/217; David Knout, *Contribution a l'histoire de la résistance juive en France,* pp.113–36. The EIF maintained its headquarters at Moissac until October, 1943, when it finally dispersed, but even the sixième had a legal front, called Service social des jeunes. After October, 1943, it was transferred to Grenoble, from where Henri Wahl, the commander, supervised seven subregions. EIF workers, in their monthly or bi-monthly visits, strengthened the children's faith "dans le judaisme et dans la France" ("Rapport sur l'activité"). EIF hid 853 children, and about 500 more were escorted into neutral territory. About one-third of the workers fell into Nazi hands and were transported to Auschwitz, but not one child was lost. Parallel to OSE's policy, the farms were maintained until early 1944 in order to keep a legal foothold. Only one farm insisted on maintaining itself until May, when it was raided and the inhabitants deported.

24. Hilberg, *Destruction of the European Jews,* pp. 413–18; Leon Poliakov, *La Condition des juifs en France sur l'occupation italienne.* Much of the material in the text is based on FSJ reports transmitted to Mayer in 1943–44 (SM-32 and SM-33), esp. those of Sept.-Oct., 1943. See also parallel OSE reports, Sept. 24-Oct. 10, 1943.

25. SM-32, esp. FSJ report, Dec. 3, 1943, in Jarblum's communication to Mayer of Dec. 27, 1943; 12-40, Dec. 30–31, 1943, Lowrie-JDC via State Dept., where Lowrie estimated the number of Jews deported from Nice at 5,000.

26. Avni, "Hahatzalah Derech Sfarad U'Portugal," p. 31.

27. The story of the crossings into Spain is based on ibid.; Keren-Patkin, "Hatzalat Yeladim"; MA, D.1.713, 732, 745. Despite the various books written about French Jewry during the Holocaust, no really satisfactory overall account exists.

28. Avni, "Hahatzalah Derech Sfarad U'Portugal," p. 154. Steinhorn went to Palestine on the S. S. *Nyassa.*

29. Jefroykin, "Le Refus," p. 20.

30. 14-1, memo (presumably by Fischer) of Dec. 5, 1944. "JDC encouraged the Jewish resistance movement morally and financially. Thus in 1943, we passed to another form of activity, we encouraged active and passive resistance."

31. SM-8, July 21, 1943, telephone Katzki-Mayer.

32. SM-32, Oct. 12, 1943, Jarblum-Schwartz; Nov. 18, 1943, Jarblum-Mayer.

33. See SM-32 and SM-33, exchange of letters between Jarblum and Mayer relating to the end of 1943 and early 1944; Conf.-47, Mar. 23, 1944, cable by Schwartz to Mayer, where Schwartz expresses his astonishment that Jarblum asked for funds from America. He received enough from JDC-Switzerland.

34. SM-35a, "Mitteilungen" of OSE, Feb. 17, 1944, transmitted to Mayer on Mar. 30; Conf.-51, May 25, 1944, Clarence E. Pickett-J. C. Hyman.

35. MA, D.1.721, report of June, 1944; MA, D.1.722. Jarblum wrote bitterly to Schwartz that JDC-Lisbon had shown no understanding of the Spanish crossing plans, apparently for budgetary reasons. He could not take the money from his aid budgets; fortunately, he had got some Palestinian money (D.1.859, Apr. 26, 1944). In a letter to Barlas in Istanbul, Jarblum complained that JA left all the work in Spain to JDC; after all, all the work had to be done with Palestinian money (D.1.867, July 28, 1944). The WJC started spending money in France from spring, 1943, at first through a clearing arrangement analogous to that of JDC. The sums were small—in June, 1943, $9,600 "at most" (monthly?). But the U. S. Treasury intervened, and WJC was given permission to transfer French francs, up to $25,000, only against the promise of repayment après. By March, 1944, only 71,600 sfr. (about $20,000) had actually been transferred (WJC, Riegner-Wise, Mar. 18, 1943; Riegner-Reagan, June 7 and 10, 1943; Reagan-Riegner, Dec. 21, 1943; Riegner's report of Mar. 23, 1944).

36. AC, June 16, 1942.

37. 12-45, Aug. 26, 1942, Schwartz-New York; 51-Switzerland, 1942–43, Aug. 18, 1942, Leavitt-James G. Vail of AFSC.

38. 12-40, Sept. 4, 1942, Baerwald internal memo.

39. *FRUS,* 1942, 2:712.

40. Ibid., p. 714.

41. Ibid., 1:466–67.

42. Ibid., p. 472.

43. 12-45, Jan. 19, 1943; for a description of the efforts made and the results achieved, see Lowrie, *Hunted Children,* p. 226.

44. For details, see 12-45, Jan. 7, 1944, memo on the evacuation of 5,000 children.

45. 14-1, July 31, 1944, Jefroykin report.

46. SM-35a, report on Drancy, n.d., no signature; 14-1, Nov. 24, 1944, Jefroykin-Leavitt; SM-35a, July 25, 1943, OSE report from Chambéry.

Chapter Eleven

1. Israel Schirman, "La Politique allemande a l'égard des juifs en Belgique, 1940–1944" (M. A. thesis, Free University of Brussels, 1971), esp. pp. 80–88. For general background, see also Betty Garfinkels, *Les Belges face à la persecution raciale, 1940–1944,* esp. the first 40 pages; Hilberg, *Destruction of the European Jews,* pp. 382–89. There is no comprehensive account of Belgian Jewry; the archives of the Association des juifs de Belgique are closed.

2. Schirman, *La Politique allemande,* pp. 36–39.

3. Garfinkels, *Les Belges,* pp. 29–40.

4. SM-29, report on Belgium, Dec., 1943.

5. Ibid.; SM-29, report of Oct. 21, 1944.

6. Cf. Leni Yahil, *Hatzalat Hayehudim Bedania,* pp. 265–71.

7. Details about CNDJ and its relationships with AJB and AJB's welfare organization, the Ouevre centrale israélite de secours, may be found in SM-29, Dec. 29, 1943, minutes of meeting at ONE; Oct. 21, 1944, CNDJ report; Feb. 10, 1944, "Rapport du CNDJ en date du Ier Janvier 1944"; Oct. 20, 1944, CNJD-WJC.

8. Garfinkels, *Les Belges,* pp. 49–78.

9. SM-29, Note of Feb. 10, 1944; 51-Switzerland, 1944– for the figure of 360,000 sfr.

10. Jacob Presser, *The Destruction of the Dutch Jews,* esp. pp. 147–51; Joseph Michman, "The Controversial Stand of the Dutch Jews," *Yad Vashem Studies* 10 (1974): 9–68; Louis de Jong, "Holland and Auschwitz," in Yisrael Gutman and Livia Rothkirchen, eds., *The Catastrophe of European Jewry,* pp. 219–34.

11. Otto Bene-Berlin, Aug. 3, 1942, in Presser, *Destruction of the Dutch Jews,* p. 151.

12. According to a list made by the Dutch Red Cross and available from the IRC's International Tracing Service at Arolsen in the Federal Republic of Germany, 103,379 were deported (letter to me of Oct. 21, 1975). I am grateful to Louis de Jong for explaining the details to me; see de Jong, *Het Koningrijk der Nederlanden in de Tweede Wereldoorlog,* vol. 6, *Den Haag* [The kingdom of the Netherlands in the second world war, The Hague].

13. Wiener Library, Jewish Central Information Office, report on Holland by Dr. Israel Taubes, June, 1945, p. 4; Gertrude van Tijn, "Contribution towards the History of the Jews in Holland," [1944], in my possession, pp. 34–36. A young Dutchman named Westerning is said by van Tijn to have managed to get exit permits from the German military, and that these were the official groups that left until August, 1941. The story is improbable, because no German military authority would have given such permits to Jews in 1941 without careful checking with the German Foreign Office, the civilian administration, and the SS. The protection of persons who had ransom payments effected in their favor was recognized officially even after such escapes had become practically impossible; they were included among the privileged Jews who got a special stamp ("120,000 plus") and were protected from deportation to Poland (ibid., p. 56; Gertrude van Tijn's memoirs, photocopy of MS in my possession, chap. 4, p. 33). The British Ministry of Economic Warfare was so worried about these payments that a campaign against them was started. The Swiss agents acting as intermediaries were put on a blacklist and a statement was issued in late 1942 warning everyone against them (FO 371-32680/W13985/4555/48, cable of Oct. 17, 1942 to Bern, and other material in the same file).

14. Van Tijn's memoirs, chap. 4, p. 39; "The difficulties with the AJDC Committee," report by van Tijn to JDC, Apr. 27, 1945. This report, and the memoirs and "Contribution" quoted above, were given to me by the late Gertrude Cohn-van Tijn in Portland, Oregon.

15. Van Tijn, "Contribution," pp. 42–44. Paraguayan, Honduran, and other Latin American visas and passports were also obtained from the autumn of 1942 on. The extent and mechanics of these rescue attempts have not yet been fully explored. Hundreds of families obtained such papers, and some were saved through them.

16. Van Tijn, Apr. 27, 1945 report. SM-37 contains an interesting note on the Polak Daniels episode, probably written by Marcus Wyler-Schmidt, of Oct. 4, 1943.

17. Some historical accounts of Yugoslav Jewry have appeared in *Vestnik*, the publication of present-day Yugoslav Jews, but only recently was a dissertation on Croatian Jewry completed by M. Shelah at Tel Aviv University. Hilberg, *Destruction of the European Jews*, pp. 452–58, gives the bare outline of Nazi policies, and there are a number of memoirs at Yad Vashem. I have relied mainly on SM-66, Dragutin Rosenberg, "Kurze Darstellung der jüdischen Verhältnisse in Jugoslawien," no signature, Apr., 1944, Switzerland.

18. Rosenberg, "Kurze Darstellung," pp. 19, 21.

19. Hilberg, *Destruction of the European Jews*, p. 457.

20. SM-66, "Falls Sie auf dessen Mithilfe reflektieren," in report by Dr. Schlesinger (?), June 5, 1942, to Valobra.

21. Between September, 1941, and September, 1942, 14 million kuna were received from the government and only 3,878,000 kuna from JDC in Budapest (Rosenberg, "Kurze Darstellung," p. 24). This does not tally with documents in the SM files that seem to show conclusively that Zagreb began receiving JDC aid from Switzerland as early as spring, 1942. Apparently the first aid came from Hehalutz out of its tiny Palestinian allocations, and then Mayer began supplying Schwalb with funds. He probably gave around 8,000 sfr. monthly, which would have been around 800,000 kuna. It is possible that part of the money went to Josef Indig's group at Lesno Brdo and Nonantola (see text, below). Later the funds were channeled through RELICO. The date of the meeting with Košak is given by Rosenberg as December, 1941 (p. 33), but Schlesinger's account is chronologically closer to the event and also seems more reliable in some financial details.

22. Rosenberg, "Kurze Darstellung," p. 27.

23. SM-66, Nov. 30, 1943, Kišicky-Silberschein; SM-67, June 14, 1944, Kišicky-Rosenberg.

24. SM-66, Oct. 22, 1942, Valobra-Mayer; Oct. 29, 1942, Mayer-Valobra.

25. See SM-66. The financial details are not clear, though the outline is present. Schwalb reported to Mayer on July 7, 1942, that Rosenberg was getting 8,700 sfr. monthly from Mayer, but was spending 3 million kuna monthly. Correspondence between Mayer and Silberschein shows that Hockey was in contact with RELICO, and Mayer proposed cutting the Zagreb budget to 3,000 sfr. to Silberschein on July 2, 1943, because of the small number of people left in the city and because those who fled to Dalmatia ought to be supported there. In September, correspondence with IRC indicates that Zagreb was getting 10,000 sfr. monthly through Hockey, under IRC supervision. Bitter reproaches by the Zagreb community were answered by indicating that there were technical difficulties in transmitting the funds, but they finally got there. In 1944, Mayer started sending parcels, milk, and clothes. Another report, in 1945, says that 800 Jews survived in mixed marriages and 700 in the two camps and the old-age homes.

26. Excom, Mar. 15, 1944; 40-Italy, 1944–45, Mar. 2, 1944, memo by Leavitt; 52-Yugoslavia, Refugees, 1939–44, June 28, 1941, report by Hugo Wollner; ibid., Apr., 1944, report, no signature.

27. SM-24, July 2, 1944, Indig-Mayer; Alexander Klein, "Zehn Jahre Jüdische Flüchtingshilfe in Jugoslawien, 1932–1942," MS in my possession. SM-25 contains a fascinating correspondence between Schwalb and Indig.

28. Hilberg, *Destruction of the European Jews*, pp. 421–32; SM-47, Settimio Sorani, "Tätigkeitsbericht . . . ab September 8, 1943," Mar., 1944 (this must be a mistake, because the report contains material up to April).

29. 45-Poland, Refugees 1939–45, May 4, 1940 report; Hilberg, *Destruction of the European Jews*, p. 424.

30. Italy-Jan., 1941-July, 1944, Mar. 24, 1941; Sorani, "Tätigkeitsbericht," p. 2.

31. 34-Germany, Refugees in Italy, June 20, 1940, report by Elizabeth Comfort (AFSC). According to this source, 54 out of 207 persons emigrated were confessing Jews. Apart from the official DELASEM activities, there was also the personal venture of Dr. Israel Kalk, a Latvian Jew married to an Italian Jewess, who lived in Milan and supported the Ferramonti refugees with parcels and money until the German occupation. He also supported many relatives of male internees (women and children could choose either internment with their men or forced residence outside the camp; in the latter case, they had to be at least partly supported), especially among the 5,000–6,000 in forced residences in the north of the country. He maintained two kitchens at Milan which served two daily meals, with help from the government, the Roman Catholic church, DELASEM, IRC, and internal fund-raising among the refugees (SM-49(3), his report to Schwartz, Feb. 15, 1945).

32. 40-Italy, Jan., 1941–July, 1944, Lichtheim-Schwartz, Nov. 12, 1941, and Schwartz-Lichtheim, Nov. 19, 1941; see also 34-Germany, Refugees in Italy, Mar. 26, 1940, Alter report. Conditions were sometimes bad enough to arouse protests by the refugees against DELASEM, which was accused of callousness. For example, Mrs. Olga Syrkus wrote to JDC on March 7, 1940, stating, probably quite truthfully, that all of the refugees were reduced to begging (ibid.).

33. SM-47, Valobra correspondence, SM-Rosen, July 19, 1942 (and copy of Rosen's letter to Troper); June 7, 1940; June 21, 1940; SM-Valobra, Dec. 29, 1942.

34. As so often, there are no reliable statistics. The lower figure is mentioned in a telephone conversation between Leavitt and Olsen (U.S. Treasury), June 7, 1943 (R-23); the higher figure is mentioned in a letter by the emissaries from Istanbul of July 20, 1943 (MA, D.1.727); also in AC, June 8, 1943; SM-47, Valobra's letter of Aug. 5, 1943. Yugoslav refugees in Italy are estimated at up to 8,200. By summer, 1943, of the Yugoslav Jews in Italian-held Dalmatia, some 1,000 were at Split, 500 at Korcula, and close to 3,000 at Rab.

35. For the figure of 8,000 Roman Jews, see Hilberg, *Destruction of the European Jews*, p. 427. 40-Italy, 1944–45, Sept. 25, 1944, report by Arthur Greenleigh, gives a different assessment: at liberation, there were 9,000 Roman Jews (thus 10,000 before deportation), 2,000 non-Italian refugees, and 1,000 Italian non-Roman Jews; cf. Sorani, "Tätigkeitsbericht," pp. 6–7. The dissident Nice group was led by a Dr. Kasterstein. The main group, under Stefano Schwarm, who seems to have fallen into German hands, were supported by Sorani.

36. Excom, Jan. 19, 1944; Mar. 15, 1944; 40-Italy, 1944–45, Aug. 20, 1944, report by Arthur Greenleigh, who states that Roman DELASEM borrowed 8 million lire ($60,000–80,000) against promises of payment after liberation.

37. SM-47, "Lage der Juden in Norditalien," n.d., Report by V(alobra); Conf.-12, Oct. 30, 1945, M. Teglio, "Relazione sull'Attivita Clandestina della Delasem."

38. SM-50(3), July 5, 1945, list of Mayer's expenditures in Italy.

39. SM-48, Oct. 1, 1945; Apr. 2, 1945, "Sylvio" reports.

40. SM-50(3), July 5, 1945, list of Mayer's expenditures in Italy.

41. The figures for Mayer's accounts in table 22 are based on SM-4; SM-50; SM-29; SM-36; SM-66; SM-67.

Chapter Twelve

1. Bauer, *My Brother's Keeper*, pp. 103–4.

2. FO 371-31084/C6767/19/55, June 1, 1942, Clark Kerr-Eden, summary of developments in Russo-Polish relations. A Polish estimate of those deported before the German-Russian hostilities began was 1 million Poles in a number of deportation sweeps. The liberation of Poles began after an agreement was signed on August 12, 1941. Of those who were liberated first and went into Soviet Asia, an estimated 45 percent were Jews. At the end of December, 1941, the Soviets gave the Poles a 100-million-ruble loan (repayable in gold) for relief. By April, 1942, a relief apparatus was set up; almost half of the officials were Jews. A total of 271,325 persons were given aid in early 1943, of whom, according to Polish figures, 106,602 were Jews. However, in June-July, 1942, most of the relief officials were arrested and, after long wrangling, deported to Iran. Money was sent to individual Jews through JA and Bund channels, and the Poles reported that they had paid out 272,257 rubles in 1941, 798,271 in 1942, and 942,100 until April, 1943—not very impressive sums (46-Poland, Refugees in Russia, 1942, Report on Deportations in Poland-USSR).

3. The quotation is from the dispatch by Halifax to the Foreign Office (FO 371-32632/W12038/87/48, Sept. 2, 1942; see also ibid., Halifax dispatch of Sept. 9). The maharajahs were those of Patiala and Nawanagar (FO 371-32635/W14184/87/48, Oct., 1942). The general correspondence about the 50,000 Polish children is in FO 371-32630.

4. FO 371-32630/W9732/87/48, Teheran report, June 26, 1942; 32632/W1142/87/48, Teheran Report, Aug. 19, 1942. According to 32633/W12487, Sept. 14, 1942, there were 25,970 civilians.

5. R-5, Apr. 12, 1941, report.

6. AJ-2, Russia Reports, 1926–46, containing summaries of developments in JDC's relations with Russia.

7. 40-Iran, 1941–45, Baerwald-Magnes, Mar. 25, 1943; AC, June 8, 1943.

8. AJ-2, Russia Reports, 1926–46, Mar. 20, 1945, resumé by Leavitt; R-1, Hyman-Warburg, May 10, 1944, for the decided opposition to the scheme by Bundist members of the JDC Executive Committee; 49-Russia Gen., Sept. 13, 1944, statement by Rosenberg. For the continued negotiations with the Soviets, see AC, Mar. 20, 1945; R-29, Apr. 18, 1945.

9. The parcel service apparently was first suggested by groups of Baltic Jews in Palestine and the United States. The first parcels went through the Polska Kasa Opieki in New York (R-4, Jan. 22, 1942, Alderstein memo). Magnes told JDC that the parcels were a feasible idea on June 23 (40-Iran, 1941–45). On June 17, Kaplan's plea was discussed in the Executive Committee. On August 31, Ben Gurion wrote to JDC asking for help for Jews in Russia, saying that the mortality was between 22 and 28 percent. The figure was probably guesswork, but was in fact not far from the truth (46-Poland, Refugees in Russia, Aug., 1941–Dec., 1942). The first allocation for the parcels was made on October 5, 1942 (AC). JDC's decision about the hospitals was reached on July 28 (40-Iran, 1941–45). Negotiations regarding what JDC still called nonsectarian relief were conducted with Ciechanowski from December, 1941, Warburg at first offered $50,000, provided that equitable distribution was assured by Jewish members of local distribution committees. By May, 1942, JDC had given $36,000 (46-Poland, Refugees in Russia, Aug., 1941–Dec., 1942, May 22, 1942). By 1944 a total of $144,500 was appropriated and spent (SM-5(3), July 17, 1944, JDC Program in the USSR, 1942–44). There was much criticism of JDC's decision to spend the $36,000 in East Africa.

10. Out of a total of 1,234 immigrants to Palestine, 834 were so-called Teheran children. Rabbi Meyer Berlin appealed to JDC to take some of them away from secular residences; see 40-Iran, 1941–45, for Baerwald's reply on Feb. 16, 1943.

11. Ibid., Dec. 31, 1942, Viteles report.

12. 46-Poland, Refugees in Russia, 1943, Sept. 20, 1943, Memo on Food and Clothing Packages.

13. 40-Iran, 1941–45, report for July 23–29, 1943.

14. Ibid., report for June 25, 1944; 42-Political Advisory Committee, July 23, 1944, report by Schwartz; Excom, Sept. 13, 1944.

15. The figures are sometimes contradictory. I have followed in the main those in 49-Russia, Food Packages. It seems that for 1944, Russian customs were paid on only 60 percent of the tonnage sent. The JA was a significant financial partner, though it had Palestinian relatives of Russian Jews pay for the parcels rather than using its own funds (the cost was $399,715 in 1944). Even the American Jewish Congress contributed $48,000; JDC also tried to organize the sending of parcels by relatives in the United States, but failed completely.

16. AC, July 28, 1942; Excom, Aug. 6, 1942.

17. For the general aspects of the Shanghai story I have relied on Herman Dicker, *Wanderers and Settlers in the Far East* and David H. Kranzler, *Japanese, Nazis, and Jews*. I am indebted to Mrs. Laura (Margolis) Jarblum, who gave me material regarding her work in Shanghai. Of special importance are her "Report of Activities in Shanghai, China, from December 8, 1941, to February 25, 1943" (hereafter LM1) and her letter to Robert Pilpel of October 28, 1941 (hereafter LM2). The figure of 20,000 refugees is mentioned in LM1 and in JDC correspondence. However, there was never a head count which resulted in more than just over 15,000 persons. In March, 1946, 13,475 persons were registered with JDC (material given to me by Gertrude van Tijn, letter to E. Dasberg, Mar. 11, 1946). It is highly unlikely that as many as 5,000 Jews were unregistered in 1941, or 7,000 in 1946. My own estimate of the Jewish refugee population in 1941 is about 17,000–18,000 (based on newspaper clippings, Wiener Library).

18. Sept. 19, 1938 lecture by Col. Senko Yasue, circulated by Prince Konoye, Oct. 13, 1938, quoted in Kranzler, *Japanese, Nazis, and Jews*, p. 223.

19. Bauer, *My Brother's Keeper*, pp. 289–92.

20. JC, Feb. 23, 1940; Alvin Mons, "A Note on the Jewish Refugees in Shanghai," *Jewish Social Studies* 31 (Oct., 1969):286–91.

21. Dicker, *Wanderers and Settlers*, pp. 84–89. On May 25, 1939, Consul Shiro Issiguro, Col. Yasue, and Inuzuka met with Sassoon and Hayim. The Japanese suggested a complicated scheme for transferring German Jewish funds to Shanghai that was similar to the Ha'avarah scheme of the 1930s, whereby German Jews could transfer capital to Palestine with Nazi agreement by buying goods in Germany and selling them in the Middle East. When nothing came of it, Consul Yoshiaki Miura in August asked the German consul at Shanghai to intervene in Germany in favor of stopping the flow of refugees. In the meantime, on July 1, an internal Japanese decision to stop the influx had been reached. What is interesting is the slow and hesitant way in which the Japanese approached the whole issue. It was obviously a strange phenomenon for them to see white refugees in their area of political interest, and one gets the impression that they did not quite know how to handle it.

22. Bauer, *My Brother's Keeper*, pp. 289–92; JDC, China, Feb. 17, 1939, Katzki-Barnes; Kranzler, *Japanese, Nazis, and Jews*, p. 68n3; JDC, Shanghai Files, Speelman report, June 21, 1939; ibid., Franklin-Alves, Dec. 23, 1938.

23. Dicker, *Wanderers and Settlers*, p. 90; on October 28, 1939, Miura advised Hayim of the relaxations.

24. Ibid., p. 99.

25. Ibid., pp. 95–96.

26. *Shanghai Herald*, Apr., 1946, special supplement in German.

27. LM1, p. 7. LM2 records: "The CFA is not a real committee. Everyone wants to be left alone, and as long as they are left alone they will accept anything

Herzberg tells them." None of the testimonies of refugees or reports by Manuel Siegel, the other JDC representative, has a good word for CFA.

28. Shanghai Files, Inuzuka memo, Sept. 17, 1941; of Kranzler, *Japanese, Nazis, and Jews*, pp. 455, 470. In his communications with Laura Margolis, Leavitt indicated that Sassoon might be persuaded to take over the refugee problem; there was no doubt that he could contribute a sizable amount of money. Margolis answered that Sassoon would brook no interference if he assumed control, which would mean further demoralization of the refugees, and she would not support such a course of action.

29. In 1943, VH gave $90,000 for the Shanghai yeshivot group (Material on the Midwest Conference of JDC at Chicago, Ill., Apr. 1, 1944, JDC Library, New York).

30. The Shanghai dollar ($CRB; Nanking Central Reserve Bank dollar) fluctuated wildly. It stood at 17 $CRB to 1 $U.S. in 1941, but fell to 20 $CRB to 1 $U.S. in 1942; by 1944 there were 193–200 $CRB to 1 $U.S. The Siberian Jew was named Zimmermann (LM1, p. 4).

31. Housing was the responsibility of Lutz Wachsner; Alfred Edel was the bookkeeper; Dr. Lang dealt with social affairs; Werner Glückmann, Margolis's secretary, was general administrator.

32. AC, May 5, 1942.

33. Dicker, *Wanders and Settlers*, p. 114. On p. 115, Dicker says that the three Nazis arrived in September; on p. 116, he says that the Jews were told of their influence in August. The dates are still unclear; cf. Kranzler, *Japanese, Nazis, and Jews*, pp. 477–88.

34. LM1, p. 19. The Japanese used the technique of forcing a conquered enemy to set up bureaucratic organs to his own detriment against the Americans as well as the Jews.

35. SM-60, "Shanghai" (detailed list of money transfers); Dicker, *Wanderers and Settlers*, p. 128. In 1945, until September 4, another 3.3 million sfr. were transferred (almost $1 million).

36. R-32, Weekly Digest, Nov. 24, 1944; SM-61, Dec. 28, 1944, Bitker report.

37. *New York Times*, Oct. 4, 1944.

Chapter Thirteen

1. The books are *Zikhrones* and *Yiddishe Alleinhilf;* the office files are in YV, AJDC, Cracow.

2. Nachman Blumenthal, *Te'udot Migetto Lublin*, p. 68.

3. Weichert, *Zikhrones*, 3:176–77, 249–51; 260–62.

4. Ibid., p. 268.

5. Ibid., pp. 272, 309–12; Weichert, *Yiddishe Alleinhilf*, p. 58.

6. Weichert, *Yiddische Alleinhilf*, p. 67.

27. 46-Poland, Refugees, 1941–44, Aug. 23, 1944, letter by Szwarcbart, quoting an American Red Cross report of May 24, 1944, which stated that the "overwhelming part of the medical supplies never reached [any] camps."

8. YV, M-2/64, July 14, 1944, Polish Ministry of Social Welfare-Szwarcbart.

9. See, for example, YV, M-2/481, Dec. 4, 1945, Szwarcbart-Brotman.

10. According to Gutman, *Yehudei Warsha*, the population of the Warsaw ghetto was 384,902 in February, 1942, 400,000 in May, and 355,514 in July. Hilberg, *Destruction of the European Jews*, gives a figure of 380,000 in July (p. 320). I am inclined to agree with Hilberg.

11. Gutman, *Yehudei Warsha*, p. 148.

12. Adam Czerniakow, *Yoman Getto Warsha*, p. 290.

13. Gutman, *Yehudei Warsha*, p. 82; see also p. 84; Kaplan, *Diary*, p. 326.

14. Emmanuel Ringelblum, *Notes from the Warsaw Ghetto,* ed. and trans. Jacob Sloane, p. 285.

15. Ibid., p. 286. In addition to the rations and the vast amounts smuggled in every month, the ghetto also continued to receive parcels of food. The numbers were of course down sharply from 1941; there had been 113,006 in June, and even in October, 30,081 arrived. Between January and July 21, 1942, however, only 13,244 arrived. They must have come from other places in the GG or perhaps from the western territories, but this has not been determined (Gutman, *Yehudei Warsha,* p. 155).

16. Haika Grossman, *Anshei Hamachteret,* p. 85.

17. Gutman, *Yehudei Warsha,* p. 250.

18. Ringelblum, *Notes from the Warsaw Ghetto,* pp. 296–98.

19. Pp. 70–71.

20. Gutman, *Yehudei Warsha,* p. 272; Hilberg, *Destruction of the European Jews,* says that 310,322 were deported and 70,000 remained (p. 320). Gutman's figure for the deportations seems more reliable, but his figure of 40,000 for those who remained in the ghetto seems much too low. If, however, there were not 355,000 people in the ghetto in July, but 380,000 or slightly fewer, then most of the number making up the difference must have been those who remained behind. Stroop gives the figure of those captured or killed in the rebellion as 56,000 (quoted in Gutman, *Yehudei Warsha,* p. 405); there were thousands who were buried in the ruins and many others who escaped into Aryan Warsaw.

21. Gutman, *Yehudei Warsha,* p. 312. Ringelblum says that Giterman tried to establish shops in order to save as many Jews as possible as workers who could not be deported because of their economic importance (*Ksavim fun Getto,* 2:184–85). This seems entirely in character, but we have no additional evidence.

22. Emmanuel Ringelblum, "Isaac Giterman, Director of the Joint in Poland," trans. Yuri Suhl (slightly edited for publication), YV, Ringelblum II archive.

23. See, for example, 46-Poland, Refugees 1941–44, Jewish National Committee report of Nov. 15, 1943.

24. Out of the wealth of material in the Foreign Office files at the Public Records Office, one might mention FO 371-31084/C6792/19/55, June 8, 1942, Minister of State in Cairo-F.O.

25. 44-2, Nov. 9, 1942, Sussman-Hyman.

26. Ibid., Sept. 23, 1942, Hyman statement. The AC, Excom, and 44-2 files contain the material on this episode.

27. 44-2, Mar. 6, 1942, Katzki-New York.

28. Ibid., Sept. 2, 1942; MA, D.1.974, Oct. 27, 1943.

29. 44-2, Jan. 4, 1943; Feb.10, 1943.

30. Conf.-26, letter from Poland by the Jewish National Committee, Jan. 21, 1943, which reached JDC on Apr. 20, 1943.

31. Conf.-27, Feb. 8, 1943, Pat-Hyman.

32. 45-Poland, Refugees, 1939–45, notes by Leavitt or Hyman on the dates mentioned in the text.

33. Cf. Adolf Berman, *Bi'yemei Hamachteret;* Batyah Temkin-Berman, *Yoman Bamachteret;* Josef Zemian, *Kikar Shloshet Hatzlavim.*

34. AC, Jan. 11, 1944.

35. Excom, Sept. 13, 1944, Schwartz.

Chapter Fourteen

1. In JDC reports the number of Rumanian Jews constantly appears as 900,000. This is completely mistaken. Rumanian statistics were not very accurate, but could certainly be taken as general indicators. The figures in the text are based

on Hilberg, *Destruction of the European Jews,* p. 486, and on statistics presented by Theodore Lavi (see n. 2 to this chapter). They tally with different counts of Jews in the Regat in 1941 and 1942: in the summer of 1942, 272,409 were counted; an earlier count had produced a figure of 248,595. The later count seems to be more accurate, though there is another figure of 234,610 for 1942. In 1944, 342,890 Jews were counted in all the areas that had been under Rumanian rule except Northern Transylvania. This seems to be possible only if the higher figure for the Regat is accepted.

2. All general descriptions in this chapter, unless otherwise indicated, closely follow Theodore Lavi, *Yahadut Romania bema'avak al hatzalata;* Theodore Lavi, "Toldot Yehudai Haregat" [The history of Old Rumania's Jews], in T. Lavi, ed., *Pinkas Hakehillot [The communities book], Rumania,* (Yad Vashem, 1970), 1:141–224 (Hebrew lettering, introduction); Doran Litani and Theodore Lavi, "Transnistria Ezor Gerushim Vehashmada" [Transnistria, the land of deportations and extermination], ibid., pp. 349–88; Hilberg, *Destruction of the European Jews,* pp. 479–509; Dora Litani, "The Destruction of the Jews of Odessa in the Light of Rumanian Documents," *Yad Vashem Studies* (1967):135–55; Alexander Safran, "The Ruler of Fascist Rumania Whom I Had to Deal with," ibid., pp. 175–81; Theodore Lavi, "The Vatican's Endeavors on Behalf of Rumanian Jewry during the Second World War," ibid., 5 (1963):405–19. Denationalization procedures were instituted against Jews in the "new" areas, and in early 1940 JDC estimated that 270,000 Jews had actually been deprived of their Rumanian citizenship, which entailed loss of professional licenses (48-Rumania, General, 1940–44, Moskowitz report, Apr., 1940). The so-called Jewish Law of August 8, 1940, provided for three categories of Jews, of which only the B category, including war veterans and other long-established citizens with special rights, was partly exempt from persecution.

3. Dora Litani, "Iasi," in *Pinkas Hakehillot,* pp. 167–72.

4. Hilberg, *Destruction of the European Jews,* pp. 492–93. Hilberg seems to think that the Tighina agreement of August 30, 1941, temporarily prevented further deportations; on the contrary, the effect was to enable the Rumanians to proceed with deportations into the Transnistrian side of the Bug.

5. Ibid., pp. 501–2 for a discussion of the deportations. Interventions by Cassulo are documented for October, 1942 (see Lavi, "Vatican's Endeavors," pp. 406–7). De Weck, the Swiss minister, and the Turkish and Swedish representatives voiced their views to Rumanian authorities. Rabbi Safran enlisted the help of Metropolitan Nicolaie Balan of Transylvania, and Filderman got the help of Dr. Stroescu, one of Antonescu's physicians, who asked for 100 million lei for his home for disabled Rumanians as his fee. In 1942, the Germans needed twenty-seven Rumanian military divisions, and the Rumanians had some measure of independence.

6. The figures are taken from Litani and Lavi, "Transnistria," in *Pinkas Hakehillot,* pp. 374–75.

7. Meir Teich, "The Jewish Self-Administration in Ghetto Shargorod (Transnistria)," *Yad Vashem Studies* 2 (1958):219–25.

8. Jean Angel, "Rumanian Jewry, 1944–1947" (Ph.D. diss., Hebrew University, 1980), p. 27. In the spring of 1945, 7,000 deportees returned to Rumania (Litani and Lavi, "Transnistria," p. 382).

9. Lavi, *Yahadut Romania,* p. 83; SM-54, Aug. 7, 1943, Fischer-Silberschein, where the arrival over the preceeding few months of a few hundred Jews from the Lwów region is reported; SM-54, Filderman report, Nov. 12, 1943, which says that 340 Polish Jews were being supported at that time at a monthly cost of 2.85 million lei (about $3,500).

10. WJC, Feb. 2, 1943, Riegner-de Pilar discussion; June 24, 1943, Pilar-Chapuissat and de Traz.

11. WJC, Nov. 27, 1942, report. Among the JDC-supported activities was

the mass child-care program run by Drs. Cornel and Mala Jancu. Their organization looked after 2,000 children, and three-fourths of their budget was covered by JDC.

12. SM-57, Note on Rumanian Subsidies, Dec. 1, 1942–Nov. 1, 1943; Mayer-Katzki telephone conversation, June 8, 1943; on July 21, Mayer told Katzki that the IRC delegate in Rumania would act in "our" behalf. The record of the conversation then says: "Herbert [Katzki]: Our behalf? SM: Not Joint's behalf, SM behalf. HK: OK. Always SM behalf."

13. SM-54, Nov. 12, 1943, Filderman report.

14. SM-54, memo, HW(elti)-MW(yler)-SM talk, Dec. 7–8, 1943.

15. 49-Transnistria, Jan. 29, 1944, and Apr. 22, 1944, reports by Schwartz and a report by IRC, June 19, 1944. See JDC official overseas expenditures for 1944; 51-Switzerland, 1944, for Mayer's accounts.

16. Lavi, *Yahadut Romania*, pp. 137–38.

17. SM-56(1), Apr. 25, 1944; May 19, 1944; June 3, 1947; Aug. 8, 1947; June 4, 1944, Silberschein-Mayer.

18. Jürgen Rohwer, *Die Versenkung der jüdischen Flüchtlingstransporter Struma und Mefkure im Schwartzen Meer*, pp. 46–96. Three small ships—the *Milka*, *Bella Citta*, and *Maritza*—plied the Black Sea until May 15, 1944, bringing up to 1,200 refugees to Istanbul; the *Milka*, with 143 passengers, reached the city first, on March 30. The *Maritza* was lost on one of her return journeys. ORAT squeezed up to 3 million lei ($3,750) per person from the Jewish passengers. Ira Hirschman said the transports should continue, "as long as the risks involved are known to the passengers" (R-25, Sept. 11, 1944).

19. 48-Rumania, 1940–44, June 30, 1944, Antonescu-Zimmer and Filderman; June 30, 1944, Filderman-Lecca; June 22, 1944, Filderman-Antonescu; conference of June 20, 1944; July 4, 1944, Filderman-Barlas.

20. R-25, Sept. 11, 1944, Hirschmann report. 48-Rumania, Reports 1943–44, report of Nov., 1944, says that there were 6,500 Hungarian and Polish Jews in Rumania at that time.

21. See Yehuda Bauer, "Hatzanchanim vetochnit hahitnagdut" [The parachutists and the resistance plan], *YM*, no. 1 (1964), pp. 91–94.

Chapter Fifteen

1. Livia Rothkirchen, *Hurban Yahadut Slovakia*, p. 9.

2. Members of the JDC committee (Zentrales Soziales Fürsorgekommittee) were Dr. Robert K. Füredi (Zionist), Dr. Karl Rosenbaum (Orthodox), Ernst Abeles (religious Zionist), Heinrich Schwarz (secretary of the Orthodox community), and Josef Blum (secretary to the committee). Schwarz became head of the Judenrat, and moved to Hungary after his dismissal in April, 1941. Blum also went to Hungary, and Leo Rosenthal, a Zionist, came to work for the committee, thus creating a Zionist majority (11-2).

3. Hilberg, *Destruction of the European Jews*, pp. 458–73.

4. Rothkirchen, *Hurban Yahadut Slovakia*, pp. 18, 59.

5. I could not locate the actual figures for dollar transfers in the JDC files, though they may have escaped my notice. On the transfers, see 11-2, Sept. 25, 1939; Oct. 10 and Oct. 17, 1939, correspondence between Füredi and Troper; R-38, June 7, 1940, Budapest cable.

6. R-6, June 4, 1941; Sept. 6, 1941; R-41, May 27, 1941.

7. 11-1, Oct. 14, 1940, report by Jacobson and Blum.

8. 11-2, Apr. 1, 1940, Neumann report; 11-4; testimony in YV by Arthur Flaum tells the story in detail.

9. 11-6.

10. NG-2586-J; Rothkirchen, *Hurban Yahadut Slovakia*, p. 19.
11. Hilberg, *Destruction of the European Jews*, pp. 464–65.
12. Michael Dov Weissmandel, *Min Hametzar*, pp. 19–27. (Weissmandel's book is probably one of the most important and profound accounts to have come out of the Holocaust, but unfortunately it was put together after Weissmandel's untimely death in 1957, and consequently is not well organized. The documents printed in it—some of them translated from German or Yiddish into rabbinical Hebrew—are not always properly placed in the text.) A protest by the Slovak bishops signed by Karol Kmetko, bishop of Nitra, was presented on February 16 (Rothkirchen, *Hurban Yahadut Slovakia*, p. 133), but as Weissmandel points out (p. 20), it was designed to protect Catholic converts rather than to protest the deportations, thus showing the true colors of the Slovak Roman Catholic church.
13. Browning, "Referat DIII of Abteilung Deutschland," p. 261; Czechoslovakia, General, Josef Blum, "Die Deportation der Juden aus der Slowakei." Blum estimated that there were 8,000 refugees in Hungary, but the figure seems exaggerated. Cf. SM-64, July 27, 1942, Fleischmann-Silberschein, where Fleischmann says that 4,000 Jews fled into Hungary. The true figure is somewhere in between. Fleischmann also reported that 6,000 Jews converted to Catholicism and to Protestant churches because they believed that conversion might save their lives. She may have wanted to play down the numbers in a letter to Switzerland; it seems to me that her figure is an understatement.
14. Aron Grünhut, *Katastrophenzeit des slowakischen Judentums*, pp. 80–82.
15. Weissmandel, *Min Hametzar*, pp. 12–16.
16. Ibid., p. 45. The other sources are Oskar Neumann, *Im Schatten des Todes*, pp. 137–40; Grünhut, *Katastrophenzeit*, p. 80. Rothkirchen quotes Wisliceny's testimony of November 18, 1946, in which he says he received $20,000 (*Hurban Yahadut Slovakia*, pp. 243–44). On p. 30 she mentions that Steiner, in his postwar testimony at the Vašek trial, spoke of $50,000 paid in installments, which would bear out Weissmandel's version.
17. Weissmandel, *Min Hametzar*, p. 45.
18. Grünhut, *Katastrophenzeit*; Czechoslovakia, General, Josef Blum, "Die Deportation der Juden aus der Slowakei"; SM-64, May 17, 1942, a handwritten note, apparently by Mayer, of a conversation with Blum. There is no indication in this note that Blum asked for a guarantee, but he may have done so on some other occasion.
19. SM-64, Sept. 28, 1942, Fleischmann-Mayer, telling him that he could write directly to her; the "detour via Blum is no longer necessary." Blum's demands were presented in his conversation of May 17 with Mayer (SM-64); SM-52, Aug. 15, 1942, the report of the Polish (Jewish) diplomat; SM-64, Aug. 27, 1942, Report from Slovakia.
20. SM-64, July 27, 1942, Fleischmann-Silberschein; Aug. 27, Report from Slovakia.
21. Ibid., Sept. 1, 1942.
22. Ibid., Sept. 10, 1942, Mayer-Schwalb. He added: "Let us not forget that the suffering is not greater than the Helper. We wish all the best for those who are so near and dear to us—whether we know them or not—they are all our brothers and sisters. Shalom, shalom." This was the way in which, all too rarely, the lonely and often desperate man let himself go.
23. Ibid., Nov. 30, 1942, Fleischmann-Mayer. Weissmandel mentions the fact that they had to place loans après with great bitterness. Even after the war he could not understand why JDC leaders could not have convinced the Americans to change the rules. Grünhut says that Blum allegedly telephoned Mayer for help for Slovakia, and Mayer twice cut him off (*Katastrophenzeit*, pp. 83–84). Weissmandel quotes from memory a letter allegedly written by Mayer in August, 1942, in which he said that "Ostjuden" (Polish or eastern Jews) always exaggerate, and

492

that the stories about the fate of Slovak Jews in Poland could not be true. Mayer is also said to have argued that it was illegal, and therefore impossible, to transfer foreign currency to Slovakia (*Min Hametzar*, p. 70). The story regarding the telephone conversations rings true in the sense that Schwalb also complained at about the same time because an angry Mayer had hung up on him (Oct. 16, 1942). Mayer was indeed a difficult person, but he could control himself, and one wonders whether his supposed anger was not in fact motivated by the knowledge that his calls were being censored. Weissmandel's account of Mayer's lack of belief in stories emanating from Poland is obviously wrong. We know of no letter by Mayer to Slovakia before November, 1942, and it is perfectly possible that Weissmandel mistook Schwalb's letter of November 11 for something written by Mayer in August. In November, it will be recalled, Mayer argued for an après arrangement. Fleischmann's and Weissmandel's disillusionment with the Jewish world parallels the Nazis' surprise at the incapability of the "all-powerful" Jewish world leadership to overcome mere international arrangements. In effect, Weissmandel unconsciously adopted some of the underlying assumptions of the antisemitic irrationalism he was fighting against.

24. NG-4407; NG-4553.

25. Himmler's ideology has been described by Josef Ackermann in *Himmler als Ideologe*; see also a description of Musy's visit to Himmler on January 15, 1945, where the problem of the power of world Jewry came up indirectly (Andreas Biss, *Stopp der Endlösung*, p. 330).

26. Weissmandel, *Min Hametzar*, pp. 64–66; Neumann, *Im Schatten des Todes*, pp. 174–77.

27. Fleischmann's original letter is in SM-64; Weissmandel's is in Weissmandel, *Min Hametzar*, pp. 67–69.

28. SM-64, Dec. 9, 1942; Jan. 14, 1943, GF(leischmann)-Switzerland.

29. Ibid., Dec. 30, 1942, Schwalb-Mayer. Schwalb suggested a meeting with Sylvain S. Guggenheim and Saly Braunschweig, who was to become president of SIG in early 1943.

30. Ibid., Jan. 29, 1943, Mayer-Fleischmann; SM-8, telephone conversations Mayer-Lisbon, Feb. 15 and Feb. 24, 1943; MA, D.1.730, Mar. 9, 1943, Bader-Bornstein.

31. SM-64, Mar. 5, 1943, Fleischmann-Schwalb.

32. SM-8, Apr. 2, 1943, telephone Mayer-Katzki.

33. Ibid., Mar. 1 and Mar. 3, 1943, telephone Mayer-Katzki.

34. On March 1, Katzki told Mayer, "Well, we cannot do this," to which Mayer wrote that he replied, "OK" (ibid.).

35. Tartakower-Goldmann et al., Apr. 12, 1943, in Weissmandel, *Min Hametzar*, pp. 81–82.

36. MA, D.1.712, letters of Mar. 10 and Apr. 25, 1943.

37. SM-64, May 11 and June 1, 1943, Fleischmann-Switzerland; Weissmandel, *Min Hametzar*, p. 162.

38. SM-8, June 8, 1943, Mayer-Schwalb telephone about Schwalb's letter of June 8.

39. SM-65, July 28, 1943, Fleischmann-Mayer; SM-8, June 10, 1943, telephone Mayer-Katzki; notes, Bern, June 17, 1943; SM-65, July 28, 1943, Fleischmann-Mayer.

40. SM-65, July 28, 1943, Fleischmann-Mayer.

41. Ibid., Aug. 4, 1943, Mayer-Fleischmann.

42. The quotation is from MA, D.1.714, Aug. 3, 1943; additional material is in MA, D.1.713, June 21 and July 8, 1943; D.1.714, Aug. 6, 1943; D.1.924; SM-8, Aug. 5, 1943, telephone Mayer-Katzki; Aug. 9, 1943, telephone Mayer-Schwalb; Aug. 10, 1943, telephone Mayer-Lichtheim.

43. SM-65, Aug. 10, 1943, Shertok cable. The money was sent in response

to Fleischmann's desperate plea for money for both the ransom plan and bribes to divert another deportation, set by the Slovaks for July 23. Funds were also needed for the fugitives from Poland, especially the Bochnia-Sosnowice area, from which about 700 people had arrived by August.

44. Ibid., Aug. 5 and Aug. 9, 1943.
45. Ibid., Aug. 10, 1943.
46. Ibid., Aug. 13, 1943, Mayer note "1026"; Sept. 22, 1943, Mayer-Fleischmann.
47. Ibid., Fleischmann letters of Sept. 1 and Sept. 13, 1943.

Chapter Sixteen

1. For some of the general background and the Brand episode I have used the following sources: Randolph L. Braham, ed., *Hungarian Jewish Studies,* vol. 1, esp. Nathaniel Katzburg, "Hungarian Jewry in Modern Times," pp. 137–66, and vol. 2, esp. Ernö Laszló, "Hungary's Jewry: A Demographic Overview," pp. 137–82, and Béla Vágo, "Germany and the Jewish Policy of the Kállay Government," pp. 183–210; Ernest Landau, ed., *Der Kastnerbericht,* (practically identical with Reszoe Kasztner, *Der Bericht des jüdischen Rettungskomittees aus Budapest, 1942–1946,* n.d. [1946]); Andreas Biss, *Der Stopp der Endlösung;* Joel Brand, *Beschlichut Nidonim Lamavet,* ed. Alex Weissberg; Brand's interrogation in Cairo in June, 1944 (PRO-FO 371-42811/WR324/3148); Yehuda Bauer, *The Holocaust in Historical Perspective.*
2. I am grateful to Dr. Frederic Goeroeg for some background information (interview of Mar. 14, 1968).
3. SM-43, Aug. 15, 1944, IRC report, "Die Situation des ungarländischen Judentums"; cf. Vágo, "Germany and the Jewish Policy." pp. 190–91.
4. R-9, Aid to Overseas Jews, 1939–June, 1940.
5. Randolph L. Braham, "The Kamenets Podolsk and Délvidék Massacres: Prelude to the Holocaust in Hungary," *Yad Vashem Studies* 9 (1973):133–56.
6. SM-38, Nov. 22, 1943, Kasztner and Springmann-Mayer, quoted in *Kastnerbericht,* p. 45. Livia Rothkirchen, "Hungary—An Asylum for the Refugees of Europe," *Yad Vashem Studies* 7 (1968):127–42, says that there were 5,000–15,000 Jews among the approximately 140,000 Polish refugees in Hungary. Most of them managed to escape to the West. She also maintains that there were 15,000 Slovak Jewish refugees in Hungary, but this figure is based on later testimonies.
7. Mayer's relationship with these students shows him from a unique angle. See, for instance, SM-38, Nov. 25, 1941, Georg Lorenz-Mayer, addressed to "Vater Saly"; ibid., Aug. 11, 1946, Laszlo Baum-Mayer, which says in part: "You, dear Mr. Mayer, were in the most difficult period a good father not only to me, but to all Hungarian students, something we all know how to value."
8. Biss, *Stopp der Endlösung,* pp. 40–49; Brand, *Beschlichut Nidonim Lamavet,* pp. 7–9. Brand's arrest and release pose something of a mystery. Eichmann must have known some of his German background when he entrusted Brand with the mission to Istanbul. On the other hand, Brand's cousin, Biss, hints in *Stopp der Endlösung* at previous contact between Brand and the Gestapo, but Biss took Kasztner's side in later disagreements between the two and may have had an axe to grind. Biss admitted Brand's courage and resourcefulness, but regarded him essentially as an adventurer, a heavy drinker, and an unstable character. The documentation quoted later in this chapter tends on the whole to support Biss's evaluation.
9. *Kastnerbericht,* p. 42; MA contain much correspondence regarding the fight between Krausz and Kasztner.
10. Béla Vágo, "The Intelligence Aspects of the Joel Brand Mission," *Yad Vashem Studies* 10 (1974):111–28.
11. Brand, *Beschlichut Nidonim Lamavet,* p. 54.

12. SM-7, Aug. 10, 1942, telephone Mayer-Schwartz.

13. SM-38, Mar. 2, 1944, Mayer-Kasztner.

14. Kasztner wrote to Istanbul on January 30, 1944, that he was helping 2,000 refugees from Poland, and that the majority of Hungarian Jews were cold and uninterested. In fact, the Va'adah was sending parcels and other aid to Theresienstadt and even to Jews hiding in Vienna (so-called *U-Boote*, "submarines"). It had spent the equivalent of $72,400, apparently since February, 1942. Mayer also received detailed reports regarding the work done. See MA, D.1.7.6 and 976; SM-38, Dec. 12, 1943, Stern-Mayer; Jan. 25, 1944, Springmann-Mayer.

15. *Kastnerbericht*, pp. 53–57, where Kasztner states, it seems wrongly, that Brand went into hiding at Winninger's apartment. He actually went to Rudi Scholz (Brand, *Beshlichut Nidonim Lamavet*, pp. 56–58). After the war he claimed $8,000 and a gold cigarette case from Winninger; the claim strengthens his contention that he did not hand the Va'adah's archive to the Abwher for safekeeping, as Kasztner alleged, but rather sacrificed his own property in order to give the Abwehr "something" (see Germany-Claims, Devecseri-Brand, 1955). The Abwehr seems to have been misled into thinking that an anti-Hitler putsch would eliminate the SS. In a discussion with the Va'adah on March 13, 1944, they hinted that the German army would soon take over all Jewish matters.

16. See the detailed documentation in Randolph L. Braham, *The Destruction of Hungarian Jewry*.

17. As, for instance, Randolph L. Braham, "The Jewish Council in Hungary," *Yad Vashem Studies* 10 (1974):69–109. Braham accuses Kasztner of not having warned Hungarian Jews of what they were to expect (he quotes Eichmann's statement that "Kasztner rendered us a great service by helping keep the deportation camps peaceful"). He establishes quite clearly that the leadership of Hungarian Jewry knew what was happening to Jews in Nazi-occupied Europe (pp. 75–77). The masses, however, "had no inkling of the mass murders committed in the German concentration camps and of the gas chambers." (The gas chambers became known in Hungary only in late April or early May, 1944, when the accounts of the Auschwtiz escapees, taken down in Slovakia, were transferred to Budapest.) In the next sentence, he admits that they had heard rumors; he then says, "They, like their leaders, deluded themselves into thinking that what had happened in Poland could not possibly happen in Hungary" (p. 77). If they had no inkling, they could not delude themselves. Braham's confusion stems from a basic error in epistemology: people had information, not knowledge.

18. The issue of armed action is discussed in *Kastnerbericht*, pp. 54–56, 67–69, and in great detail in Brand's interrogation in Cairo (PRO-FO 371-42811/WR324/3148, p. 8). The Jews had all of 2 machine guns, 3 rifles, 40 hand grenades, and 150 revolvers.

19. Rafi Benshalom, *Ne'evaknu Lema'an Ha'hayim* [We struggled for life], pp. 49–79.

20. *Kastnerbericht*, pp. 71–78; Brand, *Beshlichut Nidonim Lamavet*, pp. 61–66; excerpts from Wisliceny's testimony in Braham, *Destruction of Hungarian Jewry*, 2:922–28.

21. *Kastnerbericht*, p. 89; Brand, *Beshlichut Nidonim Lamavet*, pp. 73–78; Kasztner's version is borne out by Biss, *Stopp der Endlösung*, p. 52. It seems that Biss was present at the meeting.

22. See Brand's Cairo interrogation, PRO-FO 371-42811/WR324/3148, p. 20. In this interrogation Brand said that the first meeting took place on April 16 (p. 18) and the second on April 25. In *Beshlichut Nidonim Lamavet* (p. 73) he says the first meeting occurred on April 25, his birthday. I assume he would not make a mistake regarding an event that took place on his birthday.

23. Brand, *Beshlichut Nidonim Lamavet*, pp. 84–87. In Kasztner's confused account, Brand's two meetings with Eichmann were merged into one, and two

days later, according to Kasztner, on May 10, he was arrested. One may assume that Kasztner remembered the date on which he was arrested, and by that time he knew of the German offer of trucks for humans. That would mean that the third Brand-Eichmann meeting took place on May 8.

24. PRO-FO 371-42810, June 4, 1944, Reuben Resnik's report.

25. Vágo, "Intelligence Aspects of the Joel Brand Mission," pp. 120–21; Brand, *Beshlichut Nidonim Lamavet*, pp. 81–84, an account of Brand's meeting with Fritz Laufer and Erich Klausnitzer, two SD men. Apparently Grosz brought Brand to Laufer and also persuaded him to abandon the Abwehr people to their fate.

26. Vágo, "Intelligence Aspects of the Joel Brand Mission," pp. 123–24; interrogations of Grosz in Cairo, June, 1944, in PRO-FO 371-42811/WR422/9/G.

27. WA, D.1.719, May 27, 1944, Bader-Wenia; May 27, 1944, Bader-Brand; D.1.720, June 10, 1944, Bader-Wenia.

28. Shertok's account to the Zionist leadership in London, published in *Ma'ariv*, June 6, 1954; FO 371-42807, Hirschmann's interrogation of Brand.

29. PRO-CAB 95/15, HC cable, 683, May 26, 1944; *FRUS*, 1944, 1:1050, Steinhardt cable, May 25, 1944.

30. *FRUS* 1944, 1:1050–52; WRB materials contain all of the telegrams exchanged with Ankara, London, and Moscow. The Russian attitude was made clear in a note from Vyshinski on June 18 (ibid., p. 1074); PRO-CAB 95/15 contains the British documentation on the subject.

31. CZA, S26/1232, Gruenbaum's report on a conversation with U.S. Consul-General Pinkerton in Jerusalem on June 7, 1944. Gruenbaum thought Brand's story was just a German trick. The only thing one could do to help was use force, which in the circumstances meant using the bombing plan (S26/1284, June 21, 1944, Gruenbaum-Barlas). His colleagues in JA did not favor the bombing at that stage. Gruenbaum wrote: "They prefer not to interfere with mass murder out of a fear that Jews might be hurt by bombing. I was angry and I then understood why only in April 1943 armed resistance took place" in Warsaw. The American refusal to bomb Auschwitz is in WRB, July 4, 1944, John J. McCloy-Pehle; the British refusal is in CZA, S26. Auschwitz was bombed on September 13, 1944, according to the publications of the Auschwitz museum.

32. Veesenmayer reported on June 30 that 381,661 Jews had been deported up to then (NG-2263); on July 11, he said that 457,402 had been deported (NG-5615).

33. Braham, *Destruction of Hungarian Jewry*, 2:695, Veesenmayer message, June 29, 1944; p. 764, cable by Thomsen, Aug. 11, 1944; p. 419, Veesenmayer, July 7; p. 425, Veesenmayer on Sztojay, July 6; p. 430, Winkelmann, July 7; and documents quoted on pp. 436, 437, 441; Weissmandel, *Min Hametzar*, pp. 103–11.

34. The fact that Resnik's report (see n. 24 to this chap.) is in the Public Records Office shows that the British were given a copy immediately; it is also in the WRB files and the JDC archives.

35. WA, D.1.720, Protocol of May 29, 1944, signed by Brand and "Moledet" (Hebrew for "homeland") and transferred to Budapest, which states that the Allies had accepted the principle contained in Brand's proposal.

36. *Life*, Dec. 5, 1960, p. 146.

37. *Kastnerbericht*, pp. 126–34; cf. Weissmandel, *Min Hametzar*, pp. 123–40.

38. PS 3803, June 30, 1944, Kaltenbrunner-Blaschke. The number of people in Vienna is unclear; different sources give different figures within the margin mentioned in the text.

Chapter Seventeen

1. Blum, ed., *Morgenthau Diaries*, 2:209–11; Feingold, *Politics of Rescue*, pp. 239–44; Morse, *While Six Million Died*, pp. 71–97.

2. See WRB, 120 to Ankara, Feb. 12, 1944.
3. WRB, Presidential Press Release, Jan. 22, 1944.
4. WRB, 1023; 1805; 1806.
5. Hirschmann's rather self-aggrandizing memoirs, *Caution to the Winds*, do not give the correct picture. Resnik said some very harsh things about Hirschmann in a letter to Joseph Hyman of May 3, 1944 (Conf.-47). Similar opinions were expressed by Bader and Pomerantz. Cf. 9–45, June 9, 1944. Steinhardt-Baerwald.
6. Morse, *While Six Million Died*, p. 382.

Chapter Eighteen

1. PRO-JR 44(18), May 8, 1944.
2. FO 371-47807/W949/3/48, June 28, 1944.
3. PRO-JR 44(18), May 31, 1944.
4. PRO-JR (44)19, July 13, 1944. Brand refused to return. He had no positive answer for the Germans, and by the time the British decided to let him go in October, 1944, he had decided that there was no point in returning to Hungary. See Bauer, *Holocaust in Historical Perspective*, pp. 94–155.
5. *FRUS*, 1944, 1:1062n; ibid., p. 1047, June 19, 1944, Memorandum to the British Embassy.
6. MA, D.1.713, Bader-Wenia, June 24, 1944.
7. Feingold, *Politics of Rescue*, p. 267.
8. PRO-JR (44)21, Aug. 3 and 4, 1944; PRO-JR (44)22, Sept. 4, including McClelland's letter to WRB of Aug. 11, 1944.
9. Braham, *Destruction of Hungarian Jewry*, 1:334, NG-2234, Veesenmayer-Ribbentrop; ibid., p. 340, Apr. 14, 1944, Jägerstab protocol; ibid., 2:697, NG 2236, July 6, 1944, Berlin memo; ibid., p. 700, July 10, 1944.
10. MA, D.1.713, June 24, 1944, Bader-Wenia; D.1.746; D.1.721; WRB, July 27, 1944, Pehle-Stettinius; July 28, 1944, Stettinius-Norweb.
11. WRB, McClelland-WRB, Aug. 11, 1944 (No. 4197).
12. SM-9, telephone conversation with Lisbon, Aug. 6, 1944; SM-17, June 15, 1945, "Arba" report by Marcus Wyler-Schmidt.
13. Material in SM-4.
14. SM-9, telephone conversation with Lisbon, Aug. 1, 1944.
15. SM-17, June 15, 1945, "Arba" report by Marcus Wyler-Schmidt.
16. Ibid.
17. WRB, McClelland-WRB, Aug. 11, 1944 (No. 4197).
18. SM-13, original version of WRB No. 2867, Aug. 21,1944.
19. SM-13. Mayer tried to convince JDC to send funds to meet at least some of Becher's demands; he asked for $2 million, but in vain (ibid., Aug. 24, 1944).
20. Braham, *Destruction of Hungarian Jewry*, 2:635–36, Becher's cable of Aug. 23, which reached Himmler on Aug. 25; Himmler approved on Aug. 26 (ibid., p. 637); *Kastnerbericht*, p. 175; Braham, *Destruction of Hungarian Jewry*, 2:481.
21. WRB, No. 2990, Aug. 30, 1944, to Bern; Sept. 1, 1944. McClelland-Mayer.
22. SM-9, Sept. 10, 1944, telephone conversation with Lisbon.
23. SM-13, SM-17, Wyler-Schmidt's report. See also three small notebooks kept by Mayer and now in the JDC SM archive.
24. WRB, No. 6110 from Bern, Sept. 16, 1944, McClelland-Washington (signed Harrison). McClelland added that his personal opinion, and that of Mayer also, "is that all time possible has now been gained . . . so that these negotiations can be considered as having lapsed." His assessment differs from that of Kasztner, who expressed his disappointment at Mayer's "impossible diplomacy" ("die unmögliche Diplomatie"; *Kastnerbericht*, p. 182), which, according to him, pre-

vented the saving of many lives. Kasztner also expressed his disappointment that Joseph Schwartz did not negotiate instead of Mayer, ignoring the fact, well known to him, that Mayer acted with Schwartz's full backing. Yet Kasztner admitted that Becher's reaction was exactly what Mayer and McClelland had hoped for. "He will wait in Budapest for a telegraphic . . . answer from Saly Mayer. Until then no decision will be reached" (ibid., p. 179).

25. Biss, *Stopp der Endlösung*, p. 175.

26. *Kastnerbericht*, p. 187.

27. WRB, No. 6619 from Bern, Oct. 5, 1944, McClelland-Washington; SM-13, notebook.

28. See Trümpy's series of articles in *Sie und Er* (Switzerland), Sept. 14–Nov. 9, 1961.

29. Aug. 10, 1944; photocopy printed in *Sie und Er*, Oct. 5, 1961.

30. On November 27, 1944, Mayer paid 69,200 sfr. for four tractors to be shipped to Germany; private communication to me from Roswell McClelland regarding his lack of knowledge of tractor shipments. Freudiger did not approach Mayer directly, though he was in touch with him. He fled Hungary on August 10, and on October 13 he and Link forwarded a memorandum to Mayer in which they reported that the actual ransom was less important than the need "to urge the Jews who, it is notorious, control all operations in Britain and the USA, to compel the Allies to stop the war against Germany. Germany would be ready to undertake common action with the Western Powers against Russia" (SM-39).

31. SM-21, Musy report, n.d.; see also WRB, July 31, 1945, final report of McClelland, pp. 51–52.

32. WRB, No. 274, June 28, 1944, from Stockholm; No. 279, Oct. 18, 1944; No. 281, Mar. 28, 1945. The ghettos of Kovno and Siauliai were transferred to camps in Germany in July, 1944.

33. SM-14; SM-17; *Kastnerbericht*, p. 208.

34. OHD, Interview with Roswell McClelland, July 13, 1967; *Kastnerbericht*, pp. 211–17; SM-17.

35. WRB, No. 3932, Nov. 18, 1944; Mayer received the cable on Nov. 21.

36. WRB, No. 4014, Nov. 28, 1944, to Bern; WRB, No. 8045, Dec. 9, 1944, from Bern; also OHD, Interview with Roswell McClelland, July 13, 1967.

37. *Kastnerbericht*, p. 235.

38. SM-14; see also Trümpy, as in chap. 18, n. 27.

39. SM-14; *Kastnerbericht*, pp. 241–46.

40. *Kastnerbericht*, p. 248; this version is confirmed by Mayer's notebooks.

41. SM-21(2). On November 30, he paid 64,750 sfr. to the Willi Company for four tractors; on December 19, he paid 145,195.60, and in January, 1945, he paid 103,994.60, for a total of 313,940.20 sfr. (close to $75,000).

42. WRB, No. 8118, Dec. 13, 1944, McClelland-Pehle.

43. WRB, No. 4273, Dec. 19, 1944, to Bern; No. 8390, Dec. 28, 1944, from Bern.

44. WRB, No. 102, Jan. 6, 1945; *FRUS*, 1945, 2:1121, Jan. 6, 1945, to London.

45. SM-42; *Kastnerbericht*, pp. 260–66; NG 5230, Becher's testimony, Mar. 24, 1948.

46. WRB, Nos. 424, 605, Jan. 25 and 28, 1945, from Bern.

47. WRB, No. 881, Feb. 8, 1945, from Bern.

48. SM-21, Musy report; SM-16(2), Schellenberg trial document 50, deposition by Jean-Marie Musy, May 8, 1948.

49. YV, 0-51/DN-39/2119.

50. SM-17; *Kastnerbericht*, p. 291.

51. SM-16(2), Schellenberg trial document 51, deposition by Benoit Musy, May 8, 1948; *Kastnerbericht*, pp. 315–27.

52. WRB, No. 881, Feb. 8, 1945, from Bern; YV, 0-51/DN-39/2119; also SM-

16(2), Schellenberg trial document 40, deposition by Franz Goering; declaration of K. Becher at Nuremberg, June 24, 1948; *Tribune de Genève*, July 19, 1948, with Schellenberg's testimony of June 18, 1948; SM-21, Nov. 17, 1948, Isaac Sternbuch-military tribunal at Nuremburg; relevant correspondence in *Israelitisches Wochenblatt*, Nov.–Dec., 1948.

53. SM-42, Mar. 9, 1947, Kastzner-Steger.

54. OHD, Interview with Roswell McClelland, July 13, 1967.

Chapter Nineteen

1. Hilberg, *Destruction of the European Jews*, pp. 255, 628–29.

2. SM-21, Musy report, n.d.

3. See FO 371-WR855/49148, Mar. 22, 1943 and JR (44)16, June 29, 1944.

4. FO-JR (44)12, Memo of Sir H. Emerson, May 17, 1944.

5. 9–27, July 20, 1944, Emerson cable to JDC; Conf.-1, Feb. 27, 1945, outgoing via WRB, Emerson cable of Feb. 27, 1945; SM-6, Dec. 4, 1945, Schwartz-Mayer; SM-10, telephone conversation, Mayer-Lisbon, Mar. 11, 1945.

6. SM-23, Nov. 24, 1943.

7. Ibid., note of conversation on Aug. 10, 1944.

8. WJC, material of Kopecký meetings, Feb. 22, Mar. 5, Mar. 26, 1945.

9. Braham, *Destruction of Hungarian Jewry*, 2:740–49, esp. Veesenmayer's message of Nov. 15, 1944; for Spain, ibid., p. 755, Vessenmayer, Oct. 13, 1944.

10. Ibid., pp. 697 (NG 2236), 700 (July 10, 1944), 705 (July 24, 1944).

11. SM-43, Nov., 1944, "Note sur la situation des juifs en Hongrie, CICR."

12. Livia Rothkirchen, "The 'Final Solution' in Its Last Stages," *Yad Vashem Studies* 8 (1970): 7.

13. SM-39, Nov. 27, 1944, Peretz (Revesz)-Schwalb.

14. SM-43, Nov., 1944, "Note sur la situation des juifs en Hongrie, CICR"; Braham, *Destruction of Hungarian Jewry*, 2:528–31. On October 29, the Szálasi government announced that henceforth valid protection papers would be respected, but on November 17, it declared that protected Jews would have to leave the capital by November 20. After that date they would be treated just like all other Hungarian Jews.

15. *Kastnerbericht*, pp. 221–23, 233–38; SM-39, Kasztner's letter of Nov. 26, 1944; for the trains on Nov. 28–29, see NG-4987; SM-45, Hehalutz report, n.d.; SM-39, Schwalb-Mayer, reporting on a talk with Kasztner on Dec. 4, 1944.

16. Morse, *While Six Million Died*, pp. 363–64.

17. Ibid.; Benshalom, *Ne'evaknu Lema'an Ha'hayim*, esp. pp. 112–17; SM-39, Lutz interview in Istanbul, n.d. (Apr., 1945, with Fishzohn); ibid., Lutz reports, June 11, 1945, July 1, 1945, and letter to Mayer, Dec. 22, 1944; see also SM-43, Nov., 1944, "Note sur la situation des juifs en Hongrie, CICR."

18. SM-39, Nov. 27 and Dec. 5, 1944, Kasztner-Mayer; WJC, Nov. 9, 1944, Riegner-Schirmer conversation; SM-39, Peretz (Revesz)-Schwalb, Nov. 27, 1944.

19. SM-45, IRC, Jan. 12, 1945, on Jules Gulden; WJC, "Die Vernichtung d. Bundapester Judenheit," report; WJC, IRC letter of Nov. 27, 1944.

20. Benshalom, *Ne'evaknu Lema'am Ha'hayim*, esp. pp. 140–44, 161–75.

21. Ilona Beneschofsky, "The Position of Hungarian Jewry after the Liberation," in Braham, ed., *Hungarian Jewish Studies*, 1:237–46; cf. Erno Laszlo, "Hungary's Jewry, a Demographic Overview," ibid., 2:137–82; SM-39, "Zusammenfassender Auweis" (Aug. 31, 1945), according to which the total number of returnees from Germany was 72,104, of whom 14,025 were formerly members of labor battalions.

22. The figures in this paragraph were computed on the basis of Mayer's financial reports in SM-4.

23. Rothkirchen, *Hurban Yahadut Slovakia*, pp. 37–43; additional material may be found in Braham, *Destruction of Hungarian Jewry* and Weissmandel, *Min Hametzar*. On Gizi Fleischmann, see Chaim Kafri, "Gizi Fleischmann Kelochemet" [Gizi Fleischmann as a fighter], *YM*, no. 13 (June, 1971), pp. 46–59; WJC, IRC report of Jan. 11, 1945.

24. Mayer was accused of not providing ransom money for Slovak Jews, as in SM-38, Sept. 19, 1944, Kasztner; in fact, Mayer pressed Lisbon to permit him to pay (Sept. 26, 1944, telephone conversation with Lisbon) and then sent money anyway without asking (or telling Kasztner). On Kubala, see WJC, IRC report of Feb. 9, 1945; IRC report of Apr. 19, 1945; SM-43, Apr. 19, 1945, IRC report. For Dunant's rescue attempt, see SM-39, Apr. 13, 1945, Kasztner-Mayer; Mayer's correspondence with IRC about Slovakia, Oct. 27, Nov. 21, Dec. 4, 1944, and Jan. 26, 1945.

25. SM-39, Feb. 2, 1945, Kasztner-Mayer.

26. SM-28, Schirmer report on Vienna for Thudichum's assessment of Krumey; for Dunant's impressions, see WJC, IRC report of Apr. 27, 1945.

27. SM-23, Dec. 18, 1944, IRC-Mayer.

28. Ibid.; SM-10, Apr. 5, 1945, telephone conversation Mayer-Lisbon; Jan. 30, 1945, on the sending of parcels to Landsberg.

29. 51-Sweden, 1940–44, Margolis report for the end of 1944; ibid., Nov. 21, 1944; SM-23, June 27, 1945 report on the Göteborg parcel scheme; Jan. 1, 1945, IRC-Mayer.

30. R-32, Weekly Digest, Oct., 1944.

Chapter Twenty

1. This ideology was believed with varying degrees of fanaticism throughout the Nazi hierarchy and could be found among the German people generally; see George Mosse, *Germans and Jews* (London: Orbach and Chambers, 1971), esp. pp. 34–76; Ackermann, *Himmler als Ideologe*, pp. 157–70; Martin Broszat, *Der Staat Hitlers* (Munich: Deutscher Taschenbuch-Verlag, 1949), esp. pp. 33–40, 395–402.

2. See Alex Bein, "The Jewish Parasite," *Leo Baeck Year Book* 9 (1964):3–39; Franklin H. Littell, *The Crucifixion of the Jews* (New York: Harper and Row, 1975), pp. 24–43.

3. Andreas Hillgruber, "Die Endlösung und das deutsche Ostimperium," *Vierteljahreshefte für Zeitgeschichte* 20 (1972):133–53; see also *Hitler's Secret Book*.

4. Raphael Lemkin, *Axis Rule in Occupied Europe* (New York: Howard Fertig, 1973), pp. xi–xii.

5. PS-3358, Jan. 25, 1939.

6. Yehuda Bauer, *The Jewish Emergence from Powerlessness* (Toronto: Toronto University Press, 1979), pp. 57–60; Bernard Wasserstein, *Britain and the Jews of Europe, 1939–1945* (London: Oxford University Press, Clarendon Press, 1979).

Selected
Bibliography

Only works actually cited in this volume have been included.

Aboulker, Marcel. *Alger et ses complots,* Paris: Documents Jour et Nuit, 1945.

Ackermann, Josef. *Himmler als Ideologe.* Göttingen: Musterschmidt, 1970.

Apfelbaum, Emil, ed. *Choroba głodowa; badanie kliniczne nad glodem wykonane w getcie warszawskim z roku 1942* [Starvation illness; clinical research on starvation completed in the Warsaw ghetto in 1942]. Warsaw: American Joint Distribution Committee, 1946.

Arendt, Hannah. *Eichmann in Jerusalem.* New York: Viking Press, 1966.

Avni, Haim. *Sfarad Vehayehudim* [Spain and the Jews]. Tel Aviv: Hakibbutz Hameuchad, 1975.

Bauer, Yehuda. *My Brother's Keeper.* Philadelphia: Jewish Publication Society, 1974.

———. *The Holocaust in Historical Perspective.* Seattle, Wash.: University of Washington Press, 1948.

Barlas, Haim. *Hatzalah Bi'ymei Hashoah* [Rescue during the holocaust]. Tel Aviv: Hakibbutz Hameuchad, 1975.

Benshalom, Rafi. *Ne'evaknu Lema'an Hahayim* [We struggle for life]. Tel Aviv: Sifriat Poalim, 1977.

Berenstein, Tatiana; Eisenbach, Aron; and Rutkowski, Adam, eds. *Eksterminacja Zydow na ziemiach polskich, Zbior Dokumentow* [The extermination of the Jews in Polish lands]. Warsaw: Zydowski Institut Historyczny, 1957.

Berman, Adolf. *Bi'yemei Hamachteret* [In the underground days]. Tel Aviv: Menorah, 1971.

Biss, Andreas. *Stopp der Endlösung.* Stuttgart: Seewald Verlag, 1976.

Blum, John M., ed. *The Morgenthau Diaries.* 3 vols. Boston: Houghton Mifflin, 1967.

Blumenthal, Nahman. *Te'udot Migetto Lublin* [Documentation from the Lublin ghetto]. Jerusalem: Yad Vashem, 1957.

Braginski, Yehuda. *Am Hoter el Hof* [A people seeks a shore]. Tel Aviv: Hakibbutz Hameuchad, 1965.

Braham, Randolph L. *The Destruction of Hungarian Jewry, a Documentary Record.* 2 vols. New York: World Federation of Hungarian Jews, 1963.

501

————, ed. *Hungarian Jewish Studies*. Vols. 1 and 2. New York: World Federation of Hungarian Jews, 1966 and 1969.

Brand, Joel. *Beshlihut Nidonim Lamavet* [In the name of those condemned to death]. Tel Aviv: Ayanot, 1957.

Browning, Christopher A. "Referat DIII of Abteilung Deutschland." Ph.D. diss., University of Wisconsin, 1975.

Cerf, Paul. *Longtemps j'aurai mémoire*. Luxembourg: Letzteburger Land, 1974.

Chasmon, Raphael, et al., eds. *Sefer Yahadut Lita* [Lithuanian Jewry]. Vol. 2. Tel Aviv: Irgun Yotzei Lita, 1972.

Czerniakow, Adam. *Yoman Getto Warsha* [Warsaw ghetto diary]. Jerusalem: Yad Vashem, 1969.

Dicker, Herman. *Wanderers and Settlers in the Far East*. New York: Twayne Publishers, 1962.

Donat, Alexander. *The Holocaust Kingdom*. New York: Holt, Rinehart and Winston, 1963.

Drozdowski, Marian. *Alarm dla Warszawy* [Alarm over Warsaw]. Warsaw: Wiedza Powszech, 1964.

Feingold, Henry L. *The Politics of Rescue*. New Brunswick, N.J.: Rutgers University Press, 1970.

Fraenkel, Josef, ed. *The Jews of Austria*. London: Valentine, Mitchell and Co., 1967.

Friedman, Saul S. *No Haven for the Oppressed*. Detroit, Mich.: Wayne State University Press, 1973.

Fries, Jakob. *Uber die Gefährdung des Wohlstandes der Deutschen durch die Juden*. Heidelberg: Mohr und Zimmer, 1816.

Garfinkels, Betty. *Les Belges face à la persecution raciale, 1940–1944*. Brussels: l'Institut de sociologie de l'Université libre études juives, 1965.

Grossman, Haika. *Anshei Hamachteret* [The people of the underground]. Tel Aviv: Sifriat Poalim, 1965.

Grünhut, Aron. *Katastrophenzeit des slowakischen Judentums*. Tel Aviv: Grunhüt, 1972.

Gutman, Yisrael. *Yehudei Warsha* [The Jews of Warsaw]. Jerusalem: Yad Vashem, 1977.

———— and Rothkirchen, Livia, eds. *The Catastrophe of European Jewry*. Jerusalem: Yad Vashem, 1976.

Häsler, Alfred A. *Das Boot ist Voll*. Zürich: Ex Libris Verlag, 1967.

Hilberg, Raul. *The Destruction of the European Jews*. Chicago, Ill.: Quadrangle Books, 1961.

Hirschmann, Ira A. *Caution to the Winds*. New York: McKay, 1962.

Hitler, Adolf. *Mein Kampf*. English edition. London: Hurst and Blackett, 1942.

De Jong, Louis. *Het Koningrijk der Nederlanden in de Tweede Wereldoorlog* (The kingdom of the Netherlands during world war two). Vol. 6. s'Gravenhage: M. Nijhoff, 1975.

Kaspi, Andre. *La Mission de Jean Monnet à Alger*. Paris: Publications de la Sorbonne, 1971.

Katsh, Abraham I., ed. *The Diary of Chaim A. Kaplan*. New York: Collier Books, 1973.

Knout, David. *Contribution a l'histoire de la résistance juive en France*. Paris: Éditions de Centre, 1947.

Kotsuji, Abraham. *From Tokyo to Jerusalem*. New York: B. Geis Associates, 1964.

Kranzler, David. *Japanese, Nazis, and Jews*. New York: Yeshiva University Press, 1976.

Krausnick, Helmut, and Broszat, Martin. *Anatomy of the SS State*. Translated by Dorothy Lang and Marian Jackson. London: Paladin, 1970.

Landau, Ernest, ed. *Der Kastnerbericht*. Munich: Kindler Verlag, 1961.

Latour, Anny. *La Résistance juive en France*, Paris: Stock, 1970.

Lavi, Theodore. *Yahadut Romania Bema'avak al Hatzalah* [Rumanian Jewry's struggle for life]. Jerusalem: Yad Vashem, 1965.

Lowrie, Donald A. *The Hunted Children*. New York: W. W. Norton, 1963.

Ludwig, Karl. *Die Flüchtlingspolitik in der Schweiz*. Bern: privately published, 1957.

Madajczyk, Czeslaw. *Politika III Rzeszy w okupowanej Polsce* [The policy of the Third Reich in occupied Poland]. Warsaw: Panstwowe Wydawnictwo Naukowe, 1970.

Masur, Norbert. *En Jude Talar med Himmler* [A Jew talks with Himmler]. Stockholm: A Bonniers, 1945.

Morse, Arthur D. *While Six Million Died*. New York: Random House, 1967.

Neumann, Oskar. *Im Schatten des Todes*. Tel Aviv: Olamenu, 1956.

Opoczynski, Peretz. *Reshimot* [Notes]. Tel Aviv: Hakibbutz Hameuchad, 1970.

Poliakov, Leon. *Bréviaire de la Haine*. Paris: Calmann-Levy, 1951.

———. *La Condition des juifs en France sur l'occupation italienne*. Paris: Éditions de Centre, 1946.

Pospieszalski, Karol M., ed. *Documenta Occupationis*. 10 vols. Poznan: Instytut Zachodni, 1958–78.

Presser, Jacob. *The Destruction of the Dutch Jews*. New York: E. P. Dutton, 1969.

Rauschning, Hermann. *Gespräche mit Hitler*, New York: Europa Verlag, 1940.

Ravine, Jacques. *La Résistance organisée des juifs en France*. Paris: Julliard, 1973.

Ringelblum, Emmanuel. *Ksavim fun Getto* [Writings from the ghetto]. Warsaw: Yiddish Buch, 1961.

———. *Notes from the Warsaw Ghetto*. Edited and translated by Jacob Sloane. New York: McGraw-Hill, 1958.

Rohwer, Jürgen. *Die Versenkung der Jüdischen Flüchtlingstransporter . . .* Frankfurt am Main: Bernard and Graefe Verlag, 1964.

Rothkirchen, Livia. *Hurban Yahadut Slovakia* [The destruction of Slovak Jews]. Jerusalem: Yad Vashem, 1961.

Sefer Toldoth Hahaganah [The book of Haganah's history]. 3 vols. Tel Aviv: Am Oved, 1971–72.

Segalovitch, Zalman. *Gebrennte Tritt* [Burnt imprints]. Buenos Aires: Zentralfraband fun Poilischer Yidn, 1947.

Sheib, Israel. *Ma'aser Rishon* [The first tithe]. Tel Aviv: Hamatmid, 1960.

SIG, Festschrift zum 50 jährigen Bestehen. Zurich: Schweizerischer israelitischer Gemeindebund, n.d. [1954].

Szajkowski, Zosa. *Analytical Franco-Jewish Gazetteer, 1939–1945*. New York: The American Academy for Jewish Research, The Lucius N. Littauer Foundation, The Gustav Wurzweiler Foundation, 1966.

Temkin-Berman, Batya. *Yoman Bamachteret* [An underground diary]. Tel Aviv: Hakibbutz Hameuchad, 1957.

Trunk, Isaiah. *Judenrat*. New York: Macmillan, 1972.

Turkow, Yonas. *Hayo Hayta Warshaw Hayehudit* [Once there was a Jewish Warsaw]. Tel Aviv: Tarbut ve'Chinuch, 1969.

Waldman, Morris D. *Nor by Power*. New York: International Universities Press, 1953.

Weichert, Michael. *Yiddishe Alleinhilf* [Jewish self-help]. Tel Aviv: Menorah, 1962.

——. *Zikhrones* [Memoirs]. Vol 3. *Milchome* [War]. Tel Aviv: Menorah, 1963.

Weinberg, David H. *Les Juifs à Paris de 1933 à 1939*. Paris: Calmann-Lévy, 1974.

Werth, Alexander. *France, 1940–1955*. Boston: Beacon Press, 1966.

Weissmandel, Michael Dov-Ber. *Min Hametzar* [Out of the tribulation]. New York: Emunah Press, 1960.

Wyman, David S. *Paper Walls*. Boston: University of Massachusetts Press, 1968.

Yahadut Lita [Lithuanian Jewry]. Vol. 2. Tel Aviv: Am HaSefer, 1972.

Yahil, Leni. *Hatzalat Hayehudim Bedania* [The rescue of Danish Jewry]. Jerusalem: Magnes, 1967.

Zemian, Josef. *Kikar Shloshet Hatzlavim* [The square of the three crosses]. Jerusalem: Yad Vashem, 1962.

U.S. Department of State. *Foreign Relations of the United States. Diplomatic Correspondence*. Washington, D.C., 1963–69.

Index

520

Yehuda Bauer is a full professor, head of the Department of Holocaust Studies and former chairman of the Institute of Contemporary Jewry of the Hebrew University, Jerusalem. Born in Prague and now an Israeli citizen, he was educated at Cardiff University College of the University of Wales (B.A. Hon., 1950) and Hebrew University (Ph.D., 1960). He is the author of numerous articles and author or editor of several previous books in the area of Holocaust studies. Among his recent publications are his history of the Jewish Joint Distribution Committee before 1939 (*My Brother's Keeper*, 1974), *The Holocaust in Historical Perspective* (1978), and *The Jewish Emergence from Powerlessness* (1979).

The manuscript was edited by Sherwyn T. Carr. The book was designed by Don Ross. The typeface for the text is Mergenthaler's VIP Palatino, based on an original design by Hermann Zapf about 1950. The display face is Kabel Heavy, designed by Rudolf Koch about 1927–29.

The text is printed on 60 lb. S. D. Warren's 1854 Text paper. The book is bound in Holliston Mills' Roxite Linen over binder's boards. Manufactured in the United States of America.